JONATHAN SWIFT
JOURNAL TO STELLA

EDITING AND INTRODUCTION BY
J. K. MOORHEAD

LONDON J. M. DENT & SONS LTD
NEW YORK E. P. DUTTON & CO INC

ape 43/47

SWIFT, STELLA, AND VANESSA [1]

By Sir Walter Scott

1710/1714

At the period of Swift's residence in England, he was possessed, in an eminent degree, of many of the qualities which are the surest passports to social favour. He was not only a man of the highest talents, but he enjoyed, in full extent, all the public notice and distinction which the reputation of such talents can confer. He moved in the highest circles, was concerned in the most important business of the time, and had all the advantage of a name blown wide abroad in the world. In private society, the varied richness of his conversation, the extent of his knowledge, his unequalled powers of wit and humour, even the somewhat cynical eccentricities of his temper, joined to form a character equally interesting from its merit and originality. His manners, in these his better days, were but slightly tinged with the peculiarities which afterwards marked them more unpleasantly, and his ease and address were such as became the companion of statesmen and courtiers:

> He moved, and bow'd, and talked with too much grace,
> Nor shew'd the parson in his gait or face. . . .

Amongst the families in London where Swift was chiefly domesticated, was that of Mrs. Vanhomrigh, a widow lady of fortune and respectability, who had two sons and two daughters. The eldest daughter was Esther Vanhomrigh, better known by the poetical appellation of Vanessa. Of her personal charms we are left in some uncertainty, since Cadenus has said little upon that topic, and, by other authorities, they have been rather depreciated. But, when Swift became intimate in the family, she was not yet twenty years old, lively and graceful, yet with a greater inclination for reading and mental cultivation than is usually combined with a gay temper. This last attribute had fatal attractions for Swift, who, in intercourse with his female friends, had a marked pleasure in directing their studies, and acting as their literary Mentor; a dangerous character for him who assumes it when genius, docility, and gratitude, are combined in a young and interesting pupil. From several passages in the *Journal*, Swift's constant and intimate

---

[1] From Vol. I, section v, of Sir Walter Scott's edition of the works of Jonathan Swift (19 vols., 1814). Scott's interest in this subject had been quickened by the fact that he was able to print "the suppressed correspondence between Swift and Miss Vanhomrigh," which had been "communicated to him" by the Rev. Mr. Berwick.

familiarity in the Vanhomrigh family is manifest; and it is plain also, he soon felt that his acquaintance with Miss Esther was such as must necessarily give pain to Stella. While Vanessa was occupying much of his time, and much doubtless of his thoughts, she is never once mentioned in the *Journal* directly by name, and is only twice casually indicated by the title of Vanhomrigh's eldest daughter. There was, therefore, a consciousness on Swift's part, that his attachment to his younger pupil was of a nature which could not be gratifying to her predecessor, although he probably shut his own eyes to the consequences of an intimacy which he wished to conceal from those of Stella. Miss Vanhomrigh, in the meanwhile, sensible of the pleasure which Swift received from her society, and of the advantages of youth and fortune which she possessed, and ignorant of the peculiar circumstances in which he stood with respect to another, naturally, and surely without offence either to reason or virtue, gave way to the hope of forming a union with a man, whose talents had first attracted her admiration, and whose attentions, in the course of their mutual studies, had, by degrees, gained her affections, and seemed to warrant his own. It is easy for those who look back on this melancholy story, to blame the assiduity of Swift, or the imprudence of Vanessa. But the first deviation from the straight line of moral rectitude is, in such a case, so very gradual, and, on the female side, the shades of colour which part esteem from affection, and affection from passion, are so imperceptibly heightened, that they who fail to stop at the exact point where wisdom bids, have much indulgence to claim from all who share with them the frailties of mortality. The imprudent friends continued to use the language of friendship, but with the assiduity and earnestness of a warmer passion, until Vanessa rent asunder the veil, by intimating to Swift the state of her affections; and in this, as she conceived, she was justified by his own favourite, though dangerous maxim, of doing that which seems in itself right, without respect to the common opinion of the world. We cannot doubt that he actually felt the "shame, disappointment, guilt, surprise," expressed in his celebrated poem, though he had not courage to take the open and manly course, of avowing those engagements with Stella, or other impediments, which prevented him from accepting the hand and fortune of her rival. Perhaps he was conscious that such an explanation had been too long delayed, to be now stated without affording grounds for the heavy charge of having flattered Miss Vanhomrigh into hopes, which, from the nature of his own situation, could never be gratified. This remorseful consciousness, too, he might feel when looking back on his conduct, though until then he had blindly consulted his own gratification in seeking the pleasure of Vanessa's society, without being aware of the difficulties in which they were both becoming gradually entangled. Without, therefore, making this painful but just confession, he answered the avowal of Vanessa's passion, at first in raillery, and afterwards by an offer of devoted and everlasting friendship, founded on the basis of virtuous esteem. Vanessa seems neither to have been contented nor silenced by the result of her declaration, but, to the very close of her life, persisted in endeavouring, by entreaties and arguments, to extort a more lively return to her passion, than this cold proffer was calculated to afford. It is difficult to ascertain when this eclaircissement took place, but it seems to have preceded Swift's departure for Ireland to take possession of his deanery, though it must certainly have been made after obtaining that preferment.[1] The effect of his increasing intimacy with the fascinating Vanessa, may be plainly traced in the *Journal* to Stella, which, in the course of its progress, becomes more and more cold and indifferent—breathes fewer of those aspirations after the quiet felicity of a life devoted to M. D. and the willows at Laracor, uses less frequently the affectionate jargon, called the "little language," in which his fondness at first displays itself—and, in short, exhibits all the symptoms of waning affection. Stella was neither blind to the altered style of his correspondence, nor deaf to the rumours which were wafted to Ireland. Her letters are not preserved, but, from several passages of the *Journal*, it appears, that they intimated displeasure and jealousy, which Swift endeavours to appease. But there are two passages, in particular, worthy of notice, as illustrative of the history of Stella and Vanessa. The first occurs when Swift obtains the Deanery of St. Patrick's. "If it be worth £400 a-year," he says, "overplus shall be divided . . . besides usual . . ." an imperfect phrase, which, however, implies, that his relation with Stella was to continue on its former footing, and that she was only to share the advantage of his promotion, by an increase of her separate income. This hint was probably designed to bar any expectations of a proposal of marriage. Another ominous sentence in the *Journal* is the following intimation: "Her (Mrs. Vanhomrigh's) eldest

[1] The name Cadenus is an anagram of Decanus.

daughter is come of age, and going to Ireland to look after her fortune, and get it into her own hands." This plan, which Miss Vanhomrigh afterwards accomplished, boded no good to the unfortunate Stella.

Upon Swift's return to Ireland, we may guess at the disturbed state of his feelings, wounded at once by ungratified ambition, and harassed by his affection being divided between two objects, each worthy of his attachment, and each having great claims upon him, while neither was likely to remain contented with the limited return of friendship in exchange for love, and that friendship, too, divided with a rival. The claims of Stella were preferable in point of date, and, to a man of honour and good faith, in every respect irresistible. She had resigned her country, her friends, and even hazarded her character, in hopes of one day being united to Swift. But, if Stella had made the greater sacrifice, Vanessa was the more important victim. She had youth, fortune, fashion; all the acquired accomplishments and information in which Stella was deficient; possessed at least as much wit, and certainly higher powers of imagination. She had, besides, enjoyed the advantage of having in a manner compelled Swift to hear and reply to the language of passion. There was, in her case, no Mrs. Dingley, no convenient third party, whose presence in society and community in corre-spondence, necessarily imposed upon both a restraint, con-venient perhaps to Swift, but highly unfavourable to Stella. Vanessa could address Swift directly in her own name, and, as he was obliged to reply in the same manner, there is some-thing in the eloquence of affection that must always extort a corresponding answer. There is little doubt, therefore, that Swift, at this time, gave Vanessa a preference in his affection, although, for a reason hereafter to be hinted, it is probable, that the death or removal of one of these far-famed rivals would not have accelerated his union with the other. At least we are certain, that, could the rivals have laid jealousy and desire to sleep, the lover's choice would have been to have bounded his connection with both within the limits of Platonic affection. That he had no intention to marry Vanessa, is evident from passages in his letters, which are inconsistent with such an arrangement, as, on the other hand, their whole tenor excludes that of a guilty intimacy. Before leaving England, he acquainted her with his determination to forget everything there, and to write as seldom as he could; and in the same letter he expresses his doubts of ever visiting England again

—doubts which implied a gross insult, had he at any time held out a prospect of their union, but something still more villainous, if we suppose the parties to have passed the limits of innocence. On the other hand, his conduct with respect to Stella, was equally dubious. So soon as he was settled in the deanery-house, his first care was to secure lodgings for Mrs. Dingley and Stella, upon Ormond's Quay, on the other side of the Liffey; and to resume, with the same guarded caution, the intercourse which had formerly existed between them. But circumstances soon compelled him to give that connection a more definite character.

Mrs. Vanhomrigh was now dead. Her two sons survived her but a short time, and the circumstances of the young ladies were so far embarrassed by inconsiderate expenses, as gave them a handsome excuse for retiring to Ireland, where their father had left a small property near Celbridge. The arrival of Vanessa in Dublin excited the apprehensions of Swift, and the jealousy of Stella. However imprudently the Dean might have indulged himself and the unfortunate young lady, by frequenting her society too frequently during his residence in England, there is no doubt that he was alive to all the hazards that might accrue to the reputation and peace of both, by continuing the same intimacy in Dublin. But the means of avoiding it were no longer in his power, although his reiterated remonstrances assumed even the character of unkindness. She importuned him with complaints of neglect and cruelty, and it was obvious, that any decisive measure to break their correspondence would be attended with some such tragic consequence, as, though late, at length concluded their story. Thus engaged in a labyrinth, where perseverance was wrong and retreat seemed almost impossible, Swift resolved to temporise, in hopes probably that time, accident, or the mutability incident to violent affections, might extricate himself and Vanessa from the snare in which his own culpable imprudence had involved them. Meanwhile, he continued to bestow on her those marks of regard which it was impossible to refuse to her feelings towards him, even if they had not been reciprocal. But the conduct which he adopted as kindest to Miss Vanhomrigh, was likely to prove fatal to Stella. His fears and affections were next awakened for that early favourite, whose suppressed grief and jealousy, acting upon a frame naturally delicate, menaced her her health in an alarming manner. The feelings with which Swift beheld the wreck which his conduct had occasioned, will not bear description. Mrs. Johnson had forsaken her country, and clouded even her reputation, to become the sharer of his fortunes when at their lowest; and the implied ties by which he was bound to make her compensation, were as strong as the most solemn promise, if indeed even promises of future marriage had not been actually exchanged between them. He employed Dr. St. George Ashe, Bishop of Clogher, his tutor and early friend, to request the cause of her melancholy, and he received the answer which his conscience must have anticipated—it was her sensibility to his recent indifference, and to the discredit which her own character had sustained from the long subsistence of the dubious and mysterious connection between them. To convince her of the constancy of his affection, and to remove her beyond the reach of calumny, there was but one remedy. To this communication Swift replied, that he had formed two resolutions concerning matrimony: one, that he would not marry till possessed of a competent fortune; the other, that the event should take place at a time of life which gave him a reasonable prospect to see his children settled in the world. The independence proposed, he said, he had not yet achieved, being still embarrassed by debt; and, on the other hand, he was past that term of life after which he had determined never to marry. Yet he was ready to go through the ceremony for the ease of Mrs. Johnson's mind, provided it should remain a strict secret from the public, and that they should continue to live separately, and in the same guarded manner as formerly. To these hard terms Stella subscribed; they relieved her own mind, at least, from all scruples on the impropriety of their connection; and they soothed her jealousy, by rendering it impossible that Swift should ever give his hand to her rival. They were married in the garden of the deanery, by the Bishop of Clogher, in the year 1716.[1]

[1] The Bishop of Clogher, it is said, informed Bishop Berkeley of this secret, and by Berkeley's relict it was communicated to Mr. Monck Berkeley. *See* the Inquiry into the Life of Swift, in his *Literary Reliques*, p. 36. But I must add, that if, as affirmed by Mr. Monck Mason, Berkeley was in Italy from the period of the marriage to the death of the Bishop of Clogher, this communication could not have taken place. Dr. Madden told the same story to Dr. Johnson, upon the authority of Dr. Sheridan, to whom Stella unfolded the secret shortly before her death. And neither Mrs. Whiteway, nor any of Swift's intimate friends, excepting Dr. Lyon, doubted the fact of this unhappy marriage. Mrs. Sican's authority may also be added to the list of witnesses.

Since the first edition of this work appeared, some curious and elaborate notices concerning Swift's life have appeared in the History of the Cathedral of Saint Patrick's, Dublin, by William Monck Mason, who

Immediately subsequent to the ceremony, Swift's state of mind appears to have been dreadful. Delany (as I have learned from a friend of his relict), being pressed to give his opinion on this strange union, said, that about the time it took place, he observed Swift to be extremely gloomy and agitated, so much so, that he went to Archbishop King, to mention his apprehensions. On entering the library, Swift rushed out with a countenance of distraction, and passed him without speaking. He found the archbishop in tears, and upon asking the reason, he said, "You have just met the most unhappy man on earth; but on the subject of his wretchedness, you must never ask a question." Swift secluded himself from society for some days. When he reappeared, his intercourse with Stella and Mrs. Dingley was reassumed, with the same guarded and cautious attention, to prevent the slightest suspicion of a more intimate union with the former, as if such intimacy had not now been legal and virtuous. Stella, therefore, continued the beloved and intimate friend of Swift; the regulator of his household and table on public days, although she only appeared there as an ordinary guest; the companion of his social hours and his comforter in sickness; but his wife only in name, and even that nominal union a secret from the world. Thus situated, Stella continued to experience, in some degree, the inconveniences attached to a situation so doubtful; for though she was known to several ladies, yet their intercourse was rather formal than friendly, and her intimacies lay entirely with Swift's male friends. The obliging friend of Mrs. Delany, whom I have already mentioned, says, that Stella "went with Mrs. Dingley to Dr. Delany's villa on Wednesdays, when his men-companions dined, before he was married to my friend. She (Mrs. Delany) once saw her by accident, and was struck with the beauty of her countenance, and particularly with her fine dark eyes. She was very pale, and looked pensive, but not melancholy, and had hair black as a raven." This slight sketch of Stella, from the recollection of the venerable Mrs. Delany, will probably interest the reader as much as the editor.[1]

expresses his total disbelief of the prevailing report of a private marriage between Mrs. Esther Johnson and the Dean, with many strictures on the credulity of those previous biographers of Swift, by whom it had been received as probable. It must be conceded to both parties, in such a controversy, that it respects a doubtful and dark transaction, entered into by two persons, whose exact situation and feelings, with respect to each other, could only be known with precise accuracy to themselves.

[1] The only portrait of Stella known to exist, is in possession of my kind and respected friend, the Rev. Mr. Berwick. Dr. Tuke of St. Stephen's

If flattery and fame could have made up for domestic happiness, Stella might have been satisfied. Every year, on her birthday, the Dean addressed her in a copy of verses, in which the most elegant compliments were bestowed with an affectation of bluntness, which seemed only to warrant for their sincerity. But they contain frequent insinuations of angry passions, and virtues which

> Suspended wait,
> Till time has open'd reason's gate.

Hints which too plainly imply, that their unsatisfactory state of union neither lulled jealousy nor resentment to silence. These complaints of Stella's temper occur most frequently in the poems which precede the death of Vanessa, and the reason is sufficiently apparent.

The mind pauses on this mysterious story, with an anxious wish to ascertain its secret causes: and though time and death have destroyed the perfect clew to the labyrinth, a few speculations may be hazarded from the facts, so far as they are ascertained. The reasons alleged by Swift himself for the extraordinary conditions which he attached to his marriage, seem merely ostensible; at least they are such as never influenced any reasonable being in the same situation; for they resolve into a desire to conceal from the world his having had the weakness to break two private resolutions concerning matrimony, of which resolutions the world could know nothing. Terror for the effects the news of his marriage might produce on the irritable feelings of Vanessa, and a consciousness that his long concealment of the circumstances which led to it, placed his conduct towards her in a culpable point of view, must be allowed as one chief motive for the secrecy enjoined upon Stella. This dread would be increased to anguish, if we suppose that he married Mrs. Johnson to satisfy his own honour, and her conscience, while his heart was secretly devoted to her rival. But had such been the only cause of his distress of mind, and of the injunctions of secrecy laid upon Stella, that secrecy would have ceased to be necessary, after Vanessa was no more. A struggle there might have been between his pride and his affection; but it seems reasonable to suppose

---

Green has a lock of her hair, on the envelope of which is written, in Dean Swift's hand—"Only a woman's hair."—If Stella was dead, as is most probable, when Swift laid apart this memorial, the motto is an additional instance of his striving to veil the most bitter feelings under the guise of cynical indifference.

that the latter would have been victor, where the former had so little to support it.

After his marriage with Stella, Swift seems to have redoubled his anxiety to moderate the passion of Vanessa into friendship, or to give it, if possible, a new direction. The secret husband of another, he could not but be conscious how ill it became him to remain the object of such ardent affection. At length, about the year 1717, she retired from Dublin to her house and property near Celbridge, to nurse her hopeless passion in seclusion from the world. Swift seems to have foreseen and warned her against the consequences of this step. His letters uniformly exhort her to seek general society, to take exercise, and to divert, as much as possible, the current of her thoughts from the unfortunate subject which was preying upon her spirits. He even exhorts her to leave Ireland. But these admonitions are mingled with expressions of tenderness, greatly too warm not to come from the heart, and too strong to be designed merely to soothe the unfortunate recluse. Until the year 1720, he never appears to have visited her at Celbridge; they only met when she was occasionally in Dublin. But in that year, and down to the time of her death, Swift came repeatedly to Celbridge.

Vanessa, besides musing over her unhappy attachment, had during her residence in this solitude, the care of nursing the declining health of her younger sister, who at length died about 1720. This event, as it left her alone in the world, seems to have increased the energy of her fatal passion for Swift, while he, on the contrary, saw room for still greater reserve, when her situation became that of a solitary female, without the society or countenance of a female relation. But Miss Vanhomrigh, irritated at the situation in which she found herself, determined on bringing to a crisis those expectations of an union with the object of her affections, to the hope of which she had clung amid every vicissitude of his conduct towards her. The most probable bar was his undefined connection with Mrs. Johnson, which, as it must have been perfectly known to her, had, doubtless, long excited her secret jealousy: although only a single hint to that purpose is to be found in their correspondence, and that so early as 1713, when she writes to him, then in Ireland, "If you are very happy, it is ill-natured of you not to tell me so *except 'tis what is inconsistent with mine.*" Her silence and patience under this state of uncertainty, for no less than eight years, must have been partly owing to her awe for

Swift, and partly perhaps to the weak state of her rival's health, which, from year to year, seemed to announce speedy dissolution. At length, however, Vanessa's impatience prevailed, and she ventured on the decisive step of writing to Mrs. Johnson herself, requesting to know the nature of that connection. Stella, in reply, informed her of her marriage with the Dean; and, full of the highest resentment against Swift for having given another female such a right in him as Miss Vanhomrigh's inquiries implied, she sent to him her rival's letter of interrogation, and, without seeing him, or awaiting his reply, retired to the house of Mr. Ford, near Dublin. Every reader knows the consequence. Swift, in one of those paroxysms of fury to which he was liable, both from temper and disease, rode instantly to Marley Abbey. As he entered the apartment, the sternness of his countenance, which was peculiarly formed to express the fiercer passions, struck the unfortunate Vanessa with such terror, that she could scarce ask whether he would not sit down. He answered by flinging a letter on the table, and, instantly leaving the house, mounted his horse and returned to Dublin. When Vanessa opened the packet, she only found her own letter to Stella. It was her death-warrant. She sunk at once under the disappointment of the delayed, yet cherished hopes, which had so long sickened her heart, and beneath the unrestrained wrath of him for whose sake she had indulged them. How long she survived this last interview is uncertain, but the time does not seem to have exceeded a few weeks.

Upon the death of Miss Vanhomrigh, Swift, in an agony of self-reproach and remorse, retreated into the south of Ireland, where he spent two months, without the place of his abode being known to any one. When he returned to Dublin, Stella was easily persuaded to forgive him, judging, probably, that the anguish he had sustained, was a sufficient expiation for an offence which was now irremediable.

INTRODUCTION

SWIFT's *Journal to Stella* is misnamed. The word "Stella" was not written in the *Journal*; which was, moreover, not even addressed to Stella in any exclusive sense. Esther Johnson, to give her her real name, was the daughter of a dependant of Swift's former patron, Sir William Temple. According to a fashion of the time, Swift subsequently gave her the name "Stella"; just as he gave her unfortunate rival in his friendship, Esther Vanhomrigh, the name "Vanessa." Esther Johnson had an older companion, Rebecca Dingley, to whom most of the *Journal* Letters were directed. They were intended to amuse these two English ladies, left behind in Dublin, while Jonathan Swift, their friend and protector, was in England on political business, from the end of August in the year 1710 until the middle of 1713. But when all three were dead, Jonathan's first-cousin-once-removed, who bore the highly-confusing name of Deane Swift, somehow got possession of the earlier section of the *Journal*—about two-thirds of it—which he altered to suit his own literary taste, and then published; one Hawkesworth had already published the later section, with (it is supposed) rather less mutilation. One of Deane Swift's bright ideas was to substitute "Stella" for the formula "ppt" (probably pronounced "poppet") always used by the writer of the *Journal* to indicate Esther Johnson—it was part of their scheme of "little language," or baby-talk such as has long been deemed proper for use in conversation with girls and pussy-cats. Then came another editor, Thomas Sheridan the younger (this is the "Sherry" in regard to whose mind Dr. Johnson said "Such an excess of stupidity is not in nature"), who first issued the Letters under the title *Journal to Stella*. Then came Sir Walter Scott; who, magnetized by the romantic title, proceeded to use the *Journal* as a key to the state of Swift's affections and to the problem of his fidelity or unfaithfulness in love. At a certain point, Sir Walter detected the beginning of a cooling off, specially marked by a dwindling in the use of the little language; though it is doubtful if he ever made himself sufficiently acquainted with the originals of the later Letters to know how much of that language had been struck out of them before they were sent to the printer.

The more attention we pay to this little language, the less important it seems. The interest of the so-called *Journal to Stella* is not a love interest in any sense; whatever interest may reside in other passages between Swift and Stella, whom some say he eventually married. The interest is that of an informal and indiscreet chronicle of the time: as informal, and sometimes almost as indiscreet, as Pepys's *Diary*. Whenever an undeciphered obliterated passage, couched in the little language, was reached by the present transcriber, he found that what had gone before in the same gibberish was an almost unfailing clue to the worthless secret. It is in these passages that you will find this most original writer's most unoriginal remarks; and to add that the accompanying God-bless-you at the close of each day is also mere ritual is not to accuse Swift of any greater hypocrisy than he implicitly confessed when he said: "It is often with religion as it is with love; which, by much dissembling, at last grows real." Very far, it is certain, from any conventional piety or strained romance, is the easy confidence of Swift throughout, that the ladies will never take offence at anything he writes.

Swift left his Irish parochial cares, his Dublin lodging, and his two English-immigrant lady-companions, at the end of August, 1710, as an emissary of the Irish bishops (who were mostly English and Welsh), to transact some Church business with the Queen's Ministry in London. That business was soon disposed of; yet Swift remained in England another two-and-a-half years, and was busy all the time, as the *Journal* shows. When he arrived in London on this occasion, he was a professed Whig with High-Church reservations. He called on Sidney, Earl of Godolphin, who had just been dismissed from the office of Lord Treasurer or head of the Ministry—a moderate Tory, though most of the remaining Ministers were Whig; for in those days it was unusual for one party to have all the places. Godolphin had already told Swift that, having failed to observe any gratitude in the English Church for the bestowal of Queen Anne's Bounty, the administration would, before making a similar grant to the Irish Church, require some guarantee of a *quid pro quo*; and Swift had bluntly asked him what he meant. No doubt Godolphin meant some co-operation in easing the Occasional Conformists and other sufferers under the Test Acts: but the High-Church party had grown so strong in the country that the Minister would not be more definite; and Swift, a Tory as regarded his own cloth, refused to understand. As the mainly-Whig Ministry was now tottering, Swift expected Godolphin to be more conciliatory toward a notorious wobbler; but Godolphin was not the man to truckle. Lord Somers, the Whig Lord President of the Council, to whom Swift in his youth had dedicated his *Tale of a Tub*, was also interviewed with no better result: so Swift did what fierce and haughty souls that are not appreciated by their party frequently do—he turned his coat completely. He entered into communication with two ex-members of the Godolphin government: Robert Harley and Henry St. John: not merely with regard to the Irish Church's "first-fruits and tenths," but by way of a general political understanding. Both these statesmen had been brought up Presbyterians, and St. John—a thorough rake of the Restoration type—was now by way of becoming what we should call an agnostic; but they were prepared to lead, and *did* lead, the Church-and-Throne Tory party, whose creed in its popular form was somewhat as follows:—God has appointed the hereditary monarchy, which is not rightfully subject or answerable to any earthly authority; the divine appointment is proved by the reigning monarch's ability to cure scrofula by the mere laying-on of hands: whoever denies this doctrine, and opposes to it the theory that government derives its sanction from mere popular will, is *ipso facto* a traitor and an atheist. Thought of this kind had recently found a fair amount of expression in the pulpit of St. Paul's Cathedral. The Ministry, conceiving this to be a calling in question of the principles of the Revolution of 1688 and the Act of Settlement of the Crown, had impeached the preacher, Henry Sacheverell, before the House of Lords. Poor Sacheverell, who was not very brainy, was nevertheless very useful; and the defence he read, going back somewhat on the plain intention of his sermon—to bring in the Pretender—was prepared for him by abler heads. The bishops being mostly Low-Church so soon after King William's reign, it was possible to secure a conviction; but the sentence of the peers imposed only a trifling punishment, and their action met with such enthusiastic approval throughout the country that the Ministry never held up its head afterwards. Harley, who was a hard drinker with conscientious objections to gambling, soon replaced Godolphin, and became Earl of Oxford; St. John, becoming Secretary of State for the Northern Department, went to the House of Lords a year later as Viscount Bolingbroke.

The way for the new Ministry was smoothed at first by the Whigs having undoubtedly got into a terrible mess with their foreign policy. Because the King of France favoured Jacobitism, they had gone on with a war against him that had been started on some dispute about the succession to the throne of Spain, long after the danger of his dominating Europe had been replaced by the danger of Austria's dominating it— owing to the incalculable way in which deaths occur in royal families and make a monarchical world strongly resemble a card-party. The Duke of Marlborough had carried all before him wherever he went with a free hand; but he could not be everywhere, and the war was being fought nearly everywhere. He had frightened Queen Anne nearly out of her wits by asking to be made captain-general for life: she thought he was going to take the crown for himself. He must have seen that the war was doing England no good; but fighting was his only trade, the Whigs gave him plenty of employment in it, and so he turned Whig for the time being—although, like most prominent English statesmen of the time, he had been trying to make it all right with the Pretender, lest peradventure the Act of Settlement should not work smoothly at Queen Anne's death.

The way out, from a twentieth-century point of view, would have been to form a new party or coalition, that, while vigorously rebuking the nonsense about indefeasible divine right and the holiness of anointed royalty, would have tolerated the existence of Pretenders (at any rate in foreign parts), and, by devoting itself with sincerity to the national wellbeing, have built up a national unwillingness to change back to the bad old Stuart *régime*. But this policy, which has prevailed in our own time at least, so far as to make the Thames Valley Legitimist League explicitly loyal to King George the Fifth,[1] was impracticable in the reign of Anne; because toleration, on which all compromise must be founded, was not yet recognised as a virtue in England—indeed, was regarded as a nasty Dutch habit, as Swift's own writings disclose. The only alternative to the Whig's incompetence was the

[1] Which is at least as logical as adherence to the cause of the Stuarts, seeing that *they* derived their title from a usurper, Robert the Bruce.

Tory's bigotry; their quarrels had to go on until seas of blood had been shed and the Hanoverian dynasty had been firmly established on a basis of political corruption. Swift, who is credited with an intention to form some such party-above-party as here indicated, was obliged to retire to Ireland, and ceased to count in English politics: among other reasons because his sense of the absurdity of such people as Sacheverell, Higgins (the Irish Sacheverell, of whom you will read), and the Reverend Billy Tisdall from Carrickfergus—that Hammer of the Presbyterians!—was not accompanied by any analytic power, and because he entertained the same metaphysical assumptions as the majority of his period. If he had understood better, surely he would have been able to do more, even with the refractory material at his hand?

Even the most recent commentators on Swift have remarked that he was no metaphysician. But every man raised above the savage state who has not argued himself out of metaphysics is a metaphysician consciously or otherwise. We are entangled in a network of customs and conventions; so that we can hardly distinguish what is necessary to social life from what are mere temporary expedients, bound to undergo change. You may gather from Swift's writings that in his day property, transmissible only by bargain or gift or inheritance, and sometimes entailed beyond the scope of possible bargain or gift, was regarded not merely as a convenient human institution, but rather as something sacred and everlasting as the universe itself. The crown of a monarch, and all that it implied, was property. Those who opposed the idea of absolute monarchy, and even those who opposed all monarchy, always endeavoured to find some better and stronger property-title to supplant the monarch's, instead of merely pointing to the socially-enjoyable consequences of the change that they proposed.

This obsession explains the intolerance of even such a hater of individual instances of tyranny and such a lover of specific articles of freedom as Swift was. It explains the eighteenth-century politician's habit of laying aside all politeness and fairness upon entering the political fray. Fair-play would be resumed when the person in error—that is, the other fellow—had recanted or been put out of action.[1] The only effectual way of proving your opponent wrong was to prove him wicked. To try to prove that he was merely mistaken would not check

[1] Of course we never reason so now.

the prevalence of his error—the notion that it would involves the heresy of supposing a natural tendency in the thing that is to assimilate with the thing that ought to be: a sort of deism! It was virtuous to rage against people who did not think in the right way.

And—to descend to more personal matters—this unconscious metaphysical twist (the unconsciousness is illustrated by Swift's pained astonishment at finding himself yoked with Sacheverell) is at the root of Swift's morbid preoccupations. He had not only no belief in the possibility of progress toward better things in this world: he had no power of imagining better things. Wholly destitute of the scientific light that had begun to dawn, he never received the comforting revelation that dirt is only matter in the wrong place—or, more precisely, stagnant matter.

Shaken by a too-keen sense of the incongruous, Swift, fell between the two stools of perfect faith in revelation and interested scientific hope.

*   *   *   *   *   *

JONATHAN SWIFT was born posthumously in Dublin, 30th November, 1667; he was grandson of Thomas Swift, royalist vicar of Goodrich, Herefordshire. His mother belonged to the Erick family, of Leicester. Educated, by favour of his uncle Godwin Swift, at Kilkenny Grammar School, and Trinity College, Dublin; did not distinguish himself. Lived with his mother in Leicester. Became a member of the household of Sir William Temple about 1689, acting as secretary. There attracted the notice of King William III., who offered him a cavalry commission; which he declined, choosing to become a clergyman. Wrote verses, and was told by Dryden (who was his cousin) that he would never be a poet. Left Sir William Temple's and returned to Ireland and took orders 1694; was for less than a year prebendary of Kilroot in Connor diocese, and became suitor to a Miss Jane Waryng ("Varina") of Belfast. Returned to Temple at Moor Park, 1696. Wrote *The Battle of the Books* as a satire on the opponents of Sir William Temple in a literary controversy in which he was eventually shown to be in the wrong. Edited Temple's correspondence; and, on Temple's death in 1699, went to Ireland and became prebendary in St. Patrick's Cathedral, and vicar of Laracor, co. Meath. D.D., Dublin, 1701. Visited London, 1705 and 1707; becoming acquainted with Addison, Steele,

Congreve, and Halifax. Approached Wharton, Lord-Lieutenant of Ireland, 1708, as to the extension of Queen Anne's bounty to the Irish Church. Commissioned by the bishops to go to England on that business, 1710. Became Tory on the fall of the Godolphin cabinet that year, and worked for the new ministry in London till 1713 — this is the period covered by the *Journal*: see earlier pages as to "Stella" and Mrs. Dingley. After six months in Ireland, where he was installed Dean of St. Patrick's (the highest preferment to which Queen Anne would consent, on account of the offence she had taken at Swift's *Tale of a Tub*, published 1704), he returned to England and unsuccessfully endeavoured to compose differences in the cabinet. Returned to Ireland after Queen Anne's death, 1714. Is then reputed to have married "Stella." Came to a final rupture with Esther Vanhomrigh ("Vanessa") who had followed him from London to Ireland. Wrote the *Drapier Letters* in Dublin, 1724 — he was, ever after that, the foremost man in Ireland. Visited England, 1726; saw Pope and Gay, dined with Walpole, and was presented to the queen. Published *Gulliver's Travels*, 1726. Visited England again in 1727, for the last time. From Dublin he kept up correspondence with his friends in England, until his brain began to give way. Symptoms of the trouble became marked in 1738. In 1741 guardians were appointed to look after his affairs. He died 19th October, 1745, at the deanery. Was buried in the Cathedral beside "Stella," who had predeceased him in 1728.

After the exhaustive labours of Mr. Frederick Ryland and Mr. G. A. Aitken, no great new finds can be disclosed in footnotes. All that is attempted is a sufficient running commentary for the general reader — in which it is hoped there are no glaring errors or omissions.

EXPLANATION OF THE USE OF SQUARE BRACKETS

IN regard to Letters Nos. I., XLI. to LIII., and LV. to LXV., of which the originals are in the British Museum:—When the wording inside square brackets is preceded by the letters "*i.e.*": that means that it is an explanation of an obscurity or a correction of a mistake on Swift's part. When the wording is preceded by a query-mark, explanation or correction is merely suggested. When there is neither an "*i.e.*" nor a query-mark inside the brackets, a "superior figure" is placed at the end, outside, and a footnote deals with the

contents of the brackets. When the footnote says, "Obliterated,"
that means that the words inside the brackets have been read,
with a fair amount of certainty, through an obliterating ink-scrawl,
made usually at a period much later than the date of the Letter.

In regard to the other Letters, of which the originals are lost:—
Square brackets, *without any comment or query*, indicate that the
wording inside them is not in the earliest printed copy (Deane
Swift's compilation of Jonathan Swift's Letters, in every case
except that of No. LIV., of which the earliest copy is Hawkesworth's), but is found in Nichols's version and possibly in some
other versions. As it is not known when or by whom these original
Letters were lost, it is impossible to say whether the variations
from the earliest readings have any value; and, anyway, they
are trifling.

Where a previous annotator's footnote is adopted, square brackets
denote an interpolation by the present editor.

"Readings" of the Extant Originals

As has been pointed out in various places by Mr. Aitken, Forster's
readings of obliterated passages are often wide of the mark—he
seems never to have used a magnifying-glass. So, while Forster's
occasional astuteness is undeniable, his surmises have often been
thought unworthy even of notice here, though he is quoted nearly
always in recent versions.

Swift always spells "favor," "endeavor," "humor," &c., in what
we now call the American way—without the "u." He omits the
hyphen in "to day" and "to morrow." He uses the semicolon for
almost all purposes of punctuation; including the period, the
interrogation point, and the note of exclamation. He usually omits
the apostrophe. He sometimes doubles the full-stop, and sometimes omits it. He frequently begins a new sentence with a small
letter, and he often uses a capital to indicate a new sentence just
after a semicolon. "And" he usually writes "&"; but sometimes
"ad," and sometimes he spells it out.

As to the famous mystic letters—"MD," DD," "FW,"—"MD"
has been adhered to—though the "d" may have been the last
letter of the intended word, *i.e.*: "M—d." (The character as written
is a sort of monogram.) The [letters usually reproduced "DD"
are for a similar reason given here as "Dd," and those commonly given as "ME" are given here as "Me." It is true that
both D's are the same shape; but that shape is not specifically
capital, and the second D is always decidedly smaller than the
first. And the so-called "ME" symbol is always written Me.
Messrs. Ryland and Aitken surmise "FW" to mean "Farewell"
or "Foolish wenches"(!)—but see Letter XLIII., March 11, 1711-12.
"Ppt" is often more like "Tpt." As regards capital letters generally:
D, E, M, and S are often so written that it is uncertain whether
they are intended for capital or small. "Richar," by the way, can
scarcely be a "portmanteau" word containing "charming"—it probably means merely "little." *See* Letter XLIII., March 11, 1711-12.

Each Letter of which the original is extant has its number written *on the back* in figures, and underneath such number is a date—the date of receipt. These numbers and dates are presumed to be in the handwriting of Esther Johnson. Every letter except the first has its number written also on the front page, in the top left-hand corner, by Swift himself.

"Readings" of the Lost Letters

The "Deane Swift" small 8vo edition of 1769—corrected from the original quarto—is followed, except as to the long "f" and the old fashion of printing every proper name in italics.

Old Signed Footnotes

D.S. means Deane Swift.
Scott ,, Sir Walter Scott.
"B.," "F.," "N.," and "H." are initials used in Nichols's edition.
B. means either Bowyer or Dr. Birch.
F.   ,,   Faulkner.
N.   ,,   Nichols.
H.   ,,   Hawkesworth.
D. L. P. means D. Laing Purves.

J. K. MOORHEAD.

SELECT BIBLIOGRAPHY

COLLECTED WORKS. Works, 27 vols. Life and Notes by J. Hawkesworth, 1766–79. Works, 19 vols. Life, etc., by Sir Walter Scott, 1824; 2nd ed., 1883–4. Prose Works, ed. Temple Scott, 12 vols., 1897–1908. *The Poems of Jonathan Swift*, ed. Harold Williams, 3 vols., 1937.

A Tale of a Tub, to which is added an account of the Battle between the Ancient and Modern Books in St. James's Library, 1704; *The Predictions of, Answer to, and Vindication of Isaac Bickerstaff, Esq.*, 1708, 1709; *Miscellanies in Prose and Verse*, including "Meditations upon a Broomstick," 1711; *A Proposal for Correcting, Improving, and Ascertaining the English Tongue*, 1712; *A Proposal for the Universal Use of Irish Manufactures*, 1720; *The Drapier Letters* (concerning the brass halfpence coined by Mr. Wood), 1724; 6th and 7th in *Works*, 1735; *Cadenus and Vanessa* (poem), 1726; *Travels into Several Remote Nations of the World, in four parts, by Lemuel Gulliver, first a surgeon and then a captain of several ships*, 2 vols., 1726; *Verses on the Death of Dr. Swift*, written by himself, 1731; *Sermons : On Mutual Subjection, On the Conscience, On the Trinity, On the Difficulty of Knowing One's Self*, 1744.

Swift contributed to the *Tatler*, 1709, 1710; and to the *Examiner*, 1710, 1711.

JOURNAL TO STELLA. Besides the editions of the *Journal* included in Swift's collected works, mentioned above, the book has been several times published separately, as follows: *Swift's Journal to Stella*, 1710–13, ed. F. Ryland, 1897 (reprinted in York Library, 1904; Bohn's Popular Library, 1923); *The Journal to Stella*, ed. with Introduction and Notes, by G. A. Aitken, 1901; *The Journal to Stella, together with other Writings relating to Stella and Vanessa*, with Sir Walter Scott's Notes, 1904; *see also: Sermons of J. S.*, to which is prefixed the author's life together with his prayer for Stella, 2 vols. (1790?); *Letters written by J. S. and several of his friends, 1703–40*, ed. Hawkesworth and Deane Swift, 1766–8; *The Correspondence of J. S.*, ed. F. Elrington Ball, 6 vols., 1910–14; *Vanessa, and her Correspondence with J. S.*, ed. A. Martin Freeman, 1921; *The Journal to Stella*, ed. Harold Williams, 2 vols., 1948.

BIOGRAPHICAL. J. Boyle, Earl of Orrery: *Remarks on the Life, etc., of Jonathan Swift*, 1752 (four editions, corrected); Deane Swift: *Essays on Jonathan Swift*, 1755; Sir W. R. W. Wilde: *The Closing Years of Dean Swift's Life* (with an appendix containing some remarks on Stella), 1849; Sir H. Craik: *Life of Jonathan Swift*, 1882–97; Sir L. Stephen: *Swift, a critical biography* (English Men of Letters series), 1882; M. M. Rossi and J. M. Hone: *Swift or the Egoist*, 1934; R. Quintana: *The Mind and Art of Jonathan Swift*, 1936; B. Newman: *Jonathan Swift*, 1937; M. B. Gold: *Swift's Marriage to Stella*, 1937; B. Acworth: *Swift: a Study*, 1948.

CONTENTS

CONTENTS

LETTER I

[Endorsed: "To Mrs Dingley, at Mr Curry's House over against the Ram in Capel-street Dublin Ireland"; and by Esther Johnson—"1st MD Recd this Sepr 9"; and by Swift—"Letter to Ireld from Septr 1710 began soon after the change of Ministry. Nothing in this."]

Chester, *Septr.* 2, 1710.

Jo[1] will give you an Account of me till I got into te[2] Boat, after which the Rogues made a new bargain & forced me to give them 2 Crowns, and talkt as if we should not be able to overtake any Ship; but in half an Hour we got to te Yatcht; for the Ships lay by wait for My Ld Lt's[3] Steward. We made our Voyage in 15 hours just; last night I came to this Town, and shall leave it I believe on Monday. The first man I mett in Chestr was Dr Raymd,[4] He & Mrs Raymond were come here about levying a Fine in order to have Power to sell their Estate. They have found every Thing answer very well. They both desire to present their humble services to you: They do not think of Ireld till next Year. I got a Fall off my Horse riding here from Parkgate[5]; but no Hurt, the Horse understanding Falls very well, and lying quitely [*sic*] till I got up. My Duty to te Bp of Cl.[6] I saw him returning from Dunlary,[7] but he

[1] Mr. Joseph Beaumont, a merchant of Trim and friend of Swift, whose name often occurs in the letters; a handsome, gray-haired, intelligent man, who devoted much attention to mathematics. He invented a set of sleaing tables for the improvement of the linen trade, and received therefor, from Government, after considerable suing, a reward of £200. He chiefly used his mathematics, however, for the investigation of the longitude, in which pursuit his mind became deranged; and, after an interval of sanity, he committed suicide, about 1724.—D. L. P.

[2] The abbreviation of "the," common throughout, sometimes resembles "te" and sometimes "ye."

[3] Lord Lieutenant's.

[4] Vicar of Trim, formerly fellow of Dublin University; a particular friend of Swift, who had recommended him to Addison.—D. L. P.

[5] Formerly an important port, thirteen miles N.W. of Chester.

[6] The Bishop of Clogher, St. George Ashe (1658–1718), made Bishop of Derry in 1716.

[7] The ancient name of Kingstown. Under the Free State it has been restored.

I

saw not me. I take it ill He was not at Convocation, & that I have not His Name to My Powers. I beg y will hold yr Resolution of going to Trim, and riding there as much as y can. Let te Bp of Cloghr remind te Bp of Killala[1] to send me a Letter with one inclosd to te Bp of Lichfield.[2] Let all who write to me inclose to Richd Steele Esqr[3] at his Office at te Cockpitt, near Whitehall. But not MD. I will pay for their Lettrs at St James's Coffee house, that I may have them the sooner—My Ld Mountjoy[4] is now in te humr that we should begin our Journey this afternoon, so that I have stole here again to finish this Lettr, wch must be short or long accordingly. I write this Post to Mrs Wesly,[5] and will tell her that I have taken care she may have her Bill of 115ll whenever she pleases to send for it, and in that Case I desire you will send it her inclosed & sealed; and have it ready so in Case she should send for it otherwise keep it. I will say no more till I hear whether I go to day or no, if I do, the Lettr is almost at an end. My Cozn Abigail is grown prodigiously old—God almighty bless poodeerichar MD & for God sake be merry, gett oo health—I am perfectly resolved to return as soon as I hav done my Commission[6] whethr it succeeds or no I neer went to Engd with so little desire in my Life. If Mrs Curry[7] makes any difficulty about te Lodgings; I will quitt them, and pay her from July. 9. last, and Mrs Brent[8] must write to Parvisol with orders accordingly. The Post is come from London ad just going out; so I have only time to pray Gd to bress poor richr[9] MD[10] FW FW MD MD Me Me M.[11]

[1] William Lloyd, a Welshman. (Not the same Bishop Wm. Lloyd as is mentioned in note to Letter XLIX., July 1, 1712, as " of Worcester.")

[2] John Hough (1651–1743), successively Bishop of Oxford, Lichfield and Coventry, and Worcester; he was fifty-three years a bishop.

[3] Then Gazetteer and Commissioner of Stamps, and in cordial friendship with Swift, who had aided him in the *Tatler*.—D. L. P.

[4] Wm. Stewart (d. 1727-8), second viscount, lieut.-general and master-general of the Ordnance.

[5] Most authorities say that this Mrs. Garret Wesley was a daughter of Sir Dudley Colley; but Mr. Aitken says a daughter of Maurice Keating, of Narraghmore, Kildare.

[6] To solicit the queen to remit the first-fruits and twentieth parts, payable to the Crown by the clergy of Ireland.

[7] *See* endorsement of Letter.

[8] Swift's housekeeper at Laracor.

[9] Habits of great intimacy, and that pleasure of indulging infantine whims which is its natural consequence, had introduced between [Swift and Stella] what Swift calls a " little language," in which his fondness loved to display itself. This pretty jargon has been deciphered with considerable ability by former editors; and it is only necessary to say, that MD usually stands for Stella and Dingley, though sometimes for the former alone;

LETTER II

London [*Saturday*], *Sept.* 9, 1710.

I GOT here last Thursday after five days travelling, weary the
first, almost dead the second, tolerable the third, and well
enough the rest; and am now glad of the fatigue, which has
served for exercise; and I am at present well enough. The
Whigs were ravished to see me, and would lay hold on me as
a twig while they are drowning, and the great men making me
their clumsy apologies, &c.[1] But my lord treasurer [2] received
me with a great deal of coldness, which has enraged me so, I
am almost vowing revenge. I have not yet gone half my circle;
but I find all my acquaintance just as I left them. I hear my
lady Giffard [3] is much at Court, and lady Wharton [4] was ridiculing it t'other day; so I have lost a friend there. I have not
yet seen her, nor intend it; but I will contrive to see Stella's
mother [5] some other way. I writ to the bishop of Clogher from
Chester; and I now write to the archbishop of Dublin.[6] Every
thing is turning upside down;[7] every Whig in great office will,
to a man, be infallibly put out; and we shall have such a winter

D stands for Dingley, and DD for Dingley and Stella, yet sometimes for
Stella alone. Swift himself is represented by the letters PDFR; but this
odd and awkward combination of consonants is, in printing, usually
exchanged for "Presto"; a name given to him by the Duchess of Shrewsbury, who, being a foreigner, could not remember the English word—
Swift [for which *Presto* is the Italian].—SCOTT.

[10] The letters "MD" have long been used in print as a rendering of a
curious monogram, apparently formed of those two letters.

[11] Trails off in a scrawl here, as in other letters.

[1] For having disappointed him in the matter of preferment; principally
through the representation of Archbishop Sharpe to Queen Anne, elsewhere cited—that the author of the *Tale of a Tub* was little if at all better
than an infidel.—D. L. P.

[2] Sydney Godolphin, in 1706 created Earl of Godolphin, and in 1710
compelled to retire from office; he died in 1712.

[3] Martha (*c.* 1638-1722) daughter of Sir John and sister of Sir. Wm.
Temple (Swift's patron); married (1662) to Sir Thos. Giffard, of Castle
Jordan, co. Meath, and left a widow in less than a month. At enmity
with Swift, owing to difference of opinion over publication of Sir Wm.
Temple's works.

[4] Lucy (*c.* 1668-1715-16) daughter of George Brydges, sixth baron
Chandos of Sudeley, married to the earl of Wharton (second wife), 1692.

[5] Esther Johnson (Stella)'s mother had re-married: her husband's name
was Moss or Mose; and she still attended Lady Giffard.

[6] Wm. King (1650-1729), member of a Scottish family settled in Antrim.

[7] The great change in Queen Anne's Ministry was now going on
rapidly: Godolphin had been ordered to break his staff as Treasurer on
the 8th August.—D. L. P.

as hath not been seen in England. Every body asks me, how
I came to be so long in Ireland, as naturally as if here were
my Being; but no soul offers to make it so: and I protest I shall
return to Dublin, and the Canal at Laracor,[1] with more satisfaction than I ever did in my life. The Tatler[2] expects every
day to be turned out of his employment; and the duke of
Ormond,[3] they say, will be lieutenant of Ireland. I hope you
are now peaceably in Presto's lodgings; but I resolve to turn
you out by Christmas; in which time I shall either do my business, or find it not to be done. Pray be at Trim by the time
this letter comes to you, and ride little Johnson, who must
needs be now in good case. I have begun this letter unusually,
on the post-night, and have already written to the archbishop;
and cannot lengthen this. Henceforth I will write something
every day to MD, and make it a sort of journal; and when it
is full, I will send it whether MD writes or no; and so that will
be pretty: and I shall always be in conversation with MD, and MD
with Presto. Pray make Parvisol[4] pay you the ten pounds immediately; so I ordered him. They tell me I am grown fatter, and
look better; and, on Monday, Jervas[5] is to retouch my picture.
I thought I saw Jack Temple[6] and his wife pass by me to-day
in their coach; but I took no notice of them. I am glad I have
wholly shaken off that family. Tell the provost[7] I have obeyed
his commands to the duke of Ormond; or let it alone, if you
please. I saw Jemmey Leigh[8] just now at the Coffee-house,
who asked after you with great kindness: he talks of going in
a fortnight to Ireland. My service to the dean,[9] and Mrs. Walls
and her archdeacon.[10] Will Frankland's[11] wife is near bringing
to-bed, and I have promised to christen the child. I fancy you
had my Chester letter the Tuesday after I writ. I presented
Dr. Raymond to lord Wharton at Chester. Pray let me know

---

[1] Swift's benefice in the diocese of Meath.   [2] Richard Steele.

[3] James Butler, second Duke (1665–1745).

[4] Isaiah Parvisol, an Irishman of French extraction, Swift's agent
at Laracor.

[5] Chas. Jervas (1675?–1739) portrait painter and translator of *Don
Quixote.*   [6] Nephew to Sir William.

[7] Dr. Benjamin Pratt, then Provost of Trinity College, Dublin,
afterwards Dean of Down.   [8] A gentleman of Westmeath.—D.S.

[9] Dr. John (Mr. Aitken's index calls him Enoch—the same as the
Wicklow collector. *See* Letter IV., Sept. 29, 1710) Sterne or Stearne
(1660–1745), Dean of St. Patrick's; afterwards Bishop successively of
Dromore and of Clogher.

[10] Archdeacon Walls, rector of Castleknock.—N.

[11] In 1708, Wm. Frankland, second son of Sir Thos., was made Treasurer
of the Stamp Office. (Luttrell.) Mr. Aitken says he was at this time
Comptroller of the Inland Office at the Post Office.

when Joe gets his money. It is near ten, and I hate to send by the bellman.[1] MD shall have a longer letter in a week, but I send this only to tell I am safe in London; and so farewell, &c.

LETTER III

London, *Sept.* 9, 1710.

AFTER seeing the duke of Ormond, dining with Dr. Cockburn,[2] passing some part of the afternoon with sir Matthew Dudley[3] and Will Frankland, the rest at St. James's Coffee-house,[4] I came home and writ to the archbishop of Dublin and MD, and am going to bed. I forgot to tell you, that I begged Will Frankland to stand Manley's[5] friend with his father in this shaking season for places. He told me his father[6] was in danger to be out; that several were now soliciting for Manley's place; that he was accused of opening letters; that sir Thomas Frankland would sacrifice every thing to save himself; and in that I fear Manley is undone, &c.

10. To-day I dined with lord Mountjoy at Kensington; saw my mistress, Ophy Butler's[7] wife, who is grown a little charmless. I sat till ten in the evening with Addison and Steele: Steele will certainly lose his Gazetteer's place, all the world detesting his engaging in parties.[8] At ten I went to the Coffee-house, hoping to find lord Radnor,[9] whom I had not seen. He was there; for an hour and a half we talked treason heartily

---

[1] The night-watchman, or bellman, seems to have been a somewhat insecure depositary for belated postal correspondence.

[2] Wm. Cockburn, M.D. (1669–1739), a Scottish physician who grew very rich in London.

[3] Sir Matthew Dudley (*d.* 1721), second baronet, Commissioner of Customs.

[4] The third house (not the second as is usually supposed) from the south-western corner, in St. James's Street, was St. James's Coffee-house, kept by one Elliot—or rather, by his wife (*see* E. Beresford Chancellor's *St. James's Street*). Its windows looked right along Pall Mall. It was a Whig house.

[5] Isaac Manley, Postmaster-General of Ireland from 1703.

[6] Sir Thomas Frankland, Postmaster-General in England.

[7] Theophilus Butler, M.P. successively for Cavan and Belturbet, in Irish Parliament, became an Irish peer (Newtown-Butler) in 1715. Died in 1723.

[8] The *Examiner* charges Steele with having, "by entering into party disputes, violated the most solemn repeated promises, and that perfect neutrality which he had engaged to maintain." He had just published in the *Tatler*, No. 193, a satirical letter, purporting to be written by Downes the prompter, ridiculing the change of Ministry under the parable of a change of theatrical management. As conductor of the *London Gazette*, Steele was bound to abstain from political partisanship.—D. L. P.

[9] Chas. Bodvile Robartes (1660–1723), second earl—not of the present line.

against the Whigs, their baseness and ingratitude. And I am come home rolling resentments in my mind, and framing schemes of revenge: full of which (having written down some hints) I go to bed. I am afraid MD dined at home, because it is Sunday; and there was a little half-pint of wine: for God's sake be good girls, and all will be well. Ben Tooke[1] was with me this morning.

11. Seven morning. I am rising to go to Jervas to finish my picture, and 'tis shaving day, so good morrow MD; but don't keep me now, for I can't stay; and pray dine with the dean, but don't lose your money. I long to hear from you, &c.— Ten at night. I sat four hours this morning to Jervas, who has given my picture quite another turn, and now approves it entirely; but we must have the approbation of the town. If I were rich enough, I would get a copy of it and bring it over. Mr. Addison and I dined together at his lodgings, and I sat with him part of this evening; and I am now come home to write an hour. Patrick[2] observes that the rabble here are much more inquisitive in politicks, than in Ireland. Every day we expect changes, and the Parliament to be dissolved. Lord Wharton[3] expects every day to be out: he is working like a horse for elections; and, in short, I never saw so great a ferment among all sorts of people. I had a miserable letter from Joe last Saturday, telling me Mr. Pratt[4] refuses payment of his money. I have told it Mr. Addison, and will to lord Wharton; but I fear with no success. However, I will do all I can.

12. To-day I presented Mr. Ford[5] to the duke of Ormond; and paid my first visit to lord-president,[6] with whom I had much discourse; but put him always off when he began to talk of lord

[1] Benjamin Tooke of Temple Gate, Fleet Street, Swift's bookseller, who had printed the *Tale of a Tub*, and other works. He seems also to have acted as Swift's financial agent.

[2] Swift's Irish servant, who accompanied him on this journey.

[3] Thomas [1648–1715], then Earl, afterwards Marquis, of Wharton. He had been Lord Lieutenant of Ireland; hence Swift's acquaintance with him. Lord Wharton was deeply in the Whig interest, and was distinguished as a man of considerable talent and personal profligacy; though still more as the father of that eccentric phenomenon, Philip, Duke of Wharton, in whom his talents and profligacy were at once outstripped. —SCOTT. Swift had a strong personal animosity against Wharton, probably engendered by unfulfilled promises and disappointed hopes.—D. L. P.

[4] Deputy Vice-Treasurer of Ireland. Probably the same as "Captain Pratt" (*see* Letter VII., Oct. 26, 1710).

[5] Chas. Ford of Dublin, afterwards appointed Gazetteer.

[6] Lord Somers. Horace Walpole described Somers as "one of those divine men who, like a chapel in a palace, remains unprofaned, while all the rest is tyranny, corruption, and folly." He had, after a period of retirement, been in office since 1708.—D. L. P.

Wharton in relation to me, till he urged it: then I said, he knew I never expected any thing from lord Wharton, and that lord Wharton knew that I understood it so. He said that he had written twice to lord Wharton about me, who both times said nothing at all to that part of his letter. I am advised not to meddle in the affair of the First-Fruits, till this hurry is a little over, which still depends, and we are all in the dark. Lord-president told me he expects every day to be out, and has done so these two months. I protest upon my life, I am heartily weary of this town, and wish I had never stirred.

13. I went this morning to the city to see Mr. Stratford the Hamburgh merchant, my old schoolfellow; but called at Bull's on Ludgate-hill,[1] he forced me to his house at Hampstead to dinner among a great deal of ill company; among the rest Mr. Hoadley,[2] the whig clergyman, so famous for acting the contrary part to Sacheverell:[3] but to-morrow I design again to see Stratford. I was glad, however, to be at Hampstead, where I saw lady Lucy[4] and Moll Stanhope.[5] I hear very unfortunate news of Mrs. Long[6]; she and her comrade have broke up house, and she is broke for good and all, and is gone to the country: I should be extremely sorry if this be true.

14. To-day I saw Patty Rolt,[7] who heard I was in town; and I dined with Stratford at a merchant's in the city, where I drank the first Tockay wine I ever saw; and it is admirable, yet not to the degree I expected. Stratford is worth a plumb,

[1] Stated by Mr. Aitken to be a Whig haberdasher.

[2] Dr. Benjamin Hoadly, afterwards Bishop of Winchester, who about this time distinguished himself by opposing in the pulpit the doctrines of passive obedience and non-resistance vehemently urged by Sacheverell. —D. L. P.

[3] Henry Sacheverell (1674?-1724) the popular Tory preacher, the virtual failure of whose prosecution (1709-10) led to the downfall of the Whig Government.

[4] Catherine, second daughter of Chas. Cotton, of Beresford, Staffs., wife of Sir Berkeley Lucy (c. 1672-1759), Bart., of Facombe and Netley, Hants. She died 1740. Mr. Ryland was the identifier of Swift's "Lady Lucy"—all former annotators having been misled by the assumption that "Lucy" was a Christian name. She was cousin to Moll Stanhope.

[5] Daughter of Geo. Stanhope, dean of Canterbury.

[6] Mrs. Ann Long, once a celebrated beauty and toast of the Kitcat Club; sister to Sir James Long, and niece of Col. Strangeways; a particular friend of Swift. Through her own imprudence and the unkindness of her friends, she fell into narrow circumstances, and retired under an assumed name to Lynn, in Norfolk, where she died. Her death, noticed in the *Journal*, Dec. 25, 1711, was deeply lamented by Swift. Her comrade is supposed to have been Mrs. Barton, niece of Sir Isaac Newton.—D. L. P.

[7] A cousin, a grass-widow, apparently one of the many children of his uncle Godwin. She was afterwards widowed, and married again to one Lancelot.

and is now lending the Government forty thousand pounds; yet we were educated together[1] at the same school and university. We hear the chancellor is to be suddenly out, and sir Simon Harcourt to succeed him[2]: I am come early home, not caring for the Coffee-house.

15. To-day Mr. Addison, colonel Freind[3] and I went to see the million lottery drawn at Guildhall.[4] The jackanapes of blue-coat boys gave themselves such airs in pulling out the tickets, and shewed white hands open to the company, to let us see there was no cheat. We dined at a country-house near Chelsea, where Mr. Addison often retires; and to-night, at the Coffee-house, we hear sir Simon Harcourt is made lord-keeper; so that now we expect every moment the Parliament will be dissolved; but I forgot that this letter will not go in three or four days, and that my news will be stale, which I should therefore put in the last paragraph. Shall I send this letter before I hear from MD, or shall I keep it to lengthen? I have not yet seen Stella's mother, because I will not see lady Giffard; but I will contrive to go there when lady Giffard is abroad. I forgot to mark my two former letters; but I remember this is Number 3, and I have not yet had Number 1 from MD; but I shall by Monday, which I reckon will be just a fortnight after you had my first. I am resolved to bring over a great deal of china. I loved it mightily to-day. What shall I bring?

16. Morning. Sir John Holland, comptroller of the houshold,[5] has sent to desire my acquaintance: I have a mind to refuse him because he is a Whig, and will, I suppose, be out among the rest; but he is a man of worth and learning. Tell me, do you like this journal way of writing? Is it not tedious and dull?

---

[1] Budgell, in *Spectator*, No. 353, thus describes these schoolfellows.—"One of them was not only thought an impenetrable blockhead at school, but still maintained his reputation at the university; the other was the pride of his master, and the most celebrated person in the college of which he was a member. The man of genius is at present buried in a country parsonage of eighty-five pounds a year; whilst the other, with the bare abilities of a common scrivener, has got an estate of above an hundred thousand pounds."—But note his later history, as given in this Journal.

[2] Harcourt succeeded Sir J. Montague as Attorney-General, and not long after actually obtained the seals.—D. L. P. [He was afterwards Viscount Harcourt. Died 1727.]

[3] It has been suggested that Col. Frowde is meant. Or it may have been a relative of Dr. John Freind, hereafter introduced.

[4] See *Tatler*, No. 203.

[5] A keen Whig, and leading manager for the Commons in Sacheverell's impeachment. He had only in March (1709-10) succeeded Sir Thomas Felton in the Comptrollership.—D. L. P.

JOURNAL TO STELLA 9

Night. I dined to-day with a cousin, a printer,[1] where Patty Rolt lodges, and then came home, after a visit or two; and it has been a very insipid day. Mrs. Long's misfortune is confirmed to me; bailiffs were in her house; she retired to private lodgings; thence to the country, no-body knows where; her friends leave letters at some inn, and they are carried to her; and she writes answers without dating them from any place. I swear it grieves me to the soul.

17. To-day I dined six miles out of town, with Will Pate the learned woollen-draper[2]; Mr. Stratford went with me: six miles here is nothing: we left Pate after sun-set, and were here before it was dark. This letter shall go on Tuesday,[3] whether I hear from MD or no. My health continues pretty well; pray God Stella may give me a good account of hers: and I hope you are now at Trim, or soon designing it. I was disappointed to-night: the fellow gave me a letter, and I hoped to see little MD's hand; and it was only to invite me to a venison pasty to-day: so I lost my pasty into the bargain. Pox on these declining courtiers! Here is Mr. Brydges[4] the paymaster-general desiring my acquaintance; but I hear the queen sent lord Shrewsbury[5] to assure him he may keep his place; and he promises me great assistance in the affair of the First-Fruits. Well, I must turn over this leaf to-night, though the side would hold another line; but pray consider this is a whole sheet; it holds a plaguy deal, and you must be content to be weary; but I'll do so no more. Sir Simon Harcourt is made attorney-general, and not lord-keeper.

18. To-day I dined with Mr. Stratford at Mr. Addison's retirement near Chelsea; then came to town; got home early, and begun a letter to the *Tatler* about the corruptions of style and writing, &c. and having not heard from you, am resolved this letter shall go to-night. Lord Wharton was sent for to town in mighty haste, by the duke of Devonshire[6]: they have some project in hand; but it will not do, for every hour we expect

[1] Dryden Leach. *See* Letter VII., Oct. 26, 1710.
[2] Educated at Trinity Hall, Cambridge, where he took the degree of Bachelor of Arts, Mr. Pate became an eminent woollen-draper, lived opposite the Royal Exchange, and was known as "the learned tradesman." He died in 1746, and was buried at Lee, in Kent; Swift composed an epitaph on him.—D. L. P.
[3] Versions later than D. S. say "Thursday."
[4] James Brydges (1673–1744), afterwards successively baron and duke of Chandos.
[5] Charles Talbot (1660–1718) twelfth Earl and only Duke of Shrewsbury. He was a Whig who became Tory.
[6] William Cavendish (*c.* 1673–1729), the second Duke, a stanch Whig.

a thorough revolution, and that the Parliament will be dissolved. When you see Joe, tell him lord Wharton is too busy to mind any of his affairs; but I will get what good offices I can from Mr. Addison, and will write to-day to Mr. Pratt; and bid Joe not to be discouraged, for I am confident he will get the money under any government; but he must have patience.

19. I have been scribbling this morning, and I believe shall hardly fill this side to-day, but send it as it is; and it is good enough for naughty girls that won't write to a body, and to a good boy like Presto. I thought to have sent this to-night, but was kept by company, and could not; and, to say the truth, I had a little mind to expect one post more for a letter from MD. Yesterday at noon died the earl of Anglesey,[1] the great support of the Tories; so that employment of vice-treasurer of Ireland is again vacant. We were to have been great friends, and I could hardly have a loss that could grieve me more. The bishop of Durham[2] died the same day. The Duke of Ormond's daughter was to visit me to-day at a third place by way of advance, and I am to return it to-morrow.[3] I have had a letter from lady Berkeley, begging me for charity to come to Berkeley-castle, for company to my lord,[4] who has been ill of a dropsy; but I cannot go, and must send my excuse to-morrow. I am told, that in a few hours there will be more removals.

20. To day I returned my visits to the duke's daughters;[5] the insolent drabs came up to my very mouth to salute me; then I heard the report confirmed of removals; my lord-president Somers; the duke of Devonshire, lord-steward; and Mr. Boyle,[6]

[1] John Annesley, Earl of Anglesey, succeeded his brother James, Sept. 19, 1701. He was Joint Vice-Treasurer of Ireland.

[2] "It was not the Bishop of Durham, but of St. David's (Dr. George Bull), who died that day. He had been Archdeacon of Llandaff, and was raised to the prelacy, April 29, 1705." So says Nichols; but Mr. Aitken points out that the Bishop of Durham was dead months before this. It was probably only a rumour that Swift heard.

[3] Swift, in a letter to Miss Hoadley dated in 1734, says: "When I lived in England, once every year I issued out an edict, commanding that all ladies of wit, sense, merit, and quality, who had an ambition to be acquainted with me, should make the first advances at their peril." In this spirit was conceived the *Capitulation* with the unlucky beauty, Mrs. Long.—D. L. P.

[4] Charles Berkeley (1649–1710), second Earl of Berkeley, married (1677) Elizabeth, daughter of Baptist, third Viscount Campden. She died 1719.

[5] The Duke of Ormond's: the ladies Betty and Mary Butler. Lady Betty, says Mr. Aitken, died unmarried in 1750. As to Lady Mary, who was the younger: *see post*, Letter VII., Oct. 20.

[6] Henry Boyle, youngest son of Lord Clifford of Lanesborough, and Secretary of State for the Northern Department from 1708. Also Lord-Treasurer of Ireland; became Baron Carleton (1714). Died 1725.

secretary of state, are all turned out to-day. I never remember such bold steps taken by a Court: I am almost shocked at it, though I did not care if they were all hanged. We are astonished why the Parliament is not yet dissolved, and why they keep a matter of that importance to the last. We shall have a strange Winter here between the struggles of a cunning provoked discarded party, and the triumphs of one in power; of both which I shall be an indifferent spectator, and return very peaceably to Ireland, when I have done my part in the affair I am entrusted with, whether it succeeds or no. To-morrow I change my lodgings in Pall-mall for one in Bury-street,[1] where I suppose I shall continue while I stay in London. If any thing happens to-morrow I will add it.—Robin's Coffee-house.[2] We have great news just now from Spain; Madrid taken, and Pampeluna.[3] I am here ever interrupted.

21. I have just received your letter, which I will not answer now; God be thanked all things are so well. I find you have not yet had my second: I had a letter from Parvisol, who tells me he gave Mrs. Walls a bill of twenty pounds for me, to be given to you; but you have not sent it. This night the Parliament is dissolved: great news from Spain; king Charles and Stanhope are at Madrid, and count Staremberg has taken Pampeluna. Farewel. This is from St. James's Coffee-house. I will begin my answer to your letter to-night; but not send it this week. Pray tell me whether you like this journal way of writing.—I don't like your reasons for not going to Trim. Parvisol tells me he can sell your horse; sell it with a pox? Pray let him know that he shall sell his soul as soon. What? sell any thing that Stella loves, and may sometimes ride? It is hers, and let her do as she pleases: pray let him know this by the first that you know goes to Trim. Let him sell my grey, and be hanged.

LETTER IV

London, *Sept.* 21, 1710.

HERE must I begin another letter, on a whole sheet, for fear sawcy little MD should be angry, and think *much* that the paper is too *little*. I had your letter this night, as I told you just and no more in my last; for this must be taken up in answering

[1] St. James's.

[2] Robin's, or Robins's, was one of the coffee-houses in 'Change Alley, in the City. (Defoe.) It was of a higher class than Garraway's.

[3] The War of the Spanish Succession was just then drawing near its close.

yours, saucebox. I believe I told you where I dined to-day; and to-morrow I go out of town for two days to dine with the same company on Sunday; Molesworth the Florence envoy,[1] Stratford, and some others. I heard to-day that a gentlewoman from lady Giffard's house had been at the Coffee-house to enquire for me. It was Stella's mother, I suppose. I shall send her a penny-post letter[2] to-morrow, and contrive to see her without hazarding seeing lady Giffard, which I will not do until she begs my pardon.

22. I dined to-day at Hampstead with lady Lucy, &c. and when I got home found a letter from Joe, with one inclosed to lord Wharton, which I will send to his excellency, and second it as well as I can; but to talk of getting the queen's order, is a jest. Things are in such a combustion here, that I am advised not to meddle yet in the affair I am upon, which concerns the clergy of a whole kingdom; and does he think any body will trouble the queen about Joe? We shall, I hope, get a recommendation from the lord lieutenant to the trustees for the linen business, and I hope that will do; and so I will write to him in a few days, and he must have patience. This is an answer to part of your letter as well as his. I lied, it is to-morrow I go to the country, and I won't answer a bit more of your letter yet.

23. Here is such a stir and bustle with this little MD of ours; I must be writing every night; I can't go to-bed without a word to them; I can't put out my candle till I have bid them good night: O Lord, O Lord! Well, I dined the first time, to-day, with Will Frankland and his Fortune: she is not very handsome. Did I not say I would go out of town to-day; I hate lying abroad and clutter; I go to-morrow in Frankland's chariot, and come back at night. Lady Berkeley[3] has invited me to Berkeley-castle, and lady Betty Germain[4] to Drayton in Northamptonshire, and I'll go to neither. Let me alone, I must finish my pamphlet. I have sent a long letter to Bickerstaff:

---

[1] John Molesworth (1679-1725-6), envoy extraordinary from Queen Anne to the Grand Duke of Tuscany; afterwards from King George I., in 1720, to the King of Sardinia; and again to the States of Venice and Switzerland. A Commissioner of the Stamp Office. He became second Viscount Molesworth in May 1725, and died on the 17th of the following February.

[2] From 1680, there was a penny post (postage payable on delivery) for London and suburbs, apart from the General Post Office business. There were hourly collections, and six to ten deliveries a day.

[3] Lady of the Earl of Berkeley, to whom Swift was chaplain, and for a time private secretary, during his Lieutenancy in Ireland.—D. L. P.

[4] Lady Elizabeth Germain (1680-1769) second daughter of second Earl of Berkeley, and second wife of Sir John Germain, a soldier of fortune.

let the bishop of Clogher smoak it if he can.[1] Well, I'll write to the bishop of Killala; but you might have told him how sudden and unexpected my journey was though. Deuce take lady S——; and if I know D——y, he is a rawboned-faced fellow, not handsome, nor visibly so young as you say: she sacrifices two thousand pounds a year, and keeps only six hundred. Well, you have had all my land journey in my second letter, and so much for that. So you have got into Presto's lodgings; very fine, truly! We have had a fortnight of the most glorious weather on earth, and still continues: I hope you have made the best of it. Ballygall [2] will be a pure good place for air, if Mrs. Ashe makes good her promise. Stella writes like an emperor: I am afraid it hurts your eyes; take care of that pray, pray Mrs. Stella. Can't you do what you will with your own horse? Pray don't let that puppy Parvisol sell him. Patrick is drunk about three times a week, and I bear it, and he has got the better of me; but one of these days I will positively turn him off to the wide world, when none of you are by to intercede for him.—Stuff—how can I get her husband into the Charter-house? get, a —— into the Charter-house.[3]—Write constantly! Why, sirrah, don't I write every day, and sometimes twice a day to MD? Now I have answered all your letter, and the rest must be as it can be: send me my bill. Tell Mrs. Brent [4] what I say of the Charter-house. I think this enough for one night; and so farewel till this time to-morrow.

24. To-day I dined six miles out of town at Will Pate's, with Stratford, Frankland, and the Molesworth's,[5] and came home at night, and was weary and lazy. I can say no more now, but good night.

25. I was so lazy to-day that I dined at next door,[6] and have sat at home since six, writing to the bishop of Clogher, dean Sterne, and Mr. Manley: the last, because I am in fear

---

[1] *Tatler*, No. 230 (see *ante, Journal* Sept. 18). *Smoke* = notice or understand.

[2] A townland and estate in the eastern part of Finglas parish, of which the Rev. Dillon Ashe, younger brother of the Bishop of Clogher, was vicar; 3½ miles north of Dublin city. Francis Elrington Ball states that Ballygall House was occupied by Thomas Ashe, the bishop's elder brother —a comical diminutive person with the family weakness for punning, of which more hereafter.

[3] Swift is here abruptly disposing of the paragraphs of Stella's letter lying before him.

[4] The doctor's housekeeper.—D. S.

[5] Possibly John (mentioned on the 21st) in company with Richard Molesworth.

[6] This must have been at Mrs. Vanhomrigh's.—D. S.

for him about his place, and have sent him my opinion, what
I and his other friends here think he ought to do. I hope he
will take it well. My advice was, To keep as much in favour as
possible with sir Thomas Frankland, his master here.

26. Smoak how I widen the margin by lying in bed when
I write. My bed lies on the wrong side for me, so that I am
forced often to write when I am up. Manley you must know
has had people putting in for his place already; and has been
complained of for opening letters. Remember that last Sunday,
September 24, 1710, was as hot as Midsummer. This was written
in the morning; 'tis now night, and Presto in bed. Here's a
clutter, I have gotten MD's second letter, and I must answer it
here. I gave the Bill to Tooke, and so—Well, I dined to-day
with sir John Holland the comptroller, and sat with him till
eight; then came home and sent my letters, and writ a part of
a lampoon,[1] which goes on very slow, and now I am writing
to sawcy MD; no wonder, indeed, good boys must write to
naughty girls. I han't seen your mother yet; my penny-post
letter, I suppose, miscarried: I will write another. Mr. S——
came to see me; and said M—— was going to the country
next morning with her husband (who I find is a surly brute)
so I could only desire my service to her.

27. To-day all our company dined at Will Frankland's, with
Steele and Addison too. This is the first rainy day since I came
to town; I can't afford to answer your letter yet. Morgan,[2] the
puppy, writ me a long letter to desire I would recommend him
for purse-bearer or secretary to the next lord-chancellor that
would come with the next governor. I will not answer him;
but beg you will say these words to his father Raymond,[3] or
any body that will tell him: That Dr. Swift has received his
letter, and would be very ready to serve him, but cannot do
it in what he desires, because he has no sort of interest in the
persons to be applied to. These words you may write, and let
Joe, or Mr. Warburton,[4] give them to him: a pox on him!
However, 'tis by these sort of ways that fools get preferment.
I must not end yet, because I can't say good night without
losing a line, and then MD would scold; but now, good night.

[1] A satire on Godolphin, the fallen Treasurer, called *The Virtues of Sid
Hamet the Magician's Rod*, referring to his disrespectful breaking of his
staff.—D. L. P.
[2] Mr. Aitken suggests Marcus Antonius Morgan of Kilstrope, steward
to the Bishop of Kildare.
[3] Dr. Raymond is only called his father, because he espoused Mr.
Morgan's interest with all his power.—D. S.
[4] Swift's curate at Laracor.

28. I have the finest piece of Brazil tobacco for Dingley that ever was born.[1] You talk of Leigh; why he won't be in Dublin these two months: he goes to the country, then returns to London, to see how the world goes here in Parliament. Good night, sirrahs; no, no, not night; I writ this in the morning, and looking carelessly I thought it had been of last night. I dined to day with Mrs. Barton [2] alone at her lodgings, where she told me for certain that lady S—— was with child when she was last in England, and pretended a tympany, and saw every body; then disappeared for three weeks, her tympany was gone, and she looked like a ghost, &c. No wonder she married when she was so ill at containing. Conolly is out,[3] and Mr. Roberts in his place, who loses a better here, but was formerly a commissioner in Ireland. That employment cost Conolly three thousand pounds to lord Wharton [4]; so he has made one ill bargain in his life.

29. I wish MD a merry Michaelmas. I dined with Mr. Addison, and Jervas the painter, at Addison's country place; and then came home, and writ more to my lampoon. I made a *Tatler* since I came: guess which it is, and whether the bishop of Clogher smoaks it. I saw Mr. Sterne [5] to-day: he will do as you order, and I will give him chocolate for Stella's health. He goes not these three weeks. I wish I could send it some other way. So now to your letter, brave boys. I don't like your way of saving shillings: nothing vexes me but that it does not make Stella a coward in a coach.[6] I don't think any lady's advice about my ear signifies two-pence: however I will, in compliance to you, ask Dr. Cockburn. Radcliffe [7] I know not, and Bernard [8] I never see. Walls [9] will certainly be stingier

---

[1] This must not be construed as showing that Rebecca Dingley was a smoker. Ladies made their own snuff; a "rasp" for this purpose was a present suitable for a lady. *See* Letters: XXI., April 17; XXIV., June 7 (note), and XXXIII., Nov. 3 —— 1711.

[2] *See* Letter III., Sept. 13 (note to "Mrs. Long").

[3] A Commissioner of the Revenue, and afterwards Speaker.

[4] Who, in his Lord Lieutenancy, took gratuities on preferments and all possible occasions.

[5] Enoch Sterne, collector of Wicklow and clerk to the House of Lords in Ireland. It is not clear whether he was nearly related to Dean Sterne.

[6] In his memorandum on the death of Stella, Swift mentions that she never showed any alarm in a coach—whether this throws any light on the text the reader must judge.

[7] John Radcliffe (1650–1714), M.D.; M.P. for Bramber 1690–95, and for Buckinghamshire from 1713. Attended royal family, but was a professed Jacobite.

[8] Charles Bernard (1650–1711), surgeon; surgeon-general to Queen Anne, and Master of the Barber-Surgeons' Company (1703). Called *Barnard* in Letter XVIII., March 19, 1710-11, &c.   [9] Archdeacon.—N.

for seven years, upon pretence of his robbery. So Stella puns again; why, 'tis well enough; but I'll not second it, though I could make a dozen: I never thought of a pun since I left Ireland. —Bishop of Clogher's bill? Why, he paid it me; do you think I was such a fool to go without it? As for the four shillings, I will give you a bill on Parvisol for it on t'other side this paper; and pray tear off the two letters I shall write to him and Joe, or let Dingley transcribe and send them; though that to Parvisol, I believe, he must have my hand for. No, no, I'll eat no grapes; I ate about six t'other day at sir John Holland's; but would not give six-pence for a thousand, they are so bad this year. Yes, faith, I hope in God Presto and MD will be together this time twelvemonth: What then? Last year I suppose I was at Laracor; but next I hope to eat my Michaelmas goose at my two little gooses' lodgings. I drink no *aile* (I suppose you mean *ale*) but yet good wine every day, of five and six shillings a bottle. O Lord, how much Stella writes: pray don't carry that too far, young women, but be temperate to hold out. To-morrow I go to Mr. Harley.[1] Why; small hopes from the duke of Ormond: he loves me very well, I believe, and would, in my turn, give me something to make me easy; and I have good interest among his best friends. But I don't think of any thing further than the business I am upon: you see I writ to Manley before I had your letter, and I fear he will be out. Yes, Mrs. Owl, Blighe's corpse [2] came to Chester when I was there, and I told you so in my letter, or forgot it. I lodge in Bury-street, where I removed a week ago. I have the first floor, a dining-room, and bed-chamber, at eight shillings a week; plaguy deep, but I spend nothing for eating, never go to a tavern, and very seldom in a coach; yet after all it will be expensive. Why do you trouble yourself, Mistress Stella, about my *instrument*? I have the same the archbishop gave me; and it is as good now the bishops are away. The dean friendly; the dean be poxt: a great piece of friendship indeed, what you heard him tell the bishop of Clogher; I wonder he had the face to talk so: but he lent me money, and that's enough. Faith I would not send this these four days, only for writing to Joe and Parvisol. Tell the dean, that when the bishops send me any pacquets, they must not write to me at Mr. Steele's; but direct for Mr. Steele, at his office at the Cockpit; and let the inclosed

[1] The celebrated Robert Harley, afterwards Earl of Oxford.
[2] The Rt. Hon. Thomas Bligh, P.C., of Rathmore, co. Meath, M.P. 1704; died aged 56 on Aug. 28, 1710.

be directed for me: that mistake cost me eighteen-pence t'other day.

30. I dined with Stratford to-day, but am not to see Mr. Harley till Wednesday: 'tis late, and I send this before there is occasion for the bell; because I would have Joe have his letter, and Parvisol too; which you must so contrive as not to cost them double postage. I can say no more, but that I am, etc.

LETTER V

London, *Sept.* 30, 1710.

HAN'T I brought myself into a fine *premunire* [1] to begin writing letters in whole sheets, and now I dare not leave it off. I can't tell whether you like these journal letters: I believe they would be dull to me to read them over; but, perhaps, little MD is pleased to know how Presto passes his time in her absence. I always begin my last the same day I ended my former. I told you where I dined to-day at a tavern with Stratford: Lewis,[2] who is a great favourite of Harley's, was to have been with us; but he was hurried to Hampton-court, and sent his excuse; and that next Wednesday he would introduce me to Harley. 'Tis good to see what a lamentable confession the Whigs all make me of my ill usage: but I mind them not. I am already represented to Harley as a discontented person, that was used ill for not being Whig enough; and I hope for good usage from him. The Tories dryly tell me, I may make my fortune, if I please; but I do not understand them, or rather, I do understand them.

Oct. 1. To-day I dined at Molesworth's, the Florence envoy: and sat this evening with my friend Darteneuf,[3] whom you have heard me talk of; the greatest punner of this town next myself. Have you smoakt the *Tatler* that I writ [4]? It is much liked here, and I think it is a pure one. To-morrow I go with Delaval [5] the Portugal envoy, to dine with Lord Halifax [6] near

---

[1] A *Præmunire* was a Papal writ, overriding native jurisdiction—hence, colloquially, any formidable liability.

[2] Erasmus Lewis, secretary to the Earl of Dartmouth.

[3] This gentleman, whose name was spelt Dartiquenave, is mentioned, on account of his taste for good eating, by Mr. Pope, in his imitation of the second Epistle of the Second Book of Horace, verse 87: "When Oldfield loves what Dartineuf detests."—B. He was Paymaster of the Board of Works, and died 1737.—D. L. P.

[4] No. 230.

[5] Mr. Aitken gives his name as Captain George Delaval.

[6] Charles Montagu (1661-1715), made Baron Halifax in 1700 and Earl in 1714.

Hampton-court. Your Manley's brother,[1] a parliament-man here, has gotten an employment; and I am informed uses much interest to preserve his brother and, to-day, I spoke to the elder Frankland to engage his father, (post-master here) and I hope he will be safe, although he is cruelly hated by all the Tories of Ireland. I have almost finished my lampoon, and will print it for revenge on a certain great person.[2] It has cost me but three shillings in meat and drink since I came here, as thin as the town is. I laugh to see myself so disengaged in these revolutions. Well, I must leave off and go write to sir John Stanley,[3] to desire him to engage lady Hyde, as my mistress to engage lord Hyde,[4] in favour of Mr. Pratt.

2. Lord Halifax was at Hampton-court at his lodgings, and I dined with him there with Methuen,[5] and Delaval, and the late attorney-general.[6] I went to the drawing-room before dinner, (for the queen was at Hampton-court) and expected to see *nobody*; but I met acquaintance enough. I walked in the gardens, saw the cartons of Raphael, and other things, and with great difficulty got from lord Halifax, who would have kept me to-morrow to show me his house and park, and improvements. We left Hampton-court at sun-set, and got here in a chariot and two horses time enough by star-light. That's something charms me mightily about London; that you go dine a dozen miles off in October, stay all day, and return so quickly: you cannot do any thing like this in Dublin.[7] I writ a second penny-post letter to your mother, and hear nothing of her. Did I tell you that earl Berkeley [8] died last Sunday was se'n-night, at Berkeley-castle, of a dropsy? Lord Halifax began a health to me to-day: it was the Resurrection of the Whigs, which I refused unless he would add their Reformation too:

---

[1] This "parliament-man" is supposed to have been that cousin of Mrs. Manley, author of the *New Atalantis*, who inveigled her into a false marriage: John Manley of Truro, M.P. for Bossiney, Cornwall, 1701–1708, and for Camelford 1708–1710. Died 1714.

[2] The Earl of Godolphin.—D. S.

[3] Said by Mr. Aitken to be Sir John Stanley, Bart., of Northend, Commissioner of Customs, who married a niece of the Earl of Bath.

[4] Henry (1672–1753) only son of Laurence Hyde, first "Hyde" Earl of Rochester. He afterwards (1711) became last Earl of Rochester, and finally (1724) last Earl of Clarendon.

[5] Sir Paul Methuen, our ambassador at Lisbon, negotiator (in 1703) of the commercial treaty with Portugal, known by his name, which was abrogated in 1836.—D. L. P.

[6] Sir James Montagu (1666–1723), afterwards chief baron of the Exchequer.

[7] When this letter was written there were no turnpike roads in Ireland.

[8] *See* Letter III., Sept. 19. Swift wrote an epitaph.

and I told him he was the only Whig in England I loved, or had any good opinion of.

3. This morning Stella's sister[1] came to me with a letter from her mother, who is at Sheene; but will soon be in town, and will call to see me: she gave me a bottle of palsy water,[2] a small one, and desired I would send it you by the first convenience, as I will; and she promises a quart bottle of the same: your sister lookt very well, and seems a good modest sort of girl. I went then to Mr. Lewis, first secretary to lord Dartmouth,[3] and favourite to Mr. Harley, who is to introduce me to-morrow morning. Lewis had with him one Mr. Dyet,[4] a justice of peace, worth twenty thousand pounds, a commissioner of the stamp-office, and married to a sister of sir Philip Meadows,[5] envoy to the emperor. I tell you this, because it is odds but this Mr. Dyet will be hanged; for he is discovered to have counterfeited stampt paper, in which he was a commissioner; and, with his accomplices, has cheated the queen of a hundred thousand pounds.[6] You will hear of it before this come to you, but may be not so particularly; and it is a very odd accident in such a man. Smoak Presto writing news to MD. I dined to-day with Lord Mountjoy at Kensington, and walked from thence this evening to town like an emperor. Remember that yesterday, October 2, was a cruel hard frost, with ice; and six days ago I was dying with heat. As thin as the town is, I have more dinners than ever, and am asked this month by some people, without being able to come for pre-engagements. Well, but I should write plainer, when I consider Stella can't read,[7] and Dingley is not so skilful at my ugly hand. I had, to-night, a letter from Mr. Pratt, who tells me, Joe will have his money when there are trustees appointed by the lord lieutenant for receiving and disposing the linen fund;

[1] Ann Johnson, Esther's younger sister. She appears to have married one Filby.

[2] Cowslips used to be called palsy-wort (*Oxford Dict.*); so the suggestion that palsy-water was an infusion of cowslips is perhaps right.

[3] William Legge (1672–1750), second Baron and first Earl of Dartmouth. He was already Secretary of State for the Southern Department.

[4] Should be "Dyot."

[5] The successor of Milton as Latin secretary to Oliver Cromwell, and Cromwell's representative at the ratification of the treaty with Portugal at Lisbon, etc. Afterwards ambassador of the Commonwealth to Sweden. Born 1626; died 1718.

[6] Richard Dyot was tried at the Old Bailey, Jan. 13, 1710-11; and was acquitted; but on the 15th, a bill of indictment was found against him for a high misdemeanour.—N.

[7] Owing to the weakness of her sight, so often alluded to in the same manner in the *Journal*.

and whenever those trustees are appointed, I will solicit whoever is lord lieutenant, and am in no fear of succeeding. So
pray tell or write him word, and bid him not be cast down; for
Ned Southwell[1] and Mr. Addison both think Pratt in the right.
Do not lose your money at Manley's to-night, sirrahs.

4. After I had put out my candle last night, my landlady
came into my room, with a servant of lord Halifax, to desire
I would go dine with him at his house near Hampton-court;
but I sent him word I had business of great importance that
hindered me, &c. And, to-day, I was brought privately to Mr.
Harley, who received me with the greatest respect and kindness
imaginable: he has appointed me an hour on Saturday at four,
afternoon, when I will open my business to him; which expression I would not use if I were a woman. I know you smoakt it;
but I did not till I writ it. I dined to-day at Mr. Delaval's, the
envoy for Portugal, with Nic. Rowe[2] the poet, and other
friends; and I gave my lampoon to be printed. I have more
mischief in my heart; and I think it shall go round with them
all, as this hits, and I can find hints. I am certain I answered
your 2d letter, and yet I do not find it here. I suppose it was
in my 4th; and why N. 2d, 3d; is it not enough to say, as I do,
1, 2, 3? &c. I am going to work at another *Tatler*[3]: I'll be far
enough but I say the same thing over two or three times, just
as I do when I am talking to little MD; but what care I? they
can read it as easily as I can write it: I think I have brought
these lines pretty straight again. I fear it will be long before
I finish two sides at this rate. Pray, dear MD, when I occasionally give you any little commission mixt with my letters, don't
forget it, as that to Morgan and Joe, &c. for I write just as I
can remember, otherwise I would put them all together. I was
to visit Mr. Sterne to-day, and gave him your commission about
handkerchiefs: that of chocolate I will do myself, and send it
him when he goes, and you'll pay me when *the givers bread*,
&c.[4] To-night I will read a pamphlet, to amuse myself. God
preserve your dear healths.

5. This morning Delaval came to see me, and we went together

[1] Edward, son of Sir John Southwell, was the Duke of Ormond's secretary, and long known to Swift—as Sir John had been a friend of Sir
William Temple's.
[2] Nicholas Rowe, the dramatist, who had already produced *The
Ambitious Stepmother, Tamerlane, The Fair Penitent*, etc. He was made
Poet-Laureate on the accession of George I.; died in 1718; and was buried
in Westminster Abbey.—D. L. P.
[3] No. 238.
[4] Quotation (if it is a quotation) not traced.

to Kneller's,[1] who was not in town. In the way we met the electors for parliament-men: and the rabble came about our coach, crying A Colt, a Stanhope, &c. we were afraid of a dead cat, or our glasses broken, and so were always of their side.[2] I dined again at Delaval's; and in the evening at the Coffee-house, heard sir Andrew Fountain [*i.e.* Fountaine [3]] was come to town. This has been but an insipid sort of day, and I have nothing to remark upon it worth three-pence: I hope MD had a better, with the dean, the bishop,[4] or Mrs. Walls. Why, the reason you lost four and eight-pence last night but one at Manley's, was because you played bad games: I took notice of six that you had ten to one against you: Would any but a mad lady go out twice upon Manilio, Basto, and two small diamonds? Then in that game of spades, you blundered when you had ten-ace; I never saw the like of you: and now you are in a huff because I tell you this. Well, here's two and eight-pence half-penny towards your loss.

6. Sir Andrew Fountain came this morning, and caught me writing in bed. I went into the city with him; and we dined at the Chop-house with Will Pate, the learned woollen-draper: then we sauntered at china-shops and booksellers; went to the tavern, drank two pints of white wine, and never parted till ten: and now I am come home, and must copy out some papers I intend for Mr. Harley, whom I am to see, as I told you, to-morrow afternoon; so that this night I shall say little to MD, but that I heartily wish myself with them, and will come as soon as I either fail, or compass my business. We now hear daily of elections; and, in a list I saw yesterday of about twenty, there are seven or eight more Tories than in the last Parliament; so that I believe they need not fear a majority, with the help of those who will vote as the Court pleases. But I have been told, that Mr. Harley himself would not let the Tories be too numerous, for fear they should be insolent, and kick against him; and for that reason they have kept several Whigs in employments, who expected to be turned out every day; as

[1] Sir Godfrey Kneller's, the painter.—D. S.

[2] [*Cf.* Mr. Pickwick at Eatanswill.] There was a close contest in Westminster between Mr. Medlicot and Mr. Cross for the High Church Party, and General Stanhope and Sir Henry Dutton Colt for the Whigs; the Tory intimidated the Whig electors, and gave the Ministerial candidates a great majority.—D. L. P.

[3] Of Narford, Norfolk (1676-1753) virtuoso, knighted by William III. He died a bachelor.

[4] The Bishop of Meath, where Laracor is situate, was William Moreton, who is mentioned later in the *Journal*. He is probably the bishop referred to here.

sir John Holland the comptroller, and many others. And so get you gone to your cards, and your claret and orange, at the dean's,[1] and I'll go write.

7. I wonder when this letter will be finished: it must go by Tuesday, that's certain; and if I have one from MD before, I will not answer it, that's as certain too! 'Tis now morning, and I did not finish my papers for Mr. Harley last night; for you must understand Presto was sleepy, and made blunders and blots. Very pretty that I must be writing to young women in a morning fresh and fasting, faith. Well, good morrow to you; and so I go to business, and lay aside this paper till night, sirrahs.— At night. Jack How [*i.e.* Howe [2]] told Harley, that if there were a lower place in Hell than another, it was reserved for his porter, who tells lies so gravely, and with so civil a manner. This porter I have had to deal with, going this evening at four to visit Mr. Harley, by his own appointment. But the fellow told me no lie, though I suspected every word he said. He told me, his master was just gone to dinner, with much company, and desired I would come an hour hence, which I did, expecting to hear Mr. Harley was gone out; but they had just done dinner. Mr. Harley came out to me, brought me in, and presented me to his son-in-law, lord Doblane [3] (or some such name) and his own son,[4] and, among others, Will Penn the quaker [5]: we sat two hours drinking as good wine as you do; and two hours more he and I alone; where he heard me tell my business; entered into it with all kindness; askt for my powers, and read them; and read likewise a memorial [6] I had drawn up, and put it in his pocket to show the queen; told me the measures he would take; and, in short, said every thing I could wish: told me he must bring Mr. St. John (secretary of state) [7] and

[1] Dr. Sterne.—N.

[2] John Grubham Howe (1652–1722), an extreme Tory; privy councillor, 1702; a paymaster of the Guards and home garrison, 1702–3; joint clerk to the privy council, 1708. His heir was the first Lord Chedworth.

[3] George Henry Hay (*d.* 1758), eldest son of sixth Earl of Kinnoul; Viscount Dupplin, 1709–1719; M.P. for Fowey, 1710; made Baron Hay of Pedwardine in peerage of U.K., 1711; at this time a teller of the Exchequer. He married, about 1709, Abigail, second daughter of "the famous" Robert Harley; she died 1750. In 1719 he became seventh Earl of Kinnoul.

[4] Edward Harley (1689–1741), afterwards successively Lord Harley and second Earl of Oxford, who completed the collection of the "Harleian MSS."

[5] The celebrated founder of the colony of Pennsylvania was in great favour with Queen Anne, and often at Court. He died 1718.

[6] About the First-Fruits.

[7] For the Northern Department. Afterwards the celebrated Lord Bolingbroke.

me acquainted; and spoke so many things of personal kindness and esteem for me, that I am inclined half to believe what some friends have told me, That he would do every thing to bring me over. He has desired to dine with me (what a comical mistake was that) I mean he has desired me to dine with him on Tuesday; and after four hours being with him, set me down at St. James's Coffee-house, in a hackney-coach. All this is odd and comical, if you consider him and me. He knew my Christian name very well. I could not forbear saying thus much upon this matter, although you will think it tedious. But I'll tell you; you must know, 'tis fatal to me[1] to be a scoundrel and a prince the same day: for being to see him at four, I could not engage myself to dine at any friend's; so I went to Tooke, to give him a ballad and dine with him; but he was not at home: so I was forced to go to a blind chophouse,[2] and dine for ten-pence upon gill-ale,[3] bad broth, and three chops of mutton; and then go reeking from thence to the first minister of state. And now I am going in charity to send Steele a *Tatler*, who is very low of late. I think I am civiller than I used to be; and have not used the expression of (*you in* Ireland) and (*we in* England),[4] as I did when I was here before, to your great indignation. —— They may talk of the *you know what*[5]; but, gad, if it had not been for that, I should never have been able to get the access I have had; and if that helps me to succeed, then that *same thing* will be serviceable to the church. But how far we must depend upon new friends, I have learnt by long practice, though I think among great ministers, they are just as good as old ones. And so I think this important day has made a great hole in this side of the paper; and the fiddle faddles of to-morrow and Monday will make up the rest; and, besides, I shall see Harley on Tuesday before this letter goes.

8. I must tell you a great piece of refinement[6] of Harley. He charged me to come to him often: I told him I was loth to trouble him in so much business as he had, and desired I might have leave to come at his levee; which he immediately

---

[1] *I.e.* it is fated for me.

[2] "Blind" = out-of-the-way (*Oxford Dict.*).

[3] Malt-liquor medicated with ground-ivy (*Chelidonium*) is called "gill" by Johnson's Dictionary.

[4] Parentheses twice used as quotation-marks.

[5] *The Tale of a Tub.*—See first note to Letter II.

[6] An excessive or extravagant compliment, or a form of expression intended to impose on the hearer—in which art of statecraft Harley was an adept.—D. L. P.

refused, and said, That was not a place for friends to come to. Tis now but morning, and I have got a foolish trick, I must say something to MD when I wake, and wish them a good morrow; for this is not a shaving-day, Sunday, so I have time enough: but get you gone, you rogues, I must go write: yes, 'twill vex me to the blood if any of these long letters should miscarry: if they do, I will shrink to half sheets again; but then what will you do to make up the journal? there will be ten days of Presto's life lost; and that will be a sad thing, faith and troth.—At night. I was at a loss to-day for a dinner, unless I would have gone a great way, so I dined with some friends that board hereabout, as a spunger; and this evening sir Andrew Fountain would needs have me go to the tavern, where, for two bottles of wine, Portugal and Florence, among three of us, we had sixteen shillings to pay; but if ever he catches me so again, I'll spend as many pounds: and therefore I have put it among my extraordinaries: but we had a neck of mutton dressed *à la Maintenon*, that the dog could not eat: and it is now twelve o'clock, and I must go sleep. I hope this letter will go before I have MD's third. Do you believe me? and yet, faith, I long for MD's third too: and yet I would have it to say, that I write five for two. I am not fond at all of St. James's Coffee-house, as I used to be. I hope it will mend in winter; but now they are all out of town at elections, or not come from their country houses. Yesterday I was going with Dr. Garth[1] to dine with Charles Main,[2] near the Tower, who has an employment there: he is of Ireland; the bishop of Clogher knows him well: an honest goodnatured fellow, a thorough hearty laugher, mightily beloved by the men of wit: his mistress is never above a cook maid. And so, good night, &c.

9. I dined to-day at sir John Stanley's; my lady Stanley is one of my favourites; I have as many here as the bishop of Killala has in Ireland. I am thinking what scurvy company I shall be to MD when I come back: they know every thing of me already: I will tell you no more, or I shall have nothing to say, no story to tell, nor any kind of thing. I was very uneasy last night with ugly, nasty, filthy wine, that turned sour on my stomach. I must go to the tavern: oh, but I told you that before. To-morrow I dine at Harley's, and will finish this letter at my return; but I can write no more now, because of the

[1] Sir Samuel Garth, author of *The Dispensary*.
[2] Mr. Aitken says he was Charles Main, a fat man mentioned in a verse by Gay.

archbishop: faith 'tis true; for I am going now to write to him an account of what I have done in the business with Harley: and faith, young women, I'll tell you what you must count upon, that I never will write one word on the third side in these long letters.

10. Poor MD's letter was lying so huddled up among papers I could not find it: I mean poor Presto's letter. Well, I dined with Mr. Harley to-day, and hope some things will be done; but I must say no more: and this letter must be sent to the post-house, and not by the bell-man. I am to dine again there on Sunday next; I hope to some good issue. And so now, soon as ever I can in bed, I must begin my 6th to MD as gravely as if I had not written a word this month: fine doings, faith. Methinks I don't write as I should, because I am not in bed: see the ugly wide lines. God Almighty ever bless you, &c.

Faith, this is a whole treatise; I'll go reckon the lines on t'other sides. I've reckoned them.[1]

LETTER VI

London, *Oct.* 10, 1710.

So as I told you just now in the letter I sent half an hour ago, I dined with Mr. Harley to-day, who presented me to the attorney-general sir Simon Harcourt, with much compliment on all sides, &c. Harley told me he had shown my memorial to the queen, and seconded it very heartily; and he desires me to dine with him again on Sunday, when he promises to settle it with her majesty, before she names a governor[2]; and I protest I am in hopes it will be done, all but the forms, by that time; for he loves the church: this is a popular thing, and he would not have a governor share in it; and, besides, I am told by all hands, he has a mind to gain me over. But in the letter I writ last post (yesterday) to the archbishop, I did not tell him a syllable of what Mr. Harley said to me last night, because he charged me to keep it secret; so I would not tell it to you, but that before this goes, I hope the secret will be over. I am now writing my poetical *Description of a Shower in London*, and will send it to the *Tatler*.[3] This is the last sheet of a whole quire I have written since I came to town. Pray, now it comes

[1] Seventy-three lines in folio upon one page, and in a very small hand.—D. S.
[2] Lord Lieutenant of Ireland.
[3] No. 238.

into my head, will you, when you go to Mrs. Walls, contrive to know whether Mrs. Wesley be in town, and still at her brother's, and how she is in health, and whether she stays in town. I writ to her from Chester, to know what I should do with her note; and I believe the poor woman is afraid to write to me: so I must go to my business, &c.

11. To-day at last I dined with lord Montrath,[1] and carried lord Mountjoy and sir Andrew Fountain with me; and was looking over them at ombre till eleven this evening like a fool: they played running ombre half crowns; and sir Andrew Fountain won eight guineas of Mr. Coote [2]: so I am come home late, and will say but little to MD this night. I have gotten half a bushel of coals, and Patrick, the extravagant whelp, had a fire ready for me; but I pickt off the coals before I went to-bed. It is a sign London is now an empty place, when it will not furnish me with matter for above five or six lines in a day. Did you smoak in my last how I told you the very day and the place you were playing at ombre? But I interlined and altered a little, after I had received a letter from Mr. Manley, that said you were at it in his house, while he was writing to me; but without his help I guess'd within one day. Your town is certainly much more sociable than ours. I have not seen your mother yet, &c.

12. I dined to-day with Dr. Garth and Mr. Addison, at the Devil tavern, by Temple-bar, and Garth treated; and 'tis well I dine every day, else I should be longer making out my letters: for we are yet in a very dull state, only enquiring every day after new elections, where the Tories carry it among the new members six to one. Mr. Addison's election [3] has passed easy and undisputed; and I believe, if he had a mind to be chosen king, he would hardly be refused. An odd accident has happened at Colchester: one captain Lavallin [4] coming from Flanders or Spain, found his wife with child by a clerk of Doctors Commons, whose trade, you know, it is to prevent fornications: and this clerk was the very same fellow that made the discovery of Dyet's counterfeiting the stamp paper. Lavallin has been this fortnight hunting after the clerk to kill him; but the fellow was constantly employed at the Treasury about the discovery he made: the wife had made a shift to patch up the business,

---

[1] Charles Coote (1680?–1715), fourth Earl of Mountrath.
[2] Henry Coote (1683–1720), afterwards fifth Earl of Mountrath, brother of fourth.
[3] For Malmesbury; *vice* Farrington, deceased.
[4] Mr. Aitken says the name ought to be Lavallée.

alledging that the clerk had told her her husband was dead, and other excuses; but t'other day somebody told Lavallin his wife had intrigues before he married her: upon which he goes down in a rage, shoots his wife through the head, then falls on his sword; and, to make the matter sure, at the same time discharges a pistol through his own head, and died on the spot, his wife surviving him about two hours; but in what circumstances of mind and body is terrible to imagine. I have finished my poem on the *Shower*, all but the beginning, and am going on with my *Tatler*. They have fixt about fifty things on me since I came: I have printed but three. One advantage I get by writing to you daily, or rather you get, is, that I shall remember not to write the same things twice; and yet I fear I have done it often already: but I'll mind and confine myself to the accidents of the day; and so get you gone to ombre, and be good girls, and save your money, and be rich against Presto comes, and write to me now and then: I am thinking it would be a pretty thing to hear sometimes from sawcy MD; but don't hurt your eyes, Stella, I charge you.

13. O Lord, here's but a trifle of my letter written yet; what shall Presto do for prittle prattle to entertain MD? The talk now grows fresher of the duke of Ormond for Ireland, though Mr. Addison says he hears it will be in commission, and lord Gallaway [*i.e.* Galway[1]] one. These letters of mine are a sort of journal, where matters open by degrees; and, as I tell true or false, you will find by the event whether my intelligence be good; but I don't care two-pence whether it be or no.—At night. To-day I was all about St. Paul's, and up at the top like a fool, with sir Andrew Fountain and two more; and spent seven shillings for my dinner like a puppy: this is the second time he has served me so; but I'll never do it again, though all mankind should persuade me, unconsidering puppies! There's a young fellow here in town we are all fond of, and about a year or two come from the university, one Harrison,[2] a little pretty fellow, with a great deal of wit, good sense, and good nature; has written some mighty pretty things; that in your 6th *Miscellanea*, about the Sprig of an Orange, is his: he has

[1] Henry de Massue, Seigneur de Ruvigny (1648–1720), a French Protestant, created Viscount Galway 1692; Earl 1697. He was a general in William's army at Aughrim, where Bourke, the Jacobite Viscount Galway, was slain.

[2] Educated at Winchester, M.A. of New College, Oxford; a man of lively pleasing parts, but no great poet. Thomas Harrison was, by Swift's interest, made secretary to Lord Raby, afterwards Earl Strafford, ambassador at Utrecht.—D. L. P.

nothing to live on but being governor to one of the duke of
Queensbury's sons [1] for forty pounds a year. The fine fellows
are always inviting him to the tavern, and make him pay his
club. Henley [2] is a great crony of his: they are often at the
tavern at six or seven shillings reckoning, and always makes
the poor lad pay his full share. A colonel and a lord were at
him and me the same way to-night: I absolutely refused, and
made Harrison lag behind, and persuaded him not to go to
them. I tell you this, because I find all rich fellows have that
humour of using all people without any consideration of their
fortunes: but I'll see them rot before they shall serve me so.
Lord Halifax is always teazing me to go down to his country
house, which will cost me a guinea to his servants, and twelve
shillings coach hire; and he shall be hanged first. Is not this a
plaguy silly story? But I am vext at the heart; for I love the
young fellow, and am resolved to stir up people to do something
for him: he is a Whig, and I'll put him upon some of my cast
Whigs; for I have done with them, and they have, I hope,
done with this kingdom for our time. They were sure of the
four members for London above all places, and they have lost
three [3] in the four. Sir Richard Onslow,[4] we hear, has lost for
Surry; and they are overthrown in most places. Lookee, gentlewomen, if I write long letters, I must write you news and stuff,
unless I send you my verses; and some I dare not; and those
on the Shower in London I have sent to the *Tatler*,[5] and you
may see them in Ireland. I fancy you'll smoak me in the *Tatler* [6]
I am going to write; for I believe I have told you the hint.
I had a letter sent me to-night from sir Matthew Dudley, and
found it on my table when I came in. Because it is extraordinary
I will transcribe it from beginning to end. It is as follows [Is
the Devil in you? Oct. 13, 1710.][7] I would have answered every

[1] James Douglas (1662-1711), second Duke of Queensberry and Duke of
Dover. He had four sons, and was succeeded by the third.
[2] Anthony Henley, Whig politician and wit: he is the hero of the
ludicrous incident related in the *Spectator*, No. 494.
[3] Sir William Ashurst, Sir Gilbert Heathcote, and Sir John Ward.
They had lost the fourth seat long before this; it was held by Sir William
Withers.
[4] (1654-1717), Speaker of the House of Commons, 1708-1710; first
Baron Onslow, 1716.
[5] In No. 238.
[6] No. 258, Dec. 2; a short letter ridiculing the advocated adoption of
the title " Britain " for the United Kingdom, by the iteration of the terms
"North Briton" and "South Briton," "North British" and "South
British," for "Englishman" and "Scotchman," &c.—D. L. P.
[7] Brackets in D. S.

particular passage in it, only I wanted time. Here's enough
for to-night, such as it is, &c.

14. Is that tobacco at the top of the paper,[1] or what? I
don't remember I slobbered. Lord, I dreamt of Stella, &c. so
confusedly last night, and that we saw dean Bolton [2] and
Sterne go into a shop; and she bid me call them to her, and
they proved to be two parsons I know not; and I walked without till she was shifting, and such stuff, mixt with much melancholy and uneasiness, and things not as they should be, and
I know not how: and it is now an ugly gloomy morning.—At
night. Mr. Addison and I dined with Ned Southwell, and walkt
in the Park; and at the Coffee-house I found a letter from the
bishop of Clogher, and a pacquet from MD. I opened the
bishop's letter; but put up MD's, and visited a lady just come
to town, and am now got into bed, and going to open your
little letter: and God send I may find MD well, and happy,
and merry, and that they love Presto as they do fires. Oh,
I won't open it yet! yes I will! no I won't; I am going; I
can't stay till I turn over.[3] What shall I do? My fingers
itch; and I now have it in my left hand; and now I'll open it
this very moment.—I have just got it, and am cracking the
seal, and can't imagine what's in it; I fear only some letter
from a bishop, and it comes too late: I shall employ nobody's
credit but my own. Well, I see though—Pshaw, 'tis from sir
Andrew Fountain: What, another! I fancy that is from Mrs.
Barton [4]; she told me she would write to me; but she writes
a better hand than this: I wish you would inquire; it must be
at Dawson's [5] office at the Castle. I fear this is from Patty
Rolt, by the scrawl. Well, I'll read MD's letter. Ah, no; it is
from poor lady Berkeley, to invite me to Berkeley-castle this
winter; and now it grieves my heart: she says she hopes my
Lord is in a fair way of recovery [6]; poor lady. Well, now I go
to MD's letter: faith, 'tis all right; I hoped it was wrong. Your
letter, N. 3, that I have now received, is dated Sept. 26, and
Manley's letter, that I had five days ago, was dated Oct. 3,

[1] The upper part of the letter was a little besmeared with some such
stuff; the mark is still on it.—D. S.
[2] John Bolton, Dean of Derry. See Letter VII., p. 38, note 2.
[3] That is, to the next page; for he is now within three lines of the
bottom of the first.—D. S.
[4] Niece to Sir Isaac Newton, and widow of Colonel Barton. A favourite
among the toasts of the Kitcat Club, and named before as the comrade
of Mrs. Long in her celebrity and her misfortune.—D. L. P.
[5] Joshua Dawson, Secretary to the Lords Justices of Ireland.—D. L. P.
[6] Lord Berkeley was then dead. See Letter V., Oct. 2.

that's a fortnight difference: I doubt it has lain in Steele's office, and he forgot. Well, there's an end of that: he is turned out of his place; and you must desire those who send me pacquets, to inclose them in a paper directed to Mr. Addison, at St. James's Coffee-house: not common letters, but pacquets: the bishop of Clogher may mention it to the archbishop when he sees him. As for your letter, it makes me mad: slidikins, I have been the best boy in Christendom, and you come with your two eggs a penny.—Well; but stay, I'll look over my book; adad, I think there was a *chasm* between my N. 2 and N. 3. Faith, I won't promise to write to you every week; but I'll write every night, and when it is full I will send it; that will be once in ten days, and that will be often enough: and if you begin to take up the way of writing to Presto, only because it is Tuesday, a Monday bedad, it will grow a task; but write when you have a mind.—No, no, no, no, no, no, no, no—Agad, agad, agad, agad, agad, agad; no, poor Stellakins.[1] Slids, I would the horse were in your—chamber. Have not I ordered Parvisol to obey your directions about him? And han't I said in my former letters, that you may pickle him, and boil him, if you will? What do you trouble me about your horses for? Have I any thing to do with them?—Revolutions a hindrance to me in my business; Revolutions—to me in my business? If it were not for the revolutions, I could do nothing at all; and now I have all hopes possible, though one is certain of nothing; but to-morrow I am to have an answer, and am promised an effectual one. I suppose I have said enough in this and a former letter how I stand with new people; ten times better than ever I did with the old; forty times more caressed. I am to dine to-morrow at Mr. Harley's; and if he continues as he has begun, no man has been ever better treated by another. What you say about Stella's mother, I have spoken enough to it already. I believe she is not in town; for I have not yet seen her. My lampoon is cried up to the skies; but nobody suspects me for it, except sir Andrew Fountain: at least they say nothing of it to me. Did not I tell you of a great man who received me very coldly [2]? That's he; but say nothing; 'twas only a little revenge: I'll remember to bring it over. The bishop of Clogher has

---

[1] This word must be an invention of Swift's cousin Deane. "Stella" was not used as a name for Esther Johnson until a date later than the conclusion of the *Journal*. What was really written was probably "sluttikins"—suggested by Forster.

[2] Lord Godolphin. The lampoon was *Sid Hamet's Rod*.

smoaked my *Tatler*[1] about shortening of words, &c. But God so![2] &c.

15. I will write plainer if I can remember it; for Stella must not spoil her eyes, and Dingley can't read my hand very well; and I am afraid my letters are too long: then you must suppose one to be two, and read them at twice. I dined to-day with Mr. Harley: Mr. Prior[3] dined with us. He has left my memorial with the queen, who has consented to give the First-Fruits and Twentieth Parts, and will, we hope, declare it to-morrow in the cabinet. But I beg you to tell it to no person alive; for so I am ordered, till in publick: and I hope to get something of greater value. After dinner came in lord Peterborow[4]: we renewed our acquaintance, and he grew mightily fond of me. They began to talk of a paper of verses called *Sid Hamet*. Mr. Harley repeated part, and then pulled them out, and gave them to a gentleman at the table to read, though they had all read them often: lord Peterborow would let nobody read them but himself: so he did; and Mr. Harley bobbed me at every line to take notice of the beauties. Prior rallied lord Peterborow for author of them; and lord Peterborow said, he knew them to be his; and Prior then turned it upon me, and I on him. I am not guessed at all in town to be the author; yet so it is: but that is a secret only to you. Ten to one whether you see them in Ireland; yet here they run prodigiously. Harley presented me to lord president of Scotland,[5] and Mr. Benson,[6] lord of the treasury. Prior and I came away at nine, and sat at the Smyrna[7] till eleven, receiving acquaintance.

16. This morning early I went in a chair, and Patrick before it, to Mr. Harley, to give him another copy of my memorial, as he desired; but he was full of business, going to the queen, and I could not see him; but he desired I would send up the paper, and excused himself upon his hurry. I was a little baulkt; but they tell me it is nothing. I shall judge by next visit. I tipped

---

[1] No. 230.

[2] This appears to be an interjection of surprise at the length of his journal.—D. S.

[3] Matthew Prior (1664–1721), poet and diplomatist — first Whig, then Tory.

[4] Charles Mordaunt (1658–1735), third Earl of Peterborough; admiral, general, and diplomatist. *See post*, Letter IX., Nov. 23.

[5] Hew Dalrymple of North Berwick, Lord President of the Court of Session.—D. L. P.

[6] Robert Benson (c. 1676–1731), made Chancellor of the Exchequer in the next June; afterwards Lord Bingley.

[7] The Smyrna Coffee-house was in Pall Mall, at the corner of Crown Court, opposite Marlborough House.

his porter with half a crown; and so I am well there for a time at least. I dined at Stratford's in the city, and had Burgundy and Tockay: came back afoot like a scoundrel; then went to Mr. Addison and supt with lord Mountjoy, which made me sick all night. I forgot that I bought six pound of chocolate for Stella, and a little wooden box: and I have a great piece of Brazil tobacco for Dingley, and a bottle of palsy water for Stella: all which, with the two handkerchiefs that Mr. Sterne has bought, and you must pay him for, will be put in the box directed to Mrs. Curry's, and set [?sent] by Dr. Hawkshaw,[1] whom I have not seen; but Sterne has undertaken it. The chocolate is a present, madam, for Stella. Don't read this, you little rogue, with your little eyes; but give it to Dingley, pray now; and I'll write as plain as the skies: and let Dingley write Stella's part, and Stella dictate to her, when she apprehends her eyes, &c.

17. This letter should have gone this post, if I had not been taken up with business, and two nights being late out; so it must stay till Thursday. I dined to-day with your Mr. Sterne,[2] by invitation, and drank Irish wine[3]; but, before we parted, there came in the prince of puppies, colonel Edgworth[4]; so

---

[1] It would appear from subsequent entries that he lived in Ireland, in Swift's neighbourhood.

[2] Enoch Sterne. *See* Letter IV., Oct. 29, note.

[3] Claret.—D.S.

[4] It is reported of this Colonel Ambrose Edgworth, that he once made a visit to one of his brothers, who lived at the distance of about one day's journey from his house, and that he travelled to see him with his led horse, portmantuas, &c. As soon as he arrived at his brother's, the portmantuas were unpacked, and three suits of fine cloaths, one finer than another, hung upon chairs in his bed-chamber, together with his night-gown and shaving-plate, disposed in their proper places. The next morning, upon his coming down to breakfast, with his boots on, his brother asked him where he proposed riding before dinner: I am going directly home, said the colonel. Lord! said his brother, I thought you intended to stay some time with us. No, replied the colonel, I can't stay with you at present; I only just came to see you and my sister, and must return home this morning. And accordingly his cloaths, &c., were packed up, and off he went.

But what merit soever the colonel might have had to boast of, his son Talbot Edgworth excelled him by at least fifty bars length. Talbot never thought of any thing but fine cloaths, splendid furniture for his horse, and exciting, as he flattered himself, universal admiration. In these pursuits he expended his whole income, which, at best, was very inconsiderable: in other respects he cared not how he lived. To do him justice, he was an exceeding handsome fellow, well shaped, and of a good heighth, rather tall than of the middle size. He began very early in his life, even before he was of age, to shine forth in the world, and continued to blaze during the whole reign of George the first. He bethought himself very happily of one extravagance, well suited to his disposition: he insisted upon an exclusive right to one board at Lucas's Coffee-house,

I went away. This day came out the *Tatler* made up wholly of my *Shower*, and a preface to it. They say 'tis the best thing I ever writ, and I think so too. I suppose the bishop of Clogher will shew it you. Pray tell me how you like it. Tooke is going on with my *Miscellany*.[1] I'd give a penny the letter to the bishop of Kilaloe[2] was in it: 'twould do him honour. Could not you contrive to say you hear they are printing my Things together; and that you wish the bookseller had that letter among the rest: but don't say any thing of it as from me. I forgot whether it was good or no; but only having heard it much commended, perhaps it may deserve it. Well, I have to-morrow to finish this letter in, and then I'll send it next day. I am so vext that you should write your third to me, when you had but my second, and I had written five, which now I hope you have all: and so I tell you, you are sawcy, little, pretty, dear rogues, &c.

18. To-day I dined, by invitation, with Stratford and others, at a young merchant's in the city, with Hermitage and Tockay, and staid till nine, and am now come home. And that dog Patrick is abroad, and drinking, and I can't get my night-gown. I have a mind to turn that puppy away: he has been drunk ten times in three weeks. But I han't time to say more; so good night, &c.

19. I am come home from dining in the city with Mr. Addison, at a merchant's; and just now, at the Coffee-house, we have notice that the duke of Ormond was this day declared lord lieutenant,[3] at Hampton-court, in council. I have not seen Mr. Harley since; but hope the affair is done about First-Fruits. I will see him, if possible, to-morrow morning; but this goes to-night. I have sent a box to Mr. Sterne, to send to

where he might walk backwards and forwards, and exhibit his person to the gaze of all beholders; in which particular he was indulged almost universally: but now and then some arch fellow would usurp on his privilege, take possession of the board, meet him, and dispute his right; and when this happened to be the case, he would chafe, bluster, ask the gentleman his name, and immediately set him down in his table-book, as a man that he would fight when he came to age. With regard to the female world, his common phrase was, *They may look and die*. In short, he was the jest of the men, and the contempt of the women.—D. S.

Being neglected by his relations in his lunacy, he was taken into custody during his illness, and confined in Bridewell, Dublin, where he died. Mr. Aitken says Ambrose's father was Colonel Sir John Edgworth.

[1] Two publications, largely identical, under the title *Miscellanies*, were issued by Curll and Morphew respectively, in 1711.

[2] Thomas Lindsay. With John Hartstonge, Bishop of Ossory, he had preceded Swift upon the business of the First-Fruits.

[3] In room of the Earl of Wharton.

you by some friend: I have directed it for Mr. Curry, at his
house; so you have warning when it comes, as I hope it will
soon. The handkerchiefs will be put in some friend's pocket,
not to pay custom. And so here ends my sixth, sent when I
had but three of MD's: now I am beforehand, and will keep
so; and God Almighty bless dearest MD, &c.

LETTER VII

London, *Oct.* 19, 1710.

O FAITH, I am undone! this paper is larger than t'other, and
yet I am condemned to a sheet; but since it is MD, I did not
value though I were condemned to a pair. I told you in a letter
to-day where I had been, and how the day past; and so, &c.

20. To-day I went to Mr. Lewis, at the secretary's office, to
know when I might see Mr. Harley; and by and by comes up
Mr. Harley himself, and appoints me to dine with him to-
morrow. I dined with Mrs. Vanhomrigh,[1] and went to wait on
the two lady Butlers[2]; but the porter answered, They were
not at home; the meaning was, the youngest, lady Mary, is to
be married to-morrow to lord Ashburnham,[3] the best match
now in England, twelve thousand pounds a year, and abundance
of money. Tell me how my *Shower* is liked in Ireland: I never
knew any thing pass better here. I spent the evening with
Wortley Montague[4] and Mr. Addison, over a bottle of Irish
wine. Do they know any thing in Ireland of my greatness among
the Tories? Every body reproaches me of it here; but I value
them not. Have you heard of the verses about the *Rod of Sid
Hamet*? Say nothing of them for your life. Hardly any body
suspects me for them, only they think no-body but Prior or
I could write them. But I doubt they have not reached you.
There is likewise a Ballad, full of puns, on the Westminster
election,[5] that cost me half an hour: it runs, though it be good
for nothing. But this is likewise a secret to all but MD. If you
have them not, I'll bring them over.

21. I got MD's fourth to-day at the Coffee-house. God

---

[1] *See* Letter VIII., footnote to Nov. 8, as to Stella's curiosity about the
Vanhomrighs. There was a *Miss* Vanhomrigh—"Vanessa."

[2] Daughters of the Duke of Ormond. *See* Letter III., Sept. 20.

[3] John Ashburnham (1687–1736-7), third baron, first earl (1730). After
the death (*see post*) of his first wife Mary (Butler), he was married
again twice.

[4] Edward Wortley Montagu, grandson of first Earl of Sandwich, husband
of the famous Lady Mary Wortley Montagu. He died 1761, aged 83.

[5] *See before*, Oct. 5.

Almighty bless poor dear Stella, and her eyes and head: What shall we do to cure them, poor dear life? Your disorders are a pull-back for your good qualities. Would to Heaven I were this minute shaving your poor dear head, either here or there. Pray do not write, nor read this letter nor any thing else, and I will write plainer for Dingley to read, from henceforward, though my pen is apt to ramble when I think who I am writing to. I will not answer your letter until I tell you that I dined this day with Mr. Harley, who presented me to the earl of Sterling,[1] a Scotch lord; and in the evening came in lord Peterborow. I staid till nine before Mr. Harley would let me go, or tell me any thing of my affair. He says, the queen has now granted the First-Fruits and Twentieth Parts; but he will not yet give me leave to write to the archbishop, because the queen designs to signify it to the bishops in Ireland in form, and to take notice, That it was done upon a memorial from me, which Mr. Harley tells me he does to make it look more respectful to me, &c. and I am to see him on Tuesday. I know not whether I told you, that in my memorial which was given to the queen, I begged for two thousand pounds a year more, though it was not in my commission; but that Mr. Harley says cannot yet be done, and that he and I must talk of it further: however, I have started it, and it may follow in time. Pray say nothing of the First-Fruits being granted, unless I give leave at the bottom of this. I believe never any thing was compassed so soon, and purely done by my personal credit with Mr. Harley, who is so excessively obliging, that I know not what to make of it, unless to shew the rascals of the other party that they used a man unworthily, who had deserved better. The memorial given to the Queen from me speaks with great plainness of lord Wharton. I believe this business is as important to you as the Convocation disputes from Tisdall.[2] I hope in a month or two all the forms of settling this matter will be over, and then I shall have nothing to do here. I will only add one foolish thing more, because it is just come into my head. When this thing

---

[1] Henry, surnamed Alexander (1664–1739), fifth earl. He was also "Viscount Canada" and "Lord Alexander of Tullibody."

[2] These words, according to Deane Swift, referred to conversations, which passed between Stella and Dr. William Tisdall seven or eight years before, when he entertained her with convocation disputes. He was a native of Carrickfergus, the parish next to Kilroot, which was Swift's first cure of souls in Ireland (1695–6); so that the friendship of these two divines probably began in the North. It ceased when Tisdall became a suitor to Stella (1704). Tisdall, who was born 1669, married a Connacht woman in 1706, became Vicar of Belfast in 1712, and died 1735.

is made known, tell me impartially whether they give any of the merit to me, or no; for I am sure I have so much, that I will never take it upon me.—Insolent sluts! because I say Dublin, Ireland, therefore you must say London, England: that's Stella's malice.[1] Well, for that I won't answer your letter till to-morrow-day, and so and so: I'll go write something else, and it won't be much; for 'tis late.

22. I was this morning with Mr. Lewis, the under-secretary to lord Dartmouth, two hours talking politicks, and contriving to keep Steele in his office of stampt paper: he has lost his place of Gazetteer, three hundred pounds a year, for writing a *Tatler*,[2] some months ago, against Mr. Harley, who gave it him at first, and raised the salary from sixty to three hundred pounds. This was devilish ungrateful; and Lewis was telling me the particulars: but I had a hint given me, that I might save him in the other employment; and leave was give me to clear matters with Steele. Well, I dined with Sir Matthew Dudley, and in the evening went to sit with Mr. Addison, and offer the matter at distance to him, as the discreeter person; but found Party had so possessed him, that he talked as if he suspected me, and would not fall in with any thing I said. So I stopt short in my overture, and we parted very dryly; and I shall say nothing to Steele, and let them do as they will; but if things stand as they are, he will certainly lose it, unless I save him; and therefore I will not speak to him, that I may not report to his disadvantage. Is not this vexatious? and is there so much in the proverb of proffered service? When shall I grow wise? I endeavour to act in the most exact points of honour and conscience, and my nearest friends will not understand it so. What must a man expect from his enemies? This would vex me, but it shall not; and so I bid you good night, &c.

23. I know 'tis neither wit nor diversion to tell you every day where I dine, neither do I write it to fill my letter; but I I fancy I shall, some time or other, have the curiosity of seeing some particulars how I passed my life when I was absent from MD this time; and so I tell you now that I dined to-day at Molesworth's the Florence envoy, then went to the coffee-house, where I behaved myself coldly enough to Mr. Addison, and so came home to scribble. We dine together to-morrow and

---

[1] There is a particular compliment to Stella couched in these words. Stella was herself an Englishwoman, born at Richmond in Surry, nevertheless she respected the interest and the honour of Ireland, where she had lived for some years, with a generous patriotic spirit.—D. S.

[2] *See* Letter III., second note to Sept. 10.

next day, by invitation; but I shall not alter my behaviour
to him, till he begs my pardon, or else we shall grow bare
acquaintance. I am weary of friends, and friendships are all
monsters, but MD's.

24. I forgot to tell you that last night I went to Mr. Harley's,
hoping—faith, I am blundering, for it was this very night at
six; and I hoped he would have told me all things were done
and granted: but he was abroad, and come home ill, and was
gone to bed, much out of order, unless the porter lied. I dined
to-day at Sir Matthew Dudley's with Mr. Addison, &c.

25. I was to-day to see the duke of Ormond; and coming
out, met lord Berkeley of Stratton,[1] who told me, that Mrs.
Temple,[2] the widow, died last Saturday, which, I suppose, is
much to the outward grief and inward joy of the family. I dined
to-day with Mr. Addison and Steele, and a sister of Addison,
who is married to one Monsr. Sartre,[3] a Frenchman, Prebendary
of Westminster, who has a delicious house and garden; yet I
thought it was a sort of monastick life in those cloisters, and
I liked Laracor better. Addison's sister is a sort of a wit, very
like him. I am not fond of her, &c.

26. I was to-day to see Mr. Congreve, who is almost blind
with cataracts growing on his eyes; and his case is, that he
must wait two or three years, until the cataracts are riper,
and till he is quite blind, and then he must have them couched;
and besides he is never rid of the gout, yet he looks young and
fresh, and is as chearful as ever. He is younger by three years
or more than I,[4] and I am twenty years younger than he. He
gave me a pain in the great toe, by mentioning the gout. I find
such suspicions frequently, but they go off again. I had a second
letter from Mr. Morgan; for which I thank you: I wish you
were whipt for forgetting to send him that answer I desired
you in one of my former, that I could do nothing for him of what
he desired, having no credit at all, &c. Go, be far enough, you
negligent baggages. I have had also a letter from Parvisol, with
an account how my livings are set, and that they are fallen,
since last year, sixty pounds. A comfortable piece of news. He

[1] William Berkeley (166-?-1741) fourth baron.

[2] Possibly Mary, daughter of Duplessis Rambouillet (a Huguenot),
and widow of Sir William Temple's son John, who threw himself into the
Thames near London Bridge and was drowned, 1689.

[3] Mr. Sartre died Sept. 30, 1713. His widow (afterward married to
Daniel Combes, Esq.) died March 2, 1750.—N.

[4] Congreve was born in the year 1672: consequently he was between
four and five years younger than Dr. Swift.—D. S. He had been at school
with Swift at Kilkenny.

tells me plainly, that he finds you have no mind to part with the horse, because you sent for him at the same time you sent him my letter; so that I know not what must be done. 'Tis a sad thing that Stella must have her own horse, whether Parvisol will or no. So now to answer your letter that I had three or four days ago. I am not now in bed, but am come home by eight; and it being warm, I write up.[1] I never writ to the bishop of Killala, which, I suppose, was the reason he had not my letter. I have not time, there's the short of it.—As fond as the dean is of my letter, he has not written to me. I would only know whether dean Bolton [2] paid him the twenty pounds; and for the rest, he may kiss———. And that you may ask him, because I am in pain about it, that dean Bolton is such a *whipster*. 'Tis the most obliging thing in the world in dean Sterne to be so kind to you. I believe he knows it will please me, and makes up, that way, his other usage.[3] No, we have had none of your snow, but a little one morning; yet I think it was great snow for an hour or so, but no longer. I had heard of Will Crowe's [4] death before, but not the foolish circumstance that hastened his end. No, I have taken care that captain Pratt [5] shall not suffer by lord Anglesea's death. I'll try some contrivance to get a copy of my picture from Jervas. I'll make Sir Andrew Fountain buy one as for himself, and I'll pay him again and take it, that is, provided I have money to spare when I leave this.—Poor John! is he gone? and madam Parvisol has been in town? Humm. Why, Tighe [6] and I, when he comes, shall not take any notice of each other; I would not do it much in this town, though we had not fallen out.—I was to-day at Mr.

[1] Probably referring to the inclination of the lines. "Write up" must not be understood in the modern slang sense.

[2] This gentleman, as well as Dr. Swift, was one of the chaplains to Lord Berkeley, when Lord Lieutenant; and was promised to the deanery of Derry, which had been previously promised to Dr. Swift; but Mr. Bushe, the principal secretary, for weighty reasons best known to himself, laid Dr. Swift aside, unless he would pay him a large sum, which the doctor refused with the utmost contempt and scorn. He was afterward promoted to the archbishopric of Cashell. He was one of the most eloquent speakers of his time, and was a very learned man, especially in Church history.—F.

[3] When he became dean, he withheld from Swift the living of St. Nicholas Without, promised in gratitude for the aid rendered by Swift in his election.—D. L. P.

[4] In his essay on Wharton, Swift speaks of Wharton's "barbarous injustice" to this person—said by Mr. Aitken to have been recorder of Blessington, Wicklow.

[5] Taken to be the same as the Pratt mentioned in Letter III., Sept. 11, 1710.

[6] Richard Tighe, an Irish privy councillor.

Sterne's lodging; he was not within, and Mr. Leigh is not come
to town, but I will do Dingley's errand when I see him. What
do I know whether china be dear or no? I once took a fancy
of resolving to grow mad for it, but now 'tis off; I suppose I
told you so in some former letter. And so you only want some
salad dishes, and plates, and &c. Yes, yes, you shall. I suppose
you have named as much as will cost five pounds.—Now to
Stella's little postscript; and I am almost crazed that you vex
yourself for not writing. Can't you dictate to Dingley, and not
strain your little dear eyes? I am sure 'tis the grief of my soul
to think you are out of order. Pray be quiet, and if you will
write, shut your eyes, and write just a line, and no more, thus
[How do you do, Mrs. Stella?][1] That was written with my eyes
shut. Faith, I think it is better than when they are open[2]:
and then Dingley may stand by, and tell you when you go
too high or too low.—My letters of business, with pacquets,
if there be any more occasion for such, must be inclosed to
Mr. Addison, at St. James's Coffee-house: but I hope to hear,
as soon as I see Mr. Harley, that the main difficulties are over,
and that the rest will be but form.—Make [? Take] two or three
nutgalls, make [? take] two or three —galls; stop your receipt
in your —— I have no need on't. Here's a clutter! Well, so
much for your letter, which I will now put up in my letter
partition in my cabinet, as I always do every letter as soon as
I answer it. Method is good in all things. Order governs the
world. The Devil is the author of confusion. A general of an
army, a minister of state; to descend lower, a gardener, a
weaver, &c. That may make a fine observation, if you think it
worth finishing; but I have not time. Is not this a terrible long
piece for one evening? I dined to-day with Patty Rolt at my
cousin Leach's,[3] with a pox, in the city: he is a printer, and
prints the *Postman*, oh ho, and is my cousin, God knows how,
and he married Mrs. Baby Aires of Leicester; and my cousin
Thompson was with us: and my cousin Leach offers to bring me
acquainted with the author of the *Postman*[4]; and says, he
does not doubt but the gentleman will be glad of my acquaintance, and that he is a very ingenious man, and a great scholar,
and has been beyond sea. But I was modest, and said, May be
the gentleman was shy, and not fond of new acquaintance;

[1] Brackets in D. S.
[2] It is actually better written, and in a plainer hand.—D. S.
[3] *See* Letter III., Sept. 16, Night.
[4] A Tory newspaper. Leach was by Swift recommended to Harrison
to print the *Tatler* after Steele's withdrawal; but Harrison discarded him.

and so put it off: and I wish you could hear me repeating all
I have said of this in its proper tone, just as I am writing it.
'Tis all with with the same cadence with oh hoo, or as when
little girls say, I have got an apple, miss, and I won't give you
some. 'Tis plaguy twelve-penny weather this last week, and
has cost me ten shillings in coach and chair hire. If the fellow
that has your money will pay it, let me beg you to buy Bank
Stock with it, which is fallen near thirty *per cent*. and pays
eight pounds *per cent*. and you have the principal when you
please: it will certainly soon rise. I would to God lady Giffard
would put in the four hundred pounds she owes you,[1] and
take the five *per cent*. common interest, and give you the
remainder. I will speak to your mother about it when I see
her. I am resolved to buy three hundred pounds of it for myself,
and take up what I have in Ireland; and I have a contrivance for
it, that I hope will do, by making a friend of mine buy it as for
myself, and I'll pay him when I get in my money. I hope Stratford
will do me that kindness. I'll ask him to-morrow or next day.

27. Mr. Rowe the poet desired me to dine with him to-day.
I went to his office (he is under-secretary in Mr. Addison's place
that he had in England) and there was Mr. Prior; and they both
fell commending my *Shower* beyond any thing that has been
written of the kind: there never was such a Shower since
Danaë's, &c. You must tell me how 'tis liked among you.
I dined with Rowe; Prior could not come: and after
dinner we went to a blind tavern, where Congreve, Sir
Richard Temple,[2] Eastcourt,[3] and Charles Main were over a
bowl of bad punch. The knight sent for six flasks of his own wine
for me, and we staid till twelve. But now my head continues
pretty well; I have left off my drinking, and only take a spoon-
ful mixt with water, for fear of the gout, or some ugly distemper;
and now, because it is late, I will, &c.

28. Garth and Addison and I dined to-day at a hedge[4]
tavern; then I went to Mr. Harley, but he was denied, or not
at home; so I fear I shall not hear my business is done before
this goes. Then I visited lord Pembroke,[5] who is just come to

---

[1] Part of a legacy left Stella by Sir W. Temple.—D. L. P.

[2] Sir Richard Temple (1669?-1749), baronet, a lieut.-general, later
Baron and then Viscount Cobham, and a field-marshal.

[3] Richard Estcourt (1668-1712), actor and dramatist, mentioned in
the *Spectator*, No. 390.

[4] Depreciatory adjective—similar to "blind."

[5] Thomas Herbert, eighth of the "Herbert" Earls of Pembroke, who
had been Lord Lieutenant in 1707. "He was a nobleman of taste and
learning, and, like Swift, very fond of punning," says D. L. P.

town, and we were very merry talking of old things, and I hit him with one pun. Then I went to the ladies Butler, and the son of a whore of a porter denied them: so I sent them a threatening message by another lady, for not excepting me always to the porter. I was weary of the Coffee-house, and Ford desired me to sit with him at next door, which I did, like a fool, chatting till twelve, and now am got into bed. I am afraid the new ministry is at a terrible loss about money: the Whigs talk so, it would give one the spleen; and I am afraid of meeting Mr. Harley out of humour. They think he will never carry through this undertaking. God knows what will come of it. I should be terribly vexed to see things come round again: it will ruin the church and clergy for ever; but I hope for better. I'll send this on Tuesday, whether I hear any further news of my affair or not.

29. Mr. Addison and I dined to-day with lord Mountjoy; which is all the adventures of this day.—I chatted a while to-night in the Coffee-house, this being a full night; and now am come home to write some business.

30. I dined to-day at Mrs. Vanhomrigh's, and sent a letter to poor Mrs. Long, who writes to us, but is God knows where, and will not tell any body the place of her residence. I came home early, and must go write.

31. The month ends with a fine day; and I have been walking, and visiting Lewis, and concerting where to see Mr. Harley. I have no news to send you. Aire,[1] they say, is taken, though the Whitehall letters this morning say quite the contrary; 'tis good if it be true. I dined with Mr. Addison and Dick Stuart,[2] lord Mountjoy's brother; a treat of Addison's. They were half fuddled, but not I; for I mixt water with my wine, and left them together between nine and ten; and I must send this by the bell-man, which vexes me, but I will put it off no longer. Pray God it does not miscarry. I seldom do so; but I can put off little MD no longer. Pray give the under note to Mrs. Brent.

I'm a pretty gentleman; and you lose all your money at cards, sirrah Stella. I found you out; I did so.

I'm staying before I can fold up this letter, till that ugly *D* is dry in the last line but one. Don't you see it? O Lord, I'm loth to leave you, faith—but it must be so, till the next time. Pox take that *D*; I'll blot it to dry it.

---

[1] Aire-sur-la-Lys, now in Pas-de-Calais department.

[2] Mr Aitken says this Richard Stewart was third son of the first Lord Mountjoy, M.P. at different times for various Irish constituencies; died 1728.

LETTER VIII

London, *Oct.* 31, 1710.

So, now I have sent my seventh to your fourth, young women; and now I'll tell you what I would not in my last, that this morning, sitting in my bed, I had a fit of giddiness[1]: the room turned round for about a minute, and then it went off, leaving me sickish, but not very: and so I past the day as I told you; but I would not end a letter with telling you this, because it might vex you: and I hope in God I shall have no more of it. I saw Dr. Cockburn to-day, and he promises to send me the pills that did me good last year, and likewise has promised me an oil for my ear, that he has been making for that ailment for somebody else.

Nov. 1. I wish MD a merry new year. You know this is the first day of it with us.[2] I had no giddiness to-day, but I drank brandy, and have bought a pint for two shillings. I sat up the night before my giddiness pretty late, and writ very much; so I will impute it to that. But I never eat fruit, nor drink ale, but drink better wine than you do, as I did to-day with Mr. Addison at lord Mountjoy's: then went at five to see Mr. Harley, who could not see me for much company; but sent me his excuse, and desired I would dine with him on Friday; and then I expect some answer to this business, which must either be soon done, or begun again; and then the duke of Ormond and his people will interfere for their honour, and do nothing. I came home at six, and spent my time in my chamber, without going to the Coffee-house, which I grow weary of; and I studied at leisure, writ not above forty lines, some inventions of my own, and some hints, and read not at all, and this because I would take care of Presto, for fear little MD should be angry.

2. I took my four pills last night, and they lay an hour in my throat, and so they will do to-night. I suppose I could swallow four affronts as easily. I dined with Dr. Cockburn to-day, and came home at seven; but Mr. Ford has been with me till just now, and 'tis near eleven. I have had no giddiness

---

[1] This giddiness, which tormented Swift through life, was imputed by him to a violent indigestion brought on by a surfeit of fruit in his youth; and from this arose his continual caution and frequent warnings about eating fruit.—D. L. P.

[2] From later entries it would appear that the accounts of Swift with his two lady friends were made up always to the end of October. It was a *financial* new year.

to-day. Mr. Dopping[1] I have seen, and he tells me coldly, my *Shower* is liked well enough; there's your Irish judgment. I writ this post to the bishop of Clogher. 'Tis now just a fortnight since I heard from you. I must have you write once a fortnight, and then I'll allow for wind and weather. How goes ombre? Does Mrs. Walls win constantly, as she used to do; and Mrs. Stoite[2]? I have not thought of her this long time; how does she? I find we have a cargo of Irish coming for London: I am sorry for it; but I never go near them. And Tighe is landed; but Mrs. Wesley, they say, is going home to her husband, like a fool. Well, little monkies mine, I must go write; and so good night.

3. I ought to read these letters I write, after I have done; for looking over thus much I found two or three literal mistakes, which should not be when the hand is so bad. But I hope it does not puzzle little Dingley to read, for I think I mend: but methinks when I write plain, I do not know how, but we are not alone, all the world can see us. A bad scrawl is so snug, it looks like a PMD.[3] We have scurvy *Tatlers* of late: so pray do not suspect me. I have one or two hints I design to send him,[4] and never any more: he does not deserve it. He is governed by his wife[5] most abominably, as bad as ——. I never saw her since I came; nor has he ever made me an invitation; either he dares not, or is such a thoughtless Tisdall fellow, that he never minds[6] it. So what care I for his wit? for he is the worst company in the world, till he has a bottle of wine in his head. I cannot write straighter in bed, so you must be content.—At night in bed. Stay, let me see where's this letter to MD among these papers? Oh! here. Well, I'll go on now; but I am very

[1] Samuel Dopping. *See* Letter XI., Dec. 14. Appears to have been Irish; *see* Letter XIX., April 4, 1711.

[2] Wife of a Dublin alderman.

[3] PMD. This cypher stands for Presto, Stella, and Dingley; as much as to say, it looks like us three quite retired from all the rest of the world. —D. S.

[4] *i.e.* Steele.

[5] Lady Steele's maiden name was Mary Scurlocke; she was sole heiress of Jonathan Scurlocke, Esq., of Caermarthen. Steele's correspondence with her amply bears out Swift's account; she was, says Scott, fond of money, and totally insensible to wit; better at the active part of giving advice, than her husband at the passive department of profiting by it. It does not seem that he had the means, or she the inclination, to exercise general hospitality. She resided at a little elegant retreat, near Hampton Court, called the Hovel; the same in which Addison lodged the memorable execution for £1000.—D. L. P.

[6] *Minds:* Anglo-Irish for "remembers." It is in such little touches as this that Swift shows himself more of an Irishman than he would admit himself to be.

busy (smoak the new pen). I dined with Mr. Harley to-day, and am invited there again on Sunday. I have now leave to write to the primate and archbishop of Dublin, that the queen has granted the First-Fruits; but they are to take no notice of it, till a letter is sent them by the queen's orders from lord Dartmouth, secretary of state, to signify it. The bishops are to be made a corporation to dispose of the revenue, &c. and I shall write to the archbishop of Dublin to-morrow (I have had no giddiness to-day). I know not whether they will have any occasion for me longer to be here; nor can I judge till I see what letter the queen sends to the bishops, and what they will do upon it. If dispatch be used, it may be done in six weeks; but I cannot judge. They sent me to-day a new commission, signed by the primate [1] and archbishop of Dublin,[2] and promise me letters to the two archbishops here; but mine a— for it all. The thing is done, and has been so these ten days; though I had only leave to tell it to-day. I had this day likewise a letter from the bishop of Clogher, who complains of my not writing; and what vexes me, says he knows you have long letters from me every week. Why do you tell him so? 'Tis not right, faith: but I won't be angry with MD at [a] distance. I writ to him last post, before I had his, and will write again soon, since I see he expects it, and that lord and lady Mountjoy [3] put him off upon me to give themselves ease. Lastly, I had this day a letter from a certain naughty rogue called MD, and it was N. 5, which I shall not answer to-night, I thank you. No, faith, I have other fish to fry; but to-morrow or next day will be time enough. I have put MD's commissions in a memorandum paper. I think I have done all before, and remember nothing but this to-day about glasses and spectacles and spectacle cases. I have no commission from Stella, but the chocolate and handkerchiefs; and those are bought, and I expect they will be soon sent. I have been with, and sent to, Mr. Sterne, two or three times to know, but he was not within. Odds my life, what am I doing? I must go write and do business.

4. I dined to-day at Kensington, with Addison, Steele, &c. came home, and writ a short letter to the archbishop of Dublin, to let him know the queen has granted the thing, &c. I writ in the Coffee-house, for I staid at Kensington till nine, and am

[1] Narcissus Marsh (1638–1713), Archbishop of Armagh, an Englishman, was Primate of all Ireland, and six times a lord justice.
[2] Dr. King. See Letter II., note on p. 3.
[3] Anne (Boyle) daughter of first Viscount Blessington. After Lord Mountjoy's death, she married John Farquharson, and died 1741.

plaguy weary; for colonel Proud[1] was very ill company, and I'll never be of a party with him again; and I drank punch, and that and ill company has made me hot.

5. I was with Mr. Harley from dinner to seven this night, and went to the Coffee-house, where Dr. D'Avenant[2] would fain have had me gone and drink a bottle of wine at his house hard by, with Dr. Chamberlain[3]; but the puppy used so many words, that I was afraid of his company; and though we promised to come at eight, I sent a messenger to him, that Chamberlain was going to a patient, and therefore we would put it off till another time: so he, and the comptroller,[4] and I were prevailed on, by sir Matthew Dudley, to go to his house, where I staid till twelve, and left them. D'Avenant has been teasing me to look over some of his writings that he is going to publish; but the rogue is so fond of his own productions, that I hear he will not part with a syllable; and he has lately put out a foolish pamphlet, called, *The third part of Tom Double*; to make his court to the Tories, whom he had left.

6. I was to-day gambling[5] in the city to see Patty Rolt, who is going to Kingston, where she lodges; but to say the truth, I had a mind for a walk to exercise myself, and happened to be disengaged: for dinners are ten times more plentiful with me here than ever, or than in Dublin. I won't answer your letter yet, because I am busy. I hope to send this before I have another from MD: 'twould be a sad thing to answer two letters together, as MD does from Presto. But when the two sides are full, away the letter shall go, that's certain, like it or not like it; and that will be about three days hence, for the answering night will be a long one.

7. I dined to-day at sir Richard Temple's, with Congreve, Vanburg [*i.e.* Vanbrugh],[6] lieutenant-general Farington,[7] &c.

---

[1] This appears to be a mistake for "Froud." One of Swift's correspondents, called "Colonel Froud" in a letter from Swift to Ambrose Philips, was a poet: this seems to point to Philip Frowde (*d.* 1738), author of *The Fall of Saguntum*; who, however, is not known to history as a military man.

[2] Charles Davenant (1656–1714), political economist. "Son of the celebrated Sir William Davenant, the author of *Gondibert*; the Doctor was addicted to politics, wrote many tracts and pamphlets, went into Parliament, and when he died in 1714 was Inspector of Exports and Imports," says D. L. P.

[3] Hugh Chamberlen the younger (1664–1728), M.D. with literary pretensions.

[4] Sir John Holland. *See* Letter III., Sept. 16 (note).

[5] Some suggest this is *little* for "rambling."

[6] Sir John Vanbrugh (1664–1726), dramatist and architect.

[7] Thomas Farrington. *See* Aitken's *Life of Steele*.

Vanburg, I believe I told you, had a long quarrel with me about
those Verses on his House;[1] but we were very civil and cold.
Lady Marlborough used to teaze him with them, which had
made him angry, though he be a good-natured fellow. It was a
Thanksgiving-day,[2] and I was at Court, where the queen past
by us with all Tories about her; not one Whig: Buckingham,[3]
Rochester,[4] Leeds,[5] Shrewsbury, Berkeley of Stratton, lord
keeper Harcourt, Mr. Harley, lord Pembroke, &c. and I have
seen her without one Tory. The queen made me a curtsy, and
said, in a sort of familiar way to Presto, How does MD? I considered she was a queen, and so excused her.[6] I do not miss the
Whigs at Court; but have as many acquaintance there as formerly.

8. Here's ado and a clutter! I must now answer MD's fifth;
but first you must know I dined at the Portugal envoy's[7]
to-day, with Addison, Vanburg, admiral Wager,[8] sir Richard
Temple, Methuen, &c. I was weary of their company, and stole
away at five, and came home like a good boy, and studied till
ten, and had a fire; O ho! and now am in bed. I have no fire-
place in my bed-chamber; but 'tis very warm weather when
one's in bed. Your fine cap, madam Dingley, is too little, and
too hot: I'll have that furr taken off; I wish it were far enough;
and my old velvet cap is good for nothing. Is it velvet under
the furr? I was feeling, but can't find: if it be, 'twill do without
it, else I will face it; but then I must buy new velvet: but
may be I may beg a piece. What shall I do? Well, now to rogue
MD's letter. God be thanked for Stella's eyes mending; and
God send it holds; but faith you writ too much at a time:
better write less, or write it at ten times. Yes, faith, a long
letter in a morning from a dear friend is a dear thing. I smoke
a compliment, little mischievous girls, I do so. But who are
those *Wiggs* that think I am turned Tory? Do you mean Whigs?

[1] Alluding to some lines Swift had written comparing Vanbrugh's house
(which he had designed for himself) to a goose-pie.
[2] In connection with the progress of the war.
[3] John Sheffield (1647–1720–1), "John of Bucks," third Earl of Mulgrave,
created Duke of Buckingham (sixth of that title), 1703. He was at this
time lord steward. A writer of indifferent verse, and a soldier.
[4] Laurence Hyde (1641–2–1711) fourth Earl of Rochester (first of the
name of Hyde), second son of the great Lord Clarendon and maternal
uncle to Queen Anne; Lord President of the Council for the second time,
Sept. 1710.
[5] Sir Thomas Osborne (1631–1712), after various steps, became first
Duke of Leeds, 1694. He had been treasurer of the navy.
[6] This was, in Swift's language, a "pure bite." Swift was never introduced at Court.—D. L. P.
[7] Delaval.
[8] Sir Charles (1666–1743)

Which *Wiggs* and *wat* do you mean? I know nothing of Ray
mond, and only had one letter from him a little after I came
here. [Pray remember Morgan.][1] Raymond is indeed like to
have much influence over me in London, and to share much
of my conversation. I shall, no doubt, introduce him to Harley,
and lord keeper, and the secretary of state. The *Tatler* upon
Milton's Spear[2] is not mine, madam. What a puzzle there was
between you and your judgment? In general you may be sometimes sure of things, as that about style, because it is what I
have frequently spoken of; but guessing is mine [a]—; and
I defy mankind, if I please. Why, I writ a pamphlet when I
was last in London, that you and a thousand have seen, and
never guessed it to be mine.[3] Could you have guessed the
Shower in Town to be mine? How chance you did not see that
before your last letter went; but I suppose you in Ireland did
not think it worth mentioning. Nor am I suspected for the
lampoon; only Harley said he smoaked me, (have I told you
so before?) and some others knew it. 'Tis called *The Rod of Sid
Hamet.* And I have written several other things that I hear
commended, and nobody suspects me for them; nor you shan't
know till I see you again. What do you mean *That boards
near me, that I dine with now and then*[4]? I know no such person:
I don't dine with boarders. What the pox! You know whom
I have dined with every day since I left you, better than I do.
What do you mean, sirrah? Slids, my ailment has been over
these two months almost. Impudence, if you vex me, I'll
give ten shillings a week for my lodging; for I am almost
st[un]k out of this with the sink, and it helps me to verses in
my *Shower*.[5] Well, madam Dingley, what say you to the world
to come? What Ballad? Why go look, it was not good for
much: have patience till I come back; patience is a gay thing
as, &c. I hear nothing of lord Mountjoy's coming for Ireland.
When is Stella's Birth-day? in March? Lord bless me, my turn
at Christ-Church[6]; it is so natural to hear you write about

[1] Brackets in D. S.
[2] Later editions, *Ithuriel's Spear*. See *Tatler* No. 237.
[3] Probably on *Taste in Reading*, addressed to Sir Andrew Fountaine.
—N.
[4] Stella seems to have "smoakt" Swift's intimacy with the Vanhomrighs (which he always passes lightly by), or to have heard of a boarding-
house, mentioned Nov. 12, where Ford, Sir Richard Levinge, &c., used
to dine.
[5] "Returning home at night, you'll find the sink
Strike your offended sense with double stink."
Description of a City Shower.
[6] Christ Church Cathedral, Dublin.

that, I believe you have done it a hundred times; it is as fresh
in my mind, the verger coming to you; and why to you? Would
he have you preach for me? O, pox on your spelling of Latin,
Jonsonibus atque, that's the way. How did the dean get that
name by the end? 'Twas you betrayed me: not I, faith; I'll
not break his head. Your mother is still in the country, I
suppose, for she promised to see me when she came to town.
I writ to her four days ago, to desire her to break it to lady
Giffard, to put some money for you in the Bank, which was
then fallen thirty *per cent.* Would to God mine had been here,
I should have gained one hundred pounds, and got as good
interest as in Ireland, and much securer. I would fain have
borrowed three hundred pounds; but money is so scarce here,
there is no borrowing, by this fall of stocks. 'Tis rising now,
and I knew it would: it fell from one hundred and twenty-nine
to ninety-six. I have not heard since from your mother. Do
you think I would be so unkind not to see her, that you desire
me in a style so melancholy? Mrs. Raymond you say is with
child: I am sorry for it; and so is, I believe, her husband. Mr.
Harley speaks all the kind things to me in the world; and,
I believe, would serve me, if I were to stay here; but I reckon
in time the duke of Ormond may give me some addition to
Laracor. Why should the Whigs think I came to England to
leave them? Sure my journey was no secret? I protest sincerely,
I did all I could to hinder it, as the dean can tell you, although
now I do not repent it. But who the Devil cares what they
think? Am I under obligations in the least to any of them all?
Rot 'em, for ungrateful dogs; I'll make them repent their usage
before I leave this place. They say here the same thing of my
leaving the Whigs; but they own they cannot blame me, considering the treatment I have had. I will take care of your
spectacles, as I told you before, and of the bishop of Killala's;
but I will not write to him, I han't time. What do you mean by
my fourth, madam *Dinglibus*? Does not Stella say you have had
my fifth, goody Blunder? You frighted me till I lookt back.
Well, this is enough for one night. (Pray give my humble
service to Mrs. Stoyte and her sister, Kate is it or Sarah? I have
forgot her name,[1] faith.) I think I'll e'en (and to Mrs. Walls
Walls and the archdeacon) send this to-morrow: no, faith, that
will be in ten days from the last. I'll keep it till Saturday,
though I write no more. But what if a letter from MD should
come in the mean time? Why then I would only say, Madam,

[1] Catherine.

I have received your sixth letter; your most humble servant to command, Presto; and so conclude. Well, now I'll write and think a little, and so to bed, and dream of MD.

9. I have my mouth full of water, and was going to spit it out, because I reasoned with myself, how could I write when my mouth was full. Han't you done things like that, reasoned wrong at first thinking? Well, I was to see Mr. Lewis this morning, and am to dine a few days hence, as he tells me, with Mr. secretary St. John; and I must contrive to see Harley soon again, to hasten this business from the queen. I dined to-day at lord Montrath's, with lord Mountjoy, &c. but the wine was not good, so I came away, stayed at the Coffee-house till seven, then came home to my fire, the maidenhead of my second half-bushel, and am now in bed at eleven, as usual. 'Tis mighty warm; yet I fear I should catch cold this wet weather, if I sat an evening in my room after coming from warm places: and I must make much of myself, because MD is not here to take care of Presto; and I am full of business, writing, &c. and don't care for the Coffee-house; and so this serves for all together, not to tell it you over and over, as silly people do; but Presto is a wiser man, faith, than so, let me tell you, gentlewomen. See, I am got to the third side; but, faith, I won't do that often; but I must say something early to-day, till the letter is done, and on Saturday it shall go; so I must save something till to-morrow, till to-morrow and next day.

10. O Lord, I would this letter was with you with all my heart: If it should miscarry, what a deal would be lost? I forgot to leave a gap in the last line but one for the seal, like a puppy; but I should have allowed for night, good night; but when I am taking leave, I can't leave a bit, faith; but I fancy the seal won't come there. I dined to-day at lady Lucy's, where they ran down my *Shower*; and said *Sid Hamet* was the silliest poem they ever read, and told Prior so, whom they thought to be author of it. Don't you wonder I never dined there before? But I am too busy, and they live too far off; and, besides, I don't like women so much as I did. [MD you must know, are not women.][1] I supped to-night at Addison's, with Garth, Steele, and Mr. Dopping; and am come home late. Lewis has sent to me to desire I will dine with some company I shall like. I suppose it is Mr. secretary St. John's appointment. I had a letter just now from Raymond, who is at Bristol, and says he will be at London in a fortnight, and leave his wife behind

[1] Brackets in D. S.

him; and desires any lodging in the house where I am: but that must not be. I shan't know what to do with him in town: to be sure I will not present him to any acquaintance of mine, and he will live a delicate life, a parson and a perfect stranger. Paaast twelvvve o'clock,[1] and so good night, &c. O! but I forgot, Jemmey Leigh is come to town; says he has brought Dingley's things, and will send them with the first convenience. My parcel I hear is not sent yet. He thinks of going for Ireland in a month, &c. I cannot write to-morrow, because — what, because of the archbishop; because I will seal my letter early; because I am engaged from noon till night; because of many kind of things; and yet I will write one or two words to-morrow morning, to keep up my journal constant, and at night I will begin the ninth.

11. Morning by candlelight. You must know that I am in my night-gown every morning between six and seven, and Patrick is forced to ply me fifty times before I can get on my night-gown; and so now I'll take my leave of my own dear MD for this letter, and begin my next when I come home at night. God Almighty bless and protect dearest MD. Farewel, &c.

This letter's as long as a sermon, faith.

LETTER IX

London, *Nov.* 11, 1710.

I DINED to-day, by invitation, with the secretary of state, Mr. St. John. Mr. Harley came in to us before dinner, and made me his excuses for not dining with us, because he was to receive people who came to propose advancing money to the government: there dined with us only Mr. Lewis, and Dr. Freind (that writ lord Peterborow's *Actions in Spain*).[2] I staid with them till just now between ten and eleven, and was forced again to give my eighth to the bell-man, which I did with my own hands, rather than keep it till next post. The secretary used me with all the kindness in the world. Prior came in after dinner; and, upon an occasion, he [the secretary][3] said, the best thing he

---

[1] The watchman's call in the street outside.

[2] Dr. John Freind [1675–1728], a celebrated physician and philosopher, and an active politician and author. In 1705, he attended the Earl of Peterborough to Spain; and subsequently wrote a spirited defence of the conduct of that illustrious commander against the calumnies that assailed it. A steady Tory, he took a share in the defence of Dr. Sacheverell; and in 1722, when he sat in Parliament for Launceston, he fell under the suspicion of the Government, and was sent to the Tower. He came into favour at Court on the accession of George II., and died physician to Queen Caroline.—D. L. P.

[3] Brackets in D. S.

ever read is not yours, but Dr. Swift's on Vanbrugh; which I do
not reckon so very good neither. But Prior was damped until
I stuft him with two or three compliments. I am thinking what
a veneration we used to have for sir William Temple, because
he might have been secretary of state at fifty; and here is a
young fellow, hardly thirty,[1] in that employment. His father is
a man of pleasure, that walks the Mall, and frequents St.
James's Coffee-house, and the Chocolate-houses,[2] and the young
son is principal secretary of state. Is there not something very
odd in that? He told me, among other things, that Mr. Harley
complained he could keep nothing from me, I had the way so
much of getting into him. I knew that was a refinement; and
so I told him, and it was so: indeed it is hard to see these great
men use me like one who was their betters, and the puppies
with you in Ireland hardly regarding me: but there are some
reasons for all this, which I will tell you when we meet. At
coming home I saw a letter from your mother, in answer to
one I sent her two days ago. It seems she is in town; but cannot come out in a morning, just as you said; and God knows
when I shall be at leisure in an afternoon: for if I should send
her a penny-post letter, and afterward not be able to meet her,
it would vex me; and, besides, the days are short, and why she
cannot come early in a morning before she is wanted, I cannot
imagine. I will desire her to let lady Giffard know that she
hears I am in town, and that she would go to see me to enquire
after you. I wonder she will confine herself so much to that
old Beast's humour. You know I cannot in honour see lady
Giffard, and consequently not go into her house. This I think
is enough for the first time.

12. And how could you write with such thin paper? (I forgot
to say this in my former.) Can't you get thicker? Why that's
a common caution that writing masters give their scholars;
you must have heard it a hundred times. 'Tis this,

> If paper be thin,
> Ink will slip in;
> But if it be thick,
> You may write with a stick.[3]

---

[1] He had even been Secretary of War three years before, resigning with
Harley in 1707. Still more remarkable instances of administration by youth-
ful talent occurred in the second half of the eighteenth century.—D. L. P.

[2] Sir Henry St. John, who seems to have continued gay while life
lasted. In his youth he was tried and convicted for the murder of Sir
William Estcourt in a duel.—D. L. P.

[3] These alleged proverbs that Swift adduces are no more real quotations
than were the extracts from *Old Play* that Sir Walter Scott afterwards
headed his chapters with.

I had a letter to-day from poor Mrs. Long, giving me an account of her present life, obscure in a remote country town, and how easy she is under it. Poor creature! 'tis just such an alteration in life, as if Presto should be banished from MD, and condemned to converse with Mrs. Raymond. I dined to-day with Ford, sir Richard Levinge,[1] &c. at a place where they board, hard by. I was lazy, and not very well, sitting so long with company yesterday. I have been very busy writing this evening at home, and had a fire: I am spending my second half-bushel of coals; and now am in bed, and 'tis late.

13. I dined to-day in the city, and then went to christen Will Frankland's child; and lady Falconbridge was one of the god-mothers: this is a daughter of Oliver Cromwel,[2] and extremely like him by his pictures that I have seen. I staid till almost eleven, and am now come home and gone to bed. My business in the city was to thank Stratford for a kindness he has done me, which now I will tell you. I found Bank Stock was fallen thirty-four in the hundred, and was mighty desirous to buy it; but I was a little too late for the cheapest time, being hindered by business here; for I was so wise to guess to a day when it would fall. My project was this: I had three hundred pounds in Ireland; and so I writ Mr. Stratford in the city, to desire he would buy me three hundred pounds in Bank Stock, and that he should keep the papers, and that I would be bound to pay him for them; and if it should rise or fall, I would take my chance, and pay him interest in the mean time. I shewed my letter to one or two people, who understand those things; and they said, money was so hard to be got here, that no man would do it for me. However, Stratford, who is the most generous man alive, has done it: but it costs one hundred pounds and a half, that is ten shillings, so that three hundred pounds costs me three hundred pounds and thirty shillings. This was done about a week ago, and I can have five pounds for my bar-

[1] Speaker of the House of Commons and Lord Chief Justice of the Queen's Bench, in Ireland.

[2] Lord Fauconberg, or Falconbridge, a gentleman of hereditary loyalty, found himself notwithstanding, during the usurpations, glad to marry the Protector's youngest daughter, Mary Cromwell. She is represented as a woman of high talent and spirit, and died 14th March, 1712. A noble-man, who had seen Cromwell's remains dug up after the Restoration, venturing to tell her jeeringly that he had seen her father, and that he stunk abominably, she answered: "He was dead my Lord—had he been living, you would have stunk the worst." It was said by Cromwell's family, that "those who wore breeches deserved petticoats better; and had those who wore the petticoats had the breeches, they would have held faster."—SCOTT.

gain already. Before it fell it was one hundred and thirty pounds, and we are sure it will be the same again. I told you I writ to your mother, to desire that lady Giffard would do the same with what she owes you; but she tells your mother she has no money. I would to God all you had in the world was there. Whenever you lend money take this rule, to have two people bound, who have both visible fortunes; for they will hardly die together; and when one dies, you fall upon the other, and make him add another security: and if Rathburn (now I have his name) pays you in your money, let me know, and I will direct Parvisol accordingly: however, he shall wait on you and know. So, ladies, enough of business for one night. Paaaaast twelvvve o'clock. I must only add, that after a long fit of rainy weather, it has been fair two or three days, and is this day grown cold and frosty; so that you must give poor little Presto leave to have a fire in his chamber, morning and evening too, and he'll do as much for you.

14. What, has your chancellor [1] lost his senses, like Will Crowe? I forgot to tell Dingley, that I was yesterday at Ludgate, bespeaking the spectacles at the great shop there, and shall have them in a day or two. This has been an insipid day, I dined with Mrs. Vanhomrigh, and came gravely home, after just visiting the Coffee-house. Sir Richard Cox, [2] they say, is sure of going over lord chancellor, who is as arrant a puppy as ever eat bread: but the duke of Ormond has a natural affection to puppies, which is a thousand pities, being none himself. I have been amusing myself at home till now, and in bed bid you good night.

15. I have been visiting this morning, but nobody was at home, secretary St. John, sir Thomas Hanmer, [3] sir chancellor Cox-comb, &c. I attended the duke of Ormond with about fifty other Irish gentlemen at Skinners-hall, where the Londonderry society laid out three hundred pounds to treat us and his grace with a dinner. Three great tables with the dessert laid in mighty figure. Sir Richard Levinge and I got discreetly to the head of the second table, to avoid the crowd at the first: but it was so cold, and so confounded a noise with the trumpets and hautboys, that I grew weary, and stole away before the

[1] The Irish Lord Chancellor, Richard Freeman, who had been Chief Baron.
[2] (1650–1733). Born at Bandon, Cork, Lord Chancellor of Ireland 1703–1707. He was never Chancellor again, and lost the Chief Justiceship on the Queen's death.
[3] (1677–1746). Afterwards Speaker of the House of Commons. He edited Shakespeare.

second course came on: so I can give you no account of it, which is a thousand pities. I called at Ludgate for Dingley's glasses, and shall have them in a day or two; and I doubt it it will cost me thirty shillings for a microscope, but not without Stella's permission; for I remember she is a *virtuoso*. Shall I buy it or no? 'Tis not the great bulky ones, nor the common little ones, to impale a louse (saving your presence) upon a needle's point; but of a more exact sort, and clearer to the sight, with all its equipage in a little trunk that you may carry in your pocket. Tell me, sirrah, shall I buy it or not for you? I came home straight, &c.

16. I dined to-day in the city with Mr. Manley,[1] who invited Mr. Addison and me, and some other friends, to his lodging, and entertained us very handsomely. I returned with Mr. Addison, and loitered till nine in the Coffee-house, where I am hardly known by going so seldom. I am here soliciting for Trounce; you know him: he was gunner in the former yacht, and would fain be so in the present one: if you remember him, a good lusty fresh-coloured fellow. Shall I stay till I get another letter from MD before I close up this? Mr. Addison and I meet a little seldomer than formerly, although we are still at bottom as good friends as ever; but differ a little about party.

17. To-day I went to Lewis at the secretary's office, where I saw and spoke to Mr. Harley, who promised, in a few days, to finish the rest of my business. I reproached him for putting me on the necessity of minding him of it, and rallied him, &c. which he took very well. I dined to-day with one Mr. Gore, elder brother to a young merchant of my acquaintance, and Stratford, and my other friend merchants dined with us, where I staid late, drinking claret and burgundy, and am just got to bed, and will say no more, but that it now begins to be time to have a letter from my own little MD; for the last I had above a fortnight ago, and the date was old too.

18. To-day I dined with Lewis and Prior at an eating-house, but with Lewis's wine. Lewis went away, and Prior and I sat on, where we complimented one another for an hour or two upon our mutual wit and poetry. Coming home at seven, a gentleman unknown stopt me in the Pall-mall, and askt my advice; said he had been to see the queen (who was just come to town) and the people in waiting would not let him see her; that he had two hundred thousand men ready to serve her in the war; that he knew the queen perfectly well, and had an

[1] *See* Letter V., Oct. 1 (note).

apartment at Court, and if she heard he was there, she would send for him immediately; that she owed him two hundred thousand pounds, &c. and he desired my opinion whether he should go try again whether he could see her; or, because, perhaps, she was weary after her journey, whether he had not better stay still to-morrow. I had a mind to get rid of my companion, and begged him of all love to go and wait on her immediately; for that, to my knowledge, the queen would admit him; that this was an affair of great importance, and required dispatch: and I instructed him to let me know the success of his business, and come to the Smyrna Coffee-house, where I would wait for him till midnight; and so ended this adventure. I would have fain given the man half a crown; but was afraid to offer it him, lest he should be offended; for beside his money, he said he had a thousand pounds a year. I came home not early, and so, madams both, good night, &c.

19. I dined to-day with poor lord Mountjoy, who is ill of the gout; and this evening I christened our coffee-man Elliot's [1] child, where the rogue had a most noble supper, and Steele and I sat among some scurvy company over a bowl of punch, so that I am come home late, young women, and can't stay to write to little rogues.

20. I loitered at home, and dined with sir Andrew Fountain at his lodging, and then came home: a silly day.

21. I was visiting all this morning, and then went to the secretary's office, and found Mr. Harley, with whom I dined; and secretary St. John, &c. and Harley promised in a very few days to finish what remains of my business. Prior was of the company, and we all dine at the secretary's to-morrow. I saw Stella's mother this morning: she came early, and we talked an hour. I wish you would propose to lady Giffard to take the three hundred pounds out of her hands, and give her common interest for life, and security that will pay her: the bishop of Clogher, or any friend, would be security for you, if you gave them counter-security; and it may be argued, that it will pass better to be in your hands than hers in case of mortality, &c. Your mother says, if you write she'll second it; and you may write to your mother, and then it will come from her. She tells me lady Giffard has a mind to see me, by her discourse; but I told her what to say, with a *vengeance*. She told lady Giffard she was going to see me: she looks extremely well. I am writing in my bed like a tyger, and so good night, &c.

[1] Elliot was keeper of the St. James's Coffeehouse.—D. L. P.

22. I dined with secretary St. John; and lord Dartmouth, who is t'other secretary, dined with us, and lord Orrery[1] and Prior, &c. Harley called, but could not dine with us, and would have had me away while I was at dinner; but I did not like the company he was to have. We stayed till eight, and I called at the Coffee-house, and looked where the letters lie; but no letter directed for Mr. Presto: at last I saw a letter to Mr. Addison, and it looked like a rogue's hand, so I made the fellow give it me, and opened it before him, and saw three letters all for myself: so, truly, I put them in my pocket, and came home to my lodging. Well, and so you shall hear: well, and so I found one of them in Dingley's hand, and t'other in Stella's, and the third in Domville's.[2] Well, so you shall hear; So, said I to myself, what now, two letters from MD together? But I thought there was something in the wind; so I opened one, and I opened t'other; and so you shall hear, one was from Walls. Well, but t'other was from [my] own dear MD; yes it was. O faith, have you received my seventh, young women, already; then I must send this to-morrow, else there will be old doings at our house, faith.—Well, I won't answer your letter in this: no faith, catch me at that, and I never saw the like. Well; but as to Walls, tell him (with service to him and wife, &c.) that I have no imagination of Mr. Pratt's losing his place: and while Pratt continues Clements[3] is in no danger; and I have already engaged lord Hyde he speaks of, for Pratt and twenty others; but if such a thing should happen, I will do what I can. I have above ten businesses of other people's now on my hands, and, I believe, shall miscarry in half. It is your sixth I now have received. I writ last post to the bishop of Clogher again. Shall I send this to-morrow? Well, I will to oblige MD. Which would you rather, a short letter every week, or a long one every fortnight? A long one; well, it shall be done, and so good night. Well but is this a long one? No, I warrant you: too long for naughty girls.

23. I only ask, have you got both the ten pounds, or only the first; I hope you mean both. Pray be good housewives;

---

[1] Charles Boyle (1676–1731), fourth Earl of Orrery, whose dispute with Richard Bentley over Bentley's dispute with Sir William Temple concerning the genuineness of the " Epistles of Phalaris " led to the composition of Swift's early work, *The Battle of the Books*.

[2] William Domville, of Longman's town in the county of Dublin, Esq.—F.

[3] Robert Clements of Rathkenny, descended from a Leicestershire family settled in Ireland, and grandfather to the first Earl of Leitrim, was a Deputy Vice-Treasurer of Ireland.

and I beg you to walk when you can for health. Have you the
horse in town? and do you ever ride him? how often? Confess.
Ahhh, sirrah, have I caught you? Can you contrive to let Mrs.
Fenton [1] know, that the request she has made me in her letter,
I will use what credit I have to bring about, although I hear
it is very difficult, and I doubt I shall not succeed. Cox is not
to be your chancellor: all joined against him. I have been
supping with lord Peterborow at his house, with Prior, Lewis,
and Dr. Freind. 'Tis the ramblingest lying rogue on earth. [2]
Dr. Raymond is come to town: 'tis late, and so I bid you
good night.

24. I tell you pretty management: Ned Southwell told me
t'other day, he had a letter from the bishops of Ireland, with
an address to the duke of Ormond, to intercede with the queen,
to take off the First-Fruits. I dined with him to-day, and saw
it, with another letter to him from the bishop of Kildare, [3] to
call upon me for the papers, &c. and I had last post one from
the archbishop of Dublin, telling me the reason of this proceeding; that upon hearing the duke of Ormond was declared
lord lieutenant, they met, and the bishops were for this project, and talkt coldly of my being solicitor, as one that was
favour'd by t'other party, &c. but desired that I would still
solicit. Now the wisdom of this is admirable; for I had given
the archbishop an account of my reception from Mr. Harley,
and how he had spoken to the queen, and promised it should
be done; but Mr. Harley ordered me to tell no person alive.
Some time after he gave me leave to let the primate and archbishop know that the queen had remitted the First-Fruits; and
that in a short time they should have an account of it in form
from lord Dartmouth, secretary of state. So while their letter
was on the road to the duke of Ormond and Southwell, mine
was going to them with an account of the thing being done.
I writ a very warm answer to the archbishop immediately, and
shewed my resentments, as I ought, against the bishops, only
in good manners, excepting himself. I wonder what they will
say when they hear the thing is done. I was yesterday forced
to tell Southwell so, that the queen had done it, &c. for he
said, my lord duke would think of it some months hence when
he was going for Ireland; and he had it three years in doing

---

[1] Swift's sister Jane, who married a currier called Fenton, in Bride
Street, Dublin; for which, it is said, Swift never forgave her.
[2] Peterborough to wit.—D. L. P.
[3] Welbore Ellis (1651?-1734). Translated to Meath, 1731. He was an
Englishman.

formerly, without any success. I give you free leave to say, on occasion, that it is done, and that Mr. Harley prevailed on the queen to do it, &c. as you please. As I hope to live, I despise the credit of it, out of an excess of pride, and desire you will not give me the least merit when you talk of it; but I would vex the bishops, and have it spread that Mr. Harley had done it: pray do so. Your mother sent me last night a parcel of wax candles, and a bandbox full of small plumcakes. I thought it had been something for you; and, without opening them, sent answer by the maid that brought them, that I would take care to send the things, &c. but I will write her thanks. Is this a long letter, sirrahs? Now, are you satisfied? I have had no fit since the first: I drink brandy every morning, and take pills every night. Never fear, I an't vexed at this puppy business of the bishops, although I was a little at first. I'll tell you my reward: Mr. Harley will think he has done me a favour; the duke of Ormond, perhaps, that I have put a neglect on him; and the bishops in Ireland, that I have done nothing at all. So goes the world. But I have got above all this, and, perhaps, I have better reason for it than they know: and so you shall hear no more of First-Fruits, dukes, Harleys, archbishops, and Southwells.

I have slipt off Raymond upon some of his countrymen to shew him the town, &c. and I lend him Patrick. He desires to sit with me in the evenings; upon which I have given Patrick positive orders that I am not within at evenings.

LETTER X

London, *Nov.* 25, 1710.

I'LL tell you something that's plaguy silly: I had forgot to say on the 23d in my last, where I dined; and because I had done it constantly, I thought it was a great omission, and was going to interline it; but at last the silliness of it made me cry, Pshah, and I let it alone. I was to-day to see the Parliament meet; but only saw a great crowd: and Ford and I went to see the tombs at Westminster, and sauntered so long I was forced to go to an eating-house for my dinner. Bromley is chosen speaker, *nemine contradicente*: Do you understand those two words? And Pompey, colonel Hill's black, designs to stand speaker for the footmen.[1] I am engaged to use my interest for him,

[1] The footmen in attendance on their masters at the Houses of Parliament used to form themselves into a deliberative body, and debate the same matters with their masters. Pompey, being the servant of the

and have spoken to Patrick to get him some votes. We are now all impatient for the queen's speech, what she will say about removing the ministry, &c. I have got a cold, and I don't know how; but got it I have, and am hoarse: I don't know whether it will grow better or worse. What's that to you? I won't answer your letter to-night. I'll keep you a little longer in suspense: I can't send it. Your mother's cakes are very good, and one of them serves me for a breakfast, and so I'll go sleep like a good boy.

26. I have got a cruel cold, and staid within all this day in my night-gown, and dined on six-pennyworth of victuals, and read and writ, and was denied to every body. Dr. Raymond called often, and I was denied; and at last, when I was weary, I let him come up, and asked him, without consequence, How Patrick denied me, and whether he had the art of it? So by this means he shall be used to have me denied to him; otherwise he would be a plaguy trouble and hindrance to me: he has sat with me two hours, and drank a pint of ale cost me five pence, and smoakt his pipe, and 'tis now past eleven that he is just gone. Well, my eighth is with you now, young women, and your seventh to me is somewhere in a post-boy's bag; and so go to your gang of deans, and Stoytes, and Walls, and lose your money; go, sauce-boxes, and so good night and be happy, dear rogues. Oh, but your box was sent to Dr. Hawkshaw by Sterne, and you will have it with Hawkshaw, and spectacles, &c. &c.

27. To-day Mr. Harley met me in the court of requests,[1] and whispered me to dine with him. At dinner I told him what those bishops had done, and the difficulty I was under. He bid me never trouble myself; he would tell the duke of Ormond the business was done, and that he need not concern himself about it. So now I am easy, and they may hang themselves for a parcel of insolent ungrateful rascals. I suppose I told you in my last, how they sent an address to the duke of Ormond, and a letter to Southwell, to call on me for the papers, after the thing was over, but they had not received my letter; though the archbishop might, by what I writ to him, have expected it would be done. Well, there's an end of that; and in

brother of Mrs. Masham, the ruling favourite, had the Court and Tory interest in the footmen's parliament in his favour.—D. L. P. John Hill (d. 1735), brother of Mrs. Masham and "Mrs." (Alice) Hill, was about this time made a brigadier-general; major-general, 1712. He is often hereinafter referred to as "Jack Hill."

[1] The "Court of Requests" was no longer in existence as such. The chamber in Whitehall, where it had sat, probably retained the name.

a little time the queen will send them notice, &c. And so the methods will be settled; and then I shall think of returning, although the baseness of those bishops makes me love Ireland less than I did.

28. Lord Hallifax sent to invite me to dinner, where I staid till six, and crost him in all his Whig talk, and made him often come over to me. I know he makes court to the new men, although he affects to talk like a Whig. I had a letter to-day from the bishop of Clogher; but I writ to him lately, that I would obey his commands to the duke of Ormond. He says I bid him read the London *Shaver*, and that you both swore it was *Shaver*, and not *Shower*. You all lie, and you are puppies, and can't read Presto's hand. The bishop is out entirely in his conjectures of my share in the *Tatlers*.—I have other things to mind, and of much greater importance,[1] else I have little to do to be acquainted with a new ministry, who consider me a little more than Irish bishops do.

29. Now for your saucy good dear letter: let me see, what does it say? come then. I dined to-day with Ford, and went home early; he debauched[2] me to his chamber again with a bottle of wine till twelve: so good night. I can't write an answer now, you rogues.

30. To-day I have been visiting, which I had long neglected; and I dined with Mrs. Barton alone; and sauntered at the Coffee-house till past eight, and have been busy till eleven, and now I'll answer your letter, sauce-box. Well, let me see now again. My wax candle's almost out, but however I'll begin. Well then, don't be so tedious, Mr. Presto; what can you say to MD's letter? Make haste, have done with your preambles— Why, I say I am glad you are so often abroad; your mother thinks it is want of exercise hurts you, and so do I. (She called here to-night, but I was not within, that's by the bye.) Sure you don't deceive me, Stella, when you say you are in better health than you were these three weeks; for Dr. Raymond told me yesterday, that Smyth of the Blind-Quay had been telling Mr. Leigh, that he left you extreamly ill; and in short, spoke so, that he almost put poor Leigh into tears, and would have made me run distracted; though your letter is dated the 11th instant, and I saw Smyth in the city above a fortnight ago, as I past by in a coach. Pray, pray, don't write, Stella, until you are mighty, mighty, mighty, mighty, mighty well in

---

[1] He was writing the *Examiner* at this time.—N.
[2] Seduced.

your eyes, and are sure it won't do you the least hurt. Or come,
I'll tell you what; you, mistress Stella, shall write your share
at five or six sittings, one sitting a day; and then comes Dingley
all together, and then Stella a little crumb towards the end,
to let us see she remembers Presto; and then conclude with
something handsome and genteel, as your most humblecum-
dumble, or, &c. O Lord! does Patrick write of my not coming
till *spring*? Insolent man! he know my secrets? No; as my Lord
Mayor said, No; if I thought my shirt knew, &c. Faith, I will
come as soon as it is any way proper for me to come; but, to
say the truth, I am at present a little involved with the present
ministry in some certain things (which I tell you as a secret)
and soon as ever I can clear my hands, I will stay no longer:
for I hope the first-fruit business will be soon over in all its forms.
But, to say the truth, the present ministry have a difficult task,
and want me, &c. Perhaps they may be just as grateful as others:
but, according to the best judgment I have, they are pursuing
the true interest of the publick; and therefore I am glad to
contribute what is in my power. For God's sake, not a word of
this to any alive.—Your chancellor [1]? Why, madam, I can tell
you he has been dead this fortnight. Faith, I could hardly forbear our little language about a nasty dead chancellor, as you
may see by the blot.[2] Ploughing? A pox plough them; they'll
plough me to nothing. But have you got your money, both the
ten pounds? How durst he pay you the second so soon? Pray
be good huswives.—Aye, well, and Joe; why, I had a letter
lately from Joe, desiring I would take some care of their poor
town,[3] who, he says, will lose their liberties. To which I desired
Dr. Raymond would return answer; That the town had behaved
themselves so ill to me, so little regarded the advice I gave
them, and disagreed so much among themselves, that I was
resolved never to have more to do with them; but that what-
soever personal kindness I could do to Joe, should be done.
Pray, when you happen to see Joe, tell him this, lest Raymond
should have blundered or forgotten.—Poor Mrs. Wesley—Why
these poligyes [4] for being abroad? Why should you be at home
at all, until Stella is quite well?—So, here is mistress Stella
again with her two eggs, &c. My *Shower* admired with You;
why, the bishop of Clogher says, he has seen something of mine

---

[1] *See* Letter IX., Nov. 14.
[2] The words *this fortnight*, in the preceding sentence, were first written
in their *little language*, and afterward scratched out and written plain.
[3] Trim. Its liberties had been attacked by Wharton.
[4] So written for *apologies.*—D. S.

of the same sort, better than the *Shower*. I suppose he means *The Morning*[1]; but it is not half so good. I want your judgment of things, and not your country's. How does MD like it? and do they taste it *all*? &c.[2] I am glad dean Bolton has paid the twenty pounds. Why should not I chide the bishop of Clogher for writing to the archbishop of Cashel,[3] without sending the letter first to me? It does not signify a ——; for he has no credit at court. Stuff—they are all puppies. I'll break your head in good earnest, young woman, for your nasty jest about Mrs. Barton. Unlucky sluttikin, what a word is there? Faith, I was thinking yesterday, when I was with her, whether she could break them or no,[4] and it quite spoiled my imagination. Mrs. Walls, does Stella win as she pretends? No indeed, *doctor*; she loses always, and will play so *ventersomely*, how can she win? See here now; an't you an impudent lying slut? Do, open Domvile's letter; what does it signify, if you have a mind? Yes, faith, you write smartly with your eyes shut; all was well but the *w*. See how I can do it; *Madam Stella, your humble servant*.[5] O, but one may look whether one goes crooked or no, and so write on. I'll tell you what you may do; you may write with your eyes half shut, just as when one is going to sleep: I have done so for two or three lines now; 'tis but just seeing enough to go straight.—Now, madam Dingley, I think I bid you tell Mr. Walls, that in case there be occasion, I will serve his friend as far as I can; but I hope there will be none. Yet I believe you will have a new Parliament; but I care not whether you have or no a better. You are mistaken in all your conjectures about the *Tatlers*. I have given him one or two hints, and you have heard me talk about the *Shilling*.[6] Faith, these answering letters are very long ones: you have taken up almost the room of a week in journals; and I'll tell you what, I saw fellows wearing crosses to-day,[7] and I wondered what was the matter; but just this minute I recollect it is little Presto's birth-day; and I was resolved these three days to remember it when it came, but could rot. Pray, drink my

---

[1] A *Description of the Morning* in London, in the same strain as the *Shower*, written in 1709.

[2] He certainly means the ridicule of tripets in particular.—D. S.

[3] William Palliser (1646–1726). He was an Englishman, and had been Bishop of Cloyne.

[4] This jest is lost, whatever it was, for want of MD's letter.—D. S.

[5] Here he writ with his eyes shut, and the writing is somewhat crooked, although as well in other respects as if his eyes had been open.—D. S.

[6] *Tatler*, No. 249.

[7] St. Andrew's Day.—D. S.

health to-day at dinner; do, you rogues. Do you like *Sid Hamet's Rod*? Do you understand it all? Well, now at last I have done with your letter, and so I'll lay me down to sleep, and about fair maids; and I hope merry maids all.

Dec. 1. Morning. I wish Smyth were hanged. I was dreaming the most melancholy things in the world of poor Stella, and was grieving and crying all night.—Pshoh, 'tis foolish: I'll rise and divert myself; so good morrow, and God of his infinite mercy keep and protect you. The bishop of Clogher's letter is dated Nov. 21. He says, you thought of going with him to Clogher. I am heartily glad of it, and wish you would ride there, and Dingley go in a coach. I have had no fit since my first, although sometimes my head is not quite in good order.—At night. I was this morning to visit Mr. Pratt, who is come over with poor sick lord Shelburn; they made me dine with them, and there I staid, like a booby, till eight, looking over them at ombre, and then came home. Lord Shelburn's giddiness is turned into a colick, and he looks miserably.

2. Steele, the rogue, has done the impudentest thing in the world; he said something in a *Tatler*, that we ought to use the word Great Britain, and not England, in common conversation, as, *The finest lady in Great Britain*, &c. Upon this Rowe, Prior, and I sent him a letter, turning this into ridicule. He has to-day printed the letter, and signed it J. S. M. P. and N. R. the first letters of all our names.[1] Congreve told me to-day, he smoakt it immediately. Congreve and I and sir Charles Wager dined to-day at Delaval's, the Portugal envoy; and I staid there till eight, and came home, and am now writing to you before I do business, because that dog Patrick is not at home, and the fire is not made, and I am not in my gear. Pox take him!—I was looking by chance at the top of this side, and find I make plaguy mistakes in words; so that you must fence against that as well as bad writing. Faith, I can't nor won't read what I have written. (Pox of this puppy!) Well, I'll leave you till I am got to bed, and then I'll say a word or two.—Well, 'tis now almost twelve, and I have been busy ever since, by a fire too, (I have my coals by half a bushel at a time, I'll assure you) and now I am got to bed. Well, and what have you to say to Presto now he is a-bed? Come now, let us hear your speeches. No, 'tis a lie, I an't sleepy yet. Let us sit up a little longer, and talk. Well, where have you been to-day, that you are but just this minute come home in a coach? What have you lost? Pay

[1] No. 258. *See ante*, Oct. 13.

the coachman, Stella. No, faith, not I, he'll grumble.—What
new acquaintance have you got? come, let us hear. I have made
Delaval promise to send me some Brazil tobacco from Portugal
for you, madam Dingley. I hope you'll have your chocolate
and spectacles before this comes to you.

3. Pshaw, I must be writing to these dear saucy brats every
night, whether I will or no, let me have what business I will,
or come home ever so late, or be ever so sleepy; but an old
saying, and a true one, Be you lords, or be you earls, you
must write to naughty girls. I was to-day at Court, and saw
Raymond among the Beef-eaters, staying to see the queen:
so I put him in a better station, made two or three dozen of
bows, and went to church, and then to Court again, to pick
up a dinner, as I did with Sir John Stanley, and then we went
to visit lord Mountjoy, and just now left him, and 'tis near
eleven at night, young women, and methinks this letter comes
pretty near to the bottom, and 'tis but eight days since the
date, and don't think I'll write on t'other side, I thank you
for nothing. Faith, if I would use you to letters on sheets as
broad as this room, you would always expect them from me.
Oh, faith, I know you well enough; but an old saying, &c. Two
sides in a sheet, and one in a street. I think that's but a silly
old saying, and so I'll go to sleep, and do you so too.

4. I dined to day with Mrs. Vanhomrigh, and then came home,
and studied till eleven.[1] No adventure at all to-day.

5. So I went to the court of requests (we have had the Devil
and all of rain by the bye) to pick up a dinner; and Henley
made me go dine with him and one colonel Brag [2] at a tavern,
cost me money, faith. Congreve was to be there, but came not.
I came with Henley to the Coffee-house, where lord Salisbury
seemed mighty desirous to talk with me; and while he was
wriggling himself into my favour, that dog Henley asked me
aloud, whether I would go to see lord Somers, as I had promised
(which was a lie) and all to vex poor Lord Salisbury,[3] who is
a high Tory. He played two or three other such tricks, and
I was forced to leave my lord, and I came home at seven, and
have been writing ever since, and will now go to bed. T'other
day I saw Jack Temple [4] in the court of requests: it was the
first time of seeing him; so we talked two or three careless words,

---

[1] The first edition, and editions later than D. S., read: "till evening."
[2] Mr. Aitken says he was Lieut.-General Philip Bragg, M.P. for Armagh.
[3] James Cecil (1691–1728), fifth earl.
[4] Sir William's nephew. See Letter II.

and parted. Is it true that your recorder and mayor, and fanatick aldermen,[1] a month or two ago, at a solemn feast, drank Mr. Harley's, lord Rochester's, and other Tory healths? Let me know: it was confidently said here.—The scoundrels! It shan't do, Tom.

6. When is this letter to go, I wonder: harkee, young women, tell me that. Saturday next for certain, and not before; then it will be just a fortnight; time enough for naughty girls, and long enough for two letters, faith. Congreve and Delaval have at last prevailed on Sir Godfrey Kneller to intreat me to let him draw my picture for nothing; but I know not yet when I shall sit.—It is such monstrous rainy weather, that there is no doing with it. Secretary St. John sent to me this morning, that my dining with him to-day was put off till to-morrow; so I peaceably sat with my neighbour Ford, dined with him, and came home at six, and am now in bed as usual; and now it is time to have another letter from MD, yet I would not have it till this goes: for that would look like two letters for one. Is it not whimsical that the dean has never once written to me? And I find the archbishop very silent to that letter I sent him with an account that the business was done. I believe he knows not what to write or say; and I have since written twice to him, both times with a vengeance. Well, go to bed, sirrahs, and so will I. But have you lost to-day? Three shillings. O fye, O fye.

7. No, I won't send this letter to-day, nor till Saturday, faith; and I'm so afraid of one from MD between this and that: if it comes, I'll just say I received a letter, and that's all. I dined to-day with Mr. secretary St. John, where were lord Anglesea,[2] Sir Thomas Hanmer, Prior, Freind, &c. and then made a debauch after nine at Prior's house, and have eaten cold pye, and I hate the thoughts of it, and I am full, and I don't like it, and I'll go to bed, and it is late, and so good night.

8. To-day I dined with Mr. Harley and Prior; but Mr. St. John did not come, though he promised: he chid me for not seeing him oftener. Here's a damned libellous pamphlet come out against lord Wharton, giving the character first, and then telling some of his actions: the character is very well, but the

---

[1] The aldermen of Dublin were fanatical in those days; but, about twenty years after the date of this letter, the Protestant party so far prevailed, that they have since that period kept out fanaticks of all denominations.—D. S. [Retained for its oddity.]

[2] This was Arthur, fifth earl, Vice-Treasurer of Ireland. See Letter III., Sept. 19 (note).

facts indifferent.[1] It has been sent by dozens to several gentlemen's lodgings, and I had one or two of them, but nobody knows the author or printer. We are terribly afraid of the plague; they say it is at Newcastle. I begged Mr. Harley for the love of God to take some care about it, or we are all ruined. There have been orders for all ships from the Baltick to pass their quarantain before they land; but they neglect it. You remember I have been afraid these two years.

9. O faith, you are a saucy rogue. I have had your sixth letter just now, before this is gone; but I won't answer a word of it, only that I never was giddy since my first fit, but I have had a cold just a fortnight, and cough with it still morning and evening; but it will go off. It is, however, such abominable weather that no creature can walk. They say here three of your commissioners will be turned out, Ogle, South, and St. Quintain,[2] and that Dick Stuart and Ludlow will be two of the new ones. I am a little soliciting for another; 'tis poor lord Abercorn,[3] but that is a secret, I mean, that I befriend him, is a secret; but I believe it is too late, by his own fault and ill fortune. I dined with him to-day. I am heartily sorry you don't go to Clogher, faith, I am; and so God Almighty protect poor dear, dear, dear, dearest MD. Farewel till to-night. I'll begin my eleventh to-night; so I am always writing to little MD.

LETTER XI

London, *Dec.* 9, 1710.

So, young women, I have just sent my tenth to the post-office, and, as I told you, have received your seventh (faith I'm afraid I mistook, and said your sixth, and then we shall be all in confusion this month). Well, I told you I dined with lord Abercorn to-day, and that's enough till by and bye; for I must go write idle things; and twittle twattle. What's here to do with your little MD's? and so I put this by for a while. —'Tis now late, and I can only say MD's a dear saucy rogue, and what then? Presto loves them the better.

10. This son of a b—— Patrick is out of the way, and I can

[1] *A Short Character of the Earl of Wharton*; Swift's own writing, though at the time unsuspected; Archbishop King, writing on Jan. 9, described it to Swift as "a wound given in the dark."—D. L. P.
[2] Mr. Aitken gives their names as Samuel Ogle, John South, and Sir William St. Quintin (*c.* 1660–1723), Bart., and says none of them lost place.
[3] James Hamilton (1656–1734), sixth earl.

do nothing; am forced to borrow coals: 'tis now six o'clock, and I am come home after a pure walk in the Park; delicate weather, begun only to-day. A terrible storm last night: we hear one of your pacquet boats is cast away, and young Beau Swift[1] in it, and general Sankey[2]: I know not the truth; you will before me. Raymond talks of leaving the town in a few days, and going in a month to Ireland, for fear his wife should be too far gone, and forced to be brought to-bed here. I think he is in the right; but perhaps this pacquet-boat will fright him. He has no relish for London; and I do not wonder at it. He has got some Templars from Ireland that shew him the town. I do not let him see me above twice a week, and that only while I am dressing in the morning.—So, now the puppy's come in, and I have got my own ink, but a new pen; and so now you are rogues and sauce-boxes till I go to bed; for I must go study, sirrahs. Now I think of it, tell the bishop of Clogher he shall not cheat me of one inch of my Bell Metal. You know it is nothing but to save the town money; and Eniskilling can afford it better than Laracor: he shall have but one thousand five hundred weight. I have been reading, &c. as usual, and am now going to bed; and I find this day's article is long enough; so get you gone till to-morrow and then. I dined with sir Matthew Dudley.

11. I am come again as yesterday, and the puppy had again lockt up my ink, notwithstanding all I said to him yesterday; but he came home a little after me, so all is well: they are lighting my fire, and I'll go study. The fair weather is gone again and it has rained all day. I do not like this open weather, though some say it is healthy. They say it is a false report about the plague at Newcastle. I have no news to-day: I dined with Mrs. Vanhomrigh, to desire them to buy me a scarf; and lady Abercorn[3] is to buy me another, to see who does best; mine is all in rags. I saw the duke of Richmond[4] yesterday at Court again; but would not speak to him: I believe we are fallen out. I am now in bed; and it has rained all this evening, like wildfire: Have you so much rain in your town? Raymond was in a fright, as I expected, upon the news of this shipwreck; but I persuaded him, and he leaves this town in a week. I got him

---

[1] According to Forster, a cousin, son of William Swift.
[2] According to Mr. Aitken, Nicholas Sankey, lieut.-general, 1710.
[3] Elizabeth (c. 1668-9–1754), only child of Sir Robert Reading of Dublin, became Lady Abercorn, 1683-4.
[4] Charles Lennox (1672–1723), first duke.

acquainted with sir Robert Raymond, the solicitor general,[1] who owns him to be of his family; and I believe it may do him a kindness, by being recommended to your new lord chancellor. —I had a letter from Mrs. Long, that has quite turned my stomach against her: no less than two nasty jests in it with dashes to suppose them. She is corrupted in that country town [2] with vile conversation.—I won't answer your letter till I have leisure: so let this go on as it will, what care I? what cares saucy Presto?

12. I was to-day at the secretary's office with Lewis, and in came lord Rivers,[3] who took Lewis out and whispered him; and then came up to me to desire my acquaintance, &c. so we bowed and complimented a while, and parted; and I dined with Phil. Savage,[4] and his Irish Club, at their boarding place; and, passing an evening scurvily enough, did not come home till eight. Mr. Addison and I hardly meet once a fortnight: his Parliament [5] and my different friendships keep us asunder. Sir Matthew Dudley turned away his butler yesterday morning, and at night the poor fellow died suddenly in the streets: Was not it an odd event? But what care you; but then I knew the butler.—Why, it seems your pacquet-boat is not lost: pshah, how silly that is, when I had already gone through the forms, and said it was a sad thing, and that I was sorry for it. But when must I answer this letter of our MD's? Here it is, it lies between this paper on t'other side [of] the leaf: one of these odd-come-shortly's I'll consider, and so good-night.

13. Morning. I am to go traping with lady Kerry and Mrs. Pratt [6] to see sights all this day: they engaged me yesterday morning at tea. You hear the havock making in the army: Meredyth, Macartney, and colonel Honeywood,[7] are obliged to

---

[1] (1673-1733); afterwards Lord Chief Justice.

[2] Lynn Regis.—D. S.

[3] Richard Savage (1660?-1712), fourth Earl Rivers, envoy to Hanover. He was claimed as father by the poet "Richard Savage," the friend of Dr. Johnson.

[4] Chancellor of the Exchequer in Ireland.—D. S.

[5] i.e. his attendance in Parliament.—D. S.

[6] Lady Kerry was Anne, sister of first Earl of Shelburne and daughter of Sir William Petty, M.D.; her husband was Thomas Fitzmaurice, twenty-first Baron (and afterwards first Earl) of Kerry. Mrs. Pratt, her friend, was probably the wife of the Mr. Pratt mentioned in Letter III., Sept. 11.

[7] 1. Thomas (d. 1719), son of Arthur Meredyth of Dollardstown, co. Meath; adjt.-general of the Forces, 1701; lieut.-general, 1708-9; saw considerable service under William III. and Marlborough; M.P. for Midhurst, 1709. 2. George (d. 1730), elder son of George Maccartney of Belfast. In 1689 was serving in the Scots Guards. Had once been deprived of his command for disgraceful conduct when drunk, but rose again and

sell their commands at half value, and leave the army, for drinking Destruction to the present ministry, and dressing up a hat on a stick, and calling it Harley; then drinking a glass with one hand, and discharging a pistol with the other at the maukin,[1] wishing it were Harley himself; and a hundred other such pretty tricks, as enflaming their soldiers, and foreign ministers, against the late changes at Court. Cadogan [2] has had a little paring: his mother [3] told me yesterday he had lost the place of envoy; but I hope they will go no further with him, for he was not at those mutinous meetings. Well, these saucy jades take up so much of my time, with writing to them in a morning; but faith I am glad to see you whenever I can: a little snap and away; and so hold your tongue, for I must rise: not a word for your life. How nowww? So, very well; stay till I come home, and then, perhaps, you may hear further from me. And where will you go to-day, for I can't be with you for these ladies? It is a rainy ugly day. I'd have you send for Walls, and go to the dean's; but don't play small games [4] when you lose. You'll be ruined by Manilio, Basto, the Queen, and two small Trumps in red. I confess 'tis a good hand against the player: but then there are Spadilio, Punto, the King, strong Trumps against you, which, with one Trump more, are three tricks ten ace: for, suppose you play your Manilio—O, silly, how I prate and can't get away from this MD in a morning.

became lieut.-general, 1709-10. 3. Philip Honywood (d. 1752, with the rank of general), brigadier-general at this time.

The performance for which they were dismissed took place in Flanders. (Dalton's *Army Lists*, Vol. IV., p. 30.)

[1] Or *Malkin*; the little image, or contemptible counterfeit.—D. L. P.

[2] William Cadogan [b. 1675], the friend and confidant of Marlborough, had been in 1706 sent as plenipotentiary to the United Provinces and the Spanish Netherlands, and was promoted to his lieut.-generalship in 1709; being recalled on this occasion, and replaced by Mr. Richard Hill, he was out of public employ till, on the accession of George I., he was made Master of the Robes. In 1716 he was sent as plenipotentiary to Holland, and created Earl Cadogan in 1718. He succeeded Marlborough, on his death in 1722, in the master-generalship of the ordnance and colonelcy of the first regiment of foot guards; and died in 1726. During Marlborough's campaigns, Cadogan had the charge of marking out almost every camp; and so thoroughly did his care and skill warrant the great reliance Marlborough placed in him, that the Duke was never during the whole war surprised or attacked in his camp. The officers who suffered at the same time with Cadogan under the imputation of anti-Tory sympathies, alleged in their defence, that they had only drunk a toast to Marlborough and confusion to his enemies; but a severe example was wanted to confirm the obedience of the army, and counteract the devotion of the chief officers to the Duke and the Whigs.—D. L. P.

[3] Bridget, daughter of Sir Hardress Waller, married Henry Cadogan, a barrister. William Cadogan was their son.

[4] ? *Smell*-games. *Cf.* Letter LX., Feb. 25 and 27, 1712-13.

Go, get you gone, dear naughty girls, and let me rise. There, Patrick lockt up my ink again the third time last night: the rogue gets the better of me; but I will rise in spite of you, sirrahs.—At night. Lady Kerry, Mrs. Pratt, Mrs. Cadogan,[1] and I, in one coach; Lady Kerry's son [2] and his governor, and two gentlemen in another; maids and misses, and little master (lord Shelburn's [3] children) in a third, all hackneys, set out at ten o'clock this morning from lord Shelburn's house in Piccadilly to the Tower, and saw all the sights, lions, &c. then to Bedlam; then dined at the Chop-house behind the Exchange; then to Gresham College (but the keeper was not at home) and concluded the night at the Puppet-Shew,[4] whence we came home safe at eight, and I left them. The ladies were all in mobbs [5]; how do you call it? undrest; and it was the rainiest day that ever dript; and I'm weary, and 'tis now past eleven.

14. Stay, I'll answer some of your letter this morning in bed: let me see; come and appear, little letter. Here I am, says he, and what say you to Mrs. MD this morning fresh and fasting? Who dares think MD negligent? I allow them a fortnight, and they give it me. I could fill a letter in a week; but it is longer every day, and so I keep it a fortnight, and then 'tis cheaper by one half. I have never been giddy, dear Stella, since that morning: I have taken a whole box of pills, and keckt at them every night, and drank a pint of brandy at mornings.—Oh then, you kept Presto's little Birth-day: would to God I had been with you. I forgot it, as I told you before. Rediculous, madam; I suppose you mean Ridiculous: let me have no more of that; 'tis the author of the *Atalantis*'s [6] spelling. I have mended it in your letter. And can Stella read this writing without hurting her dear eyes? O, faith, I'm afraid not. Have a care of those eyes, pray, pray, pretty Stella.—'Tis well enough

[1] Margaretta, daughter of William Munter, Councillor of the Court of Holland.

[2] Her eldest son William (*c.* 1694–1747) was afterwards second earl.

[3] Henry Petty (1675?–1751), third baron, first earl. *See ante*, Letter X., Dec. 1.

[4] The puppet show was an institution in very high favour with the people in Swift's time; and it is believed that the passage in *Gulliver's Travels*, where the voyager is made a spectacle for the amusement of the Brobdingnagians, was intended to satirise this proclivity. Defoe, in a pamphlet published in 1713, says that Mr. Powell, the manager of the Punch Theatre, "by subscriptions and full houses, has gathered such wealth as is sufficient to buy all the poets in England."—D. L. P.

[5] *i.e.* negligée.

[6] Mrs. Mary de la Riviere Manley (1663–1724) chronicler of scandal, daughter of Sir Roger Manley, cavalier. *See* Letter V., Oct. 1, note on John Manley.

what you observe, That if I writ better, perhaps you would not read so well, being used to this manner; 'tis an alphabet you are used to: you know such a pothook makes a letter; and you know what letter, and so, and so.—I'll swear he told me so, and that they were long letters too; but I told him it was a Gasconnade of yours, &c. I am talking of the bishop of Clogher, how he forgot. Turn over.[1] I had not room on t'other side to say that, so I did it on this: I fancy that's a good Irish blunder. Ah, why don't you go down to Clogher nautinautinautideargirls; I dare not say nauti without dear: O, faith, you govern me. But, seriously, I'm sorry you don't go, as far as I can judge at this distance. No, we would get you another horse; I will make Parvisol get you one. I always doubted that horse of yours: prythee sell him, and let it be a present to me. My heart akes when I think you ride him. Order Parvisol to sell him, and that you are to return me the money: I shall never be easy until he is out of your hands. Faith, I have dreamt five or six times of horses stumbling since I had your letter. If he can't sell him, let him run this Winter. Faith, if I was near you, I would whip your —— to some tune, for your grave saucy answer about the dean and Jonsonibus; I would, young women. And did the dean preach for me? Very well. Why, would they have me stand here and preach to them? No, the *Tatler* of the *Shilling*[2] was not mine, more than the hint, and two or three general heads for it. I have much more important business on my hands: and, besides, the ministry hate to think that I should help him, and have made reproaches on it; and I frankly told them, I would do it no more. This is a secret though, Madam Stella. You win eight shillings; you win eight fiddle-sticks. Faith, you say nothing of what you lose, young women.— I hope Manley is in no great danger; for Ned Southwell is his friend, and so is sir Thomas Frankland; and his brother John Manley stands up heartily for him. On t'other side, all the gentlemen of Ireland here are furiously against him. Now, Mistress Dingley, an't you an impudent slut to expect a letter next pacquet from Presto, when you confess yourself, that you had so lately two letters in four days? Unreasonable baggage! No, little Dingley, I am always in bed by twelve; I mean my candle's out by twelve, and I take great care of myself. Pray let every body know, upon occasion, that Mr. Harley got the

[1] He seems to have written these words in a whim, for the sake of what follows.—D. S.

[2] No. 249.

First-Fruits from the queen for the clergy of Ireland, and that nothing remains but the forms, &c. So you say the dean and you dined at Stoyte's, and Mrs. Stoyte was in raptures that I remembered her. I must do it but seldom, or it will take off her rapture.—But, what now, you saucy sluts, all this written in a morning, and I must rise and go abroad. Pray stay till night: don't think I'll squander mornings upon you, pray good Madam. Faith, if I go on longer in this trick of writing in the morning, I shall be afraid of leaving it off, and think you expect it, and be in awe. Good morrow, sirrahs, I will rise.—At night. I went to-day to the court of requests (I will not answer the rest of your letter yet, that by the way) in hopes to dine with Mr. Harley: but lord Dupplin, his son-in-law, told me he did not dine at home; so I was at a loss, until I met with Mr. secretary St. John, and went home and dined with him, where he told me of a good bite.[1] Lord Rivers told me two days ago, that he was resolved to come Sunday fortnight next to hear me preach before the queen. I assured him the day was not yet fixt, and I knew nothing of it. To-day the secretary told me, that his father, sir Harry St. John, and lord Rivers, were to be at St. James's church, to hear me preach there; and were assured I was to preach; so there will be another bite; for I know nothing of the matter, but that Mr. Harley and St. John are resolved I must preach before the queen, and the secretary of state has told me he will give me three weeks warning; but I desired to be excused, which he will not. St. John, "you shall not be excused:" however, I hope they will forget it; for if it should happen, all the puppies hereabouts will throng to hear me, and expect something wonderful, and be plaguily baulkt; for I shall preach plain honest stuff.[2] I staid with St. John till eight, and then came home, and Patrick desired leave to go abroad, and by and by comes up the girl to tell me, a gentleman was below in a coach who had a bill to pay me; so I let him come up, and who should it be but Mr. Addison and Sam Dopping, to haul me out to supper, where I have staid till twelve. If Patrick had been at home I should have scaped this; for I have taught him to deny me almost as well as Mr. Harley's porter.—Where did I leave off in MD's letter: let me see. So, now I have it. You are pleased to say, Madam Dingley, that those that go for England, can

---

[1] A quiz, a sell, a spoof.
[2] The ministry never could prevail upon Dr. Swift to preach before the queen.—D. S.

never tell when to come back. Do you mean this as a reflection upon Presto, Madam? Sauce-boxes, I'll come back as soon as I can, as hope saved, and I hope with some advantage, unless all ministries be alike, as perhaps they may. I hope Hawkshaw is in Dublin before now, and that you have your things, and like your spectacles: if you do not, you shall have better. I hope Dingley's tobacco did not spoil Stella's chocolate, and that all is safe: pray let me know. Mr. Addison and I are different as black and white, and I believe our friendship will go off, by this damned business of party: he cannot bear seeing me fall in so with this ministry; but I love him still as well as ever, though we seldom meet.—Hussy, Stella, you jest about poor Congreve's eyes; you do so, hussy; but I'll bang your bones, faith.—Yes, Steele was a little while in prison, or at least in a spunging-house, some time before I came, but not since.—Pox on your convocations, and your Lamberts[1]; they write with a vengeance! I suppose you think it a piece of affectation in me to wish your Irish folks would not like my *Shower*; but you are mistaken. I should be glad to have the general applause there as I have here (though I say it) but I have only that of one or two, and therefore I would have none at all, but let you all be in the wrong. I don't know, this is not what I would say; but I am so tosticated with supper and stuff that I can't express myself—What you say of *Sid Hamet* is well enough; that an enemy should like it, and a friend not; and that telling the author would make both change their opinions. Why did not you tell Griffyth[2] that you fancied there was something in it of my manner; but first spur up his commendation to the height, as we served my poor uncle about the sconce that I mended. Well, I desired you to give what I intended for an answer to Mrs. Fenton, to save her postage, and myself trouble; and I hope I have done it, if you han't.

15. Lord, what a long day's writing was yesterday's answer to your letter, sirrahs? I dined to-day with Lewis and Ford, whom I have brought acquainted. Lewis told me a pure thing. I had been hankering with Mr. Harley to save Steele his other employment, and have a little mercy on him, and I had been saying the same thing to Lewis, who is Mr. Harley's chief favourite. Lewis tells Mr. Harley how kindly I should take it,

---

[1] Dr. Lambert was chaplain to Lord Wharton. He was censured in the Lower House of Convocation of Ireland as author of a libelling letter.—N

[2] *See* Letter LXI., March 3, 1712-13.

if he would be reconciled to Steele, &c. Mr. Harley, on my
account, falls in with it, and appoints Steele a time to let him
attend him, which Steele accepts with great submission, but
never comes, nor sends any excuse. Whether it was blundering,
sullenness, insolence, or rancor of party, I cannot tell; but I
shall trouble myself no more about him. I believe Addison
hindered him out of meer spight, being grated to the soul to
think he should ever want my help to save his friend; yet now he
is soliciting me to make another of his friends queen's secretary
at Geneva; and I'll do it if I can, it is poor Pastoral Philips.[1]

16. O, why did you leave my picture behind you at t'other
lodgings; forgot it? Well; but pray remember it now, and don't
roll it up, d'ye hear, but hang it carefully in some part of your
room, where chairs and candles, and mop-sticks won't spoil it,
sirrahs. No truly, I will not be godfather to goody Walls this
bout, and I hope she'll have no more. There will be no quiet
nor cards for this child. I hope it will die the day after the
christening. Mr. Harley gave me a paper, with an account of
the sentence you speak of against the lads that defaced the
statue,[2] and that Ingoldsby [3] reprieved that part of it of standing
before the statue. I hope it was never executed. We have got
your Broderick out [4]; Doyne [5] is to succeed him, and Cox
Doyne. And so there's an end of your letter; 'tis all answered,
and now I must go on upon my own stock; go on, did I say?
Why, I have written enough; but this is too soon to send it

[1] Ambrose Philips [1675?-1749], the poet and dramatist, whose Pastorals
drew down on him the ridicule of Pope, and provoked from the poet the
threat to thrash the satirist. He was a zealous Whig; and Swift's application in his favour came to nothing, for they soon quarrelled on the score
of "party."—D. L. P.

[2] The equestrian statue of King William III., erected after the battle
of the Boyne in College Green, Dublin; it was garlanded or insulted as
the winds of party feeling or caprice blew among the students of Trinity
College—who found a standing grievance in the position of the statue,
with its back to the College and its face to the town. In June, 1710, the
truncheon had been wrenched out of the statue's hand, and its face
bedaubed with dirt, by a disorderly crowd of students, whose offence
was warmly noticed by the House of Commons in their farewell address
to Lord Wharton. Swift's sympathies were not all against the freak of
the hot bloods of the College.—D. L. P. From the point of view of a
veterinary anatomist, the statue (if the Free State authorities have
allowed it to stand) is a remarkable specimen of sculpture. In times of
stress, King William has been blown off his horse with gunpowder, but
was always immediately refixed.

[3] Richard Ingoldsby (d. 1712). In 1707 he was made Commander of the
Forces in Ireland, being then a lieut.-general. He was member for Limerick,
and a lord-justice.

[4] Cf. Letter XXVI., July 13, 1711.

[5] Robert Doyne had been a judge since 1703.

yet, young women; faith I dare not use you to it, you'll always expect it; what remains shall be only short journals of a day, and so I'll rise; for this morning.—At night. I dined with my opposite neighbour, Darteneuf, and I was soliciting this day, to present the bishop of Clogher Vice-Chancellor[1]; but it won't do; they are all set against him, and the Duke of Ormond, they say, has resolved to dispose of it somewhere else. Well; little saucy rogues, don't stay out too late to-night, because it is Saturday night, and young women should come home soon then.

17. I went to Court to seek a dinner, but the queen was not at church, she has got a touch of the gout; so the Court was thin, and I went to the Coffee-house; and sir Thomas Frankland, and his eldest son[2] and I went and dined with his son William. I talk'd a great deal to sir Thomas about Manley, and find he is his good friend, and so has Ned Southwell been, and I hope he will be safe, though all the Irish folks here are his mortal enemies. There was a devilish bite to-day. They had it, I know not how, that I was to preach this morning at St. James's Church, and abundance went, among the rest lord Radnor, who never is abroad till three in the afternoon. I walkt all the way home from Hatton-Garden at six, by moonlight, a delicate night. Raymond called at nine, but I was denied, and now I am in bed between eleven and twelve, just going to sleep, and dream of my own dear roguish impudent pretty MD.

18. You will now have short days works, just a few lines to tell you where I am, and what I am doing; only I will keep room for the last day to tell you news, if there be any worth sending. I have been sometimes like to do it at the top of my letter, until I remark it would be old before it reached you. I was hunting to dine with Mr. Harley to-day, but could not find him; and so I dined with honest Dr. Cockburn, and came home at six, and was taken out to next door by Dopping and Ford, to drink bad claret and oranges, and we let Raymond come to us, who talks of leaving the town to-morrow, but I believe will stay a day or two longer. It is now late, and I will say no more, but end this line with bidding my own dear saucy MD good night, &c.

19. I am come down proud stomach in one instance, for I went to-day to see the duke of Buckingham; but came too late; then I visited Mrs. Barton, and thought to have dined

[1] Of the University of Dublin.—D. S.
[2] Thomas, M.P. for Harwich, who succeeded to the baronetcy, 1726. Died 1747.

with some of the ministry; but it rained, and Mrs. Vanhomrigh
was nigh, and I took the opportunity of paying her for a scarf
she bought me, and dined there; at four I went to congratulate
with lord Shelburn, for the death of poor lady Shelburn
dowager [1]; he was at his country house; and returned while
I was there, and had not heard of it, and he took it very well.
I am now come home before six, and find a pacquet from the
bishop of Clogher, with one inclosed to the duke of Ormond,
which is ten days earlier dated than another I had from Parvisol; however, 'tis no matter, for the duke has already disposed
of the vice chancellorship to the archbishop of Tuam,[2] and
I could not help it, for it is a thing wholly you know in the
duke's power; and I find the bishop has enemies about the
duke. I write this while Patrick is folding up my scarf, and doing
up the fire (for I keep a fire, it costs me twelve-pence a week)
and so be quiet till I am gone to bed, and then sit down by
me a little, and we'll talk a few words more. Well; now MD
is at my bed-side; and now what shall we say? How does Mrs.
Stoite? What had the dean for supper? How much did Mrs.
Walls win? poor lady Shelburn: well, go get you to bed, sirrahs.

20. Morning. I was up this morning early, and shaved by
candle-light, and write this by the fire-side. Poor Raymond
just came in and took his leave of me; he is summoned by
high order from his wife, but pretends he has had enough of
London. I was a little melancholy to part with him; he goes
to Bristol, where they are to be with his merchant brother,
and now thinks of staying till May; so she must be brought
to bed in England. He was so easy and manageable, that I
almost repent I suffered him to see me so seldom. But he is
gone, and will save Patrick some lies in a week; Patrick is
grown admirable at it, and will make his fortune. How now,
sirrah, must I write in a morning to your impudence? Stay
till night, And then I'll write In black and white, By candle-
light Of Wax so bright, It helps the sight, A bite a bite—
Marry come up, mistress Boldface.—— At night. Dr. Raymond
came back, and goes to-morrow. I did not come home till
eleven, and found him here to take leave of me. I went to the
court of requests, thinking to find Mr. Harley and dine with
him, and refused Henley, and every body, and at last knew

[1] Mary (c. 1672–1710), daughter of Sir John Williams, second bart.,
widow of the second Baron Shelburne, had re-married twice—her last
husband being a Colonel Dallway.
[2] John Vesey (1637 1716), Bishop of Limerick, June 11, 1672; translated to Tuam, March 18, 1678.

not where to go, and met Jemmy Leigh by chance, and he was just in the same way, so I dined at his lodging on a beef-steak, and drank your health, then left him and went to the tavern with Ben Tooke and Portlack, the duke of Ormond's secretary drinking nasty white-wine till eleven. I am sick, and ashamed of it, &c.

21. I met that beast Ferris, lord Berkeley's steward formerly; I walkt with him a turn in the Park, and that scoundrel dog is as happy as an emperor, has married a wife with a considerable estate in land and houses about this town, and lives at his ease at Hammersmith. See your confounded sect.[1]—Well; I had the same luck to-day with Mr. Harley; 'twas a lovely day, and went by water into the city, and dined with Stratford at a merchant's house, and walkt home with as great a dunce as Ferris, I mean honest colonel Caufield,[2] and came home by eight, and now am in bed, and going to sleep for a wager, and will send this letter on Saturday, and so; but first I'll wish you a merry Christmas and a happy New-Year, and pray God we may never keep them asunder again.

22. Morning. I am going now to Mr. Harley's Levee on purpose to vex him; I'll say I had no other way of seeing him, &c. Patrick says, it is a dark morning, and that the duke of Argyle [3] is to be knighted to-day, the booby means installed at Windsor. But I must rise, for this is a shaving-day, and Patrick says, there is a good fire; I wish MD were by it, or I by MD's.—At night. I forgot to tell you, madam Dingley, that I payed nine shilling for your glass and spectacles, of which three were for the bishop's case: I am sorry I did not buy you such another case; but if you like it, I will bring one over with me, pray tell me: the glass to read was four shillings, the spectacles two. And have you had your chocolate? Leigh says, he sent the petticoat by one Mr. Spencer. Pray have you no further commissions for me? I paid the glass-man but last night, and he would have made me a present of the microscope, worth thirty shillings, and would have sent it home along with me; I thought the deuce was in the man: he said I could do him more service than that was worth, &c. I refused his present, but promised him all service I could do him; and so now I am obliged in

---

[1] Sex.

[2] Mr. Aitken says he was Toby Caulfeild, third son of the fifth Lord Charlemont.

[3] John Campbell (1678-1743), second Duke of Argyll, and Duke of Greenwich. This is the duke in *The Heart of Midlothian*. Swift came to dislike him intensely.

honour to recommend him to every body.—At night. I went
to Mr. Harley's Levee; he came and asked me, what had I to
do there, and bid me come and dine with him on a family
dinner; which I did, and it was the first time I ever saw his
lady[1] and daughter[2]; at five my lord keeper came in: I told
Mr. Harley, he had formerly presented me to sir Simon Harcourt,
but now must to my lord keeper, so he laughed, &c.

23. Morning. This letter goes to-night without fail; I hope
there is none from you yet at the Coffee-house: I'll send and
see by and bye; and let you know, and so and so. Patrick goes
to see for a letter: what will you lay, Is there one from MD or
no? No, I say; done for six-pence. Why has the dean never
once written to me? I won six-pence; I won six-pence; there's
not one letter to Presto. Good morrow, dear sirrahs: Stratford
and I dine to-day with lord Mountjoy. God Almighty preserve
and bless you; farewel, &c.

I have been dining at lord Mountjoy's; and am come to
study; our news from Spain this post takes off some of our
fears. The Parliament is prorogued to-day, or adjourned rather
till after the Holy-days. Bank stock is 105, so I may get 12l.
for my bargain already. Patrick the puppy is abroad, and how
shall I send this letter? Good night, little dears both, and be
happy, and remember your poor Presto, that wants you sadly,
as hope saved. Let me go study, naughty girls, and don't keep
me at the bottom of the paper. O faith, if you knew what lies
on my hands constantly,[3] you would wonder to see how I
could write such long letters; but we'll talk of that some other
time. Good night again, and God bless dear MD with his best
blessing, yes, yes, and Dingley and Stella and me too, &c.

Ask the bishop of Clogher about the pun I sent him of lord
Stawell's brother[4] 'twill be a pure bite. This letter has 199
lines in it, beside all postscripts; I had a curiosity to reckon.

There's a long letter for you.

It is longer than a sermon, faith.

I had another letter from Mrs. Fenton, who says you were
with her; I hope you did not go on purpose. I will answer her
letter soon; it is about some money in lady Giffard's hands.

[1] His second, Sarah, daughter of Simon Middleton of Edmonton;
died 1737.
[2] Elizabeth, afterwards married to the third Duke of Leeds.
[3] Writing the *Examiner*.—D. S.
[4] Edward Stawel (1686?–1755), who succeeded the Lord Stawel here
mentioned, viz., William (1683?–1741-2), third baron. By marriage, William
acquired the fine old house at Aldermaston, Berks, burnt down in the
nineteenth century.

They say you have had eight pacquets due to you; so pray, madams, don't blame Presto, but the Wind.

My humble service to Mrs. Walls, and Mrs. Stoite; I missed the former a good while.

LETTER XII

London, *Dec. 23, 1710.*

I HAVE sent my 11th to-night as usual, and begin the dozenth, and told you I dined with Stratford at lord Mountjoy's, and I'll tell you no more at present, guess for why; because I am going to mind things, and mighty affairs, not your nasty First-Fruits: I let them alone till Mr. Harley gets the queen's letter; but other things of greater moment, that you shall know one day, when the ducks have eaten up all the dirt. So sit still a while just by me while I am studying, and do not say a word, I charge you, and when I am going to bed, I'll take you along, and talk with you a little while, so there, sit there.—Come then, let us see what we have to say to these saucy brats, that will not let us go sleep at past eleven. Why, I am a little impatient to know how you do; but that I take it for a standing maxim, that when you are silent, all is pretty well, because that is the way I will deal with you; and if there was any thing you ought to know now, I would write by the first post, although I had written but the day before. Remember this, young women, and God Almighty preserve you both, and make us happy together; and tell me how accounts stand between us, that you may be paid long before it is due, not to want. I will return no more money while I stay, so that you need not be in pain to be paid; but let me know at least a month before you can want. Observe this, d'ye hear, little dear sirrahs, and love Presto, as Presto loves MD, &c.

24. You will have a merryer Christmas-Eve than we here. I went up to Court before church, and in one of the rooms, there being but little company, a fellow in a red coat without a sword came up to me, and after words of course askt me how the ladies did. I askt, what ladies? He said, Mrs. Dingley and Mrs. Johnson: Very well, said I, when I heard from them last: And pray when came you from thence, sir? Said he, I never was in Ireland; and just at that word lord Winchelsea [1] comes up to me, and the man went off: as I went out I saw him again,

[1] Charles Finch (1672–1712), third Earl of Winchelsea and fourth holder of the title, which was first conferred on a female. A privy councillor, and President of the Board of Trade (1712).

and recollected him, it was Vedeau[1] with a pox: I then went and made my apologies that my head was full of something I had to say to lord Winchelsea, &c. and I askt after his wife, and so all was well, and he enquired after my lodging, because he had some favour to desire of me in Ireland, to recommend somebody to somebody, I know not what it is. When I came from church I went up to Court again, where sir Edmund Bacon[2] told me the bad news from Spain,[3] which you will hear before this reaches you; as we have it now, we are undone there, and it was odd to see the whole countenances of the Court changed so in two hours. Lady Mountjoy carried me home to dinner, where I staid not long after, and came home early, and now am got into bed, for you must always write to your MDs in bed, that's a maxim. Mr. White and Mr. Red, Write to MD when abed; Mr. Black and Mr. Brown, Write to MD when you're down; Mr. Oak and Mr. Willow, Write to MD on your pillow.— What's this? faith I smell fire; what can it be; this house has a thousand s[tin]ks in it. I think to leave it on Thursday, and lodge over the way. Faith I must rise, and look at my chimney, for the smell grows stronger, stay—I have been up, and in my room, and found all safe, only a mouse within the fender to warm himself, which I could not catch. I smelt nothing there, but now in my bed-chamber I smell it again; I believe I have singed the woolen curtain, and that's all, though I cannot smoak it. Presto's plaguy silly to-night; an't he? Yes, and so he be. Ay, but if I should wake and see fire. Well; I'll venture; so good night, &c.

25. Pray, young women, if I write so much as this every day, how will this paper hold a fortnight's work, and answer one of yours into the bargain? You never think of this, but let me go on like a simpleton. I wish you a merry Christmas, and many, many a one with poor Presto at some pretty place. I was at church to-day by eight, and received the sacrament, and came home by ten; then went to Court at two, it was a Collar-day, that is, when the knights of the garter wear their collars; but the queen stay'd so late at sacrament, that I came back, and dined with my neighbour Ford, because all people dine at home on this day. This is likewise a Collar-day all over

---

[1] A shopkeeper, who left his trade for the army. See *Journal*, March 28, and April 4, 1710-11.

[2] Descended from an elder brother of the famous Francis, Lord Verulam. Holder of the premier baronetcy (*cr.* 1611). Died 1704.

[3] The loss of the Battle of Villa Viciosa, and all the fruits of Peterborough's triumphs. General Stanhope and all his English were made prisoners at Brihuega, by Vendôme, Dec. 9, 1710.—D. L. P.

England in every house, at least where there is Brawn: that's very well—I tell you a good pun; a fellow hard by pretends to cure Agues, and has set out a sign, and spells it *Egoes*; a gentleman and I observing it, he said, How does that fellow pretend to cure Agues? I said, I did not know, but I was sure it was not by a Spell. That's admirable. And so you askt the bishop about that pun of lord Stawell's brother. Bite. Have I caught you, young women? Must you pretend to ask after roguish puns, and Latin ones too? Oh but you smoakt me, and did not ask the bishop. Oh but you are a fool, and you did. I met Vedeau again at Court to-day, and I observed he had a sword on; I fancy he was broke, and has got a commission, but I never askt him. Vedeau I think his name is, yet Parvisol's man is Vedel, that's true. Bank stock will fall like stock-fish by this bad news, and two days ago I could have got 12l. by my bargain; but I don't intend to sell, and in time it will rise. 'Tis odd, that my lord Peterborow foretold this loss two months ago, one night at Mr. Harley's, when I was there; he bid us count upon it, that Stanhope would lose Spain before Christmas, that he would venture his head upon it, and gave us reasons; and though Mr. Harley argued the contrary, he still held to his opinion. I was telling my lord Anglesea this at Court this morning, and a gentleman by said, he had heard my lord Peterborow affirm the same thing. I have heard wise folks say, An ill tongue may do much. And 'tis an old saying, Once I guest right, And I got credit by't; Thrice I guest wrong, and I kept my credit on. No, 'tis you are sorry, not I.

26. By the lord Harry I shall be undone here with Christmas boxes. The rogues at the Coffee-house have raised their tax, every one giving a crown, and I gave mine for shame, besides a great many half crowns to great mens porters, &c. I went to-day by water into the city, and dined with no less a man than the city printer.[1] There is an intimacy [2] between us, built upon reasons that you shall know when I see you; but the rain caught me within twelve-penny length of home. I called at Mr. Harley's, who was not within, dropt my half-crown with his porter, drove to the Coffee-house, where the rain kept me till nine. I had letters to-day from the archbishop of Dublin, and Mr. Bernage;[3] the latter sends me a melancholy account

---

[1] Mr. John Barber, afterward Lord Mayor.—N.

[2] Mr. Barber was then printing the *Examiner.*—N.

[3] A gentleman of a refugee family, to whom the interest of Swift was of great service.—D. L. P. Was his christian-name Moses? *See post*, Letter XXXI., Sept. 26, 1711.

of lady Shelburn's death, and his own disappointments, and would gladly be a captain; if I can help him I will.

27. Morning. I bespoke a lodging over the way for to-morrow, and the dog let it yesterday to another; I gave him no earnest, so it seems he could do it; Patrick would have had me give him earnest to bind him; but I would not. So I must go saunter to-day for a lodging somewhere else. Did you ever see so open a winter in England? We have not had two frosty days; but it pays it off in rain: we have not had three fair days these six weeks. O faith I dreamed mightily of MD last night; but so confused I can't tell a word. I have made Ford acquainted with Lewis, and to-day we dined together; in the evening I called at one or two neighbours, hoping to spend a Christmas evening; but none were at home, they were all gone to be merry with others. I have often observed this, That in merry times every body is abroad: where the duce are they? So I went to the Coffee-house, and talkt with Mr. Addison an hour, who at last remembered to give me two letters, which I can't answer to-night, nor to-morrow neither, I can assure you, young women, count upon that. I have other things to do than to answer naughty girls, an old saying and true. Letters from MDs Must not be answered in ten days: 'tis but bad rhyme, &c.

28. To-day I had a message from sir Thomas Hanmer to dine with him, the famous Dr. Smallridge[1] was of the company, and we sat till six, and I came home to my new lodgings in St. Alban street,[2] where I pay the same rent (eight shillings a week) for an apartment two pair of stairs; but I have the use of the parlour to receive persons of quality, and I am got into my new bed, &c.

29. Sir Andrew Fountain has been very ill this week; and sent to me early this morning to have prayers, which you know is the last thing. I found the doctors and all in despair about him. I read prayers to him, found he had settled all things; and when I came out, the nurse askt me, whether I thought it possible he could live; for the doctors thought not. I said, I believed he would live; for I found the seeds of life in him, which I observe seldom fail; (and I found them in poor dearest Stella, when she was ill many years ago) and to-night

[1] Then Canon of Christ Church. He was afterward successively Dean of Carlisle 1711, Dean of Christ Church 1713, and in 1714 Bishop of Bristol.—N.

[2] It extended from Pall Mall to St. James's Market (the turning next after Charles Street going northward), and is now covered by parts of Waterloo Place and Regent Street.

I was with him again, and he was mightily recovered, and I hope he will do well, and the doctor approved my reasons; but if he should die, I should come off scurvily. The secretary of state (Mr. St. John) sent to me to dine with him; Mr. Harley and lord Peterborow dined there too, and at night came lord Rivers. Lord Peterborow goes to Vienna in a day or two; he has promised to make me write to him. Mr. Harley went away at six, but we staid till seven. I took the secretary aside, and complained to him of Mr. Harley, that he had got the queen to grant the First-Fruits, promised to bring me to her, and get her letter to the bishops in Ireland; but the last part he had not done in six weeks, and I was in danger to lose reputation, &c. He took the matter right, desired me to be with him on Sunday morning, and promises me to finish the affair in four days; so I shall know in a little time what I have to trust to.— It is nine of clock, and I must go study, you little rogues; and so good night, &c.

30. Morning. The weather grows cold, you sauce-boxes. Sir Andrew Fountain, they bring me word, is better. I'll go rise, for my hands are starving while I write in bed.—Night. Now sir Andrew Fountain is recovering, he desires to be at ease; for I called in the morning to read prayers, but he had given orders not to be disturbed. I have lost a legacy by his living; for he told me he had left me a picture and some books, &c. I called to see my *quondam* neighbour Ford (do you know what *quondam* is? though) and he engaged me to dine with him; for he always dines at home on Opera-days. I came home at six, writ to the archbishop, then studied till past eleven, and stole to bed, to write to MD these few lines to let you know I am in good health at the present writing hereof, and hope in God MD is so too. I wonder I never write politicks to you: I could make you the profoundest politician in all the lane.—Well, but when shall we answer this letter N. 8. of MD's? Not till next year, faith. O Lord—bo—but that will be a Monday next. Cod's so, is it; and so it is: never saw the like.—I made a pun t'other day to Ben Portlack about a pair of drawers. Poh, said he, that's mine a—— all over. Pray, pray, Dingley, let me go sleep; pray, pray, Stella, let me go slumber, and put out my wax candle.

31. Morning. It is now seven, and I have got a fire, but am writing a-bed in my bed-chamber. 'Tis not shaving-day, so I shall be ready early to go before church to Mr. St. John, and to-morrow I will answer our MD's letter. Would you answer MD's letter, On New-year's-day you'll do it better: For when

the year with MD 'gins, It without MD never lins. (These proverbs have always old words in them; *lins* is leaves off.) But if on New-year you write nones, MD then will bang your bones.—But Patrick says I must rise.—Night. I was early this morning with secretary St. John, and gave him a memorial to get the queen's letter for the First-Fruits, who has promised to do it in a very few days. He told me he had been with the duke of Marlborough,[1] who was lamenting his former wrong steps in joining with the Whigs, and said he was worn out with age, fatigues, and misfortunes. I swear it pityed me; and I really think they will not do well in too much mortifying that man, although indeed it is his own fault. He is covetous as Hell, and ambitious as the Prince of it: he would fain have been general for life, and has broken all endeavours for Peace, to keep his greatness and get money. He told the queen, he was neither covetous nor ambitious. She said, if she could have conveniently turned about, she would have laughed, and could hardly forbear it in his face. He fell in with all the abominable measures of the late ministry, because they gratified him for their own designs. Yet he has been a successful general, and I hope he will continue his command. O Lord, smoak the politicks to MD. Well; but if you like them, I will scatter a little now and then, and mine are all fresh from the chief hands. Well, I dined with Mr. Harley, and came away at six: there was much company, and I was not merry at all. Mr. Harley made me read a paper of verses of Prior's. I read them plain without any fine manner, and Prior swore I should never read any of his again; but he would be revenged, and read some of mine as bad. I excused myself, and said, I was famous for reading verses the worst in the world,[2] and that every body snatcht them from me when I offered to begin. So we laughed. —Sir Andrew Fountain still continues ill. He is plagued with some sort of bile.

Jan. 1. Morning. I wish my dearest pretty Dingley and Stella a happy new-year, and health, and mirth, and good stomachs, and Fr's company. Faith, I did not know how to write Fr. I wondered what was the matter; but now I remember I always write pdfr.[3] Patrick wishes me a happy New-year and desires I would rise, for it is a good fire, and faith 'tis cold. I was so

[1] Who had arrived in England from the Low Countries on the 28th December, and had a private audience with the queen immediately after.—D. L. P.
[2] Although it be said in jest, there is some truth in this.—D. S.
[3] "Presto"—D. S. here finds it necessary to explain.

politick last night with MD, never saw the like. Get the
Examiners, and read them; the last nine or ten are full of the
reasons for the late change, and of the abuses of the last ministry;
and the great men assure me they are all true. They are written
by their encouragement and direction. I must rise and go see sir
Andrew Fountain; but perhaps to-night I may answer MD's
letter: so good morrow, my mistresses all, good morrow. I wish
you both a merry New-year, Roast beef, minced pyes, and good
strong beer, And me a share of your good cheer. That I was
there, or you were here, And you're a little saucy dear.—Good
morrow again, dear sirrahs, one cannot rise for your play.—
At night. I went this morning to visit lady Kerry and lord Shelburn, and they made me dine with them. Sir Andrew Fountain
is better. And now let us come and see what this saucy dear
letter of MD says. Come out, letter, come out from between the
sheets: here it is underneath, and it won't come out. Come
out again, I say: so there. Here it is. What says Presto to me,
pray? says it. Come, and let me answer for you to your ladies.
Hold up your head then, like a good letter. There. Pray, how
have you got up with Presto? madam Stella. You write your
eighth when you receive mine: now I write my twelfth, when
I receive your eighth. Don't you allow for what are upon the
road, simpleton? What say you to that? And so you kept
Presto's little birth-day, I warrant: would to God I had been
at the health, rather than here, where I have no manner of
pleasure, nothing but eternal business upon my hands. I shall
grow wise in time; but no more of that: only I say Amen with
my heart and vitals, that we may never be asunder again ten
days together while poor Presto lives. ⸺⸺⸺⸺⸺⸺⸺⸺
I can't be merry so near any splenetick talk; so I made that
long line, and now all's well again. Yes, you are a pretending
slut, indeed, with your fourth and fifth in the margin, and your
journal, and every thing. Wind—we saw no wind here, nothing
at all extraordinary at any time. We had it once when you
had it not. But an old saying and a true; I hate all wind, Before
and behind, From cheeks with eyes, or from blind—. Your
chimney fall down! God preserve you. I suppose you only mean
a brick or two: but that's a damn'd lie of your chimney
being carried to the next house with the wind. Don't put
such things upon us; those matters won't pass here: keep
a little to possibilities. My lord Hertford[1] would have been
ashamed of such a stretch. You should take care of what

[1] Son to the Duke of Somerset.—N.

company you converse with: when one gets that faculty, 'tis hard to break one's self of it. Jemmy Leigh talks of going over; but *quando?* I don't know when he'll go. O, now you had my ninth, now you are come up with me; marry come up with you, indeed. I know all that business of lady S——. Will nobody cut that D——y's throat? Five hundred pounds do you call poor pay for living three months the life of a king? They say she died with grief, partly, being forced to appear as witness in Court about some squabble among their servants.—The bishop of Clogher shewed you a pamphlet. Well, but you must not give your mind to believe those things; people will say any thing. The character[1] is here reckoned admirable, but most of the facts are trifles. It was first printed privately here; and then some bold cur ventured to do it publickly, and sold two thousand in two days: who the author is must remain uncertain. Do you pretend to know, impudence? How durst you think so? Pox on your parliaments: the archbishop has told me of it; but we do not vouchsafe to know any thing of it here. No, no, no more of your[2] giddiness yet; thank you, Stella, for asking after it; thank you; God Almighty bless you for your kindness to poor Presto. You write to lady Giffard and your mother upon what I advise when it is too late. But yet I fancy this bad news will bring down stocks so low, that one might buy to great advantage. I design to venture going to see your mother some day when lady Giffard is abroad. Well, keep your Rathburn and stuff. I thought he was to pay in your money upon his houses to be flung down about the what d'ye call it.—Well, madam Dingley, I sent your inclosed to Bristol, but have not heard from Raymond since he went. Come, come, young women, I keep a good fire; it costs me twelve-pence a week, and I fear something more; vex me, and I'll have one in my bed-chamber too. No, did not I tell you but just now, we have no high winds here. Have you forgot already? —Now you are at it again, silly Stella; why does your mother say, my candles are scandalous? They are good sixes in the pound, and she said, I was extravagant enough to burn them by day-light. I never burn fewer at a time than one. What would people have? The D—— burst Hawkshaw. He told me he had not the box, and the next day Sterne[3] told me he had sent it a fortnight ago; Patrick could not find him t'other day,

[1] Pamphlet (by Swift) on the character of Wharton.
[2] The "of your" (not in first edition) is, if not interpolated by mistake, expletive—like "your lion" in *A Midsummer Night's Dream*.
[3] Enoch.

but he shall to-morrow: Dear life and heart, do you teaze me? does Stella teaze Presto? That palsy-water was in the box; it was too big for a pacquet, and I was afraid of its breaking. Leign was not in town then, or I would not have trusted it to Sterne, whom yet I have befriended enough to do me more kindness than that. I'll never rest till you have it, or till it is in a way for you to have it. Poor dear rogue, naughty to think it teases me; How could I ever forgive myself for neglecting any thing that related to your health? Sure I were a Devil if I did?——————————— See how far I am forced to stand from Stella, because I am afraid she thinks poor Presto has not been careful about her little things; I am sure I bought them immediately according to order, and packt them up with my own hands, and sent them to Sterne, and was six times with him about sending them away. I am glad you are pleased with your glasses. I have got another velvet cap, a new one lord Herbert[1] bought and presented me one morning I was at breakfast with him, where he was as merry and easy as ever I saw him, yet had received a challenge half an hour before, and half an hour after fought a duel. It was about ten days ago. You are mistaken in your guesses about *Tatlers*: I did neither write that on Noses nor Religion,[2] nor do I send him of late any hints at all.—Indeed, Stella, when I read your letter, I was not uneasy at all; but when I came to answer the particulars, and found that you had not received your box, it grated me to the heart, because I thought through your little words, that you imagined I had not taken the care I ought. But there has been some blunder in this matter, which I will know to-morrow, and write to Sterne, for fear he should not be within.—And pray, pray Presto, pray now do.—No, Raymond was not above four times with me while he staid, and then only while I was dressing. Mrs. Fenton has written me another letter about some money of hers in Lady Giffard's hands, that is intrusted to me by my mother, not to come to her husband. I send my letters constantly every fortnight, and if you will have them oftener you may, but then they will be the shorter. Pray, let Parvisol sell the horse. I think I spoke to you of it in a former letter: I am glad you are rid of him, and was in pain while I thought you rode him; but if he

---

[1] Henry (*c.* 1680–1738), sixth and last Baron Herbert of Cherbury. Committed suicide.
[2] Nos. 260 and 257, both written by Addison and Steele in conjunction. —D. L. P.

would buy you another, or any body else, and that you could be often able to ride, why don't you do it?

2. I went this morning early to the secretary of state, Mr. St. John, and he told me from Mr. Harley, that the warrant was now drawn, in order for a patent for the First-Fruits: it must pass through several offices, and take up some time, because in things the queen gives they are always considerate; but that he assures me 'tis granted and done, and past all dispute, and desires I will not be in any pain at all. I will write again to the archbishop to-morrow, and tell him this, and I desire you will say it on occasion. From the secretary I went to Mr. Sterne, who said he would write to you to-night, and that the box must be at Chester, and that some friend of his goes very soon, and will carry it over. I dined with Mr. secretary St. John, and at six went to Darteneuf's house to drink punch with him, and Mr. Addison, and little Harrison, a young poet whose fortune I am making. Steele was to have been there, but came not, nor never did twice, since I knew him, to any appointment. I staid till past eleven, and am now in bed. Steele's last *Tatler*[1] came out to-day. You will see it before this comes to you, and how he takes leave of the world. He never told so much as Mr. Addison of it, who was surprized as much as I; but, to say the truth, it was time, for he grew cruel dull and dry. To my knowledge he had several good hints to go upon; but he was so lazy and weary of the work, that he would not improve them. I think I'll send this after[2] to-morrow; Shall I before 'tis full, Dingley?

3. Lord Peterborow yesterday called me into a barber's shop, and there we talkt deep politicks: he desired me to dine with him to-day at the Globe in the Strand; he said he would shew me so clearly how to get Spain, that I could not possibly doubt it. I went to-day accordingly, and saw him among half a dozen lawyers and attornies and hang-dogs, signing deeds and stuff before his journey; for he goes to-morrow to Vienna. I sat among that scurvy company till after four, but heard nothing of Spain; only I find, by what he told me before, that he fears he shall do no good in his present journey. We are to be mighty constant correspondents. So I took my leave of him, and called at sir Andrew Fountain's, who mends much. I came home, and please you, at six, and have been studying till now past eleven.

---

[1] No. 271. The *Tatler* has become obnoxious and dull from its interference with party politics; Steele dropped it to start the *Spectator*, from which politics were excluded.—D. L. P.

[2] *After* is interlined.—D. S.

4. Morning. Morrow, little dears. O, faith, I have been dreaming; I was to be put in prison, I don't know why, and I was so afraid of a black dungeon; and then all I had been enquiring yesterday of Sir Andrew Fountain's sickness I thought was of poor Stella. The worst of dreams is, that one wakes just in the humour they leave one. Shall I send this to-day? With all my heart: it is two days within the fortnight; but may be MD are in haste to have a round dozen, and then how are you come up to me in your eighth, young women? But you indeed ought to write twice slower than I, because there are two of you; I own that.—Well then, I'll seal up this letter by my morning candle, and carry it into the city with me, where I go to dine, and put it in the post-office with my own fair hands. So, let me see whether I have any news to tell MD. They say, they will very soon make some enquiries into the corruptions of the late ministry; and they must do it, to justify their turning them out. Atterbury[1] we think is to be the dean of Christ-Church in Oxford; but the college would rather have Smallridge.[2]—What's all this to you? what care you for Atterburys and Smallridges? No, you care for nothing but Presto, faith. So I'll rise, and bid you farewell; yet I'm loth to do so, because there is a great bit of paper yet to talk upon; but Dingley will have it so: Yes, says she, make your journals shorter, and send them oftener; and so I will. And I have cheated you another way too; for this is clipt paper, and holds at least six lines less than the former ones. I'll tell you a good thing I said to my lord Carteret.[3] So, says he, my lord —— came up to me, and askt me, &c. No, said I, my lord —— never did, nor ever can come up to you. We all pun here sometimes. Lord Carteret set down Prior t'other day in his chariot, and Prior thanked him for his *Charity*; that was fit for Dilly.[4] I don't remember I heard one good one from the ministry, which is really a shame. Henley is gone to the country for Christmas. The puppy comes here without his wife,[5] and keeps no house, and would have me dine with him at eating-houses; but I have only done it

[1] Francis Atterbury (1662–1732), Dean of Carlisle 1704, Dean of Christ Church 1711; made Bishop of Rochester and Dean of Westminster 1713.
[2] Atterbury succeeded.—D. L. P.
[3] John Carteret (1690–1763), second Baron C. and afterwards first Earl Granville (1744, on death of his mother, a countess in her own right). Lord Lieutenant of Ireland, 1727-1730.
[4] The Rev Dillon Ashe, younger brother of the Bishop of Clogher, and Vicar of Finglas.
[5] Mary, daughter and co-heiress of Peregrine Bertie (second son of Montague, Earl of Lindsey): she brought Henley £30,000.

once, and will do it no more. He had not seen me for some time in the Coffee-house, and asking after me, desired lord Herbert to tell me, I was a Beast for ever after the order of Melchisedec. Did you ever read the Scripture? It is only changing the word *Priest* to *Beast*.[1]—I think I am bewitched to write so much in a morning to you, little MD. Let me go, will you? and I'll come again to-night in a fine clean sheet of paper; but I can nor will stay no longer now; no, I won't, for all your wheedling: no, no, look off, don't smile at me, and say, Pray, pray, Presto, write a little more. Ah! you're a wheedling slut, you be so. Nay, but prithee turn about, and let me go, do: 'tis a good girl, and do. O faith, my morning candle is just out, and I must go now in spight of my teeth; for my bed-chamber is dark with curtains, and I'm at the wrong side. So farewel, &c. &c.

I am in the dark almost: I must have another candle, when I am up, to seal this; but I'll fold it up in the dark, and make what you can of this, for I can only see this paper I am writing upon. Service to Mrs. Walls and Mrs. Stoite.

God Almighty bless you, &c. What I am doing I can't see; but I'll fold it up, and not look on it again.

LETTER XIII

London, *January* 4, 1710-11.

I WAS going into the city (where I dined) and put my 12th, with my own fair hands, into the post-office as I came back, which was not till nine this night. I dined with people that you never heard of, nor is it worth your while to know; an authoress and a printer.[2] I walked home for exercise, and at eleven got to bed, and all the while I was undressing my self, there was I speaking monkey things in air, just as if MD had been by, and did not recollect myself till I got into bed. I writ last night to the archbishop, and told him the warrant was drawn for the First-Fruits, and I told him lord Peterborow was set out for his journey to Vienna; but it seems the lords have addressed to have him stay to be examined about Spanish affairs, upon this defeat there, and to know where the fault lay, &c. So I writ to the archbishop a lie; but I think it was not a sin.

5. Mr. secretary St. John sent for me this morning so early that I was forced to go without shaving, which put me quite out of method: I called at Mr. Ford's, and desired him to lend me a shaving, and so made a shift to get into order again. Lord! here's an impertinence: sir Andrew Fountain's mother

---

[1] Psalm cx. 4; also Heb. v.　　[2] Mrs. Manley and Mr. Barber.

and sister are come above a hundred miles from Worcester to
see him before he died. They got here but yesterday, and he
must have been past hopes, or past fears, before they could
reach him. I fell a scolding when I heard they were coming;
and the people about him wondered at me, and said what a
mighty content it would be on both sides to die when they
were with him. I knew the mother; she is the greatest Overdo[1]
upon earth, and the sister, they say, is worse; the poor man
will relapse again among them. Here was the scoundrel brother
always crying in the outer room till sir Andrew was in danger,
and the dog was to have all his estate if he died; and 'tis an
ignorant, worthless, scoundrel rake: and the nurses were comforting him, and desiring he would not take on so. I dined
to-day the first time with Ophy Butler and his wife; and you
supped with the dean, and lost two and twenty pence at
cards. And so Mrs. Walls is brought to-bed of a girl, who died
two days after it was christened; and betwixt you and me,
she is not very sorry: she loves her ease and diversions too well
to be troubled with children. I'll go to bed.

6. Morning. I went last night to put some coals on my fire
after Patrick was gone to bed; and there I saw in a closet a
poor linnet he has bought to bring over to Dingley: it cost him
six-pence, and is as tame as a dormouse. I believe he does not
know he is a bird: where you put him, there he stands, and
seems to have neither hope nor fear; I suppose in a week he will
die of the spleen. Patrick advised with me before he bought
him. I laid fairly before him the greatness of the sum and the
rashness of the attempt; shewed how impossible it was to
carry him safe over the salt sea: but he would not take my
counsel, and he'll repent it. 'Tis very cold this morning in bed,
and I hear there is a good fire in the room without, what do
you call it, the dining-room. I hope it will be good weather,
and so let me rise, sirrahs, do so.—At night. I was this morning
to visit the dean, or Mr. Prolocutor, I think you call him, don't
you? Why should not I go to the dean's as well as you? *A
little black man of pretty near fifty?* Aye, the same. *A good
pleasant man?* Aye, the same. *Cunning enough?* Yes. *One that
understands his own interests?* As well as any body. How comes
it MD and I don't meet there sometimes? A very good face,

[1] A notorious female character in Ben Jonson's play, *Bartholomew Fair*.
The "sister" mentioned next is supposed to have been Elizabeth, afterwards wife of Colonel Edward Clent of Knightwick. The "scoundrel
brother" was probably Brig Fountaine, who has a tombstone in the
churchyard of Narford, recording his death in 1746, aged 64.

and abundance of wit; do you know his lady? O Lord! whom do you mean?[1] I mean Dr. Atterbury,[2] dean of Carlisle and Prolocutor. Pshaw, Presto, you are a fool: I thought you had meant our dean of St. Patrick's.—Silly, silly, silly, you are silly, both are silly, every kind of thing is silly. As I walked into the city, I was stopt with clusters of boys and wenches buzzing about the cake-shops like flies.[3] There had the fools let out their shops two yards forward into the streets, all spread with great cakes frothed with sugar, and stuck with streamers of tinsel. And then I went to Bateman's the bookseller,[4] and laid out eight and forty shillings for books. I bought three little volumes of Lucian in French for our Stella, and so and so. Then I went to Garraway's[5] to meet Stratford and dine with him; but it was an idle day with the merchants, and he was gone to our end of the town: so I dined with sir Thomas Frankland at the post-office, and we drank your Manley's health. It was in a news-paper that he was turned out; but secretary St. John told me it was false, only that news-writer is a plaguy Tory. I have not seen one bit of Christmas merriment.

7. Morning. Your new lord chancellor[6] sets out to-morrow for Ireland: I never saw him. He carries over one Trap[7] a parson as his chaplain, a sort of pretender to wit, a second-rate pamphleteer for the cause, whom they pay by sending him to Ireland. I never saw Trap neither. I met Tighe and your Smyth of Lovet's yesterday by the Exchange. Tighe and I took no notice of each other; but I stopt Smyth, and told him of the box that lies for you at Chester, because he says he goes very soon to Ireland, I think this week: and I will send this morning to Sterne, to take measures with Smyth; so good morrow,

---

[1] Dr. Sterne, Dean of St. Patrick's, was not a married man, which seems to have been the cause of this surprise in MD.—D. S.

[2] Whom Swift very artfully characterises in the sentences here printed in italics.—N. [Atterbury was elected Prolocutor of the Lower House of Convocation in 1710. The italics are not in the first edition.]

[3] It was Twelfth Night: the cakes were twelfth-cakes.

[4] Mr. Bateman, who l¹ved in Little Britain, dealt principally in old books. He never would suffer any person whatever to look into one book in his shop; and, when asked a reason for it, would say, "I suppose you may be a physician or an author, and want some recipe or quotation; and, if you buy it, I will engage it to be perfect before you leave me, but not after; as I have suffered by leaves being torn out, and the books returned, to my very great loss and prejudice."—F.

[5] Thomas Garway, or Garraway, in Cromwell's time kept a coffee-house in Change Alley, which retained his name for about 200 years.

[6] Sir Constantine Phipps.—N.

[7] Joseph Trapp, an able and learned divine and indifferent poet; he published an unsuccessful version of Virgil and a bad Latin translation of *Paradise Lost.*—D. L. P.

sirrahs, and let me rise, pray. I took up this paper when I came
in at evening, I mean this minute, and then said I, No, no,
indeed, MD, you must stay, and then was laying it aside, but
could not for my heart, though I am very busy, till I just ask
you how you do since morning; by and bye we shall talk more,
so let me leave you softly down, little paper, till then; so there
—now to business; there, I say, get you gone: no, I won't push
you neither, but hand you on one side—So—Now I am got into
bed, I'll talk with you. Mr. secretary St. John sent for me this
morning in all haste; but I would not lose my shaving, for fear
of missing church. I went to Court, which is of late always very
full, and young Manley and I dined at sir Matthew Dudley's.
—I must talk politicks. I protest I am afraid we shall all be
embroiled with parties. The Whigs, now they are fallen, are
the most malicious toads in the world. We have had now a
second misfortune, the loss of several Virginia ships. I fear
people will begin to think that nothing thrives under this
ministry: and if the ministry can once be rendered odious to
the people, the *parliament* may be chosen Whig or Tory as the
queen pleases. Then I think our friends press a little too hard
on the duke of Marlborough. The country members[1] are
violent to have past faults enquired into, and they have reason;
but I do not observe the ministry to be very fond of it. In my
opinion we have nothing to save us but a Peace, and I am sure
we cannot have such a one as we hoped, and then the Whigs
will bawl what they would have done had they continued in
power. I tell the ministry this as much as I dare, and shall
venture to say a little more to them, especially about the duke
of Marlborough, who, as the Whigs give out, will lay down his
command; and I question whether ever any wise state laid
aside a general who had been successful nine years together,
whom the enemy so much dread; and his own soldiers cannot
but believe must always conquer; and you know that in war
opinion is nine parts in ten. The ministry hear me always with
appearance of regard, and much kindness; but I doubt they
let personal quarrels mingle too much with their proceedings.
Mean time, they seem to value all this as nothing, and are as
easy and merry as if they had nothing in their hearts or upon
their shoulders, like physicians, who endeavour to cure, but
feel no grief, whatever the patient suffers.—Pshaw, what's all
this? Do you know one thing, that I find I can write politicks

[1] These were afterward called the October Club. *See* Feb. 18, 1710-11.
—D. S.

to you much easier than to any body alive. But I swear my head is full, and I wish I were at Laracor with dear charming MD, &c.

8. Morning. Methinks, young women, I have made a great progress in four days, at the bottom of this side already, and no letter come yet from MD. (that word interlined is morning.) I find I have been writing state affairs to MD. How do they relish it? Why, any thing that comes from Presto is welcome; though really, to confess the truth, if they had their choice, not to disguise the matter, they had rather, &c. Now, Presto, I must tell you, you grow silly, says Stella. That's but one body's opinion, madam. I promised to be with Mr. secretary St. John this morning; but I am lazy and won't go, because I had a letter from him yesterday to desire I would dine there to-day. I shall be chid; but what care I?—Here has been Mrs. South[1] with me, just come from sir Andrew Fountain, and going to market. He is still in a fever, and may live or die. His mother and sister are now come up and in the house, so there's a lurry.[2] I gave Mrs. South half a pistole for a New-year's gift. So good morrow, dears both, till anon.—At night. Lord, I have been with Mr. Secretary from dinner till eight; and though I drank wine and water, I am so hot! Lady Stanley[3] came to visit Mrs. St. John,[4] and sent up for me, to make up a quarrel with Mrs. St. John, whom I never yet saw; and do you think that devil of a secretary would let me go, but kept me by main force, though I told him I was in love with his lady, and it was a shame to keep back a lover, &c. But all would not do; so at last I was forced to break away, but never went up, it was then too late; and here I am, and have a great deal to do to-night, though it be nine o'clock; but one must say something to these naughty MDs, else there will be no quiet.

9. To-day Ford and I set apart to go into the city to buy books; but we only had a scurvy dinner at an alehouse, and he made me go to the tavern, and drink Florence, four and six-pence a flask; damned wine! so I spent my money, which I seldom do, and past an insipid day, and saw no-body, and 'tis now ten o'clock, and I have nothing to say, but that 'tis a

---

[1] Mr. Aitken reasonably takes this to be Sir Andrew's housekeeper, —not the Mrs. South afterwards mentioned, wife of the commissioner South in Letter X., Dec. 9, 1710.

[2] Hubbub.

[3] See Letter V., Oct. 1, 1710 (note).

[4] Frances (d. 1718), daughter of Sir Henry Winchcombe, of Buckle-bury, Berks.

fortnight to-morrow since I had a letter from MD, but if I have
it time enough to answer here, 'tis well enough, otherwise wo
betide you, faith; I'll go to the toyman's, here just in Pall-mall,
and he sells great hugeous batoons;[1] yes, faith, and so he does.
Does not he, Dingley? Yes, faith. Don't lose your money this
Christmas.

10. I must go this morning to Mr. secretary St. John. I
promised yesterday, but failed, so I can't write any more
till night to poor dear MD.—At night. O faith, Dingley, I had
company in the morning, and could not go where I designed;
and I had a basket from Raymond at Bristol, with six bottles
of wine and a pound of chocolate, and some tobacco to snuff;
and he writ under, the carriage was paid; but he lied, or I am
cheated, or there is a mistake; and he has written to me so confusedly about some things, that Lucifer could not understand him.
This wine is to be drank with Harley's brother [2] and Sir Robert
Raymond, solicitor-general, in order to recommend the doctor
to your new lord chancellor, who left this place on Monday,
and Raymond says he is hasting to Chester to go with him.—
I suppose he leaves his wife behind; for when he left London
he had no thoughts of stirring till Summer. So I suppose he will
be with you before this. Ford came and desired I would dine
with him, because it was Opera-day, which I did, and sent
excuses to lord Shelburn who had invited me.

11. I am setting up a new *Tatler*, little Harrison, whom I
have mentioned to you. Others have put him on it, and I
encourage him; and he was with me this morning and evening,
shewing me his first, which comes out on Saturday. I doubt
he will not succeed, for I do not much approve his manner;
but the scheme is Mr. secretary St. John's and mine, and would
have done well enough in good hands. I recommended him to
a printer,[3] whom I sent for, and settled the matter between
them this evening. Harrison has just left me, and I am tired
with correcting his trash.

12. I was this morning upon some business with Mr. secretary
St. John, and he made me promise to dine with him, which
otherwise I would have done with Mr. Harley, whom I have
not been with these ten days. I cannot but think they have
mighty difficulties upon them; yet I always find them as easy

---

[1] Clubs, or batons.
[2] In all probability Edward (1664–1735), member for Leominster and
auditor of the imprest. There was another brother, Nathaniel, who was
a merchant.
[3] *See* Letter XV., Feb. 3, 1710-11.

and disengaged as schoolboys on a holiday. Harley has the procuring of five or six millions on his shoulders, and the Whigs will not lend a groat; which is the only reason of the fall of stocks: for they are like quakers and fanaticks, that will only deal among themselves, while all others deal indifferently with them. Lady Marlborough offers, if they will let her keep her employments, never to come into the queen's presence. The Whigs say the duke of Marlborough will serve no more; but I hope and think otherwise. I would to Heaven I were this minute with MD at Dublin; for I am weary of politicks, that give me such melancholy prospects.

13. O faith, I had an ugly giddy fit last night in my chamber, and I have got a new box of pills to take, and hope I shall have no more this good while. I would not tell you before, because it would vex you, little rogues; but now it is over. I dined to-day with lord Shelburn, and to-day little Harrison's new *Tatler* came out: there is not much in it, but I hope he will mend. You must understand that upon Steele's leaving off, there were two or three scrub *Tatlers* came out, and one of them holds on still, and to-day it advertised against Harrison's; and so there must be disputes which are genuine, like the straps for razors.[1] I am afraid the little toad has not the true vein for it. I'll tell you a copy of verses. When Mr. St. John was turned out from being secretary at war, three years ago, he retired to the country: there he was talking of something he would have written over his summer-house, and a gentleman gave him these verses;

> From business and the noisy world retir'd,
> Nor vex'd by love, nor by ambition fir'd;
> Gently I wait the call of Charon's boat,
> Still drinking like a fish, and —— like a stoat.

He swore to me he could hardly bear the jest; for he pretended to retire like a philosopher, though he was but twenty-eight years old: and I believe the thing was true; for he had been a thorough rake. I think the grave three lines do introduce the last well enough. Od so, but I'll go sleep; I sleep early now.

14. O faith, young women, I want a letter from MD; 'tis now nineteen days since I had the last: and where have I room to answer it, pray? I hope I shall send this away without any answer at all; for I'll hasten it, and away it goes on Tuesday,

---

[1] "The inventors of the straps for razors," says the *Tatler*, No. 224, "have written against each other this way for several years, and that with great bitterness."

by which time this side will be full. I'll send it two days sooner on purpose out of spight, and the very next day after, you must know, your letter will come, and then 'tis too late, and I'll so laugh, never saw the like! 'Tis Spring with us already. I ate asparagus t'other day. Did you ever see such a frostless winter? Sir Andrew Fountain lies still extreamly ill; it costs him ten guineas a day to doctors, surgeons, and apothecaries, and has done so these three weeks. I dined to-day with Mr. Ford; he sometimes chuses to dine at home, and I am content to dine with him; and at night I called at the Coffee-house, where I had not been in a week, and talk'd coldly a while with Mr. Addison; all our friendship and dearness are off: we are civil acquaintance, talk words of course, of when we shall meet, and that's all. I have not been at any house with him these six weeks: t'other day we were to have dined together at the comptroller's [1]; but I sent my excuses, being engaged to the secretary of state. Is not it odd? But I think he has used me ill, and I have used him too well, at least his friend Steele.

15. It has cost me three guineas to-day for a periwig. I am undone! It was made by a Leicester lad, who married Mr. Worrall's daughter, where my mother lodged [2]; so I thought it would be cheap, and especially since he lives in the city. Well, London lick-penny: I find it true. I have given Harrison hints for another *Tatler* to-morrow. The jackanapes wants a right taste; I doubt he won't do. I dined with my friend Lewis of the secretary's office, and am got home early, because I have much business to do; but before I begin I must needs say something to MD, faith—No, faith, I lie, it is but nineteen days to-day since my last from MD. I have got Mr. Harley to promise, that whatever changes are made in the council, the bishop of Clogher shall not be removed, and he has got a memorial accordingly. I will let the bishop know so much in a post or two. This is a secret; but I know he has enemies, and they shall not be gratified, if they designed any such thing, which perhaps they might; for some changes there will be made. So drink up your claret, and be quiet, and don't lose your money.

16. Morning. Faith I'll send this letter to-day to shame you, if I han't one from MD before night, that's certain. Won't you grumble for want of the third side, pray now? Yes, I warrant you; yes, yes, you shall have the third, you shall so, when you

---

[1] Sir John Holland's.

[2] Swift's mother was recently dead—she had lived many years in Leicester.

can catch it, some other time; when you be writing girls.—
O faith, I think I won't stay till night, but seal up this just
now, and carry it in my pocket, and whip it into the post-
office as I come home at evening. I am going out early this
morning.—Patrick's bills for coal and candles, &c. come sometimes to three shillings a week; I keep very good fires, though
the weather be warm. Ireland will never be happy till you get
small coal likewise; nothing so easy, so convenient, so cheap,
so pretty for lighting a fire. My service to Mrs. Stoite and Walls,
has she a boy or a girl? A girl, hmm; and died in a week,
hmmm, and was poor Stella forced to stand for godmother?—
Let me know how accounts stand, that you may have your
money betimes. There's four months for my lodging, that must
be thought on too: and so go dine with Manley, and lose your
money, do extravagant sluttikin, but don't fret.—It will be
just three weeks when I have the next letter, that's to-morrow.
Farewel, dearest beloved MD, and love poor, poor Presto, who
has not had one happy day since he left you, as hope saved—
It is the last sally I will ever make, but I hope it will turn to
some account. I have done more for these,[1] and I think they
are more honest than the last; however, I will not be disappointed. I would make MD and me easy; and I never desired
more.—Farewel, &c. &c.

LETTER XIV

London, *Jan.* 16, 1710-11.

O FAITH, young women, I have sent my letter N. 13, without
one crumb of an answer to any of MD's, there is for you now;
and yet Presto ben't angry faith, not a bit, only he will begin
to be in pain next Irish post, except he sees MD's little handwriting in the glass-frame at the bar of St. James's Coffee-house,
where Presto would never go but for that purpose. Presto's at
home, God help him, every night from six till bed-time, and has
as little enjoyment or pleasure in life at present as any body in
the world, although in full favour with all the ministry. As
hope saved, nothing gives Presto any sort of dream of happiness
but a letter now and then from his own dearest MD. I love the
expectation of it, and when it does not come, I comfort myself,
that I have it yet to be happy with. Yes faith, and when I write
to MD, I am happy too; it is just as if methinks you were here

[1] The Tory Ministry.

and I prating to you, and telling you where I have been: Well, says you, Presto, come, where have you been to-day? come, let's hear now. And so then I answer; Ford and I were visiting Mr. Lewis, and Mr. Prior, and Prior has given me a fine Plautus, and then Ford would have had me dine at his lodgings, and so I would not; and so I dined with him at an eating-house; which I have not done five times since I came here; and so I came home, after visiting sir Andrew Fountain's mother and sister, and sir Andrew Fountain is mending, though slowly.

17. I was making, this morning, some general visits, and at twelve I called at the Coffee-house for a letter from MD; so the man said, he had given it to Patrick; then I went to the court of requests and treasury, to find Mr. Harley, and after some time spent in mutual reproaches, I promised to dine with him; I staid there till seven, then called at Sterne's and Leigh's to talk about your box, and to have it sent by Smyth; Sterne says he has been making enquiries, and will set things right as soon as possible. I suppose it lies at Chester, at least I hope so, and only wants a lift over to you. Here has little Harrison been to complain, that the printer I recommended to him for his *Tatler*, is a coxcomb; and yet to see how things will happen; for this very printer is my cousin, his name is Dryden Leach; did you never hear of Dryden Leach, he that prints the *Postman*? he acted Oronoko,[1] he's in love with miss Crosse.[2]—Well, so I came home to read my letter from Stella, but the dog Patrick was abroad; at last he came, and I got my letter; I found another hand had superscribed it; when I opened it, I found it written all in French, and subscribed Bernage: faith I was ready to fling it at Patrick's head. Bernage tells me, he had been to desire your recommendation to me to make him a captain, and your cautious answer, "That he had as much power with me as you," was a notable one; if you were here I would present you to the ministry as a person of ability. Bernage should let me know where to write to him; this is the second letter I have had without any direction; however, I beg I may not have a third, but that you will ask him, and send me how I shall direct to him. In the mean time, tell him, that if regiments are to be raised here, as he says, I will speak to George Granville,[3] secretary at war, to make him a captain;

[1] "Oroonoko," in a play of that name by Thomas Southerne, founded on *Oroonoko, or the Royal Slave*, by Mrs. Aphra Behn. Oroonoko was a real person.
[2] An actress.
[3] Or Grenville (1667–1735), afterwards first Baron Lansdown. He wrote.

and use what other interest I conveniently can. I think that is enough, and so tell him, and don't trouble me with his letters, when I expect them from MD; do you hear, young women, write to Presto.

18. I was this morning with Mr. secretary St. John, and we were to dine at Mr. Harley's alone, about some business of importance; but there were two or three gentlemen there. Mr. secretary and I went together from his office to Mr. Harley's, and thought to have been very wise; but the deuce a bit, the company staid, and more came, and Harley went away at seven, and the secretary and I staid with the rest of the company till eleven; I would then have had him come away, but he was in for't; and though he swore he would come away at that flask, there I left him. I wonder at the civility of these people; when he saw I would drink no more, he would always pass the bottle by me, and yet I could not keep the toad from drinking himself, nor he would not let me go neither, nor Masham,[1] who was with us. When I got home, I found a parcel directed to me, and opening it, I found a pamphlet written entirely against myself, not by name, but against something I writ[2]: it is pretty civil, and affects to be so, and I think I will take no notice of it; 'tis against something written very lately; and indeed I know not what to say, nor do I care: and so you are a sawcy rogue for losing your money to-day at Stoite's; to let that bungler beat you, fye, Stella, an't you ashamed? Well, I forgive you this once, never do so again; no, noooo. Kiss and be friends, sirrah.—Come, let me go sleep, I go earlier to bed than formerly; and have not been out so late these two months; but the secretary was in a drinking humour. So good night, myownlittledearsaucyinsolentrogues.

19. Then you read that long word in the last line, no,[3] faith han't you. Well, when will this letter come from our MD? to-morrow or next day without fail; yes faith, and so it is coming. This was an insipid snowy day, no walking day, and I dined gravely with Mrs. Vanhomrigh, and came home, and am now got to bed a little after ten; I remember old Culpepper's maxim. Would you have a settled head, You must early go to bed; I tell you and I tell't again, You must be in bed at ten.

20. And so I went to-day with my new wig, o hoao, to visit

---

[1] Samuel Masham (1679?–1758), son of Sir Francis Masham, tnird bart., of Otes in High Laver, Essex, afterwards first Baron Masham. Chiefly known as the husband of Mrs. (afterwards Lady) Masham.

[2] Probably against the character of Lord Wharton.—N.

[3] In that word there were some puzzling characters.—D. S.

lady Worsley,[1] whom I had not seen before, although she was near a month in town; then I walkt in the Park to find Mr. Ford, whom I had promised to meet, and coming down the Mall, who should come towards me but Patrick, and gives me five letters out of his pocket. I read the superscription of the first, Pshoh, said I; of the second, Pshoh again; of the third, Pshah, Pshah, Pshah; of the fourth, A Gad, A Gad, A Gad, I'm in a rage; of the fifth and last, O hoooa; aye marry this is something, this is our MD, so truly we opened it, I think immediately, and it began the most impudently in the world, thus; Dear Presto, We are even thus far. Now we are even, quoth Stephen, when he gave his wife six blows for one. I received your ninth four days after I had sent my thirteenth. But I'll reckon with you anon about that, young women. Why did not you recant at the end of your letter when you got my eleventh, tell me that huzzies base, were we even then, were we, sirrah? But I won't answer your letter now, I'll keep it for another time. We had a great deal of snow to-day, and 'tis terrible cold. I dined with Ford, because it was his Opera-day and snowed, so I did not care to stir further. I will send to-morrow to Smyth.

21. Morning. It has snowed terribly all night, and is vengeance cold. I am not yet up, but cannot write long; my hands will freeze. Is there a good fire, Patrick? Yes, Sir; then I'll rise, come take away the candle. You must know I write on the dark side of my bed-chamber, and am forced to have a candle till I rise, for the bed stands between me and the window, and I keep the curtains shut this cold weather. So pray let me rise, and, Patrick, here take away the candle.—At night. We are now here in high frost and snow, the largest fire can hardly keep us warm. It is very ugly walking, a baker's boy broke his thigh yesterday. I walk slow, make short steps, and never tread on my heel. 'Tis a good proverb the Devonshire people have; Walk fast in snow, In frost walk slow, And still as you go, Tread on your toe: When frost and snow are both together, Sit by the fire and spare shoe-leather. I dined to-day with Dr. Cockburn, but will not do so again in haste, he has generally such a parcel of Scots with him.

22. Morning. Starving, starving, Uth, uth, uth, uth, uth.— Don't you remember I used to come into your chamber, and turn Stella out of her chair, and rake up the fire in a cold

---

[1] Frances (Thynne) (c. 1673–1750), daughter of first Viscount Weymouth, wife of Sir Robert Worsley, bart.

morning, and cry Uth, uth, uth? &c. O faith I must rise, my hand is so cold I can write no more. So good morrow, sirrahs.—At night. I went this morning to lady Giffard's house, and saw your mother, and made her give me a pint bottle of palsey water, which I brought home in my pocket; and sealed and tyed up in a paper, and sent it to Mr. Smyth, who goes to-morrow for Ireland, and sent a letter to him to desire his care of it, and that he would enquire at Chester about the box. He was not within, so the bottle and letter were left for him at his lodgings, with strict orders to give them to him; and I will send Patrick in a day or two, to know whether it was given, &c. Dr. Stratford[1] and I dined to-day with Mr. Stratford in the city, by appointment; but I chose to walk there for exercise in the frost. But the weather had *given* a little, as you women call it, so it was something slobbery. I did not get home till nine, And now I'm in bed To break your head.

23. Morning. They tell me it freezes again, but 'tis not so cold as yesterday: so now I will answer a bit of your letter.—At night. O faith, I was just going to answer some of our MD's letter this morning, when a printer came in about some business, and staid an hour; so I rose, and then came in Ben Tooke, and then I shaved and scribbled, and it was such a terrible day I could not stir out till one, and then I called at Mrs. Barton's, and we went to lady Worsley's, where we were to dine by appointment. The earl of Berkeley[2] is going to be married to lady Louisa Lenox, the duke of Richmond's daughter. I writ this night to dean Sterne, and bid him to tell you all about the bottle of palsey water by Smyth, and to-morrow morning I will say something to your letter.

24. Morning. Come now to your letter. As for your being even with me, I have spoken to that already. So now, my dearly beloved, let us proceed to the next. You are always grumbling that you han't letters fast enough, surely we shall have your tenth[3]; and yet before you end your letter, you own you have my eleventh.—And why did not MD go into the country with the bishop of Clogher? faith such a journey would have done you good; Stella should have rode [? rid],

---

[1] From Letter LX., Feb. 24, 1712-13, it seems he was a clergyman. William Stratford (*d.* 1729), son of Nicholas Stratford, Bishop of Chester, was Archdeacon of Richmond and Canon of Christ Church, Oxford.

[2] James, third earl, an admiral, whose bride was only sixteen, and who had seen much active service. He was latterly a lord justice regent. Died 1736.

[3] These are the words of MD.—D. S.

and Dingley gone in the coach. The bishop of Kilmore[1] I know nothing of; he is old and may dye; he lives in some obscure corner, for I never heard of him. As for my old friends,[2] if you mean the Whigs, I never see them, as you may find by my journals, except lord Hallifax, and him very seldom; lord Somers never since the first visit, for he has been a false deceitful rascal. My new friends are very kind, and I have promises enough, but I do not count upon them, and besides my pretences are very young to them. However, we will see what may be done, and if nothing at all, I shall not be disappointed; although perhaps poor MD may, and then I shall be sorryer for their sakes than my own.—Talk of a merry Christmas (why did you write it so then young women? sawce for the goose is sawce for the gander) I have wisht you all that two or three letters ago. Good lack; and your news, that Mr. St. John is going to Holland; he has no such thoughts to quit the great station he is in, nor if he had, could I be spared to go with him. So faith, politick Madam Stella, you come with your two eggs a penny, &c. Well, Madam Dingley, and so Mrs. Stoite invites you, and so you stay at Donnybrook,[3] and so you could not write. You are plaguy exact in your journals from Dec. 25, to Jan. 4th. Well, Smyth and the palsey water I have handled already, and he does not lodge (or rather did not, for poor man, now he is gone) at Mr. Jesse's and all that stuff; but we found his lodging, and I went to Stella's mother on my own head, for I never remembered it was in the letter to desire another bottle; but I was so fretted, so tosticated, and so impatient, that Stella should have her water (I mean decently, don't be rogues) and so vext with Sterne's carelessness.—Pray God Stella's illnesses may not return. If they come seldom, they begin to be weary; I judge by myself; for when I seldom visit, I grow weary of my acquaintance.—Leave a good deal of my tenth unanswered!—Impudent slut, when did you ever answer my tenth, or ninth, or any other number? or who desires you to answer, provided you write? I defy the D— to answer my letters; sometimes there may be one or two things I should

[1] Edward Wetenhall (c. 1635–1713) was Bishop of Kilmore from 1699. An Englishman.

[2] Swift appears from several other passages about this period to have been severely mortified by the ingratitude of his former patrons, the lords Somers, Halifax, and Wharton; and was actually introduced to Mr. Harley as "one extremely ill used by the last ministry, after some obligations, because he refused to go certain lengths they would have him"; which was in some sort Mr. Harley's own case.—D. S.

[3] About a mile from Dublin.—D. S.

be glad you would answer, but I forget them, and you never think of them. I shall never love answering letters again, if you talk of answering. Answering, quotha; pretty answerers truly.—As for the pamphlet you speak of, and call it scandalous, and that one Mr. Presto is said to write it, hear my answer. Fye, child, you must not mind what every idle body tells you. —I believe you lie, and that the dogs were not crying it when you said so; come, tell truth. I am sorry you go to St. Mary's[1] so soon, you'll be as poor as rats; that place will drain you with a vengeance: besides, I would have you think of being in the country in Summer. Indeed, Stella, pippins produced plentifully; Parvisol could not send from Laracor: there were about half a score, I would be glad to know whether they were good for any thing.—Mrs. Walls at Donnybrook with you; why is not she brought to bed? Well, well, well, Dingley, pray be satisfied; you talk as if you were angry about the bishop's not offering you conveniencies for the journey; and so he should.— What sort of Christmas? Why I have had no Christmas at all; and has it really been Christmas of late? I never once thought of it. My service to Mrs. Stoite, and Catherine, and let Catherine get the coffee ready against I come, and not have so much care on her countenance; for all will go well—Mr. Bernage, Mr. Bernage, Mr. Fiddlenage, I have had three letters from him now successively; he sends no directions, and how the D— shall I write to him? I would have burnt his last, if I had not seen Stella's hand at the bottom: his request is all nonsense. How can I assist him in buying? and if he be ordered to go to Spain, go he must, or else sell, and I believe one can hardly sell in such a juncture. If he had staid, and new regiments raised, I would have used my endeavour to have had him removed; although I have no credit that way, or very little: but if the regiment goes, he ought to go too; he has had great indulgence, and opportunities of saving; and I have urged him to it a hundred times. What can I do? whenever it lies in my power to do him a good office, I will do it. Pray draw up this into a handsome speech, and represent it to him from me, and that I would write, if I knew where to direct to him; and so I have told you, and desired you would tell him, fifty times. Yes, Madam Stella, I think I can read your long concluding word, but you can't read mine after bidding you good night. And yet, me-thinks, I mend extremely in my writing; but when Stella's eyes are well, I hope to write as bad as ever.—So now I have answered your letter, and mine is an answer; for I lay yours before me, and I look and write, and write and look, and look and write again.—So good morrow, Madams both, and I'll go rise, for I must rise; for I take pills at night, and so I must rise early, I don't know why.——

25. Morning. I did not tell you how I past my time yesterday, nor bid you good night, and there was good reason. I went in the morning to secretary St. John about some business; he had got a great Whig with him; a creature of the duke of Marlborough, who is a Go-between to make peace between the duke and the ministry[1]; so he came out of his closet; and after a few words, desired I would dine with him at three, but Mr. Lewis staid till six before he came; and there we sat talking, and the time slipt so, that at last, when I was positive to go, it was past two of clock; so I came home and went straight to bed. He would never let me look at his watch, and I could not imagine it above twelve when we went away. So I bid you good night for last night, and now I bid you good morrow, and I am still in bed, though it be near ten, but I must rise.

26, 27, 28, 29, 30. I have been so lazy and negligent these last four days that I could not write to MD. My head is not in order, and yet it is not absolutely ill, but giddyish, and makes me listless; I walk every day, and take drops of Dr. Cockburn, and I have just done a box of pills, and to-day lady Kerry sent me some of her bitter drink which I design to take twice a day, and hope I shall grow better. I wish I were with MD, I long for Spring and good weather, and then I will come over. My riding in Ireland keeps me well. I am very temperate, and eat of the easiest meats as I am directed, and hope the malignity will go off; but one fit shakes me a long time. I dined to-day with lord Mountjoy, yesterday at Mr. Stone's in the city, on Sunday at Vanhomrigh's, Saturday with Ford, and Friday I think at Vanhomrigh's, and that's all the journal I can send MD, for I was so lazy while I was well, that I could not write. I thought to have sent this to-night, but 'tis ten, and I'll go to bed, and write on t'other side to Parvisol to-morrow, and send it on Thursday; and so good night my dears, and love Presto, and be healthy, and Presto will be so too, &c.

Cut off these notes handsomely, d'ye hear, sirrahs, and give Mrs. Brent hers, and keep yours till you see Parvisol, and then

---

[1] It was strongly asserted that, to retain his command and emoluments, the Duke would have acted under the Tory Ministry; but the jealousies and quarrels of the Duchess with the Queen and Mrs. Masham prevented this arrangement.—D. L. P.

make up the letter to him, and send it him by the first opportunity, and so God Almighty bless you both, here and ever, and poor Presto.

What, I warrant you thought at first that these last lines were another letter.

Dingley, Pray pay Stella six fishes, and place them to the account of your humble servant, Presto.

Stella, Pray pay Dingley six fishes, and place them to the account of your humble servant, Presto.

There's Bills of Exchange for you.

LETTER XV

London, *Jan.* 31, 1710-11.

I AM to send you my fourteenth to-morrow, but my head having some little disorders, confounds all my journals. I was early this morning with Mr. secretary St. John about some business, so I could not scribble my morning lines to MD. They are here intending to tax all little printed penny papers a half penny every half-sheet, which will utterly ruin Grub-street, and I am endeavouring to prevent it. Besides, I was forwarding an impeachment against a certain great person; that was two of my businesses with the secretary, were they not worthy ones? It was Ford's Birth-day, and I refused the secretary and dined with Ford. We are here in as smart a frost for the time as I have seen; delicate walking weather, and the Canal and Rosamond's Pond[1] full of the rabble sliding and with skates, if you know what those are. Patrick's bird's water freezes in the gally-pot, and my hands in bed.

Feb. 1. I was this morning with poor lady Kerry, who is much worse in her head than I. She sends me bottles of her bitter, and we are so fond of one another, because our ailments are the same; don't you know that, Madam Stella? Han't I seen you conning ailments with Joe's wife,[2] and some others, sirrah? I walkt into the city to dine, because of the walk, for we must take care of Presto's health you know, because of poor little MD. But I walkt plaguy carefully, for fear of sliding against my will; but I am very busy.

2. This morning Mr. Ford came to me to walk into the city, where he had business, and then to buy books at Bateman's;

[1] The "canal" was the lake in St. James's Park. Rosamond's Pond, becoming too much used as a place of suicide, was filled in in the eighteenth century—it lay to the south of Birdcage Walk, where the barracks are.
[2] Mrs. Beaumont.—D. S.

and I laid out one pound five shillings for a Strabo and Aristophanes, and I have now got books enough to make me another shelf, and I will have more, or it shall cost me a fall; and so as we came back, we drank a flask of right French wine at Ben Tooke's chamber; and when I got home, Mrs. Vanhomrigh sent me word her eldest daughter[1] was taken suddenly very ill, and desired I would come and see her; I went, and found it was a silly trick of Mrs. Armstrong, lady Lucy's sister, who, with Moll Stanhope, was visiting there: however, I rattled off the daughter.

3. To-day I went and dined at lady Lucy's, where you know I have not been this long time; they are plaguy Whigs, especially the sister Armstrong, the most insupportable of all women, pretending to wit, without any taste. She was running down the last *Examiner*, the prettiest I had read, with a character of the present ministry.—I left them at five, and came home. But I forgot to tell you, that this morning my cousin Dryden Leach the printer, came to me with a heavy complaint, that Harrison the new *Tatler* had turned him off, and taken the last *Tatler*'s printers again. He vowed revenge; I answered gravely, and so he left me, and I have ordered Patrick to deny me to him from henceforth: and at night comes a letter from Harrison, telling me the same thing, and excused his doing it without my notice, because he would bear all the blame; and in his *Tatler* of this day he tells you the story, how he has taken his old officers, and there is a most humble letter from Morphew and Lilly to beg his pardon, &c. And lastly, this morning Ford sent me two letters from the Coffee-house (where I hardly ever go) one from the archbishop of Dublin, and t'other from ————. Who do you think t'other was from?——I'll tell you, because you are friends; why then it was, faith it was from my own dear little MD, N. 10. Oh, but won't answer it now, no noooooh, I'll keep it between the two sheets; here it is, just under; oh, I lifted up the sheet and saw it there: lie still, you shan't be answered yet, little letter; for I must go to bed, and take care of my head.

4. I avoid going to church yet, for fear of my head, though it has been much better these last five or six days, since I have taken lady Kerry's bitter. Our frost holds like a dragon. I went to Mr. Addison's, and dined with him at his lodgings; I had not seen him these three weeks, we are grown common acquaintance; yet what have not I done for his friend Steele? Mr. Harley

[1] Esther ("Vanessa").

reproached me the last time I saw him, that to please me he would be reconciled to Steele, and had promised and appointed to see him, and that Steele never came. Harrison, whom Mr. Addison recommended to me, I have introduced to the secretary of state, who has promised me to take care of him; and I have represented Addison himself so to the ministry, that they think and talk in his favour, though they hated him before.—— Well; he is now in my debt, and there's an end; and I never had the least obligation to him, and there's another end. This evening I had a message from Mr. Harley, desiring to know whether I was alive, and that I would dine with him to-morrow. They dine so late, that since my head has been wrong I have avoided being with them.—Patrick has been out of favour these ten days; I talk dry and cross to him, and have called him Friend three or four times. But, sirrahs, get you gone.

5. Morning. I am going this morning to see Prior, who dines with me at Mr. Harley's; so I cannot stay fiddling and talking with dear little brats in a morning, and 'tis still terribly cold. —I wish my cold hand was in the warmest place about you, young women, I'd give ten guineas upon that account with all my heart, faith; oh, it starves my thigh; so I'll rise, and bid you good morrow, my ladies both, good morrow. Come stand away, let me rise: Patrick, take away the candle. Is there a good fire?—So—up a-dazy.—At night. Mr. Harley did not sit down till six, and I staid till eleven; henceforth I will chuse to visit him in the evenings, and dine with him no more if I can help it. It breaks all my measures, and hurts my health; my head is disorderly, but not ill, and I hope it will mend.

6. Here has been such a hurry with the Queen's Birth-day, so much fine cloaths, and the Court so crowded that I did not go there. All the frost is gone. It thawed on Sunday, and so continues, yet ice is still on the Canal (I did not mean that of Laracor, but St. James's Park) and boys sliding on it. Mr. Ford pressed me to dine with him in his chamber.—Did not I tell you Patrick has got a bird, a linnet, to carry over to Dingley? It was very tame at first, and 'tis now the wildest I ever saw. He keeps it in a closet, where it makes a terrible litter; but I say nothing: I am as tame as a clout. When must we answer our MD's letter? One of these odd-come-shortlies. This is a week old, you see, and no further yet. Mr. Harley desired I would dine with him again to-day; but I refused him, for I fell out with him yesterday, and will not see him again till he makes me amends: and so I go to bed.

7. I was this morning early with Mr. Lewis of the secretary's office, and saw a letter Mr. Harley had sent to him, desiring to be reconciled; but I was deaf to all intreaties, and have desired Lewis to go to him, and let him know I expect further satisfaction. If we let these great ministers pretend too much, there will be no governing them. He promises to make me easy, if I will but come and see him; but I won't, and he shall do it by message, or I will cast him off. I'll tell you the cause of our quarrel when I see you, and refer it to yourselves. In that he did something,[1] which he intended for a favour; and I have taken it quite otherwise, disliking both the thing and the manner, and it has heartily vexed me, and all I have said is truth, though it looks like jest; and I absolutely refused to submit to his intended favour, and expect further satisfaction. Mr. Ford and I dined with Mr. Lewis. We have a monstrous deal of snow, and it has cost me two shillings to-day in chair and coach, and walk'd till I was dirty besides. I know not what it is now to read or write after I am in bed. The last thing I do up is to write something to our MD, and then get into bed, and put out my candle, and so go sleep as fast as ever I can. But in the mornings I do write sometimes in bed, as you know.

8. Morning. *I have desired* Apronia *to be always careful, especially about the legs.* Pray, do you see any such great wit in that sentence? I must freely own that I do not. But party carries every thing now-a-days, and what a splutter have I heard about the wit of that saying, repeated with admiration above a hundred times in half an hour. Pray read it over again this moment, and consider it. I think the word is *advised*, and not *desired*. I should not have remembered it if I had not heard it so often. Why—aye—You must know I dreamt it just now, and waked with it in my mouth. Are you bit, or are you not, sirrahs? I met Mr. Harley in the court of requests, and he askt me how long I had learnt the trick of writing to myself? He had seen your letter through the glass-case at the Coffee-house, and would swear it was my hand; and Mr. Ford, who took and sent it me, was of the same mind. I remember others have formerly said so too. I think I was little MD's writing-master.[2]—But come, what's here to do, writing to young women in a morning? I have other fish to fry; so good morrow, my ladies all, good morrow. Perhaps I'll answer your letter to-night, perhaps I

---

[1] This alludes to the £50 bank-note, which Swift indignantly returned. *See* the *Journal* of March 7, 1710-11.—N.

[2] Stella's hand had a great deal of the air of the Doctor's; but she writ more legibly, and rather better.—D. S.

won't; that's as saucy little Presto takes the humour.—At night. I walk'd in the park to-day in spight of the weather, as I do always when it does not actually rain. Do you know what? It has gone and done;[1] we had a thaw for three days, then a monstrous dirt and snow, and now it freezes, like a pot-lid, upon our snow. I dined with lady Betty Germain, the first time since I came for England; and there did I sit, like a booby, till eight, looking over her and another lady at picquet, when I had other business enough to do. It was the coldest day I felt this year.

9. Morning. After I had been a-bed an hour last night, I was forced to rise and call to the landlady and maid to have the fire removed in a chimney below stairs, which made my bed-chamber smoke, though I had no fire in it. I have been twice served so. I never lay so miserable an hour in my life. Is it not plaguy vexatious?—It has snowed all night, and rains this morning.—Come, where's MD's letter? Come, Mrs. Letter, make your appearance. Here am I, says she, answer me to my face.—Oh, faith, I am sorry you had my twelfth so soon; I doubt you will stay longer for the rest. I'm so 'fraid you have got my fourteenth while I am writing this; and I would always have one letter from Presto reading, one travelling, and one writing. As for the box, I now believe it lost. It is directed for Mr. Curry at his house in Capel street, &c. I had a letter yesterday from Dr. Raymond in Chester, who says, he sent his man every where, and cannot find it; and God knows whether Mr. Smyth will have better success. Sterne spoke to him, and I writ to him with the bottle of palsy-water; that bottle I hope, will not miscarry: I long to hear you have it. Oh, faith, you have too good an opinion of Presto's care. I am negligent enough of every thing but MD, and I should not have trusted Sterne.—But it shall not go so: I will have one more tug for it.—As to what you say of goodman Peasly and Isaac,[2] I answer as I did before. Fye, child, you must not give yourself the way to believe any such thing: and afterwards, only for curiosity, you may tell me how those things are approved, and how you like them; and whether they instruct you in the present course of affairs, and whether they are printed in your town, or only sent from hence.—Sir Andrew Fountain is recovered; so take your sorrow again, but don't keep it, fling it to the dogs. And does little MD walk, indeed?

[1] Thus D. S. Probably meaning "Do you know what it has gone and done? It," etc.
[2] He alludes to some pamphlet of which he was the suspected, and perhaps real, author.—SCOTT.

—I'm glad of it at heart.—Yes, we have done with the plague here: it was very saucy in you to pretend to have it before your betters. Your intelligence that the story is false about the officers forced to sell,[1] is admirable. You may see them all three every day, no more in the Army than you. Twelve shillings for mending the strong box; that is, for putting a farthing's worth of iron on a hinge, and gilding it; give him six shillings, and I'll pay it, and never employ him or his again.—No—indeed, I put of preaching as much as I can. I am upon another foot: no-body doubts here whether I can preach, and you are fools. —The account you give of that weekly paper[2] agrees with us here. Mr. Prior was like to be insulted in the street for being supposed the author of it; but one of the last papers cleared him. No-body knows who it is, but those few in the secret, I suppose, the ministry and the printer.—Poor Stella's eyes, God bless them, and send them better. Pray spare them, and write not above two lines a day in broad day-light. How does Stella look, madam Dingley? Pretty well; a handsome young woman still. Will she pass in a crowd? Will she make a figure in a country church?—Stay a little, fair ladies. I this minute sent Patrick to Sterne: he brings back word that your box is very safe with one Mr. Earl's sister in Chester, and that Colonel Edgworth's widow[3] goes for Ireland on Monday next, and will receive the box at Chester, and deliver it you safe: so there is some hopes now.—Well, let us go on [now] to your letter.— The warrant is passed for the First-Fruits. The queen does not send a letter; but a patent will be drawn here, and that will take up time.[4] Mr. Harley of late has said nothing of presenting me to the queen:—I was overseen[5] when I mentioned it to you. He has such a weight of affairs on him, that he cannot mind all; but he talk'd of it three or four times to me, long before I dropt it to you.[6] What, is not Mrs. Walls' business

---

[1] See Letter XI., Dec. 13.   [2] The *Examiner.*—D. S.
[3] See Letter VI., Oct. 17 (note). Perhaps Ambrose Edgworth had died meanwhile.

[4] The Queen's patent for exonerating the clergy of Ireland from paying the twentieth parts, and a grant to them of the first-fruits, payable out of all ecclesiastical benefices, in trust to be for ever applied towards purchasing glebes, and building residentiary houses for poor endowed vicars, both bear date, Feb. 7, 1710-11. The first trustees were Primate Marsh, Lord Chancellor Phipps, Archbishop King, and Archbishop Vesey.—N.

[5] Mistaken.

[6] Queen Anne's objections to the author of the *Tale of a Tub* were found invincible, both in this point and in the more important one of Swift's preferment. The ministers studiously concealed from him the Queen's aversion.—D. L. P.

over yet? I had hopes she was up and well, and the child dead before this time.—You did right, at last, to send me your accounts; but I did not stay for them, I thank you. I hope you have your bill sent in my last, and there will be eight pounds interest soon due from Hawkshaw; pray look at his bond. I hope you are good managers, and that when I say so, Stella won't think I intend she should grudge herself wine. But going to those expensive lodgings requires some fund. I wish you had staid till I came over, for some reasons. That Frenchwoman[1] will be grumbling again in a little time, and if you are invited any where to the country, it will vex you to pay in absence; and the country may be necessary for poor Stella's health: but do as you like, and don't blame Presto.— Oh, but you are telling your reasons.—Well, I have read them; do as you please.—Yes, Raymond says, he must stay longer than he thought, because he cannot settle his affairs. M—— is in the country at some friend's, comes to town in Spring, and then goes to settle in Herefordshire. Her husband is a surly ill-natured brute, and cares not she should see any body. O Lord, see how I blundered, and left two lines short; it was that ugly score in the paper[2] that made me mistake.——I believe you lie about the story of the fire, only to make it more odd. Bernage must go to Spain, and I will see to recommend him to the duke of Argyle, his general, when I see the duke next: but the officers tell me it would be dishonourable in the last degree for him to sell now, and he would never be preferred in the army; so that unless he designs to leave it for good and all, he must go. Tell him so, and that I would write if I knew where to direct to him; which I have said four-score times already. I had rather any thing almost than that you should strain yourselves to send a letter when it is inconvenient; we have settled that matter already. I'll write when I can, and so shall MD; and upon occasions extraordinary I will write, though it be a line; and when we have not letters soon, we agree that all things are well; and so that's settled for ever, and so hold your tongue.—Well, you shall have your pins; but for candles ends, I cannot promise, because I burn them to the stumps; besides, I remember what Stella told Dingley about them many years ago, and she may think the same thing of me.—And Dingley shall have her hinged spectacles.—Poor dear Stella, how durst you write those two lines by candle-light; bang your bones. Faith, this letter shall go to-morrow, I think, and that will be in ten days from the last, young women; that's too soon of all conscience: but answering yours has filled it up so quick, and I don't design to use you to three pages in folio, no nooooh. All this is one morning's work in bed;—and so good morrow, little sirrahs; that's for the rhyme.[1] You want politicks: faith, I can't think of any; but may be at night I may tell you a passage. Come, sit off the bed, and let me rise, will you?—At night. I dined to day with my neighbour Vanhomrigh; it was such dismal weather I could not stir further. I have had some threatenings with my head, but no fits. I still drink Dr. Radcliffe's[2] bitter, and will continue it.

10. I was this morning to see the secretary of state, and have engaged him to give a memorial from me to the duke of Argyle in behalf of Bernage. The duke is a man that distinguishes people of merit, and I will speak to him myself; but the secretary backing it will be very effectual, and I will take care to have it done to purpose. Pray tell Bernage so, and that I think nothing can be luckier for him, and that I would have him go by all means. I will order it that the duke shall send for him when they are in Spain; or, if he fails, that he shall receive him kindly when he goes to wait on him. Can I do more? Is not this a great deal?—I now send away this letter, that you may not stay.—I dined with Ford upon his Opera-day, and am now come home, and am going to study; don't you presume to guess, sirrahs, impudent saucy dear boxes. Toward the end of a letter I could not say saucy boxes without putting *dear* between. En't that right now? Farewel. *This* should *be* longer, *but* that *I* send *it* to-*night*,[3]

O silly, silly loggerhead!

I send a letter this post to one Mr. Staunton,[4] and I direct it to Mr. Acton's in St. Michael's-Lane. He formerly lodged there, but he has not told me where to direct. Pray send to that Acton, whether[5] the letter is come there, and whether he has sent it to Staunton.

---

[1] In the original it was, *good mollows, little sollahs*. But in these words, and many others, he writes constantly *ll* for *rr*.—D. S.

[2] *See* Letter IV., Sept. 29, 1710.

[3] Those letters which are in italicks, in the original are of a monstrous size, which occasioned his calling himself a loggerhead.—D. S.

[4] Alex. Martin Freeman, editor of the "Vanessa" correspondence, says that this was the Thomas Staunton who acted as legal agent to the younger Mr. Percival, and that Swift afterwards successfully recommended him for a post under "Harry Temple," afterwards first Viscount Palmerston. Thomas Staunton's daughter Deborah was ancestress of the Rochforts of Colgrenane, co. Carlow. As to the Percivals, *see* Letter XXXVI., Dec. 3, 1711.

[5] Presumably "to inquire whether."

If Bernage designs to sell his commission and stay at home, pray let him tell me so, that my recommendation to the duke of Argyle may not be in vain.

LETTER XVI

London, *Feb.* 10, 1710-11.

I HAVE just dispatched my fifteenth to the post; I tell you how things will be, after I have got a letter from MD. I am in furious haste to finish mine, for fear of having two of MD's to answer in one of Presto's, which would be such a disgrace, never saw the like; but before you write to me I write at my leisure, like a gentleman, a little every day, just to let you know how matters go, and so and so; and I hope before this comes to you, you'll have got your box and chocolate, and Presto will take more care another time.

11. Morning. I must rise and go see my lord keeper, which will cost me two shillings in coach-hire. Don't call them two thirteens?[1]—At night. It has rained all day, and there was no walking. I read prayers to sir Andrew Fountain in the fore-noon,[2] and dined with three Irishmen at one Mr. Cope's[3] lodgings; the other two were one Morris an archdeacon,[4] and Mr. Ford. When I came home this evening, I expected that little jackanapes Harrison would have come to get help about his *Tatler* for Tuesday: I have fixed two evenings in the week which I allow him to come. The toad never came, and I expecting him fell a reading, and left off other business.—Come, what are you doing? How do you pass your time this ugly weather? Gaming and drinking, I suppose: fine diversions for young ladies, truly. I wish you had some of our Seville oranges, and we some of your wine. We have the finest oranges for two-pence apiece, and the basest wine for six shillings a bottle. They tell me wine grows cheap with you. I am resolved to have half a hogs-head when I get to Ireland, if it be good and cheap, as it used to be; and I'll treat MD at my table in an evening, oh hoa, and laugh at great ministers of state.

12. The days are grown fine and long, —— be thanked. O faith, you forget all our little sayings, and I am angry. I dined to-day with Mr. secretary St. John: I went to the court of requests at noon, and sent Mr. Harley into the house to call

[1] A shilling passed for thirteen pence in Ireland.
[2] Thus D. S. Later editions: "afternoon."
[3] Robert Cope, Esq., a correspondent of Swift's.
[4] Unidentified.

the secretary, to let him know I would not dine with him if he dined late. By good luck the duke of Argyle was at the lobby of the house too, and I kept him in talk till the secretary came out, then told them I was glad to meet them together, and that I had a request to the duke which the secretary must second, and his grace must grant. The duke said he was sure it was something insignificant, and wished it was ten times greater. At the secretary's house I writ a memorial, and gave it [to] the secretary to give the duke, and shall see that he does it. It is, that his Grace will please to take Mr. Bernage into his protection; and if he finds Bernage answers my character, to give him all encouragement. Colonel Masham [1] and Colonel Hill [2] (Mrs. Masham's [3] brother) tell me my request is reasonable, and they will second it heartily to the duke too: so I reckon Bernage is on a very good foot when he goes to Spain. Pray tell him this, though perhaps I will write to him before he goes; yet where shall I direct? for I suppose he has left Conolly's. [4]

13. I have left off lady Kerry's bitter, and got another box of pills. I have no fits of giddiness, but only some little disorders towards it; and I walk as much as I can. Lady Kerry is just as I am, only a great deal worse: I dined to-day at lord Shelburn's, where she is, and we conn ailments, which makes us very fond of each other. I have taken Mr. Harley into favour again, and called to see him, but he was not within; I will use to visit him after dinner, for he dines too late for my head: then I went to visit poor Congreve, who is just getting out of a severe fit of the gout, and I sat with him till near nine o'clock. He gave me a *Tatler* he had written out, as blind as he is, for little Harrison. 'Tis about a scoundrel that was grown rich, and went and bought a Coat of Arms at the Herald's, and a set of ancestors at Fleet-ditch; 'tis well enough, and shall be printed in two or three days, and if you read those kind of things, this will divert you. 'Tis now between ten and eleven, and I am going to bed.

14. This was Mrs. Vanhomrigh's daughter's Birth-day, and Mr. Ford and I were invited to dinner to keep it, and we spent the evening there drinking punch. That was our way of beginning Lent; and in the morning lord Shelburn, lady Kerry,

---

[1] See Letter XIV., Jan. 18.   [2] See Letter X., Nov. 25, 1710.
[3] Abigail, daughter of Francis Hill of London, married Samuel Masham, the Prince-Consort's groom of the chambers (afterwards Lord Masham), 1707. She was cousin and successful rival to Sarah, Duchess of Marlborough, in the favour of Queen Anne, on whose death she retired from political activity. Died 1734.
[4] See Letter IV., Sept. 28, 1710.

Mrs. Pratt and I went to Hyde-park, instead of going to
church; for till my head is a little settled, I think it better not
to go; it would be so silly and troublesome to go out sick. Dr.
Duke[1] died suddenly two or three nights ago; he was one of
the wits when we were children, but turned parson, and left
it, and never writ further than a prologue or recommendatory
copy of verses. He had a fine living given him by the bishop
of Winchester[2] about three months ago; he got his living
suddenly, and he got his dying so too.

15. I walked purely to-day about the Park, the rain being
just over, of which we have had a great deal, mixt with little
short frosts, I went to the court of requests, thinking if Mr.
Harley dined early, to go with him. But meeting Leigh and
Sterne, they invited me to dine with them, and away we went.
When we got into his room, one H——, a worthless Irish
fellow, was there ready to dine with us, so I stept out and
whispered them, that I would not dine with that fellow; they
made excuses, and begged me to stay, but away to Mr. Harley's,
and he did not dine at home, and at last I dined at Sir John
Germain's, and found lady Betty but just recovered of a miscarriage. I am writing an inscription for lord Berkeley's tomb:
you know the young rake his son, the new earl,[3] is married to
the duke of Richmond's daughter, at the duke's country house,
and are now coming to town. She'll be fluxed in two months,
and they'll be parted in a year. You ladies are brave, bold
ventersome folks; and the chit is but seventeen, and is ill-
natured, covetous, vicious, and proud in extreams. And so get
you gone to Stoite to-morrow.

16. Faith this letter goes on but slow, 'tis a week old, and
the first side not written. I went to-day into the city for a
walk, but the person I designed to dine with was not at home;
so I came back and called at Congreve's, and dined with him
and Eastcourt, and laughed till six, then went to Mr. Harley's,
who was not gone to dinner; there I staid till nine, and we made
up our quarrel, and he has invited me to dinner to-morrow,
which is the day of the week (Saturday) that lord keeper and

[1] Dr. Richard Duke, of some celebrity in his day both as a poet and a
divine [he was a friend of Dryden's], was rector of Blaby in Leicestershire;
and in 1710 was presented, by Bishop Trelawny [of Winchester], to the
rich rectory of Witney, in Oxfordshire, which he enjoyed but a few months.
Feb. 10, 1710-11, having returned from an entertainment, he was found
dead next morning.—N.
[2] Sir Jonathan Trelawny (1650-1721), one of the "seven bishops"
prosecuted by James II.—he was then of Bristol. He was third baronet.
[3] See Letter XIV., Jan. 23.

secretary St. John dine with him privately, and at last they have consented to let me among them on that day. Atterbury and Prior went to bury poor Dr. Duke.[1] Congreve's nasty white wine has given me the heart-burn.

17. I took some good walks in the Park to-day, and then went to Mr. Harley. Lord Rivers was got there before me, and I chid him for presuming to come on a day when only lord keeper and the secretary and I were to be there; but he regarded me not; so we all dined together, and sat down at four; and the secretary has invited me to dine with him to-morrow. I told them I had no hopes they could ever keep in, but that I saw they loved one another so well, as indeed they seem to do. They call me nothing but Jonathan; and I said, I believed they would leave me Jonathan as they found me; and that I never knew a ministry do any thing for those whom they make companions of their pleasures; and I believe you will find it so; but I care not. I am upon a project of getting five hundred pounds, without being obliged to any body; but that is a secret, till I see my dearest MD; and so hold your tongue, and don't talk, sirrahs, for I am now about it.

18. My head has no fits, but a little disordered before dinner; yet I walk stoutly, and take pills, and hope to mend. Secretary St. John would needs have me dine with him to-day, and there I found three persons I never saw, two I had no acquaintance with, and one I did not care for: so I left them early and came home, it being no day to walk, but scurvy rain and wind. The secretary tells me he has put a cheat on me; for lord Peterborow sent him twelve dozen flasks of Burgundy, on condition that I should have my share; but he never was quiet till they were all gone, so I reckon he owes me thirty-six pound. Lord Peterborow is now got to Vienna, and I must write to him to-morrow. I begin now to be towards looking for a letter from some certain ladies of Presto's acquaintance, that live at St. Mary's,[2] and are called in a certain language our little MD. No, stay, I don't expect one these six days, that will be just three weeks; an't I a reasonable creature? We are plagued here with an October Club[3]; that is, a set of above a hundred parliament-men of the country, who drink October beer at home, and meet every evening at a tavern near the parliament, to consult affairs, and drive things on to extreams against the Whigs, to call the old ministry to account, and get off five or

six heads. The ministry seem not to regard them, yet one of
them in confidence told me, that there must be something
thought on to settle things better. I'll tell you one great state-
secret; The queen, sensible how much she was governed by
the late ministry, runs a little into t'other extream, and is
jealous in that point, even of those who got her out of the others
hands. The ministry is for gentler measures, and the other
Tories for more violent. Lord Rivers, talking to me the other
day, cursed the paper called The *Examiner*, for speaking civilly
of the duke of Marlborough; this I happened to talk of to the
secretary, who blamed the warmth of that lord and some
others, and swore, that if their advice were followed, they
would be blown up in twenty-four hours. And I have reason
to think that they will endeavour to prevail on the queen to
put her affairs more into the hands of a ministry than she does
at present; and there are, I believe, two men thought on, one
of them you have often met the name of in my letters. But
so much for politicks.

19. This proved a terrible rainy day, which prevented my
walk into the city, and I was only able to run and dine with
my neighbour Vanhomrigh, where Sir Andrew Fountain dined
too, who has just began to sally out, and has shipt his mother
and sister, who were his nurses, back to the country. This
evening was fair, and I walkt a little in the Park, till Prior made
me go with him to the Smyrna Coffee-house, where I sat a
while, and saw four or five Irish persons, who are very handsome genteel fellows, but I know not their names. I came
away at seven, and got home. Two days ago I writ to Bernage,
and told him what I had done, and directed the letter to Mr.
Curry's to be left with Dingley. Brigadiers Hill and Masham,
brother and husband to Mrs. Masham, the queen's favourite,
colonel Disney[1] and I have recommended Bernage to the
duke of Argyle; and secretary St. John has given the duke
my memorial; and besides, Hill tells me, that Bernage's colonel,
Fielding,[2] designs to make him his captain lieutenant: but

[1] There was a Henry Disney among the captains of the 1st Foot Guards
in 1709. See Dalton's *Army Lists*. Lieut.-General Withers (*see post*,
Letter XXXIX., Jan. 25, 1711-12) was lieut.-colonel of that regiment.
One of Cartwright's notes to the *Wentworth Papers* says that "Duke"
Disney (as Swift's friend was called) was a Huguenot refugee and a
friend of General Withers (as to which, *see post*, Letter LXII., April 2,
1713), and that he died in 1731. Mr. Aitken says his real name was
Desaulnais.

[2] Mr. Aitken suggests it may have been Edmund, the father of Henry
Fielding the novelist; and this seems probable—*see* Letter XXXI.,
Sept. 26, note as to Dr. Arbuthnot's brother.

I believe I said this to you before, and in this letter, but I will not look.

20. Morning. It snows terribly again, and 'tis mistaken, for I now want a little good weather; I bid you good morrow, and if it clear up, get you gone to poor Mrs. Walls, who has had a hard time of it, but it is now pretty well again; I am sorry it is a girl; the poor archdeacon too, see how simply he lookt when they told him: what did it cost Stella to be gossip? I'll rise, so d'ye hear, let me see you at night, and don't stay late out, and catch cold, sirrahs.—At night. It grew good weather, and I got a good walk, and dined with Ford upon his Opera-day: but now all his wine is gone, I shall dine with him no more. I hope to send this letter before I hear from MD, me-thinks there's—something great in doing so, only I can't express where it lies; and faith this shall go by Saturday, as sure as you're a rogue. Mrs. Edgworth was to set out but last Monday, so you won't have your box so soon perhaps as this letter; but Sterne told me since, that it is safe at Chester, and that she will take care of it. I'd give a guinea you had it.

21. Morning. Faith, I hope it will be fair for me to walk into the city, for I take all occasions of walking.—I should be plaguy busy at Laracor if I were there now, cutting down willows, planting others, scouring my canal, and every kind of thing. If Raymond goes over this summer, you must submit, and make them a visit, that we may have another eel and trout fishing; and that Stella may ride by and see Presto in his morning-gown in the garden, and so go up with Joe to the Hill of Bree, and round by Scurlock's Town; O Lord, how I remember names; faith it gives me short sighs: therefore no more of that if you love me. Good morrow, I'll go rise like a gentleman, my pills say I must.—At night. Lady Kerry sent to desire me to engage some lords about an affair she has in their house here: I called to see her, but found she had already engaged every lord I knew, and that there was no great diffi-culty in the matter, and it rained like a dog; so I took coach, for want of better exercise, and dined privately with a hang-dog in the city, and walkt back in the evening. The days are now long enough to walk in the Park after dinner; and so I do whenever it is fair. This walking is a strange remedy; Mr. Prior walks to make himself fat, and I to bring myself down; he has generally a cough, which he only calls a cold: we often [walk] round the Park together. So I'll go sleep.

22. It snowed all this morning prodigiously, and was some

inches thick in three or four hours. I dined with Mr. Lewis of
the secretary's office at his lodgings : the chairmen that carried
me squeezed a great fellow against a wall, who wisely turned
his back, and broke one of the side glasses in a thousand pieces.
I fell a scolding, pretended I was like to be cut to pieces, and
made them set down the chair in the Park, while they pickt
out the bits of glasses: and when I paid them, I quarrelled still,
so they dared not grumble, and I came off for my fare: but I
was plaguily afraid they would have said, God bless your honour,
won't you give us something for our glass? Lewis and I were
forming a project how I might get three or four hundred pounds,
which I suppose may come to nothing. I hope Smyth has
brought you your palsy drops; how does Stella do? I begin more
and more to desire to know. The three weeks since I had your
last is over within two days, and I'll allow three for accidents.

23. The snow is gone every bit, except the remainder of some
great balls made by the boys. Mr. Sterne was with me this
morning about an affair he has before the treasury. That drab
Mrs. Edgworth is not yet set out, but will infallibly next Monday, and this is the third infallible Monday, and pox take her!
So you will have this letter first; and this shall go to-morrow;
and if I have one from MD in that time, I will not answer it
till my next; only I will say, Madam, I received your letter,
and so, and so. I dined to-day with my Mrs. Butler, who
grows very disagreeable.

24. Morning. This letter certainly goes this evening, sure as
you're alive, young women, and then you'll be so shamed
that I have had none from you; and if I was to reckon like you,
I would say, I were six letters before you, for this is N. 16,
and I have had your N. 10. But I reckon you have received
but fourteen and have sent eleven. I think to go to-day a
minister-of-state-hunting in the court of requests; for I have
something to say to Mr. Harley. And 'tis fine cold sunshiny
weather; I wish dear MD would walk this morning in your
Stephen's-Green: 'tis as good as our Park, but not so large.[1]
Faith this summer we'll take a coach for six-pence [2] to the
Green Well, the two walks, and thence all the way to Stoite's.[3]
My hearty service to goody Stoite and Catherine, and I hope
Mrs. Walls had a good time. How inconstant I am? I can't

[1] It was a measured mile round the outer wall; and far beyond any
the finest square in London.—D. S.
[2] The common fare for a set-down in Dublin.—D. S.
[3] Mrs. Stoyte lived at Donnybrook, the road to which from Stephen's
Green ran into the country about a mile from the south-east corner.—D. S.

imagine I was ever in love with her. Well, I'm going; what
have you to say? *I don't care how I write now.*[1] I don't design to write on this side, these few lines are but so much
more than your due, so I'll write *large* or small as I please.
Oh, faith, my hands are starving in bed; I believe it is a hard
frost. I must rise, and bid you good bye, for I'll seal this letter
immediately, and carry it in my pocket, and put it into the
post-office with my own fair hands. Farewel.

This letter is just a fortnight's journal to-day. Yes, and so
it is, I'm sure, says you, with your two eggs a penny.

There, there, there.[2]

O Lord, I am saying There, There, to myself in all our little
keys: and now you talk of keys, that dog Patrick broke the key
general of the chest of drawers with six locks, and I have been
so plagued to get a new one, beside my good two shillings.

LETTER XVII

London, *Feb.* 24, 1710-11.

Now, young women, I gave in my sixteenth this evening.
I dined with Ford, it was his Opera-day as usual; it is very
convenient to me to do so, for coming home early after a walk
in the Park, which now the days will allow. I called on the
secretary at his office, and he had forgot to give the memorial
about Bernage to the duke of Argyle; but two days ago I met
the duke, who desired I would give it him myself, which should
have more power with him than all the ministry together, as
he protested solemnly, repeated it two or three times, and bid
me count upon it. So that I verily believe Bernage will be in
a very good way to establish himself. I think I can do no
more for him at present, and there's an end of that; and so
get you gone to bed, for it is late.

25. The three weeks are out yesterday since I had your last,
and so now I will be expecting every day a pretty dear letter
from my own MD, and hope to hear that Stella has been much
better in her head and eyes; my head continues as it was, no
fits, but a little disorder every day, which I can easily bear, if
it will not grow worse. I dined to-day with Mr. secretary St.
John, on condition I might chuse my company, which were

[1] Those words in italicks are written in a very large hand, and so is
the word in one of the next lines.—D. S.
[2] In his cipher way of writing to Stella, he writes the word *There,
Lele.*—D. S.

lord Rivers, lord Carteret, Sir Thomas Mansel,[1] and Mr. Lewis;
I invited Masham, Hill, Sir John Stanley, and George Granville,
but they were engaged; and I did it in revenge of his having
such bad company when I dined with him before; so we laughed,
&c. And I ventured to go to church to-day, which I have not
done this month before. Can you send me such a good account
of Stella's health, pray now? Yes, I hope, and better too. We
dined (says you) at the dean's, and played at cards till twelve,
and there came in Mr. French, and Dr. Travors, and Dr. Whit-
tingham,[2] and Mr. (I forget his name, that I always tell Mrs.
Walls of) the banker's son, a pox on him. And we were so
merry; I vow they are pure good company. But I lost a crown;
for you must know I had always hands tempting me to go out,
but never took in any thing, and often two black aces without a
manilio; was not that hard, Presto? Hold your tongue, &c.

26. I was this morning with Mr. secretary about some business, and he tells me, that colonel Fielding is now going to make
Bernage his captain-lieutenant, that is, a captain by commission, and the perquisites of the company, but not captain's
pay, only the first step to it. I suppose he will like it, and the
recommendation to the duke of Argyle goes on. And so trouble
me no more about your Bernage; the jackanapes understands
what fair solicitors he has got, I warrant you. Sir Andrew
Fountain and I dined, by invitation, with Mrs. Vanhomrigh.
You say they are of no consequence: why, they keep as good
female company as I do male; I see all the drabs of quality
at this end of the town with them; I saw two lady Bettys there
this afternoon, the beauty of one, the good breeding and nature
of t'other, and the wit of neither,[3] would have made a fine
woman. Rare walking in the Park now: why don't you walk in
the Green of St. Stephen? The walks there are finer gravelled
than the Mall. What beasts the Irish women are, never to walk?

27. Darteneuf and I and little Harrison, the new *Tatler*, and
Jervas the painter, dined to-day with James, I know not his
other name,[4] but it is one of Darteneuf's dining places, who is
a true epicure. James is clerk of the kitchen to the queen, and
has a little snug house at St. James's, and we had the queen's

[1] (c. 1668–1723). Afterwards Baron Mansell of Margam; Commissioner
of the Treasury, 1710.

[2] Three unidentified persons. The banker's son was perhaps Rathburn,
mentioned p. 53.

[3] *i.e.* without the wit of either.—D. S. The ladies Betty Butler and
Betty Germain.

[4] According to Chamberlayne's *Magnæ Britannia Notitia*, 1710, p. 536,
James Eckershall was "second clerk of the Queen's Privy Kitchen."

wine, and such very fine victuals, that I could not eat it.—
Three weeks and three days since my last letter from MD,
rare doings: why truly we were so busy with poor Mrs. Walls,
that indeed, Presto, we could not write, we were afraid the
poor woman would have died; and it pitied us to see the archdeacon, how concerned he was. The dean never came to see her
but once; but now she is up again, and we go and sit with her
in the evenings. The child died the next day after it was born,
and I believe, between friends, she is not very sorry for it.——
Indeed, Presto, you are plaguy silly to-night, and han't guest
one word right; for she and the child are both well, and it is
a fine girl, likely to live; and the dean was godfather, and Mrs.
Catherine and I were godmothers; I was going to say Stoite,
but I think I have heard they don't put maids and married
women together; though I know not why I think so, nor I don't
care; what care I? but I must prate, &c.

28. I walked to-day into the city for my health, and there
dined, which I always do when the weather is fair, and business
permits, that I may be under a necessity of taking a good
walk, which is the best thing I can do at present for my health.
Some bookseller has raked up every thing I writ, and published
it t'other day in one volume; but I know nothing of it, 'twas
without my knowledge or consent: it makes a four shilling book,
and is called *Miscellanies in Prose and Verse.*[1] Tooke pretends
he knows nothing of it, but I doubt he is at the bottom. One
must have patience with these things; the best of it is, I shall
be plagued no more. However, I'll bring a couple of them over
with me for MD, perhaps you may desire to see them. I hear
they sell mightily.

March 1. Morning. I have been calling to Patrick to look
in his Almanack for the day of the month; I did not know but
it might be Leap-year. The Almanack says 'tis the third after
Leap-year, and I always thought till now, that every third
year was Leap-year. I'm glad they come so seldom; but I'm
sure 'twas otherwise when I was a young man; I see times are
mightily changed since then.—Write to me, sirrahs, be sure do
by the time this side is done, and I'll keep t'other side for the
answer: so I'll go write to the bishop of Clogher; good morrow,
sirrahs.—Night. I dined to-day at Mrs. Vanhomrigh's, being a
rainy day, and lady Betty Butler knowing it, sent to let me
know she expected my company in the evening, where the

[1] "London, printed for John Morphew, near Stationers' Hall, 1711."
Octavo.

Vans (so we call them) were to be. The duchess and they do not go over this summer with the duke; so I go to bed.

2. This rainy weather undoes me in coaches and chairs. I was traipsing to-day with your Mr. Sterne, to go along with them to Moor,[1] and recommend his business to the treasury. Sterne tells me his dependence is wholly on me; but I have absolutely refused to recommend it to Mr. Harley, because I troubled him lately so much with other folks affairs; and besides, to tell the truth, Mr. Harley told me he did not like Sterne's business; however, I will serve him, because I suppose MD would have me. But in saying his dependence lies wholly on me, he lies, and is a fool. I dined with lord Abercorn, whose son Peasley [2] will be married at Easter to ten thousand pounds.

3. I forgot to tell you that yesterday morning I was at Mr. Harley's levee: he swore I came in spight, to see him among a parcel of fools. My business was to desire I might let the duke of Ormond know how the affair stood of the First-Fruits. He promised to let him know it, and engaged me to dine with him to-day. Every Saturday lord keeper, secretary St. John, and I dine with him, and sometimes lord Rivers, and they let in none else. Patrick brought me some letters into the Park; among which was one from Walls, and t'other, yes faith, t'other was from our little MD, N. 11. I read the rest in the Park, and MD's in a chair as I went from St. James's to Mr. Harley, and glad enough I was faith to read it, and see all right: Oh, but I won't answer it these three or four days, at least, or may be sooner. An't I silly? Faith your letters would make a dog silly, if I had a dog to be silly, but it must be a little dog.—I staid with Mr. Harley till past nine, where we had much discourse together after the rest were gone; and I gave him very truly my opinion where he desired it. He complained he was not very well, and has engaged me to dine with him again on Monday. So I came home afoot, like a fine gentleman, to tell you all this.

4. I dined to-day with Mr. secretary St. John; and after dinner he had a note from Mr. Harley, that he was much out of order; pray God preserve his health, every thing depends upon it.[3] The Parliament at present cannot go a step without him, nor the queen neither. I long to be in Ireland; but the ministry

---

[1] Arthur Moore, "brother to the Earl of Drogheda, and named one of the lords commissioners of trade in Sept., 1710" (D. L. P.)

[2] James, Lord Paisley (1685-6-1743-4), afterwards seventh Earl of Abercorn. His "ten thousand pounds" was Anne, daughter of Col. Plumer of Blakesware, Herts.

[3] He drank heavily.

beg me to stay: however, when this parliament lurry is over, I will endeavour to steal away; by which time I hope the First-Fruit business will be done. This kingdom is certainly ruined as much as was ever any bankrupt merchant. We must have Peace, let it be a bad or a good one, though no-body dares talk of it. The nearer I look upon things, the worse I like them. I believe the confederacy will soon break to pieces; and our factions at home increase. The ministry is upon a very narrow bottom, and stand like an Isthmus between the Whigs on one side, and violent Tories [1] on the other. They are able seamen, but the tempest is too great, the ship too rotten, and the crew all against them. Lord Somers had been twice in the queen's closet, once very lately; and your duchess of Somerset,[2] who now has the key, is a most insinuating woman, and I believe they will endeavour to play the same game that has been played against them.—I have told them of all this, which they know already, but they cannot help it. They have cautioned the queen so much against being governed, that she observes it too much. I could talk till to-morrow upon these things, but they make me melancholy. I could not but observe that lately, after much conversation with Mr. Harley, though he is the most fearless man alive, and the least apt to despond, he confessed to me, that uttering his mind to me gave him ease.

5. Mr. Harley continues out of order, yet his affairs force him abroad: he is subject to a sore throat, and was cupped last night: I sent and called two or three times. I hear he is better this evening. I dined to-day in the city with Dr. Freind at a third body's house, where I was to pass for some body else, and there was a plaguy silly jest carried on, that made me sick of it. Our weather grows fine, and I will walk like camomile.[3] And pray walk you to your dean's, or your Stoyte's, or your Manley's, or your Walls'. But your new lodgings make you so proud, you'll walk less than ever. Come, let me go to bed, sirrahs.

6. Mr. Harley's going out yesterday has put him a little backwards. I called twice, and sent, for I am in pain for him.

[1] The October Club.—D. S.

[2] Elizabeth, née Percy, daughter of last Earl of Northumberland. Swift elsewhere calls her "carrots from Northumberland." (She had red hair.) Born 1667. Married: first (1679), to Earl of Ogle (a boy of fifteen); second (1681), to Thomas Thynne, who was murdered in Pall Mall 1681-2; third, to Charles Seymour (1662–1748), sixth Duke of Somerset. A partisan of the Whigs; she became mistress of the robes to Queen Anne and retained that position till the Queen's death.

[3] A preparation of camomile was in favour for application to the feet.

Ford caught me, and made me dine with him on his Opera-day; so I brought Mr. Lewis with me, and sat with him till six. I have not seen Mr. Addison these three weeks; all our friendship is over. I go to no Coffee-house. I presented a parson of the bishop of Clogher's, one Richardson,[1] to the duke of Ormond to-day: he is translating prayers and sermons into Irish, and has a project about instructing the Irish in the protestant religion.

7. Morning. Faith, a little would make me, I could find in my heart, if it were not for one thing, I have a good mind, if I had not something else to do, I would answer your dear saucy letter. O Lord, I am going awry with writing in bed. O faith, but I must answer it, or I shan't have room, for it must go on Saturday; and don't think I'll fill the third side, I an't come to that yet, young women. Well then, as for your Bernage, I have said enough: I writ to him last week.—Turn over that leaf. Now, what says MD to the world to come? I tell you, madam Stella, my head is a great deal better, and I hope will keep so. How came yours to be fifteen days coming, and you had my fifteenth in seven? Answer me that, rogues. Your being with goody Walls is excuse enough: I find I was mistaken in the sex, 'tis a boy. Yes, I understand your cypher, and Stella guesses right, as she always does. He [2] gave me al bsadnuk lboinlpl dfaonr ufainfbtoy dpionufnad,[3] which I sent him again by Mr. Lewis, to whom I writ a very complaining letter that was shewed him; and so the matter ended. He told me he had a quarrel with me; I said I had another with him, and we returned to our friendship, and I should think he loves me as well as a great minister can love a man in so short a time. Did not I do right? I am glad at heart you have got your palsey-water; pray God Almighty it may do my dearest little Stella good. I suppose Mrs. Edgworth set out last Monday se'nnight. Yes, I do read the *Examiners*, and they are written very finely, as you judge.[4] I do not think they are too severe on the duke; they only tax him of avarice, and his avarice has ruined us. You may count upon all things in them to be true. The author has said, It is not Prior; but perhaps it may be Atterbury.—

[1] John Richardson, D.D., rector of Annult, *alias* Belturbet, and after-wards chaplain to the Duke of Ormond.
[2] Mr. Harley.—N.
[3] A bank-bill for fifty pounds. See before, *Journal* of Feb. 6 and 7, 1710-11.—N.
[4] Even to his beloved Stella he had not acknowledged himself, at this time, to be the author of the *Examiner*.—D. S.

Now, madam Dingley, says she, 'tis fine weather, says she: yes, says she, and we have got to our new lodgings. I compute you ought to save eight pounds by being in the others five months; and you have no more done it than eight thousand. I am glad you are rid of that squinting, blinking Frenchman. I will give you a bill on Parvisol for five pound for the half year. And must I go on at four shillings a week, and neither eat nor drink for it? Who the D—— said Atterbury and your dean were alike? I never saw your chancellor, nor his chaplain.[1] The latter has a good deal of learning, and is a well-wisher to be an author: your chancellor is an excellent man. As for Patrick's bird, he bought him for his tameness, and is grown the wildest I ever saw. His wings have been quilled thrice, and are now up again: he will be able to fly after us to Ireland, if he be willing.—Yes, Mrs. Stella, Dingley writes more like Presto than you; for all you superscribed the letter, as who should say, Why should not I write like our Presto as well as Dingley? You with your aukward SS[s]; cannot you write them thus, SS? No, but always SSS.[2] Spiteful sluts, to affront Presto's writing; as that when you shut your eyes you write most like Presto. I know the time when I did not write to you half so plain as I do now; but I take pity on you both. I am very much concerned for Mrs. Walls's eyes. Walls says nothing of it to me in his letter dated after yours. You say, If she recovers she may lose her sight. I hope she is in no danger of her life. Yes, Ford is as sober as I please: I use him to walk with me as an easy companion, always ready for what I please, when I am weary of business and ministers. I don't go to a Coffee-house twice a month. I am very regular in going to sleep before eleven. —And so you say that Stella's a pretty girl; and so she be, and methinks I see her just now as handsome as the day's long. Do you know what? when I am writing in our language[3] I make up my mouth just as if I was speaking it. I caught myself at it just now. And I suppose Dingley is so fair and so fresh as a lass in May, and has her health, and no spleen.—In your account you sent do you reckon as usual from the 1st of November was twelvemonth? Poor Stella, won't Dingley leave her a little day-light to write to Presto? Well, well, we'll have

[1] Mr. Trapp.—N.

[2] Print cannot do justice to whims of this kind, as they depend wholly upon the aukward shape of the letters.—D. S.

[3] " This refers to that strange spelling, &c., which abounds in these journals; but which could be no entertainment to the reader."—D. S. thus judges.

day-light shortly, spight of her teeth; and zoo[1] must cly Lele and Hele, and Hele aden. Must loo mimitate pdfr, pay? Iss, and so la shall. And so leles fol ee rettle. Dood mollow.—At night. Mrs. Barton sent this morning to invite me to dinner; and there I dined, just in that genteel manner that MD used when they would treat some better sort of body than usual.

8. O dear MD, my heart is almost broken. You will hear the thing before this comes to you. I writ a full account of it this night to the archbishop of Dublin; and the dean may tell you the particulars from the archbishop. I was in a sorry way to write, but thought it might be proper to send a true account of the fact; for you will hear a thousand lying circumstances. 'Tis of Mr. Harley's being stabbed this afternoon at three o'clock at a committee of the council. I was playing lady Catherine Morris's[2] cards, where I dined, when young Arundel came in with the story. I ran away immediately to the secretary, which was in my way: no one was at home. I met Mrs. St. John in her chair; she had heard it imperfectly. I took a chair to Mr. Harley, who was asleep, and they hope in no danger; but he has been out of order, and was so when he came abroad to-day, and it may put him in a fever: I am in mortal pain for him. That desperate French villain, Marquis de Guiscard,[3] stabbed Mr. Harley. Guiscard was taken up by Mr. secretary St. John's warrant for high treason, and brought before the lords to be examined; there he stabbed Mr. Harley. I have told all the particulars already to the archbishop. I have now at nine sent again, and they tell me he is in a fair way. Pray pardon my distraction; I now think of all his kindness to me.—The poor creature now lies stabbed in his bed by a desperate French popish villain. Good night, and God preserve you both, and pity me; I want it.

9. Morning; seven, in bed. Patrick is just come from Mr. Harley's. He slept well till four; the surgeon sat up with him:

[1] "This is one specimen of his way of writing to Stella in these journals. The meaning of this pretty language is; 'and you must cry There, and Here, and Here again. Must you imitate Presto, pray? Yes, and so you shall. And so there's for your letter. Good morrow.'"—D. S.

[2] Identified by Mr. Aitken as the wife of Sir Nicholas Morice, bart.: Catherine (eldest daughter of eighth Earl of Pembroke), who died in 1716, and was buried at Werrington, Devon.

[3] Antoine de Guiscard, abbé de la Bourlie (1658–1711), driven from France for some crime, took refuge in Holland, and roused the Protestants of the Cevennes against Louis XIV. These having been pacified, Guiscard came to England and published memoirs of his struggles for liberty. He obtained a pension from Queen Anne; but, on his being suspected of intrigue with the French Court, his papers were seized and he was brought before the council. It is believed that his motive in stabbing Harley was to avoid the disgrace of death by hanging.

he is asleep again: he felt a pain in his wound when he waked: they apprehend him in no danger. This account the surgeon left with the porter, to tell people that send. Pray God preserve him. I am rising and going to Mr. secretary St. John. They say Guiscard will die with the wounds Mr. St. John and the rest gave him. I shall tell you more at night.—Night. Mr. Harley still continues on the mending hand; but he rested ill last night, and felt pain. I was early with the secretary this morning, and I dined with him, and he told me several particularities of this accident, too long to relate now. Mr. Harley is still mending this evening, but not at all out of danger; and till then I can have no peace. Good night, &c. and pity Presto.

10. Mr. Harley was restless last night; but he has no fever, and the hopes of mending increase. I had a letter from Mr. Walls, and one from Mr. Bernage. I will answer them here, not having time to write. Mr. Walls writes about three things. First, about a hundred pounds from Dr. Raymond, of which I hear nothing, and 'tis now too late. Secondly, about Mr. Clements: I can do nothing in it, because I am not to mention Mr. Pratt; and I cannot recommend without knowing Mr. Pratt's objections, whose relation Clements is, and who brought him into the place. The third is about my being godfather to the child: that is in my power, and (since there is no remedy) will submit. I wish you could hinder it; but if it can't be helped, pay what you think proper, and get the provost to stand for me, and let his christian name be Harley, in honour to my friend, now lying stabbed and doubtful of his life. As for Bernage, he writes me word, that his colonel has offered to make him captain-lieutenant for a hundred pounds. He was such a fool to offer him money without writing to me till it was done, though I have had a dozen letters from him; and then he desires I would say nothing of this, for fear his colonel should be angry. People are mad. What can I do? I engaged colonel Disney, who was one of his solicitors to the secretary, and then told him the story. He assured me, that Fielding (Bernage's colonel) said he might have got that sum; but on account of those great recommendations he had, would give it him for nothing: and I would have Bernage write him a letter of thanks, as of a thing given him for nothing, upon recommendations, &c. Disney tells me he will again speak to Fielding, and clear up this matter; and then I will write to Bernage. A pox on him for promising money till I had it promised to me, and then making it such a ticklish point, that one cannot expostulate

with the colonel upon it: but let him do as I say, and there's
an end. I engaged the secretary of state in it; and am sure it
was meant a kindness to me, and that no money should be
given, and a hundred pounds is too much in a Smithfield
bargain,[1] as a major general told me, whose opinion I asked.
I am now hurried, and can say no more. Farewel, &c. &c.

How shall I superscribe to your new lodgings, pray madams?
Tell me but that, impudence and saucy-face.

An't you sauceboxes to write *lele* [*i.e. there*][2] like Presto?

O poor Presto;

Mr. Harley is better to night, that makes me so pert, you
saucy Gog and Magog.

LETTER XVIII

London, *March* 10, 1710-11.

PRETTY little MD must expect little from me till Mr. Harley
is out of danger. We hope he is so now; but I am subject to
fear for my friends. He has a head full of the whole business of the
nation, was out of order when the villain stabbed him, and had a
cruel contusion by the second blow. But all goes on well yet.
Mr. Ford and I dined with Mr. Lewis, and we hope the best.

11. This morning Mr. Secretary and I met at Court, where
he went to the queen, who is out of order and aguish: I doubt
the worse for this accident to Mr. Harley. We went together to
his house, and his wound looks well, and he is not feverish at
all, and I think it is foolish in me to be so much in pain as I am.
I had the penknife in my hand, which is broken within a quarter
of an inch of the handle. I have a mind to write and publish an
account of all the particularities[3] of this fact: it will be very
curious, and I would do it when Mr. Harley is past danger.

12. We have been in terrible pain to-day about Mr. Harley,
who never slept last night, and has been very feverish. But this
evening I called there, and young Mr. Harley (his only son)
tells me he is now much better, and was then asleep. They let
nobody see him, and that is perfectly right. The parliament
cannot go on till he is well, and are forced to adjourn their
money businesses, which none but he can help them in. Pray
God preserve him.

13. Mr. Harley is better to-day, slept well all night, and

---

[1] Alluding to the sharp practices in Smithfield horse-and-cattle market.
[2] D. S's brackets.
[3] Such an account, very minute, was drawn up by Mrs. Manley under
Swift's direction, and is included among his works.—D. L. P.

we are a little out of our fears. I send and call three or four
times every day. I went into the city for a walk, and dined there
with a private man; and coming home this evening broke my
shin in the Strand over a tub of sand left just in the way. I got
home dirty enough, and went straight to bed, where I have
been cooking it with gold-beaters skin, and have been peevish
enough with Patrick, who was near an hour bringing a rag
from next door. It is my right shin, where never any humour
fell when t'other used to swell; so I apprehend it less: however
I shall not stir till 'tis well, which I reckon will be in a week.
I am very careful in these sort of things; but I wish I had Mrs.
J[ohnson]'s [1] water: she is out of town, and I must make a shift
with allum. I will dine with Mrs. Vanhomrigh till I am well,
who lives but five doors off; and that I may venture.

14. My journals are like to be very diverting, now I cannot
stir abroad, between accounts of Mr. Harley's mending, and of
my broken shin. I just walkt to my neighbour Vanhomrigh at
two, and came away at six, when little Harrison the Tatler
came to me, and begged me to dictate a paper to him, which
I was forced in charity to do. Mr. Harley still mends; and I
hope in a day or two to trouble you no more with him, nor
with my shin. Go to bed and sleep, sirrahs, that you may rise
to-morrow and walk to Donnybrook, and lose your money with
Stoite and the dean; so so, dear little rogues, and drink Presto's
health. O, pray, don't you drink Presto's health sometimes with
your deans, and your Stoites, and your Walls, and your Manleys,
and your every body's, pray now? I drink MD's to myself a
hundred thousand times.

15. I was this morning at Mr. secretary St. John's for all my
shin, and he has given me for young Harrison, the Tatler, the
prettiest employment in Europe; secretary to my lord Raby,[2]
who is to be ambassador extraordinary at the Hague, where
all the great affairs will be concerted; so we shall lose the
Tatlers in a fortnight. I will send Harrison to-morrow morning
to thank the secretary. Poor Biddy Floyd [3] has got the small-
pox. I called this morning to see lady Betty Germain; and when

[1] The interpretation within square brackets is Nichols's. Perhaps the
same as the palsy-water, in the box that got lost at Chester.
[2] Thomas Wentworth (1672–1739), Baron Raby and afterwards third
Earl of Strafford, envoy to the first King of Prussia. His want of sense
led to an abortive impeachment (1715).
[3] According to Forster, a friend of Lady Betty Germain's. "Mrs. Floyd
looked out with both her eyes, and we had one day's thaw; but she drew
in her head, and it now freezes as hard as ever."—Swift to Colonel Hunter,
Jan. 12, 1708-9.

she told me so, I fairly took my leave. I have the luck of it [1];
for about ten days ago I was to see lord Carteret; and my lady
was entertaining me with telling of a young lady, a cousin, who
was then ill in the house of the small-pox, and is since dead:
it was near lady Betty's, and I fancy Biddy took the fright by
it. I dined with Mr. secretary, and a physician came in just
from Guiscard, who tells us he is dying of his wounds, and can
hardly live till to-morrow. A poor wench that Guiscard kept,
sent him a bottle of sack; but the keeper would not let him
touch it, for fear it was poison. He had two quarts of old clotted
blood come out of his side to-day, and is delirious. I am sorry
he is dying; for they have found out a way to hang him. He
certainly had an intention to murder the queen. [2]

16. I have made but little progress in this letter for so many
days, thanks to Guiscard and Mr. Harley; and it would be
endless to tell you all the particulars of that odious fact. I do
not yet hear that Guiscard is dead, but they say 'tis impossible
he should recover. I walkt too much yesterday for a man with
a broken shin; to-day I rested, and went no further than Mrs.
Vanhomrigh's, where I dined; and lady Betty Butler coming
in about six, I was forced in good manners to sit with her till
nine; then I came home, and Mr. Ford came in to visit my shin,
and sat with me till eleven: so I have been very idle and
naughty. It vexes me to the pluck [3] that I should lose walking
this delicious day. Have you seen the *Spectator* yet, a paper
that comes out every day? 'Tis written by Mr. Steele, who
seems to have gathered new life, and have a new fund of wit;
it is in the same nature as his *Tatlers*, and they have all of
them had something pretty. I believe Addison and he club.
I never see them; and I plainly told Mr. Harley and Mr. St.
John, ten days ago, before my lord keeper and lord Rivers,
that I had been foolish enough to spend my credit with them
in favour of Addison and Steele; but that I would engage and
promise never to say one word in their behalf, having been used
so ill for what I had already done.—So, now I have got into the
way of prating again, there will be no quiet for me. When
Presto begins to prate, Give him a rap upon the pate.—O Lord,
how I blot; 'tis time to leave off, &c.

[1] Swift never had the small-pox.—D. S.
[2] Guiscard concealed from the surgeons, till it had festered, one of his
most grievous wounds. He had been observed to lurk much about the
palace before his arrest; and this, and some hints in his letters of a "great
blow," led to the inference of his design on the Queen's life.—D. L. P.
[3] To the "inwards" or heart's core.

17. Guiscard died this morning at two, and the coroner's inquest have found that he was killed by bruises received from a messenger, so to clear the cabinet counsellors from whom he received his wounds. I had a letter from Raymond, who cannot hear of your box; but I hope you have it before this comes to your hands. I dined to-day with Mr. Lewis of the secretary's office. Mr. Harley has abundance of extravasated blood comes from his breast out of his wound, and will not be well so soon as we expected. I had something to say, but cannot call it to mind. (What was it?)

18. I was to-day at Court to look for the duke of Argyle, and give him the memorial about Bernage. The duke goes with the first fair wind: I could not find him, but I have given the memorial to another to give him; and, however, it shall be sent after him. Bernage has made a blunder in offering money to his colonel without my advice; however he is made captain-lieutenant, only he must recruit the company, which will cost him forty pounds, and that is cheaper than a hundred. I dined to-day with Mr. secretary St. John, and staid till seven, but would not drink his Champaign and Burgundy, for fear of the gout. My shin mends, but is not well. I hope it will by the time I send this letter, next Saturday.

19. I went to-day into the city, but in a coach, and sossed [1] up my leg on the seat; and as I came home I went to see poor Charles Barnard's [2] books, which are to be sold by auction, and I itch to lay out nine or ten pounds for some fine editions of fine authors. But 'tis too far, and I shall let it slip, as I usually do all such opportunities. I dined in a Coffee-house with Stratford upon chops, and some of his wine. Where did MD dine? Why, poor MD dined at home to-day, because of the archbishop, and they could not go abroad, and had a breast of mutton and a pint of wine. I hope Mrs. Walls mends; and pray give me an account what sort of godfather I made, and whether I behaved myself handsomely. The duke of Argyle is gone; and whether he has my memorial, I know not, till I see Dr. Arbuthnott, [3]

[1] See "soss," verb, in Oxford Dictionary, where this passage is quoted. See also Letter XXIV., June 7, 1711.
[2] Sold by auction, on the 22nd of March, at the Black-boy coffee-house, in Ave Maria Lane.—N.
[3] It is reasonable to suppose that Swift's acquaintance with Arbuthnot commenced just about this time; for in the original letter Swift misspells his name, and writes Arthburthnet in a clear large hand, that MD might not mistake any of the letters.—D. S. John Arbuthnot (1667–1735), Scottish physician and wit, the reputed originator of "John Bull" as a name for the Englishman.

to whom I gave it. That hard name belongs to a Scotch doctor, an acquaintance of the duke's and me; Stella can't pronounce it. Oh, that we were at Laracor this fine day! the willows begin to peep, and the quicks to bud. My dream's out: I was a-dreamed last night that I eat ripe cherries.—And now they begin to catch the pikes, and will shortly the trouts (pox on these ministers), and I would fain know whether the floods were ever so high as to get over the holly bank or the river walk; if so, then all my pikes are gone; but I hope not. Why don't you ask Parvisol these things, sirrahs? And then my canal, and trouts, and whether the bottom be fine and clear? But hearkee, ought not Parvisol to pay in my last year's rents and arrears out of his hands? I am thinking, if either of you have heads to take his accounts, it should be paid in to you; otherwise to Mr. Walls. I will write an order on t'other side; and do as you will. Here's a world of business; but I must go sleep, I'm drowsy: and so good night, &c.

20. This sore shin ruins me in coach hire; no less than two shillings to-day going and coming from the city, where I dined with one you never heard of, and passed an insipid day. I writ this post to Bernage, with the account I told you above. I hope he will like it; 'tis his own fault, or it would have been better. I reckon your next letter will be full of Mr. Harley's stabbing. He still mends, but abundance of extravasated blood has come out of the wound: he keeps his bed, and sees nobody. The speaker's eldest son[1] is just dead of the small-pox, and the house is adjourned a week, to give him time to wipe off his tears. I think it very handsomely done; but I believe one reason is, that they want Mr. Harley so much. Biddy Floyd is like to do well: and so go to your dean's, and roast his oranges, and lose your money, do so, you saucy sluts. Stella, you lost three shillings and four pence t'other night at Stoite's, yes, you did, and Presto stood in a corner, and saw you all the while, and then stole away. I dream very often I am in Ireland, and that I have left my cloaths and things behind me, and have not taken leave of any body; and that the ministry expect me to-morrow, and such nonsense.

21. I would not for a guinea have a letter from you till this goes; and go it shall on Saturday, faith. I dined with Mrs. Vanhomrigh, to save my shin, and then went on some business to the secretary, and he was not at home.

[1] Clobery Bromley, Esq., son of the Hon. William Bromley, by a former wife (heiress of Clobery), and M.P. for Coventry.—N.

22. Yesterday was a short day's journal: but what care I? what cares saucy Presto? Darteneuf invited me to dinner to-day. Don't you know Darteneuf? That's the man that knows every thing, and that every body knows; and that knows where a knot of rabble are going on a holiday, and when they were there last: and then I went to the Coffee-house. My shin mends, but is not quite healed: I ought to keep it up, but I don't; I e'en let it go as it comes. Pox take Parvisol and his watch. If I do not receive the ten pound bill I am to get towards it, I will neither receive watch nor chain; so let Parvisol know.

23. I this day appointed the duke of Ormond to meet him at Ned Southwell's, about an affair of printing Irish Prayer-Books, &c. but the duke never came. There Southwell had letters that two pacquets are taken; so if MD writ then, the letters are gone; for they are pacquets coming here. Mr. Harley is not yet well, but his extravasated blood continues, and I doubt he will not be quite well in a good while: I find you have heard of the fact, by Southwell's letters from Ireland: What do you think of it? I dined with sir John Percival [*i.e.* Perceval],[1] and saw his lady sitting in the bed, in the forms of a lying-in woman; and coming home my sore shin itched, and I forgot what it was, and rubbed off the s[ca]b, and blood came; but I am now got into bed, and have put on allum curd, and it is almost well. Lord Rivers told me yesterday a piece of bad news, as a secret, that the Pretender is going to be married to the duke of Savoy's daughter.[2] 'Tis very bad, if it be true. We were walking in the Mall with some Scotch lords, and he could not tell it until they were gone, and he bade me tell it to none but the secretary of state and MD. This goes to-morrow, and I have no room but to bid my dearest little MD good night.

24. I will now seal up this letter, and send it; for I reckon to have none from you ('tis morning now) between this and night; and I will put it in the post with my own hands. I am going out in great haste; so farewel, &c.

---

[1] Sir John Percival (or Perceval) (1683–1748), fifth bart., married (1710) Catharine (*c.* 1680–1749), eldest daughter of Sir Philip Parker, second bart., of Erwarton, Suffolk. He was afterwards, successively, Baron Perceval of Burton, Viscount Perceval of Kanturk, and (1733) Earl of Egmont—all in the peerage of Ireland, he being a native of co. Cork.
[2] He did not marry her; he did not marry at all until 1718.

LETTER XIX

London, *March* 24, 1710-11.

IT was a little cross in Presto not to send to-day to the Coffee-house to see whether there was a letter from MD before I sent away mine; but faith I did it on purpose, because I would scorn to answer two letters of yours successively. This way of journal is the worst in the world for writing of news, unless one does it the last day; and so I will observe henceforward, if there be any politicks or stuff worth sending. My shin mends in spite of the scratching last night. I dined to-day at Ned Southwell's with the bishop of Ossory[1] and a parcel of Irish gentlemen. Have you yet seen any of the *Spectators*?[2] Just three weeks to-day since I had your last, N. 11. I am afraid I have lost one by the pacquet that was taken; that will vex me, considering the pains MD take to write, especially poor pretty Stella, and her weak eyes, God bless them and the owner, and send them well, and little me together, I hope ere long. This illness of Mr. Harley puts every thing backwards, and he is still down, and like to be so, by that extravasated blood which comes from his breast to the wound: it was by the second blow Guiscard gave him after the pen-knife was broken. I am shocked at that villainy whenever I think of it. Biddy Floyd is past danger, but will lose all her beauty: she had them mighty thick, especially about her nose.

25. Morning. I wish you a merry New-year; this is the first day of the year, you know, with us, and 'tis Lady-day. I must rise and go to my lord keeper: it is not shaving day to-day, so I shall be early. I am to dine with Mr. secretary St. John. Good morrow, my mistresses both, good morrow. Stella will be peeping out of her room at Mrs. de Caudres' down upon the folks as they come from church;[3] and there comes Mrs. Proby,[4] and that's my lady Southwell,[5] and there's lady Betty Rochfort.[6] I long to hear how you are settled in your new lodgings.

---

[1] John Hartstonge. *See* Letter VI., Oct. 18, 1710, note on Bishop of Killaloe.

[2] The first *Spectator* was published March 1, 1710-11.—N.

[3] MD's lodgings were exactly opposite to St. Mary's church.—D. S.

[4] Mr. Aitken says she was probably a Miss Spencer, and that her husband was Thomas Proby, chirurgeon-general in Ireland from 1699 till 1761, when he died. This Proby's son, a captain in the army, was accused of popery (1724) and defended by Swift.

[5] Meliora (Coningsby), Lady of Sir Thomas Southwell of Castle Mattress, co. Limerick, afterwards Baron Southwell.

[6] Daughter of Henry Moore, third Earl of Drogheda, wife of George Rochfort, M.P. for Westmeath and son of an Irish judge.

I wish I were rid of my old ones, and that Mrs. Brent could contrive to put up my books in boxes, and lodge them in some safe place, and you keep my papers of importance. But I must rise, I tell you.—At night. So I visited and dined as I told you, and what of that? We have let Guiscard be buried at last, after shewing him pickled in a trough this fortnight for two pence apiece; and the fellow that shewed would point to his body, and, See, gentlemen, this is the wound that was given him by his grace the duke of Ormond; and this is the wound, &c. and then the show was over, and another set of rabble came in.[1] 'Tis hard that our laws would not suffer us to hang his body in chains, because he was not tried; and in the eye of our law every man is innocent till then.—Mr. Harley is still very weak, and never out of bed.

26. This was a most delicious day; and my shin being past danger, I walkt like lightning above two hours in the Park. We have generally one fair day, and then a great deal of rain for three or four days together. All things are at a stop in parliament for want of Mr. Harley; they cannot stir an inch without him in their most material affairs: and we fear by the caprice of Radcliffe, who will admit none but his own surgeon,[2] he has not been well lookt after. I dined at an alehouse with Mr. Lewis, but had his wine. Don't you begin to see the flowers and blossoms of the field? How busy should I be now at Laracor? No news of your box? I hope you have it, and are this minute drinking the chocolate, and that the smell of the Brazil tobacco has not affected it. I would be glad to know whether you like it, because I would send you more by people that are now every day thinking of going to Ireland; therefore pray tell me, and tell me soon: and I will have the strong box.

27. A rainy wretched scurvy day from morning till night: and my neighbour Vanhomrigh invited me to dine with them: and this evening I passed at Mr. Prior's with Dr. Freind; and 'tis now past twelve, so I must go sleep.

28. Morning. Oh faith, you're an impudent saucy couple of sluttekins for presuming to write so soon. Said I to myself this morning; who knows but there may be a letter from MD at the Coffee-house? Well, you must know, and so, I just now sent Patrick, and he brought me three letters, but not one from MD, no indeed, for I read all the superscriptions; and not

[1] Queen Anne no sooner heard of this indignity, than she gave orders that the assassin should be buried at once; which was done, in the common burying-place of the malefactors who die in Newgate.—D. L. P.

[2] A Mr. Green. See Letter XXVI., July 17, 1711.

one from MD. One I opened, it was from the archbishop;[1]
t'other I opened, it was from Staunton;[2] the third I took,
and lookt at the hand. Whose hand is this? says I; yes, says I,
whose hand is this? Then there was wax between the folds;
then I began to suspect; then I peeped: faith, it was Walls's
hand after all: then I opened it in a rage, and then it was little
MD's hand, dear, little, pretty, charming MD's sweet hand again.
O Lord, en't here a clutter and a stir, and a bustle, never saw
the like. Faith, I believe yours lay some days at the post-office,
and that it came before my eighteenth went, but that I did
not expect it, and I hardly ever go there. Well, and so you
think I'll answer this letter now? no faith, and so I won't. I'll
make you wait, young women; but I'll enquire immediately
about poor Dingley's exchequer trangum.[3] What, is that Vedel
again a soldier? Was he broke? I'll put it in Ben Tooke's hand.
I hope Vedel could not sell it.—At night. Vedel, Vedel, poh,
pox, I think it is Vedeau; aye, Vedeau,[4] now I have it; let
me see, do you name him in yours? Yes, Mr. John Vedeau is
the brother; but where does this brother live? I'll enquire.
This was a fast-day for the publick; so I dined late with Sir
Matthew Dudley, whom I have not been with a great while.
He is one of those that must lose his employment whenever
the great shake comes; and I can't contribute to keep him in,
though I have dropt words in his favour to the ministry; but
he has been too violent a Whig, and friend to the lord-treasurer,[5]
to stay in. 'Tis odd to think how long they let those people
keep their places; but the reason is, they have not enough to
satisfy all expecters, and so they keep them all in hopes, that
they may be good boys in the mean time; and thus the old
ones hold in still. The comptroller[6] told me, that there are
eight people expect his staff. I walkt after dinner to-day round
the Park. What, do I write politicks to little young women?
Hold your tongue, and go to your dean's.

29. Morning. If this be a fine day I will walk into the city,

---

[1] Of Dublin.

[2] *See* Letter XV., Feb. 10, 1710-11.

[3] *Trangum:* a thingumbob, a gadget. Deane Swift says he must mean
an exchequer tally: one of those curious survivals of savage accountancy,
made of wood (described and illustrated in the *Archæologia* of the Society
of Antiquaries of London, Vol. LXII., dated 1911), the cancellation of a
hoard of which, by means of burning, burned down the old Houses of
Parliament, 1834. Some specimens are on show at the Record Office,
Chancery Lane.

[4] *See* Letter XII., Dec. 24, 1710.

[5] The ex-Lord-Treasurer, Godolphin.

[6] Sir John Holland, soon after replaced by Sir Thomas Mansel.—D. L. P.

and see Charles Barnard's[1] library. What care I for your letter, saucy N. 12? I will say nothing to it yet: faith, I believe this will be full before its time, and then go it must. I will always write once a fortnight; and if it goes sooner by filling sooner, why then there is so much clear gain. Morrow, morrow, rogues and lasses both, I can't lie scribling here in bed for your play; I must rise, and so morrow again.—At night. Your friend Montgomery and his sister are here, as I am told by Patrick: I have seen him often, but take no notice of him: he is grown very ugly and pimpled. They tell me he is a gamester, and wins money.—How could I help it, pray? Patrick snufft the candle too short, and the grease ran down upon the paper.[2] It an't my fault, 'tis Patrick's fault: pray now don't blame Presto. I walkt to-day into the city, and dined at a private house, and went to see the auction of poor Charles Barnard's books; they were in the middle of the physick books, so I bought none; and they are so dear, I believe I shall buy none, and there's an end; and go to Stoite's, and I'll go sleep.

30. Morning. This is Good-Friday, you must know, and I must rise and go to Mr. secretary about some business, and Mrs. Vanhomrigh desires me to breakfast with her, because she is to intercede for Patrick, who is so often drunk and quarrelsome in the house, that I was resolved to send him over; but he knows all the places where I send, and is so used to my ways, that it would be inconvenient to me; but when I come to Ireland, I will discharge him.—[3] Sir Thomas Mansel, one of the lords of the treasury, setting me down at my door to-day, saw Patrick, and swore he was a Teaguelander.[4] I am so used to his face, I never observed it, but thought him a pretty fellow. Sir Andrew Fountain and I supped this fast-day with Mrs. Vanhomrigh. We were afraid Mr. Harley's wound would turn to a Fistula; but we think the danger is now past. He rises every day, and walks about his room, and we hope he will be out in a fortnight. Prior shewed me a handsome paper of verses he has writ on Mr. Harley's accident: they are not out; I will send them to you, if he will give me a copy.[5]

[1] See Letter XVIII., March 19.
[2] It caused a violent daub on the paper, which still continues much discoloured in the original.—D. S.
[3] He forgot here to say, "At night." See what goes before.—D. S.
[4] As, later, they bore the generic name Patrick, Irishmen were formerly known in England by various forms of another Irish name—Teague, Thigue, &c. In their native orthography it is *Tadg*, and Englishmen had better not try to pronounce it.
[5] *See* them in the *Narrative of Guiscard's Examination.*

31. Morning. What shall we do to make April fools this year, now it happens on Sunday? Patrick brings word that Mr. Harley still mends, and is up every day. I design to see him in a few days: and he brings me word too that he has found out Vedeau's brother's shop: I shall call there in a day or two. It seems the wife lodges next door to the brother. I doubt the scoundrel was broke, and got a commission, or perhaps is a voluntier gentleman, and expects to get one by his valour. Morrow, sirrahs, let me rise.—At night. I dined to-day with Sir Thomas Mansel. We were walking in the Park, and Mr. Lewis came to us. Mansel askt Where we dined? We said, Together. He said, we should dine with him, only his wife[1] desired him to bring nobody, because she had only a leg of mutton. I said, I would dine with him to chuse; but he would send a servant to order a plate or two: yet this man has ten thousand pounds a year in land, and is a lord of the treasury, and is not covetous neither, but runs out merely by slattering[2] and negligence. The worst dinner I ever saw at the dean's was better: but so it is with abundance of people here. I called at night at Mr. Harley's, who begins to walk in his room with a stick, but is mighty weak.—See how much I have lost with that ugly grease.[3] 'Tis your fault, pray; and I'll go to bed.

April 1. The duke of Buckingham's house fell down last night with an earth-quake, and is half swallowed up;—Won't you go and see it?—An April fool, an April fool, Oh ho, young women. Well, don't be angry, I'll make you an April fool no more till the next time: we had no sport here, because it is Sunday, and Easter-Sunday. I dined with the secretary, who seemed terribly down and melancholy, which Mr. Prior and Lewis observed as well as I: perhaps something is gone wrong; perhaps there is nothing in it. God bless my own dearest MD, and all is well.

2. We have such windy weather, 'tis troublesome walking, yet all the rabble have got into our Park these Easter holidays. I am plagued with one Richardson,[4] an Irish parson, and his projects of printing Irish Bibles, &c. to make you Christians in that country: I befriend him what I can on account of the arch-bishop and bishop of Clogher.—But what business have I to

[1] Sir Thomas married, while under age (1686), Martha, daughter of Francis Millington, a Commissioner of Customs under Charles II.
[2] Slovenliness.
[3] The candle grease mentioned before, which soaked through, and deformed this part of the paper on the second page.—D. S.
[4] See Letter XVII., March 6, 1710-11.

meddle, &c? Don't you remember that, sirrah Stella? what was that about, when you thought I was meddling with something that was not my business? Oh faith, you are an impudent slut, I remember your doings, I'll never forget you as long as I live. Lewis and I dined together at his lodgings. But where's the answer to this letter of MD's. O faith, Presto, you must think of that. Time enough, says saucy Presto.

3. I was this morning to see Mrs. Barton; I love her better than any body here, and see her seldomer. Why really now, so it often happens in the world, that where one loves a body best—pshah, pshah, you are so silly with your moral observations. Well, but she told me a very good story. An old gentlewoman died here two months ago, and left in her will, to have eight men and eight maids bearers, who should have two guineas apiece, ten guineas to the parson for a sermon, and two guineas to the clerk. But bearers, parson and clerk must be all true virgins; and not be admitted till they took their oaths of virginity: so the poor woman lies still unburied, and so must do till the general resurrection.—I called at Mr. secretary's, to see what the D— ailed him on Sunday; I made him a very proper speech, told him I observed he was much out of temper; that I did not expect he would tell me the cause, but would be glad to see he was in better; and one thing I warned him of, Never to appear cold to me, for I would not be treated like a school-boy; that I had felt too much of that in my life already (meaning from sir William Temple); that I expected every great minister, who honoured me with his acquaintance, if he heard or saw any thing to my disadvantage, would let me know in plain words, and not put me in pain to guess by the change or coldness of his countenance or behaviour; for it was what I would hardly bear from a crowned head, and I thought no subject's favour was worth it; and that I designed to let my lord keeper and Mr. Harley know the same thing, that they might use me accordingly. He took all right; said, I had reason, vowed nothing ailed him but sitting up whole nights at business, and one night at drinking; would have had me dined [? dine] with him and Mrs. Masham's brother, to make up matters; but I would not. I don't know, but I would not. But indeed I was engaged with my old friend Rollinson,[1] you never heard of him before.

[1] William Rollinson, Esq., formerly a wine merchant, settled afterward in Oxfordshire, where he died at a great age; a genteel agreeable man, an old acquaintance of Lord Bolingbroke, and a favourite of Mr. Pope's, who left him five pounds for a ring.—N.

4. I sometimes look a line or two back, and see plaguy mistakes of the pen; how do you get over them? you are puzzled sometimes. Why, I think what I said to Mr. secretary was right. Don't you remember how I used to be in pain when Sir William Temple would look cold and out of humour for three or four days, and I used to suspect a hundred reasons? I have pluckt up my spirit since then, faith; he spoiled a fine gentleman. I dined with my neighbour Vanhomrigh, and MD, poor MD, at home on a loin of mutton and half a pint of wine, and the mutton was raw, poor Stella could not eat, poor dear rogue, and Dingley was so vext: but we'll dine at Stoyte's to-morrow. Mr. Harley promised to see me in a day or two, so I called this evening; but his son and others were abroad, and he asleep, so I came away, and found out Mrs. Vedeau. She drew out a letter from Dingley, and said she would get a friend to receive the money. I told her I would employ Mr. Tooke in it henceforward. Her husband bought a lieutenancy of foot, and is gone to Portugal. He sold his share of the shop to his brother, and put out the money to maintain her, all but what bought the commission. She lodges within two doors of her brother. She told me, It made her very melancholy to change her manner of life thus, but trade was dead, &c. She says, she will write to you soon. I design to engage Ben Tooke, and then receive the parchment from her.—I gave Mr. Dopping a copy of Prior's verses on Mr. Harley, he sent them yesterday to Ireland, so go look for them, for I won't be at the trouble to transcribe them here. They will be printed in a day or two. Give my hearty service to Stoyte and Catherine; upon my word I love them dearly, and desire you will tell them so: pray desire goody Stoyte not to let Mrs. Walls and Mrs. Johnson cheat her of her money at ombre, but assure her from me, that she is a bungler. Dine with her to-day, and tell her so, and drink my health, and good voyage, and speedy return, and so you're a rogue.

5. Morning. Now let us proceed to examine a saucy letter from one madam MD.—God Almighty bless poor dear Stella, and send her a great many Birth-days, all happy and healthy, and wealthy, and with me ever together, and never asunder again, unless by chance. When I find you are happy or merry there, it makes me so here, and I can hardly imagine you absent when I am reading your letter, or writing to you. No, faith, you are just here upon this little paper, and therefore I see and talk with you every evening constantly, and sometimes in the morning, but not always in the morning, because that is not

so modest to young ladies.—What, you would fain palm a letter on me more than you sent; and I, like a fool, must look over all yours, to see whether this was really N. 12. or more. [Patrick has this moment brought me letters from the bishop of Clogher and Parvisol; my heart was at my mouth for fear of one from MD; what a disgrace would it be to have two of yours to answer together? But faith this shall go tonight, for fear, and then come when it will, I defy it.]¹ No, you are not naughty at all, write when you are disposed. And so the dean told you the story of Mr. Harley from the archbishop; I warrant it never spoiled your supper, or broke off your game. Nor yet, have not you the box; I wish Mrs. Edgworth had the ——. But you have it now, I suppose; and is the chocolate good, or has the tobacco spoiled it? Leigh stays till Sterne has done his business, no longer; and when that will be, God knows: I befriend him as much as I can, but Mr. Harley's accident stops that as well as all things else. You guess, Madam Dingley, that I shall stay a round twelvemonth; as hope saved, I would come over, if I could, this minute; but we will talk of that by and bye.—Your affair of Vedeau I have told you of already; now to the next, turn over the leaf. Mrs. Dobbins lies, I have no more provision here or in Ireland than I had. I am pleased that Stella the conjuror approved what I did with Mr. Harley ²; but your generosity makes me mad; I know you repine inwardly at Presto's absence; you think he has broken his word of coming in three months, and that this is always his trick; and now Stella says, she does not see possibly how I can come away in haste, and that MD is satisfied, &c. An't you a rogue to overpower me thus? I did not expect to find such friends as I have done. They may indeed deceive me too. But there are important reasons [Pox on this grease, this candle tallow!]³ why they should not.⁴ I have been used barbarously by the late ministry; I am a little piqued in honour to let people see I am not to be despised. The assurances they give me, without any scruple or provocation, are such as are usually believed in the world; they may come to nothing, but the first opportunity that offers, and is neglected, I shall depend no more, but come away. I could say a thousand things on this head, if I were with you. I am thinking why

---

¹ So bracketed in D. S.
² In relation to the bank bill. *See* Letter XVII., March 7.
³ So bracketed in D. S.
⁴ Swift was, at this time, their great support and champion.—N.

Stella should not go to the Bath, if she be told it will do her good; I will make Parvisol get up fifty pounds, and pay it you; and you may be good houswives and live cheap there some months, and return in Autumn, or visit London, as you please: pray think of it. I writ to Bernage, directed to Curry's; I wish he had the letter. I will send the bohea tea, if I can. The bishop of Kilmore,[1] I don't keep such company; an old dying fool whom I was never with in my life. So I am no godfather[2]; all the better. Pray, Stella, explain those two words of yours to me, what you mean by *Villian*, and *Dainger*,[3] and you, Madam Dingley, what is *Christianing*?—Lay your letter[s] *this way, this way*, and the devil a bit of difference between this way and t'other way. No; I'll shew you, lay them *this way, this way*, and not *that way, that way*.[4]——You shall have your aprons; and I'll put all your commissions as they come, in a paper together, and don't think I'll forget MD's orders, because they are friends; I'll be as careful, as if they were strangers. I know not what to do about this Clements.[5] Walls will not let me say any thing, as if Mr. Pratt was against him; and now the bishop of Clogher has written to me in his behalf. This thing does not rightly fall in my way, and that people never consider: I always give my good offices where they are proper, and that I am judge of; however, I will do what I can. But, if he has the name of a Whig, it will be hard, considering my lord Anglesea and Hyde[6] are very much otherwise, and you know they have the employment of deputy treasurer. If the frolick should take you of going to the Bath, I here send you a note on Parvisol; if not, you may tear it, and there's an end. Farewel.

If you have an imagination that the Bath will do you good, I say again, I would have you go; if not, or it be inconvenient, burn this note. Or, if you would go, and not take so much money, take thirty pounds, and I will return you twenty from hence. Do as you please, sirrahs. I suppose it will not be too

---

[1] *See* Letter XIV., Jan. 24.

[2] *See* Letter XVII., March 10.

[3] It may be somewhat amazing to declare; but Stella, with all her wit and good sense, spelled very ill. And Dr. Swift insisted greatly upon women's spelling well.—D. S.

[4] The slope of the letters in the words *this way, this way*, is to the left hand, but the slope of the words *that way, that way*, is to the right hand. —D. S.

[5] *See* Letter XVII., March 10.

[6] Jointly holding the offices of Vice-Treasurer, Receiver-General, and Paymaster-General in Ireland.—D. L. P.

late for the first season; if it be, I would have you resolve however to go the second season, if the doctors say it will do you good, and you fancy so.

LETTER XX

London, *April* 5, 1711.

I PUT my nineteenth in the post-office just now myself, as I came out of the city, where I dined. This rain ruins me in coach-hire; I walkt away sixpennyworth, and came within a shilling length, and then took a coach, and got a lift back for nothing; and am now busy.

6. Mr. secretary desired I would see him this morning, said he had several things to say to me, and said not one; and the duke of Ormond sent to desire I would meet him at Mr. Southwell's by ten this morning too, which I did, thinking it was some particular matter. All the Irish in town were there, to consult upon preventing a bill for laying a duty on Irish yarn; so we talkt awhile, and then all went to the lobby of the house of commons, to solicit our friends, and the duke came among the rest; and lord Anglesea[1] solicited admirably, and I did wonders. But after all, the matter was put off till Monday, and then we are to be at it again. I dined with lord Mountjoy, and lookt over him at chess, which put me in mind of Stella and Griffyth. I came home, and that dog Patrick was not within, so I fretted, and fretted, and what good did that do me? And so get you gone to your deans, You couple of queans. I can't find rhyme to Walls and Stoyte.—Yes, yes, You expect Mrs. Walls, Be dress'd when she calls, To carry you to Stoyte, Or else *honi soit*. Henley told me, that the Tories were insupportable people, because they are for bringing in French claret, and will not *sup-port*. Mr. Harley will hardly get abroad this week or ten days yet. I reckon when I send away this letter he will be just got into the house of commons. My last letter went in twelve days, and so perhaps may this. No it won't, for those letters that go under a fortnight are answerers to one of yours, otherwise, you must take the days as they happen, some dry, some wet, some barren, some fruitful, some merry, some insipid; some, &c.—I will write you word exactly the first day I see young gooseberries, and pray observe how much later you are. We have not had five fine days this five weeks, but rain or wind. 'Tis a late Spring they say here.—Go to bed, you two dear saucy brats, and don't keep me up all night.

[1] Arthur Annesley, who succeeded his brother in title, obtained the office of joint treasurer, Sept. 19, 1710.—N. [*See* Letter X., Dec. 7, 1710.]

7. Ford has been at Epsom, to avoid Good-Friday and Easter-Sunday. He forced me to-day to dine with him; and tells me, there are letters from Ireland giving an account of a great indiscretion in the archbishop of Dublin, who applied a story out of Tacitus[1] very reflectingly on Mr. Harley, and that twenty people have written of it; I do not believe it yet. I called this evening to see Mr. secretary, who has been very ill with the gravel and pain in his back, by Burgundy and Champagne, added to the sitting up all night at business; I found him drinking tea while the rest were at Champagne, and was very glad of it. I have chid him so severely that I hardly knew whether he would take it well: then I went and sat an hour with Mrs. St. John, who is growing a great favourite of mine; she goes to the Bath on Wednesday, for she is much out of health, and has begged me to take care of the secretary.

8. I dined to-day with Mr. secretary St. John; he gave me a letter to read, which was from the publisher of the newspaper called the *Post-boy*;[2] in it there was a long copy of a letter from Dublin, giving an account of what the Whigs said upon Mr. Harley's being stabbed, and how much they abuse him and Mr. secretary St. John; and at the end there was half a dozen lines, telling the story of the archbishop of Dublin, and abusing him horribly; this was to be printed on Tuesday. I told the secretary I would not suffer that about the archbishop to be printed, and so I crost it out; and afterwards, to prevent all danger, I made him give me the letter, and, upon further thought, would let none of it be published: and I sent for the printer and told him so, and ordered him, in the secretary's name, to print nothing reflecting on any body in Ireland till he had shewed it me. Thus I have prevented a terrible scandal to the archbishop, by a piece of perfect good fortune. I will let him know it by next post; and pray, if you pick it out, let me know, and whether he is thankful for it; but say nothing.

9. I was to-day at the house of commons again about their [? this] yarn, at lord Anglesea's desire, but the business is again put off till Monday. I dined with Sir John Stanley, by an assignation I had made with Mr. St. John, and George Granville, the

---

[1] *Accensis indicibus ad prodendum Faenium Rufum, quem eundem conscium et inquisitorem non tolerabant.* TACITUS, *Ann. Lib.* xv. 66. "Informers having been instigated to denounce Fænius Rufus, whom they could not suffer to be at the same time an accomplice and the collector of evidence against them"; an insinuation that Harley was engaged in intrigues with France, and denounced Guiscard to secure his own safety.—D. L. P.

[2] A Tory paper. *See* Letter XLIII., March 21, 1711-12, note on Roper (Abel).

secretary at war, but they let in other company, some ladies, and so we were not as easy as I intended. My head is pretty tolerable, but every day I feel some little disorders; I have left off snuff since Sunday, finding myself much worse after taking a good deal at the secretary's. I would not let him drink one drop of Champagne or Burgundy without water, and in compliment I did so myself. He is much better, but when he is well he is like Stella, and will not be governed. So go to your Stoyte's and I'll go sleep.

10. I have been visiting lady Worsley and Mrs. Barton to-day, and dined soberly with my friend Lewis. The dauphin is dead of an apoplexy; I wish he had lived till the finishing of this letter, that it might be news to you; Duncomb,[1] the rich alderman, died to-day, and I hear has left the duke of Argyle, who married his niece,[2] two hundred thousand pounds; I hope it is true, for I love that duke mightily. I writ this evening to the archbishop of Dublin, about what I told you; and then went to take leave of poor Mrs. St. John, who gave me strict charge to take care of the secretary in her absence, said she had none to trust but me; and the poor creature's tears came fresh in her eyes. Before we took leave, I was drawn in by the other ladies and Sir John Stanley to raffle for a fan, with a pox; it was four guineas, and we put in seven shillings apiece, several raffling for absent people; but I lost, and so mist an opportunity of shewing my gallantry to Mrs. St. John, whom I designed to have presented it to, if I had won. Is Dilly [3] gone to the Bath? His face will whizz in the water; I suppose he will write to us from thence, and will take London in his way back.—The rabble will say, There goes a drunken parson, and which is worse, they will say true. Oh, but you must know, I carried Ford to dine with Mr. St. John last Sunday, that he may brag when he goes back, of dining with a secretary of state. The secretary and I went away early, and left him drinking with the rest, and he told me, that two or three of them were drunk. They talk of great promotions to be made; that Mr. Harley is to be lord treasurer, and lord Poulet [4] master of the horse, &c.

[1] Sir Charles Duncombe, knight, Lord Mayor of London in 1709.—N. The dauphin whose death is recorded in this sentence was Louis, eldest son of Louis XIV.

[2] The daughter of Ursula [Browne], sister of Sir Charles Duncombe, and wife of John Browne, Esq. She died in 1716, without issue.—N.

[3] The Reverend Dillon Ashe.—N.

[4] John (1663–1743), fourth baron. Since Aug. 8, 1710, he had been nominally First Lord of the Treasury.

but they are only conjecture. The speaker is to make Mr. Harley a compliment the first time he comes into the house, which I hope will be in a week. He has had an ill surgeon, by the caprice of that puppy Dr. Radcliffe; which has kept him back so long; and yesterday he got a cold, but is better to-day. —What; I think I am stark mad to write so much in one day to little saucy MD; here's a deal of stuff, indeed; can't you bid those little dear rogues good night, and let them go sleep, Mr. Presto? When your tongue runs there's no ho with you, pray.

11. Again at the lobby, like a lobcock, of the house of commons, about your Irish yarn, and again put off till Friday; and I and Patrick went into the city by water, where I dined, and then went to the auction of Charles Barnard's books, but the good ones were so monstrous dear, I could not reach them, so I laid out one pound seven shillings but very indifferently, and came away, and will go there no more. Henley would fain engage me to go with Steele and Rowe, &c. to an invitation at Sir William Read's.[1] Surely you have heard of him. He has been a mountebank, and is the queen's oculist: he makes admirable punch, and treats you in gold vessels. But I am engaged, and won't go, neither indeed am I fond of the jaunt. So good night, and go sleep.

12. I went about noon to the secretary, who is very ill with a cold, and sometimes of the gravel, with his Champagne, &c. I scolded him like a dog, and he promises faithfully more care for the future. To-day my lord Anglesea, and Sir Thomas Hanmer, and Prior and I dined, by appointment, with lieutenant general Webb.[2] My lord and I staid till ten o'clock, but we drank soberly, and I always went with water. There was with us one Mr. Campain,[3] one of the October Club, if you know what that is; a Club of country members, who think the ministers are too backward in punishing and turning out the Whigs. I found my lord and the rest thought I had more credit with the ministry than I pretend to have, and would have engaged me to put them upon something that would satisfy their desires, and indeed I think they have some reason to complain;

---

[1] He lived in Durham Yard. His advertisements in the *Tatler* (which displayed his astonishing abilities in the cure of every disorder of the eye, in removing wens and hare lips, and in the curing of wry necks) conclude by a notice, "that he allowed nobody to practise in his name but his lady, whom he had instructed."—N. [He died 1715.]

[2] John Richmond Webb (1667?–1724), distinguished as the victor of Wynandaele in 1708. Cardonnel, secretary to Marlborough, assigned the credit to Webb's subordinate, which made mischief.

[3] Mr. Aitken says that Henry Campion, M.P. for Bossiney, is meant.

however, I will not burn my fingers. I'll remember Stella's chiding; What had you to do with what did not belong to you, &c. However, you will give me leave to tell the ministry my thoughts when they ask them, and other people's thoughts sometimes when they do not ask; so thinks Dingley.

13. I called this morning at Mrs. Vedeau's again, who has employed a friend to get the money; it will be done in a fortnight, and then she will deliver me up the parchment. I went then to see Mr. Harley, who I hope will be out in a few days; he was in excellent good humour, only complained to me of the neglect of Guiscard's cure, how glad he would have been to have had him live. Mr. secretary came in to us, and we were very merry till lord chamberlain (duke of Shrewsbury) came up, then colonel Masham and I went off, after I had been presented to the duke, and that we made two or three silly compliments suitable to the occasion. Then I attended at the house of commons about your yarn, and 'tis again put off. Then Ford drew me to dine at a tavern, it happened to be the day and the house where the October Club dine. After we had dined, coming down we called to enquire, whether our yarn business had been over that day, and I sent into the room for Sir George Beaumont.[1] But I had like to be drawn into a difficulty; for in two minutes out comes Mr. Finch, lord Guernsey's son,[2] to let me know, that my lord Compton,[3] the steward of this feast, desired, in the name of the Club, that I would do them the honour to dine with them. I sent my excuses, adorned with about thirty compliments, and got off as fast as I could. It would have been a most improper thing for me to dine there, considering my friendship with the ministry. The Club is about a hundred and fifty, and near eighty of them were then going to dinner at two long tables in a great ground room. At evening I went to the auction of Barnard's books, and laid out three pounds three shillings, but I'll go there no more; and so I said once before, but now I'll keep to it. I forgot to tell, that when I dined at Webb's with lord Anglesea, I spoke to him of Clements, as one recommended for a very honest

[1] (c. 1665–1737) "of Stoughton Grange," co. Leicester, M.P. for Leicester from 1702 till death. Mr. Aitken says he was acquainted with Swift's mother.
[2] Heneage Finch (c. 1683–1757), whose father (one of the counsel for the seven bishops) became Earl of Gernsey (sic) in 1702-3, and who was at this time Tory M.P. for Surrey.
[3] James Compton (1687–1754) went in 1711 to the House of Lords as Baron Compton; his father (then alive) being fifth Baron Compton and fourth Earl of Northampton. James became fifth earl in 1727.

gentleman, and good officer, and hoped he would keep him: he said, he had no thought otherwise, and that he should certainly hold his place, while he continued to deserve it; and I could not find there had been any intentions from his lordship against him. But I tell you, hunny, the impropriety of this. A great man will do a favour for me, or for my friend; but why should he do it for my friend's friend? Recommendations should stop before they come to that. Let any friend of mine recommend one of his to me for a thing in my power, I will do it for his sake; but to speak to another for my friend's friend, is against all reason; and I desire you will understand this, and discourage any such troubles given me.—I hope this may do some good to Clements, it can do no hurt; and I find by Mrs. Pratt, that her husband is his friend; and the bishop of Clogher says, Clements's danger is not from Pratt,[1] but from some other enemies, who think him a Whig.

14. I was so busy this morning that I did not go out till late. I writ to-day to the duke of Argyle, but said nothing of Bernage, who, I believe, will not see him till Spain is conquered, and that is, not at all. I was to-day at lord Shelburn's, and spoke to Mrs. Pratt again about Clements; her husband himself wants some good offices, and I have done him very good ones lately, and told Mrs. Pratt, I expected her husband should stand by Clements in return. Sir Andrew Fountain and I dined with neighbour Vanhomrigh; he is mighty ill of an Asthma, and apprehends himself in much danger; 'tis his own fault, that will rake and drink, when he is but just crawled out of his grave. I will send this letter just now, because I think my half year is out for my lodging; and, if you please, I would be glad it were paid off, and some deal boxes made for my books, and kept in some safe place, I would give something for their keeping: but I doubt that lodging will not serve me when I come back; I would have a larger place for books, and a stable, if possible. So pray be so kind to pay the lodging, and all accounts about it; and get Mrs. Brent [2] to put up my things. I would have no books put in that trunk where my papers are. If you do not think of going to the Bath, I here send a bill on Parvisol for twenty pounds Irish, out of which you will pay for the lodging, and score the rest to me. Do as you please, and love poor Presto that loves MD better than his life a thousand millions of times. Farewel, MD, &c. &c.

<hr />

[1] *See* Letter III., Sept. 11, 1710.　　　[2] *See* Letter I.

LETTER XXI

London, *April* 14, 1711.

REMEMBER, sirrahs, that there are but nine days between the dates of my two former letters. I sent away my twentieth this moment, and now am writing on like a fish, as if nothing was done. But there was a cause for my hasting away the last, for fear it should not come time enough before a new quarter began. I told you where I dined to-day, but forgot to tell you what I believe, that Mr. Harley will be lord treasurer in a short time, and other great removes and promotions made. This is my thought, &c.

15. I was this morning with Mr. secretary, and he is grown pretty well. I dined with him to-day, and drank some of that wine which the great duke of Tuscany[1] used to send to Sir William Temple: he always sends some to the chief ministers. I liked it mightily, but he does not; and he ordered his butler to send me a chest of it to-morrow. Would to God MD had it. The queen is well again, and was at chapel to-day, &c.

16. I went with Ford into the city to-day, and dined with Stratford, and drank Tockay, and then we went to the auction; but I did not lay out above twelve shillings. My head is a little out of order to-night, though no formal fit. My lord keeper has sent to invite me to dinner to-morrow, and you'll dine better with the Dean, and God bless you. I forgot to tell you that yesterday was sent me *A Narrative* printed, with all the circumstances of Mr. Harley's stabbing. I had not time to do it myself; so I sent my hints to the author of the *Atalantis*,[2] and she has cook'd it into a six-penny pamphlet, in her own style, only the first page is left as I was beginning it. But I was afraid of disobliging Mr. Harley or Mr. St. John in one critical point about it, and so would not do it myself. It is worth your reading, for the circumstances are all true. My chest of Florence was sent me this morning, and cost me seven and six-pence to two servants. I would give two guineas you had it, &c.

17. I was so out of order with my head this morning, that I was going to send my excuses to my lord keeper; but however I got up at eleven, and walked there after two, and staid till eight. There was Sir Thomas Mansel, Prior, George Granville, and Mr. Cæsar,[3] and we were very merry. My head is

---

[1] Cosimo III. [1642-1723], son of Ferdinand II., of the house of Medici, succeeded his father in 1669.—COURTENAY'S *Life of Sir Wm. Temple.*

[2] Mrs. Manley.

[3] Charles Caesar, M.P., afterwards Treasurer of the Navy.

still wrong, but I have had no formal fit, only I totter a little. I have left off snuff altogether. I have a noble roll of tobacco for grating, very good. Shall I send it to MD, if she likes that sort? My lord keeper and our this day's company are to dine on Saturday with George Granville, and to-morrow I dine with lord Anglesea.

18. Did you ever see such a blundering goose-cap as Presto? I saw the number 21 atop, and so I went on as if it were the day of the month, whereas this is but Wednesday the 18th. How shall I do to blot and alter them? I have made a shift to do it behind, but it is a great botch. I dined with lord Anglesea to-day, but did not go to the house of commons about the yarn; my head was not well enough. I know not what's the matter; it has never been thus before: two days together giddy from morning till night, but not with any violence or pain; and I totter a little, but can make shift to walk. I doubt I must fall to my pills again: I think of going into the country a little way. I tell you what you must do henceforward: you must inclose your letters in a fair half sheet of paper, and direct the outside To Erasmus Lewis, esquire, at my Lord Dartmouth's office at Whitehall: for I never go to the Coffee-house, and they will grudge to take in my letters. I forgot to tell you that your mother was to see me this morning, and brought me a flask of sweat water for a present, admirable for my head; but I shall not smell to it. She is going to Sheen with lady Giffard: she would fain send your papers over to you, or give them to me. Say what you would have done, and it shall be done; because I love Stella, and she is a good daughter, they say, and so is Dingley.

19. This morning general Webb was to give me a visit: he goes with a crutch and stick, yet was forced to come up two pair of stairs. I promised to dine with him, but afterwards sent my excuses, and dined privately in my friend Lewis's lodgings at Whitehall, with whom I had much business to talk of, relating to the publick and myself. Little Harrison the Tatler goes to-morrow to the secretaryship I got him at the Hague, and Mr. St. John has made him a present of fifty guineas to bear his charges. An't I a good friend? Why are not you a young fellow, that I might prefer you? I had a letter from Bernage from Kinsale: he tells me his commission for captain-lieutenant was ready for him at his arrival: so there are two jackanapeses I have done with. My head is something better this evening, though not well.

20. I was this morning with Mr. secretary, whose pacquets were just come in, and among them a letter from lord Peterborow to me: he writes so well, I have no mind to answer him, and so kind, that I must answer him. The emperor's[1] death must, I think, cause great alterations in Europe, and, I believe, will hasten a Peace. We reckon our king Charles[2] will be chosen emperor, and the duke of Savoy set up for Spain; but I believe he will make nothing of it. Dr. Freind and I dined in the city at a printer's, and it has cost me two shillings in coach hire, and a great deal more this week and month, which has been almost all rain, with now and then sun-shine, and is the truest April that I have known these many years. The lime-trees in the Park are all out in leaves, though not large leaves yet. Wise people are going into the country; but many think the Parliament can hardly be up these six weeks. Mr. Harley was with the queen on Tuesday. I believe certainly he will be lord treasurer: I have not seen him this week.

21. Morning. Lord keeper, and I, and Prior, and Sir Thomas Mansel have appointed to dine this day with George Granville. My head, I thank God, is better; but to be giddyish three or four days together mortified me. I take no snuff, and I will be very regular in eating little and the gentlest meats. How does poor Stella just now, with her deans and her Stoytes? Do they give you health for the money you lose at ombre, sirrah? What say you to that? Poor Dingley frets to see Stella lose that four and eleven pence, t'other night. Let us rise. Morrow, sirrahs. I will rise, spight of your little teeth; good morrow.— At night. Oh, Faith, you are little dear saucy boxes. I was just going in the morning to tell you that I began to want a letter from MD, and in four minutes after Mr. Ford sends me one that he had pickt up at St. James's Coffee-house; for I go to no Coffee-house at all. And faith, I was glad at heart to see it, and to see Stella so brisk. O Lord, what pretending? Well, but I won't answer it yet; I'll keep it for t'other side. Well, we dined to-day according to appointment; lord keeper went away at near eight, I at eight, and I believe the rest will be fairly fuddled: for young Harcourt,[3] lord keeper's son, began to prattle

[1] Joseph I. (1678–1711).

[2] Joseph's brother, the Emperor Charles VI. (1685–1740), already acknowledged by the allies as "Charles the Second of Spain." His accession to the throne of the empire led to the Peace of Utrecht with France— the English not wishing Germany and Spain to be united under one sovereign.

[3] Simon (1684–1720), second son of the Lord Keeper, elected 1710 M.P. for Wallingford. Wrote verses.

before I came away. It will not do with Prior's lean carcase. I drink little, miss my glass often, put water in my wine, and go away before the rest, which I take to be a good receipt for sobriety. Let us put it into rhyme, and so make a proverb;

> Drink little at a time;
> Put water with your wine;
> Miss your glass when you can;
> And go off the first man.

God be thanked I am much better than I was, though something of a totterer. I ate but little to-day, and of the gentlest meat. I refused ham and pigeons, pease-soup, stewed beef, cold salmon, because they were too strong. I take no snuff at all, but some herb-snuff prescribed by Dr. Radcliffe.

> Go to your deans,
> You couple of queans.

I believe I said that already, What care I? what cares Presto?

22. Morning. I must rise and go to the secretary's. Mr. Harley has been out of town this week to refresh himself before he comes into parliament.[1] Oh, but I must rise, so there is no more to be said; and so morrow, sirrahs both.—Night. I dined to-day with the secretary, who has engaged me for every Sunday: and I was an hour with him this morning deep in politicks, where I told him the objections of the October Club, and he answered all except one, That no Enquiries are made into past mismanagement. But indeed I believe they are not yet able to make any: the late ministry were too cunning in their rogueries, and fenced themselves with an Act of general Pardon. I believe Mr. Harley must be lord treasurer; yet he makes one difficulty which is hard to answer: he must be made a lord, and his estate is not large enough, and he is too generous to make it larger; and if the ministry should change soon by any accident, he will be left in the suds. Another difficulty is, that if he be made a peer, they will want him prodigiously in the House of Commons, of which he is the great mover, and after him the secretary, and hardly any else of weight.[2] Two shillings more to-day for coach and chair. I shall be ruined.

23. So you expect an answer to your letter, do you so? Yes, yes, you shall have an answer, you shall, young women. I made

[1] About this time appeared Trapp's poem to the Right Honourable Robert Harley on his appearing in publick after the wound given him by Guiscard.—N.
[2] That is, among the ministry.—D. S.

a good pun on Saturday to my lord keeper. After dinner we had coarse *Doiley*[1] napkins, fringed at each end, upon the table to drink with: my lord keeper spread one of them between him and Mr. Prior; I told him I was glad to see there was such a *Fringeship*[2] between Mr. Prior and his lordship. Prior swore it was the worst he ever heard: I said I thought so too; but at the same time I thought it was most like one of Stella's that ever I heard. I dined to-day with lord Montjoy, and this evening saw the Venetian ambassador[3] coming from his first publick audience. His coach was the most monstrous, huge, fine, rich, gilt thing that ever I saw. I loitered this evening, and came home late.

24. I was this morning to visit the duchess of Ormond, who has long desired it, or threatened she would not let me visit her daughters. I sat an hour with her, and we were good company, when in came the countess of Bellamont,[4] with a pox. I went out, and we did not know one another; yet hearing me named, she asked, What, is that Dr. Swift? said, she and I were very well acquainted, and fell a railing at me without mercy, as a lady told me that was there; yet I never was but once in the company of that drab of a countess. Sir Andrew Fountain and I dined with my neighbour Van. I design in two days, if possible, to go lodge at Chelsea for the air, and put myself under a necessity of walking to and from London every day. I writ this post to the bishop of Clogher a long politick letter to entertain him. I am to buy statues and *Harnese*[5] for them, with a vengeance. I have packt and sealed up MD's twelve letters against I go to Chelsea. I have put the last commissions of MD in my account-book; but if there be any former ones, I have forgot them. I have Dingley's pocket-book down, and Stella's green silk apron, and the pound of tea; pray send me word if you have any other, and down they shall go. I will not answer your letter yet, saucy boxes. You are with the dean just now, madam Stella, losing your money. Why don't you name what number you have received? You say you have received my letters, but don't tell the number.

25. I was this day dining in the city with very insignificant,

[1] So called from the original vender, who kept a linen-draper's shop in the Strand, a little west of Catherine Street.—*Vide* PEGGE MS.
[2] Friendship.—D. S.
[3] A special envoy, name not ascertained.
[4] Lucia Anna, wife of third Earl (second of second creation) of Bellomont (Coote), and youngest daughter of Henry, Count of Nassau and Lord of Auverquerque. Died 1744.
[5] Farnese.—D. S.

low, and scurvy company. I had a letter from the archbishop of Dublin, with a long denial of the report raised on him, which yet has been since assured to me by those who say they have it from the first hand; but I cannot believe them. I will shew it to the secretary to-morrow. I will not answer yours till I get to Chelsea.

26. *Chelsea.* I have sent two boxes of lumber to my friend Darteneuf's house, and my chest of Florence and other things to Mrs. Vanhomrigh, where I dined to-day. I was this morning with the secretary, and shewed him the archbishop's letter, and convinced him of his grace's innocence, and I will do the same to Mr. Harley. I got here in the stage coach with Patrick and my portmantua for six-pence, and pay six shillings a week for one silly room with confounded coarse sheets. We have had such a horrible deal of rain, that there is no walking to London, and I must go as I came until it mends; and besides the whelp has taken my lodgings as far from London as this town could afford, at least half a mile further than he need; but I must be content. The best is, I lodge just over-against Dr. Atterbury's house, and yet perhaps I shall not like the place the better for that. Well, I'll stay till to-morrow before I answer your letter; and you must suppose me always writing at Chelsea from henceforward, till I alter and say London. This letter goes on Saturday, which will be just a fortnight; so go and cheat goody Stoyte, &c.

27. Do you know that I fear my whole chest of Florence is turned sour, at least the two first flasks were so, and hardly drinkable. How plaguy unfortunate am I! and the secretary's own is the best I ever tasted; and I must not tell him, but be as thankful as if it were the best in Christendom. I went to town in the sixpenny stage to-day, and hearing Mr. Harley was not at home, I went to see him, because I knew by the message of his lying porter that he was at home. He was very well, and just going out, but made me promise to dine with him; and betwixt that and indeed strolling about, I lost four pound seven shillings at play——with a——a——a——bookseller, and got but half a dozen books.[1] I will buy no more books now, that's certain. Well, I dined at Mr. Harley's, came away at six, shifted my gown, cassock, and periwig, and walkt hither to Chelsea, as I always design to do when it is fair. I am heartily sorry to find my friend the secretary stand a little ticklish with the rest of the ministry; there have been one or

[1] This must have been at some raffling for books.—D. S.

two disobliging things that have happened, too long to tell: and t'other day in parliament, upon a debate of about thirty-five millions that have not been duly accounted for, Mr. secretary, in his warmth of speech, and zeal for his friend Mr. Brydges,[1] on whom part of the blame was falling, said, he did not know that either Mr. Brydges or the late ministry were at all to blame in this matter; which was very desperately spoken, and giving up the whole cause: for the chief quarrel against the late ministry was the ill management of the treasure, and was more than all the rest together. I have heard of this matter: but Mr. Foley[2] beginning to discourse to-day at table, without naming Mr. St. John, I turned to Mr. Harley, and said, If the late ministry were not to blame in that article, he [Mr. Harley][3] ought to lose his head for putting the queen upon changing them. He made it a jest; but by some words dropt, I easily saw that they take things ill of Mr. St. John, and by some hints given me from another hand that I deal with, I am afraid the secretary will not stand long. This is the fate of Courts. I will, if I meet Mr. St. John alone on Sunday, tell him my opinion, and beg him to set himself right, else the consequences may be very bad; for I see not how they can well want him neither, and he would make a troublesome enemy. But enough of politicks.

28. Morning. I forgot to tell you that Mr. Harley askt me yesterday, how he came to disoblige the archbishop of Dublin? Upon which (having not his letter about me) I told him what the bishop had written to me on that subject, and desired I might read him the letter some other time. But after all, from what I have heard from other hands, I am afraid the archbishop is a little guilty. Here is one Brent Spencer, a brother of Mr. Proby's,[4] who affirms it, and says he has leave to do so from Charles Dering,[5] who heard the words; and Ingoldsby[6] abused the archbishop, &c. Well, but now for your saucy letter: I have no room to answer it; O yes, enough on t'other side. Are you no sicker? Stella jeers Presto for not coming over by Christmas; but indeed Stella does not jeer but reproach poor Presto. And how can I come away, and the First-Fruits not finish'd? I am of opinion the duke of Ormond will do nothing

---

[1] See Letter III., Sept. 17, 1710.
[2] Thomas Foley, grandson of an iron-manufacturer and philanthropist at Stourbridge, M.P. for Stafford until made Baron Foley in 1711-12.
[3] Brackets in D. S.
[4] See Letter XIX., March 25.
[5] The uncle of Sir Cholmeley Dering, and (Mr. Aitken says) M.P. for Carlingford and Auditor of the Exchequer in Ireland.
[6] See Letter XI., Dec. 16, 1710.

in them before he goes, which will be in a fortnight, they say; and then they must fall to me to be done in his absence. No, indeed, I have nothing to print: you know they have printed the *Miscellanies* already. Are they on your side yet? If you have my snuff-box, I'll have your strong box. Hi, does Stella take snuff again? or is it only because it is a fine box? Not the *Meddle*, but the *Medley*,[1] you fool. Yes, yes, a wretched thing, because it is against you Tories: now I think it is very fine, and the *Examiner* a wretched thing.—Twist your mouth, sirrah. Guiscard, and what you will read in the *Narrative*, I ordered to be written, and nothing else. The *Spectator* is written by Steele, with Addison's help: 'tis often very pretty. Yesterday it was made of a noble hint I gave him long ago for his *Tatlers*, about an Indian supposed to write his travels into England.[2] I repent he ever had it. I intended to have written a book on that subject. I believe he has spent it all in one paper, and all the under hints there are mine too; but I never see him or Addison. The queen is well, but I fear will be no long liver; for I am told she has sometimes the gout in her bowels (I hate the word *bowels*). My ears have been, these three months past, much better than any time these two years; but now they begin to be a little out of order again. My head is better, though not right; but I trust to air and walking. You have got my letter, but what number? I suppose 18. Well, my shin has been well this month. No. Mrs. Westley[3] came away without her husband's knowledge, while she was in the country: she has written to me for some tea. They lie; Mr. Harley's wound was very terrible: he had convulsions, and very narrowly escaped. The bruise was nine times worse than the wound: he is weak still. Well, Brooks married; I know all that. I am sorry for Mrs. Walls's eye: I hope 'tis better. O yes, you are great walkers: but I have heard them say, Much talkers, Little walkers: and I believe I may apply the old proverb to you; If you talkt no more than you walkt, Those that think you wits would be baulked. Yes, Stella shall have a large printed Bible: I have put it down among my commissions for MD. I am glad to hear you have taken the fancy of intending to read the Bible. Pox take the box; is not it come yet? This is trusting to your young fellows, young women; 'tis your fault: I thought you had such power with Sterne, that he would fly over Mount

---

[1] Whig journal, engaged in answering the *Examiner*.—D. L. P.
[2] No. 50.
[3] ? Wesley—*see* Letter I.

Atlas to serve you. You say you are not splenetick; but if you be, faith you will break poor Presto's——I won't say the rest; but I vow to God, if I could decently come over now, I would, and leave all schemes of politicks and ambition for ever. I have not the opportunities here of preserving my health by riding, &c. that I have in Ireland; and the want of health is a great cooler of making one's court. You guess right about my being bit with a direction from Walls, and the letter from MD: I believe I described it in one of my last. This goes to-night; and I must now rise and walk to town, and walk back in the evening. God Almighty bless and preserve poor MD. Farewel.

Oh faith, don't think, saucy noses, that I'll fill this third side: I can't stay a letter above a fortnight: It must go then; and you would rather see a short one like this, than want it a week longer.

My humble service to the dean, and Mrs. Walls, and good kind hearty Mrs. Stoyte, and honest Catherine.

LETTER XXII

Chelsea, *April* 28, 1711.

AT night. I say at night, because I finished my twenty-first this morning here, and put it into the post-office my own self, like a good boy. I think I am a little before you now, young women: I am writing my twenty-second, and have received your thirteenth. I got to town between twelve and one, and put on my new gown and periwig, and dined with lord Abercorn, where I had not been since the marriage of his son lord Peasley,[1] who has got ten thousand pound with a wife. I am now a country gentleman. I walkt home as I went, and am a little weary, and am got into bed: I hope in God the air and exercise will do me a little good. I have been enquiring about statues for Mrs. Ashe:[2] I made lady Abercorn go with me; and will send them word next post to Clogher. I hate to buy for her: I'm sure she'll maunder. I am going to study.

29. I had a charming walk to and from town to-day: I washed, shaved and all, and changed gown and periwig, by half an hour after nine, and went to the secretary, who told me how he had differed with his friends in parliament: I apprehended this

---

[1] *i.e.* Paisley. *See* Letter XVII., March 2, 1710-11.
[2] The Bishop of Clogher's wife. *See* Letter IV., Sept. 23, 1710.

division, and told him a great deal of it. I went to Court, and there several mentioned it to me as what they much disliked. I dined with the secretary; and we proposed some business of importance in the afternoon, which he broke to me first, and said how he and Mr. Harley were convinced of the necessity of it; yet he suffered one of his under-secretaries to come upon us after dinner, who staid till six, and so nothing was done: and what care I? he shall send to me the next time, and ask twice. To-morrow I go to the election at Westminster-school, where lads are chosen for the University: they say 'tis a sight, and a great trial of wits. Our Expedition Fleet is but just sailed:[1] I believe it will come to nothing. Mr. secretary frets at their tediousness; but hopes great things from it, though he owns four or five princes are in the secret; and, for that reason, I fear it is no secret to France. There are eight regiments; and the admiral is your Walker's brother the midwife.[2]

30. Morn. I am here in a pretty pickle: it rains hard; and the cunning natives of Chelsea have outwitted me, and taken up all the three stage coaches. What shall I do? I must go to town: this is your fault. I can't walk: I'll borrow a coat. This is the blindside of my lodging out of town; I must expect such inconveniencies as these. Faith I'll walk in the rain. Morrow.— At night. I got a gentleman's chaise by chance, and so went to town for a shilling, and lie this night in town. I was at the election of lads at Westminster to-day, and a very silly thing it is; but they say there will be fine doings to-morrow. I dined with Dr. Freind, the second master[3] of the school, with a dozen parsons and others: Prior would make me stay. Mr. Harley is to hear the election to-morrow; and we are all to dine with tickets, and hear fine speeches. 'Tis terrible rainy weather again: I lie at a friend's in the city.

May 1. I wish you a merry May-day, and a thousand more. I was baulkt at Westminster; I came too late: I heard no speeches nor verses. They would not let me in to their dining place for want of a ticket; and I would not send in for one, because Mr. Harley excused his coming, and Atterbury was not

[1] To Canada, under Admiral Walker and General Hill, to expel the French from North America. The fleet was damaged by a storm in the St. Lawrence, and returned, as Swift predicted, *re infectâ*.—D. L. P.

[2] This is a little mixed. "Your Walker," the younger of the brothers, was Sir Chamberlain Walker, a celebrated accoucheur; and he stayed at home. The admiral who went to Canada was Sir Hovenden Walker (*c.* 1656–1728). *Cf.* Letter XXXII., Oct. 12, 1711, passage as to "Mrs. Colledge."

[3] Robert Freind (1667–1751), D.D., brother of John (*see* Letter IX., Nov. 11, 1710), under-master 1699, head-master 1711–1733.

there; and I cared not for the rest: and so my friend Lewis and I dined with Kit Musgrave,[1] if you know such a man: and, the weather mending, I walkt gravely home this evening; and so I design to walk and walk till I am well: I fancy myself a little better already. How does poor Stella? Dingley is well enough. Go, get you gone, naughty girl, you are well enough. O dear MD, contrive to have some share of the country this spring: go to Finglass, or Donnybrook, or Clogher, or Killala, or Lowth. Have you got your box yet? Yes, yes. Don't write to me again till this letter goes: I must make haste, that I may write two for one. Go to the Bath: I hope you are now at the Bath, if you had a mind to go; or go to Wexford: do something for your living. Have you given up my lodging according to order? I have had just now a compliment from dean Atterbury's lady,[2] to command the garden and library, and whatever the house affords. I lodge just over against them; but the dean is in town with his convocation: so I have my dean and prolocutor as well as you, young women, though he has not so good wine, nor so much meat.

2. A fine day, but begins to grow a little warm; and that makes your little fat Presto sweat in the forehead. Pray, are not the fine buns sold here in our town; was it not *Rrrrrrrrrare Chelsea buns*? I bought one to-day in my walk; it cost me a penny; it was stale, and I did not like it, as the man said, &c. Sir Andrew Fountain and I dined at Mrs. Vanhomrigh's; and had a flask of my Florence, which lies in their cellar; and so I came home gravely, and saw nobody of consequence to-day. I am very easy here, nobody plaguing me in a morning; and Patrick saves many a score lies. I sent over to Mrs. Atterbury, To know whether I might wait on her? but she is gone a visiting: we have exchanged some compliments, but I have not seen her yet. We have no news in our town.

3. I did not go to town to-day, it was so terrible rainy; nor have I stirred out of my room till eight this evening; when I crost the way to see Mrs. Atterbury, and thank her for her civilities. She would needs send me some veal, and small beer, and ale, to-day at dinner; and I have lived a scurvy, dull, splenetick day, for want of MD: I often thought how happy I could have been, had it rained eight thousand times more, if

---

[1] (166-— 1718). Second son of Sir Christopher Musgrave of Edenhall. He was clerk of the council (*Dict. Nat. Biog.*).

[2] Was a Miss Katharine Osborne, a niece of the Duke of Leeds, "a great beauty and possessed of a fortune of seven thousand pounds" (Dean Hook).

MD had been with a body. My lord Rochester[1] is dead this morning; they say at one o'clock; and I hear he died suddenly. To-morrow I shall know more. He is a great loss to us: I cannot think who will succeed him as lord president. I have been writing a long letter to lord Peterborow and am dull.

4. I dined to-day at lord Shelburn's, where lady Kerry made me a present of four India handkerchiefs, which I have a mind to keep for little MD, only that I had rather, &c. I have been a mighty handkerchief-monger, and have bought abundance of snuff ones since I have left off taking snuff. And I am resolved, when I come over, MD shall be acquainted with lady Kerry: we have struck up a mighty friendship; and she has much better sense than any other lady of your country. We are almost in love with one another: but she is most egregiously ugly; but perfectly well bred, and governable as I please. I am resolved, when I come, to keep no company but MD: you know I kept my resolution last time; and, except Mr. Addison, conversed with none but you and your club of deans and Stoytes. 'Tis three weeks, young women, since I had a letter from you; and yet, methinks, I would not have another for five pound till this is gone; and yet I send every day to the Coffee-house, and I would fain have a letter, and not have a letter: and I don't know what, nor I don't know how, and this goes on very slow; 'tis a week to-morrow since I began it. I am a poor country gentleman, and don't know how the world passes. Do you know that every syllable I write I hold my lips just for all the world as if I were talking in our own little language to MD. Faith, I am very silly; but I can't help it for my life. I got home early to-night. My solicitors,[2] that used to ply me every morning, knew not where to find me; and I am so happy not to hear *Patrick, Patrick*, called a hundred times every morning. But I lookt backward, and find I have said this before. What care I? go to the dean, and roast the oranges.

5. I dined to-day with my friend Lewis, and we were deep in politicks how to save the present ministry; for I am afraid of Mr. secretary, as I believe I told you. I went in the evening to see Mr. Harley; and, upon my word, I was in perfect joy. Mr. secretary was just going out of the door; but I made him come back, and there was the old Saturday Club, lord keeper, lord Rivers, Mr. secretary, Mr. Harley and I; the first time since his stabbing. Mr. secretary went away; but I staid till nine, and

---

[1] *See* Letter VIII., Nov. 7, 1710.
[2] Of course, by "solicitors," he means cadgers—not attorneys.

made Mr. Harley shew me his breast, and tell all the story: and I shewed him the archbishop of Dublin's letter, and defended him effectually. We were all in mighty good humour. Lord keeper and I left them together, and I walkt here after nine two miles, and I found a parson drunk fighting with a seaman, and Patrick and I were so wise to part them, but the seaman followed him to Chelsea, cursing at him, and the parson slipt into a house, and I know no more. It mortified me to see a man in my coat so overtaken. A pretty scene for one that just came from sitting with the prime ministers: I had no money in my pocket, and so could not be robbed. However, nothing but Mr. Harley shall make me take such a journey again. We don't yet know who will be president in lord Rochester's room. I measured, and found that the pen-knife would have killed Mr. Harley, if it had gone but half the breadth of my thumb-nail lower; so near was he to death. I was so curious to ask him what were his thoughts, while they were carrying him home in the chair. He said, he concluded himself a dead man. He will not allow that Guiscard gave him the second stab, though my lord keeper, who is blind, and I that was not there, are positive in it. He wears a plaister still as broad as half a crown. Smoak how wide the lines are, but faith I don't do it on purpose: but I have changed my side in this new Chelsea bed, and I don't know how, methinks, but it is so unfit, and so aukward, never saw the like.

6. You must remember to inclose your letters in a fair paper, and direct the outside thus; To Erasmus Lewis, esq., at my lord Dartmouth's office at Whitehall; I said so before, but it may miscarry you know, yet I think none of my letters did ever miscarry; faith I think never one; among all the privateers and the storms: oh faith, my letters are too good to be lost. MD's letters may tarry, but never miscarry, as the old woman used to say. And indeed, how should they miscarry, when they never come before their time? It was a terrible rainy day; yet I made a shift to steal fair weather over head enough to go and come in. I was early with the secretary, and dined with him afterwards. In the morning I began to chide him, and tell him my fears of his proceedings. But Arthur Moore came up and relieved him. But I forgot, for you never heard of Arthur Moore.[1] But when I get Mr. Harley alone, I will know the bottom. You will have Dr. Raymond over before this letter, and what care you?

[1] *See* Letter XVII., March 2, 1710-11.

7. I hope, and believe my walks every day do me good.
I was busy at home, and set out late this morning, and dined
with Mrs. Vanhomrigh, at whose lodgings I always change my
gown and periwig. I visited this afternoon, and among others,
poor Biddy Floyd, who is very red, but I believe won't be much
marked. As I was coming home I met sir George Beaumont in
the Pall-mall, who would needs walk with me as far as Buckingham house. I was telling him of my head; he said he had been
ill of the same disorder, and by all means forbid me bohea tea;
which he said always gave it him; and that Dr. Radcliffe said
it was very bad. Now I had observed the same thing, and have
left it off this month, having found my self ill after it several
times; and I mention it, that Stella may consider it for her
own poor little head: a pound lies ready packt up and directed
for Mrs. Walls, to be sent by the first convenience. Mr. secretary
told me yesterday, that Mr. Harley would this week be lord
treasurer and a peer, so I expect it every day; yet perhaps it
may not be 'till Parliament is up, which will be in a fortnight.

8. I was to-day with the duke of Ormond, and recommended
to him the care [? case] of poor Joe Beaumont, who promises
me to do him all justice and favour, and give him encouragement; and desired I would give a memorial to Ned Southwell
about it, which I will, and so tell Joe when you see him, though
he knows it already by a letter I writ to Mr. Warburton.[1] It
was bloody hot walking to-day. I dined in the city, and went
and came by water; and it rained so this evening again, that I
thought I should hardly be able to get a dry hour to walk home
in. I'll send to-morrow to the Coffee-house for a letter from MD;
but I would not have one methinks, 'till this is gone, as it shall
on Saturday. I visited the duchess of Ormond this morning;
she does not go over with the duke. I spoke to her to get a lad
touched for the evil,[2] the son of a grocer in Capel-street, one
Bell, the ladies have bought sugar and plumbs of him. Mrs.
Mary used to go there often. This is Patrick's account; and the
poor fellow has been here some months with his boy. But the
queen has not been able to touch, and it now grows so warm,
I fear she will not at all. Go, go, go to the dean's, and let him
carry you to Donnybrook, and cut asparagus. Has Parvisol
sent you any this year[3]? I cannot sleep in the beginnings of

[1] Swift's curate at Laracor.
[2] It is somewhat pleasant to see a person of Dr. Swift's turn of thinking
seriously mention a design of getting "a lad touched for the evil."—N.
[Anne was the last sovereign to "touch."]
[3] From Dr. Swift's garden at Laracor.—D. S.

the nights, the heat or something hinders me, and I am drowsy in the mornings.

9. Dr. Freind came this morning to visit Atterbury's lady and children as physician, and persuaded me to go with him to town in his chariot. He told me he had been an hour before with Sir Cholmley Dering,[1] Charles Dering's nephew, and head of that family in Kent, for which he is knight of the shire. He said he left him dying of a pistol-shot quite through the body, by one Mr. Thornhill.[2] They fought at sword and pistol this morning in Tuttle-fields,[3] their pistols so near, that the muzzles touched. Thornhill discharged first, and Dering having received the shot, discharged his pistol as he was falling, so it went into the air. The story of this quarrel is long. Thornhill had lost seven teeth by a kick in the mouth from Dering, who had first knocked him down; this was above a fortnight ago. Dering was next week to be married to a fine young lady. This makes a noise here, but you won't value it. Well, Mr. Harley, lord keeper, and one or two more are to be made lords immediately; their patents are now passing, and I read the preamble [4] to Mr. Harley's, full of his praises. Lewis and I dined with Ford; I found the wine; two flasks of my Florence, and two bottles of six that Dr. Raymond sent me of French wine; he sent it to me to drink with Sir Robert Raymond, and Mr. Harley's brother, whom I had introduced him to; but they never could find time to come; and now I have left the town, and it is too late. Raymond will think it a cheat. What care I, sirrah?

10. Pshaw, pshaw. Patrick brought me four letters to-day: from Dilly at Bath; Joe; Parvisol; and what was the fourth, who can tell? Stand away, who'll guess? Who can it be? You old man with a stick, can you tell who the fourth is from? Iss, an please your honour, it is from one madam MD, Number Fourteen. Well; but I can't send this away now, because it was here, and I was in town, but it shall go on Saturday, and this is Thursday night, and it will be time enough for Wexford. Take my method: I write here to Parvisol to lend Stella twenty pound, and to take her note promissary to pay it in half a

---

[1] Cholmeley Dering, fifth baronet, born 1679. See Letter XXI., April 28.
[2] Richard Thornhill was tried at the Old Bailey, May 18, 1711, and found guilty of manslaughter only. . . . The fatal duel is the subject of No. 84 of the *Spectator*, where Thornhill, under the name of Spinamont, bewails the misfortune of having slain his friend, and the tyranny of custom that had forced him into the field.—D. L. P.
[3] Tothill Fields, Westminster.
[4] Written by Swift himself, in a very pompous strain of laudation. Harley was made Earl of Oxford and Mortimer, Baron Wigmore.—D. L. P.

year, &c. You shall see, and if you want more, let me know afterwards; and be sure my money shall be always paid constantly too. Have you been good or ill housewives pray?

11. Joe has written to me to get him a collector's place, nothing less; he says all the world knows of my great intimacy with Mr. Harley, and that the smallest word to him will do. This is the constant cant of puppies who are at a distance, and strangers to Courts and ministers. My answer is this; which pray send; That I am ready to serve Joe, as far as I can; that I have spoken to the duke of Ormond about his money, as I writ to Warburton; that for the particular he mentions, it is a work of time, which I cannot think of at present. But if accidents and opportunities should happen hereafter, I would not be wanting; that I know best how far my credit goes; that he is at distance, and cannot judge; that I would be glad to do him good; and if Fortune throws an opportunity in my way, I shall not be wanting. This is my answer; which you may send or read to him. Pray contrive that Parvisol may not run away with my two hundred pound, but get Burton's [1] note, and let the money be returned me by bill. Don't laugh, for I will be suspicious. Teach Parvisol to inclose, and direct the outside to Mr. Lewis. I will answer your letter in my next, only what I take notice of here excepted. I forgot to tell you, that at the court of requests to-day I could not find a dinner I liked, and it grew late, and I dined with Mrs. Vanhomrigh, &c.

12. Morning. I will finish this letter before I go to town, because I shall be busy, and have neither time nor place there. Farewel, &c. &c.

LETTER XXIII

Chelsea, *May* 12, 1711.

I SENT you my twenty-second this afternoon in town. I dined with Mr. Harley and the old club, lord Rivers, lord keeper, and Mr. secretary. They rallied me last week, and said I must have Mr. St. John's leave, so I writ to him yesterday, that foreseeing I should never dine again with Sir Simon Harcourt, knight, and Robert Harley, esq.; I was resolved to do it to-day. The jest is, that before Saturday next we expect they will be lords: for Mr. Harley's patent is drawing to be earl of Oxford. Mr. secretary and I came away at seven, and he brought me to

---

[1] Burton, a famous banker in Dublin.—D. S.

our town's end in his coach; so I lost my walk. St. John read my letter to the company, which was all raillery, and past purely.

13. It rained all last night and this morning as heavy as lead; but I just got fair weather to walk to town before church. The roads are all over in deep puddle. The hay of our town is almost fit to be mowed. I went to court after church (as I always do on Sundays) and then dined with Mr. secretary, who has engaged me for every Sunday; and poor MD dined at home upon a bit of veal, and a pint of wine. Is it not plaguy insipid to tell you every day where I dine; yet now I have got into the way of it, I cannot forbear it neither. Indeed, Mr. Presto, you had better go answer MD's letter, N. 14. I'll answer it when I please, Mr. Doctor. What's that you say? The Court was very full this morning, expecting Mr. Harley would be declared earl of Oxford, and have the treasurer's staff. Mr. Harley never comes to Court at all; somebody there askt me the reason; Why, said I, the lord of Oxford knows. He always goes to the queen by the back stairs. I was told for certain, your jacka-napes, lord Santry,[1] was dead, captain Cammock[2] assured me so; and now he's alive again, they say; but that shan't do: he shall be dead to me as long as he lives. Dick Tighe[3] and I meet and never stir our hats. I am resolved to mistake him for Witherington, the little nasty lawyer that came up to me so sternly at the Castle the day I left Ireland. I'll ask the gentle-man I saw walking with him, how long Witherington has been in town.

14. I went to town to-day by water. The hail quite dis-couraged me from walking, and there is no shade in the greatest part of the way: I took the first boat; and had a footman my companion; then I went again by water, and dined in the city with a printer, to whom I carried a pamphlet in manuscript, that Mr. secretary gave me. The printer sent it to the secretary for his approbation, and he desired me to look it over, which I did, and found it a very scurvy piece. The reason I tell you so, is because it was done by your parson *Slap, Scrap, Flap,* (what

[1] Henry Barry (1680–1734·5), third Baron Barry of Santry, a Whig. His only son, the last Lord Santry, a member of the Hell-fire Club in Dublin, was convicted of murder in 1739, pardoned, and regranted his estates in 1741.

[2] There was a George Camocke (1666?–1722?), a captain in the navy, commander of the *Speedwell* frigate. He deserted to the service of Spain and became a rear-admiral in the Spanish navy 1717–18. He fought against the British fleet in 1718.

[3] *See* Letter VII., Oct. 26, 1710.

d'ye call him) *Trap*, your chancellor's chaplain. 'Tis called *A Character* of the present set of Whigs, and is going to be printed, and no doubt the author will take care to produce it in Ireland. Dr. Freind was with me, and pulled out a two-penny pamphlet just published, called, *The State of Wit*,[1] giving a character of all the papers that have come out of late. The author seems to be a Whig, yet he speaks very highly of a paper called the *Examiner*, and says the supposed author of it is Dr. Swift. But above all things he praises the *Tatlers* and *Spectators*; and I believe Steele and Addison were privy to the printing of it. Thus is one treated by these impudent dogs. And that villain Curl[2] has scraped up some trash, and calls it Dr. Swift's miscellanies[3] with the name at large: and I can get no satisfaction of him. Nay, Mr. Harley told me he had read it, and only laughed at me before lord keeper, and the rest. Since I came home I have been sitting with the prolocutor, dean Atterbury, who is my neighbour over the way; but generally keeps in town with his convocation. 'Tis late, &c.

15. My walk to town to-day was after ten, and prodigiously hot: I dined with lord Shelburn, and have desired Mrs. Pratt, who lodges there, to carry over Mrs. Walls's tea; I hope she will do it, and they talk of going in a fortnight. My way is this; I leave my best gown and periwig at Mrs. Vanhomrigh's, then walk up the Pall-mall, through the Park, out at Buckingham-house, and so to Chelsea a little beyond the Church: I set out about sun-set, and get here in something less than an hour; it is two good miles and just five thousand seven hundred and forty-eight steps; so there is four miles a day walking, without reckoning what I walk while I stay in town. When I pass the Mall in the evening it is prodigious to see the number of ladies walking there; and I always cry shame at the ladies of Ireland, who never walk at all, as if their legs were of no use, but to be *laid aside*. I have been now almost three weeks here, and I thank God, am much better in my head, if it does but continue. I tell you what, if I was with you, when we went to Stoyte at Donnybrook, we would only take a coach to the hither end of Stephen's-Green, and from thence go every step on foot, yes

[1] Gay is supposed to have been the author.—D. L. P.
[2] Edmund Curll (1675-1747), bookseller, "at the Peacock without Temple Bar," maligned by Pope in the *Dunciad* as "Dauntless Curll." He was, later, of the Pope's Head in Rose Street, Covent Garden.
[3] Four days before this, a volume of Miscellanies in prose and verse, without the name of any author, but consisting wholly of pieces written by Dr. Swift, had been published by Morphew.—N.

faith, every step; it would do: DD[1] goes as well as Presto. Every body tells me I look better already; for faith I lookt sadly, that's certain. My breakfast is milk porridge: I don't love it, faith I hate it, but 'tis cheap and wholesome; and I hate to be obliged to either of those qualities for any thing.

16. I wonder why Presto will be so tedious in answering MD's letters; because he would keep the best to the last, I suppose. Well, Presto must be humoured, it must be as he will have it, or there will be an old to do. Dead with heat, are not you very hot? My walks make my forehead sweat rarely; sometimes my morning journey is by water, as it was to-day with one parson Richardson,[2] who came to see me, on his going to Ireland; and with him I send Mrs. Walls's tea, and three books I got from the lords of the treasury for the College.[3] I dined with lord Shelburn to-day; lady Kerry and Mrs. Pratt are going likewise for Ireland.—Lord I forgot, I dined with Mr. Prior to-day at his house, with dean Atterbury and others; and came home pretty late, and I think I'm in a fuzz, and don't know what I say, never saw the like.

17. Sterne came here by water to see me this morning, and I went back with him to his boat. He tells me, that Mrs. Edgworth married a fellow in her journey to Chester; so I believe she little thought of any body's box but her own. I desired Sterne to give me directions where to get the box in Chester, which he says he will to-morrow, and I will write to Richardson to get it up there as he goes by, and whip it over. It is directed to Mrs. Curry: you must caution her of it, and desire her to send it you when it comes. Sterne says Jemmy Leigh loves London mightily; that makes him stay so long, I believe, and not Sterne's business, which Mr. Harley's accident has put much backward. We expect now every day that he will be earl of Oxford and lord treasurer. His patent is passing; but they say, lord keeper's not yet, at least his son, young Harcourt, told me so t'other day. I dined to-day privately with my friend Lewis at his lodgings at Whitehall. T'other day at Whitehall I met a lady of my acquaintance, whom I had not seen before since I came to England: we were mighty glad to see each other, and she has engaged me to visit her, as I design to do. It is one Mrs. Colledge: she has lodgings at Whitehall, having been seamstress to king William, worth three hundred a year.

[1] [Sir Henry Craik read "It would do DD good as well as Presto."] In this passage DD signifies both Dingley and Stella.—D. S.
[2] *See* Letter XVII., March 6, 1710-11.
[3] The University of Dublin.—D. S.

Her father[1] was a fanatick joiner, hanged for treason in Shaftsbury's plot. This noble person and I were brought acquainted, some years ago, by lady Berkeley. I love good creditable acquaintance: I love to be the worst of the company: I am not of those that say, For want of company welcome trumpery. I was this evening with lady Kerry and Mrs. Pratt at Vauxhall, to hear the nightingals; but they are almost past singing.

18. I was hunting the secretary to-day in vain about some business, and dined with colonel Crowe,[2] late governor of Barbadoes, and your friend Sterne was the third: he is very kind to Sterne, and helps him in his business, which lies asleep till Mr. Harley is lord treasurer, because nothing of moment is now done in the treasury, the change being expected every day. I sat with dean Atterbury till one o'clock after I came home; so 'tis late, &c.

19. Do you know that about our town we are mowing already and making hay, and it smells so sweet as we walk through the flowry meads; but the hay-making nymphs are perfect drabs, nothing so clean and pretty as further in the country. There is a mighty increase of dirty wenches in straw hats since I knew London. I staid at home till five o'clock, and dined with dean Atterbury; then went by water to Mr. Harley's, where the Saturday Club was met, with the addition of the duke of Shrewsbury. I whispered lord Rivers, that I did not like to see a stranger among us; and the rogue told it aloud: but Mr. secretary said, The duke writ to have leave; so I appeared satisfied, and so we laughed. Mr. secretary told me the duke of Buckingham had been talking to him much about me, and desired my acquaintance. I answered, It could not be; for he had not made sufficient advances. Then the duke of Shrewsbury said, he thought that duke was not used to make advances. I said, I could not help that; for I always expected advances in proportion to men's quality, and more from a duke than other men.[3] The duke replied, that he did not mean any thing of his quality; which was handsomely said enough; for he meant his pride: and I have invented a notion to believe that

---

[1] Stephen College (1635?–1681).

[2] Mitford Crow (d. 1719), governor of Barbadoes 1707–1711. Mr. Aitken says charges of bribery were brought against him in 1710—he was probably in England at this juncture to answer the accusations.

[3] Buckingham was very proud; and Swift was probably piqued that he had (as stated in a former letter) made an advance, by calling on the duke, to which there had been no response.—D. L. P.

nobody is proud. At ten all the company went away; and from ten till twelve Mr. Harley and I sat together, where we talked through a great deal of matters I had a mind to settle with him, and then walked, in a fine moon-shine night, to Chelsea, where I got by one. Lord Rivers conjured me not to walk so late; but I would, because I had no other way; but I had no money to lose.

20. By what lord keeper told me last night, I find he will not be made a peer so soon; but Mr. Harley's patent for earl of Oxford is now drawing, and will be done in three days. We made him own it, which he did scurvily, and then talkt of it like the rest. Mr. secretary had too much company with him to-day; so I came away soon after dinner. I give no man liberty to swear or talk b—dy, and I found some of them were in constraint, so I left them to themselves. I wish you a merry Whitsuntide, and pray tell me how you pass away your time: but faith, you are going to Wexford, and I fear this letter is too late; it shall go on Thursday, and sooner it cannot, I have so much business to hinder me answering yours. Where must I direct in your absence? Do you quit your lodgings?

21. Going to town this morning, I met in the Pall-mall a clergyman of Ireland, whom I love very well and was glad to see, and with him a little jackanapes of Ireland too, who married Nanny Swift, uncle Adam's[1] daughter, one Perry; perhaps you may have heard of him. His wife has sent him here to get a place from Lownds;[2] because my uncle and Lownds married two sisters, and Lownds is a great man here in the treasury[3]; but by good luck I have no acquaintance with him: however, he expected I should be his friend to Lownds, and one word of mine, &c. the old cant. But I will not go two yards to help him. I dined with Mrs. Vanhomrigh, where I keep my best gown and periwig to put on when I come to town and be a spark.

22. I dined to-day in the city, and coming home this evening, I met Sir Thomas Mansel and Mr. Lewis in the Park. Lewis whispered me, that Mr. Harley's patent for earl of Oxford was passed in Mr. secretary St. John's office; so to-morrow or next

---

[1] Adam Swift never left Ireland. He lived at Greencastle, co. Antrim. Died before May, 1704.

[2] William Lowndes (1652–1724), Secretary to the Treasury from 1695 till his death.

[3] Gay addressed some humourous verses, "To my very ingenious and worthy friend William Lownds, esq., Author of that celebrated Treatise in folio, called The Land Tax Bill."—N.

day I suppose he will be declared earl of Oxford, and have the staff. This man has grown by persecutions, turnings out, and stabbing. What waiting, and crowding, and bowing, will be at his levee? yet, if human nature be capable of so much constancy, I should believe he will be the same man still, bating the necessary forms of grandeur he must keep up. 'Tis late, sirrahs, and I'll go sleep.

23. Morning. I sate up late last night, and waked late to-day; but will now answer your letter in bed before I go to town, and I will send it to-morrow; for perhaps you mayn't go so soon to Wexford.—No, you are not out in your number; the last was Number 14, and so I told you twice or thrice; will you never be satisfied? What shall we do for poor Stella? Go to Wexford, for God's sake: I wish you were to walk there by three miles a day, with a good lodging at every mile's end. Walking has done me so much good, that I cannot but prescribe it often to poor Stella. Parvisol has sent me a bill for fifty pounds, which I am sorry for, having not written to him for it, only mentioned it two months ago; but I hope he will be able to pay[1] you what I have drawn upon him for: he never sent me any sum before but one bill of twenty pounds, half a year ago. You are as welcome as my blood to every farthing I have in the world; and all that grieves me is, I am not richer, for MD's sake, as hope saved. I suppose you give up your lodgings when you go to Wexford; yet that will be inconvenient too: yet I wish again you were under the necessity of rambling the country until Michaelmas, faith. No, let him keep the shelves, with a pox; yet they are exacting people about those four weeks, or Mrs. Brent may have the shelves, if she please. I am obliged to your dean for his kind offer of lending me money. Will that be enough to say? A hundred people would lend me money, or to any man who has not the reputation of a squanderer. O faith, I should be glad to be in the same kingdom with MD, however, although you were[2] at Wexford. But I am kept here by a most capricious fate, which I would break through, if I could do it with decency or honour.—To return without some mark of distinction, would look extremely little; and I would likewise gladly be somewhat richer than I am. I will say no more, but beg you to be easy, 'till Fortune take her course, and to believe that MD's felicity is the great end I aim at in all my pursuits. And so let us talk no more on this subject, which makes me melancholy, and that I would fain divert. Believe

---

[1] D. S. has "pay." Others have "tell."   [2] D. S. 4to; 8vo has "are."

me, no man breathing at present has less share of happiness in life than I: I do not say I am unhappy at all, but that every thing here is tasteless to me for want of being as [? where] I would be. And so, a short sigh, and no more of this. Well, come and let's see what's next, young women. Pox take Mrs. Edgworth and Sterne: I will take some methods about that box. What orders would you have me give about the picture? Can't you do with it as if it were your own? No, I hope Manley will keep his place; for I hear nothing of Sir Thomas Frankland's losing his. Send nothing under cover to Mr. Addison, but to Erasmus Lewis, Esq., at my lord Dartmouth's office at White-hall. Direct your outside so.—Poor dear Stella, don't write in the dark, nor in the light neither, but dictate to Dingley; she is a naughty healthy girl, and may drudge for both. Are you good company together? and don't you quarrel too often? Pray, love one another, and kiss one another just now, as Dingley is reading this; for you quarrelled this morning just after Mrs. Marget had poured water on Stella's head: I heard the little bird say so. Well, I have answered every thing in your letter that required it, and yet the second side is not full. I'll come home at night, and say more; and to-morrow this goes for certain. Go, get you gone to your own chambers, and let Presto rise like a modest gentleman, and walk to town. I fancy I begin to sweat less in the forehead by constant walking than I used to do; but then I shall be so sun-burnt, the ladies won't like me. Come, let me rise, sirrahs. Morrow.—At night. I dined with Ford to-day at his lodgings, and I found wine out of my own cellar, some of my own chest of the great duke's wine: it begins to turn. They say wine with you in Ireland is half a crown a bottle. 'Tis as Stella says, nothing that once grows dear in Ireland ever grows cheap again, except corn, with a pox, to ruin the parson. I had a letter to-day from the archbishop of Dublin, giving me further thanks about vindi-cating him to Mr. Harley and Mr. St. John, and telling me a long story about your mayor's election, wherein I find he has had a finger, and given way to further talk about him; but we know nothing of it here yet.[1] This walking to and fro, and dressing myself, takes up so much of my time, that I cannot go among company so much as formerly; yet what must a body do? I thank God I yet continue much better since I left the

---

[1] The Whig Corporation of Dublin had, it would seem, rejected four mayors and eight sheriffs, all regularly chosen by the city, on the ground of their political principles; and the Archbishop's letter betrayed that his heart was really with the enemies of the Ministry.—D. L. P.

town; I know not how long it may last. I am sure it has done
me some good for the present. I do not totter as I did, but
walk firm as a cock, only once or twice for a minute, I don't
know how; but it went off, and I never followed it. Does Dingley
read my hand as well as ever? do you, sirrah? Poor Stella must
not read Presto's ugly small hand. Preserve your eyes, If you
be wise. Your friend Walls's tea will go in a day or two towards
Chester by one parson Richardson. My humble service to her,
and to good Mrs. Stoyte, and Catherine; and pray walk while
you continue in Dublin. I expect your next but one will be
from Wexford. God bless dearest MD.

24. Morning. Mr. secretary has sent his groom hither to invite
me to dinner to-day, &c. God Almighty for ever bless and preserve
you both, and give you health, &c. Amen. Farewel, &c.

Don't I often say the same thing two or three times in the
same letter, sirrah?

Great wits, they say, have but short memories; that's good
vile conversation.

LETTER XXIV

Chelsea, *May* 24, 1711.

MORNING. Once in my life the number of my letters and of the
day of the month is the same; that's lucky, boys; that's a sign
that things will meet, and that we shall make a figure together.
What, will you still have the impudence to say *London, Eng-*
land, because I say *Dublin, Ireland*? Is there no difference
between London and Dublin, saucy boxes? I have sealed up
my letter, and am going to town. Morrow, sirrahs.—At night.
I dined with the secretary to-day; we sat down between five
and six. Mr. Harley's patent passed this morning: he is now
earl of Oxford, earl Mortimer, and lord Harley of Wigmore-
Castle. My letter was sealed, or I would have told you this
yesterday; but the publick news may tell it you. The queen,
for all her favour, has kept a rod for him in her closet this
week; I suppose he will take it from her though in a day or
two.[1] At eight o'clock this evening it rained prodigiously, as
it did from five; however I set out, and in half way the rain
lessened, and I got home, but tolerably wet; and this is the
first wet walk I have had in a month's time that I am here: but
however I got to bed, after a short visit to Atterbury.

25. It rained this morning, and I went to town by water;

---

[1] The treasurer's staff. The office was still in commission.

and Ford and I dined with Mr. Lewis by appointment. I ordered Patrick to bring my gown and periwig to Mr. Lewis, because I designed to go to see lord Oxford, and so I told the dog; but he never came, though I staid an hour longer than I appointed, so I went in my old gown, and sat with him two hours, but could not talk over some business I had with him; so he has desired me to dine with him on Sunday, and I must disappoint the secretary. My lord set me down at a Coffee-house, where I waited for the dean of Carlisle's chariot to bring me to Chelsea; for it has rained prodigiously all this afternoon. The dean did not come himself, but sent me his chariot, which has cost me two shillings to the coachman; and so I am got home, and Lord knows what is become of Patrick. I think I must send him over to you; for he is an intolerable rascal. If I had come without a gown, he would have served me so, though my life and preferment should have lain upon it: and I am making a livery for him will cost me four pounds; but I will order the taylor to-morrow to stop till further orders. My lord Oxford can't yet abide to be called My lord; and when I called him My lord, he called me Dr. Thomas Swift, which he always does when he has a mind to teaze me.[1] By a second hand, he proposed my being his chaplain, which I by a second hand excused; but we had no talk of it to-day: but I will be no man's chaplain alive. But I must go and be busy.

26. I never saw Patrick till this morning, and that only once, for I dressed myself without him; and when I went to town, he was out of the way. I immediately sent for the taylor, and ordered him to stop his hand in Patrick's cloaths till further orders. Oh, if it were in Ireland, I should have turned him off ten times ago; and it is no regard to him, but myself, that has made me keep him so long. Now I am afraid to give the rogue his cloaths. What shall I do? I wish MD were here to intreat for him, just here at the bed's side. Lady Ashburnham has been engaging me this long time to dine with her, and I set to-day apart for it; and whatever was the mistake, she sent me word, she was at dinner and undressed, but would be glad to see me in the afternoon; so I dined with Mrs. Vanhomrigh,

---

[1] A "little parson cousin" of Swift's, Thomas Swift, rector of Putenham, Surrey, and son of Swift's Oxford uncle Thomas, "certainly induced his uncle Davenant to make interest to procure him a war-chaplaincy on the ground of his having had some hand in the *Tale*" [*of a Tub*] (Forster). This credit was claimed for Thomas in *A Complete Key to the Tale of a Tub*, published 1710. *See also* Letter XXXVIII., Jan. 8, 1711-12, note by Nichols.

and would not go see her at all, in a huff. My fine Florence is turning sour with a vengeance, and I have not drank half of it. As I was coming home to-night, Sir Thomas Mansel and Tom Harley[1] met me in the Park, and made me walk with them till nine, like unreasonable whelps: so I got not here till ten: but it was a fine evening, and the foot-path clean enough already after this hard rain.

27. Going this morning to town, I saw two old lame fellows walking to a brandy-shop, and when they got to the door, stood a long time complimenting who should go in first. Though this be no jest to tell, it was an admirable one to see. I dined to-day with my lord Oxford and the ladies, the new countess, and lady Betty,[2] who has been these three days a lady born. My lord left us at seven, and I had no time to speak to him about some affairs; but he promises in a day or two we shall dine alone; which is mighty likely, considering we expect every moment that the queen will give him the staff, and then he will be so crowded, he will be good for nothing: for aught I know he may have it to-night at council.

28. I had a petition sent me t'other day from one Stephen Gernon, setting forth that he formerly lived with Harry Tenison,[3] who gave him an employment of gauger; and that he was turned out after Harry's death, and came for England, and is now starving, or, as he expresses it, that the staff of life has been of late a stranger to his appetite. To-day the poor fellow called, and I know him very well, a young slender fellow with freckles in his face; you must remember him; he waited at table as a better sort of servant. I gave him a crown, and promised to do what I could to help him to a service, which I did for Harry Tenison's memory. It was bloody hot walking to-day, and I was so lazy I dined where my new gown was, at Mrs. Vanhomrigh's, and came back like a fool, and the dean of Carlisle has sat with me till eleven. Lord Oxford has not the staff yet.

29. I was this morning in town by ten, though it was shaving-day, and went to the secretary about some affairs, then visited

---

[1] From later entries, it is gathered that this was a cousin-german of Robert's, who became "secretary to the treasury"—possibly assistant to Lowndes (see Letter XXIII., May 21).

[2] Elizabeth (d. 1713), daughter of "the celebrated Robert." She married (1712) Peregrine Hyde Osborne, Marquess of Caermarthen and afterwards third Duke of Leeds. She is said to have been twenty-eight at her death —although described as twenty-one years old in the marriage licence of the year before—the same age as the bridegroom.

[3] According to Mr. Aitken, M.P. for co. Louth.

the duke and duchess of Ormond; but the latter was dressing to go out, and I could not see her. My lord Oxford had the staff given him this morning; so now I must call him lord Oxford no more, but lord treasurer: I hope he will stick there: this is twice he has changed his name this week; and I heard to-day in the city (where I dined) that he will very soon have the garter. — Prithee, don't you observe how strangely I have changed my company and manner of living? I never go to a Coffee-house; you hear no more of Addison, Steele, Henley, lady Lucy, Mrs. Finch,[1] lord Somers, lord Hallifax, &c. I think I have altered for the better. Did I tell you, the archbishop of Dublin has writ me a long letter of a squabble in your town about chusing a mayor, and that he apprehended some censure for the share he had in it. I have not heard any thing of it here; but I shall not be always able to defend him. We hear your bishop Hickman is dead[2]; but nobody here will do any thing for me in Ireland; so they may die as fast or slow as they please.—Well, you are constant to your deans, and your Stoyte, and your Walls. Walls will have her tea soon; parson Richardson is either going or gone to Ireland, and has it with him. I hear Mr. Lewis has two letters for me: I could not call for them to-day, but will to-morrow; and perhaps one of them may be from our little MD, who knows, man? who can tell? Many more unlikely thing has happened.—Pshaw, I write so plaguy little, I can hardly see it myself. *Write bigger, sirrah*[3] Presto. No, but I won't. Oh, you are a saucy rogue, Mr. Presto, you are so impudent. Come, dear rogues, let Presto go to sleep: I have been with the dean, and 'tis near twelve.

30. I am so hot and lazy after my morning's walk, that I loitered at Mrs. Vanhomrigh's, where my best gown and peri-wig are, and out of mere listlessness dine there very often, so I did to-day; but I got little MD's letter, N. 15 (you see, sirrahs, I remember to tell the number) from Mr. Lewis, and I read it in a closet they lend me at Mrs. Van's, and I find Stella is a saucy rogue and a great writer, and can write finely still when her hand's in, and her pen good. When I came here to-night, I had a mighty mind to go swim after I was cool, for my lodging is just by the river, and I went down with only my

---

[1] Anne (c. 1666–1720), daughter of Sir William Kingsmill, of Sidmonton, Hants, married (1684) Heneage Finch, afterwards fourth Earl of Winchilsea. Authoress of *The Spleen* and other poems.

[2] He was not. Charles Hickman (1648–1713) was Bishop of Derry from 1703. An Englishman.

[3] These words in italicks are written in a large round hand.—D. S.

night-gown and slippers on at eleven, but came up again; however, one of these nights I will venture.

31. I was so hot this morning with my walk, that I resolve to do so no more during this violent burning weather. It is comical, that now we happen to have such heat to ripen the fruit, there has been the greatest blast that was ever known, and almost all the fruit is despaired of. I dined with lord Shelburn; lady Kerry and Mrs. Pratt are going to Ireland. I went this evening to lord treasurer, and sat about two hours with him in mixt company; he left us, and went to Court, and carried two staves with him, so I suppose we shall have a new lord steward, or comptroller to-morrow; I smoakt that state secret out by that accident. I won't answer your letter yet, sirrahs, no I won't, Madam.

June 1. I wish you a merry month of June. I dined again with the Vans and Sir Andrew Fountain. I always give them a flask of my Florence, which now begins to spoil, but 'tis near an end. I went this afternoon to Mrs. Vedeau's, and brought away Madam Dingley's parchment and letter of attorney. Mrs. Vedeau tells me, she has sent the bill a fortnight ago. I will give the parchment to Ben. Tooke, and you shall send him a letter of attorney at your leisure, inclosed to Mr. Presto. Yes, I now think your mackarel is full as good as ours, which I did not think formerly. I was bit about the two staves, for there is no new officer made to-day. This letter will find you still in Dublin, I suppose, or at Donnybrook, or losing your money at Walls' (how does she do?)

2. I missed this day by a blunder and dining in the city.[1]

3. No boats on Sunday, never: so I was forced to walk, and so hot by the time I got to Ford's lodging, that I was quite spent; I think the weather is mad. I could not go to church. I dined with the secretary as usual, and old colonel Graham[2] that lived at Bagshot-Heath, and they said it was colonel Graham's house. Pshaw, I remember it very well, when I used to go for a walk to London from Moor-park. What, I warrant you don't remember the golden farmer neither, *Figgarkick Soley?* [3]

---

[1] This is interlined in the original.—D. S.

[2] Mr. Aitken says he was James Graham (1649–1730), M.P. for Appleby and then for Westmorland.

[3] William Davis (1627–1690), ostensibly a farmer, but really a notorious highwayman, was called the Golden Farmer, and hung in chains on Bagshot Heath. Obviously, the inn at Frimley, on the hill between Bagshot and Farnborough (mentioned by Leslie Stephen, and no doubt here alluded to by Swift), was originally named the Golden Farmer (afterwards it was renamed the Jolly Farmer) in memory of Davis. Mr. Aitken's sug-

4. When must we answer this letter, this N. 15 of our little MD? Heat and laziness, and Sir Andrew Fountain made me dine to-day again at Mrs. Van's; and, in short, this weather is insupportable; how is it with you? Lady Betty Butler, and lady Ashburnham sat with me two or three hours this evening in my closet at Mrs. Van's. They are very good girls, and if lady Betty went to Ireland you should let her be acquainted with you. How does Dingley do this hot weather? Stella, I think, never complains of it, she loves hot weather. There has not been a drop of rain since Friday sennight. Yes, you do love hot weather, naughty Stella, you do so, and Presto can't abide it. Be a good girl then, and I'll love you; and love one another, and don't be quarrelling girls.

5. I dined in the city to-day, and went from hence early to town, and visited the duke of Ormond, and Mr. secretary. They say, my lord treasurer has a dead warrant in his pocket, they mean, a list of those who are to be turned out of employment, and we every day now expect those changes. I past by the treasury to-day, and saw vast crowds waiting to give lord treasurer petitions as he passes by. He is now at the top of power and favour: he keeps no levees yet. I am cruel thirsty this hot weather.—I am just this minute going to swim. I take Patrick down with me to hold my nightgown, shirt and slippers, and borrow a napkin of my landlady for a cap.—So farewel till I come up; but there's no danger, don't be frighted—I have been swimming this half hour and more; and when I was coming out I dived, to make my head and all through wet, like a cold bath; but as I dived, the napkin fell off and is lost, and I have that to pay for. O faith, the great stones were so sharp, I could hardly set my feet on them as I came out. It was pure and warm. I got to bed, and will now go sleep.

6. Morning. This letter shall go to-morrow; so I will answer yours when I come home to-night. I feel no hurt from last night's swimming. I lie with nothing but the sheet over me, and my feet quite bare. I must rise and go to town before the tide is against me. Morrow, sirrahs; dear sirrahs, morrow.—At night. I never felt so hot a day as this since I was born. I dined with lady Betty Germain, and there was the young earl of Berkeley

gestion, that "Figgarkick Soley" is *little* for "Pilgarlic" something—it may be really *sollahs* and not *soley*—seems reasonable. "Pilgarlic" was a common enough term of reproach in Ireland at one time. "Sollahs" we shall become familiar with when we get past Letter XL.: that is, beyond the influence of Deane Swift's editing.

and his fine lady.[1] I never saw her before, nor think her near
so handsome as she passes for.—After dinner Mr. Bertue [2]
would not let me put ice in my wine; but said my lord Dor-
chester [3] got the bloody-flux with it, and that it was the worst
thing in the world. Thus are we plagued, thus are we plagued;
yet I have done it five or six times this summer, and was but the
drier and the hotter for it. Nothing makes me so excessively
peevish as hot weather. Lady Berkeley after dinner clapt my
hat on another lady's head, and she in roguery put it upon
the rails. I minded them not; but in two minutes they called
me to the window, and lady Carteret [4] shewed me my hat out
of her window five doors off, where I was forced to walk to it,
and pay her and old lady Weymouth [5] a visit, with some more
beldames. Then I went and drank coffee, and made one or
two puns with lord Pembroke,[6] and designed to go to lord
treasurer; but it was too late, and beside I was half broiled,
and broiled without butter; for I never sweat after dinner, if
I drink any wine. Then I set an hour with lady Betty Butler
at tea, and every thing made me hotter and drier. Then I walkt
home, and was here by ten, so miserably hot, that I was in as
perfect a passion as ever I was in my life at the greatest affront
or provocation. Then I sat an hour, till I was quite dry and cool
enough to go swim; which I did, but with so much vexation,
that I think I have given it over: for I was every moment
disturbed by boats, rot them; and that puppy Patrick, standing
ashore, would let them come within a yard or two, and then
call sneakingly to them. The only comfort I proposed here in
hot weather is gone; for there is no jesting with those boats
after 'tis dark: I had none last night. I dived to dip my head,
and held my cap on with both my hands, for fear of losing it.
—Pox take the boats! Amen. 'Tis near twelve, and so I'll
answer your letter (it strikes twelve now) to-morrow morning.

7. Morning. Well, now let us answer MD's letter N. 15, 15,
15, 15. Now have I told you the number? 15, 15; there, impu-

[1] See Letter XIV., Jan. 23, 1710-11.

[2] Mr. Aitken surmises that the Hon. James Bertie, second son of first
Earl of Abingdon, and M.P. for Middlesex, is meant.

[3] Evelyn Pierrepont (c. 1665-1725-6), first Marquess, afterwards Duke
of Kingston-upon-Hull.

[4] Frances (1693-4-1743), daughter of Sir Robert Worsley, Bart., married
Baron Carteret (see Letter XII., Jan. 4, 1710-11), afterwards Earl
Granville, in 1710.

[5] Frances (d. 1712), first daughter of Heneage Finch, first Earl of
Winchilsea, by second wife. She married Thomas Thynne (c. 1640-1714),
first Viscount Weymouth.

[6] See Letter VII., Oct. 28, 1710.

dence, to call names in the beginning of your letter, before you say, How do you do, Mr. Presto?—There's your breeding. Where's your manners, sirrah, to a gentleman? Get you gone, you couple of jades.—No, I never sit up late now; but this abominable hot weather will force me to eat or drink something that will do me hurt. I do venture to eat a few strawberries.— Why then, do you know in Ireland that Mr. St. John talkt so[1] in parliament? Your Whigs are plaguily bit; for he is intirely for their being all out.—And are you as vicious in snuff as ever? I believe, as you say, it does neither hurt nor good; but I have left it off, and when any body offers me their box, I take about a tenth part of what I used to do, and then just smell to it, and privately fling the rest away. I keep to my tobacco still,[2] as you say; but even much less of that than formerly, only mornings and evenings, and very seldom in the day.—As for Joe, I have recommended his case heartily to my lord lieutenant; and, by his direction, given a memorial of it to Mr. Southwell, to whom I have recommended it likewise. I can do no more, if he were my brother. His business will be to apply himself to Southwell. And you must desire Raymond, if Price of Galway comes to town, to desire him to wait on Mr. Southwell, as recommended by me for one of the duke's chaplains, which was all I could do for him; and he must be presented to the duke, and make his court, and ply about and find out some vacancy, and solicit early for it. The bustle about your mayor I had before, as I told you, from the archbishop of Dublin. Was Raymond not come till May 18? So he says fine things of me? Certainly he lies. I'm sure I used him indifferently enough, and we never once dined together, or walkt, or were in any third place, only he came sometimes to my lodgings, and even there was oftener denied than admitted.— What an odd bill[3] is that you sent of Raymond's? A bill upon one Murry in Chester, which depends entirely not only upon Raymond's honesty, but his discretion; and in money matters he is the last man I would depend on. Why should Sir Alexander Cairnes[4] in London pay me a bill, drawn by God knows who, upon Murry in Chester? I was at Cairnes's, and they can do

[1] In defence of Brydges. See Letter XXI., April 27.

[2] He does not mean smoaking, which he never practised, but snuffing up cut-and-dry tobacco, which sometimes was just coloured with Spanish snuff; and this he used all his life, but would not own that he took snuff.—D. S.

[3] A bill for £200. See Letter XXV., June 30.

[4] Sir Alexander Cairnes, of Monaghan, Bart.; an eminent banker; and father to Mary Lady Blaney, the wife to Cadwallader the seventh lord.—F.

no such thing. I went among some friends, who are merchants, and I find the bill must be sent to Murry, accepted by him, and then returned back, and then Cairnes may accept or refuse it as he pleases. Accordingly I gave Sir Thomas Frankland the bill, who has sent it to Chester, and ordered the post-master there to get it accepted, and then send it back, and in a day or two I shall have an answer; and therefore this letter must stay a day or two longer than I intended, and see what answer I get. Raymond should have written to Murry at the same time, to desire Sir Alexander Cairnes to have answered such a bill, if it come. But Cairnes's clerks (himself was not at home) said, they had received no notice of it, and could do nothing; and advised me to seud to Murry.—I have been six weeks to-day at Chelsea, and you know it but just now. And so dean —— thinks I write the *Medley*. Pox of his judgment; 'tis equal to his honesty. Then you han't seen the *Miscellany* yet. Why, 'tis a four shilling book: has nobody carried it over?—No, I believe Manley [1] will not lose his place: for his friend in England [2] is so far from being out, that he has taken a new patent since the post-office act; and his brother Jack Manley [3] here takes his part firmly; and I have often spoken to Southwell in his behalf, and he seems very well inclined to him. But the Irish folks here in general are horribly violent against him. Besides, he must consider he could not send Stella wine if he were put out. And so he is very kind, and sends you a dozen bottles of wine *at a time*, and you win eight shillings *at a time*; and how much do you lose? No, no, never one syllable about that, I warrant you.—Why this same Stella is so unmerciful a writer, she has hardly left any room for Dingley. If you have such Summer there as here, sure the Wexford waters are good by this time. I forgot what weather we had May 6th; go look in my journal. We had terrible rain the 24th and 25th, and never a drop since. Yes, yes, I remember Berested's bridge; the coach sosses up and down as one goes that way, just as at Hockley in the Hole. [4] I never impute any illness or health I have to good or ill weather, but to want of exercise, or ill air, or something I have eaten, or hard study, or sitting up; and so I fence against those as well as I can: but who a deuce can

[1] Isaac. *See* Letter III., Sept. 9, 1710, note.
[2] Sir T. Frankland. *See* Letter V., Oct. 1, and Letter XI., Dec. 14, 1710.
[3] *See* Letter V., Oct. 1, 1710, note.
[4] Re-named Ray Street, Clerkenwell. Once a place of very rowdy jollification.

help the weather? Will Seymor, the general,[1] was excessively hot with the sun shining full upon him; so he turns to the sun, and says, Hearkee, friend, you had better go and ripen cucumbers than plague me at this rate, &c. Another time fretting at the heat, a gentleman by said, It was such weather as pleased God: Seymor said, Perhaps it may; but I'm sure it pleases no body else. Why, madam Dingley, the First-Fruits are done. Southwell told me they went to enquire about them, and lord treasurer said they were done, and had been done long ago. And I'll tell you a secret you must not mention, that the duke of Ormond is ordered to take notice of them in his speech in your parliament: and I desire you will take care to say on occasion, that my lord treasurer Harley did it many months ago, before the duke was lord lieutenant. And yet I cannot possibly come over yet: so get you gone to Wexford, and make Stella well.—Yes, yes, I take care not to walk late; I never did but once, and there are five hundred people on the way as I walk.—Tisdall is a puppy, and I will excuse him the half hour he would talk with me. As for the *Examiner*, I have heard a whisper, that after that of this day, which tells what this parliament has done, you will hardly find them so good. I prophecy they will be trash for the future; and methinks in this day's *Examiner* the author talks doubtfully, as if he would write no more.[2] Observe whether the change be discovered in Dublin, only for your own curiosity, that's all. Make a mouth there. Mrs. Vedeau's business I have answered, and I hope the bill is not lost. Morrow. 'Tis stewing hot, but I must rise, and go to town between fire and water. Morrow, sirrahs both, morrow.—At night. I dined to-day with colonel Crowe, governor of Jamaica, and your friend Sterne. I presented Sterne to my lord treasurer's brother,[3] and gave him his case, and engaged him in his favour. At dinner there fell the swingingest long shower, and the most grateful to me, that ever I saw: it thundered fifty times at least, and the air is so cool, that a body is able to live; and I walkt home to-night with comfort, and without dirt. I went this evening to lord treasurer, and sat with him two hours, and we were in very good humour, and he

---

[1] Lieutenant-general. Mr. Aitken says he was second son of Sir Edward Seymour, Bart., of Bury Pomeroy, and retired 1717.

[2] The *Examiner* of 7th June, 1711, the last of Swift's series, sums up the advantages gained under Harley's Ministry, and declares that the whole nation is sensible of them, and that "the main design he had in writing these papers is fully executed."—D. L. P.

[3] Edward. *See* Letter XIII., Jan. 10, 1710-11.

abused me, and called me Dr. Thomas Swift fifty times: I have
told you he does that when he has mind to make me mad. Sir
Thomas Frankland gave me to-day a letter from Murry, accepting my bill; so all is well: only by a letter from Parvisol, I find
there are some perplexities.—Joe has likewise written to me,
to thank me for what I have done for him; and desires I would
write to the bishop of Clogher, that Tom Ashe[1] may not
hinder his father[2] from being portrief. I have written, and sent
to Joe several times, that I will not trouble myself at all about
Trim. I wish them their liberty; but they do not deserve it: so
tell Joe, and send to him. I am mighty happy with this rain:
I was at the end of my patience, but now I live again. This
cannot go till Saturday; and perhaps I may go out of town
with lord Shelburn and lady Kerry to-morrow for two or three
days. Lady Kerry has written to desire it; but to-morrow I
shall know further.—O this dear rain, I cannot forbear praising
it: I never felt myself to be revived so in my life. It lasted
from three till five, hard as a horn, and mixt with hail.

8. Morning. I am going to town, and will just finish this
there, if I go into the country with lady Kerry and lord Shelburn: so morrow, till an hour or two hence.—In town. I met
Cairnes, who, I suppose, will pay me the money; though he
says, I must send him the bill first, and I will get it done in
absence. Farewel, &c. &c.

LETTER XXV

Chelsea, *June* 9, 10, 11, 12, 13, 14,
15, 16, 17, 18, 19, 20.

I HAVE been all this time at Wicomb, between Oxford and
London, with lord Shelburn, who has the squire's house at the
town's end, and an estate there in a delicious country. Lady
Kerry and Mrs. Pratt were with us, and we passed our time
well enough; and there I wholly disengaged myself from all
publick thoughts, and every thing but MD, who had the impudence to send me a letter there; but I'll be revenged: I'll
answer it. This day, the 20th, I came from Wicomb with lady
Kerry after dinner, lighted at Hyde-Park corner, and walkt:
it was twenty-seven miles, and we came it in about five hours.

[1] Elder brother of the Bishop of Clogher, a squire with an estate of
£1000 a year in co. Meath. *See* Letter IV., Sept. 23, 1710; note on "Ballygall."
[2] Even Mr. Joseph Beaumont, the son, was at this time an old man,
whose gray locks were venerable; consequently his father was very
ancient; and yet the father lived till about the year 1719.—D. S.

21. I went at noon to see Mr. secretary at his office, and there was lord treasurer: so I killed two birds, &c. and we were glad to see one another, and so forth. And the secretary and I dined at Sir William Wyndham's, who married lady Catharine Seymor,[1] your acquaintance, I suppose. There were ten of us at dinner. It seems in my absence they had erected a Club, and made me one; and we made some laws to-day, which I am to digest, and add to, against next meeting. Our meetings are to be every Thursday: we are yet but twelve: lord keeper and lord treasurer were proposed; but I was against them, and so was Mr. secretary, though their sons are of it, and so they are excluded; but we design to admit the duke of Shrewsbury. The end of our Club is to advance conversation and friendship, and to reward deserving persons with our interest and recommendation. We take in none but men of wit or men of interest; and if we go on as we begin, no other Club in this town will be worth talking of. The solicitor general, Sir Robert Raymond, is one of our Club; and I ordered him immediately to write to your lord chancellor in favour of Dr. Raymond: so tell Raymond, if you see him; but I believe this will find you at Wexford. This letter will come three weeks after the last; so there is a week lost; but that is owing to my being out of town; yet I think it is right, because it goes inclosed to Mr. Reading:[2] and why should he know how often Presto writes to MD, pray? —I sat this evening with lady Betty Butler[3] and lady Ashburnham,[4] and then came home by eleven, and had a good cool walk; for we have had no extream hot weather this fortnight, but a great deal of rain at times, and a body can live and breathe. I hope it will hold so. We had peaches to-day.

22. I went late to-day to town, and dined with my friend Lewis. I saw Will. Congreve attending at the treasury, by order, with his brethren, the commissioners of the wine licences. I had often mentioned him with kindness to lord treasurer; and Congreve told me, that after they had answered to what they were sent for, my lord called him privately, and spoke to him with great kindness, promising his protection, &c. The poor man

[1] Sir William Wyndham (c. 1688–1740), Bart., at this time master of the buckhounds, was a supporter of St. John, and his lady was second daughter of Charles Seymour, sixth Duke of Somerset—she died 1731 (misprinted 1713 in Aitken).

[2] Mr. Aitken suggests Daniel Reading, M.P. for Newcastle, co. Dublin.

[3] Her ladyship, who had a very great appetite, and ate hearty suppers every night, lived to be above ninety years of age. She never was married.—N.

[4] Her sister.

said, he had been used so ill of late years, that he was quite
astonished at my lord's goodness, &c. and desired me to tell
my lord so; which I did this evening, and recommended him
heartily. My lord assured me he esteemed him very much, and
would be always kind to him; that what he said was to make
Congreve easy, because he knew people talked as if his lordship designed to turn every body out, and particularly Congreve; which indeed was true, for the poor man told me he
apprehended it. As I left my lord treasurer, I called on Congreve (knowing where he dined) and told him what had passed
between my lord and me: so I have made a worthy man easy,
and that is a good day's work. I am proposing to my lord
to erect a society or academy for correcting and settling our
language, that we may not perpetually be changing as we do.
He enters mightily into it, so does the dean of Carlisle[1]; and
I design to write a letter to lord treasurer with the proposals
of it, and publish it[2]; and so I told my lord, and he approves it.
Yesterday's was a sad *Examiner*, and last week was very indifferent, though some little scraps of the old spirit, as if he
had given some hints; but yesterday's is all trash. It is plain
the hand is changed.

23. I have not been in London to-day: for Dr. Gastrel[3] and
I dined, by invitation, with the dean of Carlisle, my neighbour; so I know not what they are doing in the world, a meer
country gentleman. And are not you ashamed both to go into
the country just when I did, and stay ten days, just as I did,
saucy monkies? But I never rode; I had no horses, and our
coach was out of order, and we went and came in a hired one.
Do you keep your lodgings when you go to Wexford? I suppose
you do; for you will hardly stay above two months. I have
been walking about our town to-night, and it is a very scurvy
place for walking. I am thinking to leave it, and return to
town, now the Irish folks are gone. Ford goes in three days.
How does Dingley divert herself while Stella is riding? work,
or read, or walk? Does Dingley ever read to you? Had you
ever a book with you in the country? Is all that left off?
confess. Well, I'll go sleep, 'tis past eleven, and I go early to
sleep; I write nothing at night but to MD.

24. Stratford and I, and pastoral Philips (just come from

---

[1] Atterbury was still "of Carlisle."
[2] *A Proposal for Correcting, Improving and Ascertaining the English
Tongue, in a Letter to the Most Honourable Robert Earl of Oxford and
Mortimer, Lord High Treasurer of Great Britain.* Benjamin Tooke, 1712.
[3] Rev. Francis Gastrell (1662-1725), D.D., afterwards Bishop of Chester.

Denmark) dined at Ford's to-day, who paid his way, and goes
for Ireland on Tuesday. The earl of Peterborow is returned from
Vienna without one servant: he left them scattered in several
towns of Germany.[1] I had a letter from him, four days ago,
from Hanover, where he desires I would immediately send him
an answer to his house at Parson's-Green,[2] about five miles off.
I wondered what he meant, till I heard he was come. He sent
expresses, and got here before them. He is above fifty, and as
active as one of five and twenty. I have not seen him yet, nor
know when I shall, or where to find him.

25. Poor duke of Shrewsbury has been very ill of a fever:
we were all in a fright about him: I thank God, he is better.
I dined to-day at lord Ashburnham's with his lady, for he was
not at home: she is a very good girl and always a great favourite
of mine. Sterne tells me, he has desired a friend to receive your
box in Chester, and carry it over. I fear he will miscarry in his
business, which was sent to the treasury before he was recommended; for I was positive only to second his recommendations,
and all his other friends failed him. However, on your account,
I will do what I can for him to-morrow with the secretary
of the treasury.

26. We had much company to-day at dinner at lord treasurer's.
Prior never fails: he is a much better courtier than I; and we
expect every day that he will be a commissioner of the customs,
and that in a short time a great many more will be turned out.
They blame lord treasurer for his slowness in turning people
out; but I suppose he has his reasons. They still keep my neighbour Atterbury in suspense about the deanry of Christ-Church,[3]
which has been above six months vacant, and he is heartily
angry. I reckon you are now preparing for your Wexford expedition; and poor Dingley is full of carking and caring, scolding. How long will you stay? Shall I be in Dublin before you
return? Don't fall and hurt yourselves, nor overturn the coach.
Love one another, and be good girls; and drink Presto's health
in water, madam Stella; and in good ale,[4] madam Dingley.

27. The secretary appointed me to dine with him to-day,

[1] "Mordanto gallops on alone,
    The road is with his followers strown,
    This breaks a girth, and that a bone."
        SWIFT's *Verses to the Earl of Peterborough*, 1706.
[2] Fulham.
[3] Atterbury obtained Christ Church (Oxford) deanery in August, 1711.
[4] The Wexford ale is highly esteemed, which is hinted at in this passage;
and the Wexford waters were prescribed to Stella.—D. S.

and we were to do a world of business: he came at four, and brought Prior with him, and had forgot the appointment, and no business was done. I left him at eight, and went to change my gown at Mrs. Vanhomrigh's; and there was Sir Andrew Fountain at ombre, with lady Ashburnham and lady Frederick Schomberg, and lady Mary Schomberg,[1] and lady Betty Butler, and others, talking: and it put me in mind of the dean, and Stoyte, and Walls, and Stella at play, and Dingley and I looking on. I staid with them till ten, like a fool. Lady Ashburnham is something like Stella; so I helped her, and wished her good cards. It is late, &c.

28. Well, but I must answer this letter of our MD's. Saturday approaches, and I han't written down this side. O faith, Presto has been a sort of a lazy fellow: but Presto will remove to town this day sennight: the secretary has commanded me to do so; and I believe he and I shall go for some days to Windsor, where he will have leisure to mind some business we have together. To-day our Society (it must not be called a Club) dined at Mr. secretary's; we were but eight, the rest sent excuses, or were out of town. We sat till eight, and made some laws and settlements; and then I went to take leave of lady Ashburnham, who goes out of town to-morrow, as a great many of my acquaintance are already, and left the town very thin. I shall make but short journies this Summer, and not be long out of London. The days are grown sensibly shorter already, and all our fruit blasted. Your duke of Ormond is still at Chester; and perhaps this letter will be with you as soon as he. Sterne's [2] business is quite blown up: they stand to it to send him back to the commissioners of the revenue in Ireland for a reference, and all my credit could not alter it, though I almost fell out with the secretary of the treasury,[3] who is my lord treasurer's cousin-german, and my very good friend. It seems every step he has hitherto taken hath been wrong; at least they say so, and that is the same thing. I am heartily sorry for it; and I really think they are in the wrong, and use him hardly; but I can do no more.

29. Steele has had the assurance to write to me, that I would

---

[1] Lady Frederica (not "Frederick") was afterwards mother, by her first husband, of Robert D'Arcy, fourth Earl of Holderness. Lady Mary, her younger sister, born 1692, married Christoph Martin von Degenfeld. They were daughters of Meinhard Schomberg (1641–1719), Duke of Leinster.

[2] Collector of Wicklow.—F.

[3] Thomas Harley—*see* Letter XXIV., May 26.

engage my lord treasurer to keep a friend of his in an employment: I believe I told you how he and Addison served me for
my good offices in Steele's behalf; and I promised lord treasurer
never to speak for either of them again. Sir Andrew Fountain
and I dined to-day at Mrs. Vanhomrigh's. Dilly Ashe has been
in town this fortnight: I saw him twice; he was four days at
lord Pembroke's in the country, punning with him; his face
is very well. I was this evening two or three hours at lord
treasurer's, who called me doctor Thomas Swift twenty times;
that's his way of teazing. I left him at nine, and got home here
by ten, like a gentleman; and to-morrow morning I'll answer
your little letter, sirrahs.

30. Morning. I am terrible sleepy always in a morning; I
believe it is my walk over-night that disposes me to sleep;
faith 'tis now striking eight, and I am but just awake. Patrick
comes early, and wakes me five or six times, but I have excuses,
though I am three parts asleep. I tell him I sat up late, or slept
ill in the night, and often it is a lie. I have now got little MD's
letter before me, N. 16, no more, nor no less, no mistake.
Dingley says, "This letter won't be above six lines," and I was
afraid it was true, though I saw it filled on both sides. The
bishop of Clogher writ me word you were in the country, and
that he heard you were well: I am glad at heart MD rides, and
rides, and rides. Our hot weather ended in May, and all this
month has been moderate: it was then so hot, I was not able
to endure it; I was miserable every moment, and found myself
disposed to be peevish and quarrelsome; I believe a very hot
country would make me stark mad.—Yes, my head continues
pretty tolerable, and I impute it all to walking. Does Stella eat
fruit? I eat a little; but I always repent, and resolve against it.
No, in very hot weather I always go to town by water; but I
constantly walk back, for then the sun is down. And so Mrs.
Proby goes with you to Wexford; she's admirable company:
you'll grow plaguy wise with those you frequent. Mrs. Taylor,
and Mrs. Proby; take care of infection. I believe my two hundred
pounds will be paid; but that Sir Alexander Cairnes is a scrupu-
lous puppy: I left the bill with Mr. Stratford, who is to have the
money. Now, madam Stella, what say you? you ride every day;
I know that already, sirrah; and if you rid every day for a
twelvemonth, you would be still better and better. No, I hope
Parvisol will not have the impudence to make you stay an hour
for the money; if he does I'll un-parvisol him; pray let me know.
O Lord, how hasty we are, Stella can't stay writing and writing;

she must write and go a cock-horse, pray now. Well; but the
horses are not come to the door; the fellow can't find the
bridle; your stirrup is broken; where did you put the whips,
Dingley? Marg'et, where have you laid Mrs. Johnson's ribband
to tie about her? reach me my mask: sup up this before you
go. So, so, a gallop, a gallop: sit fast, sirrah, and don't ride
hard upon the stones.—Well, now Stella is gone, tell me,
Dingley, is she a good girl? and what news is that you are to
tell me?—No, I believe the box is not lost: Sterne says, it is
not.—No faith, you must go to Wexford without seeing your
duke of Ormond, unless you stay on purpose; perhaps you may
be so wise.—I tell you this is your sixteenth letter; will you
never be satisfied? No, no, I'll walk late no more; I ought less
to venture it than other people, and so I was told[1]: but I'll
return to lodge in town next Thursday. When you come from
Wexford I would have you send a letter of attorney to Mr.
Benjamin Tooke, bookseller in London, directed to me; and
he shall manage your affair. I have your parchment safely
lockt up in London.—O madam Stella, welcome home; was it
pleasant riding? did your horse stumble? how often did the man
light to settle your stirrup? ride nine miles? faith you have
galloped indeed. Well, but where's the fine thing you promised
me? I have been a good boy, ask Dingley else. I believe you
did not meet the fine-thing-man: faith you are a cheat. So
you'll see Raymond and his wife in town. Faith that riding to
Laracor gives me short sighs, as well as you. All the days I
have passed here, have been dirt to those. I have been gaining
enemies by the scores, and friends by the couples, which is
against the rules of wisdom; because they say, one enemy can
do more hurt, than ten friends can do good. But I have had
my revenge at least, if I get nothing else. And so let Fate
govern.——Now I think your letter is answered; and mine will
be shorter than ordinary, because it must go to-day. We have
had a great deal of scattering rain for some days past, yet it
hardly keeps down the dust.——We have plays acted in our
town, and Patrick was at one of them, oh, ho. He was damnably
mauled one day when he was drunk; he was at cuffs with a
brother footman, who dragged him along the floor upon his
face, which lookt for a week after as if he had the leprosy;
and I was glad enough to see it. I have been ten times sending
him over to you; yet now he has new cloaths, and a laced hat,

[1] Lest, through his obnoxiousness to the opposite political party, he
should incur the hazard of maltreatment or assassination.—D. L. P.

which the hatter brought by his orders, and he offered to pay
for the lace out of his wages.—I am to dine to-day with Dilly
at Sir Andrew Fountain's, who has bought a new house, and
will be weary of it in half a year. I must rise and shave, and
walk to town, unless I go with the dean in his chariot at twelve,
which is too late: and I have not seen that lord Peterborow yet.
The duke of Shrewsbury is almost well again, and will be abroad
in a day or two: what care you? There it is now; you don't care
for my friends. Farewell, my dearest lives, and delights, I love
you better than ever, if possible, as hope saved, I do, and ever
will. God Almighty bless you ever, and make us happy together;
I pray for this twice every day; and I hope God will hear my
poor hearty prayers.—Remember if I am used ill and ungratefully, as I have formerly been, 'tis what I am prepared for, and
shall not wonder at it. Yet, I am now envied, and thought in
high favour, and have every day numbers of considerable men
teazing me to solicit for them. And the ministry all use me
perfectly well, and all that know them, say they love me. Yet
I can count upon nothing, nor will, but upon MD's love and
kindness.—They think me useful; they pretended they were
afraid of none but me; and that they resolved to have me;
they have often confessed this: yet all makes little impression
on me.—Pox of these speculations! They give me the spleen;
and that is a disease I was not born to. Let me alone, sirrahs,
and be satisfied: I am, as long as MD and Presto are well:
Little wealth, And much health, And a life by stealth: that is
all we want; and so farewel, dearest MD; Stella, Dingley,
Presto, all together, now and for ever all together. Farewel
again and again.

LETTER XXVI

Chelsea, *June* 30, 1711.

SEE what large paper I am forced to take to write to MD;
Patrick has brought me none clipt; but faith the next shall be
smaller. I dined to-day, as I told you, with Dilly at Sir Andrew
Fountain's: there were we wretchedly punning, and writing
together to lord Pembroke. Dilly is just such a puppy as
ever; and it is so uncouth, after so long an intermission.
My twenty-fifth is gone this evening to the post. I think I will
direct my next (which is this) to Mr. Curry's, and let them
send it to Wexford, and then the next inclosed to Reading.

Instruct me how I shall do. I long to hear from you from Wexford, and what sort of place it is. The town grows very empty and dull. This evening I have had a letter from Mr. Phillips the pastoral poet, to get him a certain employment from lord treasurer. I have now had almost all the Whig poets my solicitors; and I have been useful to Congreve, Steele, and Harrison: but I will do nothing for Phillips; I find he is more a puppy than ever; so don't solicit for him. Besides, I will not trouble lord treasurer, unless upon some very extraordinary occasion.

July 1. Dilly lies conveniently for me when I come to town from Chelsea of a Sunday, and go to the secretary's; so I called at his lodgings this morning, and sent for my gown, and dressed myself there. He had a letter from the bishop, with an account that you were set out for Wexford the morning he writ, which was June 26, and he had the letter the 30th; that was very quick: the bishop says, you design to stay there two months or more. Dilly had also a letter from Tom. Ashe, full of Irish news: that your lady Linden [1] is dead, and I know not what besides, of Dr. Coghil [2] losing his drab, &c. The secretary was gone to Windsor, and I dined with Mrs. Vanhomrigh. Lord treasurer is at Windsor too; they will be going and coming all Summer, while the queen is there, and the town is empty, and I fear I shall be sometimes forced to stoop beneath my dignity, and send to the ale-house for a dinner. Well, sirrahs, had you a good journey to Wexford? did you drink ale by the way? were you never overturned? how many things did you forget? do you lie on straw in your new town where you are? Cudsho,[3] the next letter to Presto will be dated from Wexford. What fine company have you there? what new acquaintance have you got? you are to write constantly to Mrs. Walls and Mrs. Stoyte: and the dean said, Shall we never hear from you? Yes, Mr. dean, we'll make bold to trouble you with a letter. Then at Wexford; when you meet a lady; Did your waters pass well

[1] According to Mr. Aitken, widow of a Sir John Lyndon, an Irish judge who died 1699.

[2] Dr. Marmaduke Coghil was judge of the Prerogative Court in Ireland. About this time he courted a lady, and was soon to have been married to her; but unfortunately a cause was brought to trial before him, wherein a man was sued for beating his wife. When the matter was agitated, the doctor gave his opinion, "that although a man had no right to beat his wife unmercifully, yet that with such a little cane or switch as he then held in his hand, a husband was at liberty, and was invested with a power, to give his wife moderate correction"; which opinion determined the lady against having the doctor. He died an old man and a batchelor, about thirty years ago.—D. S., writing in 1768.

[3] "Cuds-ho!" ? A variant of his "God so!"

this morning, madam? Will Dingley drink them too? Yes, I warrant; to get her a stomach. I suppose you are all gamesters at Wexford. Don't lose your money, sirrah, far from home. I believe I shall go to Windsor in a few days; at least, the secretary tells me so. He has a small house there, with just room enough for him and me; and I would be satisfied to pass a few days there sometimes. Sirrahs, let me go to sleep, 'tis past twelve in our town.

2. Sterne came to me this morning, and tells me he has yet some hopes of compassing his business: he was with Tom Harley, the secretary of the treasury,[1] and made him doubt a little he was in the wrong; the poor man tells me, it will almost undo him, if he fails. I called this morning to see Will Congreve, who lives much by himself, is forced to read for amusement, and cannot do it without a magnifying-glass. I have set him very well with the ministry, and I hope he is in no danger of losing his place. I dined in the city with Dr. Freind, not among my merchants, but with a scrub instrument of mischief of mine, whom I never mentioned to you, nor am like to do. You two little saucy Wexfordians, you are now drinking waters. You drink waters! you go fiddlestick. Pray God send them to do you good; if not, faith next Summer you shall come to the Bath.

3. Lord Peterborow desired to see me this morning at nine; I had not seen him before since he came home. I met Mrs. Manley there, who was soliciting him to get some pension or reward for her service in the cause, by writing her *Atalantis*, and prosecution, &c. upon it. I seconded her, and hope they will do something for the poor woman. My lord kept me two hours upon politicks: he comes home very sanguine; he has certainly done great things at Savoy and Vienna, by his negotiations: he is violent against a Peace, and finds true what I writ to him, That the ministry seems for it. He reasons well; yet I am for a Peace.[2] I took leave of lady Kerry, who goes to-morrow for Ireland; she picks up lord Shelburn and Mrs. Pratt at lord Shelburn's house. I was this evening with lord treasurer; Tom Harley was there; and whispered me that he began to doubt about Sterne's business; I told him he would find he was in the wrong. I sat two or three hours at lord treasurer's; he rallied me sufficiently upon my refusing to take him into our Club; told a judge who was with us, that my name

was Thomas Swift. I had a mind to prevent Sir H. Bellasis [1]
going to Spain, who is a most covetous curr, and I fell a railing
against avarice, and turned it so that he smoakt me, and named
Bellasis. I went on, and said it was a shame to send him, to which
he agreed, but desired I would name some who understood
business, and do not love money, for he could not find them.
I said, there was something in a treasurer different from other
men; that we ought not to make a man a bishop who does not
love divinity, or a general who does not love war; and I wondered why the queen would make a man lord treasurer who does
not love money. He was mightily pleased with what I said. He
was talking of the First-Fruits of England: and I took occasion
to tell him, that I would not for a thousand pounds, any body
but he had got them for Ireland, who got them for England
too. He bid me consider what a thousand pounds was; I said,
I would have him to know, I valued a thousand pounds as
little as he valued a million.—Is it not silly to write all this?
but it gives you an idea what our conversation is with mixt
company. I have taken a lodging in Suffolk-street, and go to it
on Thursday; and design to walk the Park and the town to
supply my walking here: yet I will walk here sometimes too,
in a visit now and then to the dean. [2] When I was almost at
home, Patrick told me he had two letters for me, and gave
them to me in the dark, yet I could see one of them was from
saucy MD. I went to visit the dean for half an hour; and then
come home, and first read the other letter, which was from the
bishop of Clogher, who tells me the archbishop of Dublin mentioned in a full assembly of the clergy, the queen's granting the
First-Fruits; said it was done by the lord treasurer; and talked
much of my merit in it; but reading your's I find nothing of
that: perhaps the bishop lies, out of a desire to please me.
I dined with Mrs. Vanhomrigh. Well, sirrahs, you are gone
to Wexford, but I'll follow you.

4. Sterne came to me again this morning to advise about
reasons and memorials he is drawing up; and we went to town
by water together; and having nothing to do, I stole into the
city to an instrument of mine, and then went to see poor Patty
Rolt, who has been in town these two months with a cousin

[1] Mr. Aitken says (among other particulars) that he was Sir Henry
Belasyse, son of Sir Richard Belasyse, knight, of Ludworth, Durham, and
M.P. for Durham. " He was appointed a commissioner to inquire into the
number and quality of the English forces in Spain and Portugal, and to
examine the army accounts " (D. L. P.)
[2] Atterbury.

of hers. Her life passes with boarding in some country town as cheap as she can, and when she runs out, shifting to some cheaper place, or coming to town for a month. If I were rich I would ease her, which a little thing would do. Some months ago I sent her a guinea, and it patched up twenty circumstances. She is now going to Berkhamstead in Hertfordshire. It has rained and hailed prodigiously to-day, with some thunder. This is the last night I lie at Chelsea; and I got home early, and sat two hours with the dean, and eat victuals, having had a very scurvy dinner. I'll answer your letter when I come to live in town. You shall have a fine London answer: but first I'll go sleep, and dream of MD.

London, July 5. This day I left Chelsea for good (that's a genteel phrase) and am got into Suffolk-street. I dined to-day at our Society, and we are adjourned for a month, because most of us go into the country: we dined at lord keeper's with young Harcourt, and lord keeper was forced to sneak off, and dine with lord treasurer, who had invited the secretary and me to dine with him; but we scorned to leave our company, as George Granville did, whom we have threatened to expel: however, in the evening I went to lord treasurer, and, among other company, found a couple of judges with him; one of them, judge Powel,[1] an old fellow with gray hairs, was the merriest old gentleman I ever saw, spoke pleasant things, and laughed and chuckled till he cryed again. I staid till eleven, because I was not now to walk to Chelsea.

6. An ugly rainy day; I was to visit Mrs. Barton, then called at Mrs. Vanhomrigh's, where Sir Andrew Fountain and the rain kept me to dinner; and there did I loiter all the afternoon, like a fool, out of perfect laziness, and the weather not permitting me to walk; but I'll do so no more. Are your waters at Wexford good in this rain? I long to hear how you are established there, how and whom you visit, what is your lodging, what are your entertainments. You are got far southwards; but I think you must eat no fruit while you drink the waters. I eat some Kentish cherries t'other day, and I repent it already; I have felt my head a little disordered. We had not a hot day all June, nor since, which I reckon a mighty happiness. Have you left a direction with Reading for Wexford? I will, as I said, direct this to Curry's, and the next to Reading,

---

[1] Sir John Powell (1645-1713), died a bachelor. An enlightened judge, who, on a woman being accused of witchcraft before him, it being alleged that she could fly, said to her, "You may."

or suppose I send this at a venture straight to Wexford? It would vex me to have it miscarry. I had a letter to-night from Parvisol, that White has paid me most of my remaining money; and another from Joe, that they have had their election at Trim, but not a word who is chosen portrieve.[1] Poor Joe is full of complaints, says he has enemies, and fears he will never get his two hundred pounds, and I fear so too, although I have done what I could.—I'll answer your letter when I think fit, when saucy Presto thinks fit, sirrahs. I an't at leisure yet; when I have nothing to do, perhaps I may vouchsafe.—O Lord, the two Wexford ladies; I'll go dream of you both.

7. It was the dismallest rainy day I ever saw; I went to the secretary in the morning, and he was gone to Windsor. Then it began raining, and I struck in to Mrs. Vanhomrigh's, and dined, and staid till night very dull and insipid. I hate this town in Summer; I'll leave it for a while if I can have time.

8. I have a fellow of your town, one Tisdall,[2] lodges in the same house with me. Patrick told me, Squire Tisdall and his lady lodged here; I pretended I never heard of him, but I knew his ugly face, and saw him at church in the next pew to me, and he often looked for a bow, but it would not do. I think he lives in Capel-street, and has an ugly fine wife in a fine coach. Dr. Freind and I dined in the city by invitation, and I drank punch, very good, but it makes me hot. People here are troubled with agues by this continuance of wet cold weather; but I am glad to find the season so temperate. I was this evening to see Will Congreve, who is a very agreeable companion.

9. I was to-day in the city, and dined with Mr. Stratford, who tells me Sir Alexander Cairnes makes difficulties about paying my bill, so that I cannot give order yet to Parvisol to deliver up the bond to Dr. Raymond. To-morrow I shall have a positive answer: that Cairnes is a shuffling scoundrel; and several merchants have told me so: what can one expect from a Scot and a fanatick? I was at Bateman's the bookseller's, to see a fine old library he has bought; and my fingers itched, as yours would do at a china shop; but I resisted, and found every thing too dear, and I have fooled away too much money that way already. So go and drink your waters, saucy rogue, and make your self well; and pray walk while you are there: I have

---

[1] See Letter XXIV., June 7.
[2] Mr. Aitken thinks he was Richard Tisdall, registrar of the Irish Court of Chancery, who was a relative of the Rev. William, and died 1742.

a notion there is never a good walk in Ireland.[1] Do you find all places without trees? Pray observe the inhabitants about Wexford; they are old English;[2] see what they have particular in their manners, names, and language: magpies have been always there, and no where else in Ireland,[3] till of late years. They say the cocks and dogs go to sleep at noon, and so do the people. Write your travels, and bring home good eyes, and health.

10. I dined to-day with lord treasurer: we did not sit down till four. I dispatched three businesses with him, and forgot a fourth. I think I have got a friend an employment; and besides I made him consent to let me bring Congreve to dine with him. You must understand I have a mind to do a small thing, only turn out all the queen's physicians; for in my conscience they will soon kill her among them. And I must talk over that matter with some people. My lord treasurer told me, the queen and he between them have lost the paper about the First-Fruits; but desires I will let the bishops know it shall be done with the first opportunity.

11. I dined to-day with neighbour Van, and walkt pretty well in the Park this evening. Stella, hussy, don't you remember, sirrah, you used to reproach me about meddling in other folks affairs. I have enough of it now: two people came to me to-night in the Park to engage [me] to speak to lord treasurer in their behalf; and I believe they make up fifty who have asked me the same favour. I am hardened, and resolved to trouble him, or any other minister, less than ever. And I observe those who have ten times more credit than I, will not speak a word for any body. I met yesterday the poor lad I told you of, who lived with Mr. Tenison,[4] who has been ill of an ague ever since I saw him. He lookt wretchedly, and was exceeding thankful for half a crown I gave him. He had a crown from me before.

12. I dined to-day with young Manley[5] in the city, who is

---

[1] In Ireland there are not publick paths from place to place, as in England.—D. S. [Country footpaths are still scarce there.]

[2] Wexford was the first Irish city that submitted to the English and was colonised; and the county was in Camden's time "very full of English."—D. L. P.

[3] "No pies to plucke the thatch from house
  are bred in Irish grounde,
But worse than pies the same to burne,
  a thousand maie be founde."

        DERRICK, *Image of Ireland.*

They are now common everywhere.—D. S.

[4] *See* Letter XXIV., May 28.

[5] Perhaps a son of John's.

H 757

to get me out a box of books and a hamper of wine from Hamburgh. I enquired of Mr. Stratford, who tells me that Cairnes has not yet paid my two hundred pounds, but shams and delays from day to day. Young Manley's wife is a very indifferent person of a young woman, goggle-eyed, and looks like a fool: yet he is a handsome fellow, and married her for love after long courtship, and she refused him until he got his last employment.—I believe I shall not be so good a boy for writing as I was, during your stay at Wexford, unless I may send my letters every second time to Curry's; pray, let me know. This, I think, shall go there, or why not to Wexford itself? That's right, and so it shall this next Tuesday, although it costs you ten pence. What care I?

13. This toad of a secretary is come from Windsor, and I can't find him; and he goes back on Sunday, and I can't see him to-morrow. I dined scurvily to-day with Mr. Lewis and a parson; and then went to see lord treasurer, and met him coming from his house in his coach: he smiled, and I shrugged, and we smoakt each other; and so my visit is paid. I now confine myself to see him only twice a week: he has invited me to Windsor, and betwixt two stools, &c. I'll go live at Windsor, if possible, that's pozzz. I have always the luck to pass my Summer in London. I called this evening to see poor Sir Matthew Dudley, a commissioner of the customs; I know he is to be out for certain: he is in hopes of continuing: I would not tell him bad news, but advised him to prepare for the worst. Dilly was with me this morning, to invite me to dine at Kensington on Sunday with lord Mountjoy, who goes soon for Ireland. Your late chief justice Broderick[1] is here, and they say violent as a tiger. How is party among you at Wexford? Are the majority of ladies for the late or present ministry? Write me Wexford news, and love Presto, because he's a good boy.

14. Although it was shaving-day I walkt to Chelsea, and was there by nine this morning; and the dean of Carlisle and I crossed the water to Battersea, and went in his chariot to Greenwich, where we dined at Dr. Gastrell's, and passed the afternoon at Lewsham, at the dean of Canterbury's;[2] and there I saw Moll Stanhope,[3] who is grown monstrously tall,

[1] Alan Brodrick (1660?–1728), speaker of Irish House of Commons 1703; Attorney-General for Ireland 1707; Chief Justice of Queen's Bench in Ireland, May 1710; dismissed 1711; Lord Chancellor of Ireland 1714; Baron Midleton, 1715.

[2] Dr. Stanhope, then vicar of Lewisham.

[3] See Letter III., Sept. 13, 1710.

but not so handsome as formerly. It is the first little rambling journey I have had this Summer about London, and they are the agreeablest pastimes one can have, in a friend's coach, and to good company. Bank stock is fallen three or four *per cent.* by the whispers about the town of the queen's being ill, who is however very well.

15. How many books have you carried with you to Wexford? What, not one single book? Oh, but your time will be so taken up; and you can borrow of the parson. I dined to-day with Sir Andrew Fountain and Dilly at Kensington with lord Mountjoy; and in the afternoon Stratford came there, and told me my two hundred pounds was paid at last; so that business is over, and I am at ease about it: and I wish all your money was in the bank too. I'll have my t'other hundred pounds there, that is in Hawkshaw's hands. Have you had the interest of it paid yet? I ordered Parvisol to do it. What makes Presto write so crooked? I'll answer your letter to-morrow, and send it on Tuesday. Here's hot weather come again, yesterday and to-day; fine drinking waters now. We had a sad pert dull parson at Kensington to-day. I almost repent my coming to town; I want the walks I had.

16. I dined in the city to-day with a hedge acquaintance, and the day passed without any consequence. I'll answer your letter to-morrow.

17. Morning. I have put your letter before me, and am going to answer it. Hold your tongue: stand by. Your weather and ours were not alike; we had not a bit of hot weather in June, yet you complain of it on the 19th day. What, you used to love hot weather then? I could never endure it: I detest and abominate it. I would not live in a hot country to be king of it. What a splutter you keep about my bonds with Raymond, and all to affront Presto? Presto will be suspicious of every thing but MD, in spight of your little nose. Soft and fair, madam Stella, how you gallop away in your spleen and your rage about repenting my journey, and preferment here, and six-pence a dozen, and nasty England, and Laracor all my life. Hey dazy, will you never have done? I had no offers of any living. Lord keeper told me some months ago, he would give me one when I pleased; but I told him, I would not take any from him: and the secretary told me t'other day, he had refused a very good one for me; but it was in a place he did not like; and I know nothing of getting any thing here, and, if they would give me leave, I would come over just now. Addison,

I hear, has changed his mind about going over; but I have not seen him these four months.—O aye, that's true, Dingley; that's like herself: millions of businesses to do before she goes. Yes, my head has been pretty well, but threatening within these two or three days, which I impute to some fruit I ate; but I will eat no more: not a bit of any sort. I suppose you had a journey without dust, and that was happy. I long for a Wexford letter; but must not think of it yet: your last was finished but three weeks ago. It is d——d news you tell me of Mrs. F——; it makes me love England less a great deal. I know nothing of the trunk being left or taken; so 'tis odd enough, if the things in it were mine; and I think I was told that there were some things for me, that my mother left particularly to me. I am really sorry for ——; that scoundrel —— will have his estate after his mother's death. Let me know if Mrs. Walls has got her tea: I hope Richardson [1] staid in Dublin till it came. Mrs. Walls needed not have that blemish in her eye; for I am not in love with her at all. No, I don't like any thing in the *Examiner* after the 45th, except the first part of the 46th; [2] all the rest is trash; and if you like them, especially the 47th, your judgment is spoiled by ill company and want of reading; which I am more sorry for than you think: and I have spent fourteen years in improving you to little purpose. (Mr. Tooke is come here, and I must stop.)—At night. I dined with lord treasurer to-day, and he kept me till nine; so I cannot send this to-night, as I intended, nor write some other letters. Green, his surgeon, [3] was there, and dressed his breast; that is, put on a plaister, which is still requisite: and I took an opportunity to speak to him of the queen; but he cut me short with this saying, *Laissez faire à don Antoine*; which is a French proverb, expressing, *Leave that to me*. I find he is against her taking much physick; and I doubt he cannot persuade her to take Dr. Radcliffe. However, she is very well now, and all the story of her illness, except the first day or two, was a lie. We had some business, that company hindered us from doing, though he is earnest for it, yet would not appoint me a certain day, but bids me come at all times till we can have leisure. This takes up a great deal of my time, and I can do nothing I would do for them. I was with the secretary this morning, and we both think to go next week to Windsor for some days, to dis-

---

[1] *See* Letter XVII., March 6, 1710-11.
[2] *See* Letter XXIV., June 7.
[3] *See* Letter XIX., March 26, note.

patch an affair, if we can have leisure. Sterne met me just now in the street by his lodgings, and I went in for an hour to Jemmy Leigh, who loves London dearly: he asked after you with great respect and friendship.—To return to your letter. Your bishop Mills [1] hates me mortally: I wonder he should speak well of me, having abused me in all places where he went. So you pay your way. Cudsho: you had a fine supper, I warrant; two pullets, and a bottle of wine, and some currants.—It is just three weeks to-day since you set out to Wexford; you were three days going, and I don't expect a letter these ten days yet, or rather this fortnight. I got a grant of the *Gazette* for Ben Tooke this morning from Mr. secretary: it will be worth [to] him a hundred pounds a year.

18. To-day I took leave of Mrs. Barton, who is going into the country; and I dined with Sir John Stanley,[2] where I have not been this great while. There dined with us lord Rochester,[3] and his fine daughter, lady Jane,[4] just growing a top toast I have been endeavouring to save Sir Matthew Dudley, but fear I cannot. I walkt the Mall six times to-night for exercise, and would have done more; but as empty as the town is, a fool got hold of me, and so I came home, to tell you this shall go to-morrow, without fail, and follow you to Wexford, like a dog.

19. Dean Atterbury sent to me to dine with him at Chelsea: I refused his coach, and walkt, and am come back by seven, because I would finish this letter, and some others I am writing. Patrick tells me, the maid says one Mr. Walls, a clergyman, a tall man, was here to visit me. Is it your Irish archdeacon? I shall be sorry for it; but I shall make a shift to see him seldom enough, as I do Dilly. What can he do here? or is it somebody else? The duke of Newcastle is dead by the fall he had from his horse.[5] God send poor Stella her health, and keep MD happy. Farewel, and love Presto, who loves MD above all things ten million of times. God bless the dear Wexford girls. Farewel again, &c. &c.

---

[1] Bishop of Waterford, 1707-40.—N.
[2] *See* Letter V., Oct. 1, 1710.
[3] Henry, Lord Hyde (*see* Letter V., Oct. 1, 1710), had become Earl of Rochester, May 2, 1711.
[4] Lady Jane Hyde was married Nov. 27, 1718, to William, third of the "Capell" Earls of Essex; and died 1723-4.
[5] In the hunting field.—D. L. P. John Holles (1662-1711), first Duke of Newcastle-on-Tyne, Lord Privy Seal.

LETTER XXVII

London, *July* 19, 1711.

I HAVE just sent my 26th, and have nothing to say, because I have other letters to write; (pshaw, I began too high) but I must lay the beginning like a nest-egg; to-morrow I'll say more, and fetch up this line to be straight. This is enough at present for two dear saucy naughty girls.

20. Have I told you that Walls has been with me, and leaves the town in three days. He has brought no gown with him. Dilly carried him to a play. He has come upon a foolish errand, and goes back as he comes. I was this day with lord Peterborow, who is going another ramble: I believe I told you so. I dined with lord treasurer, but cannot get him to do his own business with me; he has put me off till to-morrow.

21, 22. I dined yesterday with lord treasurer, who would needs take me along with him to Windsor, although I refused him several times, having no linen, &c. I had just time to desire lord Forbes[1] to call at my lodging, and order my man to send my things to-day to Windsor by his servant. I lay last night at the secretary's lodgings at Windsor, and borrowed one of his shirts to go to court in. The queen is very well. I dined with Mr. Masham; and not hearing any thing of my things, I got lord Winchelsea to bring me to town. Here I found that Patrick had broke open the closet to get my linen and night-gown, and sent them to Windsor, and there they are; and he not thinking I would return so soon, is gone upon his rambles: so here I am left destitute, and forced to borrow a night-gown of my landlady, and have not a rag to put on to-morrow: faith, it gives me the spleen.

23. Morning. It is a terrible rainy day, and rained prodigiously on Saturday night. Patrick lay out last night, and is not yet returned: faith, poor Presto is a desolate creature; neither servant nor linen, nor any thing.—Night. Lord Forbes's man has brought back my portmantua, and Patrick is come; so I am in Christian circumstances: I shall hardly commit such a frolick again. I just crept out to Mrs. Van's, and dined, and staid there the afternoon: it has rained all this day. Windsor is a delicious place: I never saw it before, except for an hour about seventeen years ago. Walls has been here in my absence, I suppose to take his leave; for he designed not to stay above

[1] Alexander (1678–1762), fourth baron, attainted 1746.

five days in London. He says, he and his wife will come here for some months next year; and, in short, he dares not stay now for fear of her.

24. I dined to-day with a hedge friend in the city; and Walls overtook me in the street, and told me he was just getting on horseback for Chester. He has as much curiosity as a cow: he lodged with his horse in Aldersgate-street: he has bought his wife a silk gown, and himself a hat. And what are you doing? what is poor MD doing now? how do you pass your time at Wexford? how do the waters agree with you? Let Presto know soon; for Presto longs to know, and must know. Is not madam Proby curious company? I am afraid this rainy weather will spoil your waters. We have had a great deal of wet these three days. Tell me all the particulars of Wexford; the place, the company, the diversions, the victuals, the wants, the vexations. Poor Dingley never saw such a place in her life; sent all over the town for a little parsley to a boiled chicken, and it was not to be had: the butter is stark naught, except an old English woman's; and it is such a favour to get a pound from her now and then. I am glad you carried down your sheets with you, else you must have lain in sackcloth. O Lord!

25. I was this forenoon [1] with Mr. secretary at his office, and helped to hinder a man of his pardon, who is condemned for a rape. The under-secretary [2] was willing to save him, upon an old notion that a woman cannot be ravished: but I told the secretary, he could not pardon him without a favourable report from the judge; besides, he was a fiddler, and consequently a rogue, and deserved hanging for something else; and so he shall swing. What; I must stand up for the honour of the fair sex? 'Tis true, the fellow had lain with her a hundred times before; but what care I for that? What! must a woman be ravished because she is a whore?—The secretary and I go on Saturday to Windsor for a week. I dined with lord treasurer, and staid with him till past ten. I was to-day at his levee, where I went against my custom, because I had a mind to do a good office for a gentleman: so I talked with him before my lord, that he might see me, and then found occasion to recommend him this afternoon. I was forced to excuse my coming to the levee, that I did it to see the sight; for he was going to chide me away: I had never been there before but once, and that was long before he was treasurer. The rooms were all full, and as many

[1] Versions later than D. S. have "afternoon."
[2] Mr. Thomas Hare. *See* Letter XXVIII., Aug. 13.

Whigs as Tories. He whispered me a jest or two, and bid me come to dinner. I left him but just now, and 'tis late.

26. Mr. Addison and I have at last met again. I dined with him and Steele to-day at young Jacob Tonson's. The two Jacobs[1] think it is I who have made the secretary take from them the printing of the *Gazette*, which they are going to lose, and Ben. Tooke and another[2] are to have it. Jacob came to me t'other day, to make his court; but I told him, it was too late, and that it was not my doing. I reckon they will lose it in a week or two. Mr. Addison and I talked as usual, and as if we had seen one another yesterday; and Steele and I were very easy, although I writ him lately a biting letter, in answer to one of his, where he desired me to recommend a friend of his to lord treasurer. Go, get you gone to your waters, sirrah. Do they give you a stomach? Do you eat heartily?—We have had much rain to-day and yesterday.

27. I dined to-day in the city, and saw poor Patty Rolt, and gave her a pistole to help her a little forward against she goes to board in the country. She has but eighteen pounds a year to live on, and is forced to seek out for cheap places. Sometimes they raise their price, and sometimes they starve her, and then she is forced to shift. Patrick the puppy put too much ink in my standish, and carrying too many things together, I spilled it on my paper and floor. The town is dull, and wet and empty: Wexford is worth two of it; I hope so at least, and that poor little MD finds it so. I reckon upon going to Windsor to-morrow with Mr. secretary, unless he changes his mind, or some other business prevents him. I shall stay there a week, I hope.

28. Morning. Mr. secretary sent me word, he will call at my lodgings by two this afternoon, to take me to Windsor, so I must dine no where; and I promised lord treasurer to dine with him to-day; but I suppose we shall dine at Windsor at five, for we make but three hours there. I am going abroad, but have left Patrick to put up my things, and to be sure to be at home half an hour before two.—*Windsor*, at night. We did not leave London till three, and dined here between six and seven; at nine I left the company, and went to see lord treasurer, who is just come. I chid him for coming so late; he chid me for not dining with him; said, he staid an hour for me. Then I went

---

[1] Old Jacob (1656?-1736) was the celebrated bookseller of Dryden; he was a Whig, and secretary to the Kitcat Club. Young Jacob, who assisted him in the business, and predeceased him (1735), was his nephew.

[2] John Barber. *See* Letter XII., Dec. 26, 1710, note.

and sat [an hour] with Mr. Lewis till just now, and 'tis past eleven. I lie in the same house with the secretary, one of the prebendary's houses. The secretary is not come from his apartment in the Castle. Do you think that abominable dog Patrick was out after two to-day, and I in a fright every moment for fear the chariot should come? and when he came in he had not put up one rag of my things: I never was in a greater passion, and would certainly have cropt one of his ears, if I had not lookt every momentf or the secretary, who sent his equipage to my lodging before, and came in a chair from Whitehall to me, and happened to stay half an hour later than he intended. One of lord treasurer's servants gave me a letter to-night; I found it was from *****, with an offer of fifty pounds, to be paid me in what manner I pleased; because, he said, he desired to be well with me. I was in a rage[1]: but my friend Lewis cooled me, and said, it is what the best men sometimes meet with; and I have been not seldom served in the like manner, although not so grossly. In these cases I never demur a moment; nor ever found the least inclination to take any thing. Well, I'll go try to sleep in my new bed, and to dream of poor Wexford MD, and Stella that drinks water, and Dingley that drinks ale.

29. I was at Court and church to-day, as I was this day sennight; I generally am acquainted with about thirty in the drawing-room, and I am so proud I make all the lords come up to me; one passes half an hour pleasant enough. We had a dunce to preach before the queen to-day, which often happens. Windsor is a delicious situation, but the town is scoundrel. I have this morning got the *Gazette* for Ben Tooke and one Barber a printer; it will be about three hundred pounds a year between them. T'other fellow[2] was printer of the *Examiner*, which is now laid down. I dined with the secretary, we were a dozen in all, three Scotch lords, and lord Peterborow. Duke Hamilton[3] would needs be witty, and hold up my train as I walked up stairs. It is an ill circumstance, that on Sundays much company always meet at the great tables. Lord treasurer told at Court, what I said to Mr. secretary on this occasion. The secretary shewed me his bill of fare to encourage me to dine with him. Poh, said I, shew me a bill of company, for I

---

[1] The second of these "insults." *See* Letter XVII., March 7, 1710-11.
[2] This other fellow was Mr. Barber, who was afterward lord mayor.—N.
[3] James Douglas (1658–1712), fourth Duke of Hamilton, eldest son of third duke. In 1698 he married his second wife, Elizabeth, only child of Digby, Lord Gerrard.

value not your dinner. See how this is all blotted,[1] I can write no more here, but to tell you I love you MD dearly, and God bless them.

30. In my conscience I fear I shall have the gout. I sometimes feel pains about my feet and toes; I never drank till within these two years, and I did it to cure my head. I often sit evenings with some of these people, and drink in my turn; but I am now resolved to drink ten times less than before; but they advise me to let what I drink be all wine, and not to put water to it. Tooke and the printer staid to-day to finish their affair, and treated me, and two of the under-secretaries, upon their getting the *Gazette*. Then I went to see lord treasurer, and chid him for not taking notice of me at Windsor: he said, he kept a place for me yesterday at dinner, and expected me there; but I was glad I did not come, because the duke of Buckingham [2] was there, and that would have made us acquainted; which I have no mind to. However, we appointed to sup at Mr. Masham's, and there staid till past one o'clock; and that is late, sirrahs: and I have much business.

31. I have sent a noble haunch of venison this afternoon to Mrs. Vanhomrigh: I wish you had it, sirrahs: I dined gravely with my landlord the secretary. The queen was abroad to-day in order to hunt, but finding it disposed to rain, she kept in her coach; she hunts in a chaise with one horse, which she drives herself, and drives furiously, like Jehu, and is a mighty hunter, like Nimrod. Dingley has heard of Nimrod, but not Stella, for it is in the Bible. I was to-day at Eton, which is but just cross the bridge, to see my lord Kerry's son,[3] who is at school there. Mr. secretary has given me a warrant for a buck; I can't send it to MD. It is a sad thing faith, considering how Presto loves MD, and how MD would love Presto's venison for Presto's sake. God bless the two dear Wexford girls.

Aug. 1. We had for dinner the fellow of that haunch of venison I sent to London; 'twas mighty fat and good, and eight people at dinner; that was bad. The queen and I were going to take the air this afternoon, but not together; and were both hindered by a sudden rain. Her coaches and chaises all went back, and the guards too: and I scoured into the market place for shelter. I intended to have walked up the finest avenue I ever saw, two miles long, with two rows of elms on each

[1] This refers to the ink mentioned above, which blotted his paper.—D. S.
[2] Who had been appointed Lord President of the Council (*vice* Rochester, deceased), June 12, 1711.
[3] *See* Letter XI., Dec. 13, 1710.

side.[1] I walked in the evening a little upon the terrace, and came home at eight: Mr. secretary came soon after, and we were engaging in deep discourse, and I was endeavouring to settle some points of the greatest consequence; and had wormed myself pretty well into him, when his under-secretary came in (who lodges in the same house with us) and interrupted all my scheme. I have just left him; 'tis late, &c.

2. I have been now five days at Windsor, and Patrick has been drunk three times that I have seen, and oftener I believe. He has lately had cloaths that have cost me five pounds, and the dog thinks he has the whip hand of me; he begins to master me; so now I am resolved to part with him, and will use him without the least pity. The secretary and I have been walking three or four hours to-day. The duchess of Shrewsbury [2] asked him, was not that Dr. Dr. and she could not say my name in English, but said Dr. *Presto,* which is Italian for Swift. Whimsical enough, as Billy Swift says.[3] I go to-morrow with the secretary to his house at Buckleberry, twenty-five miles from hence, and return early on Sunday morning. I will leave this letter behind me lockt up, and give you an account of my journey when I return. I had a letter yesterday from the bishop of Clogher, who is coming up to Dublin to his parliament. Have you any correspondence with him at Wexford? Methinks I now long for a letter from you, dated Wexford, July 24, &c. O Lord, that would be so pretending; and then says you, Stella can't write much, because it is bad to write when one drinks the waters; and I think, says you, I find myself better already, but I cannot tell yet, whether it be the journey or the waters. Presto is so silly to-night; yes he be; but Presto loves MD dearly, as hope saved.

3. Morning. I am to go this day at noon, as I told you, to Buckleberry; we dine at twelve, and expect to be there in four hours; I cannot bid you good-night now, because I shall be twenty-five miles from this paper to-night, and so my journal must have a break; so good morrow, &c.

4, 5. I dined yesterday at Buckleberry, where we lay two

---

[1] This fine avenue in Windsor Park is still in good preservation.—N.

[2] Adelaide, or Adelhida, widow of an Italian count (?Brachiano), married the first Duke of Shrewsbury at Rome, 1705. "The duchess was daughter of the Marquis Paleotti, of Bologna, who descended by the mother's side from Robert Earl of Leicester, favourite of Queen Elizabeth. The duchess had only been a short time in England, since the duke's appointment as Lord Chamberlain." (D. L. P.)

[3] *See post,* Letter XXX., Sept. 25. It is supposed Billy was one of his cousins.

nights, and set out this morning at eight, and were here at twelve, in four hours we went twenty-six miles. Mr. secretary was a perfect country gentleman at Buckleberry; he smoakt tobacco with one or two neighbours; he enquired after the wheat in such a field; he went to visit his hounds; and knew all their names; he and his lady saw me to my chamber just in the country fashion. His house is in the midst of near three thousand pounds a year he had by his lady, who is descended from Jack [of] Newbury,[1] of whom books and ballads are written; and there is an old picture of him in the house. She is a great favourite of mine. I lost church to-day; but I dressed, and shaved, and went to Court, and would not dine with the secretary, but engaged myself to a private dinner with Mr. Lewis, and one friend more. We go to London to-morrow; for lord Dartmouth, the other secretary, is come, and they are here their weeks by turns.

6. Lord treasurer comes every Saturday to Windsor, and goes away on Monday or Tuesday. I was with him this morning at his levee, for one cannot see him otherwise here, he is so hurried: we had some talk, and I told him I would stay this week at Windsor by myself, where I can have more leisure to do some business that concerns them. Lord treasurer and the secretary thought to mortify me, for they told me, they had been talking a great deal of me to-day to the queen, and she said, she had never heard of me; I told them, That was their fault, and not hers, &c. and so we laughed. I dined with the secretary, and let him go to London at five without me; and here am I all alone in the prebendary's house, which Mr. secretary has taken; only Mr. Lewis is in my neighbourhood, and we shall be good company. The vice-chamberlain,[2] and Mr. Masham, and the green-cloth, have promised me dinners. I shall want but four till Mr. secretary returns. We have a musick meeting in our town to-night. I went to the rehearsal of it, and there was Margarita,[3] and her sister, and another drab, and a parcel of fiddlers; I was weary, and would not go to the meeting, which I am sorry for, because I heard it was

---

[1] John Winchcombe, *alias* Smalwoode (*d.* 1520), clothier, hero of chap-book stories which relate that he marched to Flodden Field at the head of his 100 or 150 workmen.

[2] Thomas Coke, M.P. for Derbyshire.

[3] Francesca Margherita de l'Epine (*d.* 1746), a native of Tuscany, a singer, who came to England with her German master, Groeber, about 1692. She became associated with the establishment of Italian opera in England, and was joined in 1703 by her sister Maria Gallia; and she retired in 1718, when she married Dr. Pepusch.

a great assembly. Mr. Lewis came from it, and sat with me till just now; and 'tis late.

7. I can do no business, I fear, because Mr. Lewis, who has nothing or little to do here, sticks close to me. I dined to-day with the gentlemen ushers, among scurvey company; but the queen was hunting the stag till four this afternoon, and she drove in her chaise above forty miles, and it was five before we went to dinner. Here are fine walks about this town. I sometimes walk up the avenue.

8. There was a drawing-room to-day at Court; but so few company, that the queen sent for us into her bed-chamber, where we made our bows, and stood about twenty of us round the room, while she looked at us round with her fan in her mouth, and once a minute said about three words to some that were nearest her, and then she was told dinner was ready, and went out. I dined at the green-cloth, by Mr. Scarborow's invitation, who is in waiting.[1] It is much the best table in England, and costs the queen a thousand pounds a month while she is at Windsor or Hampton-court; and is the only mark of magnificence or hospitality I can see in the queen's family: it is designed to entertain foreign ministers, and people of quality, who come to see the queen, and have no place to dine at.

9. Mr. Coke, the vice-chamberlain, made me a long visit this morning, and invited me to dinner, but the toast, his lady,[2] was unfortunately engaged to lady Sunderland.[3] Lord treasurer stole here last night, but did not lie in his lodgings in the Castle; and after seeing the queen, went back again. I just drank a dish of chocolate with him. I fancy I shall have reason to be angry with him very soon: but what care I? I believe I shall die with ministries in my debt.—This night I received a certain letter from a place called Wexford, from two dear naughty girls of my acquaintance; but faith I won't answer it here, no in troth. I will send this to Mr. Reading,[4] supposing it will find you returned; and I hope better for the waters.

10. Mr. vice-chamberlain lent me his horses to ride about and see the country this morning. Dr. Arbuthnott, the queen's

---

[1] Charles Scarborow, one of the two clerks.

[2] "Saturday, 9 July [1709] . . . Mr. vice chamberlain Coke is married to Mrs. Hale, one of the maids of honour."—NARCISSUS LUTTRELL'S *Brief Relation of State Affairs.*

[3] Charles Spencer (*c.* 1675–1722), fourth Earl of Sunderland, married (1699-1700) as his second wife Anne Churchill, second daughter of the famous Duke of Marlborough. She was of small stature, and known as "the little Whig." She died 1716.

[4] *See* Letter XXV., June 21.

physician and favourite, went out with me to show me the
places: we went a little after the queen, and overtook Miss
Forester, a maid of honour, on her palfry taking the air; we
made her go along with us. We saw a place they have made for
a famous horse-race to-morrow, where the queen will come.
We met the queen coming back, and Miss Forester stood, like
us, with her hat off while the queen went by. The Dr. and I
left the lady where we found her, but under other conductors,
and we dined at a little place he has taken, about a mile off.
—When I came back, I found Mr. Scarborow had sent all about
to invite me to the green-cloth, and lessened his company on
purpose to make me easy. It is very obliging, and will cost me
thanks. Much company is come to town this evening, to see
to-morrow's race. I was tired with riding a trotting mettlesome
horse a dozen miles, having not been on horse-back this twelvemonth. And Miss Forester did not make it easier; she is a silly
true maid of honour, and I did not like her, although she be a
toast, and was dressed like a man.[1]

11. I will send this letter to-day. I expect the secretary by
noon. I will not go to the race, unless I can get room in some
coach. It is now morning. I must rise, and fold up and seal my
letter. Farewel, and God preserve dearest MD.

I believe I shall leave this town on Monday.

LETTER XXVIII

Windsor, *Aug.* 11, 1711.

I SENT away my twenty-seventh this morning in an express to
London, and directed to Mr. Reading: this shall go to your
lodgings, where I reckon you will be returned before it reaches
you. I intended to go to the race to-day, but was hindered by
a visit, I believe I told you so in my last. I dined to-day at the
green-cloth, where every body had been at the race but myself,
and we were twenty in all; and very noisy company: but I
made the vice-chamberlain and two friends more sit at a side-
table, to be a little quiet. At six I went to see the secretary,
who is returned; but lord keeper sent to desire I would sup
with him, where I stayed till just now; lord treasurer and secretary were to come to us, but both failed. 'Tis late, &c.

---

[1] In a riding habit, then just coming into fashion. Miss Forester had
been married to Sir John Downing in 1701, when he was fifteen and she
but thirteen; they were divorced, by mutual consent springing from
mutual aversion.—D. L. P.

12. I was this morning to visit lord keeper, who made me reproaches that I had never visited him at Windsor. He had a present sent him of delicious peaches, and he was champing and champing, but I durst not eat one; I wished Dingley had some of them, for poor Stella can no more eat fruit than Presto. Dilly Ashe is come to Windsor; and after church I carried him up to the drawing-room, and talked to the keeper and treasurer, on purpose to shew them to him, and he saw the queen and several great lords, and the duchess of Montague[1]; he was mighty happy, and resolves to fill a letter to the bishop.[2] My friend Lewis and I dined soberly with Dr. Adams,[3] the only neighbour prebendary. One of the prebendaries here is lately a peer, by the death of his father. He is now lord Willoughby of Brook [i.e. Broke], and will sit in the house of lords with his gown.[4] I supped to-night at Masham's with lord treasurer, Mr. secretary, and Prior. The treasurer made us stay till twelve before he came from the queen, and 'tis now past two.

13. I reckoned upon going to London to-day; but by an accident the cabinet council did not sit last night, and sat to-day, so we go to-morrow at six in the morning. I miss'd the race to-day by coming out too late, when every body's coach was gone, and ride I would not; I felt my last riding three days after. We had a dinner to-day at the secretary's lodgings without him: Mr. Hare,[5] his under-secretary, Mr. Lewis, brigadier Sutton[6] and I dined together, and I made the vice-chamberlain take a snap with us, rather than stay till five for his lady, who

---

[1] John (1689–1749), second Duke of Montagu, married (1704-5) Mary Churchill (c. 1690–1751), fourth and youngest daughter of the famous Duke of Marlborough.   [2] Of Clogher.—D. S.

[3] John Adams, born in London, became fellow of King's College, in the place of John Ingelo, 1670; and travelled into Spain, Italy, France, and Ireland. He was presented to a rectory in Lincolnshire, by the Lord Chancellor, in 1687; resigned his fellowship 1688; lecturer of St. Clement's Danes, 1690; rector of St. Alban, Wood-street; chaplain to his Majesty 1697; D.D. 1704; prebendary of Canterbury, and afterwards of Windsor. Thus far from the MSS. of Mr. Baker. He published, in 1700, An Essay concerning Self Murther; and died of an apoplexy Jan. 29, 1719-20; being at that time provost of Eton, canon of Windsor, and rector of St. Bartholomew's behind the Royal Exchange.—N.

[4] The Rev. George Verney (c. 1659–1728-9), D.D., rector of Southam and canon of Windsor, twelfth holder of the baronial title of Willoughby de Broke, succeeded his father, Richard. "This is an incidental circumstance and expression; yet it marks the delight Swift took in everything that could add dignity to the clerical character." (Scott).

[5] See Letter XXVII., July 25, note. In Bolingbroke's office, Mr. Aitken says.

[6] Richard Sutton, stated by Mr. Aitken to have been nephew of Viscount Lexington (? first Baron Lexinton of Aram). Brigdr.-general, Jan 1, 1710. M.P. for Newark same year. Died lieut.-general 1737.

was gone to the race. The reason why the cabinet council was not held last night, was because Mr. secretary St. John would not sit with your duke of Somerset.[1] So to-day the duke was forced to go to the race while the cabinet was held. We have musick-meetings in our town, and I was at the rehearsal t'other day, but I did not value it, nor would go to the meeting. Did I tell you this before?

London, 14. We came to town this day in two hours and forty minutes: twenty miles are nothing here. I found a letter from the archbishop of Dublin, sent me the Lord knows how. He says some of the bishops will hardly believe that lord treasurer got the queen to remit the First-Fruits before the duke of Ormond was declared lord lieutenant; and that the bishops have written a letter to lord treasurer, to thank him. He has sent me the address of the convocation, ascribing, in good part, that affair to the duke, who had less share in it than MD; for if it had not been for MD, I should not have been so good a solicitor. I dined to-day in the city, about a little bit of mischief with a printer.—I found Mrs. Vanhomrigh all in combustion, squabbling with her rogue of a landlord; she has left her house, and gone out of our neighbour-hood a good way. Her eldest daughter is come of age, and going to Ireland to look after her fortune, and get it in her own hands.

15. I dined to-day with Mrs. Van, who goes to-night to her new lodgings. I went at six to see lord treasurer, but his company was gone, contrary to custom, and he was busy, and I was forced to stay some time before I could see him. We were together hardly an hour, and he went away, being in haste. He desired me to dine with him on Friday, because there would be a friend of his that I must see: my lord Harley told me when he was gone, that it was Mrs. Masham his father meant, who is come to town to lie-in, and whom I never saw, though her husband is one of our Society. God send her a good time; her death would be a terrible thing.—Do you know, that I have ventured all my credit with these great ministers to clear some misunderstandings betwixt them; and if there be no breach, I ought to have the merit of it? 'Tis a plaguy ticklish piece of work, and a man hazards losing both sides. 'Tis a pity the world does not know my virtue.—I thought the clergy in convocation in Ireland would have given me thanks for being their solicitor, but I hear of no such thing. Pray talk

[1] *See* Letter XVII., March 4, 1710-11, note on Duchess of Somerset.

occasionally on that subject, and let me know what you hear. Do you know the greatness of my spirit, that I value their thanks not a rush? but at my return shall freely let all people know, that it was my lord treasurer's action, wherein the duke of Ormond had no more share than a cat. And so they may go whistle, and I'll go sleep.

16. I was this day in the city, and dined at Pontack's[1] with Stratford, and two other merchants. Pontack told us, although his wine was so good, he sold it cheaper than others, he took but seven shillings a flask. Are not these pretty rates? The books he sent for from Hamburgh, are come, but not yet got out of the custom-house. My library will be at least double when I come back. I shall go to Windsor again on Saturday, to meet our Society, who are to sup at Mr. secretary's; but I believe I shall return on Monday, and then I will answer your letter, that lies safe here underneath;—I see it; lie still; I'll assure you, when the ducks have eaten up the dirt.

17. I dined to-day at lord treasurer's with Mrs. Masham, and she is extremely like one Mrs. Malolly, that was once my landlady in Trim. She was used with mighty kindness and respect, like a favourite. It signifies nothing going to this lord treasurer about business, although it be his own. He was in haste, and desires I will come again, and dine with him to-morrow. His famous lying porter[2] is fallen sick, and they think he will die: I wish I had all my half-crowns again. I believe I have told you, he is an old Scotch fanatick, and the damn'dest liar in his office alive. I have a mind to recommend Patrick to succeed him: I have trained him up pretty well. I reckon for certain, you are now in town. The weather now begins to alter to rain.

Windsor, 18. I dined to-day with lord treasurer, and he would make me go with him to Windsor, although I was engaged to the secretary, to whom I made my excuses: we had in the coach besides, his son and son-in-law, lord Harley, and lord Dupplin, who are two of our Society, and seven of us met by appointment, and supped this night with the secretary. It was past nine before we got here; but a fine moon-shiny night. I shall go back, I believe, on Monday. 'Tis very late.

[1] In Abchurch Lane. Pontack (1638?–1720?), whose christian-name is unknown, was the son of Arnaud de Pontac, president of the parliament of Bordeaux from 1653 to 1673, who died 1681. His father's vineyards contributed to the success of his house, where the Royal Society Club dined annually.
[2] His name was Read.—SCOTT.

19. The queen did not stir out to-day, she is in a little fit of the gout. I dined at Mr. Masham's; we had none but our society members, six in all, and I supped with lord treasurer. The queen has ordered twenty thousand pounds to go on with the building at Blenheim, which has been starved till now, since the change of the ministry. I suppose it is to reward his last action of getting into the French lines.[1] Lord treasurer kept me till past twelve.

London, 20. It rained terribly every step of our journey to-day; I returned with the secretary after a dinner of cold meat, and went to Mrs. Van's, where I sat the evening. I grow very idle, because I have a great deal of business. Tell me how you passed your time at Wexford; and an't you glad at heart you have got home safe to your lodgings at St. Mary's, pray? And so your friends come to visit you; and Mrs. Walls is much better of her eye; and the dean is just as he used to be: and what does Walls say of London? 'tis a reasoning coxcomb. And goody Stoyte, and Hannah what d'ye call her; no, her name en't Hannah, Catherine I mean; they were so glad to see the ladies again; and Mrs. Manley [2] wanted a companion at ombre.

21. I writ to-day to the archbishop of Dublin, and inclosed a long politick paper by itself. You know the bishops are all angry that (smoak the wax candle drop at the bottom of this paper) I have let the world know the First-Fruits were got by lord treasurer before the duke of Ormond was governor. I told lord treasurer all this, and he is very angry; but I pacified him again by telling him they were fools, and knew nothing of what passed here, but thought all was well enough, if they complimented the duke of Ormond. Lord treasurer gave me t'other day a letter of thanks he received from the bishops of Ireland, signed by seventeen, and says he will write them an answer. The dean of Carlisle sat with me to-day till three, and I went to dine with lord treasurer, who dined abroad, so did the secretary, and I was left in the suds. 'Twas almost four, and I got to Sir Matthew Dudley, who had half dined. Thornhill,[3] who killed Sir Cholmley Dering, was murdered by two men on Turnham-Green last Monday night: as they stabbed him, they bid him remember Sir Cholmley Dering. They had quarrelled at Hampton-Court, and followed and stabbed him on horseback. We have only a Grubstreet paper of it, but I believe it

[1] The capture of the lines before Bouchain; one of Marlborough's greatest exploits.—D. L. P.
[2] Mrs. *Isaac* Manley—not the authoress of the *New Atalantis*.
[3] *See* Letter XXII., May 9.

is true. I went myself through Turnham-Green the same night, which was yesterday.

22. We have had terrible rains these two or three days. I intended to dine at lord treasurer's, but went to see lady Abercorn, who is come to town, and my lord; and I dined with them, and visited lord treasurer this evening. His porter is mending. I sat with my lord about three hours, and am come home early to be busy. Passing by White's Chocolate-house,[1] my brother Masham called me, and told me his wife was brought to-bed of a boy, and both very well. (Our Society, you must know, are all brothers.) Dr. Garth told us, that Mr. Henley is dead of an apoplexy. His brother-in-law, earl Poulet,[2] is gone down to the Grange to take care of his funeral. The earl of Danby,[3] the duke of Leeds's eldest grandson, a very hopeful young man of about twenty, is dead at Utrecht of the small-pox.—I long to know whether you begin to have any good effect by your waters.—Methinks this letter goes on slowly; 'twill be a fortnight next Saturday since it was begun, and one side not filled. O fye for shame, Presto. Faith, I'm so tosticated to and from Windsor, that I know not what to say; but faith, I'll go to Windsor again on Saturday, if they ask me, not else. So lose your money again, now you are come home; do, sirrah.

Take your magnifying glass, madam Dingley.

You shan't read this, sirrah Stella; don't read it for your life, for fear of your dearest eyes.

There's enough for this side; these ministers hinder me.

Pretty, dear, little, naughty, saucy MD.

Silly, impudent loggerhead Presto.

23. Dilly and I dined to-day with lord Abercorn, and had a fine fat haunch of venison, that smelt rarely on one side: and after dinner Dilly won half a crown of me at backgammon at his lodgings, to his great content. It is a scurvy empty town this melancholy season of the year; but I think our weather begins to mend. The roads are as deep as in Winter. The grapes are sad things; but the peaches are pretty good, and there are some figs. I sometimes venture to eat one, but always repent

---

[1] At this time, White's Chocolate-house occupied its second site: on the west side of St. James's Street, three doors south of St. James's Place. The site is covered by the northern portion of Arthur's Club-house of to-day, says Mr. E. Beresford Chancellor.

[2] See Letter XX., April 10.

[3] William Henry Osborne (1690–1711), known as Viscount Latimer till 1694, and afterwards as Earl of Danby, died before his father, who was afterwards second Duke of Leeds, and who was the son of the Duke of Leeds mentioned in Letter VIII., Nov. 7, 1710.

it. You say nothing of the box sent half a year ago. I wish you would pay me for Mrs. Walls's tea. Your mother is in the country, I suppose. Pray send me the account of MD, madam Dingley, as it stands since November, that is to say, for this year, (excluding the twenty pounds lent Stella for Wexford) for I cannot look in your letters. I think I ordered that Hawkshaw's interest should be paid to you. When you think proper, I will let Parvisol know you have paid that twenty pounds, or part of it; and so go play with the dean, and I will answer your letter to-morrow. Good night, sirrahs, and love Presto, and be good girls.

24. I dined to-day with lord treasurer, who chid me for not dining with him yesterday, for it seems I did not understand his invitation: and their Club of the ministry dined together, and expected me. Lord Radnor and I were walking the Mall this evening; and Mr. secretary met us and took a turn or two, and then stole away, and we both believed it was to pick up some wench; and to-morrow he will be at the cabinet with the queen: so goes the world. Prior has been out of town these two months, nobody knows where, and is lately returned. People confidently affirm he has been in France, and I half believe it. It is said, he was sent by the ministry, and for some overtures towards a Peace. The secretary pretends he knows nothing of it. I believe your parliament will be dissolved. I have been talking about the quarrel between your lords and commons with lord treasurer; and did, at the request of some people, desire that the queen's answer to the commons address might express a dislike to some principles, &c. but was answered dubiously.—And so now to your letter, fair ladies. I know drinking is bad; I mean writing is bad in drinking the waters; and was angry to see so much in Stella's hand. But why Dingley drinks them I cannot imagine; but truly she'll drink waters as well as Stella: why not? I hope you now find the benefit of them since you returned: pray let me know particularly. I am glad you are forced upon exercise, which, I believe, is as good as the waters for the heart of them. 'Tis now past the middle of August; so by your reckoning you are in Dublin. It would vex me to the dogs that letters should miscarry between Dublin and Wexford, after scaping the salt seas. I will write no more [to] that nasty town in haste again, I warrant you. I have been four Sundays together at Windsor, of which a fortnight together; but I believe I shall not go to-morrow; for I will not, unless the secretary asks me. I know all your news about the mayor: it

devil that ever was born; and he a hot whiffling puppy, very apt to resent. I'll keep this bottom till to-morrow: I'm sleepy.

25. I was with the secretary this morning, who was in a mighty hurry, and went to Windsor in a chariot with lord keeper; so I was not invited, and am forced to stay at home; but not at all against my will; for I could have gone, and would not. I dined in the city with one of my printers, for whom I got the *Gazette*, and am come home early; and have nothing to say to you more, but finish this letter, and not send it by the bell-man. Days grow short, and the weather grows bad, and the town is splenetick, and things are so oddly contrived, that I cannot be absent; otherwise I would go for a few days to Oxford, as I promised.—They say, 'tis certain that Prior has been in France; nobody doubts it: I had not time to ask the secretary, he was in such haste. Well, I will take my leave of dearest MD for a while; for I must begin my next letter to-night: consider that, young women; and pray be merry, and good girls, and love Presto. There is now but one business the ministry wants me for; and when that is done, I will take my leave of them. I never got a penny from them, nor expect it. In my opinion, some things stand very ticklish; I dare say nothing at this distance. Farewel, dear sirrahs, dearest lives: there is peace and quiet with MD, and nowhere else. They have not leisure here to think of small things, which may ruin them: and I have been forward enough. Farewel again, dearest rogues; I am never happy, but when I write or think of MD. I have enough of Courts and ministries; and wish I were at Laracor: and if I could with honour come away this moment, I would. —Bernage [1] came to see me to-day; he is just landed from Portugal, and come to raise recruits: he looks very well, and seems pleased with his station and manner of life: he never saw London nor England before; he is ravished with Kent, which was his first prospect when he landed. Farewel again, &c. &c.

[1] Dr. Swift obtained for Mr. Bernage, who was educated in the University of Dublin, an ensign's commission from the Earl of Pembroke, when Lord Lieutenant. He was afterward made a captain, but was disbanded at the Peace of Utrecht. He sent the dean some fine medals and other curiosities from Rome.—N.

LETTER XXIX

London, *Aug.* 25, 1711.

I HAVE got a pretty small gilt sheet of paper to write to MD. I have this moment sent my 28th by Patrick, who tells me he has put it in the post-office; 'tis directed to your lodgings: if it wants more particular direction, you must set me right. It is now a solar month and two days since the date of your last, N. 18, and I reckon you are now quiet at home, and thinking to begin your 19th, which will be full of your quarrel between the two houses, all which I know already. Where shall I dine to-morrow? can you tell? Mrs. Vanhomrigh boards now, and cannot invite one; and there I used to dine when I was at a loss; and all my friends are gone out of town, and your town is now at the fullest with your parliament and convocation. But let me alone, sirrahs; for Presto is going to be very busy; not Presto, but t'other I.[1]

26. People have so left the town, that I am at a loss for a dinner. It is a long time since I have been at London upon a Sunday; and the ministers are all at Windsor. It cost me eighteen pence in coach-hire before I could find a place to dine in. I went to Frankland's, and he was abroad, and the drab his wife lookt out at window, and bowed to me without inviting me up: so I dined with Mr. Coote,[2] my lord Montrath's brother; my lord is with you in Ireland. This morning at five my lord Jersey[3] died of the gout in his stomach, or apoplexy, or both: he was abroad yesterday, and his death was sudden: he was chamberlain to king William, and a great favourite, turned out by the queen as a Tory, and stood now fair to be privy-seal; and by his death will, I suppose, make that matter easier, which has been a very stubborn business at Court, as I have been informed. I never remembered so many people of quality to have died in so short a time.

27. I went to-day into the city to thank Stratford for my books, and dine with him, and settle my affairs of my money in the bank, and receive a bill for Mrs. Wesley for some things to buy for her; and the d— a one of all these could I do. The merchants were all out of town, and I was forced to go to a little

---

[1] That is, Swift in his serious person.
[2] *See* Letter VI., Oct. 11, 1710.
[3] Edward Villiers (*c.* 1656–1711), first earl. He married (1681) Barbara, daughter of the notorious William Chiffinch, keeper of the closet to Charles II.

hedge place for my dinner. May my enemies live here in Summer!
and yet I am so unlucky that I cannot possibly be out of the
way at this juncture. People leave the town so late in Summer,
and return so late in Winter, that they have almost inverted
the seasons. It is Autumn this good while in St. James's Park;
the limes have been losing their leaves, and those remaining
on the trees are all parched: I hate this season, where every
thing grows worse and worse. The only good thing of it is the
fruit, and that I dare not eat. Had you any fruit at Wexford?
A few cherries, and durst not eat them. I do not hear we have
yet got a new privy-seal. The Whigs whisper, that our new
ministry differ among themselves, and they begin to talk out
Mr. secretary: they have some reasons for their whispers,
although I thought it was a greater secret. I do not much like
the posture of things; I always apprehended, that any falling
out would ruin them, and so I have told them several times.
The Whigs are mighty full of hopes at present; and whatever
is the matter, all kind of stocks fall. I have not yet talked with
the secretary about Prior's journey. I should be apt to think
it may fortel a peace; and that is all we have to preserve us.
The secretary is not come from Windsor; but I expect him
to-morrow. Burn all politicks!

28. We begin to have fine weather, and I walked to-day to
Chelsea, and dined with the dean of Carlisle, who is laid up
with the gout. It is now fixed that he is to be dean of Christ-
church in Oxford. I was advising him to use his interest to
prevent any misunderstanding between our ministers; but he
is too wise to meddle, though he fears the thing and the consequences as much as I. He will get into his own warm quiet
deanry, and leave them to themselves; and he is in the right.
—When I came home to-night I found a letter from Mr. Lewis,
who is now at Windsor; and in it, forsooth, another which
lookt like Presto's hand; and what should it be but a 19th
from MD? O faith, I scaped narrowly, for I sent my 28th
but on Saturday; and what should I have done if I had two
letters to answer at once? I did not expect another from Wexford, that's certain. Well, I must be contented; but you are
dear saucy girls, for all that, to write so soon again, faith;
an't you?

29. I dined to-day with lord Abercorn, and took my leave
of them; they set out to-morrow for Chester, and, I believe,
will now fix in Ireland. They have made a pretty good journey
of it: his eldest son is married to a lady with ten thousand

pounds[1]; and his second son[2] has, t'other day, got a prize in the lottery of four thousand pounds, beside two small ones of two hundred pounds each: nay, the family was so fortunate, that my lord bestowing one ticket, which is a hundred pounds, to one of his servants, who had been his page, the young fellow got a prize, which has made it another hundred. I went in the evening to lord treasurer, who desires I will dine with him to-morrow, when he will shew me the answer he designs to return to the letter of thanks from your bishops in Ireland. The archbishop of Dublin desired me to get myself mentioned in the answer which my lord would send; but I sent him word I would not open my lips to my lord upon it. He says, It would convince the bishops of what I have affirmed, that the First-Fruits were granted before the duke of Ormond was declared governor; and I writ to him, That I would not give a farthing to convince them. My lord treasurer began a health to my lord privy-seal; Prior punned, and said it was so privy, he knew not who it was; but I fancy they have fixt it all, and we shall know to-morrow. But what care you who is privy-seal, saucy sluttikins?

30. When I went out this morning, I was surprized with the news, that the bishop of Bristol is made lord privy-seal. You know his name is Robinson,[3] and that he was many years envoy in Sweden. All the friends of the present ministry are extreme glad, and the clergy above the rest. The Whigs will fret to death, to see a civil employment given to a clergyman. It was a very handsome thing in my lord treasurer, and will bind the church to him for ever. I dined with him to-day, but he had not written his letter; but told me, he would not offer to send it without shewing it to me: he thought that would not be just, since I was so deeply concerned in the affair. We had much company; lord Rivers, Marr,[4] and Kinnoul,[5] Mr. secretary, George Granville, and Masham; the last has invited me to the christening of his son to-morrow sennight, and on Saturday I go to Windsor with Mr. secretary.

[1] Lord Paisley. *See* Letter XVII., March 2, 1710-11. But he was really second son.

[2] Mr. Aitken says the Hon. John (second surviving son), who died 1714.

[3] John (1650–1723), second surviving son of John Robinson of Cleasby, north Yorkshire. He had already gained political experience as chaplain to the English Embassy in Sweden for about a quarter of a century.

[4] John Erskine (1675–1732), twenty-third Earl of Mar, "Bobbing John," attainted 1715-16 — changed sides between Hanoverian and Jacobite more than once.

[5] Thomas Hay (*c.* 1669–1719), sixth earl. *See* Letter V., Oct. 7, 1710, note on "Doblane."

31. Dilly and I walked to-day to Kensington to lady Mount-joy,[1] who invited us to dinner. He returned soon to go to a play, it being the last that will be acted for some time: he dresses himself like a beau, and no doubt makes a fine figure. I went to visit some people at Kensington; Ophy Butler's wife there lies very ill of an ague, which is a very common disease here, and little known in Ireland.—I am apt to think we shall soon have a Peace, by the little words I hear thrown out by the ministry. I have just thought of a project to bite the town. I have told you, that it is now known that Mr. Prior has been lately in France. I will make a printer of my own sit by me one day, and I will dictate to him a formal relation of Prior's journey, with several particulars, all pure inventions; and I doubt not but it will take.

Sept. 1. Morning. I go to-day to Windsor with Mr. secretary; and lord treasurer has promised to bring me back. The weather has been fine for some time, and I believe we shall have a great deal of dust.—At night. *Windsor.* The secretary and I and brigadier Sutton dined to-day at Parson's-Green, at my lord Peterborow's house, who has left it and his gardens to the secretary during his absence. It is the finest garden I have ever seen about this town, and abundance of hot walls for grapes, where they are in great plenty, and ripening fast. I durst not eat any fruit but one fig; but I brought a basket full to my friend Lewis here at Windsor. Does Stella never eat any? what, no apricocks at Donnybrook? nothing but claret and ombre; I envy people maunching and maunching [2] peaches and grapes, and I not daring to eat a bit. My head is pretty well, only a sudden turn any time makes me giddy for a moment, and sometimes it feels very stufft; but if it grows no worse, I can bear it very well. I take all opportunities of walking; and we have a delicious park here just joining to the castle, and an avenue in the great park very wide and two miles long, set with a double row of elms on each side. Were you ever at Windsor? I was once a great while ago; but had quite forgotten it.

2. The queen has the gout, and did not come to chapel, nor stir out from her chamber, but received the sacrament there: as she always does the first Sunday in the month. Yet we had a great Court, and among others, I saw your Ingoldsby, who

[1] See Letter VIII., Nov. 3, 1710.
[2] As the provincial word *maunching* echoes rather better to the action of the jaws than the proper term *munching*, it is therefore here retained.
—D. S.

seeing me talk very familiarly with the keeper, treasurer, &c.
came up and saluted me, and began a very impertinent discourse about the siege of Bouchain. I told him, I could not
answer his questions, but I would bring him one that should;
so I went and fetched Sutton (who brought over the express
about a month ago) and delivered him to the general, and bid
him answer his questions; and so I left them together. Sutton
after some time comes back in rage; finds me with lord Rivers
and Masham, and there complains of the trick I had played
him, and swore he had been plagued to death with Ingoldsby's
talk. But he told me, Ingoldsby askt him what I meant by
bringing him; so, I suppose, he smoakt me a little. So we
laughed, &c. My lord Willoughby, who is one of the chaplains,
and prebendary of Windsor, read prayers last night to the
family; and the bishop of Bristol, who is dean of Windsor,
officiated last night at the cathedral. This they do to be popular,
and it pleases mightily. I dined with Mr. Masham, because he
lets me have a select company. For the Court here have got
by the end a good thing I said to the secretary some weeks ago.
He shewed me his bill of fare to tempt me to dine with him;
Poh, said I, I value not your bill of fare, give me your bill of
company. Lord treasurer was mightily pleased, and told it
every body, as a notable thing. I reckon upon returning to-
morrow; they say the bishop will then have the privy-seal
delivered him at a great council.

3. Windsor still. The council was held so late to-day, that
I do not go back to town till to-morrow. The bishop was sworn
privy-counsellor, and had the privy-seal given him: and now
the patents are passed for those who were this long time to be
made lords or earls. Lord Raby, who is earl of Strafford, is
on Thursday to marry a namesake of Stella's; the daughter of
Sir H. Johnson in the city [1]; he has threescore thousand pounds
with her, ready money; besides the rest at the father's death.
I have got my friend Stratford [2] to be one of the directors of
the South-Sea company, who were named to-day. My lord
treasurer did it for me a month ago; and one of those whom
I got to be printer of the *Gazette*, I am recommending to be
printer to the same company. He treated Mr. Lewis and me
to-day at dinner. I supped last night and this with lord treasurer,

[1] The Lord Raby of Letter XVIII., March 15, 1710-11, became third
bearer of the title of Earl of Strafford, June 29, 1711, and on Sept. 6 married
Anne, daughter and heiress (£60,000) of Sir Henry Johnson of Bradenham,
Bucks. She died 1754.
[2] *See* Letter III., Sept. 13, 1710, and note.

JOURNAL TO STELLA

keeper, &c. and took occasion to mention the printer. I said,
It was the same printer, whom my lord treasurer has appointed
to print for the South-Sea company; he denied, and I insisted
on it; and I got the laugh on my side.

London, 4. I came as far as Brentford in lord Rivers's
chariot, who had business with lord treasurer; then I went
into lord treasurer's: we stopt at Kensington, where lord
treasurer went to see Mrs. Masham, who is now what they
call in the straw. We got to town by three, and I lighted at
lord treasurer's; who commanded me not to stir: but I was not
well; and when he went up, I begged the young lord to excuse
me, and so went into the city by water, where I could be easier,
and dined with the printer, and dictated to him some part of
Prior's journey to France. I walkt from the city, for I take all
occasions of exercise. Our journey was horrid dusty.

5. When I went out to-day, I found it had rained mightily
in the night, and the streets were as dirty as Winter: it is very
refreshing after ten days dry.—I went into the city and dined
with Stratford, thanked him for his books, gave him joy of his
being director, of which he had the first notice by a letter
from me. I ate sturgeon, and it lies on my stomach. I almost
finished Prior's journey at the printer's, and came home pretty
late with Patrick at my heels.

7.[1] Morning. But what shall we do about this letter of MD's
N. 19? not a word answered yet, and so much paper spent?
I cannot do any thing in it, sweethearts, till night.—At night.
O Lord, O Lord, the greatest disgrace that ever was has happened to Presto. What do you think; but when I was going out
this forenoon a letter came from MD, N. 20, dated at Dublin.
O dear, O dear; O sad, O sad.—Now I have two letters together
to answer: here they are, lying together. But I will only answer
the first; for I came in late. I dined with my friend Lewis at
his lodgings, and walked at six to Kensington to Mr. Masham's
son's christening. It was very private; nobody there but my
lord treasurer, his son, and son-in-law, that is to say, lord
Harley, and lord Dupplin, and lord Rivers and I. The dean of
Rochester [2] christened the child, but soon went away. Lord
treasurer and lord Rivers were godfathers, and Mrs. Hill,[3]
Mrs. Masham's sister, godmother. The child roared like a bull,

[1] Entry for 6th comes after 7th.
[2] Samuel Pratt (1659?-1723), Dean of Rochester and clerk of the
closet since 1706.
[3] Alice (*c.* 1685-1762), Mrs. Masham's younger sister, a woman of the
bedchamber.

and I gave Mrs. Masham joy of it; and she charged me to take care of my nephew; because Mr. Masham being a brother of our Society, his son you know is consequently a nephew. Mrs. Masham sat up dressed in bed, but not as they do in Ireland with all smooth about her, as if she was cut off in the middle; for you might see the counterpain (what d'ye call it?) rise about her hips and body. There's another name of the counterpain, and you'll laugh now, sirrahs. George Granville came in at supper, and we stayed till eleven, and lord treasurer set me down at my lodgings in Suffolk-street. Did I ever tell you that lord treasurer hears ill with the left ear, just as I do? he always turns the right; and his servants whisper him at that only. I dare not tell him, that I am so too, for fear he should think I counterfeited, to make my court.

6. You must read this before the other; for I mistook, and forgot to write yesterday's journal, it was so insignificant: I dined with Dr. Cockburn, and sat the evening with lord treasurer, till ten o'clock. On Thursdays he has always a large select company, and expects me. So good night for last night, &c.

8. Morning. I go to Windsor with lord treasurer to-day, and will leave this behind me to be sent to the post. And now let us hear what says the first letter, N. 19. You are still at Wexford, as you say, madam Dingley. I think no letter from me ever yet miscarried. And so *Inish-Corthy*,[1] and the river *Slainy*; fine words those in a lady's mouth. Your hand like Dingley's, you scambling, scattering, sluttekin. *Yes mighty like indeed, is not it?*[2] Pisshh, don't talk of writing or reading till your eyes are well, and long well; only I would have Dingley read sometimes to you, that you may not quite lose the desire of it. God be thanked that the ugly numming is gone. Pray use exercise when you go to town. What game is that ombra[3] which Dr. Elwood and you play at? is it the Spanish game ombre? Your card purse? you a card purse! you a fiddlestick. You have luck indeed; and luck in a bag. What a Devil is that eight shilling tea-kettle copper, or tin japanned? It is like your Irish politeness, raffling for tea-kettles. What a splutter you keep to convince me that Walls has no taste? My head continues pretty well. Why do you write, dear sirrah Stella, when you find your eyes so weak that you cannot see? wha

---

[1] Enniscorthy, Wexford.
[2] These words in *Italicks* are written in strange misshapen letters inclining to the right hand, in imitation of Stella's writing.—D. S.
[3] In Stella's spelling. It is an odd thing that a woman of Stella's understanding should spell extremely ill.—D. S.

comfort is there in reading what you write, when one knows that? So Dingley can't write because of the clutter of new company come to Wexford? I suppose the noise of their hundred horses disturbs you; or, do you lie in one gallery, as in an hospital? What; you are afraid of losing in Dublin the acquaintance you have got in Wexford; and chiefly the bishop of Rapho,[1] an old, doating, perverse coxcomb? Twenty at a time at breakfast. That is like five pounds at a time, when it was never but once. I doubt, madam Dingley, you are apt to lie in your Travels, though not so bad as Stella; she tells thumpers, as I shall prove in my next, if I find this receives encouragement. —So Dr. Elwood[2] says, There are a world of pretty things in my works. A pox on his praises! an enemy here would say more. The duke of Buckingham would say as much, though he and I are terribly fallen out; and the great men are perpetually inflaming me against him: they bring me all he says of me, and, I believe, make it worse out of roguery.—No 'tis not your pen is bewitched, madam Stella, but your old *scrawling, splay-foot, pot hooks*,[3] *s, ſ*, ay that's it: there the s, ſ, ſ, there, there, that's exact. Farewel, &c.

Our fine weather is gone, and I doubt we shall have a rainy journey to-day. Faith, 'tis shaving day, and I have much to do.

When Stella says her pen is bewitched, it was only because there was a hair in it. You know the fellow they call God-help-it had he same thoughts of his wife, and for the same reason. I think this s very well observed, and I unfolded the letter to tell you it.

Cut off those two notes above; and see the nine pounds ndorsed, and receive the other; and send me word how my iccounts stand, that they may be adjusted by Nov. 1. Pray be very particular: but the twenty pounds I lend you is not to be ncluded; so make no blunder. I won't wrong you; nor you shan't vrong me; that's the short. O Lord, how stout Presto is of late? Jut he loves MD more than his life a thousand times, for all iis stoutness; tell him that; and I'll swear it, as hope saved, en millions of times, &c. &c.

I open my letter once more to tell Stella, that if she does not se exercise after her waters, it will lose all the effects of them: should not live, if I did not take all opportunities of walking. 'ray, pray, do this to oblige poor Presto.

---

[1] John Pooley (*d.* 1712), Bishop of Raphoe since 1702. An Englishman.
[2] Senior fellow of Trinity College, Dublin, and member of Parliament r that university.—D. S.
[3] These words in *Italicks*, and the two *esses* that follow, are miserably :rawled, in imitation of Stella's hand.—D. S.

LETTER XXX

Windsor, *Sept.* 8, 1711.

I MADE the coachman stop, and put in my twenty-ninth at the post-office at two o'clock to-day, as I was going to lord treasurer, with whom I dined, and came here by a quarter past eight; but the Moon shone, and so we were not in much danger of overturning; which however he values not a straw, and only laughs when I chide at him for it. There was nobody but he and I, and we supped together, with Mr. Masham, and Dr. Arbuthnot, the queen's favourite physician, a Scotchman. I could not keep myself awake after supper, but did all I was able to disguise it, and thought I came off clear, but at parting he told me, I had got my nap already. It is now one o'clock; but he loves sitting up late.

9. The queen is still in the gout, but recovering; she saw company in her bed-chamber after church; but the crowd was so great, I could not see her. I dined with my brother, Sir William Windham, and some others of our Society, to avoid the great tables on Sunday at Windsor, which I hate. The usual company supped to-night at lord treasurer's, which was lord keeper, Mr. secretary, George Granville, Masham, Arbuthnot and I. But showers have hindred me from walking to-day, and that I don't love.—Noble fruit, and I dare not eat a bit. I ate one fig to-day, and sometimes a few mulberries, because it is said, they are wholesome, and you know, a good name does much. I shall return to town to-morrow, though I thought to have staid a week, to be at leisure for something I am doing. But I have put it off till next; for I shall come here again on Saturday, when our Society are to meet at supper at Mr secretary's. My life is very regular here: on Sunday morning I constantly visit lord keeper, and sup at lord treasurer's with the same set of company. I was not sleepy to-night I resolved I would not; yet it is past midnight at this present writing.

London, 10. Lord treasurer and Masham and I left Windsor at three this afternoon; we dropt Masham at Kensington with his lady, and got home by six. It was seven before we sat down to dinner, and I stayed till past eleven. Patrick came home with the secretary: I am more plagued with Patrick and my port mantua than with myself. I forgot to tell you, that when I went to Windsor on Saturday, I overtook lady Giffard and Mrs

Fenton in a chariot going, I suppose, to Sheen.[1] I was then in a chariot too, of lord treasurer's brother, who had business with the treasurer; and my lord came after, and overtook me at Turnham-Green, four miles from London, and then the brother went back, and I went in the coach with lord treasurer: so it happened that those people saw me, and not with lord treasurer. Mrs. F. was to see me about a week ago; and desired I would get her son into the Charter-house.

11. This morning the printer sent me an account of Prior's journey; it makes a two-penny pamphlet, I suppose you will see it, for I dare engage it will run; 'tis a formal grave lie, from the beginning to the end. I writ all but about the last page, that I dictated, and the printer writ. Mr. secretary sent to me to dine where he did; it was at Prior's; when I came in Prior shewed me the pamphlet, seemed to be angry, and said, Here is our English liberty: I read some of it, and said I liked it mightily, and envied the rogue the thought; for had it come into my head, I should have certainly done it myself. We stayed at Prior's till past ten, and then the secretary received a pacquet with the news of Bouchain being taken, for which the guns will go off to-morrow. Prior owned his having been in France, for it was past denying; it seems he was discovered by a rascal at Dover, who had positive orders to let him pass.[2] I believe we shall have a peace.

12. It is terrible rainy weather, and has cost me three shillings in coaches and chairs to-day, yet I was dirty into the bargain. I was three hours this morning with the secretary about some business of moment, and then went into the city to dine. The printer tells me he sold yesterday a thousand of Prior's journey,[3] and had printed five hundred more. It will do rarely, I believe, and is a pure bite. And what is MD doing all this while? got again to their cards, their Walls, their deans, their Stoytes, and their claret? Pray present my service to Mr. Stoyte and Catherine. Tell goody Stoyte, she owes me a world of dinners, and I will shortly come over and demand them.—Did I tell you of the archbishop of Dublin's last letter? He had been saying in several of his former, that he would shortly write to

[1] To Lady Giffard's house there. (Mrs. Fenton—see Letter IX., Nov. 23, 1710.)

[2] He was seized by the custom-house officers, who suspected him to be a French emissary, probably; he had landed from a small vessel near Deal.—D. L. P.

[3] A New Journey to Paris together with some Secret Transactions between the Fr—h K— and an Eng— Gentleman. By the Sieur du Baudrier, Translated from the French. 1711.

me something about myself, and it looked to me as if he intended
something for me: at last out it comes, and consists of two
parts. First, he advises me to strike in for some preferment
now I have friends; and secondly, he advises me, since I have
parts, and learning, and a happy pen, to think of some new
subject in Divinity not handled by others, which I should
manage better than any body. A rare spark this, with a pox!
but I shall answer him as rarely. Methinks he should have
invited me over, and given me some hopes or promises. But,
hang him! and so good night, &c.

13. It rained most furiously all this morning till about
twelve, and sometimes thundered; I trembled for my shillings,
but it cleared up, and I made a shift to get a walk in the Park,
and then went with the secretary to dine with lord treasurer.
Upon Thursdays there is always a select company; we had the
duke of Shrewsbury, lord Rivers, the two secretaries,[1] Mr.
Granville, and Mr. Prior. Half of them went to council at six;
but Rivers, Granville, Prior and I stayed till eight. Prior was
often affecting to be angry at the account of his journey to
Paris; and indeed the two last pages, which the printer [had]
got somebody to add, are so romantick, they spoil all the rest.
Dilly Ashe pretended to me that he was only going to Oxford
and Cambridge for a fortnight, and then would come back.
I could not see him, as I appointed t'other day; but some of his
friends tell me, he took leave of them as going to Ireland;
and so they say at his lodging. I believe the rogue was ashamed
to tell me so, because I advised him to stay the Winter, and he
said he would. I find he had got into a good set of scrub acquaintance, and I thought passed his time very merrily; but I suppose
he languished after Balderig,[2] and the claret of Dublin; and,
after all, I think he is in the right; for he can eat, drink and
converse better there than here. Bernage was with me this
morning: he calls now and then; he is in terrible fear of a
Peace. He said, he never had his health so well as in Portugal.
He is a favourite of his colonel.

14. I was mortified enough to-day, not knowing where in
the world to dine, the town is so empty; I met H. Coote,[3] and
thought he would invite me, but he did not: Sir John Stanley
did not come into my head; so I took up with Mrs. Van, and
dined with her and her damned landlady, who, I believe, by
her eyebrows, is a bawd. This evening I met Addison and

---

[1] St. John and Lord Dartmouth.   [2] Locality awaiting identification.
[3] See Letter VI., Oct. 11, 1710.

Pastoral Phillips in the Park, and supped with them at Addison's lodgings; we were very good company; and yet know no man half so agreeable to me as he is. I sat with them till twelve, so you may think 'tis late, young women; however, I would have some little conversation with MD before your Presto goes to bed, because it makes me sleep and dream, and so forth. Faith this letter goes on slowly enough, sirrahs, but I can't write much at a time till you are quite settled after your journey you know, and have gone all your visits, and lost your money at ombre. You never play at chess now, Stella. That puts me in mind of Dick Tighe; I fancy I told you, he used to beat his wife here; and she deserved it; and he resolves to part with her; and they went to Ireland in different coaches. O Lord, I said all this before, I'm sure. Go to bed, sirrahs.

Windsor, 15. I made the secretary stop at Brentford, because we set out at two this afternoon, and fasting would not agree with me. I only designed to eat a bit of bread and butter, but he would light, and we ate roast beef like dragons. And he made me treat him and two more gentlemen; faith it cost me a guinea; I don't like such jesting, yet I was mightily pleased with it too. To-night our Society met at the secretary's, there were nine of us; and we have chosen a new member, the earl of Jersey,[1] whose father died lately. 'Tis past one, and I have stolen away.

16. I design to stay here this week by myself, about some business that lies on my hands, and will take up a great deal of time. Dr. Adams,[2] one of the canons, invited me to-day to dinner. The tables are so full here on Sunday, that it is hard to dine with a few, and Dr. Adams knows I love to do so; which is very obliging. The queen saw company in her bed-chamber; she looks very well, but she sat down. I supped with lord treasurer as usual, and stayed till past one as usual, and with our usual company, except lord keeper, who did not come this time to Windsor. I hate these suppers mortally; but I seldom eat any thing.

17. Lord treasurer and Mr. secretary stay here till to-morrow; some business keeps them, and I am sorry for it, for they hinder me a day. Mr. Lewis and I were going to dine soberly with a little court friend at one. But lord Harley and lord Dupplin kept me by force, and said we should dine at lord

[1] William Villiers (*c.* 1682–1721), Viscount Villiers 1697–1711, M.P. for Kent 1705–1708, succeeded his father as second Earl of Jersey, Aug. 26, 1711.
[2] *See* Letter XXVIII., Aug. 12.

treasurer's, who intended to go at four to London; I stayed like a fool, and went with the two young lords to lord treasurer; who very fairly turned us all three out of doors. They both were invited to the duke of Somerset, but he was gone to a horse-race, and would not come till five: so we were forced to go to a tavern, and sent for wine from lord treasurer's, who at last we were told did not go to town till the morrow, and at lord treasurer's we supped again; and I desired him to let me add four shillings to the bill I gave him. We sat up till two, yet I must write to little MD.

18. They are all gone early this morning; and I am alone to seek my fortune; but Dr. Arbuthnot engages me for my dinners; and he yesterday gave me my choice of place, person, and victuals for to-day. So I chose to dine with Mrs. Hill, who is one of the dressers, and Mrs. Masham's sister, no company but us three, and to have a shoulder of mutton, a small one, which was exactly, only there was too much victuals besides; and the Dr.'s wife[1] was of the company. And to-morrow Mrs. Hill and I are to dine with the Doctor. I have seen a fellow often about Court, whom I thought I knew; I asked who he was, and they told me it was the gentleman porter; then I called him to mind; he was Killy's acquaintance (I won't say yours) I think his name is Lovet, or Lovel,[2] or something like it. I believe he does not know me, and in my present posture I shall not be fond of renewing old acquaintance; I believe I used to see him with the Bradleys[3]; and by the way, I have not seen Mrs. Bradley since I came to England. I left your letter in London, like a fool; and cannot answer it till I go back, which will not be until Monday next: so this will be above a fortnight from my last; but I will fetch it up in my next; so go and walk to the dean's for your health this fine weather.

19. The queen designs to have cards and dancing here next week, which makes us think she will stay here longer than we believed. Mrs. Masham is not well after her lying-in: I doubt she got some cold; she is lame in one of her legs with a rheumatick pain. Dr. Arbuthnot and Mrs. Hill go to-morrow to Kensington to see her, and return the same night. Mrs. Hill and I dined with the Doctor to-day. I rode out this morning with the Doctor to see Cranburn, a house of lord Ranelagh's,[4]

[1] Mr. Aitken says she died 1730.
[2] Lovet, gentleman porter. Mr. Aitken says a yeoman porter, named John Lovet.
[3] They seem to have been dependants of the Temples and Lady Giffard.
[4] Richard Jones (d. 1711-12) only Earl of Ranelagh.

and the duchess of Marlborough's lodge, and the park; the finest places they are for nature, and plantations, that ever I saw; and the finest riding upon artificial roads, made on purpose for the queen. Arbuthnot made me draw up a sham subscription for a book, called *A History of the Maids of honour since Harry the eighth*, shewing they make the best wives, with a list of all the maids of honour since, &c. to pay a crown in hand, and t'other crown upon delivery of the book; and all in the common forms of those things. We got a gentleman to write it fair, because my hand is known, and we sent it to the maids of honour, when they came to supper. If they bite at it, 'twill be a very good court jest; and the queen will certainly have it; we did not tell Mrs. Hill.

20. To-day I was invited to the green-cloth by colonel Godfrey,[1] who married the duke of Marlbrough's sister, mother to the duke of Berwick by king James: I must tell you those things that happened before you were born: But I made my excuses, and young Harcourt (lord keeper's son) and I dined with my next neighbour Dr. Adams. Mrs. Masham is better, and will be here in three or four days. She had need; for the duchess of Somerset is thought to gain ground daily.—We have not yet sent you over all your bills; and I think we have altered your money-bill. The duke of Ormond is censured here by those in power for very wrong management in the affair of the mayoralty. He is governed by fools; and has usually much more sense than his advisers, but never proceeds by it. I must know how your health continues after Wexford. Walk and use exercise, sirrahs both; and get somebody to play at shuttle-cock with you, madam Stella, and walk to the dean's and Donnybrook.

21. Colonel Godfrey sent to me again to-day; so I dined at the green-cloth, and we had but eleven at dinner, which is a small number there, the Court being always thin of company till Saturday night.—This new ink and pen make a strange figure; *I must write larger, yes I must, or Stella won't be able to read this*.[2] S.S.S. there's your Ss for you, Stella. The maids of honour are bit, and have all contributed their crowns, and are

[1] Charles Godfrey (*d.* 1714), lieut.-colonel of Sir T. Slingsby's regiment of foot, 1678; major and capt.-lieut. of Lord Gerard's regiment of horse, 1679; had the posts of master of the jewel house and clerk-comptroller of the board of green cloth. His wife was Arabella Churchill: maid of honour to the Duchess of York; and mistress to the Duke, to whom she bore two sons—the celebrated Marshal Berwick, and Henry Fitz-James, grand prior of France—and a daughter, who took the veil.

[2] These words in *Italicks* are written enormously large.—D. S.

teazing others to subscribe for the book. I will tell lord keeper
and lord treasurer to-morrow; and I believe the queen will have
it. After a little walk this evening, I squandered away the rest
of it in sitting at Lewis's lodging, while he and Dr. Arbuthnot
played at picquet. I have that foolish pleasure, which I believe
nobody has beside me, except old lady Berkeley.[1] But I fretted
when I came away; I will loiter so no more, for I have a plaguy
deal of business upon my hands, and very little time to do it.
The pamphleteers begin to be very busy against the ministry:
I have begged Mr. secretary to make examples of one or
two of them; and he assures me he will. They are very bold
and abusive.

22. This being the day the ministry comes to Windsor, I ate
a bit or two at Mr. Lewis's lodgings, because I must sup with
lord treasurer; and at half an hour after one, I led Mr. Lewis
a walk up the avenue, which is two miles long: we walkt in all
about five miles; but I was so tired with his slow walking, that
I left him here, and walkt two miles towards London, hoping
to meet lord treasurer, and return with him; but it grew
darkish, and I was forced to walk back, so I walkt nine miles
in all; and lord treasurer did not come till after eight; which
is very wrong, for there was no Moon, and I often tell him how
ill he does to expose himself so; but he only makes a jest of it.
I supped with him, and staid till now, when it is half an hour
after two. He is as merry, and careless, and disengaged as a
young heir at one and twenty. 'Tis late indeed.

23. The secretary did not come last night, but at three this
afternoon; I have not seen him yet; but I verily think they
are contriving a Peace as fast as they can, without which it
will be impossible to subsist. The queen was at church to-day,
but was carried in a chair. I and Mr. Lewis dined privately
with Mr. Lowman, clerk of the kitchen. I was to see lord keeper
this morning, and told him the jest of the maids of honour, and
lord treasurer had it last night. That rogue Arbuthnot puts it
all upon me. The Court was very full to-day; I expected lord
treasurer would have invited me to supper; but he only bowed
to me, and we had no discourse in the drawing-room. 'Tis now
seven at night, and I am at home; and I hope lord treasurer
will not send for me to supper; if he does not, I will reproach
him, and he will pretend to chide me for not coming.—So
farewell till I go to bed, for I am going to be busy.—'Tis now
past ten, and I went down to ask the servants about Mr.

[1] *See* Letter III., Sept. 19, 1710.

secretary; they tell me the queen is yet at council, and that she went to supper, and came out to the council afterwards. 'Tis certain they are managing a Peace. I will go to bed, and there's an end.—'Tis now eleven, and a messenger is come from lord treasurer to sup with them; but I have excused myself, and am glad I am in bed; for else I should sit up till two, and drink till I was hot. Now I'll go sleep.

London, 24. I came to town by six with lord treasurer, and have staid till ten. That of the queen's going out to sup, and coming in again, is a lie, as the secretary told me this morning: but I find the ministry are very busy with Mr. Prior, and I believe he will go again to France. I am told so much, that we shall certainly have a Peace very soon. I had charming weather all last week at Windsor; but we have had a little rain to-day, and yesterday was windy. *Prior's Journey* sells still; they have sold two thousand, although the town is empty. I found a letter from Mrs. Fenton here, desiring me in lady Giffard's name to come and pass a week at Sheen, while she is at Moorpark. I will answer it with a vengeance: and now you talk of answering, there is MD's N. 20 is yet to be answered: I had put it up so safe I could hardly find it; but here it is, faith, and I am afraid I cannot send this till Thursday; for I must see the secretary to-morrow morning, and be in some other place in the evening.

25. Stella writes likes an emperor, and gives such an account of her journey, never saw the like. Let me see; stand away, let us compute; you staid four days at Inish-Corthy; two nights at Mrs. Proby's mother's; and yet was but six days in journey; for your words are, "We left Wexford this day sennight, and came here last night." I have heard them say, that travellers may lie by authority. Make up this, if you can. How far is it from Wexford to Dublin? how many miles did you travel in a day?[1] Let me see — thirty pounds in two months, is nine score pounds a year; a matter of nothing in Stella's purse. I dreamed Billy Swift[2] was alive, and that I told him, you writ me word he was dead, and that you had been at his funeral, and I admired at your impudence, and was in mighty haste to

[1] The doctor was always a bad reckoner, either of money or any thing else; and this is one of his rapid computations. For as Stella was seven days in journey, although Dr. Swift says only six, she might well have spent four days at Inish-Corthy, and two nights at Mrs. Proby's mother's, the distance from Wexford to Dublin being but two easy days journey.—D. S.

[2] *See* Letter XXVII., Aug. 2.

run and let you know what lying rogues you were. Poor lad, he is dead of his mother's former folly and fondness, and yet now I believe as you say, that her grief will soon wear off.— O yes, madam Dingley, mightily tired of the company, no doubt of it, at Wexford? And your description of it is excellent; clean sheets, but bare walls; I suppose then you lay upon the walls.—Mrs. Walls has got her tea; but who pays me the money? Come, I shall never get it; so I make a present of it to stop some gaps, &c. Where's the thanks of the house? So, that's well; why, it cost four and thirty shillings English.— You must adjust that with Mrs. Walls; I think that is so many pence more with you.—No, Leigh and Sterne, I suppose, were not at the water-side; I fear Sterne's business will not be done; I have not seen him this good while. I hate him for the management of that box; and I was the greatest fool in nature for trusting to such a young jackanapes; I will speak to him once more about it, when I see him. Mr. Addison and I met once more since, and I supped with him: I believe I told you so somewhere in this letter. The archbishop chose an admirable messenger in Walls to send to me; yet I think him fitter for a messenger than any thing.—The D— she [1] has! I did not observe her looks. Will she rot out of modesty with lady Giffard? I pity poor Jenny [2]—but her husband is a dunce, and with respect to him she loses little by her deafness. I believe, madam Stella, in your accounts you mistook one liquor for another, and it was a hundred and forty quarts of wine, and thirty-two of water.— This is all written in the morning before I go the secretary, as I am now doing. I have answered your letter a little shorter than ordinary; but I have a mind it should go to-day, and I will give you my journal at night in my next; for I'm so afraid of another letter before this goes: I will never have two together again unanswered.—What care I for Dr. Tisdall and Dr Raymond, or how many children they have? I wish they had a hundred apiece.——Lord treasurer promises me to answer the bishops' letter to-morrow, and shew it me; and I believe it will confirm all I said, and mortify those that threw the merit on the duke of Ormond. For I have made him jealous of it; and t'other day talking of the matter, he said, I am your witness you got it for them before the duke was lord lieutenant. My humble service to Mrs. Walls, Mrs. Stoyte, and Catherine. Farewel, &c.

What do you do when you see any literal mistakes in my

---

[1] Somewhat or other which Stella's mother had consented to.—D. S.
[2] Mrs. Fenton, the dean's sister.—D. S.

letters? how do you set him right? for I never read them over
to correct them. Farewel again.

Pray send this note to Mrs. Brent, to get the money when
Parvisol comes to town, or she can send to him.

LETTER XXXI

London, Sept. 25, 1711.

I DINED in the city to-day, and at my return I put my 30th into
the post-office; and when I got home I found for me one of the
noblest letters I ever read; it was from ——, three sides and a
half in folio on a large sheet of paper; the two first pages made
up of satire upon London, and crowds and hurry, stolen from
some of his own school-boy's exercises: the side and a half
remaining is spent in desiring me to recommend Mrs. South,
your commissioner's [1] widow, to my lord treasurer for a pension. He is the prettiest, discreetest fellow that ever my eyes
beheld, or that ever dipt pen into ink. I know not what to say
to him. A pox on him, I have too many such customers on this
side already. I think I will send him word that I never saw my
lord treasurer in my life: I am sure I industriously avoided the
name of any great person when I saw him, for fear of his
reporting it in Ireland. And this recommendation must be a
secret too, for fear the duke of Bolton [2] should know it, and
think it was too mean. I never read so d——d a letter in my
life: a little would make me send it over to you.—I must send
you a pattern, the first place I cast my eyes on, I will not
pick and chuse. [In this place (meaning the Exchange in
London) which is the compendium of old Troynovant, as that
is of the whole busy world, I got such a surfeit, that I grew
sick of mankind, and resolved, for ever after, to bury myself
in the shady retreat of ——.] [3] You must know that London
has been called by some Troynovant, or New Troy.—Will you
have any more? Yes, one little bit for Stella, because she'll be
fond of it. [This wondrous Theatre (meaning London) was no
more to me than a desert, and I should less complain of solitude

[1] *See* Letter X., Dec. 9, 1710. South was one of the commissioners of
the revenue, and a ranger of Phœnix Park (Faulkner). Mr. Aitken gives
his name as John, *d.* 1711, commissioner from 1696 till death.
[2] Charles Powlett (1661-1721-2), second duke, a Lord-Justice of Ireland,
1697-1700; Lord-Lieutenant of Ireland, April 1717 till Nov. 1719.
"A most lewd, vicious man, a great dissembler and a very hard drinker."
Thrice married.
[3] Brackets in D. S.—for quotation marks.

in a Connaught shipwreck, or even the great bog of Allen.][1]
A little scrap for Mrs. Marget,[2] and then I have done. [Their
royal *Fanum*, wherein the Idol *Pecunia* is daily worshipped,
seemed to me to be just like a hive of bees working and labour-
ing under huge weights of cares.][3] *Fanum* is a temple, but he
means the Exchange; and *Pecunia* is money: so now Mrs.
Marget will understand her part. One more paragraph, and I
—Well, come, don't be in such a rage, you shall have no more.
Pray, Stella, be satisfied; 'tis very pretty; and that I must be
acquainted with such a dog as this!——Our Peace goes on fast.
Prior was with the secretary two hours this morning: I was
there a little after he went away, and was told it. I believe he
will soon be dispatched again to France; and I will put somebody to write an account of his second journey: I hope you
have seen the other. This latter has taken up my time with
storming at it.

26. Bernage has been with me these two days; yesterday
I sent for him to let him know, that Dr. Arbuthnott is putting
in strongly to have his brother [4] made a captain over Bernage's
head. Arbuthnot's brother is but an ensign; but the doctor has
great power with the queen: yet he told me, he would not do
any thing hard to a gentleman who is my friend; and I have
engaged the secretary and his colonel for him. To-day he told
me very melancholy, that the other had written from Windsor
(where he went to solicit) that he has got the company; and
Bernage is full of the spleen. I made the secretary write yesterday a letter to the colonel in Bernage's behalf. I hope it will
do yet; and I have written to Dr. Arbuthnott to Windsor, not
to insist on doing such a hardship. I dined in the city at Pontack's
with Stratford; it cost me seven shillings: he would have
treated; but I did not let him. I have removed my money from
the bank to another fund. I desire Parvisol may speak to
Hawkshaw to pay in my money when he can; for I will put it
in the funds; and in the mean time borrow so much of Mr.
secretary, who offers to lend it me. Go to the dean's, sirrahs.

[1] Brackets in D. S.—for quotation marks.
[2] Stella's maid.—D S.
[3] Brackets in D. S.—for quotation marks.
[4] This may have been the George Arbuthnot who obtained his captaincy
Sept. 10, 1712 (after Bernage had been placed on half-pay on account of
the disbanding of his regiment), in the Earl of Orrery's regiment—*see*
Dalton, vol. vi., p. 164; on p. 165 it is stated he had previously served
under Col. Edmund Fielding, who was colonel of "Brasier's" regiment,
in which one Moses Bernage was made a captain-lieutenant in Feb. 1711
—there appears to be no record of his full captaincy.

27. Bernage was with me again to-day, and is in great fear, and so was I; but this afternoon at lord treasurer's, where I dined, my brother George Granville, secretary at war, after keeping me a while in suspense, told me, that Dr. Arbuthnott had waved the business, because he would not wrong a friend of mine; that his brother is to be a lieutenant, and Bernage is made a captain. I called at his lodging, and the soldier's Coffee-house, to put him out of pain, but cannot find him; so I have left word, and shall see him to-morrow morning, I suppose. Bernage is now easy; he has ten shillings a day, beside lawful cheating. However, he gives a private sum to his colonel; but it is very cheap: his colonel loves him well, but is surprised to see him have so many friends. So he is now quite off my hands. —I left the company early to-night at lord treasurer's; but the secretary followed me, to desire I would go with him to W—. Mr. Lewis's man came in before I could finish that word beginning with a W, which ought to be Windsor, and brought me a very handsome rallying letter from Dr. Arbuthnott, to tell me, he had, in compliance to me, given up his brother's pretensions in favour of Bernage this very morning; that the queen had spoken to Mr. Granville to make the company easy in the other's having the captainship. Whether they have done it to oblige me or no, I must own it so. He says, he this very morning begged her majesty to give Mr. Bernage the company. I am mighty well pleased to have succeeded so well; but you will think me tedious, although you like the man, as I think.

Windsor, 28. I came here a day sooner than ordinary, at Mr. secretary's desire, and supped with him and Prior, and two private ministers from France, and a French priest. I know not the two ministers names; but they are come about the Peace. The names the secretary called them, I suppose, were feigned; they were good rational men.[1] We have already settled all things with France, and very much to the honour and advantage of England; and the queen is in mighty good humour. All this news is a mighty secret; the people in general know that a Peace is forwarding. The earl of Strafford [2] is to go soon to Holland, and let them know what we have been doing: and then there will be the devil and all to pay; but we'll make them swallow it with a pox. The French ministers staid with us till

[1] They were M. Mesnager and the Abbé Du Bois; the priest, the Abbé Gualtier, originally employed by Marshal Tallard (then prisoner of war) to receive and forward his letters from France.—D. L. P.

[2] *See* Letter XXIX., Sept. 3.

one, and the secretary and I sat up talking till two; so you will
own 'tis late, sirrahs, and time for your little sausy Presto to go
to bed and sleep adazy; and God bless poor little MD: I hope
they are now fast asleep and dreaming of Presto.

29. Lord treasurer came to-night, as usual, at half an hour
after eight, as dark as pitch. I am weary of chiding him; so
I commended him for observing his friends advice, and coming
so early, &c. I was two hours with lady Oglethorp[1] to-night,
and then supped with lord treasurer, after dining at the green-
cloth: I staid till two; this is the effect of lord treasurer's
being here; I must sup with him, and he keeps cursed hours.
Lord keeper and the secretary were absent; they cannot sit up
with him. This long sitting up makes the periods in my letters
so short. I design to stay here all the next week, to be at leisure
by myself, to finish something of weight I have upon my hands,
and which must soon be done. I shall then think of returning
to Ireland, if these people will let me; and I know nothing else
they have for me to do. I gave Dr. Arbuthnott my thanks
for his kindness to Bernage, whose commission is now signed.
Methinks I long to know something of Stella's health, how it
continues after Wexford waters.

30. The queen was not at chapel to-day, and all for the
better, for we had a dunce to preach: she has a little of the
gout. I dined with my brother Masham and a moderate company, and would not go to lord treasurer's till after supper at
eleven o'clock, and pretended I had mistaken the hour; so
I ate nothing: and a little after twelve the company broke up,
the keeper and secretary refusing to stay; so I saved this
night's debauch. Prior went away yesterday with his French-
men, and a thousand reports are raised in this town. Some
said, they knew one to be the Abbé de Polignac[2]: others
swore it was the Abbé du Bois.[3] The Whigs are in a rage about
the Peace; but we'll wherret them, I warrant, boys. Go, go,
go to the dean's, and don't mind politicks, young women, they
are not good after the waters; they are stark naught; they strike
up into the head. Go, get two black aces, and fish for a manilio.[4]

---

[1] Sir Theophilus Oglethorpe (1650–1702), brigadier-general, married
Eleanor, daughter of Richard Wall of Tipperary; she bore him seven
children and died 1732. James Edward Oglethorpe, colonist of Georgia
(a recent proposal for whose exhumation from Cranham and reburial in
America caused some public concern), was one of her children.

[2] Melchior de Polignac (1661–1742), French diplomat and author.

[3] Guillaume Dubois (1656–1723), French ecclesiastic and statesman.

[4] *Manilio*. In quadrille and ombre, the second best trump or honour
(being the deuce of a black suit or the seven of a red suit).

Oct. 1. Sir John Walters,[1] an honest drunken fellow, is now in waiting, and invited me to the green-cloth to-day, that he might not be behind hand with colonel Godfrey, who is a Whig. I was engaged to the Mayor's feast with Mr. Masham; but waiting to take leave of lord treasurer, I came too late, and so returned sneaking to the green-cloth, and did not see my lord treasurer neither; but was resolved not to lose two dinners for him. I took leave to-day of my friend and solicitor lord Rivers, who is commanded by the queen to set out for Hanover on Thursday. The secretary does not go to town till to-morrow: he and I and two friends more drank a sober bottle of wine here at home, and parted at twelve; he goes by seven to-morrow morning, so I shall not see him. I have power over his cellar in his absence, and make little use of it. Lord Dartmouth and my friend Lewis stay here this week; but I can never work out a dinner from Dartmouth. Masham has promised to provide for me: I squired his lady out of her chaise to-day, and must visit her in a day or two. So you have had a long fit of the finest weather in the world; but I am every day in pain that it will go off. I have done no business to-day: I am very idle.

2. My friend Lewis and I, to avoid overmuch eating, and great tables, dined with honest Jemmy Eckershall,[2] clerk of the kitchen, now in waiting; and I bespoke my dinner: but the cur had your acquaintance Lovet, the gentleman porter, to be our company: Lovet, toward the end of dinner, after twenty wrigglings, said he had the honour to see me formerly at Moor-park, and thought he remembered my face; I said, I thought I remembered him, and was glad to see him, &c. and I escaped for that much, for he was very pert. It has rained all this day, and I doubt [all] our good weather is gone. I have been very idle this afternoon, playing at twelve-penny picquet with Lewis; I won seven shillings, which is the only money I won this year; I have not played above four times, and I think always at Windsor: cards are very dear, there is a duty on them of sixpence a pack, which spoils small gamesters.

3. Mr. Masham sent this morning to desire I would ride out with him, the weather growing again very fine: I was very busy, and sent my excuses; but desired he would provide me a dinner: I dined with him, his lady, and her sister, Mrs. Hill, who invites us to-morrow to dine with her, and we are to ride

[1] Sir John Walter (c. 1673-1722), bart., the other clerk of the green cloth. M.P. for Oxford in six parliaments.
[2] See Letter XVII., Feb. 27, 1710-11 (note).

out in the morning. I sat with lady Oglethorp till eight this
evening, then was going home to write; looked about for the
woman that keeps the key of the house; she told me Patrick
had it. I cooled my heels in the cloisters till nine, then went
in to the musick-meeting, where I had been often desired to
go; but was weary in half an hour of their fine stuff,[1] and stole
out so privately that every body saw me; and cooled my heels
in the cloisters again till after ten: then came in Patrick. I went
up, shut the chamber-door, and gave him two or three swinging
cuffs on the ear, and I have strained the thumb of my left
hand with pulling him, which I did not feel until he was gone.
He was plaguily afraid and humbled.

4. It was the finest day in the world, and we got out before
eleven, a noble caravan of us. The duchess of Shrewsbury in
her own chaise with one horse, and Miss Touchet [2] with her;
Mrs. Masham and Mrs. Scarborow, one of the dressers, in one
of the queen's chaises; Miss Forester and Miss Scarborow,[3] two
maids of honour, and Mrs. Hill on horseback. The duke of
Shrewsbury, Mr. Masham, George Fielding,[4] Arbuthnott and
I on horseback too. Mrs. Hill's horse was hired for Miss Scarborow, but she took it in civility, her own horse was galled and
could not be rid, but kicked and winced: the hired horse was not
worth eighteen pence. I borrowed coat, boots and horse, and in
short we had all the difficulties, and more than we used to have
in making a party from Trim to Longfield's.[5] My coat was
light camblet, faced with red velvet, and silver buttons. We
rode in the great park and the forest about a dozen miles, and
the duchess and I had much conversation; we got home by two,
and Mr. Masham, his lady, Arbuthnott and I dined with Mrs.
Hill. Arbuthnott made us all melancholy, by some symptoms
of bloody ur[in]e: he expects a cruel fit of the stone in twelve
hours; he says he is never mistaken, and he appeared like a
man that was to be racked to-morrow. I cannot but hope it
will not be so bad; he is a perfectly honest man, and one I

[1] Swift, like some others, rather hated than loved musick.—D. S.
Music and mathematics he made the two chief pursuits of the ridiculous
Laputans.—D. L. P.

[2] Mr. Aitken surmises, a daughter of Mervyn Tuchet, fourth Earl
of Castlehaven.

[3] Henrietta Maria, daughter of Charles Scarborough (see Letter XXVII.,
Aug. 8), afterwards (Feb. 4, 1711-12) married to Sir Robert Jenkinson
(1685-1717), third baronet.

[4] One of the two commissioners for executing the office of master of
the horse (Aitken).

[5] Mr. Longfield lived at Killibride, about four miles from Trim.—D. S.
The roadless condition of Ireland must be considered.—D. L. P.

have much obligation to. It rained a little this afternoon, and grew fair again. Lady Oglethorp sent to speak to me, and it was to let me know that lady Rochester[1] desires she and I may be better acquainted. 'Tis a little too late; for I am not now in love with lady Rochester: they shame me out of her, because she is old. Arbuthnott says, he hopes my strained thumb is not the gout; for he has often found people so mistaken. I do not remember the particular thing that gave it me, only I had it just after beating Patrick, and now it is better; so I believe he is mistaken.

5. The duchess of Shrewsbury sent to invite me to dinner; but I was abroad last night when her servant came, and this morning I sent my excuses, because I was engaged, which I was sorry for. Mrs. Forester taxed me yesterday about the history of the maids of honour; but I told her fairly it was no jest of mine; for I found they did not relish it altogether well: and I have enough already of a quarrel with that brute Sir John Walters, who has been railing at me in all companies ever since I dined with him; that I abused the queen's meat and drink, and said, nothing at the table was good, and all a d——d lie; for, after dinner, commending the wine, I said, I thought it was something small. You would wonder how all my friends laugh at this quarrel. It will be such a jest for the keeper, treasurer, and secretary.——I dined with honest colonel Godfrey, took a good walk of an hour on the terrace, and then came up to study; but it grows bloody cold, and I have no waistcoat here.

6. I never dined with the chaplains till to-day; but my friend Gastrel[2] and the dean of Rochester had often invited me, and I happened to be disengaged: it is the worst provided table at court. We ate on pewter: every chaplain, when he is made a dean, gives a piece of plate, and so they have got a little,[3] some of it very old. One who was made dean of Peterborow (a small deanry) said, he would give no plate; he was only dean of *Pewterborow*. The news of Mr. Hill's miscarriage in his expedition came to-day, and I went to visit Mrs. Masham and Mrs. Hill, his two sisters, to condole with them. I advised them by all means to go to the musick-meeting to-night,

[1] Wife of the Lord Hyde mentioned in Letter V., Oct. 1, 1710, who became Earl of Rochester, May 1711. She was Jane (c. 1670–1725), daughter of Sir William Leveson-Gower, fourth baronet.

[2] See Letter XXV., June 23.

[3] This good old custom is still observed; and there is now a very handsome stock of plate.—N.

to show they were not cast down, &c. and they thought
my advice was right, and went. I doubt Mr. Hill[1] and his
admiral made wrong steps; however, we lay it all to a storm,
&c. I sat with the secretary at supper; then we both went to
lord treasurer's supper, and sat till twelve. The secretary is
much mortified about Hill; because this expedition was of his
contriving, and he counted much upon it; but lord treasurer
was just as merry as usual, and old laughing at Sir John
Walters and me falling out. I said, Nothing grieved me, but
that they would take example, and perhaps presume upon it,
and get out of my government; but that I thought I was not
obliged to govern bears, though I governed men. They promise
to be as obedient as ever, and so we laughed;—and so I go
to bed; for it is colder still, and you have a fire now, and are
at cards at home.

7. Lord Harley and I dined privately to-day with Mrs.
Masham and Mrs. Hill, and my brother Masham. I saw lord
Hallifax at Court, and we joined and talked, and the duchess
of Shrewsbury came up and reproached me for not dining with
her: I said, That was not so soon done; for I expected more
advances from ladies, especially duchesses: she promised to
comply with any demands I pleased; and I agreed to dine with
her to-morrow, if I did not go to London too soon, as I believe
I shall before dinner. Lady Oglethorp brought me and the
duchess of Hamilton together to-day in the drawing-room, and
I have given her some encouragement, but not much. Every
body has been teazing Walters. He told lord treasurer, that he
took his company from him that were to dine with him; my
lord said, I will send you Dr. Swift: lord keeper bid him take
care what he did; For, said he, Dr. Swift is not only all our
favourite, but our governor. The old company supped with
lord treasurer, and got away by twelve.

London, 8. I believe I shall go no more to Windsor; for we
expect the queen will come in ten days to Hampton-Court. It
was frost last night, and cruel cold to-day. I could not dine with
the duchess; for I left Windsor half an hour after one with lord
treasurer, and we called at Kensington, where Mrs. Masham
was got to see her children for two days. I dined, or rather
supped with lord treasurer, and staid till after ten. Tisdall[2]
and his family are gone from hence, upon some wrangle with

[1] *See* Letter XXII., April 29; also note on "Colonel Hill," Letter X.
Nov. 25, 1710.
[2] *See* Letter XXVI., July 8.

the family. Yesterday I had two letters brought me to Mr. Masham's; one from Ford, and t'other from our little MD, N. 21. I would not tell you till to-day, because I would not. I won't answer it till the next, because I slipt two days by being at Windsor, which I must recover here. Well, sirrahs, I must go to sleep. The roads were as dry as at Midsummer to-day. This letter shall go to-morrow.

9. Morning. It rains hard this morning; I suppose our fair weather is now at an end. I think I'll put on my waistcoat to-day: shall I? Well, I will then, to please MD. I think of dining at home to-day upon a chop and a pot. The town continues yet very thin. Lord Strafford is gone to Holland to tell them what we have done here towards a Peace. We shall soon hear what the Dutch say, and how they take it. My humble service to Mrs. Walls, Mrs. Stoyte and Catherine.—Morrow, dearest sirrahs, and farewell; and God Almighty bless MD, poor, little, dear MD, for so I mean, and Presto too. I'll write to you again to night, that is, I'll begin my next letter. Farewel, &c.

This little bit belongs to MD; we must always write on the margin [1]: you are saucy rogues.

LETTER XXXII

London, *October* 9, 1711.

I was forced to lie down at twelve to-day, and mend my night's sleep: I slept till after two, and then sent for a bit of mutton and pot of ale from the next cook's shop, and had no stomach. I went out at four, and called to see Biddy Floyd,[2] which I had not done these three months: she is something marked, but has recovered her complexion quite, and looks very well. Then I sat the evening with Mrs. Vanhomrigh, and drank coffee, and ate an egg. I likewise took a new lodging to-day, not liking a ground floor, nor the ill smell, and other circumstances. I lodge, or shall lodge, by Leicester-Fields, and pay ten shillings a week; that won't hold out long, faith. I shall lie here but one night more. It rained terribly till one o'clock to-day. I lie, for I shall lie here two nights, till Thursday, and then remove. Did I tell you that my friend Mrs. Barton has a brother

[1] This happens to be the only single line written upon the margin of any of his journals. By some accident there was a margin about as broad as the back of a razor, and therefore he made this use of it.—D. S.

[2] *See* Letter XVIII., March 15, 1710-11.

drowned,[1] that went on the expedition with Jack Hill? He
was a lieutenant-colonel, and a coxcomb; and she keeps her
chamber in form, and the servants say, she receives no messages.
—Answer MD's letter, Presto, d'ye hear? No, says Presto,
I won't yet, I'm busy: you're a saucy rogue. Who talks?

10. It cost me two shillings in coach-hire to dine in the city
with a printer. I have sent, and caused to be sent, three pamphlets out in a fortnight. I will ply the rogues warm, and
whenever any thing of theirs makes a noise, it shall have an
answer. I have instructed an under-spur-leather to write so,
that it is taken for mine. A rogue that writes a news-paper called
The Protestant Post-boy, has reflected on me in one of his
papers; but the secretary has taken him up, and he shall have
a squeeze extraordinary. He says, that an ambitious Tantivy,[2]
missing of his towering hopes of preferment in Ireland, is come
over to vent his spleen on the late ministry, &c. I'll *Tantivy*
him with a vengeance. I sat the evening at home, and am very
busy, and can hardly find time to write, unless it were to MD.
I am in furious haste.

11. I dined to-day with lord treasurer. Thursdays are now
his days when his choice company comes, but we are too much
multiplied. George Granville sent his excuses upon being ill;
I hear he apprehends the apoplexy, which would grieve me
much. Lord treasurer calls Prior nothing but *Monsieur Baudrier*,
which was the feigned name of the Frenchman that writ his
journey to Paris. They pretend to suspect me; so I talk freely
of it, and put them out of their play. Lord treasurer calls me now
Dr. Martin, because *Martin*[3] is a sort of swallow, and so is a
Swift. When he and I came last Monday from Windsor, we
were reading all the signs[4] on the road. He is a pure trifler;
tell the bishop of Clogher so. I made him make two lines in verse
for the *Bell and Dragon*, and they were rare bad ones. I suppose
Dilly is with you by this time: what could his reason be of

---

[1] Lieut.-Colonel Barton, of Colonel Kane's regiment, perished in the
River St. Lawrence, Aug. 22.

[2] A nickname for the High Church party in the time of Charles II. and
James II.; derived from a caricature in which they were shown riding
tantivy to Rome.—D. L. P.

[3] From this pleasantry of Lord Oxford, the appellative *Martinus
Scriblerus* took its rise.—D. S.

[4] *Vide* Swift's imitations of Horace, lib. ii. sat. 6, where he gives
an account of what sort of tattle entertained my lord Oxford and
him upon the road to Windsor; and among other whims, how, as the
chariot passed along,

> "They gravely try'd to read the lines
> Writ underneath the country signs."—D. S.

leaving London, and not owning it? 'Twas plaguy silly. I believe his natural inconstancy made him weary; I think he is the king of inconstancy. I stayed with lord treasurer till ten; we had five lords and three commoners. Go to ombre, sirrahs.

12. Mrs. Vanhomrigh has changed her lodging as well as I. She found she had got with a bawd,[1] and removed: I dined with her to-day; for though she boards, her landlady does not dine with her. I am grown a mighty lover of herrings; but they are much smaller here than with you. In the afternoon I visited an old major-general, and eat six oysters; then sat an hour with Mrs. Colledge,[2] the joiner's daughter that was hanged; it was the joiner was hanged, and not his daughter; with Thompson's wife, a magistrate.[3] There was the famous Mrs. Floyd of Chester,[4] who, I think, is the handsomest woman (except MD) that ever I saw. She told me, that twenty people had sent her the verses upon *Biddy*,[5] as meant to her: and indeed, in point of handsomeness, she deserves them much better. I will not go to Windsor to-morrow, and so I told the secretary to-day. I hate the thoughts of Saturday and Sunday suppers with lord treasurer. Jack Hill is come home from his unfortunate expedition, and is, I think, now at Windsor: I have not yet seen him. He is privately blamed by his own friends for want of conduct. He called a council of war, and therein it was determined to come back.[6] But they say, a general should not do that, because the officers will always give their opinion for returning, since the blame will not lie upon them, but the general: I pity him heartily. Bernage received his commission to-day.

13. I dined to-day with colonel Crowe,[7] late governor of Barbadoes; he is a great acquaintance of your friend Sterne, to whom I trusted the box. Lord treasurer has refused Sterne's business; and I doubt he is a rake; Jemmy Leigh stays for him, and nobody knows where to find him. I am so busy now, I have hardly time to spare to write to our little MD; but in a fortnight I hope it will be over. I am going now to be busy, &c.

[1] *See* Letter XXX., Sept. 14.
[2] *See* Letter XXIII., May 17.
[3] He ought, surely, to have appended that Thompson, and not Thompson's wife, was the magistrate.
[4] Unknown now.
[5] Written 1708.
[6] On the plea of want of provisions; the squadron, to lull suspicion, had not been victualled for so long a voyage, and the colonies had not the means of making good the want.—D. L. P.
[7] *See* Letter XXIII., May 18.

14. I was going to dine with Dr. Cockburn, but Sir Andrew Fountain met me, and carried me to Mrs. Van's, where I drank the last bottle of Raymond's wine, admirable good, better than any I get among the ministry. I must pick up time to answer this letter of MD's, I'll do it in a day or two for certain.—— I am glad I am not at Windsor, for it is very cold, and I won't have a fire till November. I am contriving how to stop up my grate with bricks. Patrick was drunk last night; but did not come to me, else I should have given him t'other cuff. I sat this evening with Mrs. Barton, it is the first day of her seeing company; but I made her merry enough, and we were three hours disputing upon Whig and Tory. She grieved for her brother only for form, and he was a sad dog. Is Stella well enough to go to church, pray? no nummings left? no darkness in your eyes? do you walk and exercise? Your exercise is ombre. ——People are coming up to town; the queen will be at Hampton-court in a week. Lady Betty Germain, I hear, is come, and lord Pembroke is coming: his new wife[1] is as big with child as she can tumble.

15. I sat at home till four this afternoon to-day writing, and ate a roll and butter; then visited Will Congreve an hour or two, and supped with lord treasurer, who came from Windsor to-day, and brought Prior with him. The queen has thanked Prior for his good service in France, and promised to make him a commissioner of the customs. Several of that commission are to be out; among the rest, my friend Sir Matthew Dudley; I can do nothing for him, he is so hated by the ministry. Lord treasurer kept me till twelve, so I need not tell you it is now late.

16. I dined to-day with Mr. secretary at Dr. Cotesworth's,[2] where he now lodges till his house be got ready in Golden-Square. One Boyer, a French dog, has abused me in a pamphlet,[3] and I have got him up in a messenger's hands: the secretary promises me to swinge him. Lord treasurer told me last night, that he had the honour to be abused with me in a pamphlet. I must make that rogue an example for warning to others. I was to see Jack Hill this morning, who made that unfortunate expedition; and there is still more misfortune; for that

---

[1] *See* 20th.

[2] Mr. Aitken says Caleb Coatesworth, who died rich, 1741.

[3] Abel Boyer (1667-1729), a Protestant native of Castres, Upper Languedoc, educated in Holland; came to England 1689, worked for Dr. Thomas Swift, wrote plays and Whig history books. He attacked Swift, calling him "a shameless and most contemptible ecclesiastical turncoat, whose tongue is as *Swift* to revile, as his mind is *Swift* to change." (D. L. P.).

ship, which was admiral of his fleet, is blown up in the Thames,[1] by an accident and carelessness of some rogue, who was going, as they think, to steal some gun-powder: five hundred men are lost; we don't yet know the particulars. I am got home by seven, and am going to be busy, and you are going to play and supper; you live ten times happier than I: but I should live ten times happier than you, if I were with MD. I saw Jemmy Leigh to-day in the street, who tells me that Sterne has not lain above once these three weeks in his lodgings, and he doubts he takes ill courses; he stays only till he can find Sterne to go along with him, and he cannot hear of him. I begged him to enquire about the box when he comes to Chester, which he promises.

17. The secretary and I dined to-day with Brigadier Britton,[2] a great friend of his. The lady of the house is very galante, about thirty-five; she is said to have a great deal of wit; but I see nothing among any of them that equals MD by a bar's length, as hope saved. My lord treasurer is much out of order; he has a sore throat, and the gravel, and a pain in his breast where the wound was: pray God preserve him. The queen comes to Hampton-Court on Tuesday next; people are coming fast to town, and I must answer MD's letter, which I can hardly find time to do, though I am at home the greatest part of the day. Lady Betty Germain and I were disputing Whig and Tory to death this morning. She is grown very fat, and looks mighty well. Biddy Floyd was there, and she is, I think, very much spoiled with the small-pox.

18. Lord treasurer is still out of order, and that breaks our method of dining there to-day. He is often subject to a sore throat, and some time or other it will kill him, unless he takes more care than he is apt to do. It was said about the town, that poor lord Peterborow was dead at Frankfort; but he is something better, and the queen is sending him to Italy, where I hope the warm climate will recover him; he has abundance of excellent qualities, and we love one another mightily. I was this afternoon in the city, eat a bit of meat, and settled some things with a printer.[3] I will answer your letter on Saturday, if

---

[1] The *Edgar* man-of-war, of 70 guns and 470 men, was blown up at Spithead, Oct. 15, and only one man saved.—N.

[2] William Breton, of first regiment of Foot Guards, became brigadier-general, Jan. 1, 1710. Appointed envoy in Prussia same year. Died 1714 or 1715. (Dalton.)

[3] Probably with Morphew, who was then publishing the genuine volume of *Miscellanies.*—N.

possible, and then send away this; so to fetch up the odd days I lost at Windsor, and keep constant to my fortnight. Ombre time is now coming on, and we shall have nothing but Manley, and Walls, and Stoytes, and the dean. Have you got no new acquaintance? Poor girls; no body knows MD's good qualities. 'Tis very cold; but I will not have a fire till November, that's pozz.—Well, but coming home to-night, I found on my table a letter from MD; faith I was angry, that is with myself; and I was afraid too to see MD's hand so soon, for fear of something, I don't know what: at last I opened it, and it was over well, and a bill for the two hundred guineas. However, 'tis a sad thing that this letter is not gone, nor your twenty-first answered yet.

19. I was invited to-day to dine with Mrs. Van, with some company who did not come; but I ate nothing but herrings: you must know I hardly ever eat of above one thing, and that the plainest ordinary meat at table; I love it best, and believe it wholesomest. You love rarities; yes you do; I wish you had all that I ever see where I go. I was coming home early, and met the secretary in his chair, who persuaded me to go with him to Britton's; for he said, he had been all day at business, and had eaten nothing. So I went, and the time past so, that we staid till two, so you may believe 'tis late enough.

20. This day has gone all wrong, by sitting up so late last night. Lord treasurer is not yet well, and can't go to Windsor. I dined with Sir Matthew Dudley, and took occasion to hint to him that he would lose his employment, for which I am very sorry. Lord Pembroke and his family [1] are all come to town. I was kept so long at a friend's this evening, that I cannot send this to-night. When I knocked at my lodgings, a fellow asked me where lodged Dr. Swift? I told him, I was the person: he gave me a letter he brought from the secretary's office, and I gave him a shilling: when I came up, I saw Dingley's hand: faith I was afraid, I do not know what. At last it was a formal letter from Dingley about her exchequer business. Well, I'll do it on Monday, and settle it with Tooke. And now, boys, for your letter, I mean the first, N. 21. Let's see; come out, little letter.—I never had the letter from the bishop that Raymond mentions; but I have written to Ned Southwel, to

---

[1] The Earl of Pembroke mentioned in Letter VII., Oct. 28, 1710, married (1708), as his second wife, Barbara, Dowager Baroness Arundell of Trerice, formerly widow of Sir Richard Mauleverer, daughter of Sir Thomas Slingsby, second baronet; she died 1722. The earl was three times married, and had a numerous family.

desire the duke of Ormond to speak to his reverence that he
may leave off his impertinence. What a pox can they think
I am doing for the archbishop here? You have a pretty notion
of me in Ireland, to make me an agent for the archbishop of
Dublin.——Why; do you think I value your people's ingratitude about my part in serving them? I remit them their First-
Fruits of Ingratitude, as freely as I got the other remitted to
them. This lord treasurer defers writing his letter to them, or
else they would be plaguily confounded by this time. For, he
designs to give the merit of it wholly to the queen and me, and
to let them know it was done before the duke of Ormond was
lord lieutenant. You visit, you dine abroad, you see friends;
you pilgarlick; you walk from Finglass, you a cat's foot. O Lord
—lady Gore[1] hung her child by the waist; what is that *waist*,[2]
I don't understand that word; he must hang on till you explain
or spell it.—I don't believe he was pretty, that's a liiii.—Pish;
burn your First-Fruits; again at it. Stella has made twenty
false spellings in her writing; I'll send them to you all back again
on the other side of this letter, to mend them; I won't miss one.
Why; I think there were seventeen bishops names to the letter
lord Oxford received.—I will send you some pamphlets by
Leigh: put me in mind of it on Monday, for I shall go then
to the printer; yes, and the *Miscellany*. I am mightily obliged
to Walls, but I don't deserve it by any usage of him here, having
seen him but twice, and once *en passant*. Mrs. Manley[3] for-
sworn ombre! What; and no blazing star appear? no monsters
born? no whale thrown up? Have you not found out some
evasion for her? She had no such regard to oaths in her younger
days. I got the books for nothing, madam Dingley; but the
wine I got not; it was but a promise.—Yes, my head is pretty
well in the main, only now and then a little threatening or so.
——You talk of my reconciling some great folks. I tell you
what. The secretary told me last night, that he had found the
reason why the queen was cold to him for some months past;
that a friend had told it him yesterday; and it was, that they
suspected he was at the bottom with the duke of Marlborough.
Then he said, he had reflected upon all I had spoken to him

[1] Uncertain. Mr. Aitken gives a selection of three ladies of three
separate Irish baronets.
[2] This was considered by Swift to be a newfangled and affected way
of spelling the word—he himself writes "wastcoat" for "waistcoat."
Also (*see* Letter LXI., March 20, 1712-13) he writes "tast" for "taste."
—as did many of his contemporaries.
[3] Mrs. Isaac Manley.

long ago; but he thought it had been only my suspicion, and my zeal and kindness for him. I said I had reason to take that very ill, to imagine I knew so little of the world as to talk at a venture to a great minister; that I had gone between him and lord treasurer often, and told each of them what I had said to the other, and that I had informed him so before: he said all that you may imagine to excuse himself, and approve my conduct. I told him, I knew all along, that this proceeding of mine was the surest way to send me back to my willows in Ireland, but that I regarded it not, provided I could do the kingdom service in keeping them well together. I minded him how often I had told lord treasurer, lord keeper, and him together, that all things depended on their union, and that my comfort was to see them love one another; and I had told them all singly, that I had not said this by chance, &c. He was in a rage to be thus suspected; swears he will be upon a better foot, or none at all: and I do not see, how they can well want[1] him in this juncture. I hope to find a way of settling this matter. I act an honest part; that will bring me neither profit nor praise. MD must think the better of me for it: nobody else shall ever know [of] it. Here's politicks enough for once; but madam D. D. gave me occasion for it. I think I told you I have got into lodgings that don't smell ill—O Lord! the spectacles: well, I'll do that on Monday too; although it goes against me to be employed for folks that neither you nor I care a groat for. Is the eight pounds from Hawkshaw included in the thirty-nine pounds five shillings and two-pence? How do I know by this how my account stands? Can't you write five or six lines to cast it up? Mine is forty-four pounds *per annum*, and eight pounds from Hawkshaw makes fifty-two pounds. Pray set it right, and let me know; you had best.— And so now I have answered N. 21, and 'tis late, and I will answer N. 22 in my next: this cannot go to-night, but shall on Tuesday: and so go to your play, and lose your money, with your two eggs a penny; silly jade: you witty? very pretty.

21. Mrs. Van would have me dine with her again to-day, and so I did, though lady Mountjoy had sent two or three times to have me see and dine with her, and she is a little body I love very well. My head has ached a little in the evenings these three or four days, but it is not of the giddy sort, so I do not much value it. I was to see lord Harley to-day, but lord treasurer

---

[1] *i.e.* "be without"—the original meaning of "want." The modern colloquial "want" would mean the very opposite.

took physick, and I could not see him. He has voided much gravel, and is better, but not well; he talks of going on Tuesday to see the queen at Hampton-Court; I wish he may be able. I never saw so fine a summer day as this was; how is it with you pray? and can't you remember, naughty packs. I han't seen lord Pembroke yet. He will be sorry to miss Dilly: I wonder you say nothing of Dilly's being got to Ireland; if he be not there soon, I shall have some certain odd thoughts; guess them if you can.

22. I dined in the city to-day with Dr. Freind, at one of my printers [1]; I enquired for Leigh, but could not find him: I have forgot what sort of apron you want. I must rout among your letters, a needle in a bottle of hay. I gave Sterne directions, but where to find him Lord knows. I have bespoken the spectacles; got a set of *Examiners*, and five pamphlets, which I have either written or contributed to, except the best, which is the *Vindication of the duke of Marlborough*; and is entirely of the author of the *Atalantis*. I have settled Dingley's affair with Tooke, who has undertaken it, and understands it. I have bespoken a *Miscellany*: what would you have me do more? It cost me a shilling coming home; it rains terribly, and did so in the morning. Lord treasurer has had an ill day, in much pain. He writes and does business in his chamber now he is ill: the man is bewitched; he desires to see me, and I'll maul him, but he will not value it a rush.——I am half weary of them all. I often burst out into these thoughts, and will certainly steal away as soon as I decently can. I have many friends, and many enemies; and the last are more constant in their nature. I have no shuddering at all to think of retiring to my old circumstances, if you can be easy; but I will always live in Ireland as I did the last time; I will not hunt for dinners there; nor converse with more than a very few.

23. Morning. This goes to-day, and shall be sealed by and bye. Lord treasurer takes physick again to-day: I believe I shall dine with lord Dupplin. Mr. Tooke brought me a letter directed for me at Morphew's the bookseller. I suppose, by the postage, it came from Ireland; it is a woman's hand, and seems false spelt on purpose; it is in such sort of verse as Harris's petition [2]; rallies me for writing merry things, and not upon divinity; and is like the subject of the archbishop's last letter,

---

[1] This probably was Morphew, in distinction from Tooke, who was then his regular publisher.—N.

[2] *Mrs. Frances Harris's Petition*, now included in Swift's works.

as I told you. Can you guess whom it came from? it is not ill written; pray find it out; there is a Latin verse at the end of it all rightly spelt; yet the English, as I think, affectedly wrong in many places.—My plaguing time is coming. A young fellow brought me a letter from judge Coote,[1] with recommendation to be a lieutenant of a man of war. He is the son of one Echlin,[2] who was minister of Belfast before Tisdall, and I have got some other new customers; but I shall trouble my friends as little as possible. Saucy Stella used to jeer me for meddling with other folks affairs: but now I am punished for it.—Patrick has brought the candle, and I have no more room. Farewel, &c. &c.

Here is a full and true account of STELLA's new spelling.

Plaguely	Plaguily.[3]	A bout	About.
Dineing	Dining.	Intellegence	Intelligence.
Straingers	Strangers.	Aboundance	Abundance.
Chais	Chase.[4]	Merrit	Merit.
Waist	Wast.	Secreet	Secret.
Houer	Hour.	Phamphlets	Pamphlets.
Immagin	Imagine.	Bussiness	Business.

Tell me truly, sirrah, how many of these are mistakes of the pen, and how many are you to answer for as real ill spelling? There are but fourteen; I said twenty by guess. You must not be angry, for I will have you spell right, let the world go how it will. Though after all, there is but a mistake of one letter in any of these words. I allow you henceforth but six false spellings in every letter you send me.

LETTER XXXIII

London, *Oct.* 23, 1711.

I DINED with lord Dupplin, as I told you I would, and put my thirty-second into the post-office my own self; and I believe there has not been one moment since we parted, wherein a letter was not upon the road going or coming to or from P MD.[5]

[1] Thomas Coote, a judge of the Queen's Bench in Ireland, removed 1715 according to Mr. Aitken.
[2] Probably one of the numerous descendants of Robert Echlin (*d.* 1635), a Scot who became Bishop of Down and Connor in 1612-13, as part of James I.'s "plantation" of Ulster. Mr. Aitken suggests a relative of Robert, Dean of Tuam, murdered 1712.
[3] This column of words, as they are corrected, is in Stella's hand.—D. S.
[4] Yet here is one word still false spelt.—D. S.
[5] That is, Presto and MD.—D. S.

If the queen knew it, she would give us a pension; for it is we bring good luck to their post-boys and their pacquets: else they would break their necks and sink. But, an old saying and a true one; Be it snow or storm or hail, P MD's letters never fail: Cross winds may sometimes make them tarry; But P MD's letters can't miscarry.——Terrible rain to-day, but it cleared up at night enough to save my twelve-pence coming home. Lord treasurer is much better this evening. I hate to have him ill, he is so confoundedly careless. I won't answer your letter yet, so be satisfied.

24. I called at lord treasurer's to-day at noon; he was eating some broth in his bed-chamber, undressed, with a thousand papers about him. He has a little fever upon him, and his eye terribly blood-shot; yet he dressed himself, and went out to the treasury. He told me, he had a letter from a lady with a complaint against me, it was from Mrs. Cutts, a sister of lord Cutts,[1] who writ to him, that I had abused her brother: you remember the *Salamander*; it is printed in the *Miscellany*. I told my lord, that I would never regard complaints, and that I expected whenever he received any against me, he would immediately put them into the fire, and forget them, else I should have no quiet.——I had a little turn in my head this morning; which, though it did not last above a moment, yet being of the true sort, has made me as weak as a dog all this day. 'Tis the first I have had this half year. I shall take my pills if I hear of it again. I dined at lady Mountjoy's with Harry Coote,[2] and went to see lord Pembroke upon his coming to town.——The Whig party are furious against a Peace, and every day some ballad comes out reflecting on the ministry on that account. The secretary St. John has seized on a dozen booksellers and publishers, into his messengers hands. Some of the foreign ministers have published the Preliminaries agreed on here between France and England; and people rail at them as insufficient to treat a Peace upon; but the secret is, that the French have agreed to articles much more important, which our ministers have not communicated, and the people, who think they know all, are discontented that there is no more. This was an inconvenience I foretold to the secretary; but we could contrive no way to fence against it.——So there's politicks for you.

25. The queen is at Hampton-Court; she went on Tuesday

[1] Joanna (unmarried). John (1661–1707), Baron Cutts, was a lieut.-general in the Low-Country wars. The *Description of a Salamander* was a scurrilous satire in verse on Lord Cutts.
[2] *See* Letter VI., Oct. 11, 1710, and note.

in that terrible rain. I dined with Lewis at his lodgings, to dispatch some business we had. I sent this morning and evening to lord treasurer, and he is much worse by going out; I am in pain about evening. He has sent for Dr. Radcliffe; pray God preserve him. The chancellor of the exchequer[1] shewed me to-day a ballad in manuscript against lord treasurer and his South-Sea project; it is very sharply written: if it be not printed, I will send it you. If it be, it shall go in your pacquet of pamphlets.—I found out your letter about directions for the apron, and have ordered to be bought a cheap, green silk work apron; I have it by heart. I sat this evening with Mrs. Barton, who is my near neighbour. It was a delicious day, and I got my walk, and was thinking whether MD was walking too just at that time that Presto was.——This paper does not cost me a farthing, I have it from the secretary's office. I long till to-morrow to know how my lord treasurer sleeps this night, and to hear he mends: we are all undone without him; so pray for him, sirrahs, and don't stay too late at the dean's.

26. I dined with Mrs. Van; for the weather is so bad, and I am so busy, that I can't dine with great folks: and besides I dare eat but little, to keep my head in order, which is better. Lord treasurer is very ill, but I hope in no danger. We have no quiet with the Whigs, they are so violent against a Peace; but I'll cool them, with a vengeance, very soon. I have not heard from the bishop of Clogher, whether he has got his statues. I writ to him six weeks ago; he's so busy with his parliament. I won't answer your letter yet, say what you will, saucy girls.

27. I forgot to go about some business this morning, which cost me double the time; and I was forced to be at the secretary's office till four, and lose my dinner; so I went to Mrs. Van's, and made them get me three herrings, which I am very fond of, and they are a light vittals: besides, I was to have supped at lady Ashburnham's; but the drab did not call for us in her coach, as she promised, but sent for us, and so I sent my excuses. It has been a terrible rainy day, but so flattering in the morning, that I would needs go out in my new hat. I met Leigh and Sterne as I was going into the Park. Leigh says he will go to Ireland in ten days, if he can get Sterne to go with him; so I will send him the things for MD, and I have desired him to enquire about the box. I hate that Sterne for his carelessness about it; but it was my fault.

29. I was all this terrible rainy day with my friend Lewis

[1] Benson. *See* Letter VI., Oct. 15, 1710 (note).

upon business of importance; and I dined with him, and came home about seven, and thought I would amuse myself a little after the pains I had taken. I saw a volume of Congreve's Plays in my room, that Patrick had taken to read; and I looked into it, and in mere loitering read in it till twelve, like an owl and a fool: if ever I do so again; never saw the like. Count Gallas, the emperor's envoy, you will hear is in disgrace with us: the queen has ordered her ministers to have no more commerce with him;[1] the reason is, the fool writ a rude letter to lord Dartmouth, secretary of state, complaining of our proceedings about a Peace; and he is always in close confidence with lord Wharton, and Sunderland, and others of the late ministry. I believe you begin to think there will be no Peace; the Whigs here are sure it cannot be, and stocks are fallen again. But I am confident there will, unless France plays us tricks; and you may venture a wager with any of your Whig acquaintance, that we shall not have another campaign. You will get more by it than by ombre, sirrah.—I let slip telling you yesterday's journal, which I thought to have done this morning, but blundered. I dined yesterday at Harry Coote's with lord Hatton,[2] Mr. Finch, a son of lord Nottingham,[3] and Sir Andrew Fountain. I left them soon; but hear they staid till two in the morning, and were all drunk; and so good night for last night, and good night for to-night. You blundering goosecap, an't you ashamed to blunder to young ladies? I shall have a fire in three or four days, now, oh ho.

30. I was to-day in the city concerting some things with a printer, and am to be to-morrow all day busy with Mr. secretary about the same.[4] I won't tell you now; but the ministers reckon it will do abundance of good, and open the eyes of the nation, who are half bewitched against a Peace. Few of this generation can remember any thing but war and taxes, and they think it is as it should be: whereas 'tis certain we are the most undone people in Europe, as I am afraid I shall make appear

[1] Johann Wenzel (1669–1719), Graf von Gallas: "He was told in a message from St. John that he should come no more to Court, that what his master had to communicate would be well received from the hands of another Minister, and that he might depart from Britain when he thought fit" (D. L P.).
[2] William Seton Hatton (1689-90–1760), second viscount. He was a sort of half-uncle to the Mr. Finch who accompanied him.
[3] The Earl of Nottingham was Daniel Finch (1647–1729-30), afterwards Earl of Winchilsea. Known as "Dismal" on account of the natural expression of his face. Left the Tories and became a Whig—see *post*.
[4] This was *The Conduct of the Allies*; see the *Journal* of the whole of the following month. It was published Nov. 27.—N.

beyond all contradiction. But I forgot; I won't tell you what I will do, nor what I will not do: so let me alone, and go to Stoyte, and give goody Stoyte and Catherine my humble service; I love goody Stoyte better than goody Walls. Who'll pay me for this green apron? I will have the money; it cost ten shillings and six pence. I think it plaguy dear for a cheap thing; but they said, that English silk would cockle, and I know not what. You have the making into the bargain. 'Tis right Italian: I have sent it and the pamphlets to Leigh, and will send the *Miscellanies* and spectacles in a day or two. I would send more; but faith I'm plaguy poor at present.

31. The Devil's in this secretary; when I went this morning he had people with him; but says he, We are to dine with Prior to-day, and then will do all our business in the afternoon; at two Prior sends word, he is otherwise engaged; then the secretary and I go and dine with brigadier Britton, sit till eight, grow merry, no business done; he is in haste to see lady Jersey, we part, and appoint no time to meet again. This is the fault of all the present ministers, teazing me to death for my assistance, laying the whole weight of their affairs upon it, yet slipping opportunities. Lord treasurer mends every day, though slowly: I hope he will take care of himself. Pray, will you send to Parvisol to send me a bill of twenty pounds as soon as he can, for I want money. I must have money; I will have money, sirrahs.

Nov. 1. I went to-day into the city to settle some business with Stratford, and to dine with him; but he was engaged, and I was so angry I would not dine with any other merchant, but went to my printer, and ate a bit, and did business of mischief with him, and I shall have the spectacles and *Miscellany* to-morrow, and leave them with Leigh. A fine day always makes me go into the city, if I can spare time, because it is exercise; and that does me more good than any thing. I have heard nothing since of my head, but a little, I don't know how, sometimes: but I am very temperate, especially now the treasurer is ill, and the ministers often at Hampton-Court, and the secretary not yet fixed in his house, and I hate dining with many of my old acquaintance. Here has been a fellow discovered going out of the East-India house with sixteen thousand pounds in money and bills; he would have escaped, if he had not been so uneasy with thirst, that he stole out before his time, and was caught. But what is that to MD? I wish we had the money, provided the East-India Company was never the worse; you know we must not covet, &c. Our weather, for this fortnight past, is checquered, a fair and a rainy day; this was very fine, and I have walked four miles, wish MD would do so, lazy sluttikins.

2. It has rained all day with a *continuendo*, and I went in a chair to dine with Mrs. Van; always there in a very rainy day. But I made a shift to come back afoot. I live a very retired life, pay very few visits, and keep but very little company; I read no news-papers. I am sorry I sent you the *Examiner*; for the printer is going to print them in a small volume: it seems the author is too proud to have them printed by subscription, though his friends offered, they say, to make it worth five hundred pounds to him. The *Spectators* are likewise printing in a larger and a smaller volume: so I believe they are going to leave them off, and indeed people grow weary of them, though they are often prettily written. We have had no news for me to send you now towards the end of my letter. The queen has the gout a little; I hoped the lord treasurer would have had it too; but Radcliffe told me yesterday it was the rheumatism in his knee and foot; however he mends, and I hope will be abroad in a short time. I am told they design giving away several employments before the parliament sits, which will be the thirteenth instant. I either do not like, or [do] not understand this policy; and if lord treasurer does not mend soon, they must give them just before the sessions. But he is the greatest procrastinator in the world.

3. A fine day this, and I walked a pretty deal; I stufft the secretary's pockets with papers, which he must read and settle at Hampton-Court, where he went to-day, and stays some time. They have no lodgings for me there, so I can't go; for the town is small, chargeable and inconvenient. Lord treasurer had a very ill night last night, with much pain in his knee and foot, but is easier to-day.—And so I went to visit Prior about some business, and so he was not within, and so Sir Andrew Fountain made me dine to-day again with Mrs. Van, and I came home soon, remembering this must go to-night, and that I had a letter of MD's to answer. O Lord, where is it? let me see; so, so, here it is. You grudge writing so soon. Pox on that bill; the woman would have me manage that money for her. I do not know what to do with it now I have it. I am like the unprofitable steward in the gospel: *I laid it up in a napkin; there thou hast what is thine own*, &c. Well, well, I know of your new mayor. (I'll tell you a pun; a fishmonger owed a man two

crowns; so he sent him a piece of bad ling and a tench, and then
said he was paid: how is that now? find it out; for I won't tell
it you: which of you finds it out?) Well, but as I was saying,
what care I for your mayor? I fancy Ford may tell Forbes
right about my returning to Ireland before Christmas, or soon
after. I'm sorry you did not go on with your story about
Pray God you be John; I never heard it in my life, and wonder
what it can be.—Ah, Stella, faith you learned upon your Bible
to think what to say when you writ that. Yes, that story of
the secretary's making me an example is true; "never heard
it before;" why how could you hear it? is it possible to tell
you the hundredth part of what passes in our companies here?
The secretary is as easy with me as Mr. Addison was. I have
often thought what a splutter Sir William Temple makes[1]
about being secretary of state; I think Mr. St. John the greatest
young man I ever knew; wit, capacity, beauty, quickness of
apprehension, good learning, and an excellent taste; the best
orator in the house of commons, admirable conversation, good
nature, and good manners; generous, and a despiser of money.
His only fault is talking to his friends in [a] way of complaint
of too great a load of business, which looks a little like affectation; and he endeavours too much to mix the fine gentleman,
and man of pleasure, with the man of business. What truth
and sincerity he may have I know not: he is now but thirty-
two, and has been secretary above a year. Is not all this extraordinary? How he stands with the queen and lord treasurer
I have told you before. This is his character; and I believe you
will be diverted by knowing it. I writ to the archbishop of
Dublin, bishop of Cloyne,[2] and of Clogher together, five weeks
ago from Windsor: I hope they had my letters; pray know if
Clogher had his.—Fig for your Physician and his advice, madam
Dingley; if I grow worse, I will; otherwise I will trust to tem-
perance and exercise: your fall of the leaf; what care I when
the leaves fall? I am sorry to see them fall with all my heart;
but why should I take physick because leaves fall off from trees?
that won't hinder them from falling. If a man falls from a
horse, must I take physick for that?—This arguing makes you
mad; but it is true right reason, not to be disproved.—I am glad
at heart to hear poor Stella is better; use exercise and walk, spend
pattens and spare potions, wear out clogs and waste claret. Have
you found out my pun of the fishmonger? Don't read a word

[1] In his writings. Historic present tense.
[2] Charles Crow, from 1702. An Englishman. Died 1726.

more till you have got it. And Stella is handsome again, you say? and is she fat? I have sent to Leigh the set of *Examiners*; the first thirteen were written by several hands, some good, some bad; the next three and thirty were all by one hand, that makes forty six:[1] then that author, whoever he was, laid it down on purpose to confound guessers; and the last six were written by a woman. Then there is an account of Guiscard by the same woman, but the facts sent by Presto. Then *An Answer to the Letter to the lords about Greg*, by Presto; *Prior's journey*, by Presto; *Vindication of the duke of Marlborough*, entirely by the same woman. *Comment* on Hare's Sermon, by the same woman, only hints sent to the printer from Presto to give her. Then there's the *Miscellany*, an apron for Stella, a pound of chocolate without sugar for Stella, a fine snuff-rasp of ivory, given me by Mrs. St. John for Dingley, and a large roll of tobacco, which she must hide or cut shorter out of modesty, and four pair of spectacles for the Lord knows who. There's the cargo, I hope it will come safe. Oh, Mrs. Masham and I are very well; we write to one another, but it is upon business; I believe I told you so before: pray pardon my forgetfulness in these cases; poor Presto can't help it. MD shall have the money as soon as Tooke gets it. And so I think I have answered all, and the paper is out, and now I have fetcht up my week, and will send you another this day fortnight.—Why, you rogues, two crowns make *tench-ill-ling*: you are so dull you could never have found it out. Farewel, &c. &c.

LETTER XXXIV

London, *November* 3, 1711.

My thirty-third lies now before me just finished, and I am going to seal and send it, so let me know whether you would have me add any thing: I gave you my journal of this day; and it is now nine at night, and I am going to be busy for an hour or two.

4. I left a friend's house to-day where I was invited, just

---

[1] In six or eight weeks after Swift became silent, the *Examiner* was laid down, although revived again the December following, and continued to be a lively and spirited paper for two or three months, the writers of it being supplied with hints from Mr. secretary St. John and Dr. Swift. But the ministry having then obtained their ends in parliament, and the peace being in great forwardness, they suffered the *Examiner* to sink again into obscurity and dulness.—D. S.

when dinner was setting on, and pretended I was engaged, because I saw some fellows I did not know, and went to Sir Matthew Dudley's, where I had the same inconvenience, but he would not let me go; otherwise I would have gone home, and sent for a slice of mutton and a pot of ale, rather than dine with persons unknown, as bad for aught I know as your deans, parsons, and curates. Bad slabby weather to-day.—Now methinks I write at ease, when I have no letter of MD's to answer. But I mistook, and have got the large paper. The queen is laid up with the gout at Hampton-Court; she is now seldom without it any long time together; I fear it will wear her out in a very few years. I plainly find I have less twitchings about my toes since these ministers are sick and out of town, and that I don't dine with them. I would compound for a light easy gout to be perfectly well in my head.—Pray walk when the [first] frost comes, young ladies, go a frost-biting. It comes into my head, that from the very time you first went to Ireland I have been always plying you to walk and read. The young fellows here have begun a kind of fashion to walk, and many of them have got swinging strong shoes on purpose; it has got as far as several young lords; if it hold, it would be a very good thing. Lady Lucy and I are fallen out: she rails at me, and I have left visiting her.

5. MD was very troublesome to me last night in my sleep; I was adreamed, methought, that Stella was here: I asked her after Dingley, and she said, she had left her in Ireland, because she designed her stay to be short, and such stuff.—Monsieur Pontchartrain,[1] the secretary of state in France, and Monsieur Fontenelle,[2] the secretary of the Royal Academy there (who writ the *Dialogues des morts*, &c.) have sent letters to lord Pembroke, that the Academy have, with the king's consent, chosen him one of their members,[3] in the room of one who is lately dead. But the cautious gentleman has given me the letters to show my lord Dartmouth and Mr. St. John, our two secretaries, and let them see there is no treason in them[4]; which I will do on Wednesday, when they come from Hampton-Court. The letters are very handsome, and it is a [very] great mark

[1] Louis Phelypeaux (1643–1727), Comte de Pontchartrain.
[2] Bernard le Bovyer de Fontenelle (1657–1757) lived to within one month of the completion of his hundredth year.
[3] An honour conferred on the earl as a man of taste and science, particularly eminent for his splendid collection of marbles and other antiquities at Wilton.—D. L. P.
[4] England and France being then at war with each other!!

of honour and distinction to lord Pembroke. I hear the two French ministers are come over again about the Peace; but I have seen nobody of consequence to know the truth. I dined to-day with a lady of my acquaintance who was sick, in her bed-chamber, upon three herrings and a chicken; the dinner was my bespeaking. We begin now to have chesnuts and Seville oranges; have you the latter yet? 'Twas a terrible windy day, and we had processions in carts of the Pope and the Devil, and the butchers rang their cleavers; you know this is the fifth of November, popery and gun-powder.

6. Since I am used to this way of writing, I fancy I could hardly make out a long letter to MD without it. I think I ought to allow for every line taken up by telling you where I dined; but that will not be above seven lines in all, half a line to a dinner. Your Ingolsby is going over, and they say here, he is to be made a lord.—Here was I staying in my room till two this afternoon for that puppy Sir Andrew Fountain, who was to go with me into the city, and never came; and if I had not shot a dinner flying, with one Mr. Murray, I might have fasted, or gone to an alehouse.—You never said one word of good Stoyte in your letter; but I suppose these winter nights we shall hear more of her.—Does the Provost laugh as much as he used to do? we reckon him here a good-for-nothing fellow. —I design to write to your dean one of these days, but I can never find time, nor what to say. I will think of something: but if DD [1] were not in Ireland, I believe seriously I should not think of the place twice a year. Nothing there ever makes the subject of talk in any company where I am.

7. I went to-day to the city on business; but stopt at a printer's and staid there; it was a most delicious day. I hear the parliament is to be prorogued for a fortnight longer; I suppose, either because the queen has the gout, or that lord treasurer is not well, or that they would do something more towards a Peace. I called at lord treasurer's at noon, and sat a while with lord Harley, but his father was asleep. A bookseller has reprinted or new-titled *A Sermon* of Tom Swift's [2] printed last year, and publishes an advertisement calling it Dr. Swift's *Sermon*. Some friend of lord Galway has, by his directions, published a four-shilling book about his conduct in Spain; to defend him; I have but just seen it. But what care you for books,

except Presto's *Miscellanies*? Leigh promised to call and see
me, but has not yet; I hope he will take care of his cargo, and
get your Chester box. A murrain take that box; every thing
is spoiled that is in it. How does the strong box do? You say
nothing of Raymond: is his wife brought to bed again; or how?
has he finished his house; paid his debts; and put out the rest
of the money to use? I am glad to hear poor Joe is like to get
his two hundred pounds. I suppose Trim is now reduced to
slavery again. I am glad of it; the people were as great rascals
as the gentlemen. But I must go to bed, sirrahs; the secretary
is still at Hampton-Court with my papers, or is come only
to-night. They plague me with attending them.

8. I was with the secretary this morning, and we dined with
Prior, and did business this afternoon till about eight, and I
must alter and undo, and a clutter: I am glad the parliament
is prorogued. I staid with Prior till eleven; the secretary left
us at eight. Prior, I believe, will be one of those employed to
make the Peace, when a Congress is opened. Lord Ashburnham
told to-day at the Coffee-house, that lord Harley was yesterday
morning married to the duke of Newcastle's daughter, the great
heiress, and it got about all the town. But I saw lord Harley
yesterday at noon in his night-gown, and he dined in the city
with Prior and others; so it is not true: but I hope it will be
so; for I know, it has been privately managing this long time:[1]
the lady will not have half her father's estate; for the duke
left lord Pelham's son his heir; the widow duchess will not
stand to the will, and she is now at law with Pelham.[2] However, at worst, the girl will have about ten thousand pounds a
year, to support the honour: for lord treasurer will never save
a groat for himself. Lord Harley is a very valuable young
gentleman; and they say the girl is handsome, and has good
sense, but red hair.

9. I designed a jaunt into the city to-day to be merry, but
was disappointed; so one always is in this life; and I could not
see lord Dartmouth to-day, with whom I had some business.
Business and pleasure both disappointed. You can go to your

---

[1] The great end, Lord Bolingbroke says, of Harley's administration,
was to marry his son to this lady.—N. She was Henrietta Cavendish Holles
(*c.* 1693–1755), only daughter and heiress of John, first "Holles" Duke
of Newcastle: *see* Letter XXVI., July 19, 1711.

[2] The widow was Margaret (Cavendish) (1661–1716), third daughter and
co-heiress of Henry, second "Cavendish" Duke of Newcastle; she was
married to the duke in 1690. The heir, Thomas Pelham-Holles (1693–
1768), was son and successor of Thomas Pelham, first Baron Pelham of
Laughton; and in 1715 he was created Duke of Newcastle-on-Tyne.

dean, and for want of him, goody Stoyte, or Walls, or Manley, and meet every where with cards and claret. I dined privately with a friend on a herring and chicken, and half a flask of bad Florence. I begin to have fires now, when the mornings are cold; I have got some loose bricks at the back of my grate for good husbandry. Fine weather. Patrick tells me, my caps are wearing out; I know not how to get others. I want a necessary woman strangely; I am as helpless as an elephant.—I had three pacquets from the archbishop of Dublin, cost me four shillings, all about Higgins,[1] printed stuff, and two long letters. His people forget to enclose them to Lewis; and they were only directed to Doctor Swift, without naming London or any thing else: I wonder how they reached me, unless the post-master directed them. I have read all the trash, and am weary.

10. Why; if you must have it out, something is to be published of great moment, and three or four great people are to see there are no mistakes in point of fact: and 'tis so troublesome to send it among them, and get their corrections, that I am weary as a dog. I dined to-day with the printer, and was there all the afternoon; and it plagues me, and there's an end, and what would you have? Lady Dupplin, lord treasurer's daughter, is brought to bed of a son.[2] Lord treasurer has had an ugly return of his gravel. 'Tis good for us to live in gravel pits,[3] but not for gravel pits to live in us: a man in this case should leave no stone unturned. Lord treasurer's sickness, the queen's gout, the forwarding the Peace, occasion putting off the parliament a fortnight longer. My head has had no ill returns. I had good walking to-day in the city, and take all opportunities of it on purpose for my health; but I can't walk in the Park, because that is only for walking sake, and loses time, so I mix it with business: I wish MD walked half as much as Presto. If I was with you, I'd make you walk; I would walk behind or before you, and you should have masks on, and be tucked up like any thing, and Stella is naturally a stout walker, and carries herself firm, methinks I see her strut, and step clever over a kennel; and Dingley would do well enough, if her petticoats were pinned up; but she is so embroiled, and so

---

[1] Francis Higgins (1669–1728), "the Irish Sacheverell." At this time he was a prebendary of Christ Church, Dublin, and had already (1706) got himself into trouble in London, preaching sedition in the supposed interests of the Church. He died archdeacon of Cashel.

[2] *See* Letter V., Oct. 7, 1710, note on "Doblane." This son (the second) was christened Robert; and, as Robert Hay Drummond, became Archbishop of York, 1761. Died 1776.

[3] Patients were sent to Kensington gravel pits for the air.

fearful, and then Stella scolds, and Dingley stumbles, and is so daggled. Have you got the whale-bone petticoats amongst you yet? I hate them; a woman here may hide a moderate gallant under them. Pshaw, what's all this I'm saying? methinks I am talking to MD face to face.

11. Did I tell you that old Frowde,[1] the old fool, is selling his estate at Pepperhara,[2] and is sculking about the town no body knows where? and who do you think manages all this for him, but that rogue Child,[3] the double squire of Farnham? I have put Mrs. Masham, the queen's favourite, upon buying it; but that is yet a great secret; and I have employed lady Oglethorp to enquire about it. I was with lady Oglethorp to-day, who is come to town for a week or two, and to-morrow I will see to hunt out the old fool; he is utterly ruined, and at this present in some blind alley with some dirty wench. He has two sons that must starve, and he never gives them a farthing. If Mrs. Masham buys the land, I will desire her to get the queen to give some pension to the old fool, to keep him from absolutely starving. What do you meddle with other people's affairs for? says Stella. O, but Mr. Masham and his wife are very urgent with me, since I first put them in the head of it. I dined with Sir Matthew Dudley, who, I doubt, will soon lose his employment.

12. Morning. I am going to hunt out old Frowde, and to do some business in the city. I have not yet called to Patrick to know whether it be fair. It has been past dropping these two days. Rainy weather hurts my pate and my purse. He tells me 'tis very windy, and begins to look dark; woe be to my shillings: an old saying and a true; Few fillings, many shillings.[4] If the day be dark, my purse will be light. To my enemies be this curse; A dark day and a light purse. And so I'll rise, and go to my fire, for Patrick tells me I have a fire; yet it is not shaving day, nor is the weather cold; this is too extravagant. What is become of Dilly? I suppose you have him with you. Stella is just now shewing a white leg, and putting it into the slipper.—Present my service to her, and tell her I am engaged to the dean; and desire she will come too: or, Dingley, can't you write a note? This is Stella's morn-

[1] Apparently the father of the Philip Frowde mentioned in note to "Colonel Proud," Letter VIII., Nov. 4, 1710. This Philip senior had been deputy Postmaster-General, 1678–1688.

[2] Peper Harrow is two and a half miles west of Godalming in Surrey.

[3] *Gent. Mag.* for 1754, p. 579. Death; Dec. 12: "Charles Child, of Farnham, Surry, Esq."

[4] In this extemporised "old saying," shilling means expense. In Ireland they say "shill out"—not "shell out" as in England.

ing dialogue, no, morning speech I mean.—Morrow, sirrahs, and let me rise as well as you; but I promise you Walls can't dine with the dean to-day, for she is to be at Mrs. Proby's just after dinner, and to go with Gracy Spencer[1] to the shops to buy a yard of muslin, and a silver lace for an under petticoat. Morrow again, sirrahs.—At night. I dined with Stratford in the city, but could not finish my affairs with him; but now I have resolved to buy five hundred pounds South-Sea stock, which will cost me three hundred and eighty ready money; and I will make use of the bill of a hundred pounds you sent me, and transfer Mrs. Walls over to Hawkshaw; or, if she dislikes it, I will borrow a hundred pounds of the secretary, and repay her. Three shillings coach-hire to-day. I have spoken to Frowde's brother,[2] to get me the lowest price of the estate, to tell Mrs. Masham.

13. I dined privately with a friend to-day in the neighbour-hood. Last Saturday night I came home, and the drab had just washed my room, and my bed-chamber was all wet, and I was forced to go to bed in my own defence, and no fire: I was sick on Sunday, and now have got a swinging cold. I scolded like a dog at Patrick, although he was out with me: I detest washing of rooms: can't they wash them in a morning, and make a fire, and leave open the windows? I slept not a wink last night for hawking and spitting: and now every body has colds. Here's a clutter: I'll go to bed and sleep if I can.

14. Lady Mountjoy sent to me two days ago, so I dined with her to-day, and in the evening went to see lord treasurer. I found Patrick had been just there with a how d'ye,[3] and my lord had returned answer, that he desired to see me. Mrs. Masham was with him when I came; and they are never disturbed: 'tis well she is not very handsome[4]: they sit alone together, settling the nation. I sat with lady Oxford,[5] and stopt Mrs. Masham as she came out, and told her what progress I had made, &c. and then went to lord treasurer: he is very well, only uneasy at rising or sitting, with some rheumatick pain in his thigh, and a foot weak. He shewed me a small paper,

[1] Mr. Aitken opines she was a sister of Mrs. Proby (Letter XIX. March 25).
[2] Possibly Colonel William Frowde, mentioned in Dalton's third vol. of *Army Lists*, p. 382, as being apparently third son of Sir Philip Frowde, Kt.,—who was grandfather of the author of *The Fall of Saguntum*.
[3] A formal inquiry by a servant.
[4] Especially she was remarkable for a very red nose, a perpetual subject of raillery in Whig lampoons.—D. L. P.
[5] *See* Letter XI., Dec. 22, 1710.

sent by an unknown hand to one Mr. Cook, who sent it to my
lord: it was written in plain large letters, thus;

> *Though G——d's knife did not succeed;*
> *A F——n's yet may do the Deed.*

And a little below; *Burn this you Dog.* My lord has frequently
such letters as these: once he shewed me one, which was a
vision describing a certain man, his dress, his sword, and his
countenance, who was to murder my lord. And he told me,
he saw a fellow in the chapel at Windsor with a dress very
like it. They often send him letters signed Your humble servant,
The Devil, and such stuff. I sat with him till after ten, and
have business to do.

15. The secretary came yesterday to town from Hampton-
Court, so I went to him early this morning; but he went back
last night again: and coming home to-night I found a letter
from him to tell me, that he was just come home from Hampton-
Court, and just returning, and will not be here till Saturday
night. A pox take him; he stops all my business. I'll beg leave
to come back when I have got over this; and hope to see MD
in Ireland soon after Christmas.—I'm weary of courts, and
want my journies to Laracor; they did me more good than all
the ministries these twenty years. I dined to-day in the city,
but did no business as I designed. Lady Mountjoy tells me,
that Dilly is got to Ireland, and that the archbishop of Dublin
was the cause of his returning so soon. The parliament was
prorogued two days ago for a fortnight, which, with the queen's
absence, makes the town very dull, and empty. They tell me
the duke of Ormond brings all the world away with him from
Ireland. London has nothing so bad in it in Winter, as your
knots of Irish folks; but I go to no Coffee-house, and so I
seldom see them. This letter shall go on Saturday; and then
I am even with the world again. I have lent money, and cannot
get it, and am forced to borrow for myself.

16. My man made a blunder this morning, and let up a
visiter, when I had ordered to see no body, so I was forced to
hurry a hang-dog instrument of mine into my bed-chamber,
and keep him cooling his heels there above an hour.——I am
going on fairly in the common forms of a great cold; I believe
it will last me about ten days in all.——I should have told you
that in those two verses sent to lord treasurer, the G——d
stands for *Guiscard*; that is easy; but we differed about F——n;
I thought it was for *Frenchman*, because he hates them, and

they him: and so it would be, That although Guiscard's knife
missed its design, the knife of a Frenchman might yet do it.
My lord thinks it stands for *Felton*, the name of him that stabbed
the first duke of Buckingham.—Sir Andrew Fountain and I
dined with the Vans to-day, and my cold made me loiter all
the evening. Stay, young women, don't you begin to owe me
a letter? just a month to-day since I had your N. 22. I'll stay
a week longer, and then I'll expect like agog; till then you may
play at ombre, and so forth, as you please. The Whigs are still
crying down our Peace, but we will have it, I hope, in spite of
them: the emperor comes now with his two eggs a penny, and
promises wonders to continue the war; but it is too late; only
I hope the fear of it will serve to spur on the French to be easy
and sincere. Night, sirrahs; I'll go early to bed.

17. Morning. This goes to-night; I will put it myself in the
post-office. I had just now a long letter from the archbishop of
Dublin, giving me an account of the ending your sessions, how
it ended in a storm; which storm, by the time it arrives here,
will be only *half nature*. I can't help it, I won't hide. I often
advised the dissolution of that parliament, although I did not
think the scoundrels had so much courage; but they have it
only in the wrong, like a bully that will fight for a whore, and
run away in an army. I believe, by several things the archbishop says, he is not very well either with the government or
clergy.—See how luckily my paper ends with a fortnight.—
God Almighty bless and preserve dearest little MD.—I suppose
your lord-lieutenant is now setting out for England. I wonder
the bishop of Clogher does not write to me; or let me know of
his statues, and how he likes them: I will write to him again,
as soon as I have leisure. Farewel, dearest MD, and love Presto,
who loves MD infinitely above all earthly things, and who
will.—My service to Mrs. Stoyte, and Catherine. I'm sitting
in my bed; but will rise to seal this. Morrow, dear rogues.
Farewel again, dearest MD, &c.

LETTER XXXV

London, *Nov.* 17, 1711.

I PUT my last this evening in the post-office. I dined with Dr.
Cockburn. This being queen Elizabeth's birth-day, we have the
D— and all to do among us. I just heard of the stir as my letter
was sealed this morning; and was so cross I would not open it

to tell you. I have been visiting lady Oglethorp and lady Worsley; the latter is lately come to town for the Winter, and with child, and what care you? This is queen Elizabeth's birth-day, usually kept in this town by 'prentices, &c. but the Whigs designed a mighty procession by midnight, and had laid out a thousand pounds to dress up the Pope, Devil, Cardinals, Sacheverell, &c. and carry them with torches about, and burn them. They did it by contribution. Garth gave five guineas, Dr. Garth I mean, if ever you heard of him. But they were seized last night, by order from the secretary: you will have an account of it, for they bawl it about the streets already. They had some very foolish and mischievous designs; and it was thought they would have put the rabble upon assaulting my lord treasurer's house, and the secretary's; and other violences. The Militia[1] was raised to prevent it, and now, I suppose, all will be quiet. The figures are now at the secretary's office at White-hall. I design to see them if I can.

18. I was this morning with Mr. secretary, who just came from Hampton-Court. He was telling me more particulars about this business of burning the Pope. It cost a good deal of money, and had it gone on, would have cost three times as much: but the town is full of it, and half a dozen Grubstreet papers already. The secretary and I dined at brigadier Britton's, but I left them at six, upon an appointment with some sober company of men and ladies, to drink punch at Sir Andrew Fountain's. We were not very merry; and I don't love rack punch, I love it better with brandy: are you of my opinion? Why then; twelve-penny weather; sirrahs, why don't you play at shuttle-cock? I have thought of it a hundred times; faith Presto will come over after Christmas, and will play with Stella before the cold weather is gone. Do you read the *Spectators*? I never do; they never come in my way; I go to no Coffee-houses. They say abundance of them are very pretty; they are going to be printed in small volumes; I'll bring them over with me. I shall be out of my hurry in a week, and if Leigh be not gone over, I will send you by him what I am now finishing. I don't know where Leigh is; I have not seen him this good while, though he promised to call: I shall send to him. The queen comes to town on Thursday for good and all.

19. I was this morning at lord Dartmouth's office, and sent out for him from the committee of council, about some business. I was asking him more concerning this bustle about the

[1] The London trained bands.—D. L. P.

figures in wax-work of the Pope, and Devil, &c. He was not at leisure, or he would have seen them. I hear the owners are so impudent, that they design to replevin[1] them by law. I am assured that the figure of the Devil is made as like lord treasurer as they could. Why; I dined with a friend in St. James's-street. Lord treasurer, I am told, was abroad to-day; I will know to-morrow how he does after it. The duke of Marlborough is come, and was yesterday at Hampton-Court with the queen; no, it was t'other day; no it was yesterday; for to-day I remember Mr. secretary was going to see him, when I was there, not at the duke of Marlborough's, but at the secretary's; the duke is not so fond of me. What care I? I won seven shillings to-night at picquet: I play twice a year or so.

20. I have been so teazed with Whiggish discourse by Mrs. Barton and lady Betty Germain, never saw the like. They turn all this affair of the pope-burning into ridicule; and indeed they have made too great a clutter about it, if they had no real reason to apprehend some tumults. I dined with lady Betty. I hear Prior's commission is passed to be ambassador extraordinary and plenipotentiary for the Peace; my lord privy-seal, who you know is bishop of Bristol, is the other; and lord Strafford, already ambassador at the Hague, the third: I am forced to tell you ignorant sluts who is who. I was punning scurvily with Sir Andrew Fountain and lord Pembroke this evening; do you ever pun now? Sometimes the dean, or Tom Leigh.[2] Prior puns very well. Od so, I must go see his excellency, 'tis a noble advancement: but they could do no less, after sending him to France. Lord Strafford is as proud as hell, and how he will bear one of Prior's mean birth on an equal character with him, I know not.[3] And so I go to my business, and bid you good night.

21. I was this morning busy with my printer; I gave him the fifth sheet, and then I went and dined with him in the city, to correct something, and alter, &c. and I walked home in the dusk, and the rain overtook me: and I found a letter here from Mr. Lewis; well, and so I opened it; and he says,

---

[1] *Replevin.* Recovery of goods in consideration of security given that their ownership shall be tried.

[2] Tom Leigh (staying in Ireland) was a brother of Jemmy's and was of Stella's acquaintance. When Swift says merely "Leigh" (or "Lee"), he usually means Jemmy.

[3] Lord Strafford absolutely refused to be joined on the commission with Prior; so the department of trade, which was to be Prior's, was entrusted to the Bishop of Bristol, much enchancing the difficulties of the negotiation.—D. L. P.

The Peace is past danger, &c. Well; and so there was another letter inclosed in his; well; and so I looked on the outside of this t'other letter. Well; and so who do you think this t'other letter was from? Well; and so I'll tell you, it was from little MD, N. 23, 23, 23, 23. I tell you it is no more, I have told you so before:[1] but I just looked again to satisfy you. Hie, Stella, you write like an emperor, a great deal together; a very good hand, and but four false spellings in all. Shall I send them to you? I am glad you did not take my correction ill. Well; but I won't answer your letter now, sirrah saucy boxes, no, no; not yet; just a month and three days from the last, which is just five weeks: you see it comes just when I begin to grumble.

22. Morning. Tooke has just brought me Dingley's money. I will give you a note for it at the end of this letter. There was half a crown for entering the letter of attorney: but I swore to stop that. I'll spend your money bravely here. Morrow, dear sirrahs.—At night. I dined to-day with Sir Thomas Hanmer; his wife, the duchess of Grafton,[2] dined with us: she wears a great high head-dress, such as was in fashion fifteen years ago, and looks like a mad-woman in it; yet she has great remains of beauty. I was this evening to see lord Harley, and thought to have sat with lord treasurer; but he was taken up with the Dutch envoy and such folks; and I would not stay. One particular in life here different from what I have in Dublin, is, that whenever I come home I expect to find some letter for me, and seldom miss; and never any worth a farthing, but often to vex me. The queen does not come to town till Saturday. Prior is not yet declared; but these ministers being at Hampton-Court I know nothing; and if I write news from common hands, it is always lies. You will think it affectation; but nothing has vexed me more for some months past, than people I never saw, pretending to be acquainted with me, and yet speak ill of me too; at least some of them. An old crooked Scotch countess, whom I never heard of in my life, told the duchess of Hamilton[3] t'other day, that I often visited her. People of worth never do that; so that a man only gets the scandal of having scurvy acquaintance. Three ladies were railing against me some time

---

[1] Nothing was ever more in Swift's style and manner of conversation than these repetitions and the words following.—D. S.

[2] His first wife, married 1698, was Isabella (c. 1667-1722-3), daughter of Henry Bennet, first Earl of Arlington; she had become suo jure Countess of Arlington in 1685, and had married, first (1672), when five years old, Henry FitzRoy, first Duke of Grafton, aged nine. He died (of wounds at Cork) 1690.

[3] See Letter XXVII., Aug. 29, note to "Duke of Hamilton."

ago, and said they were very well acquainted with me; two of
which I had never heard of; and the third [I] had only seen
twice where I happened to visit. A man who has once seen me
in a Coffee-house will ask me how I do, when he sees me talking
at Court with a minister of state; who is sure to ask me, how
I came acquainted with that scoundrel. But come, sirrahs,
this is all stuff to you, so I'll say no more on this side the
paper, but turn over.

23. My printer invited Mr. Lewis and me to dine at a tavern
to-day, which I have not done five times since I came to
England; I never will call it *Britain*, pray don't call it *Britain*.
My week is not out, and one side of this paper is out, and I
have a letter to answer of MD's into the bargain: must I write
on the third side? faith that will give you an ill habit. I saw
Leigh last night: he gives a terrible account of Sterne; he reckons
he is seduced by some wencher; he is over head and ears in debt,
and has pawned several things. Leigh says he goes on Monday next for Ireland, but believes Sterne will not go with
him; Sterne has kept him these three months. Leigh has
got the apron and things, and promises to call for the box at
Chester; but I despair of it. Good night, sirrahs; I have
been late abroad.

24. I have finished my pamphlet to-day, which has cost me
so much time and trouble; it will be published in three or four
days, when the parliament begins sitting. I suppose the queen
is come to town, but know nothing, having been in the city
finishing and correcting with the printer. When I came home
I found letters on my table as usual, and one from your mother,
to tell me, that you desire your writings and a picture should
be sent to me, to be sent over to you. I have just answered her
letter, and promised to take care of them if they be sent to me.
She is at Farnham: it is too late to send them by Leigh; besides,
I will wait your orders, madam Stella. I am going to finish a
letter to lord treasurer about reforming our language; but
first I must put an end to a ballad; and go you to your cards,
sirrahs, this is card season.

25. I was early with the secretary to-day, but he was gone
to his devotions, and to receive the sacrament; several rakes
did the same; it was not for piety, but employments; according
to act of parliament. I dined with lady Mary Dudley[1]; and
past my time since insipidly, only I was at Court at noon, and

[1] Wife of Sir Matthew; third and youngest daughter of Henry O'Brien,
seventh Earl of Thomond. She died 1735.

saw fifty acquaintance I had not met this long time: that is the advantage of a Court, and I fancy I am better known than any man that goes there. Sir John Walters' quarrel with me has entertained the town ever since; and yet we never had a word, only he railed at me behind my back. The parliament is again to be prorogued for eight or nine days; for the Whigs are too strong in the house of lords: other reasons are pretended, but that is the truth. The prorogation is not yet known, but will be to-morrow.

26. Mr. Lewis and I dined with a friend of his, and un-expectedly there dined with us an Irish knight, one Sir John St. Leger,[1] who follows the law here, but at a great distance: he was so pert, I was forced to take him down more than once. I saw to-day the Pope, and Devil, and the other figures of Cardinals, &c. fifteen in all, which have made such a noise. I have put an under-strapper upon writing a two-penny pamphlet to give an account of the whole design. My large pamphlet will be published to-morrow, copies are sent to the great men this night. Domville [2] is come home from his travels; I am vexed at it; I have not seen him yet; I design to present him to all the great men.

27. Domville came to me this morning, and we dined at Pontack's, and were all day together, till six this evening; he is perfectly as fine a gentleman as I know; he set me down at lord treasurer's, with whom I staid about an hour, till Monsieur Buys, the Dutch envoy, came to him about business. My lord treasurer is pretty well; but stiff in the hips with the remains of the rheumatism. I am to bring Domville to my lord Harley in a day or two. It was the dirtiest rainy day that ever I saw. The pamphlet [3] is published; lord treasurer had it by him on the table, and was asking me about the mottos in the title page; he gave me one of them himself. I must send you the pamphlet if I can.

28. Mrs. Van sent to me to dine with her to-day, because some ladies of my acquaintance were to be there; and there I dined. I was this morning to return Domville his visit, and went to visit Mrs. Masham, who was not within. I am turned out of my lodging by my landlady; it seems her husband and her son are coming home; but I have taken another lodging hard by, in Leicester-Fields. I presented Mr. Domville to Mr. Lewis

---

[1] He was made a judge in Ireland by King George I.—F.
[2] See Letter IX., Nov. 22, 1710.
[3] See Letter XXXIII., Oct. 30.

JOURNAL TO STELLA

and Mr. Prior this morning. Prior and I are called the
two Sosias[1] in a Whig newspaper. *Sosias,* can you read
it? The pamphlet begins to make a noise: I was asked by
several whether I had seen it, and they advised me to read it,
for it was something very extraordinary. I shall be suspected:
and it will have several paultry answers. It must take its fate,
as Savage[2] said of his sermon that he preached at Farnham
on Sir William Temple's death. Domville saw Savage in Italy,
says he is a coxcomb, and half mad: he goes in red, and with
yellow waistcoats,[3] and was at ceremony kneeling to the Pope
on a Palm Sunday, which is much more than kissing his toe;
and I believe it will ruin him here when 'tis told. I'll answer
your letter in my new lodgings: I have hardly room; I must
borrow from the other side.

29. New lodgings. My printer came this morning to tell me
he must immediately print a second edition, and lord treasurer
made one or two small additions: they must work day and night
to have it out on Saturday; they sold a thousand in two days.
Our society met to-day, nine of us were present, we dined at
our brother Bathurst's,[4] we made several regulations, and
have chosen three new members, lord Orrery, Jack Hill, who
is Mrs. Masham's brother, he that lately miscarried in the
expedition to Quebec, and one colonel Disney. We have taken
a room in a house near St. James's to meet in. I left them
early about correcting the pamphlet, &c. and am now got
home, &c.

30. This morning I carried Domville to see my lord Harley,
and I did some business with lord treasurer, and have been all
this afternoon with the printer, adding something to the second
edition. I dined with the printer; the pamphlet makes a world
of noise, and will do a great deal of good: it tells abundance of
most important facts which were not at all known. I'll answer
your letter to-morrow morning; or suppose I answer it just
now, though it is pretty late. Come then—You say you are
busy with parliaments, &c. that's more than ever I will be
when I come back; but you will have none these two years.

[1] Sosia, the servant of Amphitryon, was personated by Mercury, and
a " comedy of errors " ensued. *See* Plautus, Molière, and Dryden.
[2] Uncertain. There was a Dr. William Savage, of Emmanuel College,
Cambridge (Aitken).
[3] In view of the entry of Oct. 20th in Letter XXXII., and footnote
thereto, it must be presumed that this is D.S.'s spelling of the word, and
not that of the inditer of the Journals.
[4] Allen Bathurst (1684–1775), Tory M.P. for Cirencester, afterwards
Jan. 1, 1711-12) first Baron and (1772) Earl of Bathurst.

Lord Santry,[1] &c. yes, I have had enough on't. I am glad
Dilly is mended; does not he thank me for shewing him the
Court and the great people's faces? He had his glass out at the
queen and the rest. 'Tis right what Dilly says; I depend upon
nothing from my friends; but to go back as I came. Never fear
Laracor, 'twill mend with a Peace; or surely they'll give me the
Dublin parish. Stella is in the right; the bishop of Ossory[2] is
the silliest, best-natured wretch breathing, of as little consequence as an egg-shell.—Well, the spelling I have mentioned
before; only the next time say *at least*, and not *at lest*. Pox on
your Newbury[3]: what can I do for him? I'll give his case (I
am glad it is not a woman's) to what members I know; that's
all I can do. Lord treasurer's lameness goes off daily. Pray
God preserve poor good Mrs. Stoyte, she would be a great loss
to us all; pray give her my service, and tell her she has my
heartiest prayers. I pity poor Mrs. Manley;[4] but I think the
child is happy to die, considering how little provision it would
have had. Poh, every pamphlet abuses me, and for things that
I never writ. Joe should have written me thanks for his two
hundred pounds: I reckon he got it by my means; and I must
thank the duke of Ormond, who I dare swear will say he did it
on my account. Are they golden pippins, those seven apples?
We have had much rain every day as well as you: 7l. 17s. 8d.
old blunderer, not 18sh. I have reckoned it 18 times. Hawkshaw's eight pounds is not reckoned; and if it be secure, it may
lie where it is, unless they desire to pay it: so Parvisol may let
it drop till further orders; for I have put Mrs. Wesley's money
into the bank, and will pay her with Hawkshaw's.——I mean
that Hawkshaw's money goes for an addition to MD, you
know; but be good houswives. Bernage never comes now to
see me; he has no more to ask: but I hear he has been ill.—
A pox on Mrs. South's affair; I can do nothing in it, but by
way of assisting any body else that solicits it, by dropping a
favourable word, if it comes in my way. Tell Walls I do no more
for any body with my lord treasurer, especially a thing of this
kind. Tell him I have spent all my discretion, and have no
more to use.——And so I have answered your letter fully and
plainly—And so I have got to the third side of my paper,

---

[1] Lord Santry, an extreme Whig, prosecuted Dr. Higgins, the Irish
Sacheverell, before the Privy Council, for uttering some violent High
Church doctrines.—D. L. P.
[2] See Letter XIX., March 24, 1710-11.
[3] ? Newburgh. See *post*, Letter XLII., March 5, 1711-12.
[4] Mrs. Isaac M.

which is more than belongs to you, young women. It goes to-morrow, To nobody's sorrow. You are silly, not I; I'm a poet, if I had but,[1] &c.——Who's silly now? rogues and lasses, tinder-boxes and buzzards. O Lord, I am in a high vein of silliness; methought I was speaking to dearest little MD face to face. There; so lads, enough for to-night; to cards with the blackguards. Good night, my delight, &c.

Dec. 1. Pish, sirrahs, put a date always at the bottom of the letter as well as the top, that I may know when you send it; your last is of Nov. 3d, yet I had others at the same time written a fortnight after. Whenever you would have any money, send me word three weeks before, and in that time you will certainly have an answer, with a bill on Parvisol: pray do this; for my head is full, and it will ease my memory. Why, I think I quoted to you some of ——'s letter, so you may imagine how witty the rest was; for it was all of a bunch, as goodman Peesley[2] says. Pray let us have no more *Bussiness*, but *Busyness*: the Deuse take me if I know how to spell it, your wrong spelling, madam Stella, has put me out: it does not look right ; let me see, *Bussiness, Busyness, Business, Bisyness, Bisness, Bysness*; faith, I know not which is right, I think the second; I believe I never writ the word in my life before; yes, sure I must though; *Business, Busyness, Bisyness.*——I have perplexed myself, and can't do it. Prithee ask Walls. *Business*, I fancy that's right. Yes it is; I looked in my own pamphlet, and found it twice in ten lines, to convince you that I never writ it before. Oh, now I see it as plain as can be; so yours is only an *s* too much. The parliament will certainly meet on Friday next; the Whigs will have a great majority in the house of lords; no care is taken to prevent it; there is too much neglect; they are warned of it, and that signifies nothing: it was feared there would be some peevish address from the lords against a Peace. 'Tis said about the town, that several of the allies begin now to be content that a Peace should be treated. This is all the news I have. The queen is pretty well; and so now I bid poor dearest MD farewel till to-night, then I will talk with them again.

The fifteen images that I saw were not worth forty pounds, so I stretched a little when I said a thousand. The Grub-street account of that tumult is published. The Devil is not like lord treasurer; they were all in your odd antick masks,

---

[1] He surely means, "If I did but know it! "
[2] *See* Letter XV., Feb. 9, 1710-11.

bought in common shops. I fear Prior will not be one of the plenipotentiaries.

I was looking over this letter, and find I make many mistakes of leaving out words; so 'tis impossible to find my meaning, unless you be conjurers. I will take more care for the future, and read over every day just what I have written that day; which will take up no time to speak of.

LETTER XXXVI

London, *December* 1, 1711.

My last was put in this evening. I intended to dine with Mr. Masham to-day, and called at White's Chocolate-house [1] to see if he was there. Lord Wharton [2] saw me at the door, and I saw him, but took no notice, and was going away; but he came through the crowd, called after me, and asked me how I did, &c. This was pretty; and I believe he wished every word he spoke was a halter to hang me. Masham did not dine at home, so I ate with a friend in the neighbourhood. The printer has not sent me the second edition; I know not the reason, for it certainly came out to-day; perhaps they are glutted with it already. I found a letter from lord Harley on my table, to tell me that his father desires I would make two small alterations. I am going to be busy, &c.

2. Morning. See the blunder; I was making it the 37th day of the month from the number above. Well, but I am staying here for old Frowde,[3] who appointed to call this morning: I am ready dressed to go to church; I suppose he dare not stir out but on Sundays. The printer called early this morning, told me the second edition went off yesterday in five hours, and he must have a third ready to-morrow, for they might have sold half another: his men are all at work with it, though it be Sunday. This old fool will not come, and I shall miss church.—Morrow sirrahs.—At night. I was at Court to-day; the queen is well, and walked through part of the rooms. I dined with the secretary, and dispatched some business. He tells me, the Dutch envoy designs to complain of that pamphlet. The noise it makes is extraordinary. It is fit it should answer the pains I have been at about it. I suppose it will be printed in

---

[1] *See* Letter XXVIII., Aug. 22.
[2] *See* Letter III., Sept. 11, 1710.
[3] Philip Frowde, Esq., author of some poems and plays.— D. S.

Ireland. Some lay it to Prior, others to Mr. secretary St. John, but I am always the first they lay every thing to. I'll go sleep, &c.

3. I have ordered Patrick not to let any odd fellow come up to me; and to-day a fellow would needs speak with me from Sir George Prettyman.[1] I had never heard of him, and would not see the messenger; but at last it proved that this Sir George has sold his estate, and is a beggar. Smithers, the Farnham carrier, brought me this morning a letter from your mother, with three papers inclosed of lady Giffard's writing; one owning some exchequer business of 100l. to be Stella's; another for 100l. that she has of yours, which I made over to you for Mariston[2]; and a third for 300l.; the last is on stampt paper. I think they had better lie in England in some good hand till lady Giffard dies; and I will think of some such hand before I come over. I was asking Smithers about all the people of Farnham. Mrs. White[3] has left off dressing, is troubled with lameness and swelled legs, and seldom stirs out; but her old hang-dog husband as hearty as ever. I was this morning with lord treasurer about something he would have altered in the pamphlet; but it can't be till the fourth edition, which I believe will be soon; for I dined with the printer, and he tells me they have sold off half the third. Mrs. Percival and her daughter[4] have been in town these three weeks, which I never heard till to-day; and Mrs. Wesley is come to town too, to consult Dr. Radcliffe. The Whigs are resolved to bring that pamphlet into the house of lords to have it condemned, *so I hear*. But the printer will stand to it, and not own the author; he must say, he had it from the penny-post. Some people talk as if the house of lords would do some peevish thing; for the Whigs are now a great majority in it; our ministers are too negligent of such things: I have never slipt giving them warning; some of them are sensible of it; but lord treasurer stands too much upon his own legs. I fancy his good fortune will bear him out in every thing; but in reason I should think this ministry to stand very unsteady: if they can carry a Peace, they may hold; I believe not else.

4. Mr. secretary sent to me to-day to dine with him alone; but we had two more with us, which hindered me doing some

---

[1] Sir George Pretyman (1638–1715), second baronet. In Le Neve's *Knights*, it is said he was "living in London and goes a begging, 1712."

[2] Unidentified.

[3] We are referred by Mr. Aitken to Manning and Bray's *Surrey*, iii., 177.

[4] These were doubtless near relatives of the Sir John Perceval, of Cork, afterwards first Earl of Egmont.—*See* Letter XVIII., March 23, 1710-11.

business. I was this morning with young Harcourt,[1] secretary to our society, to take a room for our weekly meetings; and the fellow asked us five guineas a week only to have leave to dine once a week; was not that pretty? so we broke off with him, and are to dine next Thursday at Harcourt's (he is lord keeper's son). They have sold off above half the third edition, and answers are coming out: the Dutch envoy [2] refused dining with Dr. D'avenant,[3] because he was suspected to write it: I have made some alterations in every edition, and it has cost me more trouble, for the time, since the printing than before. 'Tis sent over to Ireland, and I suppose you will have it reprinted.

5. They are now printing the fourth edition, which is reckoned very extraordinary, considering 'tis a dear twelvepenny book, and not bought up in numbers by the party to give away, as the Whigs do, but purely upon it's own strength. I have got an under spur-leather to write an *Examiner* again, and the secretary and I will now and then send hints; but we would have it a little upon the Grubstreet, to be a match for their writers. I dined with lord treasurer to-day at five; he dined by himself after his family, and drinks no claret yet, for fear of his rheumatism, of which he is almost well. He was very pleasant, as he is always; yet I fancied he was a little touched with the present posture of affairs. The elector of Hanover's minister [4] here has given in a violent memorial against the Peace, and caused it to be printed. The Whig lords are doing their utmost for a majority against Friday, and design, if they can, to address the queen against the Peace. Lord Nottingham, a famous Tory and speech-maker, is gone over to the Whig side: they toast him daily, and lord Wharton says, It is *Dismal* (so they call him from his looks) will save England at last. Lord treasurer was hinting as if he wished a ballad was made on him, and I will get up one against to-morrow.[5] He gave me a scurrilous printed paper of bad verses on himself, under the name of the *English Catiline*, and made me read them to the company. It was his birth-day, which he would not tell us, but lord Harley whispered it to me.

6. I was this morning making the ballad, two degrees above Grubstreet; at noon I paid a visit to Mrs. Masham, and then

[1] *See* Letter XXI., April 21.
[2] *See* Letter XXXV., Nov. 22, etc.
[3] *See* Letter VIII., Nov. 5, 1710.
[4] *See post*, Letter XL., Feb. 3, 1711-12.
[5] Included in Swift's works. Begins: "An orator dismal of Nottingham-shire."

went to dine with our society. Poor lord keeper dined below
stairs, I suppose on a bit of mutton. We chose two members;
we were eleven met, the greatest meeting we ever had: I am
next week to introduce lord Orrery.[1] The printer came before
we parted, and brought the ballad, which made them laugh
very heartily a dozen times. He is going to print the pamphlet
in small, a fifth edition, to be taken off by friends and sent
into the country. A sixpenny answer is come out, good for
nothing, but guessing me among others for the author. To-
morrow is the fatal day for the parliament meeting, and we
are full of hopes and fears. We reckon we have a majority of
ten on our side in the house of lords; yet I observed Mrs. Masham
a little uneasy; she assures me the queen is stout.[2] The duke
of Marlborough has not seen the queen for some days past;
Mrs. Masham is glad of it, because she says, he tells a hundred
lies to his friends of what she says to him: he is one day humble,
and the next [day] on the high ropes. The duke of Ormond,
they say, will be in town to-night by twelve.

7. This being the day the parliament was to meet, and the
great question to be determined, I went with Dr. Freind[3] to
dine in the city, on purpose to be out of the way, and we sent
our printer to see what was our fate; but he gave us a most
melancholy account of things. The earl of Nottingham began,
and spoke against a Peace, and desired that in their address
they might put in a clause to advise the queen not to make a
peace without Spain; which was debated, and carried by the
Whigs by about six voices[4]: and this has happened entirely
by my lord treasurer's neglect, who did not take timely care
to make up all his strength, although every one of us gave him
caution enough. Nottingham has certainly been bribed. The
question is yet only carried in the committee of the whole house,
and we hope when it is reported to the house to-morrow, we shall
have a majority by some Scotch lords coming to town. However, it is a mighty blow and loss of reputation to lord treasurer,
and may end in his ruin. I heard the thing only as the printer
brought it, who was at the debate; but how the ministry take
take it, or what their hopes and fears are, I cannot tell until

[1] *See* Letter IX., Nov. 22, 1710.
[2] "Resolute." "Marlborough, Godolphin, Somers, and other Whig
leaders, were repeatedly closeted with the Queen, who sought to bring
them if possible to unite with her Ministry in the project of a
peace." (D. L. P.)
[3] John. *See* Letter IX., Nov. 11, 1710.
[4] The "previous question" by one voice, the main question by six
voices.—D. L. P.

I see them. I shall be early with the secretary to-morrow, and then I will tell you more, and shall write a full account to the bishop of Clogher to-morrow, and to the archbishop of Dublin, if I have time. I am horribly down at present. I long to know how lord treasurer bears this, and what remedy he has. The duke of Ormond came this day to town, and was there.

8. I was early this morning with the secretary, and talkt over this matter. He hoped, that when it was reported this day in the house of lords, they would disagree with their committee, and so the matter would go off, only with a little loss of reputation to lord treasurer. I dined with Dr. Cockburn, and after a Scotch member came in, and told us that the clause was carried against the Court in the house of lords almost two to one; I went immediately to Mrs. Masham, and meeting Dr. Arbuthnott (the queen's favourite physician) we went together. She was just come from waiting at the queen's dinner, and going to her own. She had heard nothing of the thing being gone against us. It seems lord treasurer had been so negligent, that he was with the queen while the question was put in the house: I immediately told Mrs. Masham, that either she and lord treasurer had joined with the queen to betray us, or that they two were betrayed by the queen: she protested solemnly it was not the former, and I believed her; but she gave me some lights to suspect the queen is changed. For, yesterday when the queen was going from the house, where she sat to hear the debate, the duke of Shrewsbury lord chamberlain asked her, whether he or the great chamberlain Lindsay [1] ought to lead her out; she answered short, Neither of you, and gave her hand to the duke of Somerset,[2] who was louder than any in the house for the clause against Peace. She gave me one or two more instances of this sort, which convince me that the queen is false, or at least very much wavering. Mrs. Masham begged us to stay, because lord treasurer would call, and we were resolved to fall on him about his negligence in securing a majority. He came, and appeared in good humour as usual, but I thought his countenance was much cast down. I rallied him, and desired him to give me his staff, which he did; I told him, if he would secure it me a week, I would set all right: he asked, How? I said, I would immediately turn lord Marl-

[1] Robert Bertie (1660–1723), fourth Earl of Lindsey (co. Lincoln), styled Lord Willoughby de Eresby, 1666–1701; in after years became Marquess of Lindsey, and then Duke of Ancaster and Kesteven.
[2] Charles Seymour (1662–1748), sixth duke. "A man in whom the pride of birth and rank amounted almost to a disease" (Macaulay).

borough, his two daughters, the duke and duchess of Somerset, and lord Cholmondeley [1] out of all their employments; and I believe he had not a friend but was of my opinion. Arbuthnott asked, How he came not to secure a majority? He could answer nothing, but that he could not help it, if people would lie and forswear. A poor answer for a great minister. There fell from him a scripture expression, that *the hearts of kings are unsearchable.* I told him, It was what I feared, and was from him the worst news he could tell me. I begged him to know what we had to trust to; he stuck a little; but at last bid me not fear, for all would be well yet. We would fain have had him eat a bit where he was, but he would go home, it was past six: he made me go home with him. There we found his brother and Mr. secretary. He made his son take a list of all in the house of commons who had places, and yet voted against the Court, in such a manner as if they should lose their places: I doubt he is not able to compass it. Lord keeper came in an hour, and they were going upon business. So I left him, and returned to Mrs. Masham; but she had company with her, and I would not stay.—This is a long journal, and of a day that may produce great alterations, and hazard the ruin of England. The Whigs are all in triumph; they foretold how all this would be, but we thought it boasting. Nay, they said the parliament should be dissolved before Christmas, and perhaps it may: this is all your d——d duchess of Somerset's doings. I warned them of it nine months ago, and a hundred times since: the secretary always dreaded it. I told lord treasurer, I should have the advantage of him; for he would lose his head, and I should only be hanged, and so carry my body entire to the grave.

9. I was this morning with Mr. secretary; we are both of opinion that the queen is false. I told him what I heard, and he confirmed it by other circumstances. I then went to my friend Lewis, who had sent to see me. He talks of nothing but retiring to his estate in Wales. He gave me reasons to believe the whole matter is settled between the queen and the Whigs; he hears that lord Somers is to be treasurer, and believes, that sooner than turn out the duchess of Somerset, she will dissolve the parliament, and get a Whiggish one, which may be done by managing elections. Things are now in the crisis, and a day or two will determine. I have desired him to engage lord

[1] Hugh Cholmondeley (c. 1662–1724-5), second viscount (third bearer of the viscount's title), was created Earl of Cholmondeley 1706. Treasurer of the queen's household, but unfavourable to the Ministry. "Good for nothing, as far as ever I knew" (Swift).

treasurer, that as soon as he finds the change is resolved on, he will send me abroad as queen's secretary somewhere or other, where I may remain till the new ministers recal me; and then I will be sick for five or six months till the storm has spent itself. I hope he will grant me this; for I should hardly trust myself to the mercy of my enemies while their anger is fresh. I dined to-day with the secretary, who affects mirth, and seems to hope all will yet be well. I took him aside after dinner, told him how I had served them, and had asked no reward, but thought I might ask security; and then desired the same thing of him, to send me abroad before a change. He embraced me, and swore he would take the same care of me as himself, &c. but bid me have courage, for that in two days my lord treasurer's wisdom would appear greater than ever; that he suffered all that had happened on purpose, and had taken measures to turn it to advantage. I said, God send it; but I do not believe a syllable; and as far as I can judge, the game is lost. I shall know more soon, and my letters will at least be a good history to show you the steps of this change.

10. I was this morning with Lewis, who thinks they will let the parliament sit till they have given the money, and then dissolve them in Spring, and break the ministry. He spoke to lord treasurer about what I desired him. My lord desired him with great earnestness to assure me, that all would be well, and that I should fear nothing. I dined in the city with a friend. This day the commons went to the queen with their address, and all the lords who were for the Peace went with them, to shew their zeal. I have now some further conviction that the queen is false, and it begins to be known.

11. I went between two and three to see Mrs. Masham; while I was there she went to her bed-chamber to try a petti-coat. Lord treasurer came in to see her, and seeing me in the outer room fell a rallying me: says he, You had better keep company with me, than with such a fellow as Lewis, who has not the soul of a chicken, nor the heart of a mite. Then he went in to Mrs. Masham, and as he came back desired her leave to let me go home with him to dinner. He asked, whether I was not afraid to be seen with him? I said, I never valued my lord treasurer in my life, and therefore should have always the same esteem for Mr. Harley and lord Oxford. He seemed to talk confidently, as if he reckoned that all this would turn to advantage. I could not forbear hinting, that he was not sure of the queen; and that those scoundrel, starving lords would never

have dared to vote against the Court, if Somerset had not assured them, that it would please the queen. He said, That was true, and Somerset did so. I staid till six; then de Buys, the Dutch envoy, came to him, and I left him. Prior was with us a while after dinner. I see him and all of them cast down; though they make the best of it.

12. Ford is come to town; I saw him last night; he is in no fear, but sanguine, although I have told him the state of things. This change so resembles the last, that I wonder they do not observe it. The secretary sent for me yesterday to dine with him, but I was abroad; I hope he had something to say to me. This is morning, and I write in bed. I am going to the duke of Ormond, whom I have not yet seen. Morrow, sirrahs.——At night. I was to see the duke of Ormond this morning: he asked me two or three questions after his civil way, and they related to Ireland: at last I told him, that from the time I had seen him, I never once thought of Irish affairs. He whispered me, that he hoped I had done some good things here. I said, If every body else had done half as much, we should not be as we are: then we went aside, and talked over affairs. I told him how all things stood, and advised him what was to be done. I then went and sat an hour with the duchess; then as long with lady Oglethorp, who is so cunning a devil, that I believe she could yet find a remedy, if they would take her advice. I dined with a friend at court.

13. I was this morning with the secretary; he will needs pretend to talk as if things would be well; Will you believe it, said he, if you see these people turned out? I said, Yes, if I saw the duke and duchess of Somerset out: he swore, if they were not, he would give up his place. Our Society dined to-day at Sir William Wyndham's; we were thirteen present. Lord Orrery, and two other members were introduced; I left them at seven. I forgot to tell you, that the printer told me yesterday, that Morphew, the publisher,[1] was sent for by that lord chief justice, who was a manager against Sacheverell: he showed him two or three papers and pamphlets; among the rest mine of the *Conduct of the Allies*,[2] threatened him, asked who was the author, and has bound him over to appear next term. He would not have the impudence to do this, if he did not foresee what was coming at court.

[1] *See* Letter XXXII., Oct. 23, 1711.

[2] Thomas Parker (1666?-1732), afterwards first Earl of Macclesfield, was the lord chief justice; and the *Conduct of the Allies* was Swift's pamphlet, of which he reported the call for a fourth edition on Dec. 5.

14. Lord Shelburn was with me this morning, to be informed of the state of affairs, and desired I would answer all his objections against a Peace, which was soon done, for he would not give me room to put in a word. He is a man of good sense enough; but argues so violently, that he will some day or other put himself into a consumption. He desires that he may not be denied when he comes to see me, which I promised, but will not perform. Leigh and Sterne set out for Ireland on Monday sennight: I suppose they will be with you long before this. ——I was to-night drinking very good wine in scurvy company, at least some of them; I was drawn in, but will be more cautious for the future; 'tis late, &c.

15. Morning. They say the *Occasional bill*[1] is brought to-day into the house of lords; but I know not. I will now put an end to my letter, and give it into the post-house myself. This will be a memorable letter, and I shall sigh to see it some years hence. Here are the first steps towards the ruin of an excellent ministry; for I look upon them as certainly ruined; and God knows what may be the consequences.——I now bid my dearest MD farewel; for company is coming, and I must be at lord Dartmouth's office by noon. Farewel, dearest MD; I wish you a merry Christmas; I believe you will have this about that time. Love Presto, who loves MD above all things a thousand times. Farewel again, dearest MD, &c.

LETTER XXXVII

London, *Dec.* 15, 1711.

I PUT in my letter this evening myself. I was to-day enquiring at the secretary's office of Mr. Lewis, how things went: I there met Prior, who told me, he gave all for gone, &c. and was of opinion the whole ministry would give up their places next week; Lewis thinks they will not till Spring, when the session is over; both of them entirely despair. I went to see Mrs. Masham, who invited me to dinner; but I was engaged to Lewis. At four I went to Masham's. He came and whispered me, that he had it from a very good hand, that all would be well, and I found them both very chearful. The company was going to the Opera, but desired I would come and sup with them. I did so at ten, and lord treasurer was there, and sat with us till past twelve, and was more chearful than I have seen him these ten days.

[1] The Bill against occasional conformity, aimed at those who took the sacramental test merely as qualification for offices.

Mrs. Masham told me, he was mightily cast down some days ago, and he could not indeed hide it from me. Arbuthnott is in good hopes, that the queen has not betrayed us; but only has been frightened, and flattered, &c. But I cannot yet be of his opinion, whether my reasons are better, or that my fears are greater. I do resolve, if they give up, or are turned out soon, to retire for some months, and I have pitched upon the place already: but I will take methods for hearing from MD, and writing to them. But I would be out of the way upon the first of the ferment; for they lay all things on me, even some I have never read.

16. I took courage to-day, and went to Court with a very cheerful countenance. It was mightily crowded; both parties coming to observe each other's faces. I have avoided lord Hallifax's [1] bow till he forced it on me; but we did not talk together. I could not make less than fourscore bows, of which about twenty might be to Whigs. The duke of Somerset is gone to Petworth, and, I hear, the duchess too, of which I shall be very glad. Prince Eugene,[2] who was expected here some days ago, we are now told, will not come at all. The Whigs designed to have met him with forty thousand horse. Lord treasurer told me some days ago of his discourse with the emperor's resident, that puppy Hoffman, about prince Eugene's coming; by which I found my lord would hinder it, if he could; and we shall be all glad if he does not come, and think it a good point gained. Sir Andrew Fountain, Ford and I dined to-day with Mrs. Van, by invitation.

17. I have mistaken the day of the month, and been forced to mend it thrice. I dined to-day with Mr. Masham and his lady, by invitation. Lord treasurer was to be there, but came not. It was to entertain Buys, the Dutch envoy, who speaks English well enough: he was plaguy politick, telling a thousand lies, of which none passed upon any of us. We are still in the condition of suspense, and, I think, have little hopes. The duchess of Somerset is not gone to Petworth; only the duke; and that is a poor sacrifice. I believe the queen certainly designs to change the ministry; but perhaps may put it off till the session is over: and I think they had better give up now, if she will not deal openly; and then they need not answer

[1] *See* Letter V., Oct. 1, 1710.
[2] François Eugène de Savoie-Carignan, son of Count of Soissons and a niece of Cardinal Mazarin. Austrian general—the banishment of his mother and refusal of his service by France inducing him to take up arms against that country. Co-victor with Marlborough in the Battle of Blenheim, 1704.

for the consequences of a Peace, when it is in other hands, and may yet be broken. They say, my lord privy seal[1] sets out for Holland this week: so the Peace goes on.

18. It has rained hard from morning till night, and cost me three shillings in coach-hire. We have had abundance of wet weather. I dined in the city, and was with the printer, who has now a fifth edition of the *Conduct*, &c. it is in small, and sold for six-pence; they have printed as many[2] as three editions, because they are to be sent in numbers into the country by great men, &c. who subscribe for hundreds. It has been sent a fortnight ago to Ireland; I suppose you will print it there. The Tory lords and commons in parliament argue all from it: and all agree, that never any thing of that kind was of so great consequence, or made so many converts. By the time I have sent this letter, I expect to hear from little MD: it will be a month two days hence since I had your last, and I will allow ten days for accidents. I cannot get rid of the leavings of a cold I got a month ago; or else it is a new one. I have been writing letters all this evening till I am weary, and I am sending out another little thing, which I hope to finish this week, and design to send to the printer in an unknown hand. There was printed a Grubstreet speech of lord Nottingham; and he was such an owl to complain of it in the house of lords, who have taken up the printer for it. I heard at Court, that Walpole[3] (a great Whig member) said, that I and my whimsical club writ it at one of our meetings, and that I should pay for it. He will find he lies; and I shall let him know by a third hand my thoughts of him. He is to be secretary of state, if the ministry changes: but he has lately had a bribe proved against him in parliament, while he was secretary at war. He is one of the Whigs chief speakers.

19. Sad dismal weather. I went to the secretary's office, and Lewis made me dine with him. I intended to have dined with lord treasurer. I have not seen the secretary this week. Things do not mend at all. Lord Dartmouth despairs, and is for giving up; Lewis is of the same mind; but lord treasurer only says, Poh, poh, all will be well. I am come home early to finish

---

[1] Robinson, Bishop of Bristol. *See* Letters XXIX., Aug. 30, and XXXV., Nov. 20, 1711 (note).

[2] Three times as many as are usually printed in one edition. The number at first printed was 4,000.—N.

[3] Sir Robert Walpole (1676–1745)—further on, it is spelt "Walpool" —afterwards first Earl of Orford, the famous Prime Minister of the next decade. At this time he was M.P. for Lynn and leader of the Opposition.

something I am doing; but I find I want heart and humour; and would read any idle book that came in my way. I have just sent away a penny paper to make a little mischief. Patrick is gone to the burial of an Irish footman, who was Dr. King's [1] servant; he died of a consumption, a fit death for a poor starving wit's [2] footman. The Irish servants always club to bury a countryman.

20. I was with the secretary this morning, and for aught I can see we shall have a languishing death: I can know nothing, nor themselves neither. I dined, you know, with our Society, and that odious secretary would make me president next week, so I must entertain them this day sennight at the Thatched-house Tavern,[3] where we dined to-day; it will cost me five or six pounds; yet the secretary says, he will give me wine. I found a letter when I came home from the bishop of Clogher.

21. This is the first time I ever got a new cold before the old one was going: it came yesterday, and appeared in all due forms, eyes and nose running, &c. and is now very bad, and I cannot tell how I got it. Sir Andrew Fountain and I were invited to dine with Mrs. Van.—I was this morning with the duke of Ormond; and neither he nor I can think of any thing to comfort us in present affairs. We must certainly fall, if the duchess of Somerset be not turned out; and no body believes the queen will ever part with her. The duke and I were settling when Mr. secretary and I should dine with him, and he fixt upon Tuesday; and when I came away I remembred it was Christmas day. I was to see lady ——, who is just up after lying-in; and the ugliest sight I have seen, pale, dead, old and yellow, for want of her paint. She has turned my stomach. But she will soon be painted, and a beauty again.

22. I find myself disordered with a pain all round the small of my back, which I imputed to Champagne I had drunk; but find it to have been only my new cold. It was a fine frosty day, and I resolved to walk into the city. I called at lord treasurer's at eleven, and staid some time with him. He shewed me a letter from a great presbyterian parson [4] to him,

[1] William King (1663-1712), D.C.L., connected with the Boyle-Bentley controversy; see note on Lord Orrery, Letter IX., Nov. 22, 1710. Author of *Dialogues of the Dead*, 1699. The Archbishop of Dublin was another William King.

[2] Dr. King, of the Commons, well known as a facetious bard, was miserably poor.—N.

[3] Not on the site of the Thatched House Club of to-day, but on the site of the Conservative Club: 74, St. James's Street—that is, on the west side, just south of Little St. James's Street. It stood back from the roadway. *See* Edwin Beresford Chancellor's *St. James's Street*.   [4] Mr. Shower.—N.

complaining how their friends had betrayed them by passing this *Conformity Bill*; and he shewed me the answer he had written; which his friends would not let him send; but was a very good one. He is very chearful; but gives one no hopes, nor has any to give. I went into the city, and there I dined.

23. Morning. As I was dressing to go to church, a friend that was to see me, advised me not to stir out; so I shall keep at home to-day, and only eat some broth, if I can get it. It is a terrible cold frost, and snow fell yesterday, which still remains, look, there you may see it from the pent-houses. The lords made yesterday two or three votes about Peace, and Hanover, of a very angry kind, to vex the ministry, and they will meet sooner by a fortnight than the commons: and they say, are preparing some knocking addresses. Morrow, sirrahs. I'll sit at home, and when I go to bed, I will tell you how I am.—I have sat at home all day, and eaten only a mess of broth and a roll. I have written a *Prophecy*, which I design to print; I did it to-day, and some other verses.

24. I went into the city to-day in a coach, and dined there. My cold is going. It is now bitter hard frost, and has been so these three or four days. My *Prophecy*[1] is printed, and will be published after Christmas day; I like it mightily; I don't know how it will pass. You will never understand it at your distance, without help. I believe every body will guess it to be mine,[2] because it is somewhat in the same manner with that of *Merlin* in the *Miscellanies*. My lord privy-seal set out this day for Holland: he'll have a cold journey. I gave Patrick half a crown for his Christmas-box, on condition he would be good, and he came home drunk at midnight. I have taken a memorandum of it; because I never design to give him a groat more. 'Tis cruel cold.

25. I wish MD a merry Christmas, and many a one; but mine is melancholy: I durst not go to church to-day, finding myself a little out of order, and it snowing prodigiously, and freezing. At noon I went to Mrs. Van, who had this week engaged me to dine there to-day: and there I received the news, that poor Mrs. Long[3] died at Lynn in Norfolk on Saturday last, at four in the morning; she was sick but four hours. We suppose it was the asthma, which she was subject to as well as the dropsy, as she sent me word in her last letter, written about

---

[1] *The Windsor Prophecy.*
[2] It was by some ascribed to Swift, by others to Mr. Prior.—N.
[3] *See* Letter III., Sept. 13, 1710, etc.

five weeks ago; but then said she was recovered. I never was more afflicted at any death. The poor creature had retired to Lynn two years ago, to live cheap, and pay her debts. In her last letter she told me she hoped to be easy by Christmas; and she kept her word, although she meant it otherwise. She had all sorts of amiable qualities, and no ill ones, but the indiscretion of too much neglecting her own affairs. She had two thousand pounds left her by an old grandmother,[1] with which she intended to pay her debts, and live on an annuity she had of one hundred pounds a year, and Newburg-house, which would be about sixty pounds more. That odious grandmother living so long, forced her to retire; for the two thousand pounds was settled on her after the old woman's death, yet her brute of a brother, Sir James Long,[2] would not advance it for her; else she might have paid her debts, and continued here, and lived still: I believe melancholy helped her on to her grave. I have ordered a paragraph to be put in the *Post-boy*,[3] giving an account of her death, and making honourable mention of her; which is all I can do to serve her memory: but one reason was spite; for, her brother would fain have her death a secret, to save the charge of bringing her up here to bury her, or going into mourning. Pardon all this, for the sake of a poor creature I had so much friendship for.

26. I went to Mr. secretary this morning, and he would have me dine with him. I called at noon at Mrs. Masham's, who desired me not to let the *Prophecy* be published, for fear of angering the queen about the duchess of Somerset; so I writ to the printer to stop them. They have been printed and given about, but not sold. I saw lord treasurer there, who had been two hours with the queen; and Mrs. Masham is in hopes things will do well again. I went at night again, and supped at Mr. Masham's, and lord treasurer sat with us till one o'clock. So 'tis late, &c.

27. I entertained our Society at the Thatched-house Tavern to-day at dinner; but brother Bathurst[4] sent for wine, the

[1] Dorothy, daughter of Sir Edward Leech, of Chatsworth, in Derbyshire, one of the Masters in Chancery.—N.

[2] Representative in several parliaments in the reign of Queen Anne for Chippenham in Wilts, and afterwards for the county. He died March 15, 1728.—N.

[3] The paragraph was thus worded: "On Saturday the 22d instant, about four in the morning, Mrs. Anne Long, sister of Sir James Long, Bart. died at Lynn, in Norfolk, after a sickness but of four hours. She was a lady very much celebrated here for her beauty, virtue, and good sense; and is lamented by all who knew her." *Post Boy*, Dec. 27, 1711.—N.

[4] *See* Letter XXXV., Nov. 29.

house affording none. The printer had not received my letter, and so he brought up dozens a piece of the *Prophecy*; but I ordered him to part with no more. 'Tis an admirable good one, and people are mad for it. The frost still continues violently cold. Mrs. Masham invited me to come to-night and play at cards; but our Society did not part till nine. But I supped with Mrs. Hill, her sister, and there was Mrs. Masham and lord treasurer, and stayed till twelve. He is endeavouring to get a majority against next Wednesday, when the house of lords is to meet, and the Whigs intend to make some violent addresses against a Peace, if not prevented. God knows what will become of us. —It is still prodigiously cold; but so I told you already. We have eggs on the spit, I wish they may not be addle. When I came home to-night I found, forsooth, a letter from MD, N. 24, 24, 24, 24; there, do you know the number now? and at the same time one from Joe, full of thanks: let him know I have received it, and am glad of his success, but won't put him to the charge of a letter. I had a letter some time ago from Mr. Warburton,[1] and I beg one of you will copy out what I shall tell you, and send it by some opportunity to Warburton. 'Tis as follows; The Dr. has received Mr. Warburton's letter, and desired he will let the Dr. know, where that accident [2] he mentions is like soon to happen, and he will do what he can in it.——And pray, madam, let them know, that I do this to save myself the trouble, and them the expence, of a letter.—And I think this is enough for one that comes home at twelve from a lord treasurer and Mrs. Masham. Oh, I could tell you ten thousand things of our mad politicks, upon what small circumstances great affairs have turned. But I will go rest my busy head.

28. I was this morning with brother Bathurst to see the duke of Ormond. We have given his grace some hopes to be one of our Society. The secretary and I and Bathurst are to dine with him on Sunday next. The duke is not in much hopes, but has been very busy in endeavouring to bring over some lords against next Wednesday. The duchess catched me as I was going out; she is sadly in fear about things, and blames me for not mending them by my credit with lord treasurer; and I blame her. She met me in the street at noon, and engaged me to dine with her, which I did; and we talked an hour after dinner in her closet. If we miscarry on Wednesday, I believe it will be by some strange sort of neglect. They talk of making

[1] The Doctor's curate at Laracor.—D. S.
[2] Nichols has "action" in place of "accident."

eight new lords, by calling up some peers eldest sons; but they delay strangely. I saw judge Coote[1] to-day at the duke of Ormond's: he desires to come and see me, to justify his principles.

29. Morning. This goes to-day. I will not answer yours, your 24th, till my next, which shall begin to-night, as usual. Lord Shelburn has sent to invite me to dinner, but I am engaged with Lewis at Ned Southwell's. Lord Northampton[2] and lord Aylesbury's[3] sons are both made peers; but we shall want more. I write this post to your dean. I owe the archbishop a letter this long time. All people that come from Ireland complain of him, and scold me for protecting him. Pray, madam Dingley, let me know what Presto has received for this year, or whether any thing is due to him for last: I cannot look over your former letters now. As for Dingley's own account of her ex-chequer money, I will give it on t'other side. Farewel, my own dearest MD, and love Presto; and God ever bless dearest MD, &c. &c. I wish you many happy Christmasses and New-Years.

I have owned to the dean a letter I just had from you; but that I had not one this great while before.

DINGLEY'S ACCOUNT.

	£	s	d
Received of Mr. Tooke	6	17	6
Deducted for entering the letter of attorney . .	0	2	6
For the three half crowns it used to cost you, I don't know why nor wherefore	0	7	6
For exchange to Ireland	0	10	0
For coach-hire	0	2	6

In all, just   8   0   0

So there's your money, and we are both even: for I'll pay you no more than that eight pounds Irish, and pray be satisfied.

Churchwardens' accounts, boys.

Saturday night. I have broke open my letter, and tore it into the bargain; to let you know, that we are all safe; the queen

[1] See Letter XXXII., Oct. 23.

[2] George Compton (1664-1727), fourth of the "Compton" Earls of Northampton—his eldest son James (1687-1754) was at this time styled Lord Compton and was M.P. for Warwickshire; he was summoned as Lord Compton to the House of Lords, and afterwards became fifth Earl of Northampton.

[3] Thomas Bruce (1656-1741) second Earl of Ailesbury—his eldest surviving son was M.P. for Marlborough, and was summoned in his father's barony of "Bruce of Whorlton"; he afterwards became third Earl of Ailesbury.

has made no less than twelve lords to have a majority; nine
new ones, the other three peers sons[1]; and has turned out the
duke of Somerset. She is awaked at last, and so is lord treasurer:
I want nothing now but to see the duchess out. But we shall
do without her. We are all extremely happy. Give me joy,
sirrahs. This is written in a Coffee-house. Three of the new
lords are of our Society.

LETTER XXXVIII

London, *Dec.* 29, 1711.

I PUT my letter in this evening, after coming from dinner at
Ned Southwell's, where I drank very good Irish wine, and we
were in great joy at this happy turn of affairs. The queen has
been at last persuaded to her own interest and security, and
I freely think she must have made both herself and kingdom
very unhappy, if she had done otherwise. It is still a mighty
secret that Masham is to be one of the new lords; they say he
does not yet know it himself; but the queen is to surprise him
with it. Mr. secretary will be a lord at the end of the session;
but they want him still in parliament. After all, it is a strange
unhappy necessity of making so many peers together; but the
queen has drawn it upon herself, by her confounded trimming
and moderation. Three, as I told you, are of our Society.

30. I writ the dean and you a lie yesterday; for the duke of
Somerset is not yet turned out. I was to-day at Court, and
resolved to be very civil to the Whigs; but saw few there. When
I was in the bed-chamber talking to lord Rochester,[2] he went
up to lady Burlington,[3] who asked him, who I was; and lady
Sunderland[4] and she whispered about me: I desired lord
Rochester to tell lady Sunderland, I doubted she was not as
much in love with me as I was with her; but he would not
deliver my message. The duchess of Shrewsbury came running
up to me, and clapt her fan up to hide us from the company,
and we gave one another joy of this change; but sighed, when

---

[1] The twelve new peers were Lords Compton, Bruce, Hay, Mountjoy,
Burton, Mansel, Middleton, Trevor, Lansdowne, Masham, Foley, and
Bathurst. The *Gazette* which announced their elevation or creation also
announced that "Her Majesty has removed the Duke of Marlborough
from all his employments."

[2] The new earl, formerly Lord Hyde; *see* Letter V., Oct. 1, 1710.

[3] Juliana (1672–1750), daughter of the Hon. Henry Noel of North
Ruffenham, Rutland, and widow (1703-4) of Charles Boyle, second Earl
of Burlington. Mistress of the Robes.

[4] *See* Letter XXVII., Aug. 9.

we reflected on the Somerset family not being out. The secretary
and I, and brother Bathurst, and lord Windsor,[1] dined with the
duke of Ormond. Bathurst and Windsor are to be two of the
new lords. I desired my lord Radnor's brother,[2] at Court to-day,
to let my lord know I would call on him at six, which I did,
and was arguing with him three hours to bring him over to us,
and I spoke so closely, that I believe he will be tractable; but
he is a scoundrel, and though I said I only talked for my love
to him, I told a lie; for I did not care if he were hanged: but
every one gained over is of consequence. The duke of Marlborough was at Court to-day, and no body hardly[3] took notice
of him. Masham's being a lord begins to take wind: nothing
at Court can be kept a secret. Wednesday will be a great day:
you shall know more.

31. Our frost is broken since yesterday, and it is very
slabbery; yet I walked to the city and dined, and ordered
some things with the printer. I have settled Dr. King[4] in the
Gazette; it will be worth two hundred pounds a year to him.
Our new lords patents are passed: I don't like the expedient,
if we could have found any other. I see I have said this before.
I hear the duke of Marlborough is turned out of all his employments: I shall know to-morrow, when I am to carry Dr. King
to dine with the secretary.—These are strong remedies; pray
God the patient is able to bear them. The last ministry people
are utterly desperate.

Jan. 1. Now I wish my dearest little MD many happy New-
years; yes, both Dingley and Stella, aye and Presto too, many
happy new-years. I dined with the secretary, and it is true
that the duke of Marlborough is turned out of all. The duke of
Ormond has got his regiment of Foot-guards, I know not who
has the rest. If the ministry be not sure of a Peace, I shall
wonder at this step, and do not approve it at best. The queen
and lord treasurer mortally hate the duke of Marlborough, and
to that he owes his fall, more than to his other faults; unless
he has been tampering too far with his party, of which I have

[1] Thomas Windsor (c. 1670–1738), first Viscount Windsor of Blackcastle
in the peerage of Ireland from 1699; M.P. for Bramber. He now became
Baron Mountjoy of the Isle of Wight.
[2] Russell Robartes (d. 1724), one of the tellers of the exchequer—
there were four of them.
[3] It is curious to find such an early instance of this vulgarism, so
common in modern Cockney: the use of a negative with "hardly," as if
the latter were synonymous with "almost."
[4] Dr. William King, the facetious poet [*see* Dec. 19], was at this time
appointed writer of the *Gazette*.—N.

not heard any particulars; however it be, the world abroad will blame us. I confess my belief, that he has not one good quality in the world besides that of a general, and even that I have heard denied by several great soldiers. But we have had constant success in arms while he commanded. Opinion is a mighty matter in war, and I doubt but the French think it impossible to conquer an army that he leads, and our soldiers think the same; and how far even this step may encourage the French to play tricks with us, no man knows. I do not love to see personal resentment mix with publick affairs.

2. This being the day the lords meet, and the new peers to be introduced. I went to Westminster to see the sight; but the crowd was too great in the house. So I only went into the robing-room, to give my four brothers joy, and Sir Thomas Mansel,[1] and lord Windsor; the other six I am not acquainted with. It was apprehended the Whigs would have raised some difficulties, but nothing happened. I went to see lady Masham at noon, and wish her joy of her new honour, and a happy New-year. I found her very well pleased; for peerage will be some sort of protection to her upon any turn of affairs. She engaged me to come at night, and sup with her and lord treasurer; I went at nine and she was not at home, so I would not stay.—No, no, I won't answer your letter yet, young women. I dined with a friend in the neighbourhood. I see nothing here like Christmas, except brawn or mincepies in places where I dine, and giving away my half-crowns like farthings to great men's porters and butlers. Yesterday I paid seven good guineas to the fellow at the tavern, where I treated the Society. I have a great mind to send you the bill. I think I told you some articles. I have not heard whether any thing was done in the house of lords after introducing the new ones. Ford has been sitting with me till peeast tweelve a clock.

3. This was our Society day, lord Dupplin [2] was president; we chuse every week; the last president treats and chuses his successor. I believe our dinner cost fifteen pounds beside wine. The secretary grew brisk, and would not let me go, nor lord Lansdown, who would fain have gone home to his lady, being newly married to lady Mary Thynne.[3] It was near one when

---

[1] See Letter XVII., Feb. 25, 1710-11.
[2] He was really Lord Hay of Pedwardine by this time.
[3] Lord Lansdown, formerly (see Letter XIV., Jan. 17, etc) known as George Granville, had been raised to his peerage on Jan. 1. His wife was Mary, daughter of Edward Villiers, first Earl of Jersey, and widow of one Thomas Thynne. She died 1734-5.

we parted; so you must think I can't write much to-night. The adjourning of the house of lords yesterday, as the queen desired, was just carried by the twelve new lords, and one more. Lord Radnor was not there; I hope I have cured him. Did I tell you, that I have brought Dr. King in to be Gazetteer? it will be worth above two hundred pounds a year to him: I believe I told you so before, but I am forgetful. Go, get you gone to ombre, and claret, and toasted oranges. I'll go sleep.

4. I cannot get rid of the leavings of my cold. I was in the city to-day, and dined with my printer, and gave him a ballad made by several hands, I know not whom. I believe lord treasurer had a finger in it; I added three stanzas; I suppose Dr. Arbuthnott had the greatest share. I have been over-seeing some other little prints, and a pamphlet made by one of my understrappers. Somerset is not out yet. I doubt not but you will have the *Prophecy* in Ireland, although it is not published here, only printed copies given to friends. Tell me, do you understand it? No, faith, not without help. Tell me what you stick at, and I'll explain. We turned out a member of our Society yesterday for gross neglect and non-attendance. I writ to him by order to give him notice of it. It is Tom Harley,[1] secretary to the treasurer, and cousin-german to lord treasurer. He is going to Hanover from the queen. I am to give the duke of Ormond notice of his election as soon as I can see him.

5. I went this morning with a parishioner of mine, one Nuttal, who came over here for a legacy of one hundred pounds, and a roguish lawyer had refused to pay him, and would not believe he was the man. I writ to the lawyer a sharp letter, that I had taken Nuttal into my protection, and was resolved to stand by him; and the next news was, that the lawyer desired I would meet him, and attest he was the man, which I did, and his money was paid upon the spot. I then visited lord treasurer, who is now right again, and all well, only that the Somerset family is not out yet. I hate that; I don't like it, as the man said by, &c. Then I went and visited poor Will Congreve, who had a French fellow tampering with one of his eyes; he is almost blind of both. I dined with some merchants in the city, but could not see Stratford, with whom I had business. Presto, leave off your impertinence, and answer our letter, sayth MD. Yes, yes, one of these days, when I have nothing else to do. Oh, faith, this letter is a week written, and not one side done yet.—These ugly spots are not tobacco, but

[1] *See* Letter XXIV., May 26, 1711.

this is the last gilt sheet I have of large paper, therefore hold
your tongue. Nuttal was surprised, when they gave him bits
of paper instead of money; but I made Ben Tooke put him in
his geers[1]: he could not reckon ten pounds, but was puzzled
with the Irish way. Ben Tooke and my printer have desired
me to make them stationers to the ordnance, of which lord
Rivers is master instead of the duke of Marlborough. It will
be a hundred pounds a year a-piece to them, if I can get it.
I will try to-morrow.

6. I went this morning to earl Rivers, gave him joy of his
new employment,[2] and desired him to prefer my printer and
bookseller to be stationers to his office. He immediately granted
it me; but, like an old courtier, told me it was wholly on my
account, but that he heard I had intended to engage Mr.
secretary to speak to him, and desired I would engage him to
do so; but that however he did it only for my sake. This is a
court trick, to oblige as many as you can at once. I read prayers
to poor Mrs. Wesley (who is very much out of order) instead of
going to church; and then I went to Court, which I found very
full, in expectation of seeing prince Eugene, who landed last
night, and lies at Leicester-House; but he was not to see the
queen till six this evening. I hope and believe he comes too late
to do the Whigs any good.[3] I refused dining with the secretary,
and was like to lose my dinner, which was at a private acquaintance's. I went at six to see the prince at Court; but he was
gone in to the queen; and when he came out, Mr. secretary,
who introduced him, walked so near him, that he quite screened
him from me with his great periwig. I'll tell you a good passage:
As prince Eugene was going with Mr. secretary to Court, he
told the secretary, that Hoffman, the emperor's resident, said
to his highness, that it was not proper to go to Court without
a long wig, and his was a tyed-up one; Now, says the prince,
I knew not what to do; for I never had a long periwig in my
life; and I have sent to all my valets and footmen to see whether
any of them have one, that I might borrow it; but none of them
has any.—Was not this spoken very greatly with some sort of
contempt? But the secretary said, It was a thing of no consequence, and only observed by gentlemen-ushers. I supped with
lord Masham, where lord treasurer and Mr. secretary supped

[1] Cf. Letter LVIII., Jan. 8, 1712-13.
[2] Master of the Ordnance, displacing Marlborough.
[3] He was sent by the Emperor to prevent, if possible, the negotiation
of peace between England and France; and was by all parties most
honourably received.

with us; the first left us at twelve, but the rest did not part till two; yet I have written all this, because it is fresh: and now I'll go sleep, if I can; that is, I believe I shall, because I have drank a little.

7. I was this morning to give the duke of Ormond notice of the honour done him to make him one of our Society, and to invite him on Thursday next to the Thatched-house: he has accepted it with the gratitude and humility such a preferment deserves; but cannot come till the next meeting, because prince Eugene is to dine with him that day; which I allowed for a good excuse, and will report accordingly. I dined with lord Masham, and sat there till eight this evening; and came home, because I was not very well, but a little griped: but now I am well again, I will not go, at least but very seldom, to lord Masham's suppers. Lord treasurer is generally there, and that tempts me; but late sitting up does not agree with me; there's the short and the long, and I won't do it; so take your answer, dear little young women; and I have no more to say to you to-night, because of the archbishop; for I am going to write a long letter to him; but not so politickly as formerly: I won't trust him.

8. Well; then come, let us see this letter; if I must answer it, I must. What's here now? Yes faith, I lamented my birth-day[1] two days after, and that's all; and you rhyme, madam Stella; were those verses made upon my birth-day? Faith, when I read them, I had them running in my head all the day, and said them over a thousand times; they drank your health in all their glasses, and wished, &c. I could not get them out of my head. What; no, I believe it was not: what do I say upon the eighth of December? Compare, and see whether I say so. I am glad of Mrs. Stoyte's recovery, heartily glad: your Dolly Manley's[2] and bishop of Cloyne's child I have no concern about: I am sorry in a civil way, that's all. Yes, yes, Sir George St. George[3] dead. Go, cry, madam Dingley; I have written to the dean.[4] Raymond will be rich, for he has the building itch. I wish all he has got may put him out of debt. Poh, I have fires like light'ning; they cost me twelvepence a week, besides

---

[1] Dr. Swift, upon his birthday, used always to read the third chapter of Job.—D. S.

[2] Apparently Mrs. Isaac Manley.

[3] Not the baronet of this name, for he did not die till 1735. Mr. Aitken says it was a Sir George who had been M.P. for Leitrim and for Galway counties, and who died in December 1711.

[4] Dr. Sterne.

small-coal. I have got four new caps, madam, very fine and convenient, with striped cambrick, instead of muslin; so Patrick need not mend them, but take the old ones. Stella snatched Dingley's word out of her pen; Presto a cold? why all the world here is dead with them: I never had any thing like it in my life; 'tis not gone in five weeks. I hope Leigh is with you before this, and has brought your box: how do you li[k]e the ivory rasp? Stella is angry; but I'll have a finer thing for her. Is not the apron as good? I'm sure I shall never be paid it: so all's well again. What the quarrel with Sir John Walters?[1] Why, we had not one word of quarrel; only he railed at me when I was gone. And lord keeper and treasurer teazed me for a week: it was nuts to them: a serious thing with a vengeance. The Whigs may sell their estates then, or hang themselves, as they are disposed; for a Peace there will be. Lord treasurer told me, that Conolly[2] was going to Hanover. Your provost[3] is a coxcomb. Stella is a good girl for not being angry when I tell her of spelling; I see none wrong in this. God Almighty be praised that your disorders lessen, it encreases my hopes mightily that they will go off. And have you been plagued with the fear of the plague? Never mind those reports; I have heard them five hundred times. *Replevi*; Replevin,[4] simpleton, 'tis Dingley I mean; but it is a hard word, and so I'll excuse it. I stated Dingley's accounts in my last. I forgot Catherine's sevenpenny dinner. I hope it was the beef-steaks; I'll call and eat them in Spring: but goody Stoyte must give me coffee, or green tea, for I drink no bohea. Well, aye, the pamphlet; but there are some additions to the fourth edition: the fifth edition was of four thousand, in a smaller print, sold for sixpence. Yes, I had the twenty pound bill from Parvisol; and what then? Pray now eat the Laracor apples; I beg you not to keep them, but tell me what they are. You have had Tooke's bill in my last. And so there now, your whole letter is answered. I tell you what I do; I lay your letter before me, and take it in order, and answer what is necessary; and so, and so. Well; when I expected we were all undone, I designed to retire for six months, and then steal over to Laracor; and I had in my mouth a thousand times two lines of Shakspear, where cardinal Wolsey says:

> " A weak old man, battered with storms of state,
> Is come to lay his weary bones among you."

---

[1] *See* Letter XXXV., Nov. 25, 1711.
[2] *See* Letter IV., Sept. 28, 1710.
[3] Dr. Pratt, *see* Letter II., note on "Provost."
[4] *See* Letter XXXV., Nov. 19, 1711.

I beg your pardon, I have cheated you all this margin: I did not perceive it; and I went on wider and wider like Stella; aukward sluts, *she write so so, there*:[1] that's like as two eggs a penny.—*A weak old man,* now I am saying it, and shall till to-morrow.—The duke of Marlborough says, There is nothing he now desires so much as to contrive some way how to soften Dr. Swift. He is mistaken; for those things that have been hardest against him were not written by me. Mr. secretary told me this from a friend of the duke's; and I'm sure now he is down, I shall not trample on him; although I love him not, I dislike his being out.[2]—Bernage was to see me this morning, and gave some very indifferent excuses for not calling here so long. I care not two-pence. Prince Eugene did not dine with the duke of Marlborough on Sunday, but was last night at lady Betty Germain's assemblée, and a vast number of ladies to see him. Mr. Lewis and I dined with a private friend. I was this morning to see the duke of Ormond, who appointed me to meet him at the Cockpit at one, but never came. I sat too some time with the duchess. We don't like things very well yet. I am come home early, and going to be busy. I'll go write.

9. I could not go sleep last night till past two, and was waked before three by a noise of people endeavouring to break open my window; for a while I would not stir, thinking it might be my imagination; but hearing the noise continued, I rise[3] and went to the window, and then it ceased: I went to bed again, and heard it repeated more violently; then I rise,[3] and called up the house, and got a candle: the rogues had lifted up the sash a yard; there are great sheds before my windows, although my lodgings be a story high; and if they get upon the sheds, they are almost even with my window. We observed their

[1] These words in the manuscript imitate Stella's writing, and are sloped the wrong way.—D. S.

[2] Dr. Charles Davenant, in a letter dated Sept. 22, 1705, to his son Harry, then secretary, and *chargé-d'affaires* for the queen at Frankfort, says, "I desire you to deliver the inclosed to col. Parks (aide-de-camp to the duke of Marlborough.) The chief of it is, to bespeak his kindness for *my cousin Swift* to be his chaplain against he has a regiment. My cousin has gained immortal honour by *having had the principal hand* in a book lately published, called *The Tale of a Tub*; which has made as much noise, and is as full of wit, as any book, perhaps, that has come out these last hundred years." It needs not be added, that the application was unsuccessful. To the Duke of Marlborough, however, Swift (who without scruple "libelled the whole junto round") appears to have entertained no animosity. The refusal probably was noble; and Swift's conduct to the duke was equally liberal. He disliked his principles; but "prevented many hard things being said of him."—N. *See* page 175, note. If Forster is right, Nichols has attributed Thomas's doings to Jonathan.

[3] Nichols has "rose" where D. S. has "rise," both times.

track, and panes of glass fresh broken. The watchmen told us
to-day, they saw them, but could not catch them: they attacked
others in the neighbourhood, about the same time, and actually
robbed a house in Suffolk-Street, which is the next street but
one to us. It is said, they are seamen discharged from service.
I went up to call my man, and found his bed empty; it seems
he often lies abroad. I challenged him this morning as one of
the robbers. He is a sad dog; and the minute I come to Ireland
I will discard him. I have this day got double iron bars to every
window in my dining-room and bed-chamber; and I hide my
purse in my thread stocking between the bed's head and the
wainscot. Lewis and I dined with an old Scotch friend, who
brought the duke of Douglas,[1] and three or four more Scots
upon us.

10. This was our Society day you know; but the duke of
Ormond could not be with us, because he dined with prince
Eugene. It cost me a guinea contribution to a poet, who had
made a copy of verses upon monkies, applying the story to
the duke of Marlborough; the rest gave two guineas, except
the two physicians,[2] who followed my example. I don't like
this custom; the next time I will give nothing. I sat this evening
at lord Masham's with lord treasurer: I don't like his countenance; nor I don't like the posture of things well. We cannot
be stout, Till Somerset's out; as the old saying is.

11. Mr. Lewis and I dined with the chancellor of the exchequer,[3] who eats the most elegantly of any man I know in
town: I walkt lustily in the Park by moon-shine till eight,
to shake off my dinner and wine; and then went to sup at Mr.
Domville's [4] with Ford, and staid till twelve. It is told me
to-day as a great secret, that the duke of Somerset will be out
soon; that the thing is fixt; but what shall we do with the
duchess? They say, the duke will make her leave the queen
out of spight if he be out. It has stuck upon that Fear a good
while already. Well, but Lewis gave me a letter from MD,
N. 25. O Lord, I did not expect one this fortnight, faith. You
are mighty good, that's certain; but I won't answer it, because
this goes to-morrow, only what you say of the printer being
taken up; I value it not; all's safe there; nor do I fear any
thing, unless the ministry be changed; I hope that danger is

---

[1] Archibald Douglas (1694–1761), styled Earl of Angus till 1700, he
was then third Marquess of Douglas, and in 1703 became first duke.
[2] Arbuthnot and Freind.
[3] Benson.
[4] *See* Letter IX., Nov. 22, 1710.

over. However, I shall be in Ireland before such a change; which could not be, I think, till the end of the session, if the Whigs designs had gone on. Have not you an apron by Leigh, madam Stella? have you all I mentioned in a former letter?

12. Morning. This goes to-day as usual. I think of going into the city; but of that at night. 'Tis fine moderate weather these two or three days last. Farewell, &c. &c.

LETTER XXXIX

London, *Jan.* 12, 1711-12.

WHEN I sealed up my letter this morning, I lookt upon myself to be not worth a groat in the world. Last night, after Mr. Ford and I left Domville, Ford desired me to go with him for a minute upon earnest business, and then told me that both he and I were ruined: for he had trusted Stratford with five hundred pounds for tickets for the lottery, and he had been with Stratford, who confessed he had lost fifteen thousand pounds by Sir Stephan Evans,[1] who broke last week; that he concluded Stratford must break too; that he could not get his tickets, but Stratford made him several excuses, which seemed very blind ones, &c. And Stratford had near four hundred pounds of mine, to buy me five hundred pounds in the South-Sea company. I came home reflecting a little; nothing concerned me but MD. I called all my philosophy and religion up; and, I thank God, it did not keep me awake beyond my usual time above a quarter of an hour. This morning I sent for Tooke, whom I had employed to buy the stock of Stratford, and settle things with him. He told me, I was secure; for Stratford had transferred it to me in form in the South-Sea house, and he had accepted it for me, and all was done on stampt parchment. However, he would be farther informed; and, at night, sent me a note to confirm me. However, I am not yet secure; and, besides, am in pain for Ford, whom I first brought acquainted with Stratford. I dined in the city.

13. Domville and I dined with Ford to-day by appointment: the lord Mansel told me at court to-day, that I was engaged to him: but Stratford had promised Ford to meet him and me to-night at Ford's lodgings. He did so; said he had hopes to save himself in his affair with Evans. Ford asked him for his tickets: he said he would send them to-morrow; but looking

[1] Mr. Aitken says a goldsmith of this name was knighted in 1690.

in his pocket-book, said he believed he had some of them about him, and gave him as many as came to two hundred pounds, which rejoiced us much; besides, he talked so frankly, that we [might] think there is no danger. I asked him, Was there any more to be settled between us in my affair; he said, no; and answered my questions just as Tooke had got them from others; so I hope I am safe. This has been a scurvy affair. I believe Stella would have half laughed at me, to see a suspicious fellow, like me, over-reached. I saw prince Eugene to-day at Court: I don't think him an ugly faced fellow, but well enough, and a good shape.

14. The parliament was to sit to-day; and met; but were adjourned by the queen's directions till Thursday. She designs to make some important speech then. She pretended illness; but I believe they were not ready, and they expect some opposition; and the Scotch lords are angry,[1] and must be pacified. I was this morning to invite the duke of Ormond to our Society on Thursday, where he is then to be introduced. He has appointed me at twelve to-morrow about some business: I would fain have his help to impeach a certain lord; but I doubt we shall make nothing of it. I intended to have dined with lord treasurer, but I was told he would be busy; so I dined with Mrs. Van; and at night I sat with lord Masham till one. Lord treasurer was there, and chid me for not dining with him: he was in very good humour: I brought home two flasks of Burgundy in my chair: I wish MD had them. You see it is very late; so I'll go to bed, and bid MD good night.

15. This morning I presented my printer and bookseller to lord Rivers, to be stationers to the Ordnance; *Stationers*, that's the word; I did not write it plain at first. I believe it will be worth three hundred pounds a year between them. This is the third employment I have got for them. Rivers told them, the Doctor commanded him, and he durst not refuse it. I would have dined with lord treasurer to-day again, but lord Mansel [2] would not let me, and forced me home with him. I was very deep with the duke of Ormond to-day at the Cockpit, where we met to be private; but I doubt I cannot do the mischief I intended. My friend Penn came there, Will Penn the quaker,[3]

---

[1] Because the House of Lords had refused to permit the Duke of Hamilton to sit when he had received the title of Duke of Brandon in the British peerage.—D. L. P.

[2] Sir Thomas Mansel had been made a peer—*see* Letter XXXVII., Dec. 29 (note).

[3] *See* Letter V., Oct. 7, 1710.

at the head of his brethren, to thank the duke for his kindness to their people in Ireland. To see a dozen scoundrels with their hats on, and the duke complimenting with his off, was a good sight enough. I sat this evening with Sir William Robinson,[1] who has mighty often invited me to a bottle of wine: and it is past twelve.

16. This being Fast-day, Dr. Freind and I went into the city to dine late, like good fasters. My printer and bookseller want me to hook in another employment for them in the Tower, because it was enjoyed before by a stationer, although it be to serve the Ordnance with oil, tallow, &c. and is worth four hundred pounds *per annum* more: I will try what I can do. They are resolved to ask several other employments of the same nature to other offices; and I will then grease fat sows, and see whether it be possible to satisfy them. Why am not I a stationer? The parliament sits to-morrow, and Walpool [*i.e.* Walpole], late secretary at war, is to be swinged for bribery, and the queen is to communicate something of great importance to the two houses, at least they say so. But I must think of answering your letter in a day or two.

17. I went this morning to the duke of Ormond about some business; and he told me he could not dine with us to-day, being to dine with prince Eugene. Those of our Society of the house of commons could not be with us, the house sitting late on Walpool. I left them at nine, and they were not come. We kept some dinner for them. I hope Walpool will be sent to the Tower, and expelled the house: but, this afternoon the members I spoke with in the court of requests talked dubiously of it. It will be a leading card to maul the duke of Marlborough for the same crime, or at least to censure him. The queen's message was only to give them notice of the Peace she is treating, and to desire they will make some law to prevent libels against the government; so farewel to Grub-street.

18. I heard to-day that the commons of our Society did not leave the parliament till eleven at night, then went to those I left, and stay'd till three in the morning. Walpool is expelled, and sent to the Tower. I was this morning again with lord Rivers, and have made him give the other employment to my printer and bookseller; 'tis worth a great deal. I dined with my friend Lewis privately, to talk over affairs. We want to have this duke of Somerset out, and he apprehends it will not be;

[1] (*c.* 1656–1736) of Newby, Yorks., first baronet, M.P. for York in nine parliaments. From him are derived the Earls de Grey and Marquesses of Ripon.

but I hope better. They are going now at last to change the commissioners of the customs: my friend Sir Matthew Dudley will be out, and three more, and Prior will be in. I have made Ford copy out a small pamphlet, and send it to the press, that I might not be known for author; 'tis *A Letter to the October Club*, if ever you heard of such a thing.——Methinks this letter goes on but slowly for almost a week; I want some little conversation with MD, and to know what they are doing just now. I am sick of politicks. I have not dined with lord treasurer these three weeks; he chides me, but I don't care; I don't.

19. I dined to-day with lord treasurer; this is his day of choice company; where they sometimes admit me, but pretend to grumble. And to-day they met on some extraordinary business; the keeper, steward, both secretaries, lord Rivers, and lord Anglesey [1]; I left them at seven, and came away, and have been writing to the bishop of Clogher. I forgot to know where to direct to him since Sir George St. George's death; but I have directed to the same house: you must tell me better; for the letter is sent by the bell-man. Don't write to me again till this is gone, I charge you; for I won't answer two letters together. The duke of Somerset is out, and was with his yellow liveries at parliament to-day. You know he had the same with the queen, when he was master of the horse: we hope the duchess will follow, or that he will take her away in spite. Lord treasurer, I hope, has now saved his head. Has the dean received my letter? ask him at cards to-night.

20. There was a world of people to-day at Court to see prince Eugene, but all bit, for he did not come. I saw the duchess of Somerset talking with the duke of Buckingham [2]; she looked a little down, but was extreamly courteous. The queen has the gout, but is not in much pain. Must I fill this line [3] too? well then, so let it be. The duke of Beaufort [4] has a mighty mind to come into our Society; shall we let him? I spoke to the duke of Ormond about it, and he doubts a little whether to let him in or no. They say the duke of Somerset is advised by his friends to let his wife stay with the queen; I am sorry for it. I dined with the secretary to-day, with mixt company; I don't love it. Our Society does not meet till Friday, because Thursday

[1] *See* Letter X., Dec. 7, 1710.   [2] *See* Letter VIII., Nov. 7, 1710.
[3] It is the last of the page, and written close to the edge of the paper. —D. S.
[4] Henry Somerset (1684–1714), second duke. "So zealous a Tory, that he never appeared at Court during Godolphin's Ministry, and, when he came after Godolphin's fall, told her Majesty, 'he could now call her Queen in reality'; he died in 1714, aged only thirty " (D. L. P.).

will be a busy day in the house of commons; for then the duke of Marlborough's bribery is to be examined into about the pension pay'd him by those that furnished bread to the army.

21. I have been five times with the duke of Ormond about a perfect trifle, and he forgets it: I used him like a dog this morning for it. I was asked to-day by several in the court of requests, Whether it was true that the author of the *Examiner*[1] was taken up in an action of twenty thousand pounds by the duke of Marlborough? I dined in the city, where my printer showed me a pamphlet called *Advice to the October Club*, which he said was sent him by an unknown hand; I commended it mightily; he never suspected me; 'tis a twopenny pamphlet. I came home and got timely to bed; but about eleven one of the secretary's servants came to me, to let me know that lord treasurer would immediately speak with me at lord Masham's upon earnest business; and that if I was abed, I should rise and come. I did so; lord treasurer was above with the queen; and when he came down he laughed, and said it was not he that sent for me: the business was of no great importance, only to give me a paper, which might have been done to-morrow. I stay'd with them till past one, and then got to bed again. Pize take their frolicks. I thought to have answered your letter.

22. Doctor Gastrel[2] was to see me this morning; he is an eminent divine, one of the canons of Christ-church, and one I love very well: he said, he was glad to find I was not with James Broad. I asked what he meant; Why, says he, have you not seen the Grub-street paper, that says Dr. Swift was taken up as author of the *Examiner* on an action of twenty thousand pounds, and was now at James Broad's (who, I suppose, is some bailiff). I knew nothing of this; but at the court of requests twenty people told me they heard I had been taken up. Lord Lansdown observed to the secretary and me, that the Whigs spread three lies yesterday[3]; that about me; and another, that Macartney,[4] who was turned out last Summer, is again restored to his places in the army; and the third, that Jack Hill's commission for lieutenant of the Tower is stopt, and that Cadogan[5] is to continue. Lansdown thinks they have some

[1] Upon the 10th and 17th of this month the *Examiner* was very severe upon the Duke of Marlborough, and in consequence of this report pursued him with greater virulence in the following course of his papers. But Swift was not the writer of the *Examiner* at that period.—D. S.

[2] *See* Letter XXV., June 23, 1711.

[3] These lies are all particularly mentioned by the *Examiner*, N. 10, dated Feb. 7, 1711-12.—D. S.   [4] *See* Letter XI., Dec. 13, 1710.

[5] *See* Letter XI., Dec. 13, 1710.

design by these reports; I cannot guess it. Did I tell you that Sacheverell has desired mightily to come and see me; but I have put it off: he has heard that I have spoken to the secretary in behalf of a brother whom he maintains, and who desires an employment. T'other day at the court of requests Dr. Yalden [1] saluted me by name; Sacheverell, who was just by, came up to me, and made me many acknowledgements and compliments. Last night I desired lord treasurer to do something for that brother of Sacheverell's [2]: he said he never knew he had a brother; but thanked me for telling him, and immediately put his name in his table-book. I will let Sacheverell know this, that he may take his measures accordingly; but he shall be none of my acquaintance. I dined to-day privately with the secretary, left him at six, paid a visit or two, and came home.

23. I dined again to-day with the secretary; but could not dispatch some business I had with him, he has so much besides upon his hands at this juncture; and preparing against the great business to-morrow, which we are top full of. The ministers' design is, that the duke of Marlborough shall be censured as gently as possible, provided his friends will not make head to defend him; but if they do, it may end in some severer votes. A gentleman who was just now with him, tells me he is much cast down, and fallen away; but he is positive, if he has but ten friends in the house, that they shall defend him to the utmost, and endeavour to prevent the least censure upon him; which I think cannot be, since the bribery is manifest: Sir Solomon Medina [3] paid him six thousand pounds a year to have the employment of providing bread for the army, and the duke owns it in his letter to the commissioners of accounts.[4] I was to-night at lord Masham's; lord Dupplin took out my new little pamphlet, and the secretary read a great deal of it to lord treasurer; they all commended it to the skies, and so did I, and they began a health to the author. But I doubt lord treasurer suspected: for he said, This is Dr. Davenant's [5] style; which is his cant when he suspects me. But I carried the matter very well. Lord treasurer put the pamphlet in his pocket to read at home. I'll answer your letter to-morrow.

[1] Thomas Yalden (1670–1736), poet, D.D. in 1708, lecturer in moral philosophy at Oxford.
[2] Henry Sacheverell had two brothers: one was called Thomas, the name of the other is unknown.
[3] Mr. Aitken says he was a Jew, knighted in 1700.
[4] "Accompts" in Nichols.
[5] See Letter VIII., Nov. 5, 1710. "D'Avenant was abused as the author of the Examiner, long after Swift had taken the paper in hand" (D. L. P.).

24. The secretary made me promise to dine with him to-day after the parliament was up; I said I would come; but I dined at my usual time; knowing the house would sit late on this great affair. I dined at a tavern with Mr. Domville and another gentleman; I have not done so before these many months. At ten this evening I went to the secretary, but he was not come home; I sat with his lady till twelve, then came away; and he just came as I was gone, and he sent to my lodgings, but I would not go back; and so I know not how things have passed; but hope all is well; and I will tell you to-morrow day. It is late, &c.

25. The secretary sent to me this morning to know whether we should dine together; I went to him, and there I learnt, that the question went against the duke of Marlborough by a majority of a hundred; [and] so the ministry is mighty well satisfied, and the duke will now be able to do no hurt. The secretary and I and lord Masham, &c. dined with lieutenant-general Withers,[1] who is just going to look after the army in Flanders: the secretary and I left them a little after seven, and I am come home, and will now answer your letter, because this goes to-morrow: let me see.——The box at Chester; oh, burn that box, and hang that Sterne; I have desired one to enquire for it who went towards Ireland last Monday, but [I] am in utter despair of it.—No, I was not splenetick; you see what plunges the Court has been at to set all right again. And that duchess is not out yet, and may one day cause more mischief. Somerset shews all about a letter from the queen, desiring him to let his wife continue with her. Is not that rare! I find Dingley smelt a rat; because the Whigs are *upish*; but if ever I hear that word again, I'll *uppish* you. I am glad you got your rasp safe and sound; does Stella like her apron? Your criticks about guarantees of succession are puppies; that's an answer to the objection. The answerers here made the same objection, but [it] is wholly wrong. I am of your opinion, that lord Marlborough is used too hardly: I have often scratched out passages from papers and pamphlets sent me before they were printed; because I thought them too severe. But, he is certainly a vile man, and has no sort of merit beside the military. The *Examiners* are good for little: I would fain have hindered the severity of the two or three last, but could not. I will either bring your papers over, or leave them with Tooke, for whose honesty I will engage. And I think it is best not to venture them with me at sea. Stella is a prophet, by foretelling

[1] Henry Withers; lieut.-general 1707, lieut.-colonel first foot guards 1709.

so positively that all would be well. Duke of Ormond speak against Peace? No, simpleton: he is one of the stanchest we have for the ministry. Neither trouble yourself about the printer: he appeared the first day of term, and is to appear when summoned again; but nothing else will come of it. Lord Chief Justice is cooled since this new settlement. No; I will not split my journals in half; I will write but once a fortnight: but you may do as you will; which is, read only half at once, and t'other half next week. So now your letter is answered. (Pox on these blots!) What must I say more? I will set out in March, if there be a fit of fine weather; unless the ministry desire me to stay till the end of the session, which may be a month longer; but I believe they will not: for I suppose the Peace will be made, and they will have no further service for me. I must make my canal fine this Summer, as fine as I can. I am afraid I shall see great neglects among my quicksets. I hope the cherry-trees on the river-walk are fine things now. But no more of this.

26. I forgot to finish this letter this morning, and am come home so late I must give it to the bell-man; but I would have it go to-night, lest you should think there is any thing in the story of my being arrested in an action of twenty thousand pounds by lord Marlborough, which I hear is in Dyer's letter,[1] and consequently, I suppose, gone to Ireland. Farewel, dearest MD, &c. &c.

LETTER XL

London, *Jan.* 26, 1711-12.

I HAVE no gilt paper left of this size, so you must be content with plain. Our Society dined together to-day, for it was put off, as I told you, upon lord Marlborough's business on Thursday. The duke of Ormond dined with us to-day, the first time; we were thirteen at table; and lord Lansdown came in after dinner, so that we wanted but three. The secretary proposed the duke of Beaufort, who desires to be one of our Society; but I stopt it, because the duke of Ormond doubts a little about it; and he was gone before it was proposed. I left them at seven, and sat this evening with poor Mrs. Wesley, who has been mighty ill to-day with a fainting fit: she has often convul-

---

[1] *Dyer's Letter* (a rival of Ichabod Dawks's *News Letter*), whose editor's name Mr. Aitken gives as "John." "Mr. Dyer ... is justly looked upon by all the fox-hunters in the nation as the greatest statesman our country has produced" (*Tatler*, No. 18).

sions too; she takes a mixture with *assa fœtida*, which I have now in my nose; and every thing smells of it. I never smelt it before; 'tis abominable. We have eight pacquets, they say, due from Ireland.

27. I could not see prince Eugene at Court to-day, the crowd was so great. The Whigs contrive to have a crowd always about him, and employ the rabble to give the word, when he sets out from any place. When the duchess of Hamilton[1] came from the queen after church, she whispered me that she was going to pay me a visit: I went to lady Oglethorp's, the place appointed; for ladies always visit me in third places, and she kept me till near four: she talks too much, is a plaguy detractor, and I believe I shall not much like her. I was engaged to dine with lord Masham; they staid as long as they could, yet had almost dined, and were going in anger to pull down the brass peg for my hat, but lady Masham saved it. At eight I went again to lord Masham's; lord treasurer is generally there at night: we sat up till almost two. Lord treasurer has engaged me to contrive some way to keep the archbishop of York[2] from being seduced by lord Nottingham. I will do what I can in it to-morrow. 'Tis very late, so I must go sleep.

28. Poor Mrs. Manley the author is very ill of a dropsy and sore leg; the printer tells me he is afraid she cannot live long. I am heartily sorry for her; she has very generous principles for one of her sort; and a great deal of good sense and invention: she is about forty, very homely and very fat. Mrs. Van made me dine with her to-day. I was this morning with the duke of Ormond, and the prolocutor,[3] about what lord treasurer spoke to me yesterday; I know not what will be the issue. There is but a slender majority in the house of lords; and we want more. We are sadly mortified at the news of the French taking the town in Brasil from the Portuguese.[4] The sixth edition of three thousand of the *Conduct of the Allies* is sold, and the printer talks of a seventh; eleven thousand of them have been sold; which is a most prodigious run. The little two-penny *Letter of Advice to the October Club* does not sell; I know not

---

[1] *See* Letter XXVII., Aug. 29, 1711 (note).

[2] John Sharp (1645–1714), archbishop from 1691, much disliked by Swift. The cause of offence was supposed to be Sharp's dislike of the *Tale of a Tub*; the plan of which, however, is said to have been borrowed from Sharp's *Refutation of a Popish Argument handed about in Manuscript in* 1686.   [3] *See* Letter XIII., Jan. 6, 1710-11 (note).

[4] Du Clerc's attack on Rio de Janeiro in Sept. 1710 was finally unsuccessful, but may have been reported victorious. The French took Rio a year later, the victor being Admiral Duguay-Trouin.

the reason; for it is finely written, I assure you; and, like a
true author, I grow fond of it, because it does not sell: you
know that is usual to writers, to condemn the judgment of the
world: if I had hinted it to be mine, every body would have
bought it, but it is a great secret.

29. I borrowed one or two idle books of *Contes de Fees*,[1]
and have been reading them these two days, although I have
much business upon my hands. I loitered till one at home;
then went to Mr. Lewis at his office; and the vice chamberlain
told me, that lady Ryalton [2] had yesterday resigned her employment of lady of the bed-chamber, and that lady Jane Hyde,[3]
lord Rochester's daughter, a mighty pretty girl, is to succeed;
he said too, that lady Sunderland would resign in a day or two
I dined with Lewis, and then went to see Mrs. Wesley, who is
better to-day. But you must know, that Mr. Lewis gave me two
letters, one from the bishop of Cloyne, with an inclosed from
lord Inchequin [4] to lord treasurer; which he desires I would
deliver and recommend. I am told, that lord was much in with
lord Wharton, and I remember he was to have been one of the
lords justices by his recommendation; yet the bishop recom-
mends him as a great friend to the church, &c. I'll do what
I think proper.—T'other letter was from little saucy MD,
N. 26. O Lord, never saw the like, under a cover too, and by
way of journal; we shall never have done. Sirrahs; how durst
you write so soon, sirrahs? I won't answer it yet.

30. I was this morning with the secretary, who was sick and
out of humour; he would needs drink Champagne some days
ago, on purpose to spite me, because I advised him against it,
and now he pays for it; Stella used to do such tricks formerly; he
put me in mind of her. Lady Sunderland has resigned her place
too. It is lady Catherine Hyde that succeeds lady Ryalton;
and not lady Jane. Lady Catherine is the late earl of Rochester's
daughter.[5] I dined with the secretary, then visited his lady;
and sat this evening with lady Masham; the secretary came to
us; but lord treasurer did not; he dined with the master of the

---

[1] *Contes des Fées* by Marie Catherine la Mothe, Countess d'Aulnoy.
[2] Henrietta Churchill (1681-1733), eldest daughter of John, first Duke
of Marlborough; married, 1698, Francis Godolphin (1678-1766), styled
Viscount Rialton 1706-1712, after which he was second Earl of Godolphin. From 1722 she was Duchess of Marlborough in her own right.
[3] *See* Letter XXVI., July 18, 1711.
[4] William O'Brien (*c.* 1662-1719), third Earl of Inchiquin. The bishop
was Crow—*see* Letter XXXIII., Nov. 3, 1711.
[5] Youngest daughter of Laurence, first earl, as to whom *see* Letter VIII.,
Nov. 7 (note). She never married.

rolls,[1] and staid late with him. Our Society does not meet till to-morrow sennight, because we think the parliament will be very busy to-morrow upon the state of the war; and the secretary, who is to treat as president, must be in the house. I fancy my talking of persons and things here, must be very tedious to you, because you know nothing of them; and I talk as if you did. You know Kevin's-street, and Werburgh-street, and (what do you call the street where Mrs. Walls lives?) and Ingoldsby, and Higgins, and lord Santry; but what care you for lady Catherine Hyde? Why do you say nothing of your health, sirrah? I hope it is well.

31. Trimnel, bishop of Norwich,[2] who was with this lord Sunderland at Moor-park in their travels, preached yesterday before the house of lords; and to-day the question was put to thank him, and print his sermon; but passed against him; for it was a terrible Whig sermon. The Bill to repeal the *Act for naturalizing protestant foreigners*, passed the house of lords to-day by a majority of twenty, though the Scotch lords went out, and would vote neither way, in discontent about duke Hamilton's patent, if you know any thing of it. A poem is come out to-day, inscribed to me, by way of a flirt; for it is a Whiggish poem, and good for nothing. They plagued me with it in the court of requests. I dined with lord treasurer at five alone, only with one Dutch man. Prior is now a commissioner of the customs. I told you so before, I suppose. When I came home to-night, I found a letter from Dr. Sacheverell, thanking me for recommending his brother to lord treasurer and Mr. secretary for a place. Lord treasurer sent to him about it: so good a solicitor was I, although I once hardly thought I should be a solicitor for Sacheverell.

Feb. 1. Has not your dean of St. Patrick's received my letter? you say nothing of it, although I writ above a month ago. My printer has got the gout, and I was forced to go to him to-day, and there I dined. It was a most delicious day; why don't you observe whether the same days be fine with you? To-night at six Dr. Atterbury and Prior, and I, and Dr. Freind, met at Dr. Robert Freind's [3] house at Westminster, who is

[1] Sir John Trevor (1637-1713) was Master of the Rolls from 1685, being already Speaker of the House of Commons. He was displaced at the revolution of 1688, but reinstated in 1692-3. He was expelled the House of Commons for corruption 1694-5, but retained his Mastership of the Rolls.

[2] Charles Trimnel (1663-1723), Bishop of Norwich from 1708; in 1721 translated to Winchester.

[3] *See* Letter XXII., April 30, 1711.

master of the school: there we sat till one, and were good enough company. I here take leave to tell politick Dingley, that the passage in the *Conduct of the Allies* is so far from being blameable, that the secretary designs to insist upon it in the house of commons, when the Treaty of Barrier[1] is debated there, as it now shortly will, for they have ordered it to be laid before them. The pamphlet of *Advice to the October Club* begins now to sell; but I believe it's fame will hardly reach Ireland: 'tis finely written, I assure you. I long to answer your letter; but won't yet; you know 'tis late, &c.

2. This days ends Christmas; and what care I? I have neither seen, nor felt, nor heard any Christmas this year. I passed a lazy dull day: I was this morning with lord treasurer, to get some papers from him, which he will remember as much as a cat, although it be his own business. It threatened rain, but did not much; and Prior and I walked an hour in the Park, which quite put me out of my measures. I dined with a friend hard by; and in the evening sat with lord Masham till twelve. Lord treasurer did not come; this is an idle dining day usually with him. We want to hear from Holland how our Peace goes on; for we are afraid of those scoundrels the Dutch, lest they should play us tricks. Lord Marr,[2] a Scotch earl, was with us at lord Masham's; I was arguing with him about the stubbornness and folly of his countrymen; they are so angry about the affair of duke Hamilton, whom the queen has made a duke of England, and the house of lords will not admit him: he swears he would vote for us, but dare not; because all Scotland would detest him if he did; he should never be chosen again, nor be able to live there.

3. I was at Court to-day to look for a dinner; but did not like any that were offered me; and I dined with lord Mountjoy. The queen has the gout in her knee, and was not at chapel. I hear we have a Dutch mail, but I know not what news, although I was with the secretary this morning. He shewed me a letter from the Hanover envoy, Mr. Bothmar,[3] complaining that the Barrier Treaty is laid before the house of commons; and desiring that no infringement may be made in the *Guarantee of the Succession*; but the secretary has written him a peppering answer. I fancy you understand all this, and are able states-

---

[1] Between the Netherlands and England, signed Oct. 29, 1709, whereby the former guaranteed the Protestant succession to the throne of England in exchange for a guarantee of a *barrier* against France, consisting of fifteen specified towns.　　[2] *See* Letter XXIX., Aug. 30, 1711.
[3] Johann Caspar von Bothmer (1656-1732).

girls, since you have read the *Conduct of the Allies*. We are all preparing against the birth-day, I think it is Wednesday next. If the queen's gout encreases, it will spoil sport. Prince Eugene has two fine suits made against it; and the queen is to give him a sword worth four thousand pounds, the diamonds set transparent.

4. I was this morning soliciting at the house of commons' door for Mr. Vesey, a son of the archbishop of Tuam,[1] who has petitioned for a Bill to relieve him in some difficulty about his estate; I secured him above fifty members. I dined with lady Masham. We have no pacquet from Holland, as I was told yesterday; and this wind will hinder many people from appearing at the birth-day, who expected cloaths from Holland. I appointed to meet a gentleman at the secretary's to-night, and they both failed. The house of commons have this day made many severe votes about our being abused by our allies. Those who spoke, drew all their arguments from my book, and their votes confirm all I writ; the Court had a majority of a hundred and fifty: all agree, that it was my book that spirited them to these resolutions; I long to see them in print. My head has not been as well as I could wish it for some days past, but I have not had any giddy fit, and I hope it will go over.

5. The secretary turned me out of his room this morning, and shewed me fifty guineas rolled up, which he was going to give some French spy. I dined with four Irishmen at a tavern to-day; I thought I had resolved against it before, but I broke it. I played at cards this evening at lady Masham's, but I only played for her while she was writing; and I won her a pool; and supt there. Lord treasurer was with us, but went away before twelve. The ladies and lords have all their cloaths ready against to-morrow: I saw several mighty fine, and I hope there will be a great appearance, in spite of that spiteful French fashion of the Whiggish ladies not to come, which they have all resolved to a woman; and I hope it will more spirit the queen against them for ever.

6. I went to dine at lord Masham's at three, and met all the company just coming out of Court; a mighty crowd; they staid long for their coaches: I had an opportunity of seeing several lords and ladies of my acquaintance in their fineries. Lady Ashburnham[2] looked the best in my eyes. They say, the Court was never fuller nor finer. Lord treasurer, his lady, and two daughters, and Mrs. Hill dined with lord and lady Masham;

[1] *See* Letter XI., Dec. 19, 1710.　　　[2] Lady Mary Butler that was.

the five ladies were monstrous fine. The queen gave prince Eugene the diamond sword to-day; but no body was by when she gave it, except my lord chamberlain. There was an entertainment of Opera songs at night, and the queen was at all the entertainment, and is very well after it. I saw lady Wharton,[1] as ugly as the Devil, coming out in the crowd all in an undress; she had been with the Marlborough daughters and lady Bridgwater [2] in St. James's, looking out of the window all undressed, to see the sight. I do not hear that one Whig lady was there, except those of the bed-chamber. Nothing has made so great a noise as one Kelson's chariot, that cost nine hundred and thirty pounds, the finest was ever seen. The rabble huzzaed him as much as they did prince Eugene. This is birth-day chat.

7. Our Society met to-day, the duke of Ormond was not with us; we have lessened our dinners, which were grown so extravagant, that lord treasurer and every body else cried shame. I left them at seven, visited for an hour, and then came home, like a good boy. The queen is much better after yesterday's exercise: her friends wish she would use a little more. I opposed lord Jersey's election into our Society, and he is refused: I likewise opposed the duke of Beaufort; but I believe he will be chosen in spite of me: I don't much care; I shall not be with them above two months; for I resolve to set out for Ireland the beginning of April next (before I treat them again) and see my willows.

8. I dined to-day in the city; this morning a scoundrel dog, one of the queen's musick, a German, whom I had never seen, got access to me in my chamber by Patrick's folly, and gravely desired me to get an employment in the customs for a friend of his, who would be very grateful; and likewise to forward a project of his own, for raising ten thousand pounds a year upon Operas: I used him civiller than he deserved; but it vexed me to the pluck. He was told, I had a mighty interest with lord treasurer, and one word of mine, &c.——Well; I got home early on purpose to answer MD's letter, N. 26; for this goes to-morrow. —Well; I never saw such a letter in all my life; so saucy, so journalish, so sanguine, so pretending, so every thing.—I satisfied all your fears in my last; All is gone well, as you say; yet you are an impudent slut to be so positive; you will swagger so upon your sagacity that we shall never have done.

[1] See Letter II.
[2] Elizabeth (c. 1688–1714), third daughter of the great Duke of Marlborough, married (1703) Scroop Egerton, fifth Earl and first Duke of Bridgwater.

Pray don't mislay your reply; I would certainly print it, if I had it here: how long is it? I suppose, half a sheet: was the Answer written in Ireland? Yes, yes, you shall have a letter when you come from Baligall.[1] I need not tell you again who's out and who's in: we can never get out the duchess of Somerset. —So, they say Presto writ the *Conduct*, &c. do they like it? I don't care whether they do or no; but the Resolutions printed t'other day in the Votes, are almost quotations from it; and would never have passed, if that book had not been written. I will not meddle with the *Spectator*, let him fair-sex it to the world's end.[2] My disorder is over, but blood was not from the p[i]les.——Well, madam Dingley, the frost; why we had a great frost, but I forget how long ago; it lasted above a week or ten days: I believe about six weeks ago; but it did not break so soon with us I think as December 29; yet I think it was about that time, on second thoughts. MD can have no letter from Presto, says you, and yet four days before you own you had my thirty-seventh, unreasonable sluts! The bishop of Gloucester [3] is not dead, and I am as likely to succeed the duke of Marlborough as him if he were; there's enough for that now. It is not unlikely that the duke of Shrewsbury will be your governour; at least I believe the duke of Ormond will not return.—Well, Stella again: why really three editions of the *Conduct*, &c. is very much for Ireland; it is a sign you have some honest among you.—Well; I will do Mr. Manley [4] all the service I can: but he will ruin himself. What business had he to engage at all about the city? can't he wish his cause well, and be quiet, when he finds that stirring will do it no good, and himself a great deal of hurt? I cannot imagine who should open my letter; it must be done at your side.—If I hear of any thoughts of turning out Mr. Manley, I will endeavour to prevent it. I have already had all the gentlemen of Ireland here upon my back often, for defending him. So now I have answered your saucy letter. My humble service to goody Stoyte and Catherine; I will come soon for my dinner.

9. Morning. My cold goes off at last; but I think I have got a small new one. I have no news since last. They say we hear

[1] Deane Swift had a note here, describing Ballygall as "a village near Dublin"—which note has been copied by every editor since! As stated in note to Letter IV., Sept. 23, 1710, Ballygall was Tom Ashe's place at Finglas.

[2] Swift always ridiculed the perpetual mention of the "fair sex" in the *Spectator*.—D. L. P.

[3] Edward Fowler (1632–1714), Bishop of Gloucester since 1691.

[4] Isaac.

by the way of Calais, that Peace is very near concluding. I hope
it may be true. I'll go and seal up my letter, and give it myself
to-night into the post-office; and so I bid my dearest MD farewel till to-night. I heartily wish myself with them, as hope
saved. My willows, and quicksets, and trees will be finely
improved, I hope, this year. It has been fine hard frosty weather
yesterday and to-day. Farewell, &c. &c. &c.

[Here ends the section edited by Deane Swift; and, except as to
Letter LIV., we are no longer dependent on copies, but print from the
original manuscript—as in the instance of Letter I., which is the only sur-
vivor of the Deane Swift batch. As well as an ordinary fount of type
permits, the original is followed strictly, and in this respect the
"Everyman's Library" edition of the *Journal* is unique at present.]

LETTER XLI

[Endorsed: "To Mrs. Johnson at her Lodgings over against St. Mary's
Church near Capell Street, Dublin, Ireland." (The words "Mrs. Johnson
at her" have been scored out.) The number of the Letter is repeated in
what is believed to be Esther Johnson's writing, with the addition: "Recd.
Mar. 1st." The seal on this Letter is almost entire.]

41.   London *Febr* 9. 1711[•12]

WHEN my Letter is gone, and I have none of yrs to answer,
My Conscience is so clear, and my shoulders so light, and I go on
with such courage to prate upon nothing to deerichar MD, oo
would wonder. I dined with Sr Mat Dudley, who is newly turned
out of Commissn of the Customs; he affects a good Heart, and
talks in te extremity of Whiggery, which was always his Principle, thō he was gentle a little while he kept in Employment; We
can yet get no Pacqets from Holld. I have not been with any of
te Ministry these 2 or 3 days. I keep out of their way on purpose,
for a certain Reason, for some time: thō I must dine with te
Secrty [1] to morrow, te chusing of te Company being left to me;
I have engaged Ld Anglesea and Ld Carteret, and have promised
to get 3 more but I have a mind tht none else should be admitted:
however, if I like any body at Court to morrow I may perhaps
invite them. I have got another cod [? cold]; but not very bad.
Nite [my] [2] MD

10. I saw Pr Eugene at Court to day very plain; he is plaguy
yellow, and tolerably ugly besides. The Court was very full, and
People had their Birthday Cloaths. I dined with te Secty to

---

[1] St. John.   [2] Obliterated; apparently " my."

day, I was to invite 5, but I only invited 2, Ld Anglesea & Ld
Carteret. Pshaw, I told y this but yesterday. We have no
Pacquets from Holld yet. Here are a parcel of drunken whiggish
Lds like yr Ld Santry who come into Chocolate House & rail
aloud at te Toryes, and have Challenges sent them, and te next
morning come and beg Pardon. General Ross[1] was like to
swinge te Marquis of Winchester[2] for this Trick tother day, and
we have nothing else now to talk of till te Parlmt has had another
Bout with te State of te War, as thy intend in a few days. They
have ordered te Barrier Treaty to be layd before them, and it
was talkt some time ago, as if there were a design to impeach
Ld Townshend[3] who made it. I have no more Politicks now.
[Nite * * *[4] MD][5]

11. I dined wit Ld Anglesea to day, who had 7 Irishmen to
be my Companions, of which 2 only were Coxcombs, one I did
not know, and tother was young Blith,[6] who is a Puppy of figure
here, with a fine Chariot. He askt me one day at Court, when I
had been just talking with some Lds, who stood near me, Dr,
when shll we see y in te County of Meath, I whisprd him to take
care wht he sd, for the People would think he was some Bar-
barian. He nevr would speak to me since, till we mett to day. I
went to L'dy Mashams to night, & sate with Ld Treasr & te
Secrety there till past 2 a clock, and when I came home, found
some Letters from Ireld, which I read, but can say nothing of
them till to morrow, tis so very late, but [* * *][7] must always be
[* * * d][8] late or early. [Nite delest sollahs.][9]

12. One Lettr was from te Bp of Cl.[10] last night, and tother
from Walls,[11] about Mrs Souths[12] Sallary, and his own Pension

---

[1] Charles Ross [of Balnagowan, son of eleventh Baron Ross], appointed
lieut.-general of the horse under the Duke of Ormond in Flanders, April 5,
1712.—N. [Died 1732.]

[2] Charles Pawlet, or Pawlett, (1685–1754), called Marquess of Winchester,
late M.P. for Hants, son (by second wife) and heir to second Duke of
Bolton (see Letter XXXI., Sept. 25, 1711), whom he succeeded 1722,
being at that time already in House of Lords as Baron Pawlet.

[3] Charles Townshend (1674–1738), second Viscount Townshend, ambassador to the States-General, 1709.

[4] ? "my."

[5] Obliterated.

[6] John Bligh (1687–1728), of Rathmore, co. Meath, son of the Rt. Hon.
Thomas Bligh (see Letter IV., Sept. 29, 1710, note), afterwards married
(1713) Lady Theodosia Hyde, suo jure Baroness Clifton, and was made
Baron Clifton of Rathmore; he was finally first of the "Bligh" Earls
of Darnley.

[7], [8], [9] Obliterated.

[10] "Cl." and "Clogh." stand for "Clogher."

[11] See Letter II., etc.

[12] See Letters X., Dec. 9, 1710, and XXXI., Sept. 25, 1711.

of 1811 for his Tythe of te Park. I will do nothing in either, te first I cannot serve in, & te other is a Trifle; only y may tell him I had his Lettr, and will speak to Ned Southwell[1] about what he desires me. Y say nothing of yr Deans[2] receiving my Letter. I find, Clements, whom I recommended to Ld Anglesy[3] last year at Walls desire, or rather te Bp of Clr's is mightily in Ld Anglsea's favor; Y may tell te Bp and Walls so; I sd to Ld Anglesea that I was[4] I had te good Luck to recommend him &c I dined in te City with my Printer; to consult with him about some Paprs[5] Ld Tr— gave me last night, as he always does, too late; However, I will do something with them. My third Cold is a little bettr; I never had any thing like it before, three Colds successively. I hope I shall have te 4th; [. . . .[6]][7] Those [or "Three"] Messengers came from Holld to day and they brought over te 6 Pacquets that were due; I know not the[?] particulars yet, for when I was with te Secrty at noon, they were just opening; but one thing I find, that te Dutch are playing us Tricks, and tampering with te French, they are dogs. I shll know more [tomollow * * * * * * * MD][8]

13. I dined to day privately with my Friend Lewis at His Lodgings, to consult about some Objections on te Barrier Treaty. Our News from Holland is not good; Th French raise difficultyes, and make such Offers to te Allyes as cannot be accepted. And te Dutch are uneasy that we are like to get any thing for ourselves; and te Whigs are glad at all this. I came home early, and have been very busy 3 or 4 hours. I had a Letter from Dr Prat[9] to day by a private hand, recommending te Bearer to me, for something that I shall not trouble my self about: Wesly[10] writ to recommend te same Fellow to me; His Expression is that hearing I am acquainted with My Ld Treasr, he desires I would do so, and so: A matter of nothing. What Puppyes are Mankind.. I hope I shall be wiser when I have once done with Courts. I think y han't troubled me much with yr Recommendations. I would do y all te Saairs [sic][11] I could. Pray have you got yr

---

[1] See Letter V., Oct. 4, 1710, etc.
[2] Dr. Sterne's.
[3] Secretary of State for Ireland.—F.
[4] ? "glad" omitted.
[5] Materials for his Remarks on the Barrier Treaty.—N.
[6] Read by Forster "euge, euge, euge"—but perhaps "urge, urge, urge" (see Letter XLIV., April 30).
[7, 8] Obliterated.
[9] See Letter II.
[10] Garret Wesley. See Letter I., note on Mrs. Wesley.
[11] Possibly "services."

Apron Maran[1] ppt; I pd for it but yesterday, tht puts me in mind of it. I writ an Inventory of what things I sent by Lee, in one of my Letters; did y compare it with what y got? I hear nothing of yr Cards now; do y never play; yes at Baligawl.[2] go to bed. [Nite deelest MD] [3]

14. Our Society dined to day at Mr Secrtys house; I went there at 4, but hearing te House of Comms would sit late upon th Barrier Treaty, I went for an hour to Kensington to see Ld Masham's Children. My young Nephew his son [4] of 6 months old has got a swelling in his Neck, I fear it is te Evil. We did not go to dinner till 8 at night, and I left them at 10; te Commons have been very severe on te Barrier Treaty, as y will find by their Votes. A Whig Member took out te Conduct of te Allyes,[5] and read that Passage about te Succession, with great Resentmt, but none seconded him. The Church Party carryed every Vote by a great Majority. Th A.B. Dublin [6] is so raild at by all who come from Ired,[7] that I can defend him no longer. Ld Anglesea assured me that the Story of applying Piso out of Tacitus [8] to Ld Treasrs being wounded, is true. I believe, te D. of Beaufort will be admitted to our Society next meeting; To day I published th Fable of Midas,[9] a Poem printed in a loose half sheet of Paper; I know not how it will sell. But it passd wonderfully at our Society to night; & Mr Secty read it before me tother night to Ld Tr. at Ld Mashams, where they equally approved of it. tell me how it passes with you. I think this Paper is larger than ordinary, for here is 6 days Journall and no nearer the Bottom. I fear these Journals are very dull. Nite my deelest lives.

15. Mr Lewis and I dined by Invitation with a Scotch acquaintance, after I had been very busy in my Chamb till 2 afternoon. My third Cold is now very troublesome upon my Breast, especially in te Morning; This is a great Revolution in my Health, Colds never used to return so soon with me, or last so

---

[1] Throughout, "Maran" or "Maram" is *little language* for "Madam."
[2] Ballygall: Tom Ashe's. *See* Letter IV., Sept. 23, 1710.
[3] Obliterated.
[4] Lord Masham was one of the sixteen brothers [of the Society]; which accounts for Swift's calling his son nephew.—N.
[5] That is, Swift's pamphlet of that name. Quotation marks are of course entirely absent from Swift's letters; and his underlinings (for italics) are very rare.
[6] The archbishop, Dr. King.
[7] "Ired" or "Irel" = Ireland.
[8] *See* Letter XX., April 7, 1711 (note).
[9] A cruel satire on the Duke of Marlborough, comparing his loss of place and power to that of Midas, deprived of the virtues of his touch by the streams of Pactolus.—D. L. P.

long. Tis very surprising this News to day of te Dauphin and
Dauphiness both dying within 6 day[1]; They say te old King is
almost heart-broke. He has had prodigious mortifications in his
Family. Th Dauphin has left 2 little Sons of 4 and 2 years old,
te eldest is sick. There is a foolish Story got about te Town, tht
Ld Strafford one of our Plenipotentries is in te Interests of
France; and it has been a good while sd that Ld Privy Seal[2]
and he do not agree very well. They are both long practised in
Business, but neither of them of much Parts; Strafford has
some Life and Spirit, but is infinitely proud, & wholly illiterate.
Nite MD.

16. I dined to day in te City with my Printer to finish something I am doing about te Barrier Treaty but it is not quite
done.[3] I went this Evening to Ld Masham's, where Ld Treasr
sate with us till past 12, te Lds have voted an Adress to te Qu,[4]
to tell her they are not satisfied with te K. of France's Offers.
Th Whigs brought it in of a sudden, and te Court could not
prevent it, and therefore did not oppose it. Th H. of Lds is too
strong in Whigs notwithstanding th new Creations. For they
are very diligent, and te Toryes as [lazy[5]] The side that is
down has always most Industry. The Whigs intended to have
made a Vote tht would reflect on Ld Treasr; but their Project
was not ripe: I hitt my face such a Rap by calling te Coach to
stop to night that it is plaguy sore, te bone beneath th Eye.
Nite deely, [or "deelogues."].

17. The Court was mighty full to day and has been these
many Sundays, but te Qu was not at Chappel; she has got a
little fitt of te Gout in her foot. Th good of going to Court is tht
one sees all ones Acquaintance, whom otherwise I should hardly
meet twice a year. Prince Eugene dines with te Secretary to
day, with about 7 or 8 Genall officers or forein Ministers. They
will be all drunk I am sure. I never was in company with this
Prince; I have proposed to some Lds that we should have a
sober Meal with him, but I cant compass it. It is come over in
te Dutch News Prints that I was arrested on an action of 20000ll

[1] Louis, Duc de Bourgogne, grandson of Louis XIV., born 1682,
Dauphin of France, married, 1697, Marie-Adelaide of Savoy, born 1685.
She died Feb. 12, the dauphin Feb. 18, 1712. The difference of eleven
days between the New Style and the Old accounts for Swift's knowledge
of these deaths in Old-Style England on the 15th.

[2] Robinson, Bishop of Bristol. *See* Letter XXIX., Aug. 30, 1711.

[3] It was published under the title of *Remarks on the Barrier Treaty.*—N.

[4] The queen.

[5] Former readings followed. Word rubbed out, being at outer corner
of sheet.

by D Marlbrow.[1] I did not like my Court Invitation to day; so Sr A Fountn and I went and dined with Mrs Van [2]; I came home at 6, and have been very busy till this minute, and it is past 12. So I got into bed to write to MD; for [* * * * [3]] [4] We reckon, te Dauphin's death, will put forward te Peace a good deal. Pray is Dr. Griffith [5] reconcild to me yet? have I done enough to soften him? [* * * it * * * do * * * * rove pdfr. Nite d * * * * ogues] [6]

18. Lewis had Guiscard's Picture, he bought it, and offerd it Ld Treasr who promised to send for it, but never did; so I made Lewis give it me, and I have it in my Room. & nw Ld Treasr says he will take it from me, is that fair? He designs to have it at Length in te cloathes he was [? wore] when he did te Action & a Pen knife in his hand; & Kneller [7] is to copy it from this that I have. I intended to dine with Ld Treasr to day; but he has put me off till tomorrow; so I dined with Ld Dupplin; y know Ld Dupplin very well, he is a Brother of te Society. Well, but I have receivd a Lettr from te Bp of Clogh to sollicite an Affair for him with Ld Treasr, and with te Parlnt, wch I will do as soon as fly. I am not near so keen about other Peoples affairs as [saucy ppt [8]] [9] used to reproach me about; it was a Judgnt on me. Harkee, * * * * * * * * [10] both. Meetinks I begin to want a Rettle flom MD; fais, and so I do. I doubt y have been in pain about te Report of my being arrested. Th Pamphleteers have let me alone this month, wch is a great wonder, only te 3d part of te Answer to te Conduct,[11] which is lately come out (Did I tell y of it already?) Th H. of Commons goes on in mauling te late Ministry & their Proceedings. [Nite deelest MD][12]

19. I dined with Ld Treasr to day, & sate with him till 10 inspight of my Teeth; thō my Printer waited for me to correct a Sheet. I told him of 4 lines I writt extempore with my Pencil, on a bitt of Paper in his House while he lay wounded; Some of te Servant I suppose made wastpaper of them; and he never had heard of them. Shall I tell them you; They were inscribed,

---

[1] The Duke of Marlborough.   [2] Vanhomrigh.
[3] ? "you will always . . ."   [4] Obliterated.
[5] *See* Letters XI., Dec. 14, 1710, and XX., April 6, 1911. Probably the same person.
[6] Obliterated.
[7] Sir Godfrey. *See* Letter V., Oct. 5, 1710.
[8] Forster's reading, as above, seems probable.
[9] Obliterated.
[10] This word is not obliterated, but it is illegible. It is commonly rendered "Idledearies"; but it is more like "Jutledearies"—there is no "d" in the first half of it.
[11] To the *Conduct of the Allies*.
[12] Obliterated.

324 JONATHAN SWIFT

To Mr Harleys Physicians. Thus. On Europe Britain's Safety lyes[1]; Britain is lost if Harley dyes; Harley depends upon your Skill: Think what you save, or what you kill.—Are not they well enough to be done off hand; for that is the meaning of te word extempore, wch y did not know; did you? I proposed tht some Company should dine with him on te 8th of March, which was te day h was wounded, but he says he designs tht te Lds of te Cabinet who then sate with him, should dine that day with them [? him]; however, he has invited me too. —I can not get rid of my cold, it plagues me in te morning chiefly. Nite MD.

20. Aftr waiting to catch te Secrty coming out from Sr Ts Hanmer[2] for 2 hours, in vain, about some Business I went into te City to my Printer, to correct some sheets of te Barrier Treaty and Remarks, wch must be finished to morrow; I have been horrible busy for some days past with this and some other Things; & I wanted some very necessary papers wch te Secty was to give me, and te Pamphlet must now be published without them. But they are all busy too; Sr Tho. Hanmer is Chairman of te Committee for drawing up a Representation of te State of te Nation to te Qu— where all te wrong Steps of te Allyes & late Ministry about te War will be mentiond. te Secty I suppose was helping him about it to day. I believe it will be a Pepperer. Nite dee MD.

21. I have been 6 hours to day morning writing 19 Pages of a Lettr to day to Ld Treasr, about forming a Society or Academy to correct and fix te English Language.[3] (Is English a Speech or a Language?) it will not be above five or 6 more, I will send it him to morrow, and will print it if he desires me. I dined, you know, with our Society to day, Thursday is our day, we had a new Membr admitted; it was te D. of Beaufort. We were 13 met,, Brother Ormd[4] was not there; but sent his Excuse that Prince Eugene dined with him. I left them at 7, being engaged to go to Sr Tho. Hanmer, who desired I would see him at that Hour; His business was that I would hoenlbp ihainm italoi[5] dsroanws ubpl tohne sroeqporaensiepnotlastoiqobn;[6] which I

---

[1] The above is as Swift wrote it. Hawkesworth, followed by later editors, substituted "On Britain Europe's safety lies"—which is of course what Swift meant.
[2] See Letter IX., Nov. 15, 1710.
[3] See Letter XXV., June 22, 1711.
[4] The Duke of Ormond.
[5] The letter reproduced "l" is blotted—perhaps to obliterate it.
[6] Take every second letter (not counting the "l" in "italoi"): "Help him to draw up the representation"—mentioned on the 20th.

consented to do, but know not whether I shall succeed; because it is a little out of my way. However I have taken my Share. Nite MD.

22. I finished te rest of my Lettr to Ld Treasr to day; and sent it to him about one a Clock, and then dined privately with my friend Mr Lewis, to talk over some Affairs of moment.. I have gotten te 13th volume of Rymers Collection of te Records of te Tower [1] for te University of Dublin; I have 2 Volumes now; I will write to te Provost, to know how I shall send them to him; No, I won't for I'll bring them my self among my own Books. I was with Hanmer this morning, & there was te Secrty & Chancllr of te Excheqr very busy with him laying their Heads togethr about te Representation. I went to Ld Mashams to night, & Lady Masham made me read to her a pretty 2 penny Pamphlet called te St Albans Ghost.. [2] I thought I had writt it my self; so did they, but I did not. Ld Treasr came down to us from te Queen; and we staid till 2 a Clock; That is te best night place I have, te usually [*i.e.* usual] Company are Ld & Lady Masham, Ld Treasr, Dr Arbuthnot, & I; sometimes te Secrty; & sometimes Mrs Hill of te Bedchambr, Ldy Masham's Sister.. I assure oo it im vely rate now. but zis goes to morrow; and I must have time to converse with own richar MD. [Nite deelest sollahs.] [3]

23. I have no news to tell y this last day. nor do I know where I shll dine; I hear te Secrty is a little out of order; perhaps I may dine there. phaps not. I sent Hanmer what he wanted from me, I know not how he will approve of it. I was to do more of te same sort; I am going out; & must carry zis in my Pottick to give it at some generall Posthouse. I will talk furthr with oo at night. I suppose in my next I shll answer a Lettr from MD that will be sent me: on Tuesday it will be 4 weeks since I hd yr last. N. 26. this day sennight I expect one, for that will be something more than a full month. Farewell [mine deelest rife MD * * * MD MD * * * Ppt * * * * MD MD MD MD * * Lazy all * * * lele] [4]

---

[1] Rymer's *Fœdera.* He had obtained three books (Letter XXIII., May 16, 1711) for Trinity College—the two volumes here mentioned may be part of or in addition to that lot.
[2] The title is *The Story of St. Alban's Ghost; or the Apparition of Mother Haggy, collated from the best Manuscripts.*—B.
[3, 4] Obliterated.

LETTER XLII

[Outside half of sheet, containing direction, is missing; "42 Recd.
Mar 19" is written by Esther Johnson in top left-hand corner.]

42.   London. *Feb.* 23 1711[12]

AFTER having disposed my last Lettr in te Post office, I am now
to begin this with telling MD, that I dind with te Secty to day,
who is much out of Order with a cold, and fevorish, yet he went
to te Cabinet Council to night at 6, agst my will. The Secrty is
much te greatest Commoner in Engld, and turns te whole Parlmt,
who can do nothing without him, and if he lives & has his health,
will I believe be one day at te Head of Affairs. I have told him
sometimes, that if I were a dozen years younger, I would cul-
tivate his Favor, and trust my Fortune with his. But, what care
oo for all this; I am sorry when I came first acquainted with
this Ministry, that I did not send y their Names & Characters,
and then y would have relisht would [? what] I would have writ;
especially if I had let you into te particulars of Affairs, but
enough of this. Nite deelest Logues.

24. I went early this morning to te Secrty, who is not yet
well; Sr T. Hanmer, and te Chancellr of te Excheqr came while
I was there; and he would not let me stir; so I did not go to
Church; but was busy with them till noon, about te Affairs I
told y in my last. The other two went away; & I dined with
te Secrty, and found my head very much out of Order, but no
absolute fitt, and I have not been well all this day. It has shook
me a little. I sometimes sit up very late at Ld Mashams and have
writt much for severall days [past][1]; but I will amend both;
for I have now very little Business; and hope, I shall have no
more, and I am resolved to be a great Rider this Summer in
Irel. I was to see Mrs Wesly this evening, who has been somewhat
better for this month past, and talks of returning to Bath in a
few weeks. Our Peace goes on but slowly: The Dutch are playing
Tricks, and we do not push it as strongly as we ought. The fault
of our Court is delay, of wch te Qu— has a great deal, & Ld
Tr— is not without his share.—But pay ri char MD ret us know
a little of yr Life and tonvelsesens [*i.e.* conversation], do y play
at Ombre, or visit te Dean, & goody Walls & Stoit and Manlys
as usuall. I must have a Lettr from oo to fill te other side of this
Sheet. Let me know what y do: Is my Aunt [2] alive yet. Oh, pray
now I think of it, be so kind to step to my Aunt, and take

---

[1] Traditional reading. Word entirely blotted out by damp.
[2] His uncle Godwin's widow.—N.

notice of my great Grandfathers[1] Picture. Y know he has a Ring on his finger with a Seal of an Anchor & Dolphin[2] about it; but I think there is besides at te Bottom of te Picture the same Coat of Arms quartered with another, wch I suppose was my great Grandmothers.[3] If this be so, it is a stronger Argument than th Seal. & pray see whether y think that Coat of Arms was drawn at te same time with te Picture, or whether it be of a Later hand; and ask my Aunt what she knows about it. But, perhaps there is no such Coat of Arms on te Picture and I onely dreamt it. My reason is, because I would ask some [?] Herald here, whether I should chuse that Coat, or one in Guillim's large Folio of Heraldry,[4] where my Uncle Godwin[5] is named with another Coat of Arms, of [1][6]3 Stags. This is sad stuff to rite; so Nite MD.

25. I was this morning again with te Secrty, & we were 2 hours busy; and then went together to te Park, Hide park I mean, & he walkt to cure his Cold, and we were looking at 2 Arabian Horses sent some time ago to Ld Treasr. The D. of Marlbr's Coach overtook us, with His Grace, & Ld Godolphin in it, but they did not see us, to our great Satisfaction, for neither of us desired that either of those 2 Lds should see us together. There were half a dozen Ladyes riding like Cavaliers to take te Air. My Head is bettr to day. I dind with te Secrty, but we did no Business after dinner: and at 6 I walkt into te Fields, these [?] days are grown pure and long: then I went to visit Percivll & his Family, whom I had seen but twice since they came to Town; they too are going to te Bath next Month. Countess Doll of Meath[7] is such an Owl, that wherever I visit people are asking me whether I know such an Irish Ldy., and her Figure & her Foppery. I came home early; & have been amusing my Self with looking into one of Rimer's Volumes of te Records of te Towr;[8] & am mighty easy to think I have no urgent Business upon my Hands. My 3d Cold is not yet off; I sometimes cough, and am not right with it in te morning: Did I tell y that I believe it is Ldy Masham's hot room that gives it me; I never knew

[1] William Swift, rector of St. Andrew's, Canterbury, *temp.* Elizabeth.

[2] A dolphin was anciently called a swift—at least, so Swift says in the fragment of his autobiography printed in Forster's *Life*.

[3] Her maiden name was Mary Philpot. Said to have disinherited her only son for robbing an orchard when he was a boy. [boyhood.

[4] *Display of Heraldry*, by John Guillim (1565-1621).

[5] The elder brother of Swift's father, who was benefactor to Swift in his

[6] Probably only a blot. Three is more likely than thirteen.

[7] Dorothy, daughter of James Stopford, and second wife of Edward Brabazon, fourth Earl of Meath, who died Feb. 22, 1708, without issue.

[8] *See* Letter XLI., Feb. 22.

such a Stove; and in my Conscience, I believe, both my Ld
& she; my Ld Treasr, Mr Secrty & my self, have all suffered by
it. We have all had cold together, but I walk home on foot.
Nite deelogues.

26. I was again busy with te Secrty **************** [1] We
read over some Papers, and did a good deal of Business; and I dind
with him, & we were to do more business after dinner. But after
dinner is after dinner—An old saying and a true, much drinking
little thinking. We had company with us, and nothing could be
done, & I am to go there agn to morrow. I have now nothing to
do; and te Palnt [*i.e.* Parliament] by te Qu—'s Recommendation
is to take some Method for preventing Libells &c, which will
include Pamphlets I suppose: I don't know what Method they
will take, but it comes on in a day or two. To day in te morning
I visited upwards: First I saw te D. of Ormd below stairs, and
gave him Joy of his being declared Genll in Flandrs, then I went
up one pair of Stairs, & sate with te Dutchess; then I went up
another pr of Stairs, and pd a visit to Ldy Betty, and desired
her woman to go up to te Garret, that I might pass half an hour
with her, but she was young and handsom, & would not. Th
Duke is our President [2] this week; & I have bespoke a smal
dinner on purpose for good Example. Nite mi deelest Logues.

27. I was again with te Secrty this morning: but we onely
read over some Papers with Sr T. Hanmer; then I cald at Ld
Treasr's it was his Levee day but I went up to his Bedchamber;
& sd what I had to say; I came down & peept in at te Chambr
where a hundred Fools were waiting, and 2 Streets were full of
Coaches: I dined in te City with my Printer,[3] and came back at
6 to Ld Treasr, who had invited me to dinner, but I refused him,
I sate there an hour or 2, and then went to Ld Mashams they
were all abroad; so truly I tame [*i.e.* came] home, & read whatever stuff was next me. I can sitt and be idle now. which I have
not been above a year past.. However, I will stay out te Session,
to see if they have any further Commads for me, and tht I
suppose will end in April, but I may go somewhat before, for [?]
I hope all will be ended by then & we shall have eithr a certain
Peace, or certain War. The Ministry is contriving new Funds for
Money by Lotteryes, and we go on as if the War were to continue; but I believe it will not. Tis pretty late now ung oomens,
so I bid oo [or "ee"] Nite own deedallars.

28. I have been packing up some Books in a great Box I

---

[1] Several words obliterated.   [2] Of the Society.
[3] Barber.—D. L. P.

have bought; & must by another for Cloaths & Luggage: This is a beginning towards a Removall. I have sent to Holld for a dozen Shirts,[1] & design to buy another new Gown & hat, I'll come over like a Zinkerman,[2] and lay out nothing in Cloaths in Ireld this good while. I have writt this Night to te Provost. Our Society mett to day as usuall, and we were 14, besides te E. of Arran,[3] whom his Brother te D. of Ormd brought among us agst all order. We were mightily shockt; but after some whispers it ended in chusing Ld Arran one of our Society; wch I opposed to his Face, but it was carryed by all te rest against me.

29. This is leap year, and this is leap day. Prince George[4] was born on this day. People are mistaken and some here think it is St Davids day; but they do not understand the Virtue of Leap-year. I have nothing to do now boys; & have been reading all this day like Gumdragon[5]; and yet I was dictating some Trifles this morning to a Printer. I dined with a Friend hard by; & te Weathr was so discouraging, I could not walk. I came home early, and have read 200 Pages of Arrian,[6] Alexdr te great is just dead; I do not think he was poisoned. Betwixt y and me all those are but idle Storyes, tis certain that neither Ptolomy nor Aristobulus thought so, and they were both with him when they [for "he"] died. Tis a Pity we have not their Historyes Th Bill for limiting Membrs of Parlmt to have but so many Places past te H. of Commons, & will pass te H. of Lds inspight of te Ministry wch y know is a great Lessening of te Qu—'s Power. 4 of te new Lds voted against te Court in this Point. It is certainly a good Bill in te Reign of an ill Prince; but I think things are not settled enough for it at present: & te Court may want a Majority upon a Pinch. Nite deelest Logues rove Pdfr.

Mar. 1. I went into th City to enquire after poor Stratford,[7] who has put himself a Prisonr into te Queens Bench,[8] for wch his Friends blame him much; because his Creditors designed to be very easy with him. He graspt at too many things togethr, and that was his Ruin. There is one circumstance relating to

---

[1] At that time, very little fine linen was made in Ireland.—F.
[2] Not Dutch, though it has that appearance. It is *little* for "gentleman."
[3] Charles Butler (1671–1758), second Earl of "Arran in Ireland" (son of Thomas Butler, styled Earl of Ossory, son and heir-apparent of first Duke of Ormond), colonel of third troop of Horse Guards, ennobled 1693 —the first earl, his uncle, having died without leaving male issue.
[4] The late consort of Queen Anne.
[5] Gumdragon = gum-dragant = *tragacanth* (a kind of gum) = "goat's horn." But Swift uses the word merely on account of its terrifying sound.
[6] A distinguished historian who wrote in Greek in the second century A.D.
[7] *See* Letters III., Sept. 13, 1710, and XXXIX., Jan. 12, 1711-12.
[8] *See* later in this Letter.

Lt Genrll Meredith[1] that is very melancholy. Meredith was turnd out of all his Employmts last Year, and had about ten thousd Pds left to live on; Stratford upon Friendship desired he might have te managemt of it for Meredith, to putt it into Funds & stocks for te best Advantage; and now he has lost it all. Y have heard me often talk of Stratford; we were Classfallows at School & University. I dined with some Merchants his friends to day; & they sd they expected his breaking this good while. I gave him notice of a Treaty of Peace, while it was a Secret; of wch he might have made good use, but that helpt to ruin him. for he gave money, reckoning there would be actually a Peace by this Time, & consequently Stocks rise high; Ford[2] narrowly scapt losing 500ll by him; and so did I too. Nite my two deelest Rives MD.

2. Morn. I was wakend at 3 this morning, my man & te People of te House telling me of a great Fire in te Hay-market. I slept again, and 2 hours after my man came in again and told me it was my poor Brothr Sr Wm Windham's[3] house was burnt; and that 2 maids leaping out of an upper room to avoyd te Fire, both fell on their Heads; one of them upon te Iron Spikes before te door; and both lay dead in te Streets; it is supposed to have been some Carelessness of one or both of those Maids. The D. of Ormd was there, helping to put out te Fire. Brothr Windham gave 6000 Pound, but a few Months ago, for that House, as he told me, & it was very richly furnisht. I shall know more particulars at night. He marryed Ldy Kathrine Seymor, te D. of Sommersts Daughter; y know her I believe. At Night. Windhams young Child escapt very narrowly. Ldy Kathrne escaped barefoot; they all went to Northumbld House. Mr Briges[4] house at next door is damaged much, & was like to be burnt. Windham has lost above 10000ll by this accident; His Ldy above a thousd Pds worth of Cloaths. He was not at Court to day. [It was a terrible Accidt;][5] I dined with Ld Masham. te Qu was not at Church. Nite MD.

3. Pray tell Walls: that I spoke to te D. of Ormd, & Mr Southwell about his Friends Affair; who I find needed not me for a Sollicitor; for thy both told me the thing would be done. I likewise mentiond his own Affair to Mr Southwell; & I hope

---

[1] See Letter XI., Dec. 13, 1710, and note.
[2] See Letter III., Sept. 12, 1710, etc.
[3] Wyndham. See Letter XXV., June 21, 1711.
[4] Brydges. See Letters III., Sept. 17, 1710, and XXI., April 27, 1711.
[5] Hitherto, this phrase has been printed *before* "He was not at Court to day."

that will be done too; for Southwell seems to think it reasonable, and I will mind him of it again. Tell him this nakedly; y need not know th Particulars, they are Secrets; one of them is about Mrs South having a Pension; the othr about his Sallary from te Govmnt for te Tythe of te Park[1] that ly in his Parish, to be put upon te Establishmt; but oo muss [or "must"] not know zees sings, zey are Secrets, & we must keep them flom nauty dallars. I dind in te City with my Printer, with whom I had some small Affair, but I have no large work on my Hands now. I was with Ld Treasr this morning and hat care oo for zat, oo dined with te Dean to day. Monday is Parsons holyday, and oo lost oo money at Cards & dice ze Givars[2] device. So I'll go to bed. Nite my twodeelest Logues.

4. I sate to day with poor Mrs Wesly, who made me dine with her; she is much better than she was. I heartily pray for her health out of te entire Love I bear to her worthy Husband. This day has passt very insignificantly, but it is a great Comfort to me now that I can come home & read, and have nothing upon my hands to write. I was at Ld Mashams to night and staid there till one; Ld Treasr was there; but I thought thought he lookt melancholy; just as he did at te Beginning of te Sessions; and he was not so merry as usuall. In short, te Majority in te H. of Lds is a very weak one, & he has much ado to keep it up, and he is not able to make those Removes he would, & oblige his Friends; & I doubt to [i.e. too] he does not take care enough about it. or rather cannot do all himself; and will not employ others; wch is his great Fault, as I have often told you. Tis late. Nite MD.

5. I wish y a merry Lent; I hate Lent, I hate different diets, and Furmity & Butter, & herb Porrige, and sour devout Faces of People who onely put on Religion for 7 Weeks.. I was at te Secrtys Office this morning, and there a Gentleman brought me 2 Letters dated last Octobr, one from te Bp of Cloghr; tother from Walls; The Gentleman is calld Coll Newburgh[3]; I think y mentiond him to me sometime ago; he has business in te H. of Lds; I will do him what Service I can, The Representation of te H. of Comms is printed; I have not seen it yet. It is plaguy severe they say; I dined with Dr Arbuthnott; and had a true Lenten dinner; Not in point of Vittels, but Spleen, for his Wife and a Child or two were Sick in te House, and that was

---

[1] Or "Parts."
[2] *Little* for Devil's—or rather, Divel's.
[3] *See* "Newbury," Letter XXXV., Nov. 30, 1711.

full as mortifying as Fish. We have had mighty fine cold frosty weather for some days past; I hope you take te Advantage of it, and walk now and then. Y never answer that Part of my Letters where I desire you to walk. I must keep my Breath to cool my Lenten Porridge. Tell Jemmy Leigh that his Boy that robd him now appears about te Town; Patrick has seen him once or twice. I knew nothing of his being robbd till Patrick told me he had seen te Boy. I wish it had been Stearn[1] that had been robbd to be revengd for te Box that he lost and be p—xd to him. Nite MD.

6. I hear Mr Prior has sufferd by Stratford's breaking; I was yesterday to see Prior, who is not well; and I thought he lookt melancholy, he can ill afford to lose money. I walkt before dinner in te Mall a good while with Ld Arran, & Ld Dupplin two of my Brothrs, & then we went to dinner, where te D. of Beaufort was our President. We were but eleven to day; we are now in all 9 Lds, & ten Commonrs. te D. of Beaufort had te Confidence to propose his Brother in law[2] te E. of Danby[3] to be a Membr, but I opposed it so warmly that it was waved: Danby is not above 20, and we will have no more Boys; and we want but 2 to make up our Number.. I stayd till 8, and then we all went away soberly. Th D. of Ormds treat last week cost 20 Pound; tho it was only four dishes and 4, without a Dessert; and I bespoke it in order to be cheap. Yet I could not prevail to change the House. Ld Treasr is in a Rage with us for being so extravagant, and te Wine was not reckond neither; for that is always bought by him that is President. Ld Orrery is to be Presidt next week; and I'll see whethr it cannot be cheaper, or else we will leave te House. [. . . dee . . . Sollahs.][4] Ld Masham made me go home with him to night to eat boiled Oysters. Take Oysters; wash them clean, that is wash their Shells clean; then put yr Oysters into an Earthen Pot, with their Hollow sides down. then Put this Pot into a great Kettle with Water, and so let them boil. Yr Oysters are boyld in their own Liquor, and not mixt Water. Ld Treasr was not with us, he was very ill to day with a Swimming in te Head. and is gone home to be

[1] Enoch Sterne, the collector.

[2] The Duke of Beaufort's third wife was Lady Mary Osborne, youngest daughter of the Duke of Leeds, married Sept. 14, 1711.

[3] Peregrine Hyde Osborne (1691–1731), youngest son to the second Duke of Leeds. He was summoned to Parliament in 1711, by the title of Lord Osborne of Kiveton; became "Earl of Danby" on the death of his elder brother (see Letter XXVIII., Aug. 22, 1711), and afterwards Marquess of Caermarthen and third Duke of Leeds.

[4] Obliterated.

Cuppt & sent to desire Ldy Masham to excuse him to te Qu—Nite dee MD.

7. I was to day at te H. of Lds about a Friends bill; then I crosst te Water at Westminstr Stairs, to Southvick [? Southwark], went thro St George's fields to te Mint; wch is te Dominions of te K. Bench Prison,[1] where Stratford lodges in a blind Alley, & writt to me to come to him, but he was gone to te Change. I thought he had something to say to me about his own Affairs,—I found him at his usuall Coffee house and went to his old Lodgings, & dined with him & his Wife & other Company. His Business was onely to desire I would intercede with te Ministry about his Brothr in Law Ben Burton of Dublin,[2] yr [3] Banker, who is like to come in trouble as we hear about spreading false whiggish News. I hate Burton, & told Stratford so, and I will advise te D. of O. to make use of it to keep the Rogue in aw. Mrs Stratford tells me Her husbands Creditors have consented to give him Liberty to get up his debts abroad, & she hopes he will pay them all. He was cheerfuller than I have seen him this great while. I have walkt much to day Nite deelest Logue

8. This day Twelvemonth Mr Harley was stabbd, but he is ill & takes Physick to day I hear (tis now morning) and can't have th Cabinet Councillors with him as he intended; nor me to say Grace. I am going to see him. Pray read te Representation; tis te finest that ever was writt. Some of it is pdfr's [4] Style, but not much. This is te day of te Qu—'s Accession to te Crown. So it is a great day. I am going to Court; & will dine with Ld Masham. but I must go this moment to see te Secrty about some Business: so I will seal up this, and put it in th Post my own self. Farewell deelest hearts & Souls MD. Farewell MD MD MD FW FW FW Me Me Lele Lele Lele Sollahs lele.

---

[1] He misnames the Queen's Bench, out of old habit.
[2] *See* Letter XXII., May 11, 1711.
[3] Not "the" as formerly read; but he says "your" merely because it is an Irish banker.
[4] Remember that Swift always wrote "pdfr" where Deane Swift printed "Presto." It would appear (*see* Letter LI., Aug. 7, 1712, first footnote) that the pronunciation was "Podefar."

LETTER XLIII

[Endorsed by Swift as before, except that he spells "Capel" (with
one "l"); and by Esther Johnson, "Mar. 30."]

43.   London. *Mar.* 8. 1711
                                                      12

I CARRYED my 42d Lettr in my Pocket till evening, & then put
it in te generll Post. I went in th morning to see Ld Treasr; who
had taken Physick, and was drinking his Broth; I had been with
te Secty before, to recommend a Friend one Dr Friend [1] to be
Physician Genll, & te Secrty promised to mention it to te Qu—
I can serve every body but my Self [2] then I went to Court, and
carryed Ld Keepr & te Secrty to dine with Ld Masham, where
we drank te Qu— & Ld Treasr with every health, because this
was te day of his Stabbing. Then I went and playd Pools at
Picquet with Ldy Masham & Mrs Hill, won 10 sh, gave a Crown
to te Box, & came home. I mett at my Lodgings a Lettr from
Jo, with a Bit annexed from ppt, what Jo [3] asks is entirely out
of my way; and I take it for a foolish Whim in him; Beside I
know not who is to give a Patent; if te D. of Ormd, I would
speak to him; & if it comes in my Head I will mention it to Ned
Southwell. They have no Patent that I know of for such Things
here; but good Security is all, & to think tht I would speak to
Ld Treasr for any such Matter at Random, is a Jest. Did I
tell you of a race of Rakes calld te Mohacks [*sic*] [4] that play te
devil about this Town every Night. Slitt peoples noses, & beat
them &c. Nite sollahs, and rove pdfr. Nite MD.

9. I was at Court to day, and nobody invited me to dinner,
except one or 2 whom I did not care to dine with so I dined with
Mrs Van.[5] Young D'avenant was telling us at Court how he
was sett upon by the Mohacks; and how they ran his Chair
thro with a Sword. It is not safe being in te Streets at night for

[1] Properly " Freind."

[2] At this time Swift expected the Deanery of Wells, vacant since Feb. 4;
but it was given to Dr. Brailsford, the Duke of Newcastle's chaplain.
—D. L. P.

[3] "Joe" Beaumont, often mentioned before. He seems to have begged
Swift's influence to get his invention patented.—D. L. P.

[4] [Mohocks.] A set of disorderly debauchees, who, under the various
names of nickers, scowrers, etc., infested the streets of London, insulted
passengers, attacked the watchmen, and committed great excesses. The
Spectator often mentions them.—D. L. P.

[5] [Vanhomrigh.] It is noticeable how frequently Swift mentions his
dining or spending the evening at the Vanhomrighs' with an apologetic
explanation, hardly necessary if he had not an uneasy consciousness that
Stella would not like to know the real nature of the attraction.—D. L. P.

them.. te Bp of Salsbry's [1] son [2] is sd to be of te Gang. They are
all Whigs; and a great Ldy sent to me, to speak to her Fathr and
to Ld Treasr to have a Care of them, and to be carefull likewise
of my self; for she had heard they had malicious Intentions agst
te Ministers & their Friends. I know not whether there be any
thing in this, tho others are of te same Opinion.[3] The weath [*sic*]
still continues very fine & frosty. I walkt in te Park this evening;
and came home early to avoid te Mohaks [*sic*]. Ld Treasr is
better. Nite my own two deelest MD.

10. I went this morning agn to Ld Treasr, who is quite recoverd, and I stayd till he went out. I dined with a Friend in
te City, about a little Business of printing; but not my own. Yo
must buy te small 2 penny Pamphlet calld, *Law is a bottomless
Pitt*,[4] tis very prettily written, & there will be a Second Part.
The Commons are very slow in bringing in their Bill to limit te
Press, and te Pamphleteers make good use of their Time for
there come out 3 or 4 every Day.—Well, but is not it time
methinks to have a Lettr from MD. tis now 6 weeks since I hd
yr numbr 26. I can assure oo I expect one before this goes, and
I'll make shorter days Journalls than usuall, cause I hope to
fill up a good deal of tothr side with my answer. Our fine weathr
lasts yet, but grows a little windy; we shall have rain soon I
dispose. Go to cards Sollah, & I to seep. Nite MD.

11. Ld Treasr has lent te long Lettr [5] I writt him, to Prior,
and I can't get Prior to return it; and I want to have it printd,
and to make up this Academy for te Improvemt of our Language.
Fais we nevr shall improve it as much as FW [6] has done. Sall

---

[1] Gilbert Burnet (1643–1715), consistent representative of Broad-Church
views.

[2] Thomas Burnet, the third son; a great scapegrace, who, being one
day seen by his father unwontedly grave, and asked on what he meditated,
answered: "A greater work than your Lordship's History of the Reformation—my own reformation." He did reform, and died a Justice of the
Common Pleas, 1753.—D. L. P.

[3] In the *History of the Four Last Years of Queen Anne*, Swift does not
hesitate to give it as a historical fact, that the outrages of the Mohocks
were part of an extensive plan to create riot and disturbance in the night,
under colour of which Oxford might be assassinated; and this infamous
plot he ascribes to Prince Eugene's contrivance.

[4] Or *The History of John Bull*, written by Dr. Arbuthnot.—N. Swift
has actually underlined the title!

[5] Concerning the English language.—H.

[6] In Sheridan's edition printed TW, and conjectured by Mr. Nichols
to mean Sir William Temple; but, taken in connection with the word
G[a]ngridge that follows, the symbol may perhaps be set down as one
understood only by the recipients of the letter—and Swift's reference as
being playfully to the superiority of the "little language" they had
invented.—D. L. P.

we? No fais, ourrichar Gangridge.[1] I dined privatly with my
Friend Lewis, and then went to see Ned Southwell, and talk
with him about Walls Business, & Mrs South's, te Latter will
be done; but his own not. Southwell tells me, tht it must be
layd before Ld Treasr, and te nature of it explaind; and a great
deal of Clutter, which is not worth te while, and maybe Ld
Treasr won't do it last. & it is as Walls says himself not above
fourty shill a year difference. Yo must tell Walls this, unless he
would have te Business a Secret from y; in that Case, onely say,
I did all I could with Ned Southwell, & it cant be done; [fo]r [2]
it must be layd before Ld Treasr &c, who will not do it, and
besides it is not worth troubling his Ldship. So Nite my two
deelest nuntyes nine [3] MD.

[1]2.[4] Here is te D— and all to do with these Mohocks,,[5]
Grubstreet Papers about them fly like Lightning; and a List
Printed of near 80 put into [se]vrll [6] Prisons, and all a Lye;
and I begin almost to think there is no Truth or very little in
te whole Story. He that abusd D'avenant was a drunken gentleman, none of that Gang. My Man tells me, tht one of te Lodgers
heard in a Coffee-house publickly, tht one design of te Mohocks
was upon me, if [the]y [7] could catch me. And tho I believe
nothing of it, yet I forbear walking late, and they have put me
to te Charge of some Shillings already. I dined [t]o [8] day with
Ld Treasr, and two Gentlemen of te Highlands of Scotland, yet
very polite men; I sate there till 9, and then went to Ld Mashams,
where Ld Treasr followd me, & we sate till 12, and I came home
in a Chair for fear of te Mohocks; and I have given him warning
of [it t]oo.[9] little Harrison whom I sent to Holld is now actually
made Qu—s Secrty at te Hague, it will be in te Gazett to morrow,
tis worth [1]2 [10] hundred Pounds a Year. Here is a young Fellow
has writt some Sea Eclogues, Poems of Mermen, resembling
Pastoralls of Shepherds, & they are very pretty, and te Thought
is new. Mermen are he Mermaids; Tritons; Natives of te Sea;
do y understand me. I think to recommend him to our Society
to morrow. His Name is Diaper..[11] P— on him, I must do some-

---

[1] This phrase militates against Forster's suggestion that "deerichar"
meant "dear charming." "Richar" is apparently *little* tor "little."
"Gangridge" is "language."
[2] Part of word covered by binding.
[3] Perhaps *little* for "monkeys mine" (*see* Letter VIII., Nov. 2, 1710).
[4] Part of word covered by binding.
[5] So spelt this time.
[6], [7], [8], [9], [10] Parts of words covered by binding. Former readings
followed.
[11] William Diaper was the author of *Dryades*.

thing for him, & get him out of te Way. I hate [t]o[1] have any new Witts rise; but when they do rise I would encourage them. but they tread on our Heels, & thrust us off te Stage. Nite deelest MD.

[1]3.[2] You would laugh to see our Printer constantly attending our Society after dinner, and bringing us whatever new thing he has printed, wch he seldom fails to do. Yet he had nothing to day. Ld Lansdown one of our Society was offended at a Passage in this days Examiner, wch he thinks reflects on him, as I believe it does thō in a mighty civil way, tis onely that is [i.e. his] Underlings cheat, but that he is a very fine Gentleman every way &c. Ld Orrery was President to day; but both our Dukes were absent. Brothr Windham recommended Diaper to te Society; I believe We shall make a Contribution among our selves; wch I dont like. Ld Treasr has yet done nothing for us; but we shall try him soon. Th Company parted early; but Friend & Prior & I sate a while longer, & reformed te State, and found fault with te Ministry, Prior hates his Commission of te Customs because it spoils his Witt. He says he dreams of nothing but Cockets, & Dockets and Drawbacks, and other Jargon words of te Custom house. Our good weathr went away yesterday, & te nights are now dark, & I came home before ten. Nightnown deelest Sollahs.

14. I have been plagud this Morning with Sollicitors and with no body more than my Brothr, Dr Friend; who must needs have to gett old Dr Lawrence[3] te Physician Genrll turnd out, & himself in.. He has argued with me so long upon te reasonable-ness of it; that I am fully convinced it is very unreasonable; & so I would tell te Secty, if I had not already made him speak to te Qu. Besides; I know not but my friend Dr Arbuthnott would be content to have it himself, and I love him ten times better than Friend. What's all this to y; but I must talk of things as they happen in te day, whether y know any thing of them or no. I dined in te City, & coming back. one Parson Richardson[4] of Ired overtook me, he was here last Summer upon a Project of converting te Irish, & printing Bibles &c in that Language, & is now returnd to pursue it on. He tells me, Dr Coghill came last night[5] Town; I will send to see how he does to morrow. He gave me a Lettr from Walls about his old Business. Nite deelest MD.

[1], [2] Parts of words covered by binding. Former readings followed.
[3] Thomas (d. 1714) was a son of Henry Lawrence, Lord-President of the Council during the Commonwealth.
[4] See Letter XVII., March 6, 1710-11.
[5] "To" omitted. As to Coghil: see Letter XXVI., July 1, 1711.

15. I had intended to be early with te Secrty this morning, when my man admitted up Stairs one Mr Newcomb.[1] I think indeed his Case is hard; but Gd knows whether I shall be able to do him any Service. People will not understand; I am a very good Second; but I care not to begin a Recommendation unless it be for an intimate Friend. However, I will do what I can. I misst te Secrty; and then walkt to Chelsea to dine with te Dean of Christchurch;[2] who was engagd to Ld Orrery, with some other Christ Church men. He made me go with him whethr I would or no, for they have this long time admitted me a Christ-church man. Ld Orrery generally every Winter gives his old Acquaintance of that Colledge a Dinner. There were nine Clergy-men at Table and 4 Lay men. Th Dean and I soon left them, and after a Visit or two, I went to Ld Mashams; & Ld Treasr, Arbuthnott & I sate till twelve, and now I am come home & got to bed— I came afoot, but had my man with me. Ld Treasr advised me not to go in a Chair, because te Mohocks insult Chairs more than they do those on Foot. They think there is some mischievous design in those Villains; Severall of them Ld Treasr told me, are actually taken up. I heard at dinner that one of them was killed last night—we shall know more in a Little time. I dont like them as te man sd. Nite MD.

16. This morning at te Secrtys I met Genll Ross and recom-mended Newcombs Case to him, who promises to joyn with me in working up te D. of Ormd to do something for him. Ld Winchelsea tod me to day at Court, that two of the Mohocks caught a maid of old Ldy Winchelseas just at te door of their House in te Park where sh was with a Candle, and had just lighted out somebody. They cutt all her Face, & beat her without any Provocation. I hear my Friend Lewis has got a Mohock, in one of te Messengers hands; te Qu— was at Church to day, but was carryed in an open Chair. She has got an ugly Cough, Arbuthnott her Physician says. I dined with Crow,[3] late Governr of Barbadoes; an acquaintance of Stearns; after dinner, I askt him whethr he had heard of Stearn. Here he is sd he, at

[1] Mr. Aitken suggests Sir Beverley Newcomen, who had served at Killiecrankie.

[2] Atterbury, who had succeeded in his rivalry with Smallridge for the deanery. The Christ Church men here mentioned are doubtless the "Christ Church Wits" who aided Orrery in his controversy with Bentley. Boyle (the Earl of Orrery), in taking up the cudgels for Phalaris, assigned as a chief reason for so doing the disrespect with which Bentley had treated Temple. He was assisted in the controversy by Aldrich, Atterbury, and the "Christ Church Wits"—a number of residents at Oxford, illustrious by genius and learning.—D. L. P.

[3] *See* Letter XXIII., May 18, 1711.

te Door in a Coach, and in came Stearn, he has been here this Week; he is byying a Captainship in his Cousin Stearns[1] Regimt. He told me, he left Jemmy Leigh playing cards with y. He is to give 800 Guinneas for his Commission. I suppose y know all this better than I. How shall I have room to answer oo Rettle hen I get it. I am gone so far already. Nite deelest Logues MD.

17. Dr. Sachevrell came this morning to give me thanks for getting his Brothr an Employmt; it was but 6 or 7 weeks since I spoke to Ld Treasr for him. Sachevll brought Trap along with him, we dined togeth at my Printers, and I sate with them till 7. I little Thought, & I believe so did he, that ever I should be his Sollicitor to te present Ministry, when I left Ireld. this is te 7th I have now provided for since I came, & can do nothing for my self. I dont care: I shall have Ministryes & other People obliged to me, Trap is a Coxcomb, and te tothr is not very deep, and their Judgment in things of Witt or Sense is miraculous Th 2d Part of *Law is a bottomless Pitt*[2] is just now printed, and better I think than te first. Nite my two deel sawcy dallars.

18. There is a Proclamation out against te Mohocks, one of those that are taken is a Baronet. I dined with poor Mrs Wesley who is returning to te Bath.[3] Mrs Percivlls[4] young Daughter has got te Small Pox but will do well. I walkt this evening in te Park, & mett Prior, who made me go home with him, where I staid till past 12, and could not get a Coach, and was alone, and was afraid enough of te Mohocks; I will do so no more, thō I got home safe. Prior & I were talking discontentedly of some Managemts; that no more People are turnd out, wch get Ld Tr— many Enemyes; but whethr te Fault be in him or te Qu— I know not. I doubt, in both. Ung oomens it is now 7 weeks since I receivd oor last: but I expect one next Irish Pacquet, to fill te rest of this Paper; but if it dont come, I'll do without it. So I wish oo good Luck at Ombre with te Dean. Nite nuntyes nine.[5]

19. Newcomb came to me this morning, & I went to te D. of Ormd to speak for him, but te D. was just going out to take te

---

[1] A Lieut.-Colonel Robert Stearne is mentioned in the list of Colonel Fred. Hamilton's regiment, 1695, with a note that he became master of Kilmainham Hospital, Dublin, in 1728. *See also* Percy Fitzgerald's *Life of Laurence Sterne.*

[2] Title underlined.

[3] Bath he always writes "the Bath."

[4] *See* Letter XXXVI., Dec. 3, 1711.

[5] *See* March 11.

Oaths for Genrll.[1] Th D. of Shrewsbury is to be Ld Lt of Ireld.
I walkt with Domvill & Ford to Kensington, Where we dined
and it cost me above a Crown. I dont like it, as the man sd. I
saw there Ld Masham's Children. th youngest my Nephew, I
fear has got te Kings evil, te othr 2 are Daughters of 3 and 4
years old. Twas very windy walking, te Gardens there are mighty
fine. I passt te evening at Ld Mashams with Ld Treasr &
Arbuthnot, as usuall, and we stayd till past one; but I had my
Man to come with me. & at home I found 3 Letters, one from one
Fetherston a Parson, with a Postscript of Tisdalls [2] to recommend
him; & Fetherston whom I never saw has been so kind to give
me a Lettr of Attorney to recover a debt for him Another from
Ld Abercorn, to get him te Dukedom of Chattelheraut from te
K. of France; in wch I will do what I can. For his Pretensions
are very just.[3] te third I warrant from our MD. Tis a great
Stir this of getting a Dukedom from te K. of France; but it is
onely to speak to te Secty; & get te D. of Ormd to engage in it;
& mention te Case to Ld Treasr &c & this I shall do. Nite deelest
richar MD.

20. I was with te D. of Ormd this morning about Ld Abercorn, Dr Friend & Newcomb; some will do, & some will not do:
that's wise Maram: te D. of Shrewsbury is certainly to be yr
Governr. I ll go in a day or two, & give te Dutchess Joy &
recommend te A.B. of Dublin to her. I writt to te A.Bp some
Months ago that would be so; & told him I would speak a good
word for him to te Dutchess; & he says he has a great respect
for her &c. I made our Society change their House; & we met to
day at te Star & Garter in te Pallmall. Ld Arran was President.
Th other Dog was so extravagant in his Bills, that for four
dishes and four 1st & Second Course, without wine or Dessert;
he charged 21ll 6s 8d to te D. of Ormd; We design when all have
been Presidents this turn, to turn it into a Reckoning of so much
a Head; but we shall break up when te Session ends. Nite
deelest MD.

---

[1] In Marlborough's stead.—D. L. P.
[2] *See* Letter VII., Oct. 21, 1710.
[3] This dukedom was conferred on the Earl of Arran, during Queen
Mary's (of Scots) minority; the eldest son of the first duke died childless;
the second son fell at Worcester in 1651; and the succession then passed
to the House of Hamilton in the female line—a daughter of the second
son having married the Earl of Selkirk, the issue of the marriage being
the fourth Duke of Hamilton, mentioned in the *Journal*. But the Earl
of Abercorn was the direct descendant in the male line of the third son
of the first Duke of Chatelherault; and the question was whether, as a
male fief, the title should not have passed to him.—D. L. P.

21. Morning. Now I will answr MD s Rettle. N. 27. Y that are adding to yr Numbers, & grumbling; had made it 26; & then cobled[1] it to 27. Y[2] believe it is above a Month since yr last; yes, it is above 7 weeks since I had yr last, but I ought to consider that this was 12 days right [? writing], so that makes it pretty even. O the Sirry Zade with her excuses of a fortnight at Balligawl, seeing their Friends, & landLord running away. O Rold hot a Cruttle & a Bustle—No—if y will have it, I am not Dean of Wells, nor know any thing of being so; nor is there any thing in te Story; & that's enough. It was not Roper[3] sent that News. Roper is my humble Slave. Yes, I heard of yr Resolves, & that Burton[4] was embroyld. Stratford spoke to me in his behalf; but I sd I hated te Rascal. Poor Catherine[5] gone to Wales. but she'll come back again I hope; I would see her in my Journey if she wear near te Road; & bring her over. Jo is a Fool; that sort of Business is not at all in my way: Pray put him off it. People laugh when I mention it. Bed ee [or "oo"] puudon Maram, I'm drad oo rike ee [or "oo"] Aplon, no harm I hope—And so [te ung][6] Dd wonders she has not a Letter at te day; oo'll have it soon [marn][7]—te D— he is! marryed to that Vengeance! Men are not to be believed. I don't think her a Fool. Who would have her? Dilly will be governd like an Ass, & she will govern like a Lyon. En't that true ppt.—Why; Stearn told me he left y at Ombre with Lee,[8] & yet y never saw him. I know nothing of his Wife being here. It may cost her a C—[9] (I dont care to write that Word plain) He is a little in doubt about buying his Commission. Iss [for "Yes"]. I'll bring oo over all te little Papers I can think on; I thought I sent y by Lee[10] all that were good at that time. Th Authr of te Sea Eclogues, sent Books to te Society yesterday; & we give him Guinneas a piece, & may [? maybe] will do furthr from him. for him I mean. So te Bp of Cl. & Ldy were yr Guests for a Night or two.—Why, Ppt, y are grown a great Gamester, & Company-keeper. I did say to my self when I read those Names, just what

---

[1] This is Forster's reading, and a likely one. Or it may be "called" —in which case the next word but one ("to") is redundant. The reading "altered" is certainly wrong.
[2] "Y" means "you." "I" is usually read here.
[3] Abel Roper (1665-1726), Tory journalist, started the Post-boy (see Letter XX., April 8, 1711) in 1695.
[4] See Letter XXII., May 11, 1711.
[5] Catherine Stoyte.
[6], [7] ? (Scarcely decipherable.)
[8] For "Leigh."
[9] Smudged by Swift.
[10] For "Leigh."

y guess, & y clear up te matter wonderfully. Y may converse
with those 2 Nymphs if y please but te —— take me if I ever do.
Iss fais it is delightfull to hear tht Ppt is every way Ppt now,
in Health & looks, and all. Pray Gd keep her so many many
many Years. . I doubt te Session will not be over till towards te
End of April. However I shall not wait for it, if te Ministry will
let me go sooner. I wish I were just now in my Garden at
Laracor; I would set out for Dublin early on Monday, & bring
y an Account of my young Trees, which y are better acquainted
with than te Ministry, and so am I. Oh, now y have got numbr
41, have y so? Why perhaps I forgot & kept it to te next Post
in my Pocket; I have done such Tricks. My Cold is better, but
not gone. I want Air and Riding. Hold ee Tongue oo ppt about
Colds at Moorpark; te Case is quite different. I will do what
y desire me for Tisdal when I next see Ld Anglesea. Pray give
him my Service. The Weath is warm these 3 or 4 days and rainy.
I am to dine to day with Lewis and Dartenuff at Sommers's te
Clerk of te Kitchen at Court. Dartenuff [1] loves good Bits and
good Sups.—Good mollows richar Sollahs.—At Night.—I dined
as I sd, & it cost me a shilling for a Chair. It has raind all day,
and is very warm. Ldy Mashams young Son my Nephew is very
ill, & she is [out of **d**] [2] with grief. I pity her mightily. I am
got home early, and going to write to te Bp of Cl— but have no
Politicks to send him. Nite my own two deelest sawcy [d ones]. [3]

22. I am going into the City this morning with a Friend about
some Business, so I will immediatly seal up this, and keep it in
my Pottick till evening, & zen put it in te Post. Th Weathr
continues warm and gloomy; I have heard no news since I went
to bed, so can say no more. Pray send [*** ** *** ***] [4] that
I may have time to write to [****] [5] about it. I have here underneath given order for fourty Shill for Mrs Brent, [6] wch y will
send to Parvisol. Farewell deelest deel MD, and rove pdfr dearly
dearly. farewell MD MD FW FW FW Me Me Me—Lele lele
lele lele lele⌣lele—and lele aden.

---

[1] Dartineuf. *See* Letter V., Oct. 1, 1710, etc.
[2] Obliterated.
[3] Or perhaps "doxes"—for "doxies."
[4,] [5] Obliterated.
[6] *See* Letter I.

LETTER XLIV

[Endorsed: " To Mrs. Dingley, at " same lodgings as before. Date of receipt, " Apr. 14."]

44.   London. *Mar.* 22*d.* 1711-12.

UGLY nasty Weather. I was in te City to day with Mrs Wesly & Mr [1] Percivll to get money from a Banker for Mrs Wesly, who goes to te Bath on Thursday. . I left them there, & dined with a friend, & went to see Ld Treasr; but he had People with him I did not know, so I went to Ldy Mashams, and lost a Crown with her at Picquet, and then sate with Ld Masham, & Ld Treasr &c there till past one, but I had my Man with me to come hom; I gave in my 43d and one for te Bp of Cl. to te Post office as I came from te City, and so oo know tis late now, and I have nothing to say for this day, Our Mohocks are all vanisht; however I shall take care of my Person. Nite my own two deelest nuntyes MD.

23. I was this morning before Church with te Secrty about Ld Abercorn's Business, & some others. My Solliciting Season is come, and will last as long as te Sessions [*sic*]. I went late to Court, and te Company was almost gone. Th Court serves me for a Coffee-house, once a week I meet acquaintance there that I should not otherwise see in a quarter. There is a flying Report that te French have offerd a Cessation of Arms, and to give us Dunkerk, & te Dutch Namur for security till te Peace is made. Th D. of Ormd thy say goes in a week. Abundance of his Equipage is already gone. Is [*i.e.* His] Friends are afraid te Expence of this Employmt will ruin him, since he must lose te Governmt of Ireld. I dined privately with a Friend, and refused all Dinners offerd me at Court, wch however were but two, and I did not like eithr Did I tell y of a Scoundrel about te Court, that sells Employnts to ignorant People, and cheats them of their Money. he lately made a Bargain for te Vicechamberlns Place for 7000ll, and had received some Guinneas Earnest, but te whole Thing was discoverd tothr day, and Examination taken of it by Ld Dartmouth, & I hope he will be swingd. Th Vicechambrln [2] told me sevll Particulars of it last night at Ld Mashams. Can Dd play at Ombre yet? enough hod [? to hold] te Cards while ppt steps into next Room—Nite deelest sollahs. [3]

---

[1] Former readings, "Mrs"—but there is no " s."
[2] Mr. Thomas Coke. *See* Letter XXVII., Aug. 6, 1711 (note).
[3] From the interrogation point after "yet " to here is slightly obliterated.

24. This morning I recommended Newcomb agn to te D. of Ormd, and left Dick Stewart[1] to [do][2] it furthr; then I went to visit te Dutchess of Hamilton who was not awake; so I went to te Dutchess of Shrewsbury and sate an hour at her Toilet. I [talkt][3] to her about the Dukes being Ld Lt; she sayd she knew nothing of it, but I rallyd her out of that, and she resolves not to stay behind te Duke. I intend to recommd te Bp of Cl— to her for an Acquaintance. He will like her very well. She is indeed a most agreeable woman, & a great Favorite of mine. I know not whethr te Ladyes in Ireld will like her. I was at te Court of Requests to get some Lds to be at a Commtee to morrow about a Friends Bill; & then [? there] te Duke of Beaufort gave me a Poem finely bound in Folio, printed at Stamford, & writt by a Country Squire. Ld Exetr[4] desired te Duke to give it te Qu— because te Authr is his Friend: but te Duke desird I would let him know whethr it was good for any thing; I brought it home & will return it to morrow, as te dullest thing I ever read; & advise te Duke not to present it. I dined with Domvile at his Lodgings by Invitation, for he goes in a few days for Ireld. Nite dee MD.

25. There is a mighty Feast at a Tory Sheriffs[5] to day in te City,[6] 12 hundred dishes of meat, about[7] 5 Lds, and sevll hundrd Gentlemen will be there, and give 4 or 5 Guinneas a Piece, according to Custom. Dr Coghill[8] & I dined by Invitation at Mrs Van's. It has raind or mizzled all day as my Pockets feel. There are two new Answers come out to te Conduct of te Allyes Th last years Examiners printd togethr in a small Volume, go off but slowly. Th Printer overprintd himself by at least a thousand, so soon out of Fashion are Party papers however so well writt. Th Medlys[9] are coming out in te same Volume, & perhaps may sell better. Our news about a Cessation of Arms begins to flag; and I have not these two[10] days since [? seen] any body in Business, to ask them about it. We had a terrible Fire last night in Drury lane, or thereabouts, and 3 or

---

[1] *See* Letter VII., Oct. 31, 1710.
[2], [3] As well as can be read—there is a hole in the paper.
[4] John Cecil (1674–1721), sixth Earl of Exeter.
[5] John Case and Henry Lamb, Esqrs., were then sheriffs.—N.
[6] This day the sheriffs gave a noble feast at Merchant Taylors' Hall; His Grace the Duke of Ormond, the Earl of Oxford, and several of the nobility doing them the honour to be present. (*Dawks's News Letter*, March 25, 1712.)—N.
[7] Former reading "above."
[8] *See* Letter XXVI., July 1, 1711.
[9] *See* Letter XXI., April 28, 1711.
[10] Former reading "three."

4 People destroyd.[1] One of te Maids of Honor has te Small-pox, but the best is, she can lose no Beauty, & we have one new handsom Md of Honr. Nite MD.

26. I forgot to tell y that on Sunday last about 7 at night, it lightend above 50 times as I walkt te Mall, wch I think is extdy at this time of te Year. & te Weathr was very hot. Had y any thing of this in Dublin? I intended to dine with Ld Treasr to day: but Ld Mansel & Mr Lewis made me dine with them at Kit Musgrave's. Now y don't know who Kit Musgrave is.[2] I sate te Evening with Mrs Wesley who goes to morrow morning to te Bath. She is much better than she was. Th News of te French desiring a Cessation of Arms &c was but Town talk.. We shall know in a few days as I am told, whethr there will be a Peace or no. Th D. of Ormd will go in a Week for Flanders, they say: Our Mohawks[3] go on still, & cut Peoples faces every night; fais they shan't cut mine, I like it better as it is, the Dogs will cost me at least a Crown a Week in Chairs. I believe te souls of yr Houghers of Cattle have gott into them, and now they don't distinguish between a Cow and a Christian. I forgot to wish y yesterday a happy new Year, y know te 25 of March is te first day of te Year,[4] And now y must leave of [i.e. off] Cards, and put out yr fire: I'll put out mine th 1st of April, cold or not cold. I believe I shall lose Credit with y by not coming over at te Beginning of April: but I hoped te Session would be ended, and I must stay till then, & yet I would fain be at te Beginning of my Willows growing. Percivall[5] tells me that te Quicksetts upon te flatt in te Garden, do not grow so well as those famous ones on te Ditch. They want digging about them; The Cherry trees by te River side my Heart is sett upon. Nite MD.

27. Society day. Y know that I suppose. Dr Arthburnett [sic] was Presidt. His dinner was dresst in te Qu—s Kitchin, and was mighty fine; & we eat it at Ozinda's Chocolate house[6] just by St James's. We were never merryer nor bettr company, and did not part till after 11 I did not summon Ld Lansdown: He and

---

[1] This fire was at a grocer's in Drury Lane; and three or four lives were lost, of persons that leaped out of the windows.—N.
[2] See Letter XXII., May 1, 1711.
[3] Spelling varied again.
[4] The Gregorian New Year's Day, Jan. 1, was not fully recognised in England until 1752.
[5] See Letter XXXVI., Dec. 3, 1711.
[6] Ozinda's was "at the bottom" of St. James's Street, "next door to the Palace"—but whether on the east side or on the west is unknown. It was a resort of the extreme Tories.

I are fallen out. There was something in an Examiner a fortnight ago that he thought reflected on te Abuses in his Office, (he is Secrtry at War) & he writt to te Secty that he had heard I had inserted that Paragraph. This I resented highly, that he should comlain of me before he spoke to me; and I sent him a peppering Letter, and would not summon him by a Note as I do the rest; nor ever will have any thing to say to him till he begs my Pardon. I mett Ld Treasr to day at Ldy Masham's he would have fain carryed me home to dinner, but I beggd his Pardon; what? upon a Society day? No no. Tis rate Sollahs; I ant dlunk. Nite MD.

28. I was with my Friend Lewis to day getting Materials for a little Mischief; and I dined with Ld Treasr, and 3 or 4 fellows I never saw before; I left them at 7, and came home, and have been writing to te A.Bp Dubln, and Cozn Dean[1] in answer to one of his of 4 months old, that I spied by chance routing among my Papers. I have a Pain these 2 days exactly upon te Top of my left Shouldr, I fear it is something Rheumatick, it winches[2] now and then. Shall I putt Flannell to it? Domvile is going to Ireld; he came here this morning to take leave of me; but I shall dine with him tomorrow. Does te Bp of Cl talk of coming for Engd this Summer? I think Ld Molesworth[3] told me so about 2 Months ago. Th weathr is bad again, rainy and very cold this Evening. Do y know what te Longitude is? a Projector has been applying himself to me to recommend him to te Ministry, because he pretends to have found out te Longitude[4] I believe he has no more found it out, than he has found out mine ***[5] However I will gravely hear what he says, and discover him a Knave or Fool. Nite MD.

29. I am plagued with these Pain in my Shouldr; I believe it is Rheumatick; I will do something for it to Night. Mr Lewis & I dined with Mr Domvile to take our Leave of him; I drunk

---

[1] He refers to his uncle Godwin's son Deane; who assisted an elder brother, Willoughby Swift, in a merchant's business at Lisbon, and was father to the Deane Swift who afterwards issued the earlier portion of this journal.

[2] Twinges.

[3] This is puzzling. The first Lord Molesworth (viscount and baron) was not ennobled until 1716—he was, before that, Robert Molesworth of Brackanstown, co. Dublin. He was born 1656, died 1725; and he was the father of John and Richard, mentioned in notes to Letter IV., Sept. 21 and 24, 1710.

[4] Mr. Aitken suggests William Whiston (1667–1752), vicar of Lowestoft, deprived (1710) of a Cambridge professorship for heresy. An enthusiastic student of natural science.

[5] Obliterated word.

3 or 4 Glasses of Champigne by perfect teazing; thô it is bad for
my Pain; but if it continues I will not drink any wine without
Water till I am well. The Weathr is abominably cold and wet.—
I am got into bed and have put some old Flannel for want of
new to my Shouldr, and rubbd it with Hungary water.[1]—Tis
plaguy hard; I never would drink any Wine if it were not for
my Head, and drinking has given me this Pain. I will try
Abstemiousness for a while. How does MD do now? how does
Dd & ppt? You must know I hate Pain, as te old woman sd—But
I'll try to go seep; My Flesh sucks up Hungary water rarely.
My Man's an awkward Rascal, and makes me peevish. Do yo
know that tother day he was forced to beg my Pardon that he
could not shave my Head, his Hand shook so. He is drunk
every day & I design to turn him off soon as ever I get to Ireld.
I ll write no more now, but go to Sleep, and see whether Sleep
& Flannell will cure my Shouldr. Nite deelest MD.

30. I was not able to go to Church or Court to day, for my
Shouldr; th Pain has left my Shouldr and crept to my neck and
Collar bone. It makes me think of pooppt's bladebone. Urge,
urge, urge, dogs gnawing.. I went in a Chair at 2 and dined with
Mrs Van, where I could be easy; & came back at 7, My Hungary
water is gone, & to night I use Spirits of wine, wch my Landlady
tells me is very good. It has raind terribly all day long; & is
extreemly [or "extreamly"] cold: I am very uneasy, and such
cruell Twinges every moment. Nite deelest MD.

31. Ap. 1, 2, 3, 4, 5, 6, 7,—8. All these days I have been
extreemly [or "extreamly"] ill, tho I twice crawld out a week
ago; but am now recovering, thô very weak. The violence of
my Pain abated the night before last; I will just tell y how I
was & then send away this Lettr wch ought to have gone
Saterday last. Th Pain encreasd with mighty Violence in my
left Shouldr & Collar bone & that side of my Neck. On Thursday
morning appeared great Red Spots in all those Places where my
Pain was, & te violence of te Pain was confined to my Neck
behind a little on te left side; which was so violent that I [2] not
a minutes ease nor hardly a minutes sleep in 3 days & nights.
te Spots encreasd every day & had little Pimples which are now
grown white & full of corruption [thô] [3] small. te Red still continues too, and most prodigious hott & inflamed. The Disease

---

[1] "A distilled water, denominated from a Queen of Hungary, made
of rosemary flowers infused with rectified spirit of wine, and thus distilled."
—*Chambers's Encyclopædia*.
[2] "Had" omitted.
[3] Former reading. (Hole in paper.)

is te Shingles I eat nothing but Water gruell; I am very weak but out of all violent Pain. Th Doctrs say it would have ended in some violent Disease if it had not come out thus. I shall now recover fast. I have been in no danger of Life, but miserable Torture. I must not write too much—so adieu deelest MD MD MD FW FW Me Me Me Lele I can say lele yet oo see —Fais I dont conceal a bitt. as hope savd

[Note written at end of cover]

I must purge & clystr after this; and my next Letter will not be in te old order of Journall till I have done with Physick. An't oo surprisd to see te Lettr want half a side

LETTER XLV

[Endorsed: " Mrs. Johnson, att" same lodgings, but not in Swift's writing. Date of receipt, " May 1st."]

45.   London. *Apr.* 24. 1712

I HAD yr 28th 2 or 3 days ago. I can hardly answer it now— Since my last I have been extremely ill. Tis this day just a Month since I felt a small pain on te tip of my left Shoulder, which grew worse & spread for 6 days; then broke all out by my collar, & left side of my neck in monstrous red Spotts, inflamed, & these grew to small Pimples. for 4 days I had no rest nor nights for a Pain in my neck; then I grew a little bettr; afterwards, where my Pains were a cruell Itching seised me beyond what ever I could imagine, & kept me awake severall Nights. I rubbd it vehemently but did not scratch it. Then it grew into three or for [*sic*] great Sores like Blisters and run; at last I advised te Dr to use it like a Blister; so I did, with Melilot Plaisters,[1] which still run, and I am now in pain enough; but am daily mendeng: I kept my Chambr a fortnight; then went out a day or 2; but then confined my self again. 2 days ago, I a went to a Neighbr to dine, but yesterday again kept at home: to day I will venture abroad a little; and hope to be well in a week or ten days. I never suffered so much in my life; I have taken my Breeches in above 2 Inches, so I am leaner, wch answers one Question in yr Letter. Th Weathr is mighty fine, I write in te morning, because I am better then. I will go and try to walk a little; I will give Dd's Certificate to Took to morrow farewell MD MD MD Me Me FW FW Me M—.

[1] The dried flowers of the yellow melilot (*Melilotus officinalis*) were formerly in favour for making plasters.

LETTER XLVI

[Endorsed: " To Mrs. Dingley, att " same lodgings. Date of receipt, " May 15."]

46   London. *May.* 10. 1712.

I HAVE not yet ease or Humor enough to go on in my Journall Method, thō I have left my Chambr these 10 days. My Pain continues still in my Shouldr and Collar I keep Flannel on it, and rub it with Brandy; and take a nasty dyet Drink I still Itch terribly, & have some few Pimples; I am weak & sweat, & then te Flannell makes me mad with Itching; but I think my Pain lessens. A Journall while I was sick would have been a noble thing, made up of Pain; and Physick, & Visits & Messages. The 2 last were almost as troublesome as te 2 first. One good Circumstance is that I am grown much leaner, I believe I told you, that I have taken in my Breeches 2 Inches. I had yr N. 29 last night. In answer to yr good opinion of my disease, te Drs sd they never saw any thing so odd of the Kind; they were not properly Shingles, but Herpes miliaris, and 20 other hard names.. I can never be sick like othr People, but always something out of te common way; and as for yr notion of it coming without Pain, it neither came, nor stayd, nor went without Pain, & th most pain I ever bore in my Life—Madameris[1] is retired in te Country with te Beast her Husband long ago—I thank te Bp of Cl for his Proxy; I will write to him soon. Here is Dilly's Wife[2] in Town, but I have not seen her yet—No, Sinkerton[3] tis not a Sign of Health, but a Sign that if it had not come out some terrible Fitt of Sickness would have followd. I was at our Society last Thursday, to receive a new Membr, te Chancellor of th Exchequr[4]; but I drink nothing above wine & water—We shall have a Peace I hope soon, or at least entirely broke, but I believe te first. My Lettr to Ld Treasr about te Engl. Tongue is now printing; and I suffer my name to be put at te End of it, wch I nevr did before in my Life.[5] The Appendix to th 3d Part of John Bull was published yesterday[6]; tis equall to te rest. I hope y read John Bull. It was a Scotch Gentleman

---

[1] Interpreted, by various annotators, "Madame Ayris" and "Madame Ayres," without further explanation. There was Baby Aires of Leicester; but she became Mrs. Leach. Was Dryden Leach (*see* Letter VII., Oct. 26, 1710) a beast?

[2] *See* Letter XLIII., March 21.

[3] "Simpleton."

[4] Benson.

[5] *See* Letters XLI., Feb. 21, and XLIII., March 11.

[6] *An Appendix to John Bull still in his Senses: or, Law is a Bottomless Pit.*

a friend of mine that writ it; but they put it upon me. The Parlmt will hardly be up till June. We were like to be undone some days ago with a Tack,[1] but we carryed it bravely, and the Whigs came in to help us. Poor Ldy Masham I am afraid will lose her onely son, about a twelve Month old, with te King's Evil. I never would let Mrs Fenton [2] see me in my Illness, tho she often came, but she has been once here since I recovered.. Bernage has been twice to see me of late. His Regimt will be broke, and he onely upon half pay; so perhaps he thinks he will want me again. I am told here that te Bp of Cloghr & Family are coming over, but he says nothing of it himself.—I have been returning th Visits of those that sent Howdees in my Sickness, particularly te Dutchess of Hamilton, who came & satt with me 2 hours; I make Bargains with all People that I dine with, to let me scrub my Back agst a Chair, & te Dutchess of Ormd was forced to bear it tother day: Many of my Friends are gone to Kensington where te Qu— has been removed for some time—This is a long Lettr for a kick [3] body; I will begin te next in te Journall way, thô my Journals will be sorry ones.— My left Hand is very weak & trembles; but my right side has not been toucht This is a pitifull Letter for want of a better, but plagud with a Tetter, my Fancy does fetter—Ah my poor willows & Quicksets,—Well, but y must read John Bull. Do y understand it all? Did I tell y that young Parson Geree [*i.e.* Gery] [4] is going to be marryed, and asked my Advice when it was too late to break off. He tells me Elwick has purchasd 4oll a year in Land adjoyning to his Living. Ppt does not say one word of her own little Health. I'm angry almost; but I won't tause see im a dood dallar in odle sings,[5] iss and so im Dd too. Gd bless MD & FW & Me, ay & pdfr too. farewell MD MD MD FW FW FW Me Me. Lele I can say lele it ung oomens iss I tan, well as oo.

---

[1] A tack is a bill tacked to a money bill, that as both must be passed or rejected together, the tacked bill may pass, because the money bill must.—H. The procedure has long been obsolete, and is now contrary to parliamentary rules.

[2] His sister Jane. *See* Letter IX., Nov. 23, 1710, etc.

[3] "Sick."

[4] Mr. Gery, rector of Letcombe, in Berks, to whose house Dr. Swift retired about ten weeks before Queen Anne's death, on occasion of the incurable breach between the Earl of Oxford and Lord Viscount Bolingbroke.—B.

[5] "She is a good girl in other things."

LETTER XLVII

Endorsed as last—except that " at " is spelt with one " t." Date of receipt, "June 5."]

47   London *May* 31 1712.

I CANNOT yet arrive to my Journall Letters, My Pains continuing still thō with less Violence; but I don't love to write Journals while I am in pain, and above all, not Journalls to MD; But however I am so much mended that I intend my next shall be in te old way; and yet I shall perhaps break my Resolution when I feel Pain. I believe I have lost Credit with you in relation to my coming over; but I protest, it is impossible to one who has any thing to do with this Ministry, to be certain, when he fixes any time. There is a Business which till it takes some Turn or other, I cannot leave this Place in Prudence or Honr. And I never wished so much as now that I had staid in Ireld, but the Dye is cast, and is now a spinning, and till it settles I can not tell whethr it be an Ace or a Sise.[1] I am confident by what you know yourselves, that you will justify me in all this. The moment I am used ill, I will leave them; but know not how to do it while things are in suspense. The Session will soon be over (I believe in a fortnight) and the Peace we hope will be made in a short time; and then there will be no further Occasion for me, nor I have any thing to trust to but Court Gratitude; so that I expect to see my Willows a Month after the Parlmt is up; but I will take MD in the way, and not go to Laracor like an unmannerly Spreenekick Ferrow.[2] Have y seen my Ld [3] to Ld Treasr; there are 2 Answers come out to it already, thō tis no Politicks, but a harmless Proposall about te Improvemt of th Engl. Tongue. I believe if I writt an Essay upon a Straw some Fool would answer it. About ten days hence I expect a Lettr from MD N.30. Y are now writing it near the End as I guess. I have not received Dd's money; but I will give y a Note for it on Parvisol, & bed a [or "oo"] Paadon I have not done it before —I am just now thinking to go lodge at Kensington for te Air. Ldy Masham has teazd me to do it, but Business had hindred me; but now Ld Treasr has removed thither. Fifteen of our Society dined togethr under a Canopy in an Arbour at Parsons Green [4] last Thursday: I never saw any Thing so fine and Romantick. We got a great Victory last Wednesday in th H. of Lds by

[1] A six.
[2] "Splenetic fellow."
[3] ? "Ld" intended for "Letter."
[4] At Lord Peterborough's house. *See* Letter XXV., June 24, 1711.

a Majority I think of 28, And the Whigs had desired their
Friends to bespeak Places to see Ld Treasr carryed to the Tower.
I mett yr Higgins [1] here yesterday: He roars at te Insolence of
te Whigs in Ireld, talks much of his own Sufferings and expences
in asserting th Cause of the Church; and I find he would fain
plead merit enough to desire that his Fortune should be mended.
I believe he designs to make as much noise as he can in order
to Prefermt. Pray let te Provost, [2] when he sees you, give y ten
English Shillings, and I will give as much here to te Man that
delivrd me Rimers Books [3] he knows te meaning: Tell him I
will not trust him, but that y can order it to be pd me here;
And I will trust you till I see y; Have I told y that te Rogue
Patrick has left me these two Months, to my great Satisfaction.
I have got anothr, who seems to be much better, if he continues
it. I am printing a threepenny Pamphlet, [4] and shall print
anothr in a fortnight; and then I have done, unless some new
Occasion starts. Is my Curate Warburton marryed to Mrs
Malthrop [? Melthrop] in my Parish: So I heeear; Or is [5] a Lye.
·Has Raymd got to his new House: Do y see Jo now and then.
What luck have you at Ombre; How stands it with te Dean?
************ [6] My Service to Mrs Stoit, and Catharine if she
be come from Wales. I have not yet seen Dilly Ash's wife I calld
once but she was not at home; I think she is under th Doctor's
Hand; ********** [7] I believe this News of te D. of Ormd pro-
ducing Letters in te Council of War, with orders not to fight,
will surprise y in Ireld. Ld Treasr sd in te House of Lds that in
a few days te Treaty of Peace should be layd before them; And
our Court thought it wrong to hazard a Battle, and sacrifice
many Lives in such a Juncture. [8] If te Peace holds all will do
well: otherwise.. I know not how we shall weather it. And it was
reckoned as a wrong Step in Politicks for Ld Treasr to open
himself so much. The Secrty would not go so far to satisfy the
Whigs in the H. of Commons; but there all went swimmingly.—
I'll say no more to oo to nite sollohs [9]; becase I must send away

---

[1] *See* Letter XXXIV., Nov. 9, 1711.
[2] Dr. Benjamin Pratt. *See* Letter II.
[3] *See* Letters XXIII., May 16, 1711, and XLI., Feb. 22, 1711-12.
[4] *Some Reasons to prove that no person is obliged, by his Principles as a Whig, to oppose her Majesty or the present Ministry.*—N.
[5] "it" omitted.
[6], [7] Several words obliterated.
[8] Ormond's private instructions were not to hazard a battle, or undertake a siege; and he was obliged, in justice to his own character, to make
them known to the council of war, when it was proposed to attack the
camp of Marshal Villars.—D. L. P.
[9] So spelt this time.

te Lettr, not by th Bell,[1] but early; and besides I have not
much more to say, at zis plasant [or "plesent"] liting. Does
MD never read at all now, pee? but oo walk plodigiousry I
suppose, oo make nothing of walking to too to to ay, to Doni-
brook: I walk too as much as I can: because Sweating is good;
but I'll walk more if I go to Kensington. I suppose I shall have
no Apples this year neithr; for I dined tothr day with Ld Rivers
who is sick, at his Country house; and he shewd me all his
Cherryes blasted; Nite deelest Sollahs; farwell deelest Rives;
rove poopoopdfr farwell deelest richar MD, MD MD FW FW
FW FW FW Me Me Lele, Me, lele lele richar MD.

LETTER XLVIII

[Endorsed: "For Mrs. Rebecca Dingley att " same lodgings. Date of
receipt, "June 23d "]

48   Kensington, *Jun.* 17. 1712.

I HAVE been so tosticated [2] about since my last, that I could
not go on in my Journall manner, thō my Shoulder is a great
deal better; However I feel constant pain in it, but I think it
diminishes, and I have cutt off some slices from my Flannel.
I have lodged here near a fortnight, partly for the Air and
Exercise; partly to be near the Court, where dinners are to be
found. I generally get a lift in a Coach to Town, and in the
evening I walk back. On Saterday I dined with te Dutchess of
Ormd at her Lodge near Sheen; and thought to get a Boat back
as usuall; I walkt by te Bank to Cue [*i.e.* Kew]; but no Boat;
then to Mortlack, but no boat; & it was 9 a clock; at last a
little sculler calld, full of nasty People; I made him sett me down
at Hammersmith; so walkt 2 miles to this Place, & got here by
11. Last night I had anothr such difficulty; I was in the City
till past 10 at night; it raind hard; but no Coach to be had;
It gave over a little and I walkt all te way here and gott home
by 12. I love these shabby difficultyes when they are over; but
I hate them because they rise from not having a thousd pd a
year—I had yr N. 30 about 3 days ago. wch I will now Answer.
And first, I did not relapse; but found [or "second" [3]] I came
out before I ought, and so and so, as I have told you in some of
my last. The first coming abroad made People think I was quite

---

[1] *See* Letter II., and note as to bellman.
[2] Originally a mispronunciation of "intoxicated," it came to mean
perplexed or bewildered.
[3] Mr. Ryland's reading—but it seems suggested less by the appearance
of the word than by considerations of style.

recovered; & I had no more messages afterwards.—Well but John Bull is not writt by te Person y imagine, as hope [1]—It is too good for anothr to own, had it been Grubstreet, I would have let People think as they please; and I think that's right, is not it now? so flap ee hand, & make wry mouth ee self sawci doxi. Now comes Dd: why sollah I did write in a fortnight, my 47th, and if it did not come in due time, can I help Wind and Weathr; am I a Laplander, am I witch, can I work Miracles, can I make Easterly winds. Now I am agst Dr Smith; I drink little water with my Wine: yet I believe he is right; Yet Dr Cockburn told me a little wine would not hurt me: But it is so hot and dry, and water is so dangerous. The worst thing here is my Evenings at Ld Mashams, where Ld Treasr comes, and we sitt till after 12, but it is convenient I should be among them for a while as much as possible; I need not tell ee why. But I hope that will be at an end in a Month or two one way or othr; and I am resolvd it shall. But I can't go to Tunbridge nor any where else out of te way in this Juncture. So Ppt designs for Templeoag [2] (what a name is that) whereabouts is that place; I hope not very far from—— [3] [Higgins is here roaring that all is wrong in Ireld; & would have me gett him an Audience of Ld Treasr to tell him so. But I will have nothing to do in it; no not I fais.] Dublin. We have had no Thundr till last night; and till then we were dead for want of rain; but there fell a great deal. No field lookt green. I reckon te Qu— will go to Windsor in 3 or 4 weeks; and if te Secty takes a House there, I shall be sometimes with him. but how affecteedly ppt talks of my being here all Summer; wch I do not intend; nor to stay one Minute longer in Engld than becomes te Circumstances I am in. I wish y would go soon into te Country, & take a good deal of it; & where bettr than Trim. Jo will be yr humble Servt; Parvisol yr Slave, & Raymd at yr Command, for he picques himself on good manners. I have seen Dilly's wife,—And I have seen once or twice old Bradly [4] here. He is very well, very old, and very wise: I believe I must go see his Wife when I have Leisure. I should be glad to see Goody Stoit, and her Husband; pray give them my humble Service; and to Katharine; and to Mrs Walls; I am not

---

[1] "saved" is understood.

[2] Templeogue. A village in the parish of Tallaght, four miles south-west of Dublin city.

[3] Apparently he had turned the sheet over here; for the word "Dublin" is at top of second page, while the sentence here placed in square brackets has been added later at foot of first page.

[4] *Cf.* Letter XXX., Sept. 18, 1711.

te least bit in love with Mrs Walls. I suppose te Cares of te
Husband encrease with te fruitfullness of te Wife. I am grad at
halt[1] to hear of Ppts good Health: pray let her finish it by
drinking Waters. I hope Dd had her Bill, & has her money.
Remembr to write a due time before Me money is wanted;
& be good galls, dood dallars I mean, & no crying dallars.. I
heard somebody coming up Stairs, and forgot I was in te
Country; & I was afraid of a Visitor; that's one Advantage of
being here; that I am not teazd with Sollicitors.—My Service
to Dr Smith; [Molt the Chymist is my Acquaintance.][2] I sent
te Questions to him about Sr W. Raleighs Cordial, and the
Answer he returned is in these words *It is directly after Mr
Boyle's Receit.*[3] That Commission is performd; If he wants any
of it, Molt shall use him fairly. I suppose Smith is one of yr
Physicians. So now oor Lettr is fully and impartially answerd,
not as rascals answr me: I believe if I writt an Essay upon a Straw,
I should have a Shoal of Answerers; but no mattr for that;
Y see I can answr y without making any Reflections, as becomes
men of Learning. Well; but now for te Peace: why, we expect
it daily; but te French have te Staff in their own Hands, & we
trust to their Honesty: I wish it were otherwise. Things are now
in te way of being soon in te Extreams of well or ill. I hope and
believe the first. Ld Wharton is gone out of Town in a Rage,
and curses himself & friends for ruining themselves in defending
Ld Marl— and Godolphin, & taking Nottinghm into their favor.
He swears he will meddle no more during this Reign, a pretty
Speech at 66, & te Qu— is 20 years youngr; & now in very
good Health. For y must know her Health is fixt by a certain
Reason, that she has done with Braces (I must use te Expression)
and nothing ill has happend to her since; so she has a new
Lease of her Life. Read te Lettr to a Whig Lord.[4] Do y ever
read; why dont y say so; I mean does Dd read to ppt. Do y
walk. I think ppt should walk to Dd, as Dd reads to ppt. for
ppt oo must know is a good walker; but not so good as pdfr. I
intend to dine. to day with Mr Lewis but it threatens rain, &
I shall be too late to get a Lift; & I must write to te Bp of Cl.
tis now 10 in te morning, & this is all writt at a heat. Farewell
deelest lole deelest MD MD MD MD MD FW FW FW Me
Me Lele Me lele Me lele Me lele lele lele Me.

[1] "Glad at heart."
[2] Former versions put this before "My service to Dr Smith." Correct
position above.
[3] Underlined passage.
[4] *See* Letter XL.: *Some Reasons to Prove*, etc.

LETTER XLIX

[Endorsed: " To Mrs Dingley " &c., as before. Date of receipt, "July 8."]
49   Kensington. *Jul.* 1. 1712

I NEVER was in a worse Station for writing Letters, than this,
especially for writing to MD, since I left off my Journals; For I
go to Town early, and when I come home at night, I generally
go to Ld Masham, where Ld Tr. comes and we stay till past
twelve. But I am now resolved to write Journals again, thō
my Shouldr is not yet well, for I have still one or two itching
Pimples, and a little Pain now and then. It is now high Cherry
time with us; ·take notice is it so soon with you; & we have
early Apricocks, & Goseburyes are ripe. On Sunday Archdeacon
Parnel [1] came here to see me. It seems he has been ill for grief
of his Wives death, & has been 2 months at te Bath. He has a
mind to go to Dunkirk with Jack Hill, and I persuade him to
it, & have spoke to Hill to receive him; but I doubt he wont
have spirit to go. I have made Ford Gazeteer, and got 200ll a
year settled on the Employmt by te Secrtys of States [*sic*]
beside the Perquisites. It is te prettyest Employmt in Engd of
its bigness; yet te Puppy does not seem satisfyed with it. I
think People keep some Follyes to themselves till they have
Occasion to produce them. He thinks it not genteel enough, &
makes 20 difficultyes. Tis impossible to make any man easy:
His salary is pd him every week if he pleases, without Taxes
or Abatemts; he has little to do for it, He has a pretty Office,
with Coals, Candles, Paper &c; can frank what Lettrs he will;
and his Perquisites if he takes Care may be worth 100ll more.
I hear te Bp of Cl is landing, or landed in Engld; & I hope to
see him in a few days. I was to see Mrs Bradley [2] on Sunday
night. Her youngest son is marry [*sic*] to somebody worth
nothing; & her Daughtr was forced to leave Ldy Giffrd [*i.e.*
Giffard]; because she was striking up an Intrigue with a Footman,, who playd well upon the Flute. This is the Mothers
Account of it. Yesterday the old Bp of Worcester, [3] who pretends
to be a Prophet, went to te Queen by Appointmt, to prove to
Her Majesty out of Daniel and the Revelations, that 4 years
hence there would be a War of Religion: that the K. of France

---

[1] This amiable man, and elegant poet, was at this time Archdeacon of
Clogher, to which dignity Swift's friend the bishop had preferred him.
—D. L. P.

[2] *Cf.* Letters XXX., Sept. 18, 1711, and XLVIII.

[3] William Lloyd (1627–1717), Bishop of Worcester, one of the "seven
bishops."

would be a Protestant, and fight on their side, that th Popedom would be destroyd, &c, and declared he would be content to give up His Bishoprick if it were not true; Ld Tr. who told it me was by, and some others; and I am told, Ld Treasr confounded him sadly in his own Learning, wch made te old Fool very quarrelsom; he is near ninety years old. Old Bradley is fat and lusty, and has lost his Palsy: Have y seen Toland's Invitation to Dismal[1];? How do y like it? but it is an Imitation of Horace, and perhaps y don't understand Horace. Here has been a great Sweep of Employmts; and we expect still more Removalls. the Court seems resolved to make thorow work. Mr Hill[2] intended to sett out to morrow for Dunkirk of wch he is appointed Governr, but He tells me to day, that he can not go till Thursday or Fryday. I wish it were over. Mr Secrty tells me he is [? has] no fear at all that France will play tricks with us; If we have Dunkirk once, all is safe. We rayl now all against the Dutch, who indeed have acted like Knaves Fools and Madmen. Mr Secrty is soon to be made a Viscount; He desired I would draw te Preamble of his Patent; but I excused my self from a Work that might lose me a great deal of Reputation, and get me very little. we would fain have te Court make him an Earl, but it will not be, and therefore he will not take te Title of Bullenbrook,[3] which is lately extinct in the elder Branch of his Family. I have advised him to be called Ld Pomfret; but he thinks that Title is already in some other Family, and besides he objects that it is in Yorkshire where he has no Estate, but there is nothing in that; And I love Pomfret; Don't y love Pomfret? Why, tis in all our Historys, they are full of Pomfret Castle.[4] But what's all this to y; y dont care for this. Is goody Stoit come to London; I have not heard of her yet. Yr Dean of St Patr—[5] never had th manners to answer my Letter. I was tothr day to see Stearn[6] and his Wife; she is

[1] *T-l-nd's Invitation to Dismal to dine with the Calves-head club, imitated from Horace, Epist. V. Lib.* 1. John Toland (1670–1722) was a deist and a Whig; a native of Inishowen, co. Donegal. He was brought up a Catholic, but became a Protestant at sixteen. He was educated at Glasgow, Edinburgh, and Leyden, and became unpopular because of his unorthodox leanings. He wrote *Christianity not Mysterious.* "Dismal" is the Earl of Nottingham.

[2] Major-General John Hill: "Jack."

[3] Bolingbroke.

[4] The old Norman castle of Pomfret or Pontefract in the West Riding was the scene of the violent deaths of the Earl of Lancaster (1322), Richard II. (1400), and Earl Rivers (1483), besides sustaining two sieges in the Commonwealth wars.

[5] Dean Sterne.

[6] Enoch.

not half so handsom, as when I saw her with y in Dublin. They design to pass the Summer at a House Near Ld Sommers's, about a dozen miles off. Y never told me how my Lettr to Ld Treasr passes in Ireld. I suppose y are drinking at this time Temple-somethings Waters. Steel was arrested tother day for making a Lottery, directly agst an Act of Parlmt. He is now under Prosecution, but they think it will be droppt out of Pity. I believe he will very soon lose his Employmt, for he has been mighty impertinent of late in his Spectators, and I will never offer a Word in his behalf. Raymd writes me Word, that te Bp of Meath,[1] was going to summon me in order to Suspension, for absence ; if the Provost [2] had not prevented him. I am prettily rewarded for getting them their first fruits with a P—. We have had very little hot weathr during te whole Month of June; And for a Week past we have had a great deal of rain ; tho not every day. I am just now told that the Governr of Dunkirk has not orders yet to deliver up te Town to Jack Hill and his Forces, but expects them daily, this must putt off Hills Journy a while, and I do not like these Stoppings in such an Affair— Go get ee gone & drink ee waters if this Rain has not spoild [?] them, sawci doxi I have no more to say to oo at plesent but rove Pdfr; & MD, & Me, & Podefr will rove pdfr & MD & Me—I wish y had taken any Account when I sent mony to Mrs Brent, I believe I hant done it a great while Farewell dearest MD FW FW FW Me Me Me.

LETTER L

[Endorsed as last. Date of receipt, "July 23."]

50   Kensington. *July.* 17. 1712.

I AM weary of living in this Place, and glad I am to leave it so soon. Th Qu— goes on Tuesday to Windsor, and I shall follow in 3 or 4 days after. I can do nothing here, going early to London, and coming late from it and supping at Ldy Mashams. I din'd to day with te D. of Argyle [3] at Cue, and would not go to te Court to night because of writing to MD. te Bp of Clogher has been here this fortnight ; I see him as often as I can. poor Master Ash [4] has a sad Redness in his Face, it is St Anthony's fire, his face all swelld ; and will break in his Cheek, but no danger.—

---

[1] Moreton. *See* Letter V., Oct. 5, 1710 (note).
[2] Dr. Benjamin Pratt.
[3] *See* Letter XI., Dec. 22, 1710.
[4] Son of the Bishop of Clogher.

Since Dunkirk has been in our Hands, Grubstreet has been very fruitfull; pdfr has writt 5 or 6 Grubstreet papers this last week.. Have y seen Tolands Invitation to Dismal, or a Hue & cry after Dismal, or a Ballad on Dunkirk, or an Argument that Dunkirk is not in our Hands Poh, y have seen nothing.—I am dead here with th Hot weathr, yet I walk every night home, & believe it does me good. but my Shouldr is not yet right, itchings, & scratchings, and small akings. Did I tell y that I have made Ford Gazeteer, with 200ll a year Salary, besides Perquisites. I had a Lettr lately from Parvisol, who says my Canal looks very finely; I long to see it; but no Apples; all blasted again. He tells me there will be a Triennial Visitation in August. I must send Raymd anothr Proxy. So now will answr ee [or "oo"] Rettle, N. 33, dated June 17. Ppt writes as well as ever for all her waters I wish I had never come here, as often and as heartily as Ppt, what had I to do here? I have heard of te Bp's making me uneasy, but I did not think it was because I never writt to him. A little would make me write to him; but I don't know what to say. I find I am obliged to the Provost for keeping the Bp from being impertinent.—Yes Maram Dd, but oo would not be content with Letters flom pdfr of 6 lines, or 12 either fais. I hope Ppt will have done with te waters soon, and find benefit by them; I believe if they were as far off as Wexford they would do as much good; For I take the Journy to contribute as much as any thing. I can assure y te Bp of Cloghers being here does not in te least affect my staying or going. I never talkt to Higgins but once in th Street; and I believe he and I shall hardly meet but by chance. What care I whethr my Lettr to Ld Treasr be commended there or no? why does not somebody among y answer it, as 3 or 4 have done here (I am now sitting with nothing but my Nightgown for heat). Ppt shall have a great Bible. I have put it down in my memlandums, just now. and Dd shall be repaid her tother Book; but patience, all in good time; y are so hasty a dog would &c. So Ppt has neither won nor lost. Why mun, I play sometimes too, at Picket that is, Picquett I mean; but very seldom.—Out late, why 'tis onely at Ldy Mashams, and that's in our Town: but I never come late here from London, except once in rain when I could not get a Coach.—We have had very little Thunder here; none these 2 Months; Why pray, Madam Philosopher, how did th Rain hinder te Thunder from doing harm, I suppose it ssquencht it.—So here comes ppt aden with her little watry postscript; o Rold, dlunken Srut drink pdfrs health ten times in a molning; you are a whetter, fais I sup MDs 15 times evly molning in milk porridge. lele's fol oo now, and lele's fol ee Rettle, & evly kind of sing; and now I must say something else.—Y hear Secty St John is made Vicount Bullinbrook; I could hardly persuade him to take that Title, because te eldest Branch of his Family had it in an Earldom, & it was last year extinct; If he did not take it I advised him to be Ld Pomfret; wch I think is a noble Title; y hear of it often in te *Chronicles* [1] Pomfret Castle; but we believed it was among te Titles of some other Ld. Jack Hill sent his Sister a Pattern of a head-dress from Dunkirk; it was like our Fashion 20 years ago, onely not quite so high, and lookt very ugly. I have made Trap [2] Chapln to Ld Bullinbroke, and he is mighty happy & thankfull for it.—Mr Addison returnd me my visit this morning; He lives in our Town.. I shall be mighty retired and mighty busy for a while at Windsor. Pray why dont MD go to Trim, and see Laracor; and give me an Account of te Garden & te River, & te Holly, & te Cherry trees on te River walk.—[3]

19. I could not send this Lettr last Post, being called away before I could fold or finish it. I dined yesterday with Ld Treasr, satt with him till 10 at night, yet could not find a Minute for some Business I had with him. He brought me to Kensington, and Ld Bulingbrook would not let me go away till 2, and I am now in bed very lazy and sleepy at nine. I must shave head & Face, & meet Ld Bullinbrook [4] at 11; and dine again with Ld Tr. To day there will be anothr Grub; a Letter from te Pretendr to a Whig Ld.[5] Grubstreet has but ten days to live, then an Act of Parlmt takes place, that ruins it, by taxing every half Sheet a halfpenny: We have news just come, but not te Particulars, that te Earl of Albermarle [6] at te head of 8 thousd Dutch is beaten lost te greatest part of his men, & himself a Prisoner. This perhaps may cool their Courage, & make them think of a Peace. te D. of Ormd has got abundance of Credit by

---

[1] Underlined.

[2] *See* Letter XIII., Jan. 7, 1710-11.

[3] After a long dash, he begins "19" on same line.

[4] He had again spelt it with only one "l," but scratched that form out in favour of this.

[5] *A Supposed Letter from the Pretender to another Whig Lord*, according to Mr. Aitken.

[6] Arnold Joost van Keppel (1670-1718), Heer van der Voorst in Guelderland, Baron van Keppel, made Earl of Albemarle 1696-7. On the death of King William hé returned to Holland and took his place among the nobles of that country. His defeat was "at Denain; where the Confederates—being weakened by the absence of the Duke of Ormond, with the British forces, taking possession of Dunkirk—were attacked in their camp by Marshal Villars" (D. L. P).

his good Conduct of Affairs in Flanders. We had a good deal
of Rain last night, very refreshing—Tis late & I must rise.
Don't play at Ombre in yr waters Sollah, Farwell dealest MD
MD MD MD FW FW Me Me Me lele lele lele —

LETTER LI

[Endorsed as last. Date of receipt, " Augst 14."]

51.   London. *Aug.* 7.[1] 1712.

I HAD yr N. 32 at Windsor: I just read it, and immediatly seald
it up again, and shall read it no more this twelvemonth at least.
the Reason of my Resentmt at it is, because you talk as glibly
of a Thing as it if were done, which for ought I know, is further
from being done than ever, since I hear not a word of it; thō
the Town is full of it, and the Court always giving me Joy and
Vexation. You might be sure I would have let you know as
soon as it was done; but I believe you fancyed I would affect
not to tell it you, but let you learn it from News Papers, and
Reports. I remember onely there was something in yr Letter
about Me's money, and that shall be taken care of on the other
side. I left Windsor on Monday last, upon Ld Bolingbroke's
being gone to France, and comebodyes being here that I ought
often to consult with in an Affair I am upon; but that Person
talks of returning to Windsor again and I believe I shall follow
him. I am now in a hedge Lodging, very busy, as I am every day
till noon; so that this Lettr is like to be short, and you are not
to blame me these 2 Months, for I protest If I study ever so
hard, I believe I can not in that time compass what I am upon.[2]
We have a Feaver both here and at Windsor, which hardly any
body misses, but it lasts not above 3 or 4 days, and kills nobody.[3]
The Qu— had 40 Servants down of it at once. I dined yesterday
with Ld Tr— but could do no Business, thō he sent for me, I
thought on purpose; but he desires I will dine with him again
to day. Windsor is a most delightfull Place, and at this time
abounds in Dinners. My Lodgings there look upon Eaton and
the Thames, I wish I were Owner of them, they belong to a

[1] The figure originally written is obliterated; and "7" is written above,
in the watery ink in which Esther Johnson has hitherto written her
endorsements. Above that again, in same ink, are the explanatory words:
"Podefar was misken" (*sic*)—apparently meaning Swift was mistaken.
[2] His *History of the Four last Years of Queen Anne.*—D. L. P [This
received its title later—it was published after Swift's death.]
[3] Mr. Aitken suggests it was influenza.

Prebend. Gd knows what is in your Letter, and if it be not answered, whose fault is it sawcidallars..—Do you know, that Grubstreet is dead and gone last Week; No more Ghosts or Murders now for Love or Money. I played it pretty close the last Fortnight, and publisht at least 7 penny Papers of my own, besides some of other Peoples. But now, every single half Sheet pays a half-penny to te Qu—. The Observator is fallen, the Medleys are jumbled together with the Flying-post, the Examiner is deadly sick, the Spectator keeps up, and doubles it [*i.e.* its] price. I know not how long it will hold. Have you seen the red Stamp the Papers are marqued with. Methinks it is worth a halfpenny the stamping it. Ld Bolinbroke & Prior set out for France last Saterday, My Lds business is to hasten te Peace before the Dutch are too much mauld; and to hinder France from carrying the Jest of beating them, too far. Have you seem the 4th part of John Bull; it is equall to te rest, and extremely good. Th Bp of Cloghrs son[1] has been ill of St Anthony's Fire, but is now quite well; I was afraid his Face would be spoild, but it is not. Dilly is just as he used to be, and puns as plentifully and as bad; the two Brothers see one another, but I think not te two Sisters.[2] Raymd writ to me, that he intended to invite you to Trim. are you, have you, will you be there? won't oo pool laratol[3]; Parvisol says I shall have no fruit. Blasts have taken away all. Pray observe te Cherry Trees on te River walk; but oo are too lazy to take such a Journy. If you have not your Letters in due time for 2 Months hence, impute it to my being tosticated between this and Windsor. And pray send me again te State of MD's money; for I will not look to yr Lettr for it; Poor Ld Winchelsea is dead,[4] to my great Grief, he was a worthy honest Gentleman, & particular Friend of mine; and what is yet worse, my old Acquaintance Mrs Finch[5] is now Countess of Winchelsea, the Title being fallen to her Husband, but without much Estate.—I have been poring my Eyes all this morning, and it is now past 2 afternoon, so I shall take a little walk in te Park. Do y play at Ombre still, or is that off by Mrs Stoits absence, and Mrs Manly's Grief Somebody was telling me of a strang [? strange] Sister that Mrs Manly has got in Ireld, who disappointed you all, about her

---

[1] Master Ashe. *See* Letter L.
[2] In-law: Mrs. Dilly and the bishop's wife.
[3] "Poor Laracor."
[4] *See* Letter XII., Dec. 24, 1710. Died Aug. 5, according to " G. E C." 's *Complete Peerage.*
[5] *See* Letter XXIV., May 29, 1711.

being handsom; My Service to Mrs Walls—Farewell deelest
MD MD MD FW FW FW Me Me Me Me Me lele logues both,
rove pdfr.

LETTER LII

[Endorsed as last. The postmark " WINDSOR SE/20 " is very plain.
Date of receipt, " Oct. 1st At Portraune." Portraune, or Portraine, is
twelve miles north of Dublin City, on the coast, just south of Rogerstown
Inlet, and directly opposite Lambay Island.]

52   Windsor. *Septr*. 15th. 1712.

I NEVER was so long without writing to MD as now, since I left
them, nor ever will again while I am able to write. I have
expected from one week to anothr, that something would be
done in my own Affairs, but nothing at all is nor I dont know
when any thing will, or whethr ever at all, so slow are people at
doing Favors.—I have been much out of order of late with te
old giddyness in my Head. I took a vomit for it 2 days ago, and
will take another about a day or two hence. I have eat mighty
little Fruit, yet I impute my disorder to that little, and shall
henceforth wholly forbear it. I am engaged in a long work, and
have done all I can of it, and wait for some Papers from th
Ministry for materialls for the rest, & they delay me as if it
were a Favor I asked of them; so that I have been idle here
this good while, and it happened in a right time, when I was
too much out of order to study. One is kept constantly out of
humor by a thousand unaccountable things in publick Proceedings[1] and when I reason with some Friends, we cannot
conceive how Affairs can last as they are; God only knows; but
it is a very melancholy Subject for those who have any near
concern in it. I am again endeavoring as I was last year to
keep People from breaking to pieces, upon a hundred misunderstandings. One cannot withold them from drawing different ways
while the Enemy is watching to destroy both. See how my
Stile is altered by living & thinking & talking among these
People., instead of my Canal & river walk, and Willows. I lose
all my money here among te Ladyes, so that I never play when
I can help it, being sure to lose; I have lost 5ll the five weeks
I have been here, I hope Ppt is luckyer at Picquet with te Dean &
Mrs Walls. The Dean never answerd my Letter thō. I have
clearly forgot whethr I sent a Bill for Me in any of my last Letters;
I think I did; pray let me know, & always give me timely Notice.
I wait here but to see what they will do for me; and whenever
Prefermts are given from me, as hope saved I will come over.——[2]

---

[1] ? semicolon worn off paper.   [2] He begins "18th" on same line.

18. I have taken a Vomit to day; and hope I shall be bettr. I have been very giddy since I writ what is before; yet not as I used to be, more frequent, but not so violent. Yesterday we were allarmed with te Queens being ill. She had and [*i.e.* an] Aguish & feaverish Fitt and you never saw such Countenances as we all had; such dismal Melancholy. Her Physicians from Town[1] were sent for; but towards night she grew better, to day she misst her Feet [? Fit], and was up; We are not now in any Fear It will be at worst but an Ague; and we hope even that will not return. Ld Treasr would not come hear [*i.e.* here] from London because it would make a Noise, if he came before his usuall time, which is Saterday, & he goes away on Mondays. The Whigs have lost a great support in te E. of Godolphin.[2] Tis a good Jest to hear te Ministers talk of him now with Humanity and Pity, because he is dead, and can do them no more hurt. Ldy Orkney te late King's Mistress,[3] who lives at a fine place 5 miles from hence calld Cliffden, and I are grown mighty Acquaintance. She is te wisest woman I ever saw, & Ld Treasr made great use of her Advise [*sic*] in te late change of Affairs. I hear, Ld Marlbrow is growing ill of his Diabetis, which if it be true, may soon carry him off; and then te Ministry will be something more at ease. MD has been a long time without writing to pdfr thō they have not the same Cause; tis seven weeks since yr last came to my hands, wch was N. 32, that y may not be mistaken; I hope ppt has not wanted her health; Y were then drinking waters. The Doctor tells me I must go into a Course of Steel, tho I have not te Spleen; for that they can never give me thō I have as much Provocation to it as any man alive. Bernage's Regimt is broke, but he is upon half pay: I have not seen him this long time; but I suppose he is overrun with Melancholy. My Ld Shrewsbury is certainly designed to be Governor of Ireld; and I believe te Dutchess will please te people there mightily. The Irish Whig Leaders promise great Things to themselves from His Governmt; but care shall be taken, if possible, to prevent them. Mrs Fenton has writ to me that she has been forced to leave Ldy G— [*i.e.* Giffard] and come to Town for a Rheumatism; that Ldy does not love to be

---

[1] Arbuthnot and Freind.

[2] He died Sept. 15, 1712.

[3] Lady Elizabeth Villiers; on whom King William settled an estate in Ireland worth 25,995*l.* a year.—N. She was daughter to Sir Edward Villiers, knight-marshal, and sister to the first Earl of Jersey; and in 1695 she had married Lord (christian name) George Hamilton (fifth son of William, third Duke of Hamilton), who was soon afterwards made Earl of Orkney. He was born 1666, and died 1737.

troubled with Sick People. Mrs Fenton writes to me as one dying, & desires I would think of her son; I have not answered her Lettr; She is retired to Mrs Povey's.—Is my Aunt[1] alive yet; and do you ever see her. I suppose she has forgot te Loss of her son. Is Raymds new house quite finished; and does he squander as he used to do? Has he yet spent all his Wive's Fortune? I hear there are 5 or 6 People putting strongly in for my Livings; God help them. But if ever te Court should give me any thing, I woud recommend Raymd to te D. of Ormd, not for any particular Friendship to him, but because it would be proper for te Ministr of Trim to have Laracor. You may keep te gold studded Snuffbox now, for my Brothr Hill, Governr of Dunkirk has sent me te finest that ever you saw; tis allowed at Court, that none in Engld comes near it, thō it did not cost above 30ll[2] And te Dutchess of Hamilton has made me Pockets for[3] like a womans, with a Belt and Buckle, for y know I wear no wastcoat in Summer; & there are severall divisions, and one on purpose for my box, oh ho,— We have had most delightfull Weathr this whole week, but illness and vomiting have hindred me from sharing in a great Part of it. Ldy Masham made te Queen send to Kensington for some of her preserved Ginger for me, wch I take in te morning, and hope it will do me good. Mrs Brent sent me a Letter by a young Fellow a Printer, desiring I would recommend him here, which you may tell her, I have done; but I cannot promise what will come of it, for it is necessary they should be made free here[4] before they can be employd; I remembr I put te Boy prentice to Brent. I hope Parvisol has sett my Tyths well this year: He has writt nothing to me about it; pray talk to him of it when y see him: & lett him give me an Account how Things are. I suppose te Corn is now off th Ground. I hope he has sold that great ugly Horse. Why don't you sell to him? He keeps me at Charges for Horses that I can never ride; yrs is lame, and will never be good for any thing. The Qu will stay here about a Month longer I suppose, but Ldy Masham will go in ten days to lye in at Kensington, poor Creature she fell down in te Court here t'other day, she woud needs walk a cross it, upon some displeasure with her

---

[1] See Letter XLII., Feb. 24.

[2] "This is the box," says "B," "on the bottom of which the goose and snail were painted, that gave occasion to the jest and repartee between Swift and Lord Oxford." A particular discription of the box is contained in a letter to General Hill, dated Aug. 12, 1712.

[3] ? "it" omitted.

[4] Obtain the freedom of the city of London.—N.

Chairmen; and was like to be spoild, so near her time, but we hope all is over, for a black Eye and a sore side; tho I shall not be at ease till she is brought to bed.—I find I can fill up a Lettr some way or other without a Journall. If I had not a Spirit naturally cheerfull, I should be very much discontented at a thousand Things. Pray God preserve MD's Health, & Pdfrs; and that I may live far from te Envy and discontent that attends those who are thought to have more Favor at Courts than they really possess. Love pdfr, who loves MD above all things. farewell deelest ten thousand times deelest MD MD MD FW FW Me Me Me Me lele lele lele

lele [in position of signature]

LETTER LIII

[Endorsed as last. Date of receipt, " Octr. 18 At Portraune."]

53　　　　　　　　　　　　　　　London. *Octbr.* 9. 1712.

I HAVE left Windsor these ten days, and am deep in Pills with Assa fetida, and a Steel bitter drink; and I find my Head much better than it was; I was very much discouraged, for I used to be ill for 3 or 4 days together, ready to totter as I walked. I take 8 pills a day; and have taken I believe 150 already. Th Qu, Ld Treasr, Ldy Masham and I were all ill togethr; but we are now all better; onely Ldy Masham expects every day to ly in att Kensington. There was never such a Lump of Lyes spread about te Town togethr as now; I doubt not, but you will have them in Dublin before this comes to y; and all without te least grounds of Truth.— I have been mightily put backward in something I am writing, by my Illnesss, but hope to fetch it up so as to be ready when te Parlmt meets. Ld Treasr has hd an ugly fit of te Rheumatism, but is now qnear uite well, I was playing at one and thirty [1] with him and his Family tother night. he gave us all 12 pence apiece to begin with: it put me in mind of Sr W T [*i.e.* Sir Wm. Temple]. [2] I askt both him & Ldy Masham seriously whethr te Qu— were at all inclined to a Dropsy, and they positively assured me she was not, so did Her Physician

---

[1] An ancient and very favourite game at cards, much resembling vingt-un.—Halliwell (*Century Dictionary*).

[2] " Sir William Temple treated Swift with so little liberality, after encouraging him to hope he would provide for him, that it was like giving him a shilling to begin the world with." Thus Hawkesworth; but another story (by Lord Macaulay) is that Sir William used to start everybody with a supply of money—just as Harley did here.

Arbuthnot who always attends her. yet these Devils have spread, that she has holes in her Legs, and runs at her Navel; and I know not what. Arbuthnot has sent me from Windsor a pretty Discourse upon Lying, and I have ordered te Printer to come for it. It is A Proposall for publishing a curious Piece called te Art of Politicall Lying. in two Volumes &c. and then there is an Abstract of the first Volume,[1] just like those Pamphlets thy call te works of te Learned.[2] Pray get it when it comes out. Th Qu has a little of te Gout in one of her Hands; I believe she will say [*i.e.* stay] a Month still at Windsor. Ld Tr shewd me te kindest Lettr from her in te World. by which I pickt out one Secret, that there will be soon made some Knights of te Garter; y know anothr is fallen by Ld Godolphin's Death; He will be buryed in a day or two at Westminster Abby. I saw Tom Leigh[3] in Town once; te Bp Cl. has taken his[4] Lodging for th Winter; they are all well.. I hear there are in Town abundance of People from Ireld; half a dozen Bishops at least. Th poor old Bp of London[5] at past fourscore fell down backwards, going up Stairs, and I think broke or crackt his Scull; yet is now recovering. Th Town is as empty as at Midsummr; & if I had not occasion for Physick I would be at Windsor still. Did I tell y of Ld Rivers's[6] Will; He has left Legacy to about 20 paultry old whores by name, and not a Farthing to any Friend, Dependent or Relation; he has left from his onely Child Ldy Barrimore[7] her Mothers Estate, and given th whole to his Heir Male a Popish Priest, a Second Cousin, who is now Earl Rivers,[8] and whom he used in his Life like a Footman. after him it goes to his chief Wench and Bastard. Ld Treasr & Ld Chambrln[9] are Executors of this

---

[1] This is part of the *Miscellany*, which the dean printed in conjunction with Mr. Pope. . . .—N.

[2] *The History of the Works of the Learned: or, An Impartial Account of Books lately printed in all parts of Europe. Done by several hands.* A periodical publication that appeared from 1699 till 1711.

[3] See Letter XXXV., Nov. 20, 1711.

[4] Word slightly scratched over.

[5] See Letter XXVIII., Aug. 24, 1711. " He fought for Charles I., and at the Revolution took command of the volunteer troop that escorted the Princess Anne to Nottingham " (D. L. P.).

[6] See Letter XI., Dec. 12, 1710.

[7] Elizabeth (*d.* 1713-14), daughter of Richard Savage, fourth Earl Rivers (whose death has just been recorded), married, unknown to her father (1706), James Barry, fourth Earl of Barrymore: she was his second wife, and he had a third.

[8] John Savage (1665-*c.* 1735), son of Richard, younger son of second earl, was a Catholic priest who became fifth and last Earl Rivers.

[9] The Duke of Shrewsbury. See Letter XX., April 13, 1711.

hopefull Will. I loved te Man, and detest his Memory. We hear nothing of Peace yet. I believe verily the Dutch are so wilfull because they are told te Qu— cannot live.—I had poor MD Letters N. 3 at Windsor; [but I could not answr it then poopdfr wam vely kick then, and besides it was a very inconvenient place to send Lettrs from. Oo thought to come home te same day, and stayd a month; that was a sign your Place was agreeable;] [1] I should love such a sort of Jaunt. Is that lad Swanton [2] a little more fixed than he used to be? I think you like te Girl very well. She has left off her grave airs I suppose.— I am now told Ld Godolphin was buryed last night—[O poo ppt,[3] lay down ee [4] heads aden; fais I flodive [5] ee: I always reckon if y are ill I shall hear it; & therefore hen oo are silent, I reckon all is well.] [6]—I believe I scaped te new feaver for te same reason that pappt [or "poppt," or "pooppt"] did because I am not well, but why should Dd scape it pray. she is melthigal [7] oo know and ought to have te Feavr; but I hope it is now too late & she won't have it at all. Some Physicians here talk very melancholy, & think it foreruns te Plague; wch is actually at Hamburgh. I hoped ppt would have done with her illness; but I think we both have tht Faculty never to part with a Disorder for ever; we are very constant. I have had my Giddiness 23 years by fits—Will Mrs Raymd never have done lying in. He intends to leave Beggars enough; for I dare say he squandred away te best part of his Fortune already, & is not out of debt. I had a Lettr from him lately

Oct. 11. Ld Tr sent for me yesterday & te day before to sit with him, because he is not quite well enough to go abroad; & I could not finish my Lettr—How te duce come I to be so exact in Me Money; just 17s & 8d more than due. I believe y cheat me. If Hawkshaw [8] does not pay te Interest, I will have te Principle. pray speak to Parvisol, & have his Advice what I should do about it. Service to Mrs Stoit & Catharine & Mrs Walls—Ppt makes a petition with meny Apologyes. John Danvers you know is Ldy

[1] Obliterated.

[2] Mrs. Swanton was his cousin Willoughby's eldest daughter; but her only child was a daughter, Honoria.

[3] Ppt is the symbol which Deane Swift renders "Stella"—a name Swift never used for Esther Johnson till long after the *Journal* was finished. The pronunciation would appear to have been "poppet" or "pappet."

[4] Or "oo."

[5] "Forgive." Word hitherto undeciphered.

[6] Obliterated.

[7] Probably signifying "an healthy gal."

[8] *See* Letter VI., Oct. 16, 1710.

G—'s [*i.e.* Giffard's] Friend. Th rest I never heard of. I tell you what. as things are at present I cannot possibly speak to Ld Tr for any body. I need tell you no more.—Something or nothing will be done in my own Affairs: if te former, I will be a Sollicitr for yr Sistr. if te Latter, I have done with Courts for ever. Opportunityes will often fall in my way if I am us'd well. and I will then make it my business. It is my delight to do good Offices for people who want & deserve, and a tenfod delight to do it to a relation [of Ppts whose Affairs she has so at heart.][1] I have taken down his name & his Case (not her Case) and whenever a proper time comes. I will do all I can—zats enough to say when I can do no more. and I beg ee [or "oo"] pardon a sousand times that I cannot [2] do bettr. I hope te Dean of St P— [3] is well of his Feaver. He has never writ to me; I am glad of it, pray don't desire him to write.—I have dated yr Bill late, because it must not commence ung oomens till te 1st of November next. O [fais].[4] I must be [ise iss fais must I, else Me will cheat pdfr] [5] Arc y good Huswifes, & Readers, are y walkers? I know you are Gamesters; Are you drinkers? Are you—[O Rold, I must go no further [6] fear of aboozing fine Radyes] [7]—Parvisol has never sent me one word how he sett this years Tyths; pray ask whethr Tyths sett well or ill this year. Bp Killaloo tells me Wool bears a good rate in Ired; but how is Corn.[8] I dined yestrday with Ldy Orkney, & we sate alone from 2 till 11 at night. Y have heard of her I suppose.[9] I have 20 Lettrs on my hands, & am so lazy & so busy I cant answer them; & they grow upon me for severall months. Have I any Apples at Laracor? Tis strange every year should blast them when I took so much care for Shelter. Ld Bolingbroke has been idle at his Country house this Fortnight wch puts me backwards in a Business I have. I am got into an ordinary room two pair of Stairs, & see no body if I can help it, yet some Puppyes have found me out, and my Man is not such an Artist as Patrick at denying me. Patrick has been solliciting to come to me again: but in vain—The Printer has been here with some of te new whims printd; & has taken up my time. I am just going out, &

---

[1] Obliterated.
[2] A slight scratch over the words from and including "I beg" to here.
[3] Dr. Sterne.
[4], [5] Obliterated.
[6] "for" omitted.
[7] Obliterated.
[8] On the price of which the value of the Doctor's tithes depended. —D. L. P. For Bishop of Killaloe, *see* Letter VI., Oct. 17, 1710.
[9] *See* Letter LII., Sept. 18.

can only bid ee [or "oo"] farewell. [Farewell deelest ickle MD
MD MD MD FW FW FW FW Me Me Me
Me lele deel Me lele lele
lele sollahs bose][1]

LETTER LIV

[The original of this Letter is missing; therefore we follow the text of
Hawkesworth—quarto edition, 1766.]

London, *Oct.* 28, 1712.

I HAVE been in physic this month, and have been better these
three weeks. I stop my physic, by the doctor's orders, till he
sends me farther directions. D.D. grows [a] politician, and
longs to hear the peace is proclaimed. I hope we shall have it
soon, for the Dutch are fully humbled; and Prior is just come
over from France for a few days; I suppose, upon some important affair. I saw him last night, but had no private talk
with him. Stocks rise upon his coming. As for my stay in
England, it cannot be long now, and so tell my friends. The parliament will not meet till after Christmas, and by that time the
work I am doing will be over, and then nothing shall keep
me. I am very much discontented at Parvisol, about neglecting
to sell my horses, &c.

Lady Masham is not yet brought to-bed; but we expect it
daily. I dined with her to-day. Lord Bolingbroke returned about
two months ago, and Prior about a week; and goes back (Prior
I mean) in a few days. Who told you of my snuff-box and
pocket? Did I?[2] I had a letter to-day from Dr. Coghill,[3] desiring
me to get Rapho for dean Sterne, and the deanery for myself.
I shall indeed; I have such obligations to Sterne. But, however,
if I am asked, who will make a good bishop, I shall name him
before any body. Then comes another letter, desiring I would
recommend a provost, supposing that Pratt[4] (who has been
here about a week) will certainly be promoted; but, I believe,
he will not. I presented Pratt to lord treasurer, and truly young
Molyneux[5] would have had me present him too; but I directly
answered him I would not, unless he had business with him.

---

[1] Obliterated.
[2] *See* Letter LII., Sept. 18.
[3] *See* Letter XXVI., July 1, 1711.
[4] *See* Letter II., etc.
[5] Samuel, son of William Molyneux, Esq., the friend and correspondent
of Mr. Locke. Mr. Samuel Molyneux was afterwards secretary to George,
Prince of Wales. He married Lady Elizabeth Capell, daughter of Algernon,
Earl of Essex, and died about 1782.—B.

He is the son of one Mr. Molyneux, of Ireland. His father wrote a book[1]; I suppose you know it. Here is the duke of Marlborough going out of England (Lord knows why) which causes many speculations. Some say he is conscious of guilt, and dare not stand it. Others think he has a mind to fling an odium on the government, as who should say, that one, who has done such great services to his country, cannot live quietly in it, by reason of the malice of his enemies. I have helped to patch up these people together once more. God knows how long it may last. I was to-day at a trial between lord Lansdown[2] and lord Carteret,[3] two friends of mine. It was in the Queen's-Bench, for about six thousand pounds a year (or nine I think). I sat under lord chief justice Parker, and his pen falling down, I reached it up. He made me a low bow; and I was going to whisper him, that *I had done good for evil, for he would have taken mine from me.*[4] I told it to lord treasurer and Bolingbroke. Parker would not have known me, if several lords on the bench, and in the court, bowing, had not turned every body's eyes, and set them a whispering. I owe the dog a spite, and will pay him in two months at farthest, if I can. So much for that. But you must have chat, and I must say every sorry thing that comes into my head. They say the queen will stay a month longer at Windsor. These devils of Grubstreet rogues, that write the *Flying-Post* and *Medley*, in one paper, will not be quiet. They are always mauling lord treasurer, lord Bolingbroke, and me. We have the dog under prosecution, but Bolingbroke is not active enough; but I hope to swinge him. He is a Scotch rogue, one Ridpath.[5] They get out upon bail, and write on. We take them again, and get fresh bail; and so it goes round. They say some learned Dutchman has wrote a book, proving, by civil law, that we do them wrong by this peace; but I shall shew, by plain reason, that we have suffered the wrong, and not they. I toil like a horse, and have hundreds of letters still to read: and squeeze a line perhaps out of each, or at least the seeds of a line. Strafford[6] goes back to Holland in a day or two, and I hope our peace is very near. I have about thirty pages

---

[1] *The Case of Ireland's being bound by Acts of Parliament in England* stated, 1698, 8vo.—B.

[2] George Granville. *See* Letters XIV., Jan. 17, 1710-11, and XXXVII., Dec. 29, 1711 (note).

[3] *See* Letter XII., Jan. 4, 1710-11.

[4] *See* Letter XXXVI., Dec. 13, 1711.

[5] George Ridpath (*d.* 1726), Whig journalist, editor of the *Flying Post*, or *Postman.* He afterwards escaped to Holland.

[6] Formerly Lord Raby. *See* Letter XVIII., March 15, 1710-11.

more to write (that is to be extracted) which will be sixty in print. It is the most troublesome part of all, and I cannot keep myself private, tho' I stole into a room up two pair of stairs, when I came from Windsor; but my present man has not yet learned his lesson of denying me discreetly.

30th. The duchess of Ormond found me out to-day, and made me dine with her. Lady Masham is still expecting. She has had a cruel cold. I could not finish my letter last post for the soul of me. Lord Bolingbroke has had my papers these six weeks, and done nothing to them. Is Tisdall yet in the world? I propose writing controversies, to get a name with posterity. The duke of Ormond will not be over these three or four days. I design to make him join with me in settling all right among our people. I have ordered the duchess to let me have an hour with the duke at his first coming, to give him a true state of persons and things. I believe the duke of Shrewsbury will hardly be declared your governor yet; at least, I think so now; but resolutions alter very often. Duke Hamilton gave me a pound of snuff to-day, admirable good. I wish D.D. had it; and Ppt. too, if she likes it. It cost me a quarter of an hour of his politick, which I was forced to hear. Lady Orkney is making me a writing table of her own contrivance, and a bed night-gown. She is perfectly kind, like a mother. I think the d[evil] was in it the other day, that I should talk to her of an ugly squinting cousin of her's; and the poor lady herself, you know, squints like a dragon. The other day we had a long discourse with her about love; and she told us a saying of her sister Fitzharding,[1] which I thought excellent, that *in men desire begets love*; and *in women love begets desire*. We have abundance of our old criers still hereabouts. I hear every morning your woman with the old sattin and taffata, &c. the fellow with old coats, s s suits,[2] or cloaks. Our weather is abominable of late. We have not two tolerable days in twenty. I have lost money again at ombre, with lord Orkney[3] and others; yet, after all, this year I have lost but three and twenty shillings; so that, considering card-money, I am no loser.

Our society hath not yet renewed their meetings. I hope we shall continue to do some good this winter; and lord treasurer promises the academy for reforming our language shall soon go

---

[1] Barbara (c. 1656–1708), eldest daughter of Sir Edward Villiers, Knight-Marshal, married John Berkeley, fourth Viscount Fitzhardinge of Bere-haven, who died 1712.

[2] The three S's probably represent the hawker's drawl.

[3] *See* Letter LII., Sept. 18, note to "Lady Orkney."

forward. I must now go hunt those dry letters for materials. You will see something very notable I hope. So much for that. God Almighty bless you.

LETTER LV

[Endorsed as Letter LIII. Date of receipt, " Nov. 26 just come from Portraine." Further note: " The band box plot. D. Hamilton's Murther."]

55   London. *Novbr.* 15th, 1712.

BEFORE this comes to your Hands, you will have heard of the most terrible Accident that hath almost ever happened. This morning at 8, my man brought me word that D. [*i.e.* the Duke of] Hamilton [1] had fought with Ld Mohun,[2] & killd him, and was brought home wounded. I immediatly sent him to the Dukes house in St James's Square, but the Porter could hardly answer for tears; and a great Rabble was about te House. In short, they fought at 7 this morning the Dog Mohun was killd on the Spot, and will [? while] the Duke was over him Mohun shortening his Sword stabbd him in at the Shoulder to te heart: the Duke was helpt towards the Cake-house [3] by th Ring in Hide park (where they fought [4], and dyed on te Grass before he could reach te House, & was brought home in his Coach by 8, while te poor Dutchess was asleep. Mackartney [5] & one Hamilton [6] were te Seconds; who fought likewise, and are both fled. I am told, that a footman of Ld Mohun's stabbd D. Hamilton, & some say Macartney did so too. Mohun gave te affront, & yet sent te Challenge. I am infinitly concerned for th poor duke who was a frank honest good natured man, I loved him very well, & think he loved me better, He that [? had] te greatest mind in te world to have me go with him to France,[7] but durst not tell it me; & those he did sd I could not be spared, wch was true. They have removed te poor Dutchess to a Lodging in te Neighborhood,

[1] *See* Letter XXVII., July 29, 1711, and note.

[2] Charles Mohun (*c.* 1675–1712), fourth Baron Mohun of Okehampton. Twice tried for murder, by the House of Peers, before he was twenty. Colonel of a regiment of foot. His second wife was widow of a Colonel Griffith, and daughter of "old Dr. Lawrence" (*see* Letter XLIII., March 14, 1711-12). His first wife and Hamilton's second were nieces and co-heiresses of the first Earl of Macclesfield, and there had been protracted litigation in Chancery between Hamilton and Mohun.

[3] Of this house, still [*i.e.* in Nichols's time] known by the name of *The Cheesecake-house*, see two views in *Gent. Mag.*, vol. lxxi., p. 401, and vol. lxxii., p. 105.—N.

[4] The close of the parenthesis omitted.

[5] *i.e.* Maccartney. *See* Letter XI., Dec. 13, 1710, and note.

[6] *See* next Letter.

[7] The duke was about to be sent as ambassador to Paris.

where I have been with her two hours, and am just come away. I never saw so melancholy a Scene For indeed all Reasons for real grief belong to her, nor is it possible for any one to be a greater loser in all regards. She has moved my very soul. The Lodging was inconvenient, & they would have removed her to anothr; but I would not suffer it; because it had no room backwards; and she must have been tortured with te noise of te Grubstreet Screamers, mention [*sic*] her Husbands murder to her Ears. I believe you have heard te Story of my Escape in opening te Banbox sent to Ld Treasr, te Prints have told a thousand Lyes of it but at last we gave them a true account of it at length, printed in te Evening: onely I would not suffer them to name me, having been so often named before, & teazed to death with Questions.[1] I wonder how I came to have so much presence of mind, which is usually not my talent; but so it pleased God, and I saved my self and him. for there was a Bullet a piece. A Gentleman told me, that if I had been killed, te Whigs would have calld it a Judgmt, because th Barrells were of Inkorns [*i.e.* Inkhorns], with which I had done them so much mischief. There was a pure Grubstreet of it full of Lyes

---

[1] The truth of the fact concerning the band-box sent to the lord treasurer, we are informed, is as followeth:—"On Tuesday morning, the 4th instant, the penny-post man delivered a small parcel at the lord treasurer's house, directed to his lordship's porter, in which upon opening was found inclosed a band-box, directed to the lord treasurer. The box was carried up to my lord's bed-chamber, and delivered to his lordship, who, stretching up the lid as far as the packthread that tied it would give way, said, he saw a pistol; whereupon a gentleman in the room desired the box might be given to him; he took it to the window, at some distance from my lord, and opened it, by cutting with a penknife the packthreads that fastened the lid. The first thing that appeared was the stock and lock of a pocket pistol, lying across the middle of the band-box, and fastened at each end with two nails. On each side of the firelock were laid the middle pieces of two large ink-horns charged with powder and ball, and touch-holes bored at the butt-ends of them, to which were fastened two linen bags of gunpowder; and at the other end of the bags were two quills filled with wild fire. These two artificial barrels were placed with the muzzles contraryways, and the quill of one of them directed to the pan of the pistol, as the other probably was, though disordered by the carriage. The gentleman who opened the box, apprehending some mischief was intended, would not touch the pistol-stock till he had removed all the other machines; then gently widening the box, the nails which fastened the stock at either end gave way. He found the firelock primed and cocked, and a piece of thread fastened to the trigger, which he conceived he had cut in the opening. The small nails which fastened the stock at either end were so contrived, that by taking it up at the first view, as it was natural to do with all the implements about it, the cock would have gone down and fired the whole train, which would have immediately discharged both barrels different ways; this could not have been avoided, had the pistol-stock been pulled out with any force before the nails were loosened, and the thread cut which was tied to the trigger" (*Postboy*, Nov. 13, 1712).—N.

and Inconsistencyes. I do not like these things at all; and I
wish my self more and more among my Willows: There is a
Devilish Spirit among People; & te Ministry must exert themselves or sink. [Nite dee sollahs, I'll go seep.] [1]

16. I thought to have finished this yesterday but was too
much disturbed. I sent a Letter early this morning to Ldy
Masham to beg her to write some comforting words to te poor
Dutchess; I dined to [? "too" or "to-day"] with Ldy Masham,
at Kensington where she is expecting these 2 months to lye in
she has promised me to get te Qu— to write to te Dutchess
kindly on this Occasion; and to morrow I will beg Ld Treasr to
visit and comfort her. I have been with her 2 hours again; and
find her worse. Her violence not so frequent, but her melancholy
more formal and settled. She has abundance of witt and Spirit;
about 33 year old, handsom, and airy, and seldom spared any
body that gave her te least Provocation; by which she had many
Envyers [2] and few Friends: Ldy Orkney her Sister in Law [3]
is come to Town on this Occasion, and has been to see her;
and behaved her self with great humanity; They have been
always very ill togethr ad te poor Dutchess could not have
Patience when people told her I went often to Ldy Orkneys.
But I am resolved to make them Friends; for te Dutchess is
now no more an object of Envy, and must learn humility from
te severest Master Affliction. I design to make te Ministry put
out a Proclamation (if it can be found proper) against that
Villain Maccartney: What shall we do with these Murderers?
I cannot end this letter to night; and there is no occasion, for
I cannot send it till Tuesday, and te Crowner's inquest on te
Duke's Body is to be tomorrow, and I shall know more: but
what care oo for all this; [iss poo] [4] MD im sorry for [poopdfrs] [5]
friends; and this is a very surprising Event. Tis late, and I'll
go to bed. This looks like Journalls. [Nite.] [6]

17. I was to day at Noon with te Dutchess of Hamilton again,
after I had been with Ldy Orkney, & chargd her to be kind to
her Sister in hr Affliction; te Dutchess told me Ldy Orkney had
been with her, & tht she did not treat her as gently as she ought.
They hate one anothr; but I will try to patch it up. I have been
drawing up a Paragraph for te Post boy, to be out to morrow,
and as malicious as possible; and very proper for Abel Roper

[1] Slightly obliterated.
[2] Hitherto erroneously read "many Enemies."
[3] The Earl of Orkney was a younger brother of the slain Duke of
Hamilton.
[4], [5], [6] Obliterated.

te Printer of it.[1] I Dined at Ld Treasrs at 6 in te Evening; wch
is his usuall hour returning from Windsor. he promises to visit
te Dutchess to morrow, and say he has a message to her from
te Qu—.[2] I have stayd till past one with him; [so Nite deelest
MD.][3]

18. The Commttee of Council is to sitt this afternoon upon te

[1] The paragraph, as dictated or written by Swift, was in these words:
"On Saturday morning last, about seven of the clock, the duke of Hamilton
and the lord Mohun fought a duel in Hyde-park. His grace's second was
colonel Hamilton; and his lordship's, major-general Macartney. The Lord
Mohun died on the spot; and my lord duke, soon after he was brought
home, who received the following wounds; one, on the right side of his
leg, about seven inches long; another, in his right arm; the third, in the
upper part of his left breast, running downwards into his body, which was
looked upon to be the immediate occasion of his death; the fourth wound
was on the outside of his left leg. My lord Mohun received a very large
wound in his groin; another, on the right side through his body, up to
the hilt of his sword; and the third in his arm; and other wounds." *Post-
boy*, Nov. 18.—In the same publication, Nov. 20, was the following
article, evidently written by Dr. Swift: "Major-general Macartney went
three times to the duke's house with a challenge from the lord Mohun.
On Friday last at four in the afternoon he delivered it to the duke, and
was at the bagnio all night with my lord Mohun, who was observed to
be seized with fear and trembling at that time. They met at seven the
next morning, with their seconds, colonel Hamilton of the foot-guards
for the duke, and Macartney for the lord Mohun. There the duke told
Macartney, that his grace knew this was all of his contrivance, but that
he should have a share in the dance; for his friend Hamilton resolved to
entertain him. On Tuesday last a committee of council sate at the earl
of Dartmouth's office, and the spectators of the duel were examined;
and we hear, that my lord duke and the lord Mohun did not parry, but
gave thrusts at each other, and the latter shortening his sword stabbed
the duke in the upper part of his left breast, running downwards into
his body (which wound, upon probing, was about fourteen inches long),
who expired soon after he was put into the coach. Colonel Hamilton
received a wound in his right leg, and, going afterwards to the half-moon
tavern in Cheapside, was dressed by Mr. Woodward the chirurgeon. His
grace is universally lamented by all men of honour and honesty, or who
have the least regard for their queen and country, being a faithful subject,
a true friend, a kind master, and a loving husband; and, as a just reward
for his services and sufferings, was preferred to the greatest honours and
employments of the crown. His grace is succeeded in honour and estates
by his eldest son, who is about twelve years of age. It is to be remembered,
that the lord Mohun was the person who gave the affront, which the duke,
observing him to be in drink, disdained to regard. But the faction, weary
of him, resolved to employ him in some real service to their cause, and
valued not what became of him, provided he did their drudgery: for the
dispute at law between the duke and his lordship had continued many
years, without any personal quarrel of consequence. But this is the new
expedient of the faction, band-boxes and bullies. Macartney is absconded;
but it is hoped a proclamation will soon be issued out for apprehending
him, in order to bring him to justice.—This is the fourth person that my
lord Mohun had the misfortune to kill." The title is extinct.—N.

[2] After this, former versions read "Thank God"; but all that is visible
through an obliteration is "Th Cour[t]"—part of a sentence never
completed.

[3] Obliterated.

te [sic] Affair of D. Hamiltons murder: and I hope a Proclamation will be out agst Macartney. I was just now (tis now Noon) with te Dutchess to let her know, Ld Tr will see her. She is mightily [out of order.]¹ Th Jury have not yet brought in their Verdict upon te Crowners Inquest; we suspect Macartney stabbd te Duke while he was fighting. te Qu— ad Ld Treasr are in great Concern at this Event. I dine to day agn with Ld Tr; but must send this to te Post office before; because else I shall not have time, he usually keeping me so late. Ben Took ² bid me write to Dd ³ to send her Certificate, for it is high time it should be sent, he says. Pray make Parvisol write to me & send me a generll account of my Affairs and to let him know tht I shall be over in Spring. & tht by all means he sells te Horses. Prior has kisst te Qu— hand & will return to France in a few days, & Ld Straffd to Holld: & now te K. of Spain has renounced his Pretensions to France, te Peace must follow very soon unavoidably. You must no more call Philip Duke of Anjou, for we now acknoledge him K. of Spain. Dr Prat tells me y are all mad in Ireld with yr Play-house Frolicks & Prologues; & I know not what. Bp Cl. & Family are well; They have heard from you, or y from them lately, I have forgot which; I dined there tothr day; but te Bp came not till after dinner; & our meat & drink was very so so. Mr Vedeau ⁴ was with me yesterday; & inquired aftr you he was a Lieutenant, and is now broke & upon half pay: He asked me nothing for himself; but wanted an Employmt for a Friend, who would give a handsom pair of Gloves: One Hales sent me up a Letter tothr day; which sd y lodged in his House, & therefore desired I would get him a civil Employmt; I would not be within; and have directed my man to give him an answer, that I never open Letter brought me by te Writers &c. I was complaining to a Lady that I wanted to mend an Employmt from fourty to 6oll a year in th Salt Office; & thought it hard I could not do it. She told me one Mr Griffin ⁵ should do it, & afterwards I mett Griffin at her Lodgings, & he was as I found, one I had been acquainted with; I named Filby ⁶ to him, & his abode somewhere near Nantwich: He said

¹ Obliterated.
² *See* Letter III., Sept. 10, 1710.
³ Rebecca Dingley is "Dd." The letters are of similar and nondescript form, but the initial D is always larger than the second one.
⁴ *See* Letter XII., Dec. 24, 1710.
⁵ Mr. Aitken thinks this means Humphrey *Griffith*, a Commissioner of Salt.
⁶ Filby is said to have been a baker, and to have married Ann Johnson *See* Letter V., Oct. 3, 1710.

frankly, he had formerly examined te man, & found he understood very little of his Business; but if he heard he mended, he would do what I desired. I will let it rest awhile, & then resume it, and if ppt [?] writes to Filby she may advise him to diligence &c. I told Griffin positively I would have it done, if te man mended. This is an account of [pooppt's][1] Commission to her most humble [Servant Pdfr.][2] I have a world of writing to finish: & little time; these Toads of Ministers are so slow in their helps. This makes me sometimes steal a week from te exactness I used to write to [MD. Farewell dee logues deelest MD MD MD **** FW FW FW Me Me Me lele.][3]

Smoak te folding of my Letters of late.

LETTER LVI

[Endorsed as last, save that " at " has but one " t." Date of receipt, " Decr. 18."]

56   London, *Decbr* 12. 1712.

HERE is now [a stlange ting,[4] 2 Rettles flom MD unanswered, never was before; I am slower & MD is faster;][5] but the last was owing to [Dd's Certificate][6]; why could it not be sent before pay now; is it so hard for Dd to prove she is alive: I protest solemnly I am not able to write to MD for othr Business: but I will resume my Journall method next time; I find it is easyer, thō it contains nothing but where I dine, & te occurrences of te day: I will write now but once in 3 weeks till this Business is off my hands which must be in six I think at furthest. Oh Ppt [7] I remembr yr Reprimnding me for medling in othr Peoples Affairs I have enough of it now with a Wannion.[8] Two Women have been here 6 times a piece, I never saw them yet: te first I have dispatcht with a Lettr; the othr I must see and tell her I can do nothig for her. She is wife of one Mr Connor an old College Acquaintance,[9] and comes on a foolish Errand for some old Pretensions that will succeed when I am Ld Treasr. I am got[10] 2 pair of Stairs in a private Lodging; & have orderd all

[1], [2], [3] Obliterated more or less.
[4] Or "sing."
[5] Somewhat obliterated.
[6] Obliterated.
[7] Here, as in many other instances, the word looks more like "Tpt."
[8] A word whose etymology is unknown, but which is always used as meaning vengeance.
[9] Mr. Aitken identifies him as Charles Connor, a scholar of Trinity College, Dublin, who took his degree in the same year as Swift.
[10] ? "up" omitted.

my Friends not to discovr where I am; yet every mornig 2 or 3 Sotts are plaguing me, & my present Servant has not yet his Lesson perfect of denying me. I have written 130 Pages in folio to be printed, & must write 30 more, which will make a large Book of 4s [1]—I wish I knew an Opportunity of sending y some Snuff I will watch who goes to Ired, & do it if possible. I had a Lettr from Parvisol, & find he has sett my Livings very low. Coll Hamilton [2] who was second to D. Hamilton is tryed to day; I suppose he is come off, but have not heard. I dined with Ld Treasr; but left him by nine, & visited some People. Ldy Betty is [for "his"] Daughtr will be marryed on Monday next (as I suppose) to te Marquis of Caermarthen.[3]—I did not know yr Country place had been Portrain [4] till y tod me so in yr last. Has Swanton [or "Swenton"] taken it of Wallis. that Wallis was a grave wise Coxcomb. Gd be thankd that Ppt im bettr of her disoddles; pray God keep her so. th Pamphlet of Politicall Lying [5] is writt by Dr Arbuthnot [6] te Authr of John Bull, tis very pretty; but not so obvious to be understood—Higgins first Chapln to D. Hamilton—why D. Hamilton never dreamt of a Chapln, nor I believe ever heard of Higgins: you are glorious newsmongers in Ireld—Dean Francis [7] Sr R. Leving [8] Stuff Stuff! & Prat more Stuff. We have lost our fine Frost here, & Abel Roper tells us y have had flouds in Dublin, ho brave you.[9] Oh ho Swanton seised Portrain, now I understand ee [or "oo"]. Ay ay, now I see Portraune [10] on te top of yr Lettr. I never minded it before. Now to yr second, N. 36. So you read one of te Grub-streets about te Bandbox: Th Whig Papers have abused me about te Bandbox; God help me; what could I do; I fairly ventured my Life; there is a particular Account of it in te

---

[1] This seems to be his *History of the Peace of Utrecht*, not published till after his death.—B.

[2] Colonel John Hamilton. His evidence against Maccartney was shaken, and he was discredited. He lost his commission in the next reign, and died (rumour said "by God's vengeance") Oct. 17, 1716.

[3] *See* Letter XLII., March 6, 1711-12, note to "Earl of Danby." Peregrine Osborne, the bridegroom, was now twenty-one; and Elizabeth Harley, his bride, was described as of the same age in the marriage certificate—although at her death, in 1713, she was said to be twenty-eight.

[4] *See* note at head of Letter LII.

[5] *See* Letter LIII., Oct. 9.

[6] He was going to write it "Arthburnett" again, and got as far as "Arthb" (deleted).

[7] Mr. Aitken says John Francis, rector of St. Mary's (opposite MD's lodging), was made Dean of Leighlin in 1705.

[8] *See* Letter IX., Nov. 12, 1710.

[9] Read sometimes "ho, have you?"—but it is more Irish than that.

[10] Spelt both "Portraune" and "Portrain(e)" by both Swift and Esther Johnson.

Post boy, & evening Post of that day. Ld Treasr has had te Seal sent him that seald te Box, and directions where to find te tothr Pistol in a Tree in St James's Park, which Ld Bolinbrokes Messengrs found accordingly; but who sent te Present is not yet known. D. Hamilton avoided te quarrell as much as possible according to te foppish Rules of Honor in practice. What signifyed your writing angry to Filby: I hope y said nothing of hearing any thing from me. High[1] do oo write by tandle light nautinautinauti dallar a hundled times fol doing so. O fais Dd, I'll take care of my Self. te Queen is in Town, & Lady Mashams month of lying in is within 2 days of being out. I was at te Christnig a [or "on"] Monday; I could not get te Child[2] namd Robin aftr Ld Treasr; it is Samuel after te Father. My Brothr Ormd sent me some Chocolate to day; I wish y had share of it. but thy say tis good for me, & I design to drink some in a morning. Our Society meets next Thursday now te Qu is in town. & Ld Treasr assures me that te Society for reform-ing te Language shall soon be established I have given away ten shill to day, to Servants; tant be help if one should cry ones Eyes out. Hot a stir is here about yr Company & visits; charmig company no doubt. [Now][3] I keep no Company at all. nor have I any desire to keep any; I never go to a Coffee-house nor a Tavern, nor have touched a Card since I left Windsor. I make few Visits, nor go to Levees; My onely debauhig [? debauching] is sitting late when I dine if I like te Company; I have almost dropt te Dutchesses of Shrewsbury & Hamilton & sevrll othrs Ld Treasr, te D. of Ormd & Ldy Orkney are all that I see very often, o yes, & Ldy Masham, & Ld Bolinbroke. & one or 2 private Friends. I make no figure but at Court, where I affect to turn from a Lord to te meanest of my Acquaintance; and I love to go there on Sundays, to see te World. But to say te truth I am growing weary of it. I dislike a million of things in te course of publick Affairs; & if I were to stay here much longr I am sure I shoud ruin my self with endeavoring to mend them. I am every [? day] invited into Schemes of doing this, but I cannot find any that will probably succeed. Tis impossible to save People against their own will; and I have been too much engaged in Patch-work already. Do y understand all this Stuff?—No—well zen you are now returnd to Ombre & te Dean, & Christmas, I wish oo a very merry one, & pray don't lose oo money, nor play upon Watt Welch's Game. Nite Sollahs, tis rate, I'll go to

seep, I don't seep well, & therefore never dare to drink Coffee
or Tea after dinner; but I am very seepy in a molning.[1] This
is te Effect of Time & Years. Nite deelest MD.

13. Morn. I am so very seepy in mornings, that my man
wakens me above ten times, and now I can tell oo [or "ee"]
no News of this day (here is a restless dog crying Cabbages and
Savoys plagues me every morning about this time, he is now at
it, I wish his largest Cabbage was sticking in his Throat) I lodge
over against te House in little Rider street where Dd lodged,
dont oo lememble Maram.—To night I must see te Abbè[2]
Gaultier,[3] to get some particulars for my History: it was he
who was first employd by France in te Overtures of Peace. &
I have not had time this month to see him. He is but a Puppy
too—Ldy Orkney has just sent to invite me to dinner. She has
not given me to Bed nightgown; besides I am come very much
off from writing in bed tho I am doing it this Minute, but I
stay till my fire is burnt up. My grate is very largely [sic], 2
bushell of Coals a week, but I save it in lodgings. Ld Abercorn
is come to London, & will plague me,[4] & I can do him no Service—D. Shrewsbury goes in a day or 2 for France, perhaps
to day; We shall have a Peace very soon, te Dutch are almost
entirely agreed, & if they stop we shall make it without them;
that has been long resolved. One Squire Jones,[5] a scoundrel
in my Parish has writt to me to desire I would engage Jo Beaumont to give him his Interest for Parlmt man for Trim: pray
tell Jo this; & if he designed to vote for him already, then he
may tell Jones, that I received his Letter, & that I writt to Jo
to do it; if Jo be engaged for any othr, then he may do what he
will; & Parvisol may say he spoke to Jo, but Jo's engaged &c.
I receivd 3 pair of fine thread Stockins from Jo lately, Pray
thank him when you see him, & that I say they are very fine
& good (I never lookt at them yet, but that's no matter) This
is a fine day. I am ruined with Coaches & Chairs this 12 penny
weathr. I must see my Brothr Ormd at 11, & then te Dutchess
of Hamilton, with whom I doubt I am in disgrace, not having
seen her these ten days.—I send this to day, and must finish it
now, & phaps some People may come & hindr me, for it im ten

---

[1] Morning.
[2] He writes it thus, with the wrong accent.
[3] The French priest mentioned in Letter XXXI., Oct. 28, 1711: François Gauthier (165-?-1720), a person of obscure origin, who assisted Nicolas
le Mesnager (1658-1714), the other "private minister."
[4] About the French dukedom. See Letter XLIII., March 19, 1711-12.
[5] Thomas Jones, M.P. for Trim 1713-14, says Mr. Aitken.

a Clock (but not shaving day) & I must be abroad at 11. Abbe
Gautier sends me word I can't see him to night pots cake him.
I don't value any thing but one Letter he has, of Petcum's,[1]
shewing te Roguery of te Dutch. Did not te Conduct of te
Allyes make y great Politicians, fais I believe y are not quite
so ignorant as I thought you. I am glad to hear oo walked so
much in te Country; does Dd ever read to you ung ooman. O
fais I shall find strange doings hen I tum ole [2] [or "orb"].
Here is somebody coming that I must see, that wants a little
place, te Son of Coz Rooks [3] eldest Daughter, tht dyed many
years ago.—He's here;—farewell deelest MD MD MD Me Me
Me FW FW FW lele—

LETTER LVII

[Endorsed as last: save for an " att " with two " t " s, and a hyphen at
" Capel-street." Date of receipt, " Decr. 18."]

57.   London. *Decbr* 18. 1712.

OUR Society was to meet to day, but Ld Harley, who was
President this week could not attend, being gone to Wimbleton
with his new Brothr in Law te young Marquess of Caermarthen,
who marryed Ldy Betty Harley on Monday last, and Ld Treasr
is at Wimbleton too. However half a dozen of us mett, & I
proposed our meetings should be onely once a fortnight, for
betwixt y & me, we do no good. It cost me 13 Shillings to day
for my Club at Dinner; I don't like it fais. We have terrible
snowey slobbery weathr. Ld Abercorn is come to Town, & will
see me whethr I will or no. Y know he has a Pretence to a
Dukedom in France; wch D. Hamilton was solliciting for; but
Abercorn resolves to spoil their Title if they will not allow him a
4th Part; and I have advised te Dutchess to compound with
him, & have made te Ministry of my Opinion. Nite dee sollahs
MD MD.

19. [Ay mally zis im sumsing rike a [4] pdfr to write] [5] Journals

---

[1] This seems to refer to Edzard Adolf von Petkum (*d.* 1721), a native
of East Friesland; who was the principal tool of Karl Leopold, Grand
Duke of Mecklenburg-Schwerin.

[2] "When I come home"—usual reading; but it may be " orb," for
"when I come over."

[3] Cousin Rook is unidentified.

[4] Or "oo."

[5] This phrase is more or less obliterated. It means, "Ay marry! this is
something like *** pdfr." Messrs. Ryland and Aitken read "sumsing
rike for pdfr," etc. This attribution of modern slang to the early eighteenth
century is emphasised by Mr Aitken, who puts a comma after "rike"!
What lies between "rike" and "pdfr" is uncertain, but certainly not "for."

again, tis as naturall as Mothers milk, now I am got into it. Ld Tr. is returned from Wimbleton (tis not above 8 miles off) and sent for me to dine with him at 5, but I had te Grace to be abroad and dined with some othrs with honest Ben Took by Invitation. te Dutchess of Ormd promised me her Picture, & comig home to night I found hers & te Dukes both in my Chamber, was not that a pretty civil surprise; yess & thy are in fine gilded Frames too. I am writing a Letter to thank her, which I will send to morrow morning. I'll tell her she is such a Prude that she will not let so much as her Picture be alone in a room with a MAN, unless te Dukes be with it, and so forth.—We are all full of snow, & dabbling; Ldy Masham has come abroad these 3 days, and seen te Qu. I dined with her tothr day at her Sister Hill's. I hope she will remove in a few days to her new Lodgings at St James's from Kensington. Nite dee logues MD.

20. I lodge[1] 2 pair of Stairs, have but one Room, & deny my self to every body almost, yet I cannot be quiet and all my mornings are lost with People who will not take answers below stairs, such as Dilly, & te Bp & Provost &c. Ldy Orkney invited me to dinner to day, wch hindred me from dining with Ld Tr this is his day that his chief Friends in te Ministry dine with him. However I went there about 6, and sate with them till past nine when thy all went off; but he kept me back; and told me te Circumstances of Ldy Betty's Match.[2] te young Fellow has 60 thousand Pounds ready money; 3 great Houses furnished, 7 thousand Pounds a year at present, and aboute [or "above "] 5 more after his Father & Mother dye. I think Ldy Betty's Prtion [*i.e.* portion] is not above 8 thousd Pd. I remembr eithr Tisdal writt to me in somebody's Lettr, or y did it for him, that I should mention him on occasion to Ld Anglesea, with whom he sd, he had some little Acquaintance; Ld Anglesea was with us to night at Ld Treasr and there I asked him about Tisdal, & described him, he sd he never saw him, but that he had sent him his Book.[3] See what it is to be a Puppy Pray tell Mr Walls, that Ld Anglesea thankd me for recommending Clements [4] to him, that he says he is 20 thousand Pds th better for knowing Clements. But pray don't let Clements go and write a Lettr of thanks, & tell My Ld that he hears so & so &c. Why, tis but

---

[1] ? "up" omitted.

[2] Lady Betty Harley's, with the Marquess of Caermarthen.

[3] Tisdall, the rejected of Esther Johnson, had written to prove that the Dissenters, and especially the Presbyterians, of Ireland, were no better than they should be.

[4] *See* Letter IX., Nov. 22, 1710.

like an Irish Understanding to do so. Sad weathr, 2 Shill in Coaches to day, and yet I am dirty. I am now going to read over somethig & correct it [1] so Nite.

21. Puppyes have got a new way of plaguing me; I find Lettrs directed for me at Ld Tr's, sometims with inclosed ones to him, & sometimes with Projects & sometimes with Libels. I usually keep them 3 or 4 days without opening—I was at Court to day, as I allways am on Sundays instead of a Coffee house, to see my Acquaintance This day sennight after I had been talking at Court with Sr Wm Windham [2] te Spanish Ambasdr [3] came to him, & sd he heard that was Dr S— and desired him to tell me, that His Mastr & te K. of Fr, and te Qu— were more obliged to me than any man in Europe, so we bowd & shook hands &c I took it very well of him I dined with Ld Tr., & must again to morrow, thō I had rather not (as Dd says) but now te Qu. is in Town he does not keep me so late. I have not had time to see Fanny Manly [4] since she came, but intend it one of these days. Her Uncle Jack Manly, I hear can not live a Month, which will be a great loss to Her Father In Ireld; for I believe he is one of his chief Supports. Our Peace now will be soon determind; for Ld Bolinbroke tells me this morning, that 4 Provinces of Holland have complyd with te Qu, & we expect the rest will do so immediatly. Nite MD.

22. Ld Keepr promised me yesterday te first convenient Living to poor Mr Geree,[5] who is marryed, & wants some Addition to what he has; he is a very worthy Creature. I had a Letter some weeks ago from Elwick [6] who marryed Betty Geree. It seems te poor woman dyed some time last Summer. Elwick grows rich, and purchases lands. I dined with Ld Treasr to day, who has engaged me to come again to morrow. I gave Ld Bolinbroke a Poem of Parnels,[7] I made Parnel insert some Complimts in it to His Ldship; He is extreamly pleasd with it, & read some parts of it to day to Ld Treasr who liked it as much; & indeed he outdoes all our Poets here a Barrs Length. Ld Bolingbr— has ordered me to bring him to dinner on Christmas Day, & I made Ld Tr— promise to see him; and it may one

---

[1] Morphew published, on the 27th, *The Parliament of Birds*; and *A Letter to the Marquis de ****, concerning a book, intituled "The Sighs of Europe."*—N.

[2] *See* Letter XXV., June 21, 1711.

[3] Monteleon—see *post*.

[4] Isaac Manley's daughter, apparently.

[5] *See* Letter XLVI.

[6] *Ibid.*

[7] *See* Letter XXVIII., Aug. 24, 1711.

day do Parnel a Kindness. Y know Parnel; I believe I have told y of that Poem. Nite deel MD.

23. This morning I presented one Diaper[1] a Poet to Ld Bolinbroke, with a new Poem, which is a very good one; and I am to give him a Sum of mony from my Ld; & I have contrivd to make a Parson of him; for he is half a one already, being in Deacons Orders, and serves a small Cure in te Country, but has a sword at his A— here in Town. Tis a poor little short Wretch, but will do best in a Gown, & we will make Ld Keepr give him a Living. Ld Bolingbroke writ to Ld Treasr to excuse me to day, so I dined with te former, and Monteleon the Spanish Ambassador, who made me many Complimts, I staid till nine; and now it is past ten and my man has lockt me up, and I have just called to mind that I shall be in disgrace with Tom Leigh; That Coxcomb had got into Acquaintance with one Eckershall[2] Clerk of te Kitchin to te Qu— who was civil to him at Windsor on my Account; for I had donc some scrvice to Eckershall. Leigh teises [*sic*] me to pass an Evening at His Lodgings with Eckershall; I put it off sevrall times but was forced at last to promise I would come to night, and it never was in my head till I was lockt up, and I have called and called; but my Man is gone to bed; so I will write an Excuse to morrow. I detest that Tom Leigh and am as formal to him as I can when I happen to meet him in te Park. Th Rogue frets me if he knew it. He asked me why I did not wait on te Bishop of Dromore,[3] I answrd I had not te Honr to be acquaintd with him; & would not presume &c. He takes me seriously, says te Bishop is no proud man &c. He tells me of a Judge in Ireld that has done ill things, I ask why he is not out: Says he, I think te Bishops & you & I, and te rest of te Clergy shoud meet & consult about it; I beg his Pardon, & say I cannot be serviceable that way, he answers, yes, every body may help something. Don't you see how curiously he contrives to vex me, for te dog knows that with half a word I could no more than all of them together. Butt[4] he onely does it from te Pride & envy of his own heart, and not out of a humorous design of teazing, he is one of those, that would rather Service should not be done, than done by a

---

[1] *See* Letter XLIII., March 13, 1711-12.
[2] *See* Letter XVII., Feb. 27, 1710-11. Tom Leigh seems to have been in town some little time—*see* Letter LIII., Oct. 9.
[3] Tobias Pullen (*d.* 1713), succeeded to the bishopric of Dromore 1695.
[4] The common reading is "But." But the first letter is not very like a "B," and Swift does not elsewhere spell "butt"—*i.e.* with a double " t." It is perhaps "Tutt!"

private man and of his own Country. You take all this, don't you. Nite dee sollahs, I'll go seep a dozey [or "dazy"].

24. I dined to day with te Chancllr of te Excheqr in order to look over some of my Papers, but nothing was done. I have been also mediatig between te Hamilton Family & Ld Abercorn, to have them compound with him, and I believe they will do it. Ld Selkirk[1] te late Duke's Brother is to be in Town in order to go to France to make te demands: & te Ministry are of Opinion thy will get some Satisfaction, and they empowred me to advise te Hamilton side to agree with Abercorn, who asks a 4th Part, & will go to France & spoil all if they won't yield it. Nite sollahs.

25. [A melly Tlismas; melli Tlismas,[2] I sd it first. I wish oo a sousand' zoll,[3] with halt and soul.][4] I carryed Parnel[5] to dine at Ld Bolingb— and he behaved himself very well, & Ld Bol— is mighily pleased with him. I was at St James Chappel by 8 this morning, and Church & Sacramt were done by ten. Th Qu— has te Gout in her Hand, & did not come to Church to day; and I stayd so long in my Chambr that I misst going to Court. Did I tell y that te Qu— designs to have a drawing Room and Company every day. Nite deelogues.

26. I was to wish th D. Ormd a happy Christmas, & give half a Crown to his Porter. it will cost me a dozen half Crowns among such Fellows; I dind with Ld Treasr, who chid me for being absent 3 days, mighty kind with a P— less of Civility and more of his Interest. We here [i.e. hear] Maccartney is gone over to Ireld. Was not it Comical, for a Gentleman to be sett upon by Highway men, & to tell them he was Macartney; upon wch they brought him to a Justice of Peace in hopes of te reward; and te Rogues were sent to Gail [sic]; was it not great Presence of Mind. But may be y heard this already, for there was a Grub-street of it. Ld Bol— told me I must walk away to day when dinner was done, because Ld Tr and he and anothr were to enter on Business! but I sd it was as fit I should know their Business as any body; for I was to justify; so te rest went, and

[1] Charles Douglas (1662-3–1738-9), second Earl of Selkirk, was third son of the first earl (who became third Duke of Hamilton, 1660), and succeeded to the peerage after his father's resignation (1688), under a *novodamus*.
[2] Messrs. Ryland and Aitken both read "All melly Titmasses." It is submitted that they have mistaken part of an obliterating scratch for letters or parts of letters.
[3] "Zoll" is doubtful: some read "zoth." If "zoll" is right, it may mean "fold." The next phrase means, of course, "with heart and soul."
[4] Obliterated.
[5] *See* Letter XXVIII., Aug. 24, 1711.

I stayd and it was so important I was like to sleep over it. I left them at nine & tis now 12. Nite MD.

27. I dined to day with Genrll Hill, Governr of Dunkirk, Ldy Masham & Mrs Hill his 2 Sisters were of te Company; & some others; and there have I been sitting this evening till 11 looking over others at Play; for I have left off loving play my self, and I think ppt is now a great Gamester. I have a great Cold on me, not quite at its height. I have them seldom, and therefore ought to be Patient. I mett Mr Addison and pastorall Philips [1] on te Mall to day, & took a Turn with them; But they both looked terrible dry and cold; a Curse of Party; and do y know that I have taken more pains to recommend th Whig Witts to te Favor & Mercy of te Ministers than any other People. Steel I have kept in his Place; Congreve I have got to be used kindly and secured. Row [2] I have recommended, and got a Promise of a Place; Philips I shoud certainly have provided for if he had not run Party-mad and made me withdraw my Recommendation; and I sett Addison so right at first that he might have been employd; and have partly secured him te Place he has. Yet I am worse used by that Faction than any man. Well, go to Cards sollah, ppt, & dress te Wine & Olange sollah MD; and I'll go seep tis rate—Nite MD.

28. My Cold is so bad that I could not go to Church to day, nor to Court. but, I was engaged to Ld Orkney's with D. Ormd at dinner, and ventured; because I could cough & spitt there as I pleased: te Duke and Ld Arran [3] left us, and I have been sitting ever since with Ld & Ldy Orkney, till past 11, and my Cold is worse, & makes me giddy, I hope it is onely my Cold; Oh, says ppt, every body is giddy with a Cold; I hope it is no more; but I'll go to bed, for te fellow has bawld past 12. Nite deels.

29. I got out early to day, & scaped all my Duns. I went to see Ld Bolinbroke about some Business, & truly he was gone out too; I dined in te City upon te boild leg of a Goose, & a bitt of Brawn, with my Printer.[4] did I tell you; that I forbeer [sic] printing what I have in hand, till te Court decides something about me: I will contract no more Enemyes, at least I will not imbitter worse those I have already, till I have got under Shelter; & te Ministers know my Resolutions; so that you may be disappointed in seeing this Thing as soon as y expected: I

[1] See Letter XI., Dec. 15, 1710.
[2] Nicholas Rowe. See Letter V., Oct. 4, 1710.
[3] See Letter XLII., Feb. 28.　　[4] John Barber.

hear Ld Treasr is out of order. My Cold is very bad: Every [1]
has one. [Nite two dee logues.] [2]

30. I suppose this will be full by Saterday; [zen it sall go.] [3]
D. Ormd, Ld Arran & I dined privatly to day at an old Servants
house of his. the Council made us part at 6. one Mrs Ramsy
dined with us, an old Lady of about 55 that we are all very fond
of.. I calld this Evening at Ld Treasrs, and sate with him 2
hours; he has been cupped for a cold, & has been very ill. He
cannot dine with Parnel & me at Ld Bol—'s to morrow; but says
he will see Parnel some other time. I hoise up Parnel partly to
spight the envious Irish folks here, particularly Tom Lee [4]; I
saw te Bp Cloghrs Family to day. Miss [5] is mighty ill of a Cold
coughs incessantly. Nite MD.

31. To day Parnel & I dined with Ld Bolinbrokle,[6] to correct
Parnel's Poem, I made him shew all te Places he disliked, and
when Parnel has corrected it fully, he shall print it. I went this
evening to sitt with Ld Treasur, he is better, & will be out in a
day or two. I sate with him while te young Folks went to
Supper; and then went down, & there were te young Folks
merry togethr, having turnd Ldy Oxford up to my Ld; and I
stayd with them till 12. There was te young Couple Ld & Lady
Caermarthen, & Ld & Lady Dupplin,[7] & Ld Harley and I;
& th old Folks were togethr above; It lookd like what I have
formerly done so often, stealing togethr from te old Folks;
thō indeed it was not from poor Ld Tr—who is as young a
Fellow as any of us; but Lady Oxford [8] is a silly meer old Woman.
My Cold is still so bad that I have not te least Smelling. I am
just got home, & tis past 12; and I'll go to bed, & settled [*sic*]
my head, heavy as Lead. Nite MD.

Janr. 1. [a sousand melly new eels to deelest richar MD pray
Gd almighty bless you and] [9] send [you ever happy.][10] I forgot
to tell you, tht yesterday Ld Abercorn was here teazing me about
his French Dutchy; and suspectig my Partiality to te Hamilton
Family in such a whimsicall Manner, tht Dr Prat who was by
thought he was made [? mad]. He was no soonr gone, but Ld
Orkney sent to know whethr he night come and sitt with me

---

[1] "body" omitted.   [2], [3] Obliterated.
[4] Leigh.   [5] Bishop Ashe's daughter.
[6] The name Bolingbroke seems to have presented almost insuperable
difficulties to Swift whenever he ventured to write it in full. Here he spelt
it, at first, with two "o's"; then, writing a "k" crookedly over the
second "o," succeeded in transforming the original "k" into an "l."
[7] Or rather Lord Hay.
[8] *See* Letter XI., Dec. 22, 1710.
[9], [10] Obliterated.

half an hour about some Business. I returnd answer, that I would wait on him; which I did, we discoursed a while, and he left me with Lady Orkney: and in came th Earl of Selkirk[1] whom I had never seen before; he is anothr Brothr of D. Hamilton, and is going to France by a Power from his Mother te old Dutchess, to negotiate their Pretensions to this Dutchy of Chattellerault [*i.e.* Chatelherault]. He teazed me for 2 hours in spight of my Teeth, and held my hand when I offerd to stir, would have had me engage te Ministry to favor him agst Ld Abercorn, & to convince them that Ld Abercorn had no Pretensions; and desired I would also convince Ld Abercorn himself so, & concluded he was sorry I was a greater Friend to Abercorn than Hamilton. I had no Patience, & used him with some Plainness. Am not I purely handled between a couple of Puppyes.. Ay says [Ppt, y][2] must be medling in other Folks Affairs. I appeal to te Bp of Cl, whethr Abercorn did not complain that I [would][3] not let him see me last year, and tht he swore he would take no denyals from my Servant when he came again. The Ministers gave me leave to tell te Hamilton Family it was their Opinion that they ought to agree with Abercorn. Ld Anglesea was then by; & told Abercorn, upon which he gravely tells me I was Commissioned by te Ministers, & ought to perform my Commission &c—But I'll have done with them I have warned Ld Tr & Ld Bol— to beware of Selkirks teazing.—'x on him. Yet Abercorn vexes me more; The Whelp owes to me all te kind Receptions he has had from te Ministry.—I dined to day at Ld Treasurers with te young Folks; & sate with Ld Treasr till 9. and then was forced to Ldy Masham's and sate there till 12. talking of Affairs till I am out of humor, as every one must that knows them inwardly; A thousand things wrong, most of them easy to mend; yet our Scheams availing at best but little, & sometimes nothing at all. One evil[4] which I twice patched up with te hazard of all te Credit I had, is now spread more than ever.— But burn Politicks. & send me from Courts & Ministers. [Nite deelest richar MD.][5]

2. I sauntrd about this morning, and went with Dr Prat to a Picture Auction where I had like to be drawn in to buy a Picture that[6] was fond of, but it seems was good for nothing. Prat was there to buy some Pictures for te Bp Clr who resolves

[1] *See* Dec. 24, **1712**. [2] Obliterated.
[3] Or "did." Paper torn.
[4] Bolingbroke was a more genuine Tory and Jacobite than Harley, and became impatient of Harley's slowness.
[5] Obliterated. [6] ? "I" omitted.

to lay out ten pound to furnish his House with curious Peeces.
we dined with te Bp, I being by chance disengaged: & this
Evening I sate with Bp Ossory, who is layd up with te Gout
te French Ambasd Duke D'Aumont[1] came to Town to night;
& te Rabble conducted him home with Shouts[2]; I cannot smell
yet thō my Cold begins to break; it continues cruell hard frosty
Weathr. Go and be [melly & nite sollahs.][3]

3. Ld Dupplin & I went with Ld & Ldy Orkney this morning
at ten to Wimbleton 6 miles off; to see Ld & Ldy Caermarthen,
It is much te finest place about this Town; did oo never see it.
I was once there before about 5 years ago. You know Ldy
Caermarthen is Ld Treasr Daughter, marryed about 3 weeks
ago. I hope te young Fellow will be a good Husband.—I must
send this away now. I came back just by night fall. cruell cold
weathr. I have no smell yet. but my cold something better.
[. . . sollahs; I'll take my reave.][4] I forgett how [MD Accounts
are; pray let me know allways timely before MD wants;][5] &
pray give te Bill on tothr side to Mrs Brent as usuall. I believe
I have not payed her this great while. [Go play Cards & be melly
dee sollahs, & rove pdfr who roves MD bettle zan his Rife.[6]
Farewell deelest MD MD MD MD MD . . . Me Me Me FW
FW FW FW Me Me

lele
Lele   Lele   Lele][7]

The six odd Shillings tell Mrs B—[8]
are for her Newyears gift.

I am just now told that poor dear Lady Ashburnham,[9] te Duke
of Ormd's daughter dyed yesterday at her Country House; th
poor creature was with Child. She was my greatest Favorite,
and I am in excessive Concern for her Loss. I hardly knew a
more valuable Person on all Accounts: y must have heard me
tell of her. I am afraid to see te Duke and Dutchess; she was
naturally very healthy; I am afraid she has been thrown away
for want of care. Pray condole with me; tis extreemly moving,
Her Lord's a Puppy, and I shall never think it worth my while
to be troubled with him, now he has lost all that was valuable

---

[1] Louis (1667–1723), Duc d'Aumont.

[2] He entered the city in prodigious state; scattering money among
the populace.—SCOTT.

[3], [4], [5] Obliterated.

[6] "Who loves MD better than his Life" (see Letter XX., April 14,
1711). No complete reading of this sentence has been submitted heretofore.

[7] Obliterated.

[8] Mrs. Brent.

[9] Lady Mary Butler that was. See Letter III., Sept. 20, 1710 (note).

in his Possession. Yet I think he used her pretty well.—I hate Life, when I think it exposd to such Accidents. and to see so many thousand wretches burthening te Earth while such as her dye, makes me think God did never intend Life for a Blessing —Farewell.

LETTER LVIII

[Endorsed as last: save that " at " is reverted to, and it is "St. Marye's." Date of receipt, " Febr. 4."]

58.   London. *Janr.* 4. 1712-13.

I ENDED my last with te melancholy news of poor Ldy Ashburnhams death.. Th Bp Cl. & Dr Prat made me dine with them to day at Ld Mountjoys[1] pursuant to an Engagemt wch I had forgot. Ldy Mountjoy[2] told me that Maccartney was got safe out of our Clutches, for she had spoke with one who had a Lettr from him from Holland; others say te same thing. Tis hard such a dog should escape. As I left Ld Mountjoy's I saw te Duke d'Aumont th Fr. Ambassador going from Ld Bolingbrokes where he dined, to have a private Audience of te Qu— I followd & went up to Court, where there was a great Croud. I was talking with te Duke of Argyle by te Fireside in te Bedchambr, when te Ambassador came out from te Qu— Argyle presented me to him, & Ld Bolingb & we talked togethr awhile. He is a fine Gentleman, something like te D. Ormd, and just such an expansive[3] man. After Church to day I shewd te Bp of Cl. at Court who was who.—[Nite my too dee logues & lastles.][4]

5. Our Frost is broke, but it is bloody cold. Ld Treasr is recoverd, & went out this evening to te Qu— I dined with Ldy Oxford & then sate with Ld Trr while he went [?] out. he gave me a Letter from an unknown Hand relating to Dr Brown Bp of Cork,[5] recommending him to a better Bishoprick as a Person who opposed Ld Wharton, and was made a Bp on that Account; celebrating him for a great Politician &c, in that all directly contrary to His Character; which I made bold to explain— What dogs there are in te World. I was to see te poor Duke &

---

[1] *See* Letter I.

[2] *See* Letter VIII., Nov. 3, 1710.

[3] "Expensive" is the common reading; the letter is as likely an "a" as an "e."

[4] Obliterated—especially the last word; read " lastalls " by Forster, *i.e.* " rascals." " Ledles," Mr. Aitken's reading, is not concurred in.

[5] Peter Brown (*d.* 1735), a bishop since 1709.

Dutchess of Ormd this morning, te Duke was in his publick Room with Mr Southwell,[1] and two more Gentlemen, when Southwell and I was [sic] alone with them [sic], he talked something of Ld Ashburnham: that he was afraid te Whigs would get him again, he bore up as well as he could, but something accidentally falling in discourse, th Tears were just falling out of his Eyes, and I looked off to give him an Opportunity (which he took) of wiping them with his Hankerchief. I never saw any thing so moving, nor such a mixture of greatness of mind and Tenderness and Discretion. [Nite MD.] [2]

6. Ld Bolinbr— & Parnel & I dined by Invitation with my Friend Dartinuff, whom y have heard me talk of. Ld Bolinbr. likes Parnel mightily, and tis pleasant to see that one who hardly passt for any thing in Ireld makes his way here with a little friendly forwarding. It is scurvy rainy weathr, & I have hardly been abroad to day. nor know any thing that passes. Ld Treasr is quite recovered, and I hope will be carefull to keep himself well. Dutchess of Marlbrough is leaving Engld to go to her Duke, and makes Presents of Rings to severall Friends, they say worth 200ll a piece. I am sure she ought to give me one, Though te Duke pretended to think me his greatest Enemy, & got People to tell me so, and very mildly to let me know how gladly he would have me softned towards him. I bid a Lady of his Acquaintance & mine let him know, that I had hindred many a bitter thing against him, not for his own sake, but because I thought it looked base; and I desired every thing should be left him except Power. [Nite M.D.] [3]

7. I dined with Ld & Ldy Masham to day; & this Evenig playd at Ombre with Mrs Vanhom— merely for Amusemt; te Ministers have got my Papers & will neithr read them nor give them to me, & I can hardly do any thing.—Very warm slabby weather; but I made a shift to get a walk, yet I lost half of it. by shaking of [?off] Ld Rochester,[4] who is a good civil simple Man.—Th Bp of Ossory [5] will not be Bp of Hereford, to te great grief of himself and his Wife.—And [hat is MD doing now I wonder; playing at Cards] [6] with te Dean & Mrs Walls;— I think it is not certain yet that Macartney is escaped.— I am plagued with bad Authors, Verse and Prose, who send me their Books and Poems; the vilest Trash I ever saw. but I have given their names to my man, never to let them see me. I have got

[1] See Letter V., Oct. 3, 1710.   [2, 3] Obliterated.
[4] See Letter XXVI., July 18, 1711.   [5] Hartstonge.
[6] Obliterated.

new Ink, & tis very white,[1] & I don't see that it turns black at all—I'll go to seep tis past 12. [Nite MD.][2]

8. [Oo][3] must understad tht I am in my Geers[4] and have got a Chocolate pot a present from Mrs Ash of Clogher, and some Chocolate from my Brothr Ormd; & I treat Folks sometimes. I dined with Ld Treasr at 5 a Clock to day, & was by while He & Ld Bol— was [sic] at Business; for it is fit I should know all that passes now because—&c. te D. of Ormd emplyd me to speak to Ld Treasr to day about an Affair, and I did so; & te Duke had spoke himself 2 hours before; which vext me, and I will chide te Duke about it. I tell you a good Thing: there is not one of te Ministry but what will employ me as gravely to speak for them to Ld Tr—as if I were their Brother or his; and I do it as gravely: thō I know they do it onely because they will not make themselves uneasy, or had rathr I should be denyed than they—I believe our Peace will not be finished these 2 Months; For I think we must have a return from Spain by a Messenger who will not go till Sunday next. Ld Treasr has invited me to dine with him again to morrow. Your Commissnr Keatly[5] is to be there [Nit dee richar MD.][6]

9 Dr Prat drunk Chocolate with me this morning & then we walkt. I was yestrday with him to see Ldy Betty Butler grieving for her Sister Ashburnham: te Jade was in bed in form; and she did so cant she made me sick. I meet Tom Lee every day in te Park to preserve his Health; he is as ruddy as a Rose, & tells me his Bp of Dromore[7] recovers very much. that Bp has been very near dying. To day's Examiner talks of te Play of what is it like? and y will think it to be mine, and be bit, for I have no hand in those Papers at all. I dined with Ld Treasr. & shall again to morrow, wch is his day when all te Ministers dine with him. He calls it whipping day; it is always on Saterday; and we do indeed usually railly [i.e. rally] him about his Faults on that day. I was of te Originall Clubb when onely poor Lord Rivers, Ld Keepr, & Ld Bolinbr—came, but now Ormd, Anglesea, Ld Steward,[8] Dartmouth,[9] &

---

[1] The pale ink begins at the word "morning" on the 5th.
[2], [3] Obliterated.
[4] "In harness." Perhaps "put wise" is the modern equivalent.
[5] Mr. Aitken says Thomas Keightley, a Commissioner of the Great Seal in Ireland.
[6] Obliterated.
[7] Dr. Pullen. See Letter LVII., Dec. 23, 1712.
[8] Lord Poulett (see Letter XX., April 10, 1711). He was Lord Steward since June, 1711.
[9] See Letter V., Oct. 3, 1710.

other Rabble intrude, and I scold at it, but now they pretend
as good a Title as I, & indeed many Saterdays. I am not there:
te Company being too many I don't love it. Nite MD.

10. At 7 this Evening as we sate [or "satt"] after dinnr
at Ld Treasrs, a Servant sd Ld Peterborow[1] was at te door.
Ld Tr & Ld Bol— went out to meet him, and brought him in.
He was just returnd from abroad, where he has been above
a year. Soon as he saw me, he left te D. Ormd, & othr Lds,
and ran and kisst me before he spoke to them, but chid me
terribly for not writing to him; which I never did this last
time he was abroad, not knowing where he was; and he changed
places so often, it was impossible a Letter should overtake
him. he left Engd with a Bruise by his Coach overturning, that
made him spitt Blood, & was so ill we expected any Post to
hear of his Death: But he outrode it, or outdrunk[2] it,
or something: & is come home lustyer than ever; he is at
least 60, & has more Spirits than any young fellow I know
in Engld: He has got th old Oxford Regimt of horse; & I
believe will have a Garter, I love te hangdog dearly. [Nite
dee MD.][3]

11. Th Court was crammd to day to say [? see] te Fr Ambassdr; but he did not come. Did I never tell y tht I go to
Court on Sundays as to a Coffee-house to see acquaintance,
whom I should otherwise not see twice a year.[4] Th Provost
& I dined with Ned Southwell by appointment; in order to
settle your Kingdom, if my Scheam can be followed, but I
doubt our Ministry will be too tedious; You must certainly
have a new Parlmt, but they would have that a Secret yet.
Our Parlmt here will be prorogued for 3 weeks. those Puppyes
te Dutch will not yet come in, thō they pretend to submit to
te Qu— in every thing; but they would fain try first how our
Session begins, in hopes to embroyl us in te House of Lds.
& if my advice had been taken, te Session should have begun,
& we would have trusted te Parlmt to approve te Steps already
made towards te Peace, & had an Address perhaps from them
to conclude without te Dutch, if they would not agree. Others
are of my mind; but it is not reckoned so safe, it seems. Yet

[1] See Letter VI., Oct. 15, 1710.
[2] Not "outdrank" as heretofore read.
[3] Obliterated.
[4] It is hard to understand the constant iteration of this statement,
unless we infer that Esther Johnson's letters in reply (which are not
extant) contained some condemnation of its triteness—which would
impel Swift to "say it aden and aden."

I doubt whethr te Peace will be ready so soon as 3 weeks, but that's a Seret [*sic*].[1] [Nite MD.][2]

12. Prat and I walkt into te City to one Bateman's[3] a famous Bookseller for old books; there I layd out 4ll like a fool, and we dined at a hedge alehouse for 2sh and 2 pence like Emperors. Let me see: I bought Plutarch 2 Vollumes for thirty shillings.[4] [Well I'll tell y no][5] more, [oo don't understand Greek;][6] We have no news, and I have nothing more to say to day. I can't finish my Work, these Ministers will not find time to do what I would have them. [So Nite nown dee dallars.][7]

13. I was to have dined to day with Ld Keepr; but would not, because that Brute Sr John Walter[8] was to be one of te Company; Y' may remembr he raild at me last Summer was twelvemonth at Windsor, and has never beggd my pardon, thô he promised to do it; and Ld Mancol[9] who was one of te Company, would certainly have sett us togethr by te Ears out of pure roguish mischief. So I dined with Ld Treasr. where there was none but Ld Bol— I stayd till 8, and then went to Lady Orkney's who has been sick, and sate with her till 12, from whence y may conclude it is late Sollahs. Te Parlmt was prorogued to day as I told y, for 3 weeks.—Our weathr is very bad & slobbery; and I shall spoil my new Hatt (I have bought a new Hat) or empty my Pockets. Does Hawkshaw[10] pay te Interest he owes?[11] Ld Abercorn plagues me to death I have now not above six People to provide for, and about as many to do good offices to, and thrice as many that I will do nothing for, nor can if I would. Nite dee MD.

14. To day I took te Circle of morning Visits I went to te

---

[1] [A secret.] The ministry were sorely distracted between the reluctance of the Dutch to treat at all, and the artifices used by the French to make the most they could of the necessity of concluding peace to which the English administration were reduced. Bolingbroke, in a letter to Prior at Paris, urged that France should "depart from that shameful expedient, by which they thought to bubble us out of the advantages they had solemnly yielded"; else they and the Government were alike undone. "Make the French ashamed," he says elsewhere, "of their sneaking chicane; by Heaven, they treat like pedlars, or, which is worse, like attornies."—D. L. P.

[2] Obliterated.

[3] *See* Letter XIII., Jan. 6, 1710-11.

[4] Former editions add here "&c."—but the obliteration at this point seems to cover a note of odd pence.

[5], [6], [7] Obliterated.

[8] *See* Letter XXXI., Oct. 1 and 5, 1711.

[9] *See* Letters XVII., Feb. 25, 1710-11, and XXXVII., Dec. 29, 1711 (note).

[10] *See* Letter VI., Oct. 16, 1710.

[11] An uncertain line seems intended for interrogation point.

Dutchess of Ormd; & there was she & Ldy Betty, & Ld Ashburnham together: this was te first time te Mothr & Daughtr
saw each othr since Ldy Ashburnham's death; they were both
in Tears, and I chid them for being together, & made Ldy
Betty go to her own Chambr, then sate a while with te Dutchess,
& went after Lady Betty, & all was well. there is something of
Farce in all these Mournings let them be ever so serious. People
will pretend to grieve more than they really do, & that takes
off from their true Grief. I then went to Dutchess Hamilton,
who never grieved but raged & stormed & railed.[1] She is pretty
quiet now, but has a diabolicall Temper, Ld Keepr & his son,
and their two Ladyes and I dined to day with Mr. Cesar,[2]
Treasurer of te Navy at his House in te City where he keeps
his Office—We happened to [3] talk of Brutus, and I sd something
in his Praise, when it struck me immediatly that I had made
a Blunder in doing so, and therefore I recollected my self,
& sd, Mr Cesar I beg yr Pardon. So we laughd &c. [Nite my
own deelest richar logues MD.] [4]

15. I forgot to tell y tht last Night I had a present sent me
(I found it when I came home. in my Chambr) of te finest wild
fowl I ever saw. with the vilest Letter and from te vilest Poet
in te World, who sent it me as a bribe to get him an Employmt;
I knew not where te Scoundrel lived, so I could not send them
back, & therefore I gave them away as freely as I got them,
and have ordered my man never to let up te Poet when he comes,
te Rogue should have kept te Wings at least for his Muse. One
of his foul [i.e. fowl] was a large Capon Pheasant, as fat as a
Pullet. I eat share of it to day with a friend. We have now a
drawing room every Wednesday, Thursday and Saterday at
one a Clock: th Qu— does not come out, but all her Ministers,
Foreignrs & Persons of Quality are at it. I was there to day,
& as Ld Treasr came towards me I avoyded him, & he hunted
me thrice about te Room. I affect never to take notice of him
at Church or Court. He knows it, for I have told him so; and
to night at Ld Mashams he gave an Account of it to te Company, but my Reasons are, that People seeing me speak to
him causes me a great deal of teazing—I tell y what comes
into my head; that I never knew whether [MD] [5] were Whigs

---

[1] The Dean expresses very different sentiments of this lady in a preceding letter [Letter LV., Nov. 16, 1712]; but it is probable he had then
very little acquaintance with her.—B.
[2] See Letter XXI., April 17, 1711.
[3] Here ends the very pale ink he complained of.
[4], [5] Obliterated.

or Toryes; and I value our Conversation te more, that it never turnd on that Subject. I have a [Fancy that ppt][1] is a Tory, and a violent one; I don't know why; but methinks she looks like one; and Dd a sort of a Trimmer. Am I right.—I gave te Examiner a hint about this Prorogation, & to praise te Qu— for her tenderness to te Dutch in giving them still more time to submitt. It fitted te Occasions at present. [Nite MD.][2]

16. I was busy to day at te Sertys Office and stayd till past 3; te D. of Ormd & I were to dine at Ld Orkneys. te Duke was at te Committee: so I thought all was safe; when I went there they had almost dined; for te Duke had sent to excuse himself, which I never knew. I came home at 7, & began a little whim wch just came into my Head, & will make a threepenny Pamphlet. it shall be finished and out in a Week, and if it succeds y shall know what it is, otherwise not. I cannot send this to morrow and will put it off till next Saterday cause I have much business; so my Journalls shall be short, & MD must have Patience; so [Nite dee sollahs.][3]

17. This Rogue Parnel has not yet corrected his Poem, & I would fain have it out. I dined to day with Ld Treasr, and his Saterday company, nine of us in all. they went away at 7, and Ld Treasr & I sate talking an hour after. After dinner he was talking to te Lds about te Speech te Qu— must make when Parlmt meets. He asked me how I would make it. I was going to be serious; because it was seriously put; but I turned it to a Jest, and because they had been speaking of te Dutchess of Marlbr going to Flanders after te Duke, I sd, te Speech should begin thus. My Lds & Gentlemen; In order to my own Quiet, and that of my Subjects I have thought fit to send te Dutchess of Marlbr abroad after te Duke—This took well, & turned of [i.e. off] te discourse. I must tell y, I do not at all like te present Situation of Affairs; and remembr I tell y so. Things must be on anothr foot, or we are all undone. I hate this driving always to an Inch. [Nite MD.][4]

18. We had a mighty full Court to day. Dilly was with me at te French-church, and edifyed mightily. D. Ormd & I dined at Ld Orkney's, but I left them at 7, and came home to my whim. I have made a great Progress. My large Treatise[5] stands stock still; some think it too dangerous to publish, and would have me print onely what relates to te Peace. I can't tell what I shall do. The Bp of Dromore is dying. thy thought

1, 2, 3, 4 Obliterated.   5 His *History of the Peace of Utrecht.*—B.

yesterday he could not live 2 hours, yet he is still alive, but is utterly past all hopes. Go to Cards [sollahs, and Nite.] [1]

19. I was this morning to see te D. & Dutchess of Ormd, te Duke D. [sic] Aumont came in while I was with te Duke of Ormond, and we complimentd each other like Dragons. A poor Fellow calld at the door where I lodge, with a Parcel of Oranges for a Present for me; I bed my man know what his name was, & whence he came; he sent word his Name was Bun, and I knew him very well. I bid my Man tell him I was busy, & he could not speak to me, & not to let him leave his Oranges. I know no more of it But I am sure I never heard th Name, and I shall take no such Presents from Strangers; Perhaps he might be onely some Beggar who wanted a little Money; perhaps it might be something worse. Let them keep their Poison for their Rats. I dont love it. [Almost a whole line blotted out.] that blot is a Blundr. nite dee MD.

20. A Committee of our Society dined to day with te Chancllr of te Exchequr [2]; Our Society does not meet now as usuall; for wch I am blamed, but till Ld Tr will agree to give us money & Employmts to bestow, I am averse to it; & he gives us nothing but promises. Bp of Dromore is still alive, & that is all: we expect every day he will dy, & then Tom Leigh must go back, which is one good thing to te Town. I belive [sic] Prat will drive at one of these Bishopricks. Our English Bishoprick [3] is not yet disposed of. I believe te Peace will not be ready by te Session. Nite MD.

21. I was to day with my Printer, to give him a little Pamphlet I have written; but not Politicks; it will be out by Monday: if it succeeds I will tell you of it, otherwise not. we had a prodigious Thaw to day, as bad as rain, yet I walked like a good Boy all te way: Bp of Dromore still draws Breath, but cannot live 2 days longer. My large Book lyes flat; some people think, a great part of it ought not to be now printed; I believe I tod you so before. This Lettr shll not go till Saterday which makes up te 3 weeks exactly, and I allow MD 6 weeks, which are now almost out, so, oo must now [i.e. know] I expect a Rettle vely soon; & tht MD is vely werr,[4] and so Nite dee MD.

22. This is one of our Court days; and I was there. I told you, there is a drawing room Wednesday, thursday & Saterday:

---

[1] Obliterated.   [2] Benson.
[3] That of Hereford, vacant by the death of Dr. Humphrey Humphreys, Nov. 20, 1712, who was succeeded by Dr. Philip Bisse, translated from the see of St. David's.—B.
[4] "Very well."

the Hamiltons and Abercorns have done teising[1] me; te
latter I heer [sic] is actually going to France. Ld Tr quarrelld
with me at Court for beig 4 days without dining with him,
so I dined there to day. And he has at last fallen in with my
Project (as he calls it) of coining Halfpence & Farthings, with
devices like Medals, in honor of te Q, evry year changing te
Device: I wish it may be done. Nite MD.

23. D. Ormd & I appointd to dine with Ned Southwell to
day, to talk of settling yr Affairs of Parlmt in Ireld; but there
was a mixture of Company, & te D. Ormd was in hast, & nothing
was done. If yr Parlmt meets this Summer it must be a new
one; but I find some are of opinion there should be none at all
these 2 years. I will trouble my self no more about it. my
design was to serve th D. Ormd. Dr Prat & I sate this Evenig
with Dp Cl. & playd at Ombre for threepences. that I suppose
is but low with you. I found at comig home a Lettr flom MD.
N. 37; I shall not answr it zis bout, but will te next. I am sorry
for [poo poo ppt;][2] pray walk hen oo can. I have got a terrible
new Cold before my old one was quite gone; and dont know
how. [Pay**********][3] I shll have Dd's mony soon from te
Exchequr. Bp Dromore is dead now at last. [Nite dee MD.][4]

24. I was at Court to day, & it was comicall to see Ld Abercorn bowing to me, but not speaking. & Ld Selkirk th same.
I dined with Ld Treasr, & his Saterday Club, & sate with him
2 hours after te rest were gone, & spoke freer to him of affairs
than I am afraid others do, who might do more good. All his
Friends repine, & shrug their shoulders, but will not deal with
him so freely as they ought. Tis an odd Business. te Parlnt
just going to sit, and no Employmts given; they say they will
give them in a few days. There is a new Bishop made of Hereford; so Ossory[5] is disappointed; I hinted so to his Friends
2 Months ago, to make him leave of [i.e. off] deluding himself,
and being indiscreet as he was.—I have just time to send this
without going to te Bellman. [Nite deelest richr MD, farewell
dee MD MD MD FW FW FW Me Me Me lele lele lele.][6]

My second Cold is better now. lele lele lele   lele.

---

[1] Sic. See Letter LVII., Dec. 23: "teises."
[2] Obliterated.
[3] The words obliterated here are read by Forster: "Pay can oo walk
oftener—oftener still?" More probably they are "Pay aah well of oo
Helth?"—i.e. "Pray are [you] well of your health?"
[4] Obliterated.   [5] Hartstonge.   [6] Obliterated.

LETTER LIX

[Endorsed as last: save for reversion to " att," and that we have "St. Marye Church." Date of receipt, " Febr. 26."

59.   London. *Janry*. 25th. 1712-13.

WE had such a Terrible Storm to day, that going to Ld Bolin-brokes I saw a hundred Tiles fallen down, & one Swinger fell about 40 yards before me, that would have killd a Horse. So after Church & Court, I walked through te Park, & took a Chair to Ld Treasrs, next door to his House, a Tin Chimney top had fallen down, with a hundred Bricks. It is grown calm this Evening, I wonder had you such a Wind to day. I hate it as much as any Hog does. Ld Treasr has engagd me to dine with him again to morrow. He has those Tricks sometimes, of inviting me [or "one"] from day to day, wch I am forced to break through; My little Pamphlet[1] is out, tis not Politicks; if it takes I say again, y shll hear of it. [Nite dee logues.][2]

26. This morning I felt a little Touch of my Giddyness, which has disorderd & weakend me with its ugly remains all this day, [poo poo pdfr.][3, 4] After dinner at Ld Treasr, te Fr Ambassdr Duke d'Aumont sent Ld Tr word that his House was burnt down to te Ground, it took fire in te upper rooms while he was at Dinner with Monteleon the Span. Ambassdr, & other Persons, & soon after Ld Bolinbroke came to us with te same story.[5] We are full of Speculations upon it, but I believe it was te Carelessness of his French Rascally Servts. Tis odd that this very day Ld Sommers, Wharton, Sunderld Hallifax, and te whole Club of Whig Lords dined at Pontacks in te City, as I received private Notice; Thy have some damned design. I tell y anothr odd thing: I was observing it to Ld Treasr: that he was stabbed on te day K. Willm dyed, and the day I saved his life with opening te Banbox,[6] was K. Wms

---

[1] *See* Letter LVIII., Jan. 21.

[2, 3] Obliterated.

[4] Other versions: "Pity pdfr."

[5] At a dinner given by [? to] several of the nobility, by the duke d'Aumont, Jan. 26, between three and four in the afternoon, a fire broke out in the upper part of his excellency's house in Ormond-street, and burnt with such violence, that in two hours the house and chapel, consisting of three houses made into one, were laid in ashes. A great part of two adjoining houses, wherein the Lady Atteskew on the west side, and Hugh Parker, Esq., on the east, lived, were likewise burnt. A great quantity of goods of the Duke of Powis, which were locked up in the upper part of the house, were burnt, but the most valuable of the ambassador's furniture were saved.—*Evening Post*, Jan. 27, 1712-13.—N.

[6] He had already written "Band," but chose to obliterate the "d" by writing "b" over it.

birth-day. My Friend Mr. Lewis has had a Lye spread on him
by te mistake of a Man who went to anothr of his name to give
him thanks for passing his privy seal to come from France;
that tother Lewis, spread about that te Man brought him
thanks from Ld Perth,[1] & Ld Melfort,[2] (two Lds with te Pretender) for his great Services &c. te Lds will examine that
tother Lewis to morrow in Council, and I believe y will hear
of it in te Prints, for I will make Abel Roper give a Relation
of it. Pray tell me if it be necessary to write a little plainer;
for I lookt over a bit of my last Letter, & could hardly read it;
I'll med my Hand if oo please; but y are more used to it
NOR[3] I; as Mr Raymd says. [Nite MD][4]

27. I dined to day with Ld Treasr, this is 4 days togethr,
& he has invited me again to morrow, but I absolutely refused
him, I was this evening at a Christnig with him of Ld Dupplin's[5]
Daughter, he went away at 10, but thy kept me & some others
till past 12, so yr [*sic*] may be sure tis late as they say; We
have now stronger Suspicions that te D. D'aumonts [*sic*] House
was sett on fire by malice. I was to day to see Ld Keeper, who
has quite lost his Voice with a Cold, there Dr. Ratcliff[6] told
me, that it was te Ambassdrs Confectionr sett te House on fire
by boiling Sugar, & going down & letting it boyl over; yet others
still think differently, so I know not what to judge. [Nite my
own dearest[7] MD. rove pdfr.][8]

28. I was to day at Court, where te Span. Ambassdr talked
to me as if he did not suspect any design in burning D'Aumont's
House, but te Abbè[9] Gautier, Secrty for France here, sd
quite otherwise; & that D'Aumont had a Letter te very same
day to let him know his House should be burnd and thy tell
severall other Circumstances too tedious to write: one is that
a fellow mending te Tiles just when te fire broke out, saw a
Pot with wild fire in te room. I dined with Ld Orkney; neithr
Ld Abercorn nor Selkirk will now speak with me. I have dis-
obliged both sides. [Nite dear[7] MD][10]

[1] James Drummond (1648-1716), fourth earl, attended James II. in
his exile. His titles were forfeited on his death.
[2] John Drummond (c. 1650-1714-15), first earl, second son of third Earl
of Perth, attended James II. Outlawed, etc., 1694.
[3] Written large, and underlined.
[4] Obliterated.
[5] Lord Hay's.
[6] Radcliffe. *See* Letter IV., Sept. 29, 1710.
[7] Apparently not misspelt this time.
[8] Obliterated.
[9] He again accents it wrongly.
[10] Obliterated.

29. Our Society mett to day, 14 of us,, and at a Tavern,
We now resolve to meet but once a fortnight, and have a
Commttee every other week of 6 or 7, to consult about doing
some good. I proposed anothr Message to Ld Tr by 3 principall
Membrs to give 100 Guinneas to a certain Person, & they are
to urge it as well as they can. We also raised 60 Guinneas upon
our own Society; but I made them do it by Sessers,[1] and
I was one of them, & we fitted our Tax to the severall Estates;
te D. Ormd pays 10 Guinneas, & I the 3d part of a Guinnea;
at that Rate they may tax as often as they please. Well; but
I must answer [oo Rettle ung oomens;][2] not yet; tis [rate][3]
now, and I can't tind it. [Nite deelest MD.][4]

30. I have drank Spaw Waters[5] this 2 or 3 days, but they
do not pass, and mak me feel very giddy: I an't well [fais,][6]
I'll take them no more; I sauntrd aftr Church with te Provost
to day to see a Library to be sold, and dined at 5 with Ld
Orkney. We still think there was malic[7] in burnig D'Aumonts
house. I hear little Harrison[8] is come over; it was he I sent
to Utrecht; He is now Queens Secretary to the Ambassy; and
has brought with him te Barrier Treaty as it is now corrected
by us; and yielded to by te Dutch; which was te greatest difficulty to retard te Peace. I hope he will bring over te Peace
a month hence; for we will send him back as soon as possible;
I long to see te little Brat; my own Creature; his pay is in all
a thousand Pourids a Year, & they have never paid him a Groat,
though I have teazed their Hearts out. He must be 3 or 4
hundred Pounds in debt at least, te Brat. Let me go to [bed
sollahs; Nite dee richar MD.][9]

31. Harrison was with me this morning, we talked 3 hours,
and then I carryed him to Court. When we went down to te
door of my Lodging; I found a Coach waited for him, I chid
him for it, but he whisperd me, it was impossible to do otherwise; and in te Coach he told me[10] had not one farthing
in his Pocket to pay it; and therefore took te Coach for te
whole day, and intended to borrow money somewhere or other,
So there was te Queens Minister, entrusted in Affairs of greatest
Importance, without a Shilling in his Pocket to pay a Coach.
I payd him while he was with me 7 Guinneas, in part of a dozen
of Shirts he bought me in Holland. I presented him to te D.
Ormd, & sevrall Lds at Court. And I contrivd it so, that Ld

---

[1] Assessors.   [2, 3, 4] Obliterated.
[5] Originally from Spa, in the province of Liège, Belgium.
[6] Obliterated.   [7] Sic.
[8] See Letter VI., Oct. 13, 1710.   [9] Obliterated.   [10] " he " omitted.

Treasr came to me & asked (I had Parnel by me) whethr that was Dr Parnel, and came up and spoke to him with great kindness, & invited him to his House. I value my self upon making te Ministry desire to be acquainted with Parnel; & not Parnel with te Ministry; His Poem is almost fully corrected, and shall soon be out. Here's enough for to day, onely to tell y, that I was in te City with my Printer to alter an Examiner about my Friend Lewis's Story, which will be told with Remarks.[1] [Nite MD.][2]

Febr. 1. I could no nothig till to day about te Examinr; but te Printer came this morning, and I dictated to him what was fitt to be sd, and then Mr Lewis came and corrected as he would have it. So I was neither at Church nor Court. D. Ormd & I dined at Ld Orkney's. I left them at 7, and sate with Sr A. Fountain, who has a very bad core Logj for wch he designs to go to France. [Fais][3] here's a Week gone, and one side of this Letter not finished. oh, but I write now but once in 3 weeks; [iss fais],[4] this shall go sooner. Th Parlmt is to sitt on te 3d but will adiourn for 3 or 4 days: for te Qu— is layd up with te Gout. and both Speakers out of order, thō one of them te Ld Keepr is almost well. I spoke to D. Ormd a good deal about Ireld; we do not altogethr agree, nor am I judge enough of Irish Affairs; but I will speak to Ld Tr— to morrow, that we 3 may settle them some way or other. [Nite sollahs both, rove pdfr.][5]

2. I had a Lettr some days ago from Mol Geree, her name is now Wigmore,[6] & her Husbd is turned Parson, she desires nothing but that I would get Ld Keepr to give him a Living, but I will send her no answer, thō she desires it much, she still makes mantuas at Farnham. It raind all this day; & Dilly came to me, and was coaching it into te City, so I went with him for a shaking, because it would not cost me a Farthing; thus I mett my Friend Stratford te Merchant, who is going abroad to gathr up his Debts, & be clear in te World. he beggd me I would dine with some Merchant friends of ours there, because it was te last time I should see him, so I did, & thought to have se [?en][7] Ld Treasr in te Evening; but he happend to go out at 5, so I visited some Friends, and came home. and now I have te

[1] See *A complete Refutation of the falsehoods alledged against Erasmus Lewis, esq.*
[2], [3], [4], [5] Obliterated.
[6] Supposed to be sister of the "parson Geree" mentioned at end of Letter XLVI.
[7] Rubbed out by thumbing.

greatest part of yr Lettr to answer; & yet I will not to it to
night, say what [oo][1] please. The Parlmt meets to morrow,
but will be prorogued for a fortnight, which disappointmt will,
I believe vex abundance of them though they are not whigs;
For they are forced to be in Town at Expence for nothing.
But we want an answer from Spain, before we are sure of every
thing right for th Peace; and God knows whethr we can have
that Answer this Month. It is a most ticklish juncture of
Affairs; We are always driving to an Inch. I am weary of it.
[Nite MD][2]

3. Th Parlnt mett & was prorogued as I sd; and I found
some cloudy faces, & heard some grumbling; We have got
over all our Difficultyes with France, I think. They have now
settled all the Articles of Commerce between us and them,
wherein they were very much disposed to play te Rogue if we
had not held thcm to. and this Business we wait from Spain
is to prevent some other Rogueryes of te French, who are
finding an Evasion to trade to te Spanish West Indyes; but
I hope, we shall prevent it; I dined with Ld Treasr, and he was
in good humor enough. I gave him that Part of my Book in
Manuscript to read, where his Character was, and drawn pretty
freely; he was reading & correcting it with his Pencil, when
te Bp of St Davids (now removing to Hereford)[3] came ın,
& interrupted us; I left him at 8. & satt till 12 with te Provost,
& Bp of Cl. at te Provost's [Nite MD.][4]

4. I was to day at Court, but kept out of Ld Trr's way.
because I was engagd to te D. Ormd, where I dined, and I
think eat and drank too much. I sate this Evenig with Ldy
Masham, & then with Ld Masham & Ld Treasr at Ld Mashams:
it was last year, you may remembr, my constant evening
Place. I saw Ldy Jersey [5] with Ldy Masham, who has been
laying out for my Acquaintance, and has forced a Promise for
me to drink Chocolate with her in a day or two, which I know
not whether I shall perform, (I have just mended my Pen you
see) for I do not much like her Character, but she is very
malicious, and therefore I think I must keep fair with her.
I can not send this Letter till Saterday next I find. So I will
answer oors now. I see no different days of te Month; yet it is
dated Janr. 3d, so it was long a coming.—I did not write to

---

[1], [2] Obliterated.   [3] Philip Bisse.   [4] Obliterated.
[5] Judith (d. 1735), daughter of Frederick Herne, of London, was married
(1704-5) to William Villiers, second Earl of Jersey. See Letter XXX.,
Sept. 15, 1711.

Dr Coghill that I would have nothing in Ireld; but that I was
solliciting nothing any where, & that is true: I have named
Dr. Stearn to Ld Tr, Ld Bolingbr and D. Ormd for a Bishoprick: and I did it heartily; I know not what will come of it;
but I tell y as a great Secret, that I have made D. Ormd promise
me to recommend nobody till he tells me; and this for some
Reasons too long to mention. My head is still in no good Order,
I am heartily sorry for [pooppt][1] I am sure, [her][2] head is
good for [sumsing][3, 4]—I'll answer more to mo[llow. Nite ***
dee Sollahs MD.][5]

5. I must go on with [oo][6] Letter. I dined to day with
Sr B. Fountain, & Provost[7] & I playd at Ombre with him all
te afternoon, I wone yet Sr Andrw is an admirable Player. Ld
Pembroke[8] came in, & I gave him 3 or 4 scurvy Dilly-Puns,
that begin with an *if*.[9] Woll but oor Lettor; well, ret me see.
No, I believe I shll write no more this good while, nor publish
what I have done.—[Maram ppt *** oo ****[10] *****][11] I did
not suspect [oo][12] would tell Filby.[13] [oo][14] are so [*****][15, 16]
[********][17, 18] Turns and Visitations, what are those; I'll
preach & visit as much for Mr Walls.—Pray Gd mend poopts
Health, mine is but very indifferent; I have left Spaw-water:
it makes my leg swell. [Nite deelest MD.][19]

6. This is te Qu—'s birthday, and I never saw it celebrated
with so much Luxry. and fine Cloaths, I went to Court to see
them; & I dined with Ld Keeper, where te Ldyes were fine to
admiration; I passt te Evenig at Mrs Vanhomrighs, and came
home pretty early; to answer [oo][20] Rettle again. Pray Gd
keep te Qu—. She was very ill about ten days ago, & had te
Gout in her Stomach; when I came from Ld Keeprs, I calld
at Ld Treasrs, because I heard he was very fine, and that was
a new Thing; & it was true, for his Coat & Westcoat were
embroyderd. I have seen te Provost, often since, & never spoke

[1, 2, 3] Obliterated.
[4] Forster reads "something," but all readings are doubtful.
[5, 6] Obliterated.
[7] Dr. Pratt.
[8] *See* Letter VII., Oct. 28, 1710.
[9] Underlined word.
[10] ? "only." Forster reads "Nauty ppt oo are vely tempegant." But
the first word is certainly "Maram."
[11, 12] Obliterated.
[13] *See* Letter LV., Nov. 18, 1712.
[14, 15] Obliterated.
[16] Forster reads " 'recise"—which seems unlikely.
[17] Obliterated.
[18] "How is oo health?" seems possible.
[19, 20] Obliterated.

to him to speak to te Temples about Daniel Corr [or "Carr"],
nor will; I don't care to do it. I have writt lately to Parvisol.
[Oo][1] did well to let him make up his Accounts. All things grow
dear in Ireld but Corn to te Paasons. For my Livings are fallen
much this Year by Parvisol's Account. [Nite dee logues MD.] [2]

7 [? 8.][3] I was at Court to day, but saw no Birthday
Cloaths, the great Folks never wear them above once or twice
I dined with Ld Orkney: and sate te Evening with Sr A. Fountain, whose Leg is in a very dubious Condition Pray let me
know when [Dd's][4] money is near due; allways let me know
it before hand; this I believe will hardly go till Saturday [5];
for I tell y what; being not very well, I dare not study much;
so I let Company come in a morning; & te afternoon pass in
dining & sitting some where. Ld Tr— is angry if I dont dine
with him every 2d day; & I cannot part with him till late; he
kept me last night till near 12. Our Weathr is constant rain
above these 2 Months, which hinders walking, so that our
Spring is not like yours. I have not seen Fanny Manly [6] yet.
I cannot find time. I am in rebellion with all my Acquaintance;
but I will mend with my Health and the Weather.—Cloghr
make a Figure! Cloghr make a —— Colds; why we have been
all dying with Colds, but [now] [7] they are a little over, & my
Second is almost off. I can do nothing for Swanton [8] indeed.
This a thing impossible, and wholly out of my way; if he buys
he must buy. So now I have answrd oo [or "ee"] Rettle, and
there's an end of that now: and I'll say no more but bid [oo
Nite dee MD.] [9]

8. [? 9.] It was terrible rainy to day from morning till night.
I intendd to have dined with Ld Treasr; but went to see Sr
A. Fountain, & he kept me at dinner, which saved Coachhire,
& [10] stayd with him all te afternoon, & lost 13s-6d at Ombre,
there was managmt, & Ld Tr will chide, but I'll dine with him
to morrow: Bp Cl's Daughtr has been ill some days,[11] and it
proves te Small Pox, she is very full, but it comes out well,

---

[1], [2] Obliterated.
[3] A day was dropped somewhere between 6th and 12th (*see* latter
date). The uncertainty is indicated by figures in square brackets. Queen
Anne was born 6th.
[4] Obliterated.
[5] First correct spelling of this word.
[6] *See* Letter LVII., Dec. 21, 1712.
[7] Former readings followed. Paper torn and mended.
[8] *See* Letter LIII., Oct. 9, 1712.
[9] Obliterated.　　　　　　　　[10] "I" omitted.
[11] *See* Letter LVII., Dec. 30, 1712.

& they apprehend no danger. Ldy Orkney has given me her Picture a very fine Originall of Sr Godfrey Knellers it is now a mending. He has favored her squint admirably, & you know I love a Cast in te Eye; I was to see Ldy Worsley[1] to day, who is just come to Town, She is full of Rumatick pains, all my Acquaintance grow old & sickly. She lodges in te very house in Kingstreet between St. James's Street & St. James square where Dd's Brothr brought[2] te Sweetbread, when I lodged there, & [Dd][3] came to see me. Short [sighs.[4] Nite MD.][5]

9. [? 10.] I thought to have dined with Ld Tr to day, but he dined abroad at Tom Harley's.[6] So I dined at Ld Masham's. and was winning all I had lost with playing with Ldy Masham at Crown Picket, when we went to Pools, & I lost it again. Ld Tr— came in to us, and chid me for not following him to Tom Harley's. Miss Ash is still te same, & they think her not in dangr: my man calls there daily; after I am gone out, and tells me at night. I was this morning to see Ldy Jersey,[7] & we have made twenty partyes about dining together, & I shall hardly keep one of them. She is reduced after all her greatness, to Seven Servants, and a small House; & no Coach: I like her tolerably as yet. [Nite MD.][8]

10. [? 11.] I made visits this Morning, to te D. & Dutchess Ormd, & Ldy Betty,[9] & Dutchess Hamilton (when I was writing this near 12 a Clock te Dutchess Hamilton sent to have me dine with her to morrow, I am forced to give my answer thro te door, for my Man has got te Key, & is gone to bed; but I can not obey her, for our Society meets to morrow) I stole away from Ld Tr by 8, and intended to have passed te Evening with Sr Thomas Clarges[10] & his Ldy, but met them in anothr Place, & there have sate till now. my Head has not been ill to day; I was at Court, & made Ld Mansel walk with me in te Park before we went to dinner. yesterday & to day have been fair, but yet it rained all last night. I saw Stearne[11] staring at

---

[1] *See* Letter XIV., Jan. 20, 1710-11.
[2] Former reading, "bought."
[3] Obliterated.
[4] Forster's reading. *See* Letter XVI., Feb. 21, 1710-11.
[5] Obliterated.
[6] *See* Letter XXIV., May 24, 1711.
[7] *See* 4th.   [8] Obliterated.
[9] Butler (her daughter).
[10] Sir Thomas Clarges (1688-1759), second baronet, married Barbara, second daughter of John Berkeley, fourth Viscount Fitzhardinge, by his wife Barbara (daughter of Sir Edward Villiers), one of whose sayings is recorded in Letter LIV., Oct. 30, 1712. He was afterwards M.P. for Lostwithiel.
[11] Enoch.

Court to day; He has been often to see me he says; but my
Man has not yet let him up; he is in deep mourning; I hope it
is not for his Wife: I did not ask him. [Nite MD.][1]

12. I have reckond days wrong all this while for this is te 12,
I don't know when I lost it I dined to day with our Society,
te greatest dinner I have ever seen; it was at Jack Hills te
Governr of Dunkirk. I gave an Account of 60 Guinneas I had
collectd, & am to give them away to 2 Authors to morrow.
and Ld Tr has promised us 100ll to reward some others. I
found a Letter on my Table last night to tell me that poor
little Harrison te Queens Secrty that came lately from Utrecht
with te Barrier Treaty was ill & desired to [? see][2] me at
Night but it was late & I could not go till to day. I have often
mentiond him in my Letters. you may remembr ***[3] I went
in te morning, & found him mighty ill, & got 30 Guinneas for
him from Ld Bolinbroke; & an order for a 100ll from te Treasury
to be pd him to morrow. & I have got him removed to Knights
bridge for Air. He has a Feaver & Inflammation on his Lungs;
but I hope will do well. [? Nite.][4]

13. I was to see a poor Poet one Mr. Diaper,[5] in a nasty
Garret, very sick; I gave him 20 Guinneas from Ld Bolingbrok,
& disposed the othr 60 to 2 other Authors, & desird a Friend
to receive te 100ll for poor Harrison; and will carry it him to
morrow morning. I sent to see how he did, & he is extreamly
ill, & I very much afflicted for him, for he is my own Creature,
& in a very honorable Post, and very worthy of it. I dined in
te City. I am in much concern for this poor Lad. His Mothr
& Sister attend him, & he wants nothing. [Nite poo dee MD.][6]

14. I took Parnel this morning and we walkt to see poor
Harrison, I had te 100ll in my Pocket. I told Parnel I was
afraid to knock at te door; my mind misgave me. I knockt,
& his man in Tears told me his Master was dead an hour before.
Think what Grief this[7] to me; I went to his Mothr, & have
been ordering things for his Funerall with as little Cost as
possible, to morrow at ten at night. Ld Treasr was much con-
cernd when I told him. I could not dine with Ld Tr nor any
where, but got a bit of meat towards Evening. no loss ever

---

[1] Obliterated.
[2] Sheet mended here
[3] Obliterated word.
[4] Obliterated. Doubtful.
[5] *See* Letter XLIII., March 12, 1711-12.
[6] Obliterated.
[7] Sheet mended here—probably obliterating an "is."

grieved me so much. poor Creature.—Pray Gd Almighty bless poor [MD][1]—adieu—

I send this away to night and am sorry it must go while I am in so much Grief.

LETTER LX

[Endorsed as last: save for spelling, "St. Mary's." Date of receipt, "Mar. 7."]

60.   London. *Febr.* 15 [2]

I DINED to day with Mr Row [3] and a Projector, who has been teazing me wit 20 Scheams, to get Grants, and I don't like one of them. and besides I was out of humour for te Loss of poor Harrison. at ten this night I was at his Funerall, wch I ordered to be as private as possible, we had but one Coach, with 4 of us, and when it was carrying us home after te Funerall te Braces broke, and we were forced to sitt in it and have it held up, till my Man went for chairs, at 11 at night, in terrible rain. I am come home very melancholy; and will go to bed. [Nite my *** [4] deelest MD.] [5]

16. I dined to day with Ld Dupplin, & some company to divert me, but left them early, & have been reading a foolish book for amusement. I shall never have courage again to care for making any body's Fortune. Th Parlmt meets to morrow, and will be prorogued anothr fortnight; at wch sevrall of both Partyes are angry, but it cannot be helped, though every thing about te Peace is past all danger I never saw such a Continuance of rainy weathr, we have not had 2 fair days together these 10 weeks. I have not dined with Ld Tr these 4 days, nor can till Saterday, for I have severall engagements till then, & he will chide me to some purpose. I am perplexed with this iooll of poor Harrisons, wht to do with it, I cannot pay his Relatives till thy administer, for he is much in debt; but I will have te Staff in my own hands; and venture nothing. [Nite poo dee MD.] [6]

17. Lady Jersey & I dined by Appointmt to day with Ld Bolinbr— He is sending his Brothr [7] to succeed Mr. Harrison; It is te prettyest Post in Europe for a young Gentleman I lose my money at Ombre sadyl; I make a thousand Blunders. I play

---

[1] Obliterated.   [2] "1712-13" omitted.
[3] *See* Letter V., Oct. 4, 1710.   [4] Forster reads "own."
[5] Obliterated. It is, by the way, oddly characteristic of the epistolary habits of the time, that Swift does not mention *where* they buried Harrison. And it does not appear to be known.   [6] Obliterated.
[7] His younger half-brother, George St. John (*d.* 1715-16).

putt [*sic*] threepenny Ombre, but it is wht y call running
Ombre. Lady Clarges & a drab I hate, won a dozin shillings of
me last night. The Parlnt was prorogud to day, and people
grumble. & te good of it is, te Peace can not be finished by te
Time they meet; there are so many fidlig things to do.—Is
[Ppt][1] an Ombre Lady yet. you know all te Tricks of it now
I suppose. I reckon y have all yr Cards from France; for ours
pay 6 pence a Pack taxes, wch goes deep to te Box. I have given
away all my Spaw water, and take some nasty steel drops,
& may [*i.e.* my] head has been bettr this week past. I send
every day to see how Miss Ash does; she is very full they say,
but in no danger. I fear she will lose some of her Beauty;
The son lyes out of te House, I wish he had them too, while
he is so young. [Nite MD.][2]

18. te Earl of Abingdon[3] had been teazing me these 3 Months
to dine with him, & to day was appointd about a week ago;
and I named my Company, Ld Stawell,[4] Coll Disney,[5] & Dr
Arbuthnott; but te 2 last slippt out their Necks & left Stawel
and me to dine there. we did not dine till 7, because it is Ash-
wednesday, we had nothing but Fish, which Ld Stawel could
not eat, and gott a broyld leg of a Turkey. Our wine was
Poison; yet te Puppy has 12 thousd pd a year. His Carps were
raw, & his Candles tallow. I [*i.e.* He] shall not catch me again
in hast, and every body has laughd at me for dining with him.
I was to day to let Harrisons mothr know I coud not pay her
till she administers, wch she will do; I belive she is [an old
Bawd][6] & her Daughter [a —— [7]][8] There were more whigs
to day at Court than Toryes; I believe they think te Peace must
be made, and so come to please te Qu. She is still lame with
te Gout. [Nite MD.][9]

19. I was at Court to day to speak to Ld Bolinbroke to look
over Parnels Poem since it is corrected, & Parnel & I dined
with him to day & he had shewn him 3 or 4 more Places to after
a little. Ldy Bolinbr— came down to us while we were at
dinner, & Parnel stared at her as if she were a Goddess. I thought
she was like Parnels wife; & he thought so too. Parnel is much
pleased with Ld Bolinbrs favor to him, & I hope it may one day

[1, 2] Obliterated.

[3] Montague Bertie (afterwards Venables-Bertie) (167-?-1743), second
earl; Lord-Lieutenant of Oxfordshire, Chief-Justice in Eyre, and Recorder
of Oxford.

[4] *See* Letter XI., Dec. 23, 1710 (note).

[5] *See* Letter XVI., Feb. 19, 1710-11.

[6] Obliterated.

[7] No substantive was written—only a dash.   [8, 9] Obliterated.

turn to his Advantage. His Poem will be printed in a few days. Our Weather continues as fresh raining as if it had not rained at all. I sate to night at Ldy Masham's where Ld Tr— came, and scolded me for not dining with him, I told him I could not till Saterday. I have staid there till past 12. So [Nite dee sollahs MD.]¹

20. Ldy Jersey, Ldy Catherine Hide,² te Spanish Ambassdr,³ te Duke d'Atree⁴ anothr Spaniard, & I, dined to day by appointment with Ld Bolinbrok, but thy fell a drinking so many Spanish Healths in Champagne, that I stole away to te Ladyes, and drank Tea, till 8, and then went and lost my money at Ombre with Sr A. Fountain, who has a very bad Leg: Miss Ash is past all danger, and her Eye which was lately bad (I suppose one Effect of her distemper) is now better. I do not let te Bishop see me, nor shll this goodwhile. Good luck, when I came home I warrant I found a Letter from [MD]⁵ N. 38 and [oo]⁶ write so small now [a days]⁷ I hope [oo poor eyes are better.]⁸ Well, this shll go to morrow sennight, with a Bill for [MD.]⁹—I will speak to Mr. Griffin¹⁰ to morrow about [ppt]¹¹ Brothr, Filby, and desire, whethr he deserves or no, that his Employmt may be mended; that is to say if I can see Griffin, otherwise not. & I'll answr [oo Rettle hen I Pdfr]¹² think fitt. [Nite MD.]¹³

21. Mesinks I writt a little sawcy last night, I mean [te last words God ***]¹⁴ I saw Griffin at Court, he says he knows nothing of a salt work at Recton, but that he will give Filby a better Employmt, & desires Filby will write to him; If I knew how to write to Filby I would; but pray do you: bid him make no mention of you; but only let Mr. Griffin know, that he had had te honr to be recommended by Dr. S— &c, that he will endeavr to deserve &c; and if you dictated a whole Letter for him it would be bettr; I hope he can write & spell well. I'll enquire for a direction to Griffin before I finish this. I dined with Ld Treasr, & 7 Lords to day; y know Saturday¹⁵ is his great day; but I sat with them [? him] alone till 8, & then came home and have been writing a Lettr to Mrs. Davis at York, she took care to have a Lettr deliverd for me at Ld Tr's, for

---

¹ Obliterated.
² See Letter XL., Jan. 30, 1711-12. Afterwards Duchess of Queensberry
³ Monteleon.
⁴ Victor-Marie (1660-1737), Maréchal et Duc d'Estrees — a French nobleman. A comma is "understood" after his name.
⁵, ⁶, ⁷, ⁸, ⁹ Obliterated. ¹⁰ See Letter LV., Nov. 18, 1712.
¹¹, ¹², ¹³, ¹⁴ Obliterated. ¹⁵ Spelt correctly here.

I would not own one she sent by Postt: She reproaches me for not writing to her these 4 Years; & I have honestly told her, it was my way never to write to those whom I never am likely to see, unless I can serve them, wch I cannot her &c. Davis te Schoolmastrs Widow. [Nite MD.]¹

22. I dined to day at Ld Orkneys with D. Ormd & Sr T. Hanmer; have y ever heard of te latter. He marryed te Dutchess of Grafton ² in his Youth (she dined with us too) he is te most considerable Man in te H. of Commons, He went last Spring to Flanders with D. Ormd, from thence to France, & was going to Italy, but te Ministry sent for him, & he has been come over about ten days. He is much out of Humor with things, he thinks the Peace is kept off too long; & is full of Fears ³ and doubts; It is thought he is designed for Secrty of State instead of Ld Dartmouth. We have been acquainted these 2 years, and I intend in a day or two to have an Hours talk with him on Affairs. I saw Bp Cloghr at Court; Miss is recovering, I know not how much she will be marked. Th Qu— is slowly mending of her Gout, & intends to be brought in a Chair to Parlmt when it meets. wch will be Mar. 3, for I suppose they will prorogue no more; yet te Peace will not be signed then; & we apprehend te Toryes themselves will many of them be discontented. [Nite dee MD.]⁴

23. It was ill weath to day, & I dined with Sr A. Fountain, & in te Evenig playd at Ombre with him & te Provost, & won 25 shillings; so I have recovered my self pretty well. Dilly has been dunning me to see Fanny Manley, but I have not yet been able to do it. Miss Ash is now quite out of danger, and they hope will not be much marked. I cannot tell how to direct to Griffin, & think he lives in Bury Street near St. James's Street, hard by me; but I suppose yr Brothr may direct to him to te Salt Office and as I remembr he knows his Christian name because you sent it me in te list of te Commissioners. [Nite dee MD.]⁵, ⁶

24. I walkd this morning to Chelsea to see Dr. Atterbury Dean of Christ-church. I had business with him about entering Mr Fitsmorris ⁷ My Ld Kerry's son into his Colledge, & Ldy

¹ Obliterated.
² See Letters IX., Nov. 15, 1710, and XXXV., Nov. 22, 1711.
³ Looks more like "Feers."
⁴, ⁵ Obliterated.
⁶ Former readings followed, the passage being much thumbed.
⁷ Probably William Fitzmaurice. See Letters XI., Dec. 13, 1710, and XXVII., Aug. 31, 1711.

Kerry is a great Favorite of mine. Ld Harley, Ld Dupplin Young Bromly te Speakers son,[1] and I dined with Dr Stratford[2] and some othr Clergymen, but I left them at 7, to go to Ldy Jersey to see Monteleon te Span. Ambassdr play at Ombr. Ldy Jersey was abroad, & I chid te Servants, and made a Rattle, but since I came home, she sent me a Message, that I was mistaken, & that te meeting is to be to morrow. I have a worse memory than when I left y, and every day forget Appointments, but here my memory was by chance too good.[3] But I'll go to morrow, for Ldy Kath. Hide & Ldy Bolinbroke are to be there by my Appointmt and I tifted [4] up my Perewig and all, to make a Figure; Well. who [tan help it. not I. vow to **** Nite MD.] [5]

25. Ld Tr met me last night at Ld Mashams, & thanked me for my company in a Jear because I had not dined with him in 3 days; He chides if I stay but two days away togethr. what will this come to——nothing. My Grandmothr [6] used to say, More of yr Lining, and less of yr dining. Howevr I dind with him, & coud hardly leave him at 8 to go [7] Ldy Jerseys, wher 5 or 6 foreign Ministers were, & as many Ladyes. Monteleon playd like te English, & cryed gacco,[8] and knocked his knuckles for Jump [9]; and playd at smell-Games [10] like [Ppt.] [11] Ldy Jersey whisperd me to stay & sup with te Ldys when te

[1] Apparently William Bromley (?1699–1732), second son of the Speaker of the same name.

[2] See Letter XIV., Jan. 22, 1710-11.

[3] As it stands, this is a bull, worthy of the stage-Irishman; but perhaps he means that Lady Jersey was fibbing and had put off the party till to-morrow.

[4] Mr. Ryland hesitates between "lifted" and "listed." Mr. Aitken adopts "listed," and offers an ingenious explanation—which is rendered unnecessary by the plain fact that the first letter is not an "l" but a "t." To tift anything up is to smarten it: the expression is a Northern one, and Swift probably acquired it while he lived at Kilroot. See *Oxford Dictionary*—"tift," *verb*.

[5] Obliterated.

[6] Probably a mythical grandmother. His paternal grandmother was Elizabeth Dryden; the name of his maternal one is unknown.

[7] "to" omitted.

[8] "Gacco" it certainly looks like, and so Messrs. Ryland and Aitken read; but they do not say what "gacco" means, if it means anything. The old reading is "game"; and it may be merely "game" badly written.

[9] Former reading, "trump"—which is certainly wrong. "Jump" is probably the same as "Pass."

[10] Former reading, "small games"—and that without the hyphen, which is distinct in the manuscript. *Cf.* Letter XI., Dec. 13, 1710, where the context gives some hint of a possible meaning, if "smell" is read, and not "small." Experienced card-players can best judge. Anyway, the word *looks* more like "smell."

[11] Obliterated.

Fellows were gone, but thy playd till 11, and I woud not stay;
—I think this Lettr must go on Saterday thts certain, & it is
not half full yet. Ldy Katherine Hide had a mighty mind
I shoud be acquainted with Ldy Dalkeith her Sister, te D. of
Monmouths eldest son's Widow;[1] who was of te Company
to night; but I did not like her, she paints too much. [Nite
MD.][2]

26. This day our Society met at te D. Ormond's but I had
Business tht calld me anothr way, so I sent my Excuses, and
dind privately with a Friend. Besides Sr T. Hanmer whisprd
me last night at Ldy Jersey's that I must attend Ld Tr and
D. Ormd at Supper at his House to night, which I did at 11
and stayd till 1. so [oo][3] may be sure tis late enough there
was te Dutchess of Grafton; & te Duke her son,[4] nine of us
in all. D. Ormd chid me for not beig at Society to day, & sd
16 was [sic] there; I sd I never knew 16 People good Company
in my Life; no [fais][5] nor 8 neither.—We have no news in
this Town at all; I wonder why I don't write you news; I know
less of what passes than any body: because I go to[6] no Coffee
House; nor see any but Ministers and such People, and Ministers
never talk Politicks in Conversation; the Whigs are forming
great Schemes against te meeting of Parlmt, wch will be next
Tuesday I still think, without fail. and we hope to hear by then,
tht te Peace is ready to sign. te Qu—'s Gout mends daily.
[Nite MD.][7]

27. I passed a very insipid day, and dined privately with a
Friend in te Neighborhood, did I tell you, tht I have a very
fine Picture of Ldy Orkney,[8] an Originall by Sr Godfrey
Kneller, 3 quarters length. I have it now at home with a fine
Frame. Ld Bolingbr— & Ldy Masham have promised to sit
for me, but I despair of Ld Tr, onely I hope he will give me
a Copy, and then I shall have all te Pictures of those I really
love, here; just half a dozen. onely I'll make Ld Keepr give
me his Print in a frame. this Lettr must go to morrow. because
of sending Me a Bill, else it should not till next week, I assure

[1] Henrietta (c. 1677–1730), married, 1693-4, James Scott (1674–1704-5), second (but first surviving) son of James, Duke of Monmouth, who rebelled against James II. Scott was *styled* Earl of Dalkeith.
[2, 3] Obliterated.
[4] Charles FitzRoy (1683–1757), second duke.
[5] Obliterated.
[6] He had written "frequent," but substituted "go to."
[7] Obliterated.
[8] Dr. Swift left this picture to John, Earl of Orrery, who married Lady Orkney's daughter.—N.

[oo].[1] I have little to do now with my Pen; for my grand Business[2] stops [?] till they are more pressing, and till something or othr happens, and I belive I shall return [? retain] with disgust to finish it. it is so very laborious. Sr T. Hanmer has my Papers now. And [hat][3] is [MD][4] doing now; oh, at Ombre with te Dean always on Friday night, with Mrs Walls, pray don't play at smell[5] Games. I stood by tothr night while te Duke d'Atree lost 6 times with malilio [sic], basto,[6] and 3 small Trumps. and Ldy Jersey won above 2oll [Nite dee richr MD.][7]

28. I was at Court to day when te Abbè Gautier whisperd me that a Courier was just come with an Account tht te F. King had consented to all te Qu—'s demands, and His Consent was carryed to Utrecht, and te Peace will be signed in a few days; I suppose te Genrll Peace cannot be so soon ready but that is no matter. Th News presently ran about te Court. I saw te Qu carryed out in her Chair to take te Air in te Garden. I met Griffin at Court, & he told me, that Orders were sent to examine Filby, and if he be fitt, to make him (I think he calld it) an Assistant; I don't know what, Supervisor, I think; but it was some Emplymt a good deal bettr than his own. The Parlmt will have anothr short Prorogation, thõ it is not known yet— I dined with Ld Treasr and his Saterday company, and left him at 8 to putt this into te Post Office time enough. And now I must bid ee [or "oo"] farewell [deelest richr MD. God bless ... ever, & rove pdfr.][8] farewell [MD MD MD FW FW FW FW Me Me   lele - lele   —][9]

LETTER LXI

[Endorsed as last: only hyphen omitted. Date of receipt, " Mar. 27."]

61.   Lond. *Mar.* 1. 1712-13.

TIS out of my head whether I answerd all yr Lettr in my last yesterday or no. I think I was in hast and could not but now I see I answerd a good deal of it, no, onely about y- Brothr,

---

[1] Obliterated.
[2] His *History of the Peace of Utrecht.*—B.
[3], [4] Obliterated.
[5] The third letter is not so distinct here, and there is no hyphen before "Games"; but the reading of Feb. 25 is followed.
[6] The ace of clubs.   [7], [8], [9] Obliterated.

and Me Bill. I dined with Ldy Orkney, and we talkt Politicks
till 11 at night—and as usuall, found every thing wrong, &
put our selves out of humor.—Yes I have Ldy G's [*i.e.* Giffard's]
Picture, sent me by yr Mothr; It is Boxed up at a Place where
my other things are; I have goods in 2 or 3 Places; & when
I leave a Lodging, I box up the Books I get (for I always get
some) and come naked into a new Lodging; and so on.—Talk
not to me of Deanry's I know less of that than ever by much
[Nite MD.] [1]

2. I went to day into te City to see Pat Rolt,[2] who lodges
with a City Cozen, a daughter of Coz Cleve (y are much te wiser)
I had never been at her House before. My He Coz Tompson te
Butchr is dead or dying. I dined with my Printer, and walked
home, and went to sitt with Ldy Clarges, I found 4 of them at
Whist, Ldy Godolphin [3] was one. I sat by her, & talked of her
Cards &c, but she would not give one Look, nor say a word
to me. She refused some time ago to be acquainted with me.
Y know, she is Ld Marlbroughs eldest Daughter. She is a fool
for her Pains, & I'll pull her down.——What can I do for Dr
Smiths [4] daughters husband: I have no personall Credit with
any of te Commissionrs. I'll speak to Keightly,[5] but I believe
it will signify nothing. in te Customs people must rise by
degrees; and he must at first take what is very low, if he be
qualifyed for that. [Ppt] [6] mistakes me; I am not angry at
your recommending any one to me, provided y will take my
Answer. Some things are in my way; & then I serve those
I can: But People will not distinguish, but take things ill when
I have no Power. . but Ppt is wiser. And Employmts in genrll
are very hard to be got. [Nite MD.] [7]

3. I dined to day with Ld Tr; who chid me for my absence,
wch was onely for Saterday last. Th Parlmt was again prorogued for a week; and I suppose te Peace will be ready by
then, & te Qu— will be able to be brought to te House, and make
her Speech.—I saw Dr. Griffith [8] 2 or three Months ago at a
Latin Play at Westminstr; but did not speak to him: I hope
he will not dye. I should be sorry for [ppt's] [9] sake, He is very

---

[1] Obliterated.
[2] Patty. *See* Letter III., Sept. 14, 1710.
[3] Formerly Lady Rialton. *See* Letter XL., Jan. 29, 1711-12.
[4] *See* Letter XLVIII., June 17, 1712.
[5] *See* Letter LVIII., Jan. 8.
[6] [7] Obliterated.
[8] *See* Letter XLI., Feb. 17, 1711-12.
[9] Obliterated.

tender of her. I have long lost all my Colds; and te weathr mends a little—I take some steel drops; & my Head is pretty well, & I walk when I can, but am grown very idle, and not finishing my thing, I gamble abroad, & play at Ombre. I shall be more carefull in my Physick than Mrs Price; tis not a farthing matter her death, I think; and so I say no more to night, but will read a dull book and go sleep. [Nite dee MD.]¹

4. Mr Ford ² has been this half year inviting me to dine at his Lodgings, so I did it to day & brought te Provost and Dr Parnel with me, & my Friend Lewis was their [sic], Parnel went away, & te othr 3 playd at Ombre, & I lookt on; wch I love; & would not play. Tisdal is a pretty fellow as you say; & when I come back to Ireld with nothing, he will condole with me with abundance of secret Pleasure. I believe I told y wht he writ to me, that I have saved Engld, & he Ireld.³ but I can bear that: I have learnt to hear and see and say nothing. I was to see Dutchess Hamilton to day. and met Blyth ⁴ of Ireld just going out of her House into his Coach; I asked her how she come [sic] to receive young Fellows; It seems he had a Ball in D. Hamilton's House where [or 'when']⁵ te D. dyed; and te Dutchess got an Advertismt put in te Post-boy reflecting on te Ball, because te Marl-brow daughtrs were there. and Blith came to beg te Dutchess's pardon, & clear himself; He's a sad dog. [Nite poo dearest MD.] ⁶

5. Ldy Masham has miscarryed but is well. almost again. I have pd many Visits to day. I met Blith at te D. Ormd's & he beggd me to carry him to Dutchess Hamilton to beg her Pardon again. I did, on purpose to see how te Blunderbuss behave himself; but I beggd te Dutchess to use him mercifully, for she is te devil of a Teazer. te good of it is; she ought to beg his Pardon, for he meant no Harm, yet she woud not allow him to put in an Advertisemt to clear himself from hers, thō hers was all A Lye,. he appealed to me, & I gravely gave it against him. I was at Court to day; & te Forein Ministers have got a Trick of employing me to speak for them to Ld Tr & Ld Bolingbroke; which I do when te Case is reasonable. te College

¹ Obliterated.
² The discontented Gazetteer.
³ With his pamphlet against the Dissenters.
⁴ Bligh. See Letter XLI., Feb. 11, 1711-12.
⁵ "When" is the common reading; but the word looks more like "where." Besides, the Postboy advertisement referred to immediately afterwards dates the ball, Feb., 1712-13.
⁶ Obliterated.

need not fear, I will not be their Governr.[1] I dined with Sr
T. Hanmer & his Dutchess; D. Ormd was there; but we parted
soon, & I went to visit Ld Pembroke for te first time; but it
was to see some curious Books. Ld Chomley [2] came in; but
I would not talk to him tho he made many advances. I hate
te Scoundrel, for all he is yr Griffiths [3] friend.—Yes yes, I am
abused enough, if that be all. [Nite sollahs.] [4]

6. I was to day at an auction of Pictures with Pratt,[5] & layd
out 2ll; 1 for a Picture of Titian, & if it were a Titian it would
be worth twice as many Pounds; if I am cheated I'll part with
it to Ld Masham, if it be a bargain I'll keep it my self; that's
my Conscience. but I made Prat buy severall Pictures for Ld
Masham; Prat is a great Virtuoso that way. I dined with Ld
Tr; but made him go to Court, at 8, I allways teaze him to be
gone. I thought to have made Parnel dine with him but he
was ill, his Head is out of order like mine, but more constant,
poor boy. I was at Ld Tr's Levee, with te Provost, to ask a
Book for te Colledge: I never go to his Levee unless to present
somebody:—for all oor Raillying [Mrs Ppt],[6] as hope [savd] [7]
I expected they would have decided about me long ago; & as
hope [saved],[8] as soon as ever things are given away, & I not
provided for, I will be gone with te very first Opportunity,
& put up bag and Baggage. But People are slower than can be
thought. [Nite MD.] [9]

7. Yes I hope Leigh [10] will soon be gone a P— on him. I met
him once, & he talked gravely to me of not seeing te Irish
Bps here & te Irish Gentlemen; but I believe my Answers
fretted him enough; I would not dine with Ld Tr to day though
it was Saterday, (for he has engaged me for to morrow) but went
and dine [11] with Ld Masham; & playd at Ombre 6 penny
running Ombre for 3 hours, there were 3 Voles [12] against me,
& I was once a great Loser, but came off for 3s-6d. one may
easily lose 5 Guinnees at it. Ldy Orkney is gone out of Town
to day; and I could not see her for Lazyness; but writ to her.
She has left me some Physick. [Fais] [13] I never knew [MD's] [14]
Politicks before, and I think it pretty extrdy, & a great Com-
plment to y; & I believe never 3 People conversed so much
with so little Politicks. I avoid all Conversation with te othr

---

[1] Provost of Trinity College.
[2] Cholmondeley. *See* Letter XXXVI., Dec. 8, 1711.
[3] *See* 3rd.
[4] Obliterated.
[5] Dr. Benjamin, the provost.
[6], [7], [8], [9] Obliterated.
[10] Tom, obviously.
[11] *Sic.*
[12] A vole is the winning of all the tricks.
[13], [14] Obliterated.

Party. it is not to be born,[1] & I am sorry for it, Oh yes
things.[2] very dear. [ppt][3] must come in at last with
[? her][4] 2 Eggs a Penny, there te Proverb was well applyed;
Parvisol has sent me a Bill of 50ll. as I orderd him; wch I hope
will serve me & bring me over, pray Gd [*****5][6] does not
be delayd for it; but I have had very little from him this long
time. I was not at Court to day. a Wonder. [Nite sollahs b***
& *** Pdfr.][7]

8. [Oo][8] must know, I give Chocolate almost every day, to
2 or 3 People tht I suffr to come to see me in a morning. My
Man begins to lye pretty well. tis nothing for people to be
denyed ten times. My Man knows all I will see, and denyes me
to every body else. This is te day of th Qu—'s coming to te
Crown, & te day Ld Tr was stabbd by Guiscard. I was at
Court, where every body had their Birth-day Cloaths on, &
I dined with Ld Treasr, who was very fine; He shewd me some
of te Qu—'s Speech, wch I corrected in sevrall Places and ponned
te vote of Address of thanks for te Speech; but I was of opinion
te House should not sit on Tuesday next, unless they hear te
Peace is signed. that is, provided they are sure it will be signed
te Week after, and so have one Scolding for all. Nite MD.

9. Ld Tr woud have had me dine with him to day, he desired
me last night, but I refused; because he would not keep te day
of his Stabbing, with al te Cabinet, as he intended. so I dined
with my friend Lewis, & te Provost, & Parnel & Ford was [sic]
with us; I lost 16s at Ombre; I dont like it, as &c at Night Lewis
brought me word that te Parlnt does not sit to morrow; I hope
they are sure of te Peace by next week, and then they are right
in my opinion, otherwise I think they have done wrong &
might have sate 3 weeks ago. People will grumble, but Ld Tr
cares not a rush. Ld Keepr is suddenly taken ill of a Quinzy
and some Lds are commission [? commissioned], I think Ld
Trevor, to prorogue te Parlmt in his Stead.[9] Y never saw a
Town so full of Ferment & Expectation. Mr. Pope has publishd
a fine Pòem calld Windsor Forrest; read it.[10] [Nite.][11]

10. I was early this morning to see Ld Bolinb— I find he

---

[1] *Sic.*   [2] ? "are" omitted.   [3], [4] Obliterated.
[5] Former readings, "MD," but quite illegible.
[6], [7], [8] Obliterated.
[9] The Lord Keeper (Sir Simon Harcourt — Baron Harcourt, since
Sept., 1711) presided over the House of Lords.
[10] This is the only mention of Pope in the *Journal*. He was just
becoming known.
[11] Obliterated.

was of Opinion te Parlmt should sitt; and says they are not
sure the Peace will be signed next Week. te Prorogation is to
this day Sennight. I went to look on a Library, I am going to
buy, if we can agree; I have offerd 12oll, and will give ten
more; Ld Boling— will lend me te money; I was two hours
poring on te Books, I [I][1] will sell some of them & keep te
rest; but I doubt thy wont take te money. I dined in te City,
and sate an hour in te Evening with Ld Tr, who was in very
good humor, but reproached me for not dining with him yesterday and to-day, What will all this come to — Ld Keepr had a
pretty good night and is better, I was in pain for him. [How
do oo do sollahs, ****[2]][3]

11. I was this morning to visit D. & Dutchess of Ormd;
& Duthss Hamilton; & went with te Provost to an Auction of
Pictures, & Layd out fourteen shillings; I am in for it, if I had
money, but I doubt I shall be undone; for Sr Andr Fountain
invited te Provost and me to dine with him, & play at Ombr;
where I fairly lost 14 Shillings; [fais][4] it won't do; and I shall
be out of conceit with Play this good while; I am come home,
& this late, & my Puppy let out my Fire; & I am gone to bed;
& writing there, & it is past twelve a good while. went out 4
Matidorees[5] and a Trump in black, & was beasted; [vely bad
fais. Nite my two dee logues MD.][6, 7]

12. I was at anothr Auction of Pictures to-day,[8] and a great
Auction it was: I made Ld Masham lay out 4oll, there were
Pictures sold of twice as much value a piece. Our Society met
to day at te D. of Beauforts; a prodigious fine dinner, which
I hate; but we did some Business; our Printer was to attend
us as usuall, & te Chancellr of te Exchequr sent to Authr of te
Examiner[9] 20 Guinneas. He is an ingenious fellow, but te
most confounded vain Coxcomb in te World; so that I dare
not let him see me, nor am acquainted with him. I had much
discourse with D. Ormd this morning, and am driving some
Points to [secure us all in case of Accidents &c.].[10, 11] I left te

[1] Repeated at beginning of a line.
[2] The rest is conjecture: "Poo Pdfr, MD MD MD"—or something
like that.
[3, 4] Obliterated.
[5] Matadors are "killing" cards: spadillio, manillio, and basto.
[6] Obliterated.
[7] Former readings: "my deelest logues," etc.
[8] The first instance of a hyphen in this connection.
[9] Mr. Oldisworth.—B.
[10] Obliterated.
[11] Forster's reading; regarded by some as conjectural, but pretty plain

Society at 7, I can't drink now at all with any Pleasure; I love white Portugall wine better than Claret Champain or Burgundy: I have a sad vulgar appetite. I remembr [Ppt] [1] used to maunder when I came from a great dinner, and [MD] [2, 3] had but a bit of Mutton: I cannot endure above one dish; nor ever could since I was a Boy and loved Stuffing. It was a fine day; wch is a rarity with us I assure, [4] never fair 2 days together. [Nite dee MD.] [5]

13. I had a Rabble of Irish Parsons this morning drinking my Chocolate. I cannot remembr Appointments: I was to have suppd last night with te Swedish Envoy at his House, & some othr Company; but forgot it; & He raillyd me to day at Ld Bolingbr's; who excused me by saying te Envoy ought not to be angry, because I serve Ld Tr, and him te same way: for that reason I very seldom promise to go any where; I dined with Ld Tr; who chid me for being absent so long, as he always does if I miss a day: I sate 3 hours this evening with Ldy Jersey but te two first hours she was at Ombre with some Company: I left Ld Treasr at 8, I fancyed he was a little thoughtfull, for he was playing with an Orange by fits, wch I told him among common men looked like te Spleen. This Letter shall not go to morrow; no hast [ung oomens] [6]; nothing that presses. I promised but once in 3 weeks, & I am better than my word. I wish te Peace may be ready I mean, that we have notice it is signed before Tuesday; otherwise te grumbling will much encrease. [Nite logues.] [7]

14. It was a lovely day this, and I took te Advantage of walking a good deal in te Park: before I went to Court. Coll Disney [8] one of our Society is ill of a Feaver; and we fear, in great Danger: We all love him mightily, and he woud be a great Loss. I doubt I shall not buy te Library, [9] for a Roguy Bookseller has offered 60ll more than I designed to give; so yo see I meant to have a good Bargain. I dined with Ld Tr and his Saterday company; but there were but 7 at Table. Ld Peterborow is ill, and spits blood with a Bruise he got before he left Engld; but I believe, an Italian Lady he has brought over, is te Cause that his Illness returns. Y know old Ldy

---

[1, 2] Obliterated.
[3] Usually read "DD"—it being assumed that MD and Ppt were the same.
[4] "You" omitted.
[5, 6, 7] Obliterated.
[8] See Letter XVI., Feb. 19, 1710-11.
[9] He first wrote "Liberty."

Bellesis [1] is dead at last. She has left Ld Berkeley of Stratton [2] one of her Executors, and it will be of great Advantage to him, they say above ten thousd Pounds. I stayd with Ld Tr upon Business after te Company was gone; but I dare not tell y upon wht. My Letters would be good Memoirs, if I durst venture to say a thousd things that pass; but I hear so much of Letters opening at yr Post Office, that I am fearfull &c. and so [good nite sollahs & rove pdfr*** MD.] [3]

15. Ld Tr engaged me to dine with him again to day; & I had ready what he wanted, but he would not see it. but put me off till to morrow, Th Qu goes to Chappell now; she is carryed in an open Chair, and will be well enough to go to Parlmt on Tuesday if te Houses meet, wch is not yet certain, neither indeed can te Ministers themselves tell, for it depends on Winds and Weather, and Circumstances of Negotiation; however we go on as if it was certainly to meet, and I am to be at Ld Tr's tomorrow upon that Supposition, to settle some things relating that way [Now [4] ppt y] [5] understand me, th Doctors tell me, that if poor Coll Disney does not get some sleep to night he must dye. What care you; ah but I do care; he is one of our Society, a fellow of abundance of humor, an old battered Rake, but very honest, not an old man but an old Rake. It was he that sd of Jinny Kingdom [6] te maid of honor, who is a little old, that since she could not get a Husband te Qu— should give her a Brevet to act as a married woman; Y [7] don't understand this. they give Brevets to Majors & Captains to act as Collonells in te Army; Brevets are Commissions, ask Soldiers [dull sollahs, Nite MD.] [8]

16. I was at Ld Tr's before he came, and as he entered he told me te Parlmt was prorogued till thursday sennight. They

---

[1] Susan, daughter of Sir William Armyne, Bart., married, firstly (1662), Sir Henry Belasyse, heir of first Lord Belasyse. Sir Henry being killed in a duel (1667), she was created baroness for life. She married, secondly, James Fortrey of Chequers.

[2] *See* Letter VII., Oct. 25, 1710.

[3] Obliterated.

[4] "Now" is uncertain; but the rest means "Ppt you" etc. The reading initiated by Forster, "Yes, ppt may" is quite wrong.

[5] Obliterated.

[6] Mentioned in the *Wentworth Papers*, p. 207.

[7] The usual reading of the remainder of this paragraph ("You don't understand," etc.) is here followed, but it is doubtful. The character rendered "Y" is such that it might be an "I"; and the ironical sense thus interpreted would be consistent with the substitution of "for" for "ask." The word "ask" looks like part of a scheme of tampering; so does "dull." It may be an eighteenth-century editor's reading——and writing.   [8] Obliterated.

have had some Expresses by wch they count that te Peace
may be signed by that time, or at least, that France, Holland
& we will sign some Articles by which we shall engage to sign
te Peace when it is ready; but Spain has no Minister there, for
Monteleon, who is to be their Ambassdr at Utrecht is not yet
gone from hence, and till he is there te Spaniards can sign no
Peace: and one thing take notice, that a generall Peace can
hardly be finished these two Months, so as to be proclaimed
here. for after signing it must be ratifyed, that is, confirmed
by the Severall Princes at their Courts, which to Spain will
cost a Month, for we must have notice that it is ratifyed in
all Courts before we can proclaim it. So be not in too much
hast. [Nite MD.] [1]

17. Th Irish Folks were disappointed that te Parlmt did not
meet to day, because it was St. Patricks day, and te Mall was
so full of Crosses, that I thought all te world was Irish. Miss
Ash is almost quite well. and I see te Bishop, but shall not
yet go to his House. [2] I dined again with Ld Tr, but te Parlmt
being prorogued I must keep what I have till next week, for
I believe he will not see it till just te Evening before te Session.
He has engaged me to dine with him again to morrow, thô
I did all I could to put it off; but I don't care to disoblige him.
[Nite dee sollahs, tis late. Nite MD.] [3]

18. I have now dined 6 days successively with Ld Tr; but to
night I stole away, while he was talking with some body else,
and so am at liberty to morrow. there was a flying report of
a geneall [sic] Cessation of Arms, every body had it at Court,
but I believe there is nothing in it. I asked a certain French
Minister, how thinks [i.e. things] went, and he whispered me in
French, Yr Plenipotentys and ours play te fool. None of us
indeed approve the Conduct of either at this time. but Ld Tr
was in full good humor for all that. He had invited a good
many of his Relations, and of a dozen at table, they were all
of te Harley family but my self. Disney is recovering, tho y
don't care a straw. Dilly murders us with his If-Puns. y know
them. [Nite my own dee *** st *** [4] MD.] [5]

19. Bp Cl. has made an If-Pun that he is mighty Proud of,
and designs to send it over to his Brothr Tom, but Sr A. Fountain, has writ to Tom Ash last post, and told him te Pun, &

[1] Obliterated.
[2] Swift never had the smallpox.—H
[3] Obliterated.
[4] Forster reads "dee sollahs. Pdfr roves"—which seems guesswork.
[5] Obliterated.

desired him to send it over to te Bp as his own, and if it succeeds will be a pure bite, te Bp will tell it us as a Wonder, that he & his Brothr should jump so exactly. I'll tell y te Pun. If there was a Hackney Coach at Mr. Pooley's door, what Town in Ægypt would it be; why it would be *Hecatompolis, Hack at Tom Poley's* [1]—Silly, says ppt.[2] I dined with a private Friend to day, for our Society, I told you meet but once a fortnight. I have not seen Fanny Manley [3] yet, I can't help it. Ldy Orkney is come to Town, why, she was at her Country house, hot care you. [Nite darling [4] dee MD] [5]

20. Dilly read me a Letter to day from ppt; she seems to have scratched her head when she writt it; tis a sad thing to write to People without tast [6]: There [y say] [7] y hear I was going to te Bath, no such thing. I am pretty well, I thank God; the Town is now sending me to Savoy. fourty People have given me joy of it; yet there is not te least Truth that I know in it. I was at an Auction of Pictures but bought none. I was so glad of my Liberty, that I would dine no where; but te weathr being fine, I sauntred into te City, and eat a Bitt about 5, and then supped at Mr. Burk's [8] yr Accountant generall, how [*i.e.* who] had been engaging me this month, Bp Cl. was to have been there. but was hindred by Ld Paget's [9] Funerall. te Provost & I sate till one a Clock, and if that be not late, I don't know what is late. Parnels Poem will be published on Monday, & to morrow I design he shall present it to Ld Tr & Ld Boling— at Court. the poor Lad is almost always out of order with his head. Burk's Wife is his Sister,[10] she has a little of te pert Irish way. [Nite ***] [11]

---

[1] Underlined. It is presumed that Tom Pooley was some relation of the late Bishop of Raphoe's.

[2] Usual reading, but very like "tpt."

[3] This is the third mention of Fanny, and it appears he did not see her at all.

[4] "Darling" is Mr. Aitken's surmise—from the tail of a "g."

[5] Obliterated.

[6] *i.e.* "taste." Messrs Ryland and Aitken have both wrongly read "tact." The old editions, including Scott's, are right. "Tast" was a common spelling. "Tact," in the sense of delicacy, was not introduced into English (from the French) until the latter end of the eighteenth century.

[7] Obliterated.

[8] William Burgh (*d.* 1744), son of Ulysses Burgh, Bishop of Ardagh, was Comptroller and Accountant-General for Ireland.

[9] William (1637–1712-13), sixth baron, ambassador to Vienna and Constantinople.

[10] Margaret, daughter of Thomas Parnell of Congleton, Cheshire, married William Burgh, and died 1744.

[11] Obliterated.

21. Morning—I will now finish my Letter; for Company will come, and a Stir and. Clutters: and I ll keep te Letter in my P[ottic]¹k & give it into te Post my self—I must go to Court, & y know on Saterdays, I dine with L. Tr of course. Farewell [deelest MD MD MD FW FW FW *** Me Me Me lele sollahs.] ²

LETTER LXII
[Endorsed as last. Date of receipt, "Apr. 13."]

62   London. *Mar.* 21. 1712-13.

I GAVE yr Lettr in this night. I dined with Ld Tr to day; and find he has been at a meeting at Ld Hallifax's³ House with 4 principall whigs. But he is resolved to begin a Speech agst them when te Parlmt sitts, and I have beggd that the Ministrs may have a meeting on purpose to settle that matter, and let us be te Attackers; and I believe it will come to something; for te Whigs intend to attack te Ministers, & if instead of that, te Ministers attack te Whigs, it will be better; and further I believe we shall attack them on those very Points they intend to attack us. te Parlmt will be again prorogued for a fortnight, because of Passion week. I forgot to tell y that Mr Griffin has given [Ppts] ⁴ Brothr a new Employmt about 10ll a year better than his former, but more remote, and consequently cheaper; I wish I could have done better; and hope [oo] ⁵ will take what can be done in good part. and that [oo] ⁶ Brothr will not dislike it. [Nite own dear **** MD.] ⁷

22. I dined to day with Ld Steward ⁸ .. there Frank Annesly ⁹ (a Parlnt man) told me, he had heard that I had writt to my Friends in Ireld to keep firm to te Whig Interest, for tht Ld Tr would certainly declare for it after the Peace: Annesly sd 20 People had told him this, Yo must know this is what they endeavor to report of L.T. that he designs to declare for te Whigs, and a Scotch Fellow has writt te same to Scotland, and his meeting with those Lds gives occasion to such Reports.

¹, ² Obliterated.
³ *See* Letter V., Oct. 1, 1710.
⁴, ⁵, ⁶, ⁷ Obliterated.
⁸ Earl Poulett.
⁹ An ancestor of the Earls of Annesley, one Francis Annesley (1663-1750) of Thorganby, Yorks, was a member of both the English and the Irish Parliament. In the former, he was one of the members for Westbury, according to Mr. Aitken—unless there was another Frank Annesley, M.P.

let me henceforth call Ld Tr, *eltee*,[1] because possibly my Letters
may be opened; pray remember Eltee; you know th Reason,
L.T. and Eltee p[l][2] onounced te same way—Stay, tis 5 weeks
since I had a Lettr flom MD; I allow oo[3] six. Y see why I
cannot come over te beginning of April, whoever has to do with
this Ministry can fix no time but has [*i.e.,* as] hope [saved][4]
it is not [poopdfrs fault, pay dont blame poopdfr. Nite deelest
logues MD.][5]

23. I dined to day at Sr T. Hanmer's by an old Appointmt,
there was D. Ormd, & Ld & Ldy Orkney; I left them at 6,
Every body is as sower as vinegar. I endeavor to keep a firm
friendship between D. Ormd & Eltee ([oo][6] know who Eltee
is have [oo flodot[7] it][8] already?[9] I have great designs if I
can compass them. But delay is rooted in Eltee's heart. yet
the Fault is not altogether there that things are no better.
Here is te cursedest Libel in Verse come out, that ever was
seen, called te Ambassadress[10]; it is very dull too. It has been
printed in 3 or 4 different ways, and is handed about, but not
sold: it abuses te Qu— horribly. The Examiner has cleard me
to day of being Author of his Paper, and done it with great
Civilityes to me. I hope it will stop peoples mouths, if not,
they must go on, and be hangd, I care not. Tis terrible rainy
weathr. I'll go seep.[11] [Nite deelest MD.][12]

24. It rained all this day, & ruind me in Coach-hire. I went
to see Coll Disney, who is past danger; then I visited Ld Keepr,
who was at dinner; but I could [or "would"] not dine with him,
but drove to Ld Tr— (Eltee I mean) payd te Coachman, &
went in, but he dined abroad, so I was forced to call te Coachman again, & went to Ld Bol— he dined abroad to[13]; and at
Ld Dupplins I lighted, and by good Luck got a dinner there,
& then went to te Latin play at Westminster School, acted by
te Boys & Ld Tr— (Eltee I mean again) honored them with

---

[1] Underlined.   [2] Obliterated.   [3] Afterwards altered to "you."
[4], [5], [6] Obliterated.   [7] "Forgot."
[8] Obliterated.
[9] He remembered the interrogation point this time, but forgot the
close of the parenthesis.
[10] It was entitled *The British Ambassadress's Speech to the French King.*
For publishing it, Mr. William Hart, the printer of the *Flying Post*, was
tried in the court of Queen's Bench, June 27, 1713, and sentenced to
stand twice in the pillory, to pay a fine of 50l. to her majesty, to be
imprisoned two years, and till he should pay the said fine; and to find
sufficient sureties for his good behaviour during life.—B.
[11] Afterwards altered to "sleep."
[12] Obliterated.
[13] For "too."

his Presence. Ldy Masham's eldest boy, about 2 years old is ill, and I am afraid will not live; she is full of grief, and I pity and am angry with her. 4 shillings to day in Coachhire; [fais] [1] it won't do. Our Peace will certainly be ready by Thursday fortnight. but our Pleniptyes were to blame that it was not done already; they thought their Powers were not full enough to sign te Peace, unless every Prince was ready; wch cannot yet be, for Spain has no Minister yet at Utrecht. but now ours have new Orders. [Nite MD.] [2]

25. Weather worse than ever, terrible rain all day. but I was resolved I would spend no more money. I went to an Auction of Pictures with Dr Prat, & there met te D. of Beaufort, who promised to come with me to Court, but did not, so a Coach I got, & went to Court, and did some little Business there; but was forced to go home; for [oo] [3] must understand: I take a little Physick over night, wch works me next day; Ldy Orkney is my Physician. 'Tis Hiera picra 2 spoonfull, devilish Stuff. I thought to have dined with Eltee but would not, merely to save a Shilling; but I dined privatly with a Friend, and playd at Ombre, & won Six Shillings. Here are severall people of Quality lately dead of te Small Pox. I have not yet seen Miss Ash; but hear she is well. Th Bp. Cl. has bought abundance of Pictures; & Dr Prat has got him very good Pennyworths. I can get no Walks, te Weathr is so bad. Is it so with ₍oo Sollahs. Nite **** MD] [4, 5]

26. Tho it was shaving day head & beard, yet I was out early to see Ld Bol— and talk over Affairs with him. & then I went to te D. Ormds, & so to Court, where te Ministers did not come, because te Parlnt was this day prorogued till this day fortnight. We had terrible Rain and Hail to day. Our Society mett this day; but I left them before 7, and went to Sr A. F; & playd at Ombre with him and Sr T. Clarges [6] till ten, & then went to Sr T. Hanmer, His Wife te Dutchess of Grafton left us after a little while, and I stayd with him about an Hour upon some Affairs &c. Ld Bol— left us at te Society before I went, for there is an Express from Utrecht, but I know not yet what it contains. onely I know the Ministers expect te Peace will be signed in a week; which is a week before te Session. [Nite MD.] [7]

1, 2, 3, 4 Obliterated.
5 Possibly "deelest" is the missing word.
6 See Letter LIX., Feb. 10[11], 1712-13.
7 Obliterated.

27. Parnels Poem is mightily esteemed, but Poetry sells ill, I am plagued with that [Nasty Bawd][1, 2] poor Harrison's mother, Y would laugh to see how cautious I am of paying her te 100ll I received for her son from te Treasury; I have asked every Creature I know, whethr I may do it safely; yet durst not venture, till my Ld Keeper assured me there was no danger. yet I have not payd her; but will in a day or two. tho I have a great mind to stay till [Ppt][3] sends me [her][4] Opinion, because [ppt][5] is a great Lawyer. I dined to day with a mixture of People at a Scotchmans, who made te Invitation to Mr. Lewis & me, and has some design upon us wch we know very well. I went afterwards to see a famous moving Picture,[6] & I never saw any thing so pretty. Y see a Sea ten miles wide, a Town on tothr end, & Ships sailing in te Sea, & discharging their Canon. Y see a great Sky with Moon & Stars &c. I'm a fool. [Nite dee MD.][7]

28. I had a mighty Levee to day, I deny my self to every body except about half a dozen, & they were all here, & Mr Addison was one, & I had Chocolate twice, wch I don't like. Our rainy weather continues, Coach hire goes deep, I dined with Eltee, & his Saterday company us usuall, & could not get away till 9. Ld Peterborow was making long Harangues, & Eltee kept me in spight; then I went to see Bp Ossory, who had engagd me in te morning, he is going to Ireld. Bp of Killaloo[8] & T. Leigh was with us, te Latter had wholly changd his Stile,[9] by seeing how te Bps behaved themselves; & he seemed to think me one of more Importance than I really am. I put te ill conduct of te Bps about Firstfruits with relation to Eltee and me, strongly upon Killaloo; & shewd how it had hindred me from getting a better thing for them calld te Crownrents, wch te Qu— had promised. He had nothing to say, but was humble, & desired my Interest in that & some othr things. This Letter is half done in a week; I believe [oo][10] will have it next. [Nite MD.][11]

29. I have been employd in endeavoring to save one of yr

---

[1] Obliterated.
[2] The only reading hitherto is Forster's: "devil's brood." Mr. Aitken *surmised* "bawd." *See* Feb. 18.
[3, 4, 5] Obliterated.
[6] A moving picture is referred to in the *Tatler*, No. 129.
[7] Obliterated.
[8] Killaloe. Thomas Lindsay. *See* Letter VI., Oct. 17, 1710.
[9] *See* Letter LVII., Dec. 23, 1712.
[10, 11] Obliterated.

Junior fellows,[1] who came [or "comes"] over here for a dispensation from taking Orders, and in solliciting it, has run out his time, and now his Fellowship is void if te College pleases, unless te Qu— suspends te Execution, and gives him time to take Orders. I spoke to all te Ministers yesterday about it; but thy say te Qu— is angry, & thought it was a Trick to deceive her, & she is positive, & so te Man must be ruined, for I can not help him. I never saw him in my Life, but te Case was so hard, I could not forbear interposing; Yr Governmt recommended him to D. Ormd, & he thought they would grant it, and by te time it was refused, th Fellowship by rigor is forfeited. I dined with Dr Arbuthnot (one of my Brothers) at his Lodgings in Chelsea, and was there at Chappel, and te Altar put me in mind of Tisdal's outlandish would [2] at yr Hospital for te Soldiers. I was not at Court to day; and I hear te Qu was not at Church; perhaps te Gout has seised her again. Terrible rain all day, have oo such Weathr. [Nite MD.] [3]

30. Morning. I was naming some time ago to a certain Person, another certain Person, that was very deserving, and poor and sickly; and tother, that first certain Person gave me a hundred Pounds to give te other [4]; which I have not yet done. Th Person who is to have it, never saw te Giver, nor expects one farthing, or has te least Knoledge or Imagination of it; so I believe it will be a very agreeable Surprize. For I think it a handsom present enough.—At Night [5] I dined in te City at Pontacks, with Ld Dupplin & some others, we were treated by one Coll Cleland,[6] who has a Mind to be governr of Barbadoes, and is laying these long Trapps for me and others to engage our Interests for him. He's a true Scotchman. I paid te 100ll this evening, and it was an agreeble [sic] surprise to te Receiver. we reckon te Peace is now signed, and that we shall have it in 3 days—I believe it is pretty sure. [Nite MD.] [7]

31. I thought to day on [Ppt] [8] when she told me she

---

[1] Mr. Charles Grattan, afterward master of the Royal Free-School at Inniskilling, founded, with seven more in the province of Ulster, by King Charles I. and afterward nobly endowed by Erasmus Smith, Esq.—N.

[2] Sic. He may have intended to write "one."

[3] Obliterated.

[4] Maybe the hundred guineas mentioned in Letter LIX., Jan. 29, 1712-13

[5] A full-stop omitted.

[6] See 27th. Sir Walter Scott suggested that this was a son of the Presbyterian poet, Cleland, killed at the head of the Cameronian regiment at Bothwell Bridge in 1689. Mr. Aitkin disputes this, but allows that he was probably the William Cleland who was intimate with the wits of Queen Anne's reign. Pope inscribed the letter preliminary of the Dunciad to Cleland.   [7, 8] Obliterated.

suppose[1] I was acquainted with te Steward, when I was giving my self Airs of being at some Lds House. Sr. A. Fountain invited Bp Cl. & me & some othrs to dine where he did, & he carryed us to te D. of Kents,[2] who was gone out of Town; but te Steward treated us nobly; & shewed us te fine Pictures &c. I have not yet seen Miss Ash; I wait till she has been abroad & taken te Air. This Evening Ldy Masham Dr. Arbuthnott & I were contriving a Lye for to morrow; that Mr. Noble, who was hangd, last Saterday,[3] was recovered by His Friends, and then seised again by te Sheriff, & is now in a Messenger's hands at the black Swan in Holborn; We are all to send to our Friends to know whethr they have heard any thing of it, and so we hope it will spread. However we shall do our Endeavors, nothing shall be wanting on our Parts & leave te rest to Fortune. [Nite MD.][4]

Apr. 1. We had no Success in our Story, thô I sent my Man to sevrll Houses to enquire among te Footmen, without letting him into te Secret, but I doubt my Colleagues did not contribute as they ought. Parnell & I dined with Dartenuff to day: y have heard of Dartenuff, I have told you of Dartenuff. after dinner we all went to Ld Bol— who had desired me to dine with him, but I would not, because I heard it was to look over a dull Poem of one Parson Trap,[5] upon te Peace. Th Swedish Envoy told me to day at Court, that he was in great Apprehensions about his Master: and indeed we are afraid that Prince[6] is dead[7] among those Turkish Dogs. I prevaild on Ld Bol— to invite Mr Addison to dine with him on good Friday; I suppose we shall be mighty mannerly. Addison is to have a play of his acted on Friday in Easter week; tis a Tragedy called Cato, I saw it unfinished some Years ago: did I tell y, tht Steel has begun a new daily Paper calld te Guardian,[8] they say good for nothing; I have not seen it. [Nite dee MD.][9]

2. I was this morning with Ld Boling— and he tells me a

---

[1] "d" omitted.

[2] Henry Grey (1671–1740), first duke.

[3] Richard Noble, an attorney at New Inn, executed at Kingston, for the murder of John Sayer, Esq., whose wife, the daughter of Admiral Nevill, he had seduced from her husband. In Bishop Fleetwood's works, p. 657, is a sermon on the death of Mr. Noble, printed without his name.—N.

[4] Obliterated.

[5] See Letter XIII., Jan. 7, 1710-11.

[6] Charles the Twelfth, then a refugee at Bender, in Turkey, whither he had fled after the defeat at Pultawa.—D. L. P.

[7] Might be read "died."

[8] That paper began to be published on Thursday, March 12, 1712-13.—B.

[9] Obliterated.

Spanish Courier is just come with te News that te K. of Spain has agreed to every thing te Qu— desires, and te Duke d'Ossuna has left Paris in order to his Journy to Utrecht. I was prevaild on to come home with Trap, and read his Poem, & correct it, but it was good for nothing; while I was thus employd, Sr T. Hanmer came up to my Chamber, and baukt me of a Journy he & I intended this week to Ld Orkney's at Cliffden [1]: But he is not well & his Physicians will not let him undertake such a Journey. I intended to dine with Ld Lr— but going to see Coll Disney, who lives with Genrll Withers, I liked te Genrll's little dinner so well, that I staid & took share of it, & did not go to Ld Tr— till 6, where I found Dr Sacheverell, who told us that te Bookseller had given him 100ll for his Sermon preached last Sunday,[2] & intended to print thirty thousd: I believe he will be confoundedly bit; & will hardly sell above half I have fires still though April is begun, agst my old maxim, but te Weathr is wett & Cold, I never saw such a long run of ill weather in my Life. [Nite dee logues MD.] [3]

3. I was at te Qu—'s Chappel to day, but she was not there. Mr St John Ld Bol—'s Brother,[4] came this day at noon with an Express from Utrecht that te Peace is signed by all te Ministers there but those of te Empr, who will likewise sign in a few days: so that now the great Work is in effect done, and I believe it will appear a most excellent Peace for Europe, particularly for Engld. Addison & I & some others dined with Ld Bol— and sate with him till 12; we were very Civil, but yet when we grew warm, we talkt in a friendly manner of Party, Addison raised his Objections, & Ld Bol— answered them with great Complaisance. Addison began Ld Sommers Health, wch went about; but I bid him not name Ld Wh—'s [i.e. Wharton's] for I would not pledge it, and I tod Ld Bol— frankly that Addison loved Ld Wh— as little as I did. so we laughd &c—Well, but y are glad of te Peace, y [Ppt] [5] te Trimmer, are not y? as for Dd I don't doubt [her] [6]; Why now,

[1] See Letter LII., Sept. 18, 1712.
[2] His (Sacheverell's) sermon; preached at St. Saviour's Church, in Southwark, of which he was one of the chaplains, on Luke xxiii., 34, on occasion of the expiration of the three years' silence imposed upon him by the House of Lords, in consequence of his impeachment in 1709. The sermon was published under the title of *The Christian Triumph, or the duty of praying for our enemies*. In April, 1713, he was presented by the queen to the rectory of St. Andrew's, Holborn, which had been held *in commendam*, by Dr. Thomas Manningham, with the bishoprick of Chichester.—B.
[3] Obliterated.
[4] See Letter LX., Feb. 17, 1712-13.
[5, 6] Obliterated.

if I did not think [Ppt][1] had been a violent Tory, & [Dd][2] te
greater Whig of te two; tis late. [Nite MD][3]

4. This Passion week People are so demure, especially this
last day, that I told Dilly who calld here, that I would dine
with him, and so I did [fais][4], & had a small shouldr of Mutton
of my own bespeaking. It rained all day; I came home at 7,
and have never stirrd out, but have been reading Sacheverell's
long dull Sermon wch he sent me, It is his first sermon since
his Suspension is expired; but not a word in it upon te Occasion,
except two or three remote Hints. Bp Cl has been sadly bit
by Tom Ash, who sent him a Pun, wch te Bp had made &
designed to send to him, but delayd it, and Ld Pembr & I
made Sr A. Fountain write it to Tom. I believe I told y or it
in my last.[5] It succeeded right, & te Bp was wondring to Ld
Pembr how he and his Brothr coud hit on te same thing. I ll
go to bed soon, for I must be at Church by 8 to morrow morning.
Easter day. [Nite dee MD.][6]

5. Warburton[7] writt to me 2 Lettrs about a Living of one
Foulks who is lately dead in te County of Meath; my Answer
is, that before I received te first Genrll Gorge[8] had recommended a friend of his to te D. Ormd, wch was te first time I
heard of it's vacancy, & it was te Provost told me of it. I believe
verily that Foulks was not dead when Gorge recommended te
other; for Warburtons last Letter sd that Foulks was dead te
day before te date; this has prevented me from serving Warburton as I woud have done, if I had received early notice
enough; pray say or write this to Warburton to justify me to
him.—I was at Church at 8 this morning; and dresst & shaved
after I come [sic] back, but was too late at Court, & Ld Abingdon[9] was like to have snappt me for dinner, & I believe will
fall out with me for refusing him; but I hate dining with them,
& I dined with a private friend, & took 2 or 3 good walks, for it
was a very fine day, the first we have had a great while. Remembr was Easter day a fine day with you. I have sate with
Ldy Worsley[10] till now. [Nite dee MD.][11]

[1], [2], [3], [4] Obliterated.
[5] *See* Letter LXI., March 19, 1712-13.
[6] Obliterated.
[7] *See* Letter IV., Sept. 27, 1710.
[8] Richard Gorges (*d.* 1728), lieut.-general. Son of Dr. Robert Gorges
of Kilbrew, co. Meath. Served in the Irish campaign. He married Countess
Doll of Meath; as to whom *see* Letter XLII., Feb. 25, 1711-12.
[9] *See* Letter LX., Feb. 18, 1712-13.
[10] *See* Letter XIV., Jan. 20, 1710-11.
[11] Obliterated.

6. I was this morning at te Rehearsall of Mr Addisons Play called Cato, which is to be acted on Friday, there were not above half a score of us, to see it; we stood on te Stage & it was foolish enough to see te Actors prompted every moment, & te Poet directing them, & te drab that Acts Catos daughter [1] out in te midst of a passionate Part, & then calling out, What's next? Bp of Cl was there too, but he stood privatly in a Gallery. I went to dine with Ld Tr, but he was gone to Wimbleton his Daughter Caermarthen's Country Seat, 7 miles off, so I went back and dined privatly with Mr. Addison, whom I had left to go to Ld Tr. I keep fires yet; I'm very extravagant. I sate this Evening with Sr A. Fountain, & we amused our selves with making If's for Dilly. It is rainy weather again, nevle saw [ze rike] [2]. This Lettr shall go to morrow. remembr [ung oomens] [3] it is 7 weeks since oor last, and I allow [oo] [4] but 5 weeks; but [oo] [5] have been galloping into te Country to Swentons [i.e. Swanton's]; o Pray tell Swanton I had his Letter, but can not contrive how to serve him. If a Govrnr [6] were to go over; I would recommend him as far as lay in my Power, but I can do no more; & y know all Employmts in Ireld at least almost all, are engaged in reversions. If I were on te Spot, & had Credit with a Ld Lt I would very heartily recommend him, but Emplymts here are no more in my Powr than te Monarchy it self. [Nite dee MD.] [7]

7. Morning. I have had a Visiter here that has taken up my time. I have not been abroad [oo] [8] may be sure, so I can say nothing to day but tht I [rove MD, bettle zan] [9] ever if possibere [or "possibur"]. I will put this in te Post office, so I say no more. I write by this Post to te Dean, but it is not above 2 Lines, & one inclosed to you, but that enclosed to y is not above 3 Lines, & then one inclosed to te Dean,[10] which He must not have but under Conditions of burning it immediatly after reading, & that before yr Eyes; for there are some things in it, I would not have lyable to Accident. Y shall onely know in generall, that it is an Account of what I have done to serve him in his Pretensions on these Vacancyes &c.—but he must not know, that y know so much. [Does this perplex y, hat care I, but rove pdfr, sawcy pdfr. Farewell deelest MD MD MD FW FW FW Me Me Me Lele.] [11]

---

[1] Mrs. Oldfield.
[2], [3], [4], [5] Obliterated.
[6] Lord-lieutenant.

[7], [8], [9] Obliterated.
[10] Dr. Sterne.
[11] Obliterated.

LETTER LXIII

[Endorsed as last: save for reversion to " att." Date of receipt, "Apr. 13.ᵘ"]

63   London. *Apr* 7. 1713

I FANCY I marked my last which I sent this day, wrong, onely
61 & it ought to be 62, I dined with Ld Tr. and thō te Business
I had with him is something agst Thursday when te Parlmt
is to meet, & this is Tuesday yet he put it off till to morrow,
I dare not till [*i.e.* tell] y what it is, lest this Lettr should miscarry or be opend; but I never saw his Fellow for delays. te
Parlnt will now certainly sitt, and every body's Expectations
are ready to burst. At a Council to night, te Ld Ch Justice
Parker,[1] a Whig, spoke agst te Peace, so did Ld Chomley,[2]
anothr Whig, who is Treasur of te Houshold. My Ld Keeper
was this night made Ld Chancellr We hope there will soon be
some Removes. [Nite dee sollahs both,[3] rove Pdfr.] [4]

8. Ld Chomley the right name is Cholmondeley, is this day
removed from his Employmt for his last nights Speech, & Sr
Richd Templ Lt Genrll, te greatest Whig in te Army [5] is turned
out, & Lt Genrll Palmes [6] will be obliged to sell his Regimt,
This is te first fruits of a Friendship I have established between
two great men. I dined with Ld Tr, and did te Business I had
for him to his Satisfaction, I won't tell [? MD] [7] what is was.
[Sankee for zat.][8, 9] te Palnt sitts to morrow for certain. Here
is a Letter printed in Macartneys name vindicating himself
from te murder of D. Hamilton. I must give some hints to have
it answred; tis full of Lyes and will give an Opportunity of
exposing that Party. To morrow will be a very important day;
all te World will be at Westminster; Ld. Tr is as easy as a Lamb;
They are mustring up te Proxyes of te absent Lds;[10] but they

---

[1] *See* Letter XXXVI., Dec. 13, 1711.
[2] Cholmondeley. *See* Letter XXXVI., Dec. 8, 1711.
[3] Mr. Aitken reads, not "both," but " Late."
[4] Obliterated.
[5] *See* Letter VII., Oct. 27, 1710.
[6] Francis Palmes was made a lieut.-general in 1709. He had been in
Parliament, and had also been employed in Savoy and at Vienna as a
diplomat.
[7], [8] Obliterated.
[9] "Thank you for that." Forster read "so much for that"—which
was a mere guess; and Mr. Aitken reads (with diffidence) "so heed for
zat"—ignoring a very obvious " n."
[10] It was once one of the privileges of the members of the House of
Lords to be able to vote by proxy. Each lord present might vote for
himself and two absent ones who authorised him. For this purpose of
proxies, the temporal lords were strictly segregated from the bishops.

are not in any fear, of wanting a Majority, wch Death & Accidents have increased this year. [Nite MD] [1]

9. I was this morning with Ld Tr to present to him a young son of the late E. of Jersey [2] at the desire of the Widow. there I saw te Mace & great Coach ready for Ld Tr who was going to Parlmt. Our Society met to day, but I expected te Houses would sitt longer than I cared to fast; so I dined with a Friend, and never enquired how matters went till 8 this evening, when I went to Ld Orkneys where I found Sr T. Hanmer, Th Qu. delivered her Speech very well, but a little weaker in her Voice; the Crowd was vast Th Order for an Address was moved; & opposed by Ld Notingham, Halifax & Cowper [3]—Ld Tr spoke with great Spirit and Resolution; Ld Peterborow flirted agst D. Marlbrow, (who is in Germany y know) but it was in answer to one of Halifax's Impertinences. Th Order for an Address passd by a Majority of 33, & te Houses rise [? rose] before 6 This is te account I heard at Ld Orkneys. te Bp of Chester [4] a high Tory was agst te Court; te Dutchess of Marlbrow sent for him some Months ago to justify her self to him in relation to te Qu— and shewd him Letters, & told him Storyes, which te weak man believed, & was perverted. [Nite MD.] [5]

10. I dined with a Cousin in te City, & poor Pat Rolt [6] was there; I have got her Rogue of a Husband leave to come to Engld from Port-mahòn; te Whigs are much down; but I reckon they have some Scheam in agitation. This Parlmt time hinders our Court meetings on Wednesdays, Thursdays, & Saterdays. I had a great deal of Business to night, which gave me a Temptation to be idle, & I lost a dozen Shillings at Ombre with Dr Prat & anothr. I have been to see tothr day te Bp Cl. & Lady, but did not see Miss. It rains every day, & yet we are all over dust. Ldy Mashams eldest boy is very ill, I doubt he will not live; & she stays at Kensington to nurse him, which vexes us all. She is so excessively fond it makes me mad; she should never leave te Qu, but leave every thing to stick to

---

[1] Obliterated.

[2] Henry Villiers (d. 1743), second son of first earl. The widow was Barbara (Chiffinch). See Letter XXIX., Aug. 26, 1711.

[3] William Cowper (c. 1665–1724), first baron, and later (1717-18) first Earl Cowper. Son of Sir William Cowper, Bart., of Ratling Court, Nonington, Kent. He had been Lord Keeper.

[4] Dr. Francis Gastrell, consecrated to that see April 4, 1713. — B. See Letter XXV., June 23, 1711.

[5] Obliterated.

[6] See Letter III., Sept. 14, 1710.

what is so much te Interest of te Publick as well as her own. This I tell her, but talk to te Winds. [Nite MD.][1]

11. I dined at Ld Tr with his Saterdays company; we had ten at Table, all Lds but my self & te Chancellr of te Exchequer. Argyle went off at 6, & was in very indifferent humor, as usuall. D. Ormd & Ld Bolingbr— were absent. I stayd till near ten, Ld Tr shewd us a small Picture enamelld work, & sett in gold, worth about 20ll, a Picture I mean of te Qu; which sh gave to Dutchess Marlbrough sett in diamonds. When te Dutchess was leaving Engld, she took of [2] all te Diamonds, & gave te Picture to one Mrs Higgins; (an old intriguing woman whom every body knows) bidding her to make te best of it she could. Ld Tr sent to Mrs Higgins for this Picture, & gave her a hundred Pounds for it. was ever such an ungratefull Beast as that Dutchess?—or did yu ever hear such a Story. I suppose te Whigs will not believe it, pray try them. takes off te diamonds & gives away te Picture to an insignificant woman as a thing of no consequences [sic], & gives it her to sell, like a piece of old fashiond plate. Is she not a detestable Slut. [Nite deelest MD.][3]

12. I went to Court to day on purpose to present Mr Berkeley one of Your Fellows of Dublin Colldge,[4] to Ld Berkeley of Stratton.[5] that Mr Berkeley is a very ingenious man, & great Philosophr; & I have mentioned him to all te Ministers, & given them some of his writings, & I will favor him as much as I can. This I think I am bound to in honor & Conscience, to use all my little Credit towards helping forward Men of Worth in te world.[6] Te Qu was at Chappell to day, & looks well. I dined at Ld Orkneys with D. Ormd, Ld Arran & Sr T. Hanmer, Mr St John, Secrty at Utrecht expects every moment to return there with th Ratification of te Peace. Did I tell y in my last, of Addison's Play called Cato, & that I was at te Rehearsall of it. [Nite MD.][7]

13. This Morning My Friend Mr Lewis came to me, and shewed me an Order for a Warrant for te 3 vacant Deanryes, but none of them to me; this was what I always foresaw., and

---

[1] Obliterated.
[2] For "off."
[3] Obliterated.
[4] George Berkeley (1685-1753), afterwards Bishop of Cloyne; famous in the philosophic world for having laid down the maxim "Nothing can exist unperceived," which influences philosophy to this day.
[5] See Letter VII., Oct. 25, 1710.
[6] Swift procured him to be sent secretary and chaplain to Sicily, with the Earl of Peterborow.—H.
[7] Obliterated.

receive [sic] te notice of it better I believe than he expected. I bid Mr Lewis tell Ld Tr that I took nothing ill of him, but his not giving me timely notice, as he promised to do, if he found te Qu would do nothing for me. at Noon Ld Tr hearing, I was in Mr Lewis's Office, came to me, & sd many things too long to repeat. I told him I had nothing to do but go to Ireld immediatly, for I could not with any Reputation stay longer here, unless I had somethink [sic] honorable immediatly given to me: we dined togethr at D. Ormds, he there told me, he had stopt te Warrants for te Deans, that what was done for me, might be at te same time, & he hoped to compass it to night; but I believe him not. I told te D. Ormd my Intentions; He is content Stearn [1] should be a Bp, & I have St Patricks; but I believe nothing will come of it; for stay I will not; and so I believe for all [oo ******* [2] oo may] [3] see me in Dublin before April ends. I am less out of humor than y would imagine, & if it were not that impertinent People will condole with me, as they used to give me Joy, I would value it less: but I will avoid company, & muster up my Baggages & send them next Monday by te Carrier to Chester, and come & see my Willows, agst te Expectation of all te World. [hat care I. Nite deelest logues MD.] [4]

14. I dined in te City to day, and ordered a Lodging to be got ready for me agst I come to pack up my things; for I will leave this end of te Town as soon as ever te warrants for te Deanryes are out, wch are yet stopt: Ld Tr told Mr Lewis, that it should be determined to night; & so he will for a hundred nights, so he said yesterday; but I value it not. my daily journall shall be but short, till I gett into te City; & then I will send away this; and follow it my self, and design to walk it all the way to Chester my man & I by 10 miles a day; it will do my Health a great deal of good; I shll do it in 14 days. [Nite dee MD.] [5]

15. Ld Bol— made me dine with him to day, I [6] was as good company as ever; & told me te Qu would determine something for me to night, te dispute is Windsor or St Patricks: I told him I would not stay for their disputes, & he thought I

---

[1] Dr. John Sterne, the Dean of St. Patrick's.
[2] Nothing can be read with certainty; though something like "govnmt" may be half-seen, half-fancied. Forster read "oo saucy ppt can say oo," etc.—which is pure imagination.
[3, 4, 5] Obliterated.
[6] Mr. Aitken substitutes "he." But the phrase is obviously parenthetical: Swift means that, in spite of his disappointment, *he* was good company. The "I" is not a mistake.

was in te right. Ld Masham told me that Ldy Masham is angry
I have not been to see her since this Business; & desires I will
come to morrow. [Nite deelest MD.][1]

16. I was this noon at Ldy Mashams, who was just come
from Kensington where her eldest son is sick; she said much
to me of what she had talkt to Qu— & Ld Tr. te poor Ldy
fell a [crying][2] shedding tears openly; She coud not bear to
think of my having St Patricks &c. I was never more moved
than to see so much Friendship: I woud not stay with her,
but went and dined with Dr Arbuthnot, with Mr. Berkeley
one of yr Fellows, whom I have recommended to te Dr, & to
Ld Berkeley of Stratton Mr Lewis tells me, that D. Ormd has
been to day with Qu— & she was content that Dr Stearn should
be Bp of Dromore and I Dean of St Patricks, but then out
came Ld Tr, & sd he would not be satisfied, but that I must
be Prebend of Windsor, thus he perplexes things—I expect
neither; but I confess, as much as I love Engld, I am so angry
at this Treatmt, that if I had my Choice I would rather have
St Patricks. Ldy Masham says she will speak to purpose to
Qu— tomorrow. [Nite ****[3] MD][4]

17. I went to dine at Ldy Mashams to day, & she was taken
ill of a sore throat, & Aguish; She spoke to Qu last night, but
had not much time. Qu— says she will determine to morrow
with Ld Tr— Th warrants for te Deanry's are still stopt, for
fear I should be gone. Do y think any thing will be done; I don't
care whethr it is or no, In te mean time I prepare for my Journy;
and see no great People; nor will see Ld Tr any more, if I go.
Ld Tr tod [sic] Mr Lewis it should be done to night, so he sd
5 nights ago. [Nite MD.][5]

18. This morning Mr Lewis sent me word that Ld Tr told
him, Qu would determine at noon. at 3 Ld Tr sent to me to
come to his Lodgings at St James's, and tod me te Qu was at
last resolved, that Dr Stearn should be Bp Dromore, and I
Dean of St Patrick; and tht Stearns warrant should be drawn
immediatly. Y know te Deanry is in te D. Ormonds gift, but this
is concerted between te Qu— Ld Tr, & D. Ormd, to make room
for me. I do not know whethr it will yet be done, some unlucky
Accident may yet come; neither can I feel Joy at passing my
days in Ireld: and I confess I thought te Ministry would not
let me go; but perhaps thy cant help it. [Nite MD][6]

19. I forgot to tell y that Ld Tr forced me to dine with him

---

[1], [2] Obliterated.   [3] Apparently "dee" or "dee dee."
[4], [5], [6] Obliterated.

yesterday as usuall with his Saterday company, wch I did after
frequent refusals; to day I dined with a private Friend, & was
not at Court. after dinner Mr Lewis sent me a note, that Qu—
staid till she knew whether duke Ormd approved of Stearn
for Bp; I went this Evening and found D. Ormd. at te Cockpit,
& told him, and desired he would go to Qu, and approve of
Stearn. He made Objections, desired I would name any other
Deanry, for he did not like Stearn, that Stearn never went to
see him, that he was influenced by Ar. B. Dublin[1] &c; so all
is now broken again. I sent out for Ld Tr, and told him this.
He says all will do well, but I value not what he says. This
Suspense vexes me worse than any thing else. [Nite MD.][2]

20. I went to day by appointmt to te Cockpit, to talk with
D. Ormd; he repeated te same Proposall of any othr Deanry
&c. I desired, he would put me out of te Case, & do as he
pleased; then with great kindness he said he would consent,
but woud do it for no man alive but me &c, and he will speak
to te Qu— to day or to morrow. So perhaps something will
come of it. I can't tell. [Nite *** dee logues MD.][3]

21. D. Ormd has told Qu— he is satisfied that Stearn should
be Bp, & she consents I shall be Dean, and I suppose te
Warrants will be drawn in a day or two. I dined at an Alehouse with Parnel & Berkeley; for I am not in te humor to go
among te Ministers, thō Ld Dartmouth invited me to dine with
him to day, & Ld Tr was to be there. I sd I would if I were out
of suspense. [Nite sollahs MD][4]

22. Qu says Warrant shall be drawn, but she will dispose of
all in Engld & Ireld at once, to be teazed no more, this will
delay it sometime; & while it is delayd I am not sure of te
Qu— my Enemyes being busy; I hate their [sic] Suspense—
[Nite sollahs ***][5, 6]

23. I dined yesterday with Genll Hamilton[7] I forgot to tell
oo; I write short Journals now, I have Eggs on te Spit. This
Night te Qu— has signed all te Warrants, among which Stearn
is Bp of Dromore, & D. Ormd is to send over an Order for
making me Dean of St Patricks. I have no doubt of him at all;

---

[1] King, the Archbishop of Dublin.

[2, 3, 4, 5] Obliterated.

[6] "Sollahs" is plain enough on this day and the 21st. How Forster
could read "Nite dee logues. Poo Pdfr," and how later editors read "dee"
and "deelest," is surprising.

[7] A George Hamilton was made lieut.-general in 1709; but Mr. Aitken thinks Swift's acquaintance was Gustavus Hamilton, afterwards
Viscount Boyne.

I think tis now past; and I suppose MD is malicious enough to be glad & rathr have it than Wells. But y see what a Condition I am in. I thought I was to pay but 600ll for te House but Bp Cl. says 800ll. First Fruits 150ll and so with Patent, a thousand Pounds in all, so that I shall not be te better for this Deanery these 3 years. I hope in some time they will be persuaded here to give me some money to pay off these debts I must finish te Book I am writing,[1] before I can come over; & thy expect I shall pass next winter here, and then I will dun them to give me a Summ of money; however I hope to pass 4 or five months [with MD, and whatever comes on it. MD's Allowance must be encreased, & shall be too fais, ***][2] I received [oo *****[3] N. 39][4] to night, just 10 weeks since I had yr last. I shall write next Post to Bp Stearn; never man had so many Enemyes of Ireld as he. I carryed it with te Strongest hand possible: If he does not use me well and gently in what dealings I shall have with him, he will be te most ungratefull of Mankind. A.Bp York,[5] my mortall Enemy, has sent by a third hand that he would be glad to see me; Shall I see him or not?—I hope to be over in a Month; & that [MD][6] with their Raillery, will be mistaken that I shall make it 3 years. I will answr oor Rettle soon; but no more Journals; I shall be very busy. Short letters from henceforward. I shall not part with Laracor: that is all I have to live on; except te Deanry be worth more than 400ll a year; is it? if it be, te overplus shall be divided [between MD & **[7], besides te usuall allowance of MD & ****[8]][9] Pray write to me a good humored Lettr immediatly, let it be ever so short. This Affair was carryed with great difficulty, wch vexes me, but they say here tis much to my Reputation, that I have made a Bp in spight of all te Wor[l]d, to get te best Deanry in Ireld. [Nite dee sollahs.][10]

24. I forgot to tell y, I had Stearns Lettr yestrday in answr to mine. [oo performd oor Commission, well, dood Dallars both.][11] I made mistakes te 3 last days and am forced to

---

[1] The *History of the Peace of Utrecht*.
[2] Obliterated.
[3] Either "rettle" or "letter."
[4] Obliterated.
[5] Sharp. *See* Letter XL., Jan. 27, 1711-12.
[6] Obliterated.
[7] Mr. Aitken reads "FW."
[8] Forster read: " of MD dee rogues "—for which there is not room—besides, there is almost certainly an "&." Perhaps " & wages."
[9, 10, 11] Obliterated.

JOURNAL TO STELLA 441

alter te Numbr.[1] I dined in te City to day with my Printer,
and came home early; & am going to [2] busy with my Work.
I will send this to morrow, & I suppose te warrants will go then.
I write [3] to Dr Coghill [4] to take care of passing my Patent,
& to Parvisol to attend him with money, if he has any; or to
borrow some where he can. [Nite MD] [5]

25. Morn. I know not whethr my Warrant be yet ready from
te D. Ormd; I suppose it will by to night: I am going abroad,
& will keep this unsealed till I know whethr all be finisht:
[mollow Sollahs.] [6]——I had this Letter all day in my Pocket,
waiting till I heard te Warrants were gone over. Mr Lewis sent
to Southwells Clerk at 10, & he sd te Bp Killaloo had desired
they shoud be stoppt till next post, he sent again that Bp
Killaloo's [7] Business had nothing to do with ours; then I went
my self; but it was past 11, & asked te Reason. Killaloo is
removed to Rapho, and he has a mind to have an Order for the
Rents of Rapho that have fallen [8] since te Vacancy, & he
would have all stop till he has got that. a pretty Request; but
the Clerk at Mr Lewis's message sent te Warrants for Stearn
& me. but it was then too late to send this, wch fretts me heartily,
[tht MD shoud not have Intelligence first from Pdfr.] [9] I think
to take a hundrd Pound a year out of the Deanry, & divide it
[between MD & Pr.[10] & so be one year longer be [11] paying te
Debt, but we'll talk of zis hen I come over, so Nite dee sollahs
lele.] [12]

26. I was at Court to day; & a thousand People gave me
joy, so I ran out. I dined with Ldy Orkney—Yesterday I dined
with Ld Treasur & his Saterday People as usuall, & was
bedean'd—A.B. York says he will never more speak agst me—
Pray see that Parvisol stirs about getting my Patent. I have
given Took Dd's note to prove she is alive. I'[ll answer MD
Rettle anoddle time—Nite.] [13, 14]

---

[1] He had dated entry for 22nd, "23"—and so on. Corrected now.
[2] "be" omitted.
[3] Former versions, "wrote." If that is right, it is the first time " wrote "
is found in these letters, for Swift preferred "writt." Even here, the third
letter looks like an undotted "i."
[4] See Letter XXVI., July 1, 1711.
[5, 6] Obliterated.
[7] Thomas Lindsay.
[8] There is no "due" written after "fallen"—though no doubt it is meant.
[9] Obliterated.
[10] "Pr" is common reading—though perplexing.
[11] ? for "in."
[12, 13] Obliterated.
[14] Differs from former readings. Not quite certain as to "Rettle."

27. Nothing new to day. I dined with **Tom Harley** &c. I'll seal up this to night. pray write soon.—

[* *********** ** MD MD FW FW FW Me Me Me
Lele lele.] [1]

LETTER LXIV

[Endorsed as last. Messrs. Ryland and Aitken both record a date of receipt, "May 22," of which the present editor can find no trace.]

64   Lond. *May.* 16 [2]

I HAD yrs N. 40 yesterday. Yr new Bp acts very ungratefully, I cannot say so bad of it as he deservd. I beggd at te same Post his warrant & mine went over. that he would leave those Livings to my disposal—I shall write this post to him, to let him know how ill I take it. I have Letters to tell me, that I ought to think of employing [? Parvisol] [3] somebody to sett te Tyths of te Deanry. I know not what to do at this distance: I can not be in Ireld under a Month; I will write two Orders one to Parvisol & tother to Parvisol & a Blank for whatever Fellow it is whom te last Dean employd, & I would desire y to advise with Frends which to make use of & if te latter, let the Fellow's name be inserted, and both act by Commission. If te former, then speak to Parvisol, & know whethr he can undertake it. I doubt it is hardly to be done by a perfect Stranger alone, as Parvisol is. He may perhaps venture at all, to keep up his Interest with me, but that is needless, for I am willing to do him any good that will do me no harm. Pray advise with Walls & Raymd, & a little with Bp Stearn for form. Tell Raymd I cannot succeed for him to get that Living of Maymed [or "Moymed"]; It is represented here as a great Sinecure, sevrll Chaplns have sollicited for it, & it has vexed me so, that if I live, I will make it my Business to serve him bettr in something else: I am heartily sorry for his Illness, and that of te other two If it be not necessary to let the Tyths till a month hence, You may keep te 2 Papers, and advise well in te mean time, and whenevr it is absolutely necessary, then give that Paper wch you are most advised to. I thank Mr Walls for his Lettr, tell him that must serve for an Answr, with my Service to him & her. I shall buy Bp Stearns Hair as soon as his Houshold goods. I shll be ruined or at least sadly crampt unless te Qu— will give me 1000ll I am sure she owes me a great deal more. Ld Tr raillyes me upon it, and I believe

---

[1] Obliterated.   [2] "1713" omitted.   [3] Obliterated word

intends it; but, quando? I am advised to hasten over as soon
as possible; & so I will, & hope to sett out te beginnig of June.
Take no Lodging for me. What at yr old Tricks again? I can
ly somewhere after I land, & I care not where nor how, I will
buy yr Eggs & Bacon, [yr whadeecallit,][1, 2] yr Cups[3] & Bible,
& pray think immediatly, & give me some Commissions, & I
will perform them [as far as a poopdfr can][4]. Th Lettr I sent
before this was to have gone a Post before, but an accident
hindrd it; & I assure ee I wam vely [****[5] MD][6] did not write
to Dean pdfr. & I think oo might have had a Dean under yr
Girdle for te Superscription.[7] I have just finisht my Treatise[8]
& must be ten days correcting it. [Farewell deelest MD MD
FW FW FW Me Me Me lele.][9]

You'll seal the 2 Papers after my name.

London. *May*. 16. 1713.

I appoint Mr Isaiah Parvisol and Mr   to Sett and
let the Tyths of the Deanry of St Patricks for this present year
in witness whereof I have hereunto sett my Hand and Seal the
day and year above written.

[*The signature is cut off.*]

London. *May*. 16. 1713.

I do hereby appoint Mr Isaiah Parvisol my Proctor to sett and
let the Tyths of the Deanry of St Patricks. In witness whereof
I have hereunto sett my Hand and Seal, the Day and Year
above written.

JONAT: SWIFT.

[1] Obliterated.
[2] Forster read: "DD and dee deelest Ppt"! Mr. Aitken confirms "DD"
and declares the rest to be illegible.
[3] Former reading: "Caps."
[4] Obliterated.
[5] Messrs. Ryland and Aitken profess to read "akklee" or "akkrea"
—*i.e.* "angry."
[6] Obliterated.
[7] The joke is now unfathomable.
[8] His *History of the Peace of Utrecht.*
[9] Obliterated.

LETTER LXV

[Endorsed as last, save that the hyphen is restored to " Capel-Street.
No date of receipt marked; but Esther Johnson has written " 65 ", and,
under that, " Chester Letter."]

Chester. Jun. 6. 1713.

I AM come here after 6 days; I sett out on Monday last, and
gott here to day about 11 in the morning. A Noble Rider
[fais][1]; and all the Ships and People went off yesterday with
a rare wind. This was told me to my Comfort upon my Arrivall.
Having not used riding these 3 years, made me terrible weary;
yet I resolve on Monday to sett out for Holyhead, as weary as
I am. Tis good for my Health mun. When I came here I
found [MD's][2] Letter of te 26th of May sent down to me,—
had y writt a Post sooner, I might have brought some Pins;
but yo were lazy, & would not write yr orders immediatly as
I desired you— I will come when God Pleases, perhaps I may
be with you in a week; I will be 3 days going to Holyhead;
I cannot ride faster; say [hat oo][3] will. I am upon Stay-
behind's mare. I have te whole Inn to my self, I would fain
scape this Holy-head Journy, but I have no Prospect of Ships,
and it will be almost necessary I shoud be in Dublin before
te 25th instant, to take the others [? oaths]; otherwise I must
wait to a quarter Sessions. I will lodge as I can; therefore take
no lodgings for me, to pay in my absence, the poor Dean can't
afford it. I spoke again to D. Ormd about Moimed for Raymd,
& hope he may yet have it. for I laid it strongly to te Duke,
& gave him te Bp of Meath's Memoriall: I am sorry for Raymd's
Fistula, tell him so. I will speak to Ld Tr— about Mrs South
to morrow—Odso, I forgot; I thought I had been in London.
Mrs Tisdal is very big, ready to ly down. Her Husband is a
puppy. Do his feet stink still.—The Letters to Ireld go at so
uncertain an Hour, that I am forced to conclude—farewell
MD MD MD FW FW FW Me Me Me

　　　　　　　lele lele
　　　　　　　lele Logues ad
　　　　　　　Ladies bose fais
　　　　　　　and ******] [4, 5]

[1, 2, 3, 4] Obliterated.

[5] The last two lines of the farewell have been read: "Ladies bose fair
and slender"; but the last letter of the former line is *not* "r," and the
last word of all is *not* "slender"—whatever it may be. If Swift were in
the habit of using Irish, it might be taken for "slante" ("slainte")
="health."

[*On the Inside of Cover*]:—

I mightily approve ppt's Project of *hanging te blind* Parson[1]
—when I read that Passage upon Chester walls, as I was coming
into Town, & just receivd te Lettr: I sd aloud — Agreable
B—tch—

[1] This joke also wants its key.

THE END